ACCOUNTING AND FINANCE
for Non-Specialists

Res

Visit the *Accounting and Finance for Non-Specialists, fifth edition*
Companion Website at www.pearsoned.co.uk/atrillmclaney to find
valuable **student** learning material including:

- Multiple choice questions to test your learning
- Solutions to end of chapter review questions
- Revision questions to help you check your understanding
- Extensive links to valuable resources on the web
- An online glossary to explain key terms

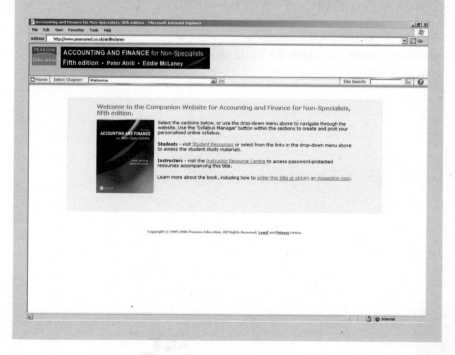

PEARSON
Education

We work with leading authors to develop the strongest
educational materials in business and finance, bringing
cutting-edge thinking and best learning practice to a
global market.

Under a range of well-known imprints, including
Financial Times Prentice Hall, we craft high quality print
and electronic publications which help readers to
understand and apply their content, whether studying
or at work.

To find out more about the complete range of our
publishing, please visit us on the World Wide Web at:
www.pearsoned.co.uk

Fifth Edition

ACCOUNTING AND FINANCE
for Non-Specialists

Peter Atrill and **Eddie McLaney**

FINANCIAL TIMES

An imprint of **Pearson Education**

Harlow, England • London • New York • Boston • San Francisco • Toronto • Sydney • Singapore • Hong Kong
Tokyo • Seoul • Taipei • New Delhi • Cape Town • Madrid • Mexico City • Amsterdam • Munich • Paris • Milan

Pearson Education Limited

Edinburgh Gate
Harlow
Essex CM20 2JE
England

and Associated Companies throughout the world

Visit us on the World Wide Web at:
www.pearsoned.co.uk

First published in 1995 by Prentice Hall Europe
Second edition in 1997
Third edition published in 2001 by Pearson Education Limited
Fourth edition in 2004
Fifth edition in 2006

ISBN-13: 978-0-273-70244-3
ISBN-10: 0-273-70244-0

British Library Cataloguing-in-Publication Data
A catalogue record for this book is available from the British Library

Library of Congress Cataloging-in-Publication Data
A catalogue record for this book is available from the Library of Congress

10 9 8 7 6 5 4 3 2
10 09 08 07 06

Typeset in 9/12.5pt Stone Serif by 35
Printed and bound by Mateu Cromo Artes Graficas, Madrid, Spain

The publisher's policy is to use paper manufactured from sustainable forests.

Contents

5 Measuring and reporting cash flows

6 Analysing and interpreting financial statements

9 Budgeting 280

Part 3 FINANCIAL MANAGEMENT

Supporting resources

Visit **www.pearsoned.co.uk/atrillmclaney** to find valuable online resources

Companion Website for students
- Multiple choice questions to test your learning
- Solutions to end of chapter review questions
- Revision questions to help you check your understanding
- Extensive links to valuable resources on the web
- An online glossary to explain key terms

For instructors
- Complete, downloadable Instructor's manual
- PowerPoint slides that can be downloaded and used as OHTs
- Progress tests, consisting of various questions and exercise material with solutions
- Tutorial/seminar questions and solutions
- Solutions to individual chapter exercises

Also: The Companion Website provides the following features:
- Search tool to help locate specific items of content
- E-mail results and profile tools to send results of quizzes to instructors
- Online help and support to assist with website usage and troubleshooting

For more information please contact your local Pearson Education sales representative or visit **www.pearsoned.co.uk/atrillmclaney**

OneKey: All you and your students need to succeed

OneKey is an exclusive new resource for instructors and students, giving you access to the best online teaching and learning tools 24 hours a day, 7 days a week.

OneKey means all your resources are in one place for maximum convenience, simplicity and success.

OneKey
OneKey is
all you need

Convenience. Simplicity. Success.

A OneKey product is available for *Accounting and Finance for Non-Specialists, fifth edition* for use with Blackboard™, WebCT and CourseCompass. It contains:

- Interactive Study Guide with exercises to enhance your understanding and assess your progress
- Interactive online flashcards that enable you to check definitions against key terms during revision
- All resources available to students through the Companion Website
- All teaching resources available to instructors

For more information about the OneKey product please contact your local Pearson Education sales representative or visit **www.pearsoned.co.uk/onekey**

Preface

This text provides an introduction to accounting and finance. It is aimed primarily at students who are not majoring in accounting or finance but who are, nevertheless, studying introductory level accounting and finance as part of their course in business, economics, hospitality management, tourism, engineering or some other area. Students who are majoring in either accounting or finance should, however, find the book useful as an introduction to the main principles, which can serve as a foundation for further study. The text does not focus on the technical aspects, but rather examines the basic principles and underlying concepts, and the ways in which accounting statements and financial information can be used to improve the quality of decision making. To support this practical approach, there are, throughout the text, numerous illustrative extracts with commentary from company reports, survey data and other sources.

The text is written in an 'open-learning' style. This means that there are numerous integrated activities, worked examples and questions throughout the text to help you to understand the subject fully. You are expected to interact with the material and to check your progress continuously in a way not typically found in textbooks. Irrespective of whether you are using the book as part of a taught course or for personal study, we have found that this approach is more 'user-friendly' and makes it easier for you to learn.

We recognise that most of you will not have studied accounting or finance before, and we have therefore tried to write in a concise and accessible style, minimising the use of technical jargon. We have also tried to introduce topics gradually, explaining everything as we go. Where technical terminology is unavoidable we try to provide clear explanations. In addition, you will find all the key terms highlighted in the text, and then listed at the end of each chapter with a page reference to help you rapidly revise the main techniques and concepts. All these key terms are also listed alphabetically with a concise definition in the glossary towards the end of the book, so providing a convenient and single point of reference from which to revise.

A further important consideration in helping you to understand and absorb the topics covered is the design of the text itself. The page layout and colour scheme have been carefully considered to allow for the easy navigation and digestion of material. The layout features a large page format, an open design, and clear signposting of the various features and assessment material.

How to use this book

We have organised the chapters to reflect what we consider to be a logical sequence and, for this reason, we suggest that you work through the text in the order in which it is presented. We have tried to ensure that earlier chapters do not refer to concepts or terms that are not explained until a later chapter. If you work through the chapters in the 'wrong' order, you will probably encounter concepts and terms that were explained previously.

Irrespective of whether you are using the book as part of a lecture/tutorial-based course or as the basis for a more independent mode of study, we advocate following broadly the same approach.

Integrated assessment material

Interspersed throughout each chapter are numerous **Activities**. You are strongly advised to attempt all these questions. They are designed to simulate the sort of quick-fire questions that your lecturer might throw at you during a lecture or tutorial. Activities serve two purposes:

■ to give you the opportunity to check that you have understood what has been covered so far;
■ to encourage you to think about the topic just covered, either to see a link between that topic and others with which you are already familiar, or to link the topic just covered to the next.

The answer to each Activity is provided immediately after the question. This answer should be covered up until you have deduced your solution, which can then be compared with the one given.

Towards the middle/end of each chapter, except for Chapter 1, there is a **Self-assessment question**. This is more comprehensive and demanding than any of the activities, and is designed to give you an opportunity to check and apply your understanding of the core coverage of the chapter. The solution to each of these questions is provided at the end of the book. As with the activities, it is important that you attempt each question thoroughly before referring to the solution. If you have difficulty with a self-assessment question you should go over the chapter again.

End-of-chapter assessment material

At the end of each chapter there are four **Review questions**. These are short questions requiring a narrative answer or discussion within a tutorial group. They are intended to help you assess how well you can recall and critically evaluate the core terms and concepts covered in each chapter. Solutions to all of these questions can be found at the end of the book.

At the end of each chapter, except for Chapter 1, there are five **Exercises**. These are mostly computational, and are designed to reinforce your knowledge and understanding. The exercises are graded according to their level of difficulty. The basic-level questions are fairly straightforward; the more advanced ones can be quite demanding, but are capable of being successfully completed if you have worked conscientiously through the chapter and have attempted the basic exercises. Solutions to three of the exercises in each chapter are provided at the end of the book and are identified by a coloured question number. Here, too, a thorough attempt should be made to answer each question before referring to the solution. Solutions to the other two exercises are available to lecturers on the Companion Website.

Guided tour of the book

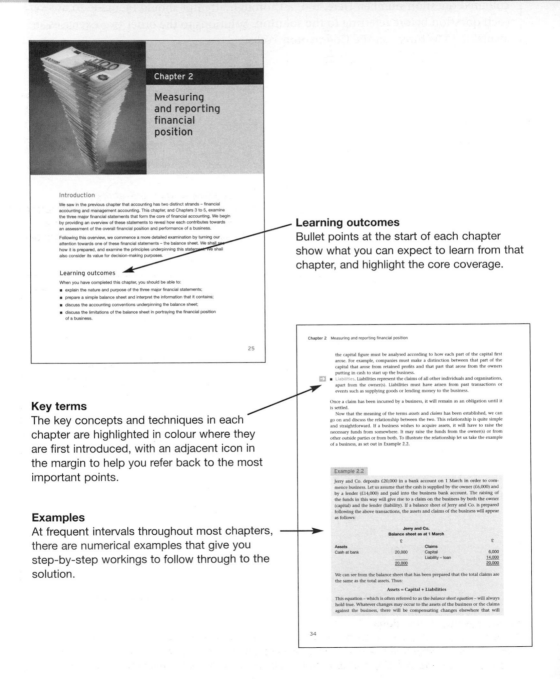

Chapter 2

Measuring and reporting financial position

Introduction

We saw in the previous chapter that accounting has two distinct strands – financial accounting and management accounting. This chapter, and Chapters 3 to 5, examine the three major financial statements that form the core of financial accounting. We begin by providing an overview of these statements to reveal how each contributes towards an assessment of the overall financial position and performance of a business.

Following this overview, we commence a more detailed examination by turning our attention towards one of these financial statements – the balance sheet. We shall see how it is prepared, and examine the principles underpinning this statement. We shall also consider its value for decision-making purposes.

Learning outcomes

When you have completed this chapter, you should be able to:

■ explain the nature and purpose of the three major financial statements;
■ prepare a simple balance sheet and interpret the information that it contains;
■ discuss the accounting conventions underpinning the balance sheet;
■ discuss the limitations of the balance sheet in portraying the financial position of a business.

25

Learning outcomes
Bullet points at the start of each chapter show what you can expect to learn from that chapter, and highlight the core coverage.

Key terms
The key concepts and techniques in each chapter are highlighted in colour where they are first introduced, with an adjacent icon in the margin to help you refer back to the most important points.

Examples
At frequent intervals throughout most chapters, there are numerical examples that give you step-by-step workings to follow through to the solution.

Chapter 2 Measuring and reporting financial position

the capital figure must be analysed according to how each part of the capital first arose. For example, companies must make a distinction between that part of the capital that arose from retained profits and that part that arose from the owners putting in cash to start up the business.

■ Liabilities. Liabilities represent the claims of all other individuals and organisations, apart from the owner(s). Liabilities must have arisen from past transactions or events such as supplying goods or lending money to the business.

Once a claim has been incurred by a business, it will remain as an obligation until it is settled.

Now that the meaning of the terms *assets* and *claims* has been established, we can go on and discuss the relationship between the two. This relationship is quite simple and straightforward. If a business wishes to acquire assets, it will have to raise the necessary funds from somewhere. It may raise the funds from the owner(s) or from other outside parties or from both. To illustrate the relationship let us take the example of a business, as set out in Example 2.2.

Example 2.2

Jerry and Co. deposits £20,000 in a bank account on 1 March in order to commence business. Let us assume that the cash is supplied by the owner (£6,000) and by a lender (£14,000) and paid into the business bank account. The raising of the funds in this way will give rise to a claim on the business by both the owner (capital) and the lender (liability). If a balance sheet of Jerry and Co. is prepared following the above transactions, the assets and claims of the business will appear as follows:

Jerry and Co.
Balance sheet as at 1 March

	£		£
Assets		**Claims**	
Cash at bank	20,000	Capital	6,000
		Liability – loan	14,000
	20,000		20,000

We can see from the balance sheet that has been prepared that the total claims are the same as the total assets. Thus:

Assets = Capital + Liabilities

This equation – which is often referred to as the *balance sheet equation* – will always hold true. Whatever changes may occur to the assets of the business or the claims against the business, there will be compensating changes elsewhere that will

34

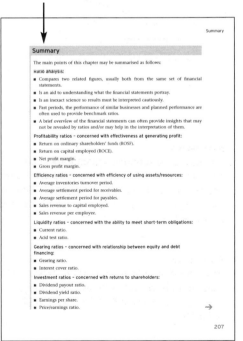

'Real World' illustrations
Integrated throughout the text, these illustrative examples highlight the practical application of accounting concepts and techniques by real businesses, including extracts from company reports and financial statements, survey data and other interesting insights from business.

Activities
These short questions, integrated throughout each chapter, allow you to check your understanding as you progress through the text. They comprise either a narrative question requiring you to review or critically consider topics, or a numerical problem requiring you to deduce a solution. A suggested answer is given immediately after each activity.

Bullet point chapter summary
Each chapter ends with a 'bullet point' summary. This highlights the material covered in the chapter and can be used as a quick reminder of the main issues.

Self-assessment questions
Towards the end of most chapters you will encounter one of these questions, allowing you to attempt a comprehensive question before tackling the end-of-chapter assessment material. To check your understanding and progress, solutions are provided at the end of the book.

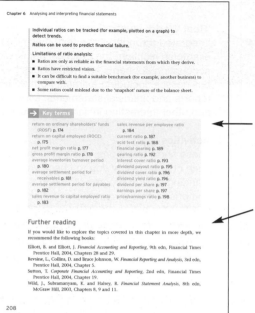

Key terms summary
At the end of each chapter, there is a listing (with page reference) of all the key terms, allowing you to easily refer back to the most important points.

Further reading
This section comprises a listing of relevant chapters in other textbooks that you might refer to in order to pursue a topic in more depth or gain an alternative perspective.

Review questions
These short questions encourage you to review and/or critically discuss your understanding of the main topics covered in each chapter, either individually or in a group. Solutions to these questions can be found at the end of the book.

Exercises
These comprehensive questions appear at the end of most chapters. The more advanced questions are separately identified. Solutions to some of the questions (those with coloured numbers) are provided at the end of the book, enabling you to assess your progress. Solutions to the remaining questions are available online for lecturers only. Additional exercises can be found on the Companion Website at **www.pearsoned.co.uk/atrillmclaney.**

Acknowledgements

We are grateful to the following for permission to reproduce copyright material:

Newcastle United Plc for an extract adapted from the Newcastle United Plc Annual Report 2004; Marks and Spencer Plc for an extract adapted from the Marks and Spencer Annual Report 2004; O2 Plc for an extract from the O2 Plc Annual Report and Accounts 2003; Thorntons Plc for an extract from the Thorntons Plc Annual Report 2004; Aurum Press for an extract from *Arnold Weinstock and the Making of GEC 1997* by Stephen Aris; and Rolls Royce Plc for an extract from the Rolls Royce Plc Annual Report and Accounts 2004.

Figure 9.4 from *Financial Management and Working Capital Practices in UK SMEs* by Chittenden, F., Michaelas, N., and Poutziouris, P. 1999, Fig. 16 on Page 22. Reproduced by permission © Francis Chittenden.

p. 1 Corbis/Thom Lang; p. 23 Corbis/L. Clarke; p. 25 Corbis/Matthias Kulka; p. 61 Getty/Royalty Free; p. 100 Corbis/James Leynse; p. 139 Corbis/Gary Houlder; p. 167 Alamy/Lisa Moore; p. 215 Getty/Taxi/Charly Franklin; p. 217 Corbis/George B. Diebold; p. 249 Corbis/Setboun; p. 280 Alamy/Royalty Free; p. 325 D. & T. Hebden Photography/PhotographersDirect.com; p. 327 Corbis/Rob Howard; p. 367 Getty/Kelvin Murray; p. 406 Comstock.

We are grateful to the Financial Times for permissions to reprint the following material:

Tsunami: finding the right figures for disaster, © *Financial Times*, 7 March 2005; Morrison in an uphill battle to integrate Safeway, © *Financial Times*, 27 May 2005; Fair shares?, FT Weekend Magazine, © *Financial Times*, 11 June 2005; Profit without honour, Financial Times Weekend, © *Financial Times*, 29/30 June 2002; CRH purchase of Cementbouw gets approval, © *Financial Times*, 1 October 2003; Household debt adds to rise in bank write-offs, © *Financial Times*, 28 March 2005; Monotub industries in a spin as founder gets Titan for £1, © *Financial Times*, 23 January 2003; Markets week world 'Clinton Cards', © *Financial Times*, 4 October 2003; Eurotunnel takes £1.3bn impairment charge, FT.com, © *Financial Times*, 9 February 2004; WaterfordWedgwood face some intense questions over its cash flow, © *Financial Times*, 17 June 2004; Sony sets more steps to raise profit margins, FT.com, © *Financial Times*, 6 October 2003; Jaguar struggles to break even, © *Financial Times*, 6 May 2005; Shell's Sakhalin-2 gas project hit by eight-month delay and $10bn cost rise, © *Financial Times*, 15 July 2005; Satellites need space to earn, © *Financial Times*, 14 July 2003; New appetite develops for Eurobonds, © *Financial Times*, 18 September 2004; Bulmer warns of breach of covenants, © *Financial Times*, 25 January 2003; Travelodge to raise £400m via sale and leaseback plan, © *Financial Times*, 12 July 2004; Tesco raises £810m in placing as sales rise, FT.com, © *Financial Times*, 13 January 2004; Benfield earmarks almost 10 per cent for fees in £100m flotation, © *Financial Times*, 9 June 2003.

In some instances we have been unable to trace the owners of copyright material, and we would appreciate any information that would enable us to do so.

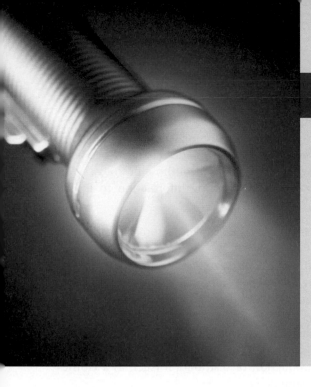

Chapter 1

Introduction to accounting and finance

Introduction

Welcome to the world of accounting and finance! In this opening chapter, we provide a broad outline of these subjects. We begin by considering the roles of accounting and finance and we shall see that both can be valuable tools for decision-making purposes. We shall identify the main users of accounting information and discuss the ways in which accounting can improve the quality of the decisions that they make. In subsequent chapters, we develop this decision-making theme by considering in some detail the kinds of financial reports and methods used to aid decision making.

For many of you, accounting and finance are not the main focus of your studies and you may well be asking 'Why do I need to study these subjects?' So, after we have considered the key features of accounting and finance, we shall go on to discuss why some understanding of these subjects is likely to be relevant to you.

Learning outcomes

When you have completed this chapter, you should be able to:

■ explain the nature and roles of accounting and finance;

■ identify the main users of financial information and discuss their needs;

■ distinguish between financial and management accounting;

■ explain why an understanding of accounting is likely to be relevant to your needs.

What are accounting and finance?

Let us start our study of accounting and finance by trying to understand the purpose of each. Accounting is concerned with collecting, analysing and communicating financial information. This information is useful for those who need to make decisions and plans about businesses, and for those who need to control those businesses. For example, the managers of businesses may need accounting information to decide whether to:

- develop new products or services (such as a computer manufacturer developing a new range of computers);
- increase or decrease the price or quantity of existing products or services (such as a telecommunications business changing its mobile phone call and text charges);
- borrow money to help finance the business (such as a supermarket wishing to increase the number of stores it owns);
- increase or decrease the operating capacity of the business (such as a beef farming business reviewing the size of its herd);
- change the methods of purchasing, production or distribution (such as a clothes retailer switching from UK to overseas suppliers).

The information provided should help in identifying and assessing the financial consequences of such decisions.

Though managers working within a particular business are likely to be significant users of accounting information about that particular business, they are by no means the only ones. There are those outside the business (whom we shall identify later) who may need information to decide whether to:

- invest or disinvest in the ownership of the business;
- lend money to the business;
- offer credit facilities;
- enter into contracts for the purchase of products or services.

Sometimes the impression is given that the purpose of accounting is simply to prepare financial reports on a regular basis. While it is true that accountants undertake this kind of work, the preparation of financial reports does not represent an end in itself. The ultimate purpose of the accountant's work is to give people better information on which to base their decisions. This decision-making perspective of accounting fits in with the theme of this book and shapes the way in which we deal with each topic.

Finance, like accounting, exists to help decision makers. It is concerned with the ways in which funds for a business are raised and invested. This lies at the very heart of what a business is about. In essence, a business exists to raise funds from investors (owners and lenders) and then to use those funds to make investments (equipment, premises, inventories and so on) in an attempt to make the business, and its owners, wealthier. It is important that funds are raised in a way that is appropriate to the particular needs of the business and an understanding of finance should help in identifying:

- the main forms of finance available;
- the costs and benefits of each form of finance;
- the risks associated with each form of finance;
- the role of financial markets in supplying finance.

Once the funds are raised, they must be invested in a way that will provide the business with a worthwhile return. An understanding of finance should help in evaluating:

- the returns from an investment;
- the risks associated with an investment.

Businesses tend to raise and invest funds in large amounts for long periods of time. The quality of the investment decisions made can, therefore, have a profound impact on the fortunes of the business.

There is little point in trying to make a sharp distinction between accounting and finance. We have already seen that both are concerned with the financial aspects of decision making. There is considerable overlap between the two subjects and, in this book, we shall not emphasise the distinctions.

Accounting and user needs

For accounting information to be useful, the accountant must be clear *for whom* the information is being prepared and *for what purpose* the information will be used. There are likely to be various groups of people (known as 'user groups') with an interest in a particular organisation, in the sense of needing to make decisions about it. For the typical private sector business, the most important of these groups are shown in Figure 1.1. Take a look at this figure and then try Activity 1.1 below.

Activity 1.1

Ptarmigan Insurance plc (PI) is a large motor insurance business. Taking the user groups identified below, suggest what sort of decisions each group is likely to make about PI.

Your answer may be as follows:

User group	Decision
Customers	Whether to take further motor policies with PI. This would probably involve an assessment of PI's ability to continue in business and to supply customers' needs. Customers (policy holders) would be concerned about the ability of PI to be able to meet any claims made by them.

$\rightarrow$

Competitors	How best to compete against PI or, perhaps, whether to leave the market on the grounds that it is not possible to compete profitably with PI. This might involve using PI's performance in various aspects as a 'benchmark' when evaluating their own performance. They might also try to assess PI's competitive strength and to identify significant changes that may signal PI's future actions (for example, expanding its ability to provide its service as a prelude to market expansion).
Employees	Whether to take up or to continue in employment with PI. Employees might assess this by considering the ability of the business to continue to provide employment and to reward employees adequately for their labour.
Government	Whether PI should pay tax and, if so, how much, whether it complies with agreed pricing policies, whether financial support is needed and so on. In making these decisions an assessment of its profits, sales revenues and financial strength would be made.
Community representatives	Whether to allow PI to expand its premises or whether to provide economic support for PI. To assess these, PI's ability to continue to provide employment for the community, to use community resources and to help fund environmental improvements might be considered.
Investment analysts	Whether or not to advise clients to invest in PI. This would involve an assessment of the likely risks and returns associated with PI.
Suppliers	Whether to continue to supply PI and, if so, whether to supply on credit. This would involve an assessment of PI's ability to pay for any goods and services supplied.
Lenders	Whether to lend money to PI and/or whether to require repayment of any existing loans. To assess this, PI's ability to meet its obligations to pay interest and to repay the principal would be considered.
Managers	Whether the performance of the business requires improvement. Here performance to date would be compared with earlier plans or some other 'benchmark' to decide whether action needs to be taken. Whether there should be a change in PI's future direction. In making such decisions, management will need to look at PI's ability to perform and at the opportunities available to it.
Owners	Whether to invest more in PI or to sell all, or part, of the investment currently held. This would involve an assessment of the likely risks and returns associated with PI. Owners would also be involved with decisions on the employment of senior managers. Here past performance of the business would be assessed.

You may have thought of other reasons why each group would find accounting information useful.

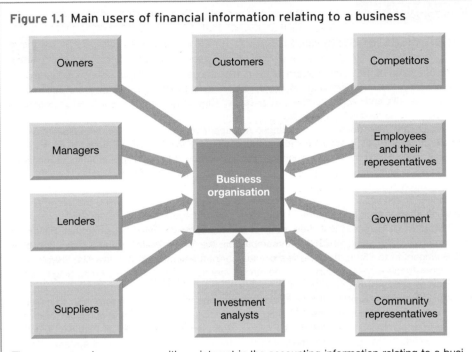

Figure 1.1 Main users of financial information relating to a business

There are several user groups with an interest in the accounting information relating to a business. The majority of these are outside the business but, nevertheless, they have a stake in it. This is not meant to be an exhaustive list of potential users; however, the groups identified are normally the most important.

Not-for-profit organisations

Though the focus of this book is accounting as it relates to private sector businesses, there are many organisations that do not exist mainly for the pursuit of profit. Examples include charities, clubs and associations, universities, local government authorities, churches and trades unions. Such organisations also need to produce accounting information for decision-making purposes. User groups need accounting information about these types of organisation to help them to make decisions. These groups are often the same as, or similar to, those identified for private sector businesses. They may have a stake in the future viability of the organisation and may use accounting information to check that the wealth of the organisation is being properly controlled and used in a way that is consistent with its objectives.

Real World 1.1 provides an example of the importance of accounting to relief agencies.

Real World 1.1

When disaster strikes

FT

In the aftermath of the Asian tsunami at the turn of the year, one of the most important issues was ensuring the huge amounts of money raised were providing necessary aid and reconstruction as efficiently and effectively as possible. That does not just mean medical staff and engineers. It also means accountants.

The charity that does this is Mango: Management Accounting for Non-Governmental Organisations (NGOs). It provides accountants in the field and it provides the back-up, such as financial training, and all the other services that should result in really robust financial management in the disaster area.

'In January we had 40 requests for placements,' says Denise Joseph, director of placements at Mango, 'and it was not just for the tsunami. It is an indication of the value that aid agencies place on management accountants. They play a very important role in relief efforts.'

That role will increase. The sheer scale of the money now involved ensures that. Funds for tsunami relief now stand at £365m. In comparison, the funds raised for the Kosovo appeal in 1999 amounted to £53m. 'It is vastly more than previous sums raised,' says Ms Joseph, 'and coupled with this is the pressure to spend money very quickly. So the strain on existing financial controls and management creates extra pressures.'

Mango's work is twofold. It recruits accountants and keeps them on a register to enable a rapid response to the needs of NGOs. And it provides training courses and guidance for them.

For example, Mango has devised a Financial Management Health Check that can be downloaded by NGOs, through which they can gauge the strength of their financial systems. So far, 47,000 copies of the Health Check have been downloaded. 'Aid agencies,' says Ms Joseph, 'achieve different levels of cost effectiveness. We find that if you have someone knowledgeable about financial reporting and that person is separate from the programme manager, it leads to cost savings and efficiencies.'

It is a simple principle. But it is one that can be easily forgotten in the chaos and speed of getting relief to disaster victims. Management accountants can make a huge difference both in making sure the money is spent effectively in the field and that accountability back to the donors is of a high standard.

Source: 'Tsunami: finding the right figures for disaster', Robert Bruce, *FT.com*, 7 March 2005

Accounting as a service function

One way of viewing accounting is as a form of service. Accountants provide economic information to their 'clients', who are the various users identified in Figure 1.1. The quality of the service provided would be determined by the extent to which the information needs of the various user groups have been met. It can be argued that, to be useful, accounting information should possess certain key qualities, or characteristics. These are:

■ Relevance. Accounting information must have the ability to influence decisions. Unless this characteristic is present, there is really no point in producing the information. The information may be relevant to the prediction of future events (for example, in predicting how much profit is likely to be earned next year) or relevant in helping confirm past events (for example, in establishing how much profit was earned last year). The role of accounting in confirming past events is important because users often wish to check on the accuracy of earlier predictions that they have made. The accuracy (or inaccuracy) of earlier predictions may enable users to judge the likely accuracy of current predictions.

→ ■ Reliability. Accounting should be free from significant error or bias. It should be capable of being relied upon by users to represent what it is supposed to represent. Though both relevance and reliability are very important, the problem that we often face in accounting is that information that is highly relevant may not be very reliable, and that which is reliable may not be very relevant. Activity 1.2 illustrates this point.

Activity 1.2

A manager has to sell a custom-built machine owned by the business and has recently received a bid for it. What information would be relevant to the manager when deciding whether to accept the bid? How reliable would that information be?

The manager would probably like to know the current market value of the machine before deciding whether or not to accept the bid. The current market value would be highly relevant to the final decision, but it might not be very reliable because the machine is unique and there is likely to be little information concerning market values.

Where a choice has to be made between providing information that has either more relevance or more reliability, the maximisation of relevance tends to be the guiding rule.

→ ■ Comparability. This quality will enable users to identify changes in the business over time (for example, the trend in sales over the past five years). It will also help users to evaluate the performance of the business in relation to other similar businesses. Comparability is achieved by treating items that are basically the same in the same manner for accounting purposes. Comparability tends also to be enhanced by making clear the policies that have been adopted in measuring and presenting the information.

→ ■ Understandability. Accounting reports should be expressed as clearly as possible and should be understood by those at whom the information is aimed. Consider Activity 1.3 below.

Activity 1.3

Do you think that accounting reports should be understandable to those who have not studied accounting?

It would be useful if anyone could understand accounting reports, but realistically, this is not likely to be the case. Complex financial events and transactions cannot always be reported easily. It is probably best that we regard accounting reports in the same way as we regard a report written in a foreign language. To understand either of these, we need to have had some preparation. Generally speaking, accounting reports assume that the user not only has a reasonable knowledge of business and accounting, but is also prepared to invest some time in studying the reports.

The threshold of materiality

The qualities, or characteristics, that have just been described will help us to decide if a particular piece of financial information is potentially useful. However, in order to make a final decision, we also have to consider whether the information is material, or significant. This means that we should ask whether its omission or misrepresentation in the financial reports would really alter the decisions that users make. Thus, in addition to possessing the characteristics mentioned above, financial information must also achieve a threshold of materiality. If the information is not regarded as material, it should not be included within the reports as it will merely clutter them up and, perhaps, interfere with the users' ability to interpret the financial results. The type of information and amounts involved will normally determine whether it is material.

Costs and benefits of accounting information

Having read the previous sections you may feel that, when considering a piece of financial information, provided the four main qualities identified are present, and it is material, it should be included in the financial reports. Unfortunately, there is one more hurdle to jump. A piece of financial information may still be excluded from the financial reports even when it is considered to be useful. Consider Activity 1.4 below.

Activity 1.4

Suppose an item of information is capable of being provided. It is relevant to a particular decision, it is also reliable, comparable, understandable and material.

Can you think of a reason why, in practice, you might choose not to produce the information?

The reason that you may decide not to produce, or discover, the information is that you judge the cost of doing so to be greater than the potential benefit of having the information. This cost–benefit issue will place limits on the extent to which accounting information is provided.

In theory, financial information should only be produced if the costs of providing a particular item of information are less than the benefits, or value, to be derived from its use.

To illustrate the cost/benefit relationship, suppose that we wish to buy a particular DVD system that we have seen in a local shop for sale at £250. We believe that other local shops may have the same system on offer for a lower price. The only way of finding out the prices at other shops are either to telephone them or to visit them. Telephone calls cost money and involve some of our time. Visiting the shops may not involve the outlay of money, but more of our time will be involved. Is it worth the cost of finding out the price of the system at various shops? The answer, as we have seen, is that if the cost of discovering the price is less than the potential benefit, it is worth having that information.

To identify the various selling prices of the DVD system, there are various points to be considered including:

■ How many shops shall we telephone or visit?
■ What is the cost of each telephone call?
■ How long will it take to make all the telephone calls or visits?
■ How much do we value our time?

The economic benefit of having the information on the price of the system is probably even harder to assess and the following points need to be considered:

■ What is the cheapest price that we might be quoted for the DVD system?
■ How likely is it that we shall be quoted prices cheaper than £250?

The answers to these questions may be far from clear. When assessing the value of accounting information we are confronted with similar problems. It is possible to apply some 'science' to the problem of weighing the costs and benefits, but a lot of subjective judgement is likely to be involved. No one would seriously advocate that a typical business should not produce accounting information but at the same time, no one would advocate that every item of information that could be seen as possessing one or more of the key characteristics should be produced, irrespective of the cost of producing it.

The key characteristics that influence the usefulness of accounting information, and which have been discussed in this section and the preceding section, are set out in Figure 1.2.

Accounting as an information system

Accounting is a part of the business's total information system, whose role is to provide information to 'clients' (the users identified in Figure 1.1). Users, both inside and outside the business, have to make decisions concerning the allocation of scarce resources. To try to ensure that these resources are allocated in an efficient manner, users require financial information on which to base decisions. It is the role of the accounting system to provide that information and this will involve information gathering and communication.

The accounting information system has certain features that are common to all information systems within a business. These are:

■ identifying and capturing relevant information (in this case financial information);
■ recording in a systematic manner the information collected;
■ analysing and interpreting the information collected;
■ reporting the information in a manner that suits the needs of users.

The relationship between these features is set out in Figure 1.3.

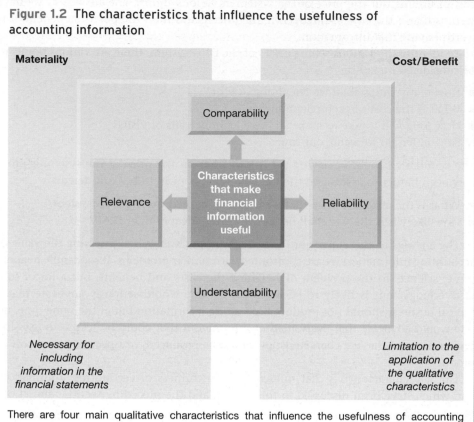

Figure 1.2 The characteristics that influence the usefulness of accounting information

There are four main qualitative characteristics that influence the usefulness of accounting information. In addition, however, accounting information should be material and the benefits of providing the information should outweigh the costs.

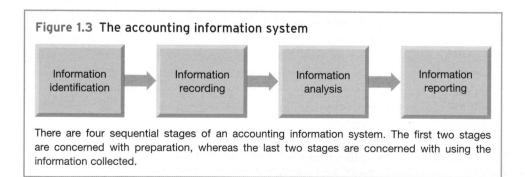

Figure 1.3 The accounting information system

There are four sequential stages of an accounting information system. The first two stages are concerned with preparation, whereas the last two stages are concerned with using the information collected.

Given the decision-making emphasis of this book, we shall be concerned primarily with the final two elements of the process – the analysis and reporting of financial information. We shall consider the way in which information is used by, and is useful to, users, rather than the way in which it is identified and recorded. In this context, information technology is playing an increasingly important role. It has created opportunities for analysis and reporting that were not possible before.

Efficient accounting systems are an essential ingredient of an efficient business. When the accounting systems fail, the results can be disastrous. Real World 1.2 provides an example of a systems failure when two businesses combined and then attempted to integrate their respective systems.

Real World 1.2

Blaming the system   **FT**

When Sir Ken Morrison bought Safeway for £3.35bn in March 2004, he almost doubled the size of his supermarket chain overnight and went from being a regional operator to a national force. His plan was simple enough. He had to sell off some Safeway stores – Morrison has to date sold-off 184 stores for an estimated £1.3bn – and convert the remaining 230 Safeway stores into Morrison's. Sir Ken has about another 50 to sell. But, nearly 15 months on, and the integration process is proving harder in practice than it looked on paper. Morrison, once known for its robust performance, has issued four profit warnings in the past 10 months. Each time the retailer has blamed Safeway. Last July, it was because of a faster-than-expected sales decline in Safeway stores. In March – there were two warnings that month – it was the fault of Safeway's accounting systems, which left Morrison with lower supplier incomes. This month's warning was put down to higher-than-expected costs from running parallel store systems. At the time of the first warning last July, Simon Procter, of the stockbrokers Charles Stanley, noted that the news 'has blown all profit forecasts out of the water and visibility is very poor from here on out'. But if it was difficult then to predict where Morrison's profits were heading, it is impossible now. Morrison itself cannot give guidance. 'No one envisaged this,' says Mr Procter. 'When I made that comment about visibility last July, I was thinking on a 12-month time frame, not a two-year one.' Morrison says the complexity of the Safeway deal has put a 'significant strain' on its ability to cope with managing internal accounts. 'This is impacting the ability of the board to forecast likely trend in profitability and the directors are therefore not currently in a position to provide reliable guidance on the level of profitability as a whole,' admits the retailer.

Source: 'Morrison in uphill battle to integrate Safeway', Elizabeth Rigby, *FT.com*, 26 May 2005

Planning and control

We saw earlier that managers are important users of financial information. They need financial information to help them to plan and control the activities of the business. Planning and control can be seen as a sequence of logical steps that we shall now briefly describe; however, this topic will be considered in more depth in Chapter 9.

It is vital that businesses plan their future. Each business must have a clear view of where it is going and how it is going to get there.

We shall now consider the seven steps in the planning and control system and see where accounting and finance has a vital role to play in each step.

- *Step 1* of the process is identifying the objectives of the business. Objectives tend to be framed in broad terms and, once established, they are likely to remain in force for a long period, say, five or ten years. As we shall see later, a key objective of private-sector businesses is to increase the wealth of their owners. It is important, therefore, that we have suitable financial indicators, such as profit, that can be used to help set the objectives.

- *Step 2* is considering the various options available to achieve the objectives of the business. To achieve the objectives that have been identified, a number of possible options (strategies) may be available. Each option must be considered carefully to see how closely it fits with the objectives that have been set, and to see whether the resources to pursue the options are available. Financial information should help to quantify the likely costs and benefits associated with each option in financial terms. As a result, we should see more clearly whether an option is worth pursuing.

- *Step 3* involves the preparation of long-term plans, based on the most appropriate option available. These long-term plans set out how the business will work towards the achievement of its objectives over a period of, say, five years. Financial information should lie at the heart of these plans. It is important to set out the financing and investment requirements for the business and the expected levels of sales revenues and expenses over the planning period. By doing so, the managers will have clear, quantifiable targets to be achieved.

- *Step 4* is the development of short-term plans, within the framework of the long-term plans. The business will usually prepare short-term plans (budgets) covering a period of one year. The role of budgets is to convert the long-term plans into actionable blueprints for the immediate future. The role of financial information here is basically the same as in the third step.

- *Step 5* in the process involves collecting information on actual performance. However well planned the activities of the business may be, they will come to nothing unless steps are taken to achieve them. The process of ensuring that planned events actually occur is known as *control*. To exercise control, there must be a timely flow of information available to managers to help them compare actual performance with earlier planned performance. As many aspects of planning will normally be expressed in financial terms, information regarding actual performance, which is required to exercise control, should also be couched in financial terms. This will make it easier for managers to compare differences between planned and actual performance, and to assess the extent to which plans have been achieved.

- *Step 6* is responding to divergences from planned performance with appropriate action. Where things have not gone according to plan, the size of the differences between planned and actual performance, expressed in financial terms, can help managers to set their priorities for action.

- *Step 7* is to revise the plans or budgets, if necessary. This will involve going through the main steps of the process once again and so will require the financial information already identified.

The planning, decision-making and control process is depicted in Figure 1.4.

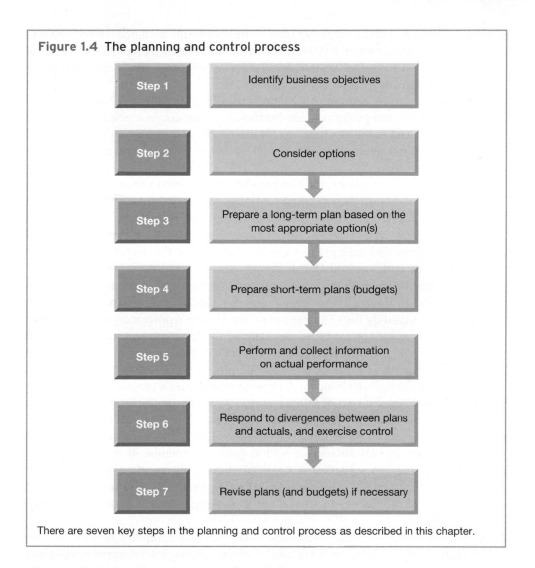

Figure 1.4 The planning and control process

Step 1	Identify business objectives
Step 2	Consider options
Step 3	Prepare a long-term plan based on the most appropriate option(s)
Step 4	Prepare short-term plans (budgets)
Step 5	Perform and collect information on actual performance
Step 6	Respond to divergences between plans and actuals, and exercise control
Step 7	Revise plans (and budgets) if necessary

There are seven key steps in the planning and control process as described in this chapter.

Management and financial accounting

Accounting is usually seen as having two distinct strands:

- Management accounting, which seeks to meet the needs of managers.
- Financial accounting, which seeks to meet the accounting needs of all of the other users that were identified in Figure 1.1, earlier in the chapter.

The differences between the two types of accounting reflect the different user groups that they address. Briefly, the major differences are as follows:

- *Nature of the reports produced.* Financial accounting reports tend to be general purpose. That is, they contain financial information that will be useful for a broad range of users and decisions rather than being specifically designed for the needs of a particular group or set of decisions. Management accounting reports, on the other hand, are often for a specific purpose. They are designed either with a particular decision in mind or for a particular manager.

■ *Level of detail*. Financial accounting reports provide users with a broad overview of the performance and position of the business for a period. As a result, information is aggregated and detail is often lost. Management accounting reports, however, often provide managers with considerable detail to help them with a particular operational decision.

■ *Regulations*. Financial reports, for many businesses, are subject to accounting regulations that try to ensure they are produced with standard content and in a standard format. Law and accounting rule setters impose these regulations. Since management accounting reports are for internal use only, there are no regulations from external sources concerning the form and content of the reports. They can be designed to meet the needs of particular managers.

■ *Reporting interval*. For most businesses, financial accounting reports are produced on an annual basis, though many large businesses produce half-yearly reports and a few produce quarterly ones. Management accounting reports may be produced as frequently as required by managers. In many businesses, managers are provided with certain reports on a monthly, weekly or even daily basis, which allows them to check progress frequently. In addition, special-purpose reports will be prepared when required (for example, to evaluate a proposal to purchase a piece of machinery).

■ *Time horizon*. Financial accounting reports reflect the performance and position of the business for the past period. In essence, they are backward looking. Management accounting reports, on the other hand, often provide information concerning future performance as well as past performance. It is an oversimplification, however, to suggest that financial accounting reports never incorporate expectations concerning the future. Occasionally, businesses will release projected information to other users in an attempt to raise capital or to fight off unwanted takeover bids.

■ *Range and quality of information*. Financial accounting reports concentrate on information that can be quantified in monetary terms. Management accounting also produces such reports, but is also more likely to produce reports that contain information of a non-financial nature such as measures of physical quantities of inventories (stocks) and output. Financial accounting places greater emphasis on the use of objective, verifiable evidence when preparing reports. Management accounting reports may use information that is less objective and verifiable, but they provide managers with the information they need.

We can see from this that management accounting is less constrained than financial accounting. It may draw on a variety of sources and use information that has varying degrees of reliability. The only real test to be applied when assessing the value of the information produced for managers is whether or not it improves the quality of the decisions made.

The distinction between the two areas reflects, to some extent, the differences in access to financial information. Managers have much more control over the form and content of information they receive. Other users have to rely on what managers are prepared to provide or what the financial reporting regulations state must be provided. Though the scope of financial accounting reports has increased over time, fears concerning loss of competitive advantage and user ignorance concerning the reliability of forecast data have led businesses to resist providing other users with the detailed and wide-ranging information that is available to managers.

Activity 1.5

Are the information needs of managers and those of other users so very different?
Is there any overlap between the information needs of managers and the needs of other users?

The distinction between management and financial accounting suggests that there are differences between the information needs of managers and those of other users. Whilst differences undoubtedly exist, there is also a good deal of overlap between these needs. For example, managers will, at times, be interested in receiving an historical overview of business operations of the sort provided to other users. Equally, the other users would be interested in receiving information relating to the future, such as the planned level of profits and non-financial information such as the state of the sales order book and the extent of product innovations.

The scope of this book

This book covers both financial accounting and management accounting topics. Broadly speaking, the next five chapters (Chapters 2 to 6) are concerned with financial accounting topics, and the three thereafter (Chapters 7 to 9) with management accounting topics. The final part of the book, comprising Chapters 10 to 12, is concerned with financial management. That is, the chapters examine issues relating to the financing and investing activities of the business. Accounting information is usually vitally important for these kinds of decisions.

Has accounting become too interesting?

In recent years, accounting has become front-page news both in the USA and Europe and has become a major talking point among those connected with the world of business. Unfortunately, the attention that accounting has attracted has been for all the wrong reasons. We have seen that investors rely on financial reports to help to keep an eye on both their investment and the managers. However, what if the managers provide misleading financial reports to investors? Recent revelations suggest that the managers of some large companies have been doing just this.

Two of the most notorious cases have been those of Enron, an energy-trading business based in Texas, which was accused of entering into complicated financial arrangements in order to obscure losses and to inflate profits, and WorldCom, a major long-distance telephone operator in the US, which was accused of reclassifying $3.9 billion of expenses so as to falsely inflate the profit figure that the business reported to its owners (shareholders) and to others. In the wake of these scandals, there was much closer scrutiny by investment analysts and investors of the financial reports that businesses produce. This has led to further businesses, in both the US and Europe, being accused of using dubious accounting practices to bolster profits.

Various reasons have been put forward to explain this spate of scandals. Some may have been caused by the pressures on managers to meet unrealistic expectations of investors for continually rising profits, others by the greed of unscrupulous executives whose pay is linked to financial performance. However, they may all reflect a particular economic environment.

The US authorities have made it plain that they view the actions of unscrupulous executives with some hostility. In July 2005, Bernie Ebbers, the former chief executive of WorldCom was sentenced to 25 years in prison for his part in the fraud.

Real World 1.3 gives some comments suggesting that when all appears to be going well with a business, people can be quite gullible and over-trusting.

Real World 1.3

The thoughts of Warren Buffett

Warren Buffett is one of the world's shrewdest and most successful investors. He believes that the accounting scandals mentioned above were perpetrated during the 'new economy boom' of the late 1990s when confidence was high and exaggerated predictions were being made concerning the future. He states that during that period:

> You had an erosion of accounting standards. You had an erosion, to some extent, of executive behaviour. But during a period when everybody 'believes', people who are inclined to take advantage of other people can get away with a lot.

> He believes that the worst is now over and that the 'dirty laundry' created during this heady period is being washed away and that the washing machine is now in the 'rinse cycle'. However, he points out that: 'It's only in the rinse cycle that you find out how dirty the laundry has been.'

Source: *The Times*, Business Section, 26 September 2002, p. 25

Whatever the causes, the result of these accounting scandals has been to undermine the credibility of financial statements and to introduce much stricter regulations concerning the quality of financial information. We shall return to this issue in later chapters when we consider the financial statements.

Why do I need to know anything about accounting and finance?

At this point you may be asking yourself 'Why do I need to study accounting and finance? I don't intend to become an accountant!' Well, from the explanation of what accounting and finance is about, which has broadly been the subject of this chapter so far, it should be clear that the accounting/finance function within an organisation is a central part of its management information system. On the basis of information provided by the system, managers make decisions concerning the allocation of resources. These decisions may concern whether to:

- continue with certain business operations;
- invest in particular projects;
- sell particular products.

Such decisions can have a profound effect on all those connected with the organisation. It is important, therefore, that *all* those who intend to work in organisations should have a fairly clear idea of certain important aspects of accounting and finance. These aspects include:

- how financial reports should be read and interpreted;
- how financial plans are made;
- how investment decisions are made;
- how businesses are financed.

Many, perhaps most, students have a career goal of being a manager within an organisation – perhaps a personnel manager, production manager, marketing manager or IT manager. If you are one of these students, an understanding of accounting and finance is very important. When you become a manager, even a junior one, it is almost certain that you will have to use financial reports to help you to carry out your management tasks. It is equally certain that it is largely on the basis of financial information and reports that your performance as a manager will be judged.

As a manager, it is likely that you will be expected to help in forward planning for the organisation. This will often involve the preparation of projected financial statements and setting of financial targets.

If you do not understand what the financial statements really mean and the extent to which the financial information is reliable, you will find yourself at a distinct disadvantage to others who know their way round the system. As a manager, you will also be expected to help decide how the limited resources available to the business should be allocated between competing options. This will require an ability to evaluate the costs and benefits of the different options available. Once again, an understanding of accounting and finance is important to carrying out this management task.

This is not to say that you cannot be an effective and successful personnel, production, marketing or IT manager unless you are also a qualified accountant. It does mean, however, that you need to acquire a bit of 'street wisdom' in accounting and finance in order to succeed. This accounting and finance book aims to give you just that.

Business objectives

A business seeks to enhance the wealth of its owners, and throughout this book we shall assume that this is its main objective. This may come as a surprise, as there are other objectives that a business may pursue that are related to the needs of others associated with the business. For example, a business may seek to provide good working conditions for its employees, or it may seek to conserve the environment for the local community. While a business may pursue these objectives, it is normally set up with a view to increasing the wealth of its owners, and in practice the behaviour of businesses over time appears to be consistent with this objective.

Real World 1.4 provides an example of how many clothes retailers pursue the search for profit.

Real World 1.4

From rags to riches

Progress in the search for profit is reported by the accounting information system. If managers find that the reported profits are inadequate, this can be an important driver for change within a business. This change can, in turn, have a profound effect on the working lives of those both inside and outside the business.

Many clothes retailers have been concerned with profit levels in recent years. This has led them to make radical changes to the ways in which they operate. Low inflation and increased competition in the high street have forced the retailers to keep costs under strict control in order to meet their profit objectives. This has been done in various ways, including:

■ moving production to cheaper countries and closing inflexible manufacturing offshoots;
■ using fewer manufacturers and working more closely with manufacturers in the design of clothes. This has enabled the retailers to add details, such as embroidery or unusual design features, and to command a higher price for relatively little cost;
■ improving communication to suppliers of materials and to manufacturers so that design and sourcing decisions can be made faster and more accurately. This has meant that the time to make garments has been reduced from as much as nine months to just a few weeks;
■ predicting more accurately what customers want in order to avoid being left with inventories of unwanted items.

The effect of implementing these changes has been to reduce costs, and thereby improve profits, and to have more flexibility in the cost structure so that the clothes retailers are more able to weather a downturn.

Source: Adapted from 'Margin of success for clothing retailers', *The Times*, 20 November 2002, p. 30

The objective of increasing owners' wealth does not mean that other groups associated with the business (employees, customers, suppliers, the community and so on) can be ignored. If a business wishes to survive and prosper over the longer term, satisfying the needs of other groups will normally be necessary to increase the wealth of the owners over the longer term. A dissatisfied workforce, for example, may result in low productivity, strikes and so forth, which will in turn have an adverse effect on the wealth of the owners. Similarly, a business that upsets the local community by polluting the environment may attract bad publicity, resulting in a loss of customers and heavy fines. Real World 1.5 provides an example of how two businesses responded to potentially damaging allegations.

Real World 1.5

The price of clothes   **FT**

US clothing and sportswear manufacturers, Gap and Nike, have much of their clothes produced in Asia where labour tends to be cheap. However, some of the contractors that produce clothes on behalf of the two companies have been accused of unacceptable practices:

> Campaigners visited the factories and came up with damaging allegations. The factories were employing minors, they said, and managers were harassing female employees.
>
> Nike and Gap reacted by allowing independent inspectors into the factories. They promised to ensure their contractors obeyed minimum standards of employment. Earlier this year, Nike took the extraordinary step of publishing the names and addresses of all its contractors' factories on the internet. The company said it could not be sure all the abuse had stopped. It said that if campaigners visited its contractors' factories and found examples of continued malpractice, it would take action.
>
> Nike and Gap said the approach made business sense. They needed society's approval if they were to prosper. Nike said it was concerned about the reaction of potential US recruits to the campaigners' allegations. They would not want to work for a company that was constantly in the news because of the allegedly cruel treatment of those who made its products.

Source: 'Fair shares?', Michael Skapinker, *Financial Times*, 11 June 2005, FT.com

To generate as much wealth as possible for its owners, a business must do more than just maximise the current year's profit. Wealth is a longer-term concept, since it relates not only to this year's profit, but to that of future years as well. In the short term, corners can be cut and risks taken that improve current profit at the expense of future profit. Real World 1.6 gives some examples of how emphasis on short-term profit can be damaging.

> **Real World 1.6**
>
> ## Short-term gains, long-term problems   **FT**
>
> In recent years, many businesses have been criticised for failing to consider the long-term implications of their policies on the wealth of the owners. John Kay argues that some businesses have achieved growth in short-term increases in wealth by sacrificing their longer-term prosperity. He points out that:
>
> > . . . The business of Marks and Spencer, the retailer, was unparalleled in reputation but mature. To achieve earnings growth consistent with a glamour rating the company squeezed suppliers, gave less value for money, spent less on stores. In 1998, it achieved the highest (profit) margin in sales in the history of the business. It had also compromised its position to the point where sales and profits plummeted.
> >
> > Banks and insurance companies have taken staff out of branches and retrained those that remain as sales people. The pharmaceuticals industry has taken advantage of mergers to consolidate its research and development facilities. Energy companies have cut back on exploration.
> >
> > We know that these actions increased corporate earnings. We do not know what effect they have on the long-run strength of the business – and this is the key point – do the companies themselves know? Some rationalisations will genuinely lead to more productive businesses. Other companies will suffer the fate of Marks and Spencer.
>
> *Source*: 'Profit without honour', John Kay, *Financial Times Weekend*, 29/30 June 2002

Summary

The main points of this chapter may be summarised as follows:

What are accounting and finance?

- Accounting provides financial information for a range of users to help them make better judgements and decisions concerning a business.

- Finance also helps users to make better decisions and is concerned with the financing and investing activities of the business.

Accounting and user needs:

- For accounting to be useful, there must be a clear understanding of *for whom* and *for what purpose* the information will be used.

- Accounting can be viewed as a form of service as it involves providing financial information required by the various users.

- To provide a useful service, accounting must possess certain qualities, or characteristics. These are relevance, reliability, comparability and understandability. In addition, accounting information must be material.

- Providing a service to users can be costly and financial information should be produced only if the cost of providing the information is less than the benefits gained.

Accounting information:

- Accounting is part of the total information system within a business. It shares the features that are common to all information systems within a business, which are the identification, recording, analysis and reporting of information.
- Managers are among the most important users of financial information and they use financial information in planning and controlling business activities.
- Planning involves having a clear view of where the business is going and how it is going to get there. Controlling involves comparing planned performance with actual performance and taking corrective action where necessary.

Management and financial accounting:

- Accounting has two main strands – management accounting and financial accounting.
- Management accounting seeks to meet the needs of the business's managers and financial accounting seeks to meet the needs of the other user groups.
- These two strands differ in terms of the types of reports produced, the level of reporting detail, the time horizon, the degree of standardisation and the range and quality of information provided.

Is accounting too interesting?

- In recent years, there has been a wave of accounting scandals in the US and Europe.
- This appears to reflect a particular economic environment, although other factors may also play a part.

Why study accounting?

- Everyone connected with business should be a little 'streetwise' about accounting and finance. Financial information and decisions exert an enormous influence over the ways in which a business operates.

Accounting and business objectives:

- A business may pursue a variety of objectives but the main objective for virtually all businesses is to enhance the wealth of its owners. This does not mean, however, that the needs of other groups connected with the business, such as employees, should be ignored.

→ **Key terms**

accounting p. 2
finance p. 2
relevance p. 6
reliability p. 7
comparability p. 7
understandability p. 7

materiality p. 8
accounting information
    system p. 9
management accounting p. 13
financial accounting p. 13
financial management p. 15

Further reading

If you would like to explore the topics covered in this chapter in more depth, we recommend the following books:

Drury, C. *Management and Cost Accounting*, 6th edn, Thomson Learning, 2004, Chapter 1.

Elliot, B. and Elliot, J. *Financial Accounting and Reporting*, 9th edn, Prentice Hall, 2004, Chapter 30.

McLaney, E. *Business Finance: Theory and Practice*, 7th edn, Prentice Hall, 2006, Chapters 1 and 2.

McLaney, E. and Atrill, P. *Accounting: An Introduction*, 3rd edn, Prentice Hall, 2005, Chapter 1.

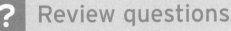

? Review questions

Answers to these questions can be found at the back of the book (pp. 486–7).

1.1 What is the purpose of producing accounting information?

1.2 Identify the main users of accounting information for a university. Do these users differ very much from the users of accounting information for private-sector businesses? Is there a major difference in the ways in which accounting information for a university would be used compared with that of a private-sector business?

1.3 Management accounting has been described as 'the eyes and ears of management'. What do you think this expression means?

1.4 Financial accounting statements tend to reflect past events. In view of this, how can they be of any assistance to a user in making a decision when decisions, by their very nature, can only be made about future actions?

Part 1

FINANCIAL ACCOUNTING

Chapter 2

Measuring and reporting financial position

Introduction

We saw in the previous chapter that accounting has two distinct strands – financial accounting and management accounting. This chapter, and Chapters 3 to 5, examine the three major financial statements that form the core of financial accounting. We begin by providing an overview of these statements to reveal how each contributes towards an assessment of the overall financial position and performance of a business.

Following this overview, we commence a more detailed examination by turning our attention towards one of these financial statements – the balance sheet. We shall see how it is prepared, and examine the principles underpinning this statement. We shall also consider its value for decision-making purposes.

Learning outcomes

When you have completed this chapter, you should be able to:

- explain the nature and purpose of the three major financial statements;
- prepare a simple balance sheet and interpret the information that it contains;
- discuss the accounting conventions underpinning the balance sheet;
- discuss the limitations of the balance sheet in portraying the financial position of a business.

The major financial statements – an overview

The objective of the major financial accounting statements is to provide a picture of the overall financial position and performance of the business. To achieve this objective, the business's accounting system will normally produce three particular statements on a regular, recurring basis. These three are concerned with answering the following questions:

- What cash movements (that is, cash in and cash out) took place over a particular period?
- How much wealth (that is, profit) was generated, or lost, by the business over that period?
- What is the accumulated wealth of the business at the end of that period?

These questions are addressed by the following three financial accounting statements, with each one addressing a particular question. The financial statements are:

- The cash flow statement
- The income statement (also known as the profit and loss account)
- The balance sheet.

Taken together, they provide an overall picture of the financial health of the business.

Perhaps the best way to introduce these financial statements is to look at an example of a very simple business. From this we shall be able to see the sort of information that each of the statements can usefully provide. It is, however, worth pointing out that, whilst a simple business is our starting point, the principles that we consider apply equally to more complex businesses. This means that we shall frequently encounter these principles again in later chapters.

Example 2.1

Paul was unemployed and unable to find a job. He therefore decided to embark on a business venture. Christmas was approaching, and so he decided to buy gift wrapping paper from a local supplier and to sell it on the corner of his local high street. He felt that the price of wrapping paper in the high street shops was excessive, and that this provided him with a useful business opportunity.

He began the venture with £40 in cash. On the first day of trading, he purchased wrapping paper for £40 and sold three-quarters of his inventories for £45 cash.

What cash movements took place during the first day of trading?

On the first day of trading, a *cash flow statement* showing the cash movements for the day can be prepared as follows:

Cash flow statement for day 1

	£
Opening balance (cash introduced)	40
Add Cash from sales of wrapping paper	45
	85
Less Cash paid to purchase wrapping paper	40
Closing balance of cash	45

How much wealth (that is, profit) was generated by the business during the first day of trading?

An *income statement* can be prepared to show the wealth (profit) generated on the first day. The wealth generated will represent the difference between the value of the sales made and the cost of the goods (that is, wrapping paper) sold:

Income statement for day 1

	£
Sales revenue	45
Less Cost of goods sold ($^3/_4$ of £40)	30
Profit	15

Note that it is only the cost of the wrapping paper *sold* that is matched against the sales revenue in order to find the profit, and not the whole of the cost of wrapping paper acquired. Any unsold inventories (in this case $^1/_4$ of £40 = £10) will be charged against the future sales revenue that it generates.

What is the accumulated wealth at the end of the first day?

To establish the accumulated wealth at the end of the first day, we can draw up a *balance sheet*. This will list the resources held at the end of that day:

Balance sheet at the end of day 1

	£
Cash (closing balance)	45
Inventories of goods for resale ($^1/_4$ of £40)	10
Total business wealth	55

We can see from the financial statements in Example 2.1 that each statement provides part of a picture that sets out the financial performance and position of the business. We begin by showing the cash movements. Cash is a vital resource that is necessary for any business to function effectively. Cash is required to meet debts that may become due and to acquire other resources (such as inventories). Cash has been described as the 'lifeblood' of a business, and movements in cash are usually given close scrutiny by users of financial statements.

However, it is clear that reporting cash movements alone would not be enough to portray the financial health of the business. The changes in cash over time do not give an insight into the profit generated. The income statement provides us with information concerning this aspect of performance. For day 1, for example, we saw that the cash balance increased by £5, but the profit generated, as shown in the income statement, was £15. The cash balance did not increase by the amount of the profit made because part of the wealth generated (£10) was held in the form of inventories.

A balance sheet can be drawn up at the end of the day, which should provide an insight to the total wealth of the business. Cash is only one form in which wealth can be held. In the case of this business, wealth is also held in the form of inventories (also known as stocks). Hence, when drawing up the balance sheet, both forms of wealth held will be listed. In the case of a large business, there may be many other forms in which wealth will be held, such as land and buildings, equipment, motor vehicles and so on.

Let us now continue with our example.

Example 2.1 (continued)

On the second day of trading, Paul purchased more wrapping paper for £20 cash. He managed to sell all of the new inventories and all of the earlier inventories, for a total of £48.

The cash flow statement on day 2 will be as follows:

Cash flow statement for day 2

	£
Opening balance (from the end of day 1)	45
Add Cash from sales of wrapping paper	48
	93
Less Cash paid to purchase wrapping paper	20
Closing balance	73

The income statement for day 2 will be as follows:

Income statement for day 2

	£
Sales revenue	48
Less Cost of goods sold (£20 + £10)	30
Profit	18

The balance sheet at the end of day 2 will be:

Balance sheet at the end of day 2

	£
Cash (closing balance)	73
Inventories	–
Total business wealth	73

We can see that the total business wealth increased to £73 by the end of day 2. This represents an increase of £18 (that is, £73 − £55) over the previous day – which, of course, is the amount of profit made during day 2 as shown on the income statement.

Activity 2.1

On the third day of his business venture, Paul purchased more inventories for £46 cash. However, it was raining hard for much of the day and sales were slow. After Paul had sold half of his total inventories for £32, he decided to stop trading until the following day.

Have a go at drawing up the three financial statements for day 3 of Paul's business venture.

Cash flow statement for day 3

	£
Opening balance (from the end of day 2)	73
Add Cash from sales of wrapping paper	32
	105
Less Cash paid to purchase wrapping paper	46
Closing balance	59

Income statement for day 3

	£
Sales revenue	32
Less Cost of goods sold ($^{1}/_{2}$ of £46)	23
Profit	9

Balance sheet at the end of day 3

	£
Cash (closing balance)	59
Inventories ($^{1}/_{2}$ of £46)	23
Total business wealth	82

Note that the total business wealth had increased by £9 (that is, the amount of the day's profit) even though the cash balance had declined. This is because the business is holding more of its wealth in the form of inventories rather than cash, compared with the end of day 2.

We can see that the income statement and cash flow statement are both concerned with measuring flows (of wealth and cash respectively) during a particular period (for example, a particular day, a particular month or a particular year). The balance sheet, however, is concerned with the financial position at a particular moment in time.

Figure 2.1 illustrates this point. The financial statements (income statement, cash flow statement and balance sheet) are often referred to as the final accounts of the business.

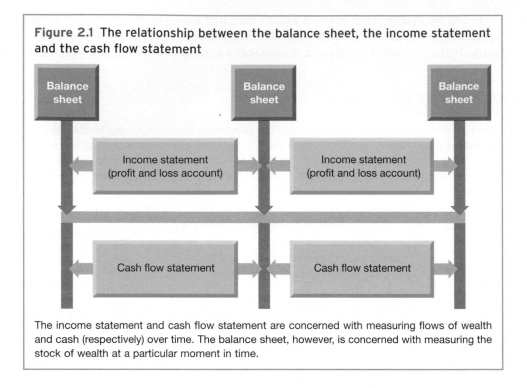

Figure 2.1 The relationship between the balance sheet, the income statement and the cash flow statement

The income statement and cash flow statement are concerned with measuring flows of wealth and cash (respectively) over time. The balance sheet, however, is concerned with measuring the stock of wealth at a particular moment in time.

For external users, these statements are normally backward looking because they are based on information concerning past events and transactions. This can be useful in providing feedback on past performance, and in identifying trends that provide clues to future performance. However, the statements can also be prepared using projected data to help assess likely future profits, cash flows and so on. The financial statements are normally prepared on a projected basis for internal decision-making purposes only. Managers are usually reluctant to publish these projected statements for external users, as they may reveal valuable information to competitors.

Now that we have an overview of the financial statements, we shall consider each statement in more detail. We shall go straight on to look at the balance sheet. Chapter 3 looks at the income statement, Chapter 5 goes into more detail on the cash flow statement. (Chapter 4 considers the balance sheets and income statements of limited companies.)

The balance sheet

The purpose of the balance sheet is simply to set out the financial position of a business at a particular moment in time. (The balance sheet is sometimes referred to as the *position statement*, because it seeks to provide the user with a picture of financial position.) We saw above that the balance sheet will reveal the forms in which the wealth of the business is held and how much wealth is held in each form. We can, however, be more specific about the nature of the balance sheet by saying that it sets out the assets of the business on the one hand, and the claims against the business on the other. Before looking at the balance sheet in more detail, we need to be clear about what these terms mean.

Assets

An asset is essentially a resource held by the business. For a particular item to be treated as an asset for accounting purposes it should have the following characteristics:

- *A probable future benefit must exist.* This simply means that the item must be expected to have some future monetary value. This value can arise through its use within the business or through its hire or sale. Thus, an obsolete piece of equipment that could be sold for scrap would still be considered an asset, whereas an obsolete piece of equipment that could not be sold for scrap would not be regarded as one.
- *The business must have an exclusive right to control the benefit.* Unless the business has exclusive rights over the resource it cannot be regarded as an asset. Thus, for a business offering holidays on barges, the canal system may be a very valuable resource, but as the business will not be able to control the access of others to the canals, it cannot be regarded as an asset of the business. (However, the barges owned by the business would be regarded as assets.)
- *The benefit must arise from some past transaction or event.* This means that the transaction (or other event) giving rise to the business's right to the benefit must have already occurred, and will not arise at some future date. Thus an agreement by a business to purchase a piece of machinery at some future date would not mean the item is currently an asset of the business.
- *The asset must be capable of measurement in monetary terms.* Unless the item can be measured in monetary terms, with a reasonable degree of reliability, it will not be regarded as an asset for inclusion on the balance sheet. Thus, the title of a magazine (for example *Hello!* or *Vogue*) that was created by its publisher may be extremely valuable to the business, but this value is usually impossible to quantify. It will not, therefore, be treated as an asset.

Note that all four of these conditions must apply. If one of them is missing, the item will not be treated as an asset, for accounting purposes, and will not appear on the balance sheet.

We can see that these conditions will strictly limit the kind of items that may be referred to as 'assets' in the balance sheet. Certainly not all resources exploited by a business will be assets of the business for accounting purposes. Some, like the canal system or the magazine title *Hello!*, may well be assets in a broader sense, but not for accounting purposes. Once an asset has been acquired by a business, it will continue to be considered an asset until the benefits are exhausted or the business disposes of it in some way.

Activity 2.2

Indicate which of the following items could appear as an asset on the balance sheet of a business. Explain your reasoning in each case.

1 £1,000 owing to the business by a customer who is unable to pay.
2 The purchase of a patent from an inventor that gives the business the right to produce a new product. Production of the new product is expected to increase profits over the period during which the patent is held.
3 The business hiring a new marketing director who is confidently expected to increase profits by over 30 per cent over the next three years.
4 The purchase of a machine that will save the business £10,000 each year. It is currently being used by the business but it has been acquired on credit and is not yet paid for.

Your answer should be along the following lines:

1 Under normal circumstances a business would expect a customer to pay the amount owed. Such an amount is therefore typically shown as an asset under the heading 'receivables' or 'debtors'. However, in this particular case the customer is unable to pay. Hence the item is incapable of providing future benefits, and the £1,000 owing would not be regarded as an asset. Debts that are not paid are referred to as 'bad debts'.
2 The purchase of the patent would meet all of the conditions set out above and would therefore be regarded as an asset.
3 The hiring of a new marketing director would not be considered as the acquisition of an asset. One argument against its classification as an asset is that the business does not have exclusive rights of control over the director. (Nevertheless, it may have an exclusive right to the services that the director provided.) Perhaps a stronger argument is that the value of the director cannot be measured in monetary terms with any degree of reliability.
4 The machine would be considered an asset even though it is not yet paid for. Once the business has agreed to purchase the machine, and has accepted it, the machine is legally owned by the business even though payment is still outstanding. (The amount outstanding would be shown as a claim, as we shall see below.)

The sorts of items that often appear as assets in the balance sheet of a business include:

■ freehold premises;
■ machinery and equipment;
■ fixtures and fittings;
■ patents and trademarks;
■ receivables (debtors);
■ investments.

Activity 2.3

Can you think of three additional items that might appear as assets in the balance sheet of a business?

You may be able to think of a number of other items. Some that you may have identified are:

- motor vehicles;
- inventories (stocks);
- computer equipment;
- cash at bank.

Note that an asset does not have to be a physical item – it may also be a non-physical right to certain benefits. Assets that have a physical substance and can be touched are referred to as tangible assets. Assets that have no physical substance but which, nevertheless, provide expected future benefits (such as patents) are referred to as intangible assets.

Claims

A claim is an obligation on the part of the business to provide cash, or some other form of benefit, to an outside party. A claim will normally arise as a result of the outside party providing funds in the form of assets for use by the business. There are essentially two types of claim against a business:

- Capital. This represents the claim of the owner(s) against the business. This claim is sometimes referred to as the *owner's equity*. Some find it hard to understand how the owner can have a claim against the business, particularly when we consider the example of a sole-proprietor-type business where the owner *is*, in effect, the business. However, for accounting purposes, a clear distinction is made between the business (whatever its size) and the owner(s). The business is viewed as being quite separate from the owner and this is equally true for a sole proprietor like Paul, the wrapping-paper seller, in Example 2.1, or a large company like Marks and Spencer plc. It is seen as a separate entity with its own separate existence and when financial statements are prepared, they are prepared for the business rather than for the owner(s). This means that the balance sheet should reflect the financial position of the business as a separate entity. Viewed from this perspective, any funds contributed by the owner will be seen as coming from outside the business and will appear as a claim against the business in its balance sheet.

  As we have just seen, the business and the owner are separate for accounting purposes, irrespective of the type of business concerned. It is also true that the operation of the capital section of the balance sheet is broadly the same irrespective of the type of business concerned. As we shall see in Chapter 4, with limited companies the capital figure must be analysed according to how each part of the capital first arose. For example, companies must make a distinction between that part of the capital that arose from retained profits and that part that arose from the owners putting in cash to start up the business.

→   ■ Liabilities. Liabilities represent the claims of all other individuals and organisations, apart from the owner(s). Liabilities must have arisen from past transactions or events such as supplying goods or lending money to the business.

Once a claim has been incurred by a business, it will remain as an obligation until it is settled.

Now that the meaning of the terms *assets* and *claims* has been established, we can go on and discuss the relationship between the two. This relationship is quite simple and straightforward. If a business wishes to acquire assets, it will have to raise the necessary funds from somewhere. It may raise the funds from the owner(s) or from other outside parties or from both. To illustrate the relationship let us take the example of a business, as set out in Example 2.2.

Example 2.2

Jerry and Co. deposits £20,000 in a bank account on 1 March in order to commence business. Let us assume that the cash is supplied by the owner (£6,000) and by a lender (£14,000) and paid into the business bank account. The raising of the funds in this way will give rise to a claim on the business by both the owner (capital) and the lender (liability). If a balance sheet of Jerry and Co. is prepared following the above transactions, the assets and claims of the business will appear as follows:

Jerry and Co.
Balance sheet as at 1 March

	£		£
Assets		Claims	
Cash at bank	20,000	Capital	6,000
		Liability – loan	14,000
	20,000		20,000

We can see from the balance sheet that has been prepared that the total claims are the same as the total assets. Thus:

$$\text{Assets} = \text{Capital} + \text{Liabilities}$$

This equation – which is often referred to as the *balance sheet equation* – will always hold true. Whatever changes may occur to the assets of the business or the claims against the business, there will be compensating changes elsewhere that will ensure that the balance sheet always 'balances'. By way of illustration, consider the following transactions for Jerry and Co.:

2 March	Purchased a motor van for £5,000, paying by cheque.
3 March	Purchased inventories (that is, goods to be sold) on one month's credit for £3,000. (This means that the inventories will be bought on 3 March, but payment will not be made to the supplier until 3 April.)
4 March	Repaid £2,000 of the loan from the lender.
6 March	Owner introduced another £4,000 into the business bank account.

A balance sheet may be drawn up after each day in which transactions have taken place. In this way, the effect can be seen of each transaction on the assets and claims of the business. The balance sheet as at 2 March will be as follows:

Jerry and Co.
Balance sheet as at 2 March

Assets	£	Claims	£
Cash at bank (20,000 – 5,000)	15,000	Capital	6,000
Motor van	5,000	Liabilities – loan	14,000
	20,000		20,000

As can be seen, the effect of purchasing a motor van is to decrease the balance at the bank by £5,000 and to introduce a new asset – a motor van – to the balance sheet. The total assets remain unchanged. It is only the 'mix' of assets that will change. The claims against the business will remain the same because there has been no change in the way in which the business has been funded.

The balance sheet as at 3 March, following the purchase of inventories, will be as follows:

Jerry and Co.
Balance sheet as at 3 March

Assets	£	Claims	£
Cash at bank	15,000	Capital	6,000
Motor van	5,000	Liabilities – loan	14,000
Inventories (stock)	3,000	Liabilities – trade payable	3,000
	23,000		23,000

The effect of purchasing inventories has been to introduce another new asset (inventories) to the balance sheet. In addition, the fact that the goods have not yet been paid for means that the claims against the business will be increased by the £3,000 owed to the supplier, who is referred to as a *trade payable* (or trade creditor) on the balance sheet.

Activity 2.4

Try drawing up a balance sheet for Jerry and Co. as at 4 March.

The balance sheet as at 4 March, following the repayment of part of the loan, will be as follows:

Jerry and Co.
Balance sheet as at 4 March

Assets	£	Claims	£
Cash at bank (15,000 – 2,000)	13,000	Capital	6,000
Motor van	5,000	Liabilities – loan (14,000 – 2,000)	12,000
Inventories (stock)	3,000	Liabilities – trade payable (creditor)	3,000
	21,000		21,000

The repayment of £2,000 of the loan will result in a decrease in the balance at the bank of £2,000 and a decrease in the loan claim against the business by the same amount.

Activity 2.5

Try drawing up a balance sheet as at 6 March for Jerry and Co.

The balance sheet as at 6 March, following the introduction of more funds, will be as follows:

Jerry and Co.
Balance sheet as at 6 March

Assets	£	Claims	£
Cash at bank (13,000 + 4,000)	17,000	Capital (6,000 + 4,000)	10,000
Motor van	5,000	Liabilities – loan	12,000
Inventories (stock)	3,000	Liabilities – trade payable (creditor)	3,000
	25,000		25,000

The introduction of more funds by the owner will result in an increase in the capital of £4,000 and an increase in the cash at bank by the same amount.

Example 2.2 illustrates the point that the balance sheet equation (assets equals capital plus liabilities) will always hold true, because it reflects the fact that, if a business wishes to acquire assets, it must raise funds equal to the cost of those assets. The funds raised must be provided by the owners (capital), or by others (liabilities) or by both the owners and others. Hence the total cost of assets acquired should always equal the total capital plus liabilities.

It is worth pointing out that in real life businesses do not normally draw up a balance sheet after each day, as shown in the example above. Such an approach is not likely to be useful, given the relatively small number of transactions each day. We have done this in our examples to see the effect on the balance sheet transaction by transaction. In real life a balance sheet for the business is usually prepared at the end of a defined reporting period.

Determining the length of the reporting interval will involve weighing up the costs of producing the information against the perceived benefits of the information for decision-making purposes. In practice, the reporting interval will vary between businesses, and could be monthly, quarterly, half-yearly or annually. For external reporting purposes, an annual reporting cycle is the norm (although certain businesses, typically larger ones, report more frequently than this). However, for internal reporting purposes to managers, many businesses produce monthly financial statements.

The effect of trading operations on the balance sheet

In the example we considered earlier, we dealt with the effect on the balance sheet of a number of different types of transactions that a business might undertake. These transactions covered the purchase of assets for cash and on credit, the repayment of a loan, and the injection of capital. However, one form of transaction, trading, has not yet been considered. To deal with the effect of trading transactions on the balance sheet, let us return to our earlier example.

Example 2.2 (continued)

The balance sheet that we drew up for Jerry and Co. as at 6 March was as follows:

Jerry and Co.
Balance sheet as at 6 March

Assets	£	Claims	£
Cash at bank	17,000	Capital	10,000
Motor van	5,000	Liabilities – loan	12,000
Inventories (stock)	3,000	Liabilities – trade payable (creditor)	3,000
	25,000		25,000

Let us assume that, on 7 March, the business managed to sell all of the inventories for £5,000 and received a cheque immediately from the customer for this amount. The balance sheet on 7 March, after this transaction has taken place, will be as follows:

Jerry and Co.
Balance sheet as at 7 March

Assets	£	Claims	£
Cash at bank (17,000 + 5,000)	22,000	Capital [10,000 + (5,000 – 3,000)]	12,000
Motor van	5,000	Liabilities – loan	12,000
Inventories (stock) (3,000 – 3,000)	–	Liabilities – trade payable (creditor)	3,000
	27,000		27,000

→

We can see that the inventories (£3,000) have now disappeared from the balance sheet, but the cash at bank has increased by the selling price of the inventories (£5,000). The net effect has therefore been to increase assets by £2,000 (that is £5,000 – £3,000). This increase represents the net increase in wealth (the profit) that has arisen from trading. Also note that the capital of the business has increased by £2,000, in line with the increase in assets. This increase in capital reflects the fact that increases in wealth, as a result of trading or other operations, will be to the benefit of the owners and will increase their stake in the business.

Activity 2.6

What would have been the effect on the balance sheet if the inventories had been sold on 7 March for £1,000 rather than £5,000?

The balance sheet on 7 March would be as follows:

Jerry and Co.
Balance sheet as at 7 March

Assets	£	Claims	£
Cash at bank (17,000 + 1,000)	18,000	Capital [10,000 + (1,000 – 3,000)]	8,000
Motor van	5,000	Liabilities – loan	12,000
Inventories (stock) (3,000 – 3,000)	–	Liabilities – trade payable (creditor)	3,000
	23,000		23,000

As we can see, the inventories (£3,000) will disappear from the balance sheet, but the cash at bank will rise by only £1,000. This will mean a net reduction in assets of £2,000. This reduction represents a loss arising from trading and will be reflected in a reduction in the capital of the owner.

We can see that any decrease in wealth (loss) arising from trading or other transactions will lead to a reduction in the owner's stake in the business. If the business wished to maintain the level of assets as at 6 March, it would be necessary to obtain further funds from the owner or from lenders, or both.

What we have just seen means that the balance sheet equation can be extended as follows:

Assets = Capital (at the start of the period) + Profit/– Loss (for the period) + Liabilities

As we have seen, the profit or loss for the period impacts on the balance sheet as an addition to capital. Any funds introduced or withdrawn by the owner for living expenses or other reasons also affect capital, but are shown separately. By doing this, we provide more comprehensive information for users of the financial statements. If we assume that the above business sold the inventories for £5,000, as in the earlier example, and further assume that the owner withdrew £1,500 for his or her own use, the capital of the owner would appear as follows on the balance sheet:

		£
Capital (owner's equity)		
Opening balance		10,000
Add Profit		2,000
		12,000
Less Drawings		1,500
Closing balance		10,500

If the drawings were in cash, the balance of cash would decrease by £1,500 in the balance sheet.

Note that, like all balance sheet items, the amount of capital is cumulative. This means that any profit made that is not taken out as drawings by the owner(s) remains in the business. These retained (or 'ploughed-back') profits have the effect of expanding the business.

The classification of assets

If the items on the balance sheet are listed haphazardly, with assets listed on one side and claims on the other, it can be confusing. To help users to understand more clearly the information that is presented, assets and claims are usually grouped into categories. Assets may be categorised as being either current or non-current.

Current assets

Current assets are basically assets that are held for the short term. To be more precise, they are assets that meet any one of four criteria. These are:

- they are held for sale or consumption in the normal course of a business's operating cycle;
- they are for the short term (that is, to be sold within the next year);
- they are held primarily for trading;
- they are cash, or near cash such as easily marketable, short-term investments.

The most common current assets are inventories (or stock), customers who owe money for goods or services supplied on credit (known as trade receivables or debtors), and cash.

Perhaps it is worth making the point here that most sales made by most businesses are made on credit. This is to say that the goods pass to, or the service is rendered to, the customer at one point but the customer pays later. Retail sales are the only significant exception to this general point.

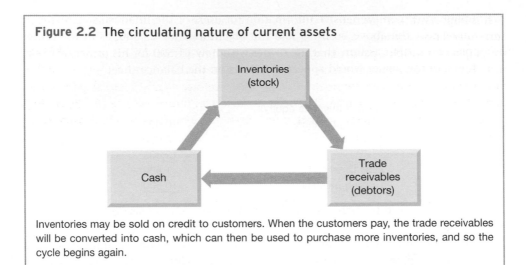

Figure 2.2 The circulating nature of current assets

Inventories may be sold on credit to customers. When the customers pay, the trade receivables will be converted into cash, which can then be used to purchase more inventories, and so the cycle begins again.

For businesses that sell goods, rather than render a service, the current assets of inventories, trade receivables and cash are interrelated. They circulate within a business as shown in Figure 2.2. We can see that cash can be used to purchase inventories, which is then sold on credit. When the credit customers (trade receivables) pay, the business receives an injection of cash, and so on.

For service businesses, the situation is similar, except that inventories are not bought in.

Non-current assets

Non-current assets (also called fixed assets) are assets that do not meet the above criteria. They are held for the long-term operations of the business. Essentially, they are the 'tools' of the business and are held with the objective of generating wealth.

This distinction between assets that are continuously circulating within the business and assets used for long-term operations may be helpful when trying to assess the appropriateness of the mix of assets held. A business will need a certain amount of both types of asset to operate effectively.

Activity 2.7

Can you think of two examples of assets that may be classified as non-current assets?

Examples of assets that may be defined as being non-current are:

- freehold premises;
- plant and machinery;
- motor vehicles;
- patents.

This is not an exhaustive list. You may have thought of others.

It is important to appreciate that how a particular asset is classified (that is, between current and non-current) varies according to the nature of the business. This is because the *purpose* for which a particular type of asset is held may differ from business to business. For example, a motor vehicle manufacturer will normally hold inventories of the motor vehicles produced for resale, and would therefore classify them as part of the current assets. On the other hand, a business that uses motor vehicles for delivering its goods to customers (that is, as part of its long-term operations) would classify them as non-current assets.

Activity 2.8

The assets of Kunalun and Co., a large advertising agency, are as follows:

- cash at bank;
- fixtures and fittings;
- office equipment;
- motor vehicles;
- freehold office premises;
- computer equipment;
- work-in-progress (that is, partly completed work for clients).

Which of these do you think should be defined as non-current assets, and which should be defined as current assets?

Your answer should be as follows:

Non-current assets	Current assets
Fixtures and fittings	Cash at bank
Office equipment	Work-in-progress
Motor vehicles	
Freehold office premises	
Computer equipment	

The classification of claims

As we have already seen, claims are normally classified into capital (owner's claim) and liabilities (claims of outsiders). Liabilities are further classified into two groups:

- **Current liabilities** are basically amounts due for settlement in the short term. To be more precise, they are liabilities that meet any one of four criteria:
  - they expect to be settled within the normal course of the business's operating cycle;
  - they are due to be settled within 12 months of the balance sheet date;
  - they are held primarily for trading purposes;
  - the business does not have the right to defer settlement beyond 12 months after the balance sheet date.
- **Non-current liabilities** represent those amounts due to outside parties that are not current liabilities.

This classification of liabilities can help gain an insight into the ability of the business to meet its maturing obligations (that is, claims that must shortly be met). The value of the current liabilities (that is the amounts that must be paid within the normal operating cycle), can be compared with the value of the current assets (that is the assets that are either cash or will turn into cash within the same period).

The classification of liabilities should also help to highlight how the long-term finance of the business is raised. If a business relies on long-term loans to finance the business, the financial risks associated with the business will increase. This is because these loans will bring a commitment to make interest payments and capital repayments and the business may be forced to stop trading if this commitment is not fulfilled. Thus, when raising long-term finance, a business must strike the right balance between non-current liabilities and owner's capital. We shall consider this issue in more detail in Chapter 6.

Activity 2.9

Can you think of one example of a current liability and one of a non-current liability?

An example of a non-current liability would be a long-term loan. An example of a current liability would be amounts owing to suppliers for goods supplied on credit (known as trade payables or trade creditors) or a bank overdraft (a form of bank borrowing that is repayable on demand).

Balance sheet formats

Now that we have looked at the classification of assets and liabilities, we shall consider the format of the balance sheet. Although there is an almost infinite number of ways in which the same balance sheet information could be presented, we shall consider two basic formats. The first of these follows the style we adopted with Jerry and Co. earlier. A more comprehensive example of this style is shown in Example 2.3.

Within each category of asset (non-current and current) shown in Example 2.3, the items are listed in reverse order of liquidity (nearness to cash). Thus, the assets that are furthest from cash are listed first and the assets that are closest to cash are listed last. In the case of non-current assets, freehold premises are listed first as these assets are usually the most difficult to turn into cash and motor vans are listed last as there is usually a ready market for them. In the case of current assets, we have already seen that inventories are converted to receivables and then receivables are converted to cash. Hence, under the heading of current assets, inventories are listed first, followed by receivables and finally cash itself.

This ordering of assets is a normal practice, which is followed irrespective of the format used. Note also that the current assets are listed individually in the first column, and a subtotal of current assets (£53,000) is carried out to the second column to be

Example 2.3

Brie Manufacturing
Balance sheet as at 31 December 2005

	£000	£000		£000
Non-current assets			**Capital**	
Freehold premises		45	Opening balance	50
Plant and machinery		30	*Add* Profit	14
Motor vans		19		64
		94	*Less* Drawings	4
				60
			Non-current liabilities	
			Loan	50
Current assets			**Current liabilities**	
Inventories (stock)	23		Trade payables (creditors)	37
Trade receivables (debtors)	18			
Cash at bank	12			
		53		
		147		147

added to the subtotal of non-current assets (£94,000). This convention is designed to make the balance sheet easier to read.

An obvious change to the format illustrated in Example 2.3 is to show claims on the left and assets on the right. Some people prefer this approach because the claims can be seen as the source of finance for the business, and the assets show how that finance has been deployed. It could be seen as more logical to show sources first and uses second.

The format shown above is sometimes referred to as the *horizontal layout*. However, in recent years, a more common form of layout for the balance sheet is the *vertical* (or *narrative*) form of layout. This format is really based on a rearrangement of the balance sheet equation. With the horizontal format above, the balance sheet equation is set out as in Figure 2.3. The vertical format merely rearranges this equation as shown in Figure 2.4.

Figure 2.3 The horizontal balance sheet

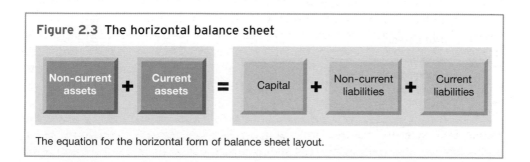

The equation for the horizontal form of balance sheet layout.

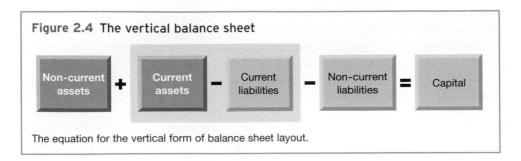

Figure 2.4 The vertical balance sheet

The equation for the vertical form of balance sheet layout.

The vertical layout not only rearranges the equation but, as the name suggests, presents the information vertically rather than horizontally. The balance sheet starts with non-current assets and works downwards towards capital at the end. The balance sheet of Brie Manufacturing that was arranged in horizontal format in Example 2.3 can be rearranged in vertical format as shown in Example 2.4.

Example 2.4

Brie Manufacturing
Balance sheet as at 31 December 2005

	£000	£000
Non-current assets		
Freehold premises		45
Plant and machinery		30
Motor vans		19
		94
Current assets		
Inventories (stock)	23	
Trade receivables (debtors)	18	
Cash at bank	12	
	53	
Less **Current liabilities**		
Trade payables (creditors)	37	
		16
Total assets *less* current liabilities		110
Less **Non-current liabilities**		
Loan		50
Net assets		60
Capital		
Opening balance		50
Add Profit		14
		64
Less Drawings		4
		60

Some people find the vertical format of Example 2.4 easier to read than the horizontal format as it usefully highlights the relationship between current assets and current liabilities. The figure derived from deducting current liabilities from the current assets is sometimes referred to as *net current assets* or *working capital*. We can see that for Brie Manufacturing this figure is £16,000, indicating that the short-term liquid assets more than cover the short-term claims against the business.

? Self-assessment question 2.1

The following information relates to Simonson Engineering as at 30 September 2005:

	£
Plant and machinery	25,000
Trade payables (creditors)	18,000
Bank overdraft	26,000
Inventories (stock)	45,000
Freehold premises	72,000
Long-term loans	51,000
Trade receivables (debtors)	48,000
Capital at 1 October 2004	117,500
Cash in hand	1,500
Motor vehicles	15,000
Fixtures and fittings	9,000
Profit for the year to 30 September 2005	18,000
Drawings for the year to 30 September 2005	15,000

Required:
Prepare a balance sheet in the vertical format.

The balance sheet as a position at a point in time

As we have already seen, the balance sheet is a statement of the financial position of the business at *a specified point in time*. The balance sheet has been compared to a photograph. A photograph 'freezes' a particular moment in time and will represent the situation only at that moment. Hence, events may be quite different immediately before and immediately after the photograph was taken. Similarly, the balance sheet represents a 'snapshot' of the business at a particular moment. When examining a balance sheet, therefore, it is important to establish the date at which it has been drawn up. This information should be prominently displayed in the balance sheet heading, as shown above in Example 2.4. The more recent the balance sheet date, the better when we are trying to assess the current financial position.

A business will normally prepare a balance sheet as at the close of business on the last day of its accounting year. In the UK, businesses are free to choose their accounting year. When making a decision on which year-end date to choose, commercial convenience can often be a deciding factor. Thus, a business operating in the retail trade may choose to have a year-end date early in the calendar year (for example 31 January) because trade tends to be slack during that period and more staff time is available to help with the tasks involved in the preparation of the annual financial statements (such as checking the amount of inventories held). Since trade is slack, it is also a time when the amount of inventories held by the retail business is likely to be unusually low as compared with other times of the year. Thus the balance sheet, though showing a fair view of what it purports to show, may not show a picture of what is more typically the position of the business over the rest of the year.

Accounting conventions and the balance sheet

Accounting is based on a number of rules or conventions that have evolved over time. They have evolved as attempts to deal with practical problems experienced by preparers and users, rather than to reflect some theoretical ideal. In preparing the balance sheets earlier, we have followed various accounting conventions, although they have not been explicitly mentioned. We shall now identify and discuss the major conventions that we have applied.

Business entity convention

For accounting purposes, the business and its owner(s) are treated as being quite separate and distinct. This is why owners are treated as being claimants against their own business in respect of their investment in the business. The business entity convention must be distinguished from the legal position that may exist between businesses and their owners. For sole proprietorships and partnerships, the law does not make any distinction between the business and its owner(s). For limited companies, on the other hand, there is a clear legal distinction between the business and its owners. (As we shall see in Chapter 4, the limited company is regarded as having a separate legal existence.) For accounting purposes these legal distinctions are irrelevant, and the business entity convention applies to all businesses.

Money measurement convention

Accounting normally deals with only those items that are capable of being expressed in monetary terms. Money has the advantage that it is a useful common denominator with which to express the wide variety of resources held by a business. However, not all such resources are capable of being measured in monetary terms and so will be excluded from a balance sheet. The money measurement convention, therefore, limits the scope of accounting reports.

Activity 2.10

Can you think of resources held by a business that cannot be quantified in monetary terms?

In answering this activity you may have thought of the following:

- the quality of the workforce;
- the reputation of the business's products;
- the location of the business;
- the relationship with customers;
- the ability of the managers.

Over the years, attempts have been made to measure, and then include on the balance sheet, resources of a business that have been previously excluded. For example, there have been attempts to measure the 'human assets' of the business. It is often claimed that employees are the most valuable 'assets' of a business. By measuring these assets and putting the amount on the balance sheet, it is sometimes argued that we have a more complete picture of the financial position. However, these attempts are resisted because they involve softening the recognition criteria for an asset that we discussed earlier in the chapter. It is feared by some that such a softening of the rules could lead to uncertainty and inconsistency, which in turn could cause the financial statements to lack credibility. Real World 2.1 shows how one business has succeeded in putting people on the balance sheet.

Real World 2.1

On the team sheet and on the balance sheet

It may be surprising to learn that although human 'assets' are not shown on the balance sheet of a business as a general rule, there are exceptions to this rule. The most common exception arises with professional football clubs. Although football clubs cannot own players, they can own the rights to the players' services. Where these rights are acquired by compensating other clubs for releasing the players from their contracts, the amounts paid provide a reliable basis for measurement. This means that the rights to services can be regarded as an asset of the club for accounting purposes (assuming, of course, the player will also bring benefits to the club).

Newcastle United Football Club (NU) has acquired several key players as a result of paying transfer fees. In common with most UK football clubs, NU reports the cost of acquiring those rights to the players' services in its balance sheet. The balance sheet for 2004 shows the cost of registering its current squad of players as being nearly £80 million. The item of players' registrations is shown as an intangible asset in the balance sheet as it is the rights to services not the players that are the assets. The figure of £80 million includes the cost of bought-in players such as James Milner (for £3.5m from Leeds United) but not 'home-grown' players or those who came to the club on a free transfer from another club, such as Patrick Kluivert. These players are not included because Newcastle United did not pay a transfer fee for them and so no clear-cut value can be placed on their services. These two players have now left the club, but were both there at the 2004 balance sheet date.

Source: Newcastle United PLC Annual Report 2004

Historic cost convention

Assets are shown on the balance sheet at a value that is based on their historic cost (that is, acquisition cost). This method of measuring asset value has been adopted by accountants in preference to methods based on some form of current value. Many people find the historic cost convention difficult to support, as outdated historic costs are unlikely to help in the assessment of current financial position. It is often argued that recording assets at their current value would provide a more realistic view of financial position and would be relevant for a wide range of decisions. However, a system of measurement based on current values can present a number of problems.

Activity 2.11

Can you think of reasons why current value accounting may pose problems for both preparers and users of financial statements?

The term 'current value' can be defined in a number of ways. For example, it can be defined broadly as either the current replacement cost or the current realisable value (selling price) of an asset. These two types of valuation may result in quite different figures being produced to represent the current value of an item. (Think, for example, of second-hand car values: there is often quite a difference between buying and selling prices.) In addition, the broad terms 'replacement cost' and 'realisable value' can be defined in different ways. We must therefore be clear about what kind of current value accounting we wish to use. There are also practical problems associated with attempts to implement any system of current value accounting. For example, current values, however defined, are often difficult to establish with any real degree of objectivity. This may mean that the figures produced are heavily dependent on the opinion of managers. Unless the current value figures are capable of some form of independent verification, there is a danger that the financial statements will lose their credibility among users.

By reporting assets at their historic cost, it is argued that more reliable information is produced. Reporting in this way reduces the need for subjective judgements, as the amount paid for a particular asset is usually a matter of demonstrable fact. However, information based on past costs may not always be relevant to the needs of users.

Later in the chapter, we shall consider the valuation of assets in the balance sheet in more detail. We shall see that the historic cost convention is not always rigidly adhered to, and that departures from this convention often occur.

Going concern convention

The going concern convention holds that the financial statements should be prepared on the assumption that the business will continue operations for the foreseeable future, unless this is known not to be true. In other words, it is assumed that there is no intention, or need, to sell off the non-current assets of the business. Such a sale may arise where the business is in financial difficulties and needs to pay amounts borrowed that are due for repayment. This convention is important because the market (sale) value of non-current assets is often low in relation to the values at which they appear in the balance sheet. This means that were a forced sale to occur, there is the likelihood that assets will be sold for less than their balance sheet value. Such anticipated losses should be fully recorded as soon as the business's going concern status is called into question. However, where there is no expectation of a need to sell off the assets, the value of non-current assets can continue to be shown at their recorded values (that is, based on historic cost). This convention therefore provides some support for the historic cost convention under normal circumstances.

Dual aspect convention

The dual aspect convention asserts that each transaction has two aspects, both of which will affect the balance sheet. Thus the purchase of a motor car for cash results in an increase in one asset (motor car) and a decrease in another (cash). The repayment of a loan results in the decrease in a liability (loan) and the decrease in an asset (cash/bank).

Activity 2.12

What are the two aspects of each of the following transactions?

- Purchase £1,000 inventories on credit.
- Owner withdraws £2,000 in cash.
- Repayment of a loan of £3,000.

Your answer should be as follows:

- Inventories increase by £1,000, payables increase by £1,000.
- Capital reduces by £2,000, cash reduces by £2,000.
- Loan reduces by £3,000, cash reduces by £3,000.

Recording the dual aspect of each transaction ensures that the balance sheet will continue to balance.

Prudence convention

The prudence convention holds that financial statements should err on the side of caution. The convention represents an attempt to deal with the uncertainty surrounding many events reported in the financial statements, and evolved to counteract the excessive optimism of some managers and owners, which resulted in an overstatement of financial position. This convention requires the recording of all losses in full, and applies to both actual losses and expected losses. For example, if certain goods purchased for resale proved to be unpopular with customers and, as a result, the goods are to be sold below their original cost, the prudence convention requires that the expected loss from the future sales should be recognised immediately rather than when the goods are eventually sold. Profits, on the other hand, are not recognised until they are realised (that is, when the goods are actually sold). When the prudence convention conflicts with another convention, it is prudence that will normally prevail.

Activity 2.13

Can you think of a situation where certain users might find a prudent view of the financial position of a business will work to their disadvantage?

Applying the prudence convention can result in an understatement of financial position as unrealised profits are not recognised but expected losses are recognised in full. This may result in owners selling their stake in the business at a price that is lower than they would have received if a more balanced approach to valuation were employed.

The degree of bias towards understatement may be difficult to judge. It is likely to vary according to the views of the individual carrying out the valuation.

Stable monetary unit convention

The stable monetary unit convention holds that money, which is the unit of measurement in accounting, will not change in value over time. However, in the UK and throughout much of the world, inflation has been a persistent problem. This has meant that the value of money has declined in relation to other assets. In past years, high rates of inflation have resulted in balance sheets, which are drawn up on an historic cost basis, reflecting figures for assets that were much lower than if current values were employed. This sparked a big debate within the accounting profession and business community and there were calls to abandon historic costs in favour of current values in accounting. In more recent years, however, there have been lower rates of inflation and the debate has lost its intensity.

Objectivity convention

The objectivity convention seeks to reduce personal bias in financial statements. As far as possible, financial statements should be based on objective verifiable evidence rather than on matters of opinion.

Activity 2.14

Which of the above conventions does the objectivity convention support and which does it conflict with?

The objectivity convention provides further support (along with the going concern convention) for the use of historic cost as a basis of valuation. It can conflict, however, with the prudence convention, which requires the use of judgement in determining values.

Accounting for goodwill and product brands

Some intangible non-current assets are similar to tangible non-current assets, in so far as they have a clear and separate identity and the cost of the asset can be reliably determined. Patents, trademarks, copyrights and licences would normally fall into this category. Some intangible non-current assets, however, are quite different in nature. They lack a clear and separate identity and are really a hotchpotch of attributes that form part of the essence of the business. Goodwill and product brands fall into this category.

The term 'goodwill' is often used to cover various attributes of the business such as the quality of the products, the skill of the workforce and the relationship with customers. Product brands are similar to goodwill in that they are made up of various attributes, such as the brand image, the quality of the product, the trademark and so on. Although goodwill and product brands may be valuable to a business, this does not mean that they meet the recognition criteria for accounting assets that were discussed earlier in the chapter. Where they have been generated internally by the business it is often difficult to measure their cost or even to verify their existence. They are, therefore, excluded from the balance sheet.

When these items are acquired through an arm's-length transaction, however, the problems of verification and measurement are resolved. (An 'arm's-length' transaction is one that is undertaken between two unconnected parties.) If goodwill is acquired when taking over another business, or if a business acquires a particular product brand from another business, these items will be clearly identified and a price agreed for them. Under these circumstances, they should be reported as assets by the business that acquired them. Real World 2.2 provides an example of a purchase of goodwill.

Real World 2.2

Where there's goodwill

CRH is a Dublin-based building materials business that has expanded its operations in recent years. In October 2003 it was reported that it had purchased Cementbouw, Handel and Industrie, a Dutch building materials business. CRH paid €646m for Cementbouw's distribution and building products operations. This was made up of €354m for the net assets (that is, assets less liabilities taken over) leaving a payment of €292m for goodwill. The payment for goodwill, which represents around 45 per cent of the total purchase price, will be recorded as an asset on the balance sheet of CRH.

Source: Based on information in 'CRH purchase of Cementbouw gets approval', *Financial Times*, 1 October 2003, FT.com

The basis of valuation of assets on the balance sheet

It was mentioned earlier that, when preparing the balance sheet, the historic cost convention is normally applied for the reporting of assets. However, this point requires further elaboration as, in practice, it is not simply a matter of recording each asset on the balance sheet at its original cost. We shall see that things are a little more complex than this. Before discussing the valuation rules in some detail, however, we should point out that these rules are based on international accounting standards. These are rules that are generally accepted world-wide. The nature and role of accounting standards will be discussed in detail in Chapter 4.

Tangible non-current assets (property, plant and equipment)

Tangible non-current assets tend to be referred to as property, plant and equipment, and we shall use this terminology from now on. Items of property, plant and equipment should be measured initially at their historic cost. However, they will normally be used up over time as a result of wear and tear, obsolescence and so on. The amount used up, which is referred to as *depreciation*, must be measured for each accounting period that the assets are held. Although we shall leave a detailed examination of depreciation until Chapter 3, we need to know that when an asset has been depreciated, this fact should be reflected in the balance sheet. The total depreciation that has accumulated over the period since the asset was acquired must be deducted from its cost. This net figure (that is, the cost of the asset less the total depreciation to date) is referred to as the *net book value, written down value* or *carrying amount*. The procedure described is not really a contravention of the historic cost convention. It is simply recognition of the fact that a proportion of the historic cost of the non-current asset has been consumed in the process of generating benefits for the business.

Although using depreciated cost is the 'benchmark treatment' for these assets, an alternative is allowed. Property, plant and equipment can be measured using fair values provided that these values can be measured reliably. The 'fair values', in this case, are usually the current market values (that is, the exchange values in an arm's-length transaction). By using fair value, a more up-to-date figure than the depreciated cost figure is provided to users, which may be more relevant to their needs. It may also place the business in a better light, as assets such as freehold property may have increased significantly in value over time. Of course, increasing the balance sheet value of an asset does not make that asset more valuable. However, perceptions of the business may be altered by such a move.

One consequence of revaluing non-current assets is that the depreciation charge will be increased. This is because the depreciation charge is based on the increased value of the asset.

Real World 2.3 shows that one well-known business revalued its land and buildings and, by doing so, greatly improved the look of its balance sheet.

Real World 2.3

Retailer marks up land and buildings

The balance sheet of Marks and Spencer plc, a major high street retailer, as at 3 April 2004 reveals land and buildings at a net book value, or carrying amount, of £2,151.9m. These land and buildings are shown at an open market value and were valued by a firm of independent surveyors. If the land and buildings of the business had not been valued in this way, the net book value at 3 April 2004 would have been £1,482.8m. The effect of using market values was, therefore, to increase the net book value of these assets by £669.1m. This represents almost 20% of the net book value of all the tangible non-current assets of the business.

Source: Marks and Spencer plc, Annual Report 2004, www.marksandspencer.com

Activity 2.15

Refer to the vertical format balance sheet of Brie Manufacturing shown earlier (page 44). What would be the effect of revaluing the freehold land to a figure of £110,000 on the balance sheet?

The effect on the balance sheet would be to increase the freehold land to £110,000 and the gain on revaluation (that is, £110,000 – £45,000 = £65,000) would be added to the capital of the owner, as it is the owner who will benefit from the gain. The revised balance sheet would therefore be as follows:

Brie Manufacturing
Balance sheet as at 31 December 2005

	£000	£000
Non-current assets		
Freehold premises		110
Plant and machinery		30
Motor vans		19
		159
Current assets		
Inventories (stock)	23	
Trade receivables (debtors)	18	
Cash at bank	12	
	53	
Less **Current liabilities**		
Trade payables (creditors)	37	
		16
Total assets *less* current liabilities		175
Less **Non-current liabilities**		
Loan		50
Net assets		125
Capital		
Opening balance		50
Add Revaluation gain		65
Profit		14
		129
Less Drawings		4
		125

Once assets are revalued, the frequency of revaluation then becomes an important issue as assets recorded at out-of-date values can mislead users. Using out-of-date revaluations on the balance sheet is the worst of both worlds. It lacks the objectivity and verifiability of historic cost; it also lacks the realism of current values. Revaluations should therefore be frequent enough to ensure that the net book value, or carrying amount, of the revalued asset does not differ materially from its fair value at the balance sheet date.

When an item of property, or plant, or equipment is revalued on the basis of fair values, all assets within that particular group must be revalued. Thus, it is not acceptable to revalue some property but not others. Although this provides some degree of consistency within a particular group of assets, it does not, of course, prevent the balance sheet from containing a mixture of valuations.

Intangible non-current assets

For these assets, the balance sheet treatment used for tangible non-current assets broadly applies. The 'benchmark treatment' is that they are measured initially at historic cost and any depreciation (or *amortisation* as it is usually termed in the context of intangible non-current assets) incurred following acquisition will be deducted to obtain a net book value. Once again, the alternative of revaluing intangible assets using fair values is available. However, this can only be used where fair values can be properly determined by reference to an active market. In practice, this is likely to be a rare occurrence.

The impairment of non-current assets

There is always a risk that both types of non-current asset (tangible and non-tangible) may suffer a significant fall in value. This may be due to factors such as changes in market conditions, technological obsolescence and so on. In some cases, this fall in value may lead to the net book value, or carrying amount, of the asset being higher than the amount that could be recovered from the asset through its continued use or through its sale. When this situation arises, the asset figure on the balance sheet should be reduced to its recoverable amount. Unless this is done, the asset will be overstated on the balance sheet.

Activity 2.16

With which of the accounting conventions, described earlier, is this accounting treatment consistent?

The answer is the prudence convention, which states that actual or anticipated losses should be recognised in full.

We have seen that, under normal circumstances, a business may have a choice of using either depreciated cost or a value-based measure when reporting its non-current assets. However, where the former is greater than the latter, the business has no choice; the use of depreciated cost is not an option. Real World 2.4 provides an example of where the application of this 'impairment rule' as it is called, resulted in huge write-downs (that is, reductions in the balance sheet value of the assets) for a business.

Real World 2.4

Talking telephone numbers

mmO_2 plc is a major mobile phone operator. During the year to 31 March 2003, the business was badly affected by a downturn in market conditions, which led to a review of the carrying amounts of its non-current assets. Following this review, the business decided to reduce the value of its intangible non-current assets by a total of £8,300m on the year-end balance sheet. This amount included write-downs for licences and goodwill in its operations in the UK and Germany of £2,300m and £4,700m respectively, and a write-down of goodwill in its operations in Ireland of £1,300m.

Source: mmO_2, Annual Report 2003

Inventories (stocks)

It is not only non-current assets that run the risk of a significant fall in value. The inventories, or stocks, of a business could also suffer this fate, which could be caused by factors such as obsolescence, deterioration, damage and so on. Where a fall in value means that the amount likely to be recovered from the sale of the inventories will be lower than their cost, this loss must be reflected in the balance sheet. Thus, if the net realisable value (that is, selling price less any selling costs) falls below the cost of inventories held, the former should be used as the basis of valuation. This reflects, once again, the influence of the prudence convention on the balance sheet.

Real World 2.5 shows how inventories may be reported in the financial statements of large businesses.

Real World 2.5

Reporting the valuation basis of inventories (stocks)

The published financial statements of large businesses normally show the basis on which the inventories of the business are valued. For example, Unilever plc, a large business selling food and home- and personal-care products, stated in its 2004 financial statements that inventories are: '. . . stated at the lower of cost and estimated net realisable value'.

In some cases, the way in which the cost of inventories has been derived (usually when the goods are manufactured by the business rather than bought in) will be stated and, in a few cases, the basis for deriving net realisable value is stated. For example, the published financial statements of Thorntons plc, the chocolate makers, include the following statement:

> Cost includes materials, direct labour and an attributable proportion of manufacturing over-heads according to the stage of production reached. Net realisable value is the estimated value which would be realised after deducting all costs of completion, marketing and selling.

Source: Unilever plc, Annual Report 2004; Thorntons plc, Annual Report 2004

Interpreting the balance sheet

We have seen that the conventional balance sheet has a number of limitations. This has led some users of financial information to conclude that the balance sheet has little to offer in the way of useful information. However, this is not really the case. The balance sheet can provide useful insights into the financing and investing activities of a business. We shall consider this in detail in Chapter 6 when we deal with the analysis and interpretation of the financial statements.

Summary

The main points of the chapter may be summarised as follows:

The major financial statements:

- There are three major financial statements – the cash flow statement, the income statement (profit and loss account) and the balance sheet.
- The cash flow statement shows the cash movements over a particular period.
- The income statement shows the wealth (profit) generated over a particular period.
- The balance sheet shows the accumulated wealth at a particular point in time.

The balance sheet:

- This sets out the assets of the business, on the one hand, and the claims against those assets, on the other.
- Assets are resources of the business that have certain characteristics, such as the ability to provide future benefits.
- Claims are obligations on the part of the business to provide cash, or some other benefit, to outside parties.
- Claims are of two types – capital and liabilities.
- Capital represents the owner's claim and liabilities represent the claims of others, apart from the owner.

Classification of assets and liabilities:

- Assets are normally categorised as being current or non-current (fixed).
- Current assets are held for sale or consumption in the normal course of business or are held for the short term.
- Non-current assets are held for use within the business for long-term operations.
- Liabilities are normally categorised as being current or non-current liabilities.
- Current liabilities represent amounts due in the normal course of the business's operating cycle or due for repayment within 12 months.
- Non-current liabilities represent amounts due that are not current liabilities.

Balance sheet formats:

- The horizontal format sets out the assets on one side of the balance sheet and the capital and liabilities on the other side.
- The vertical format begins with the assets at the top of the balance sheet and deducts the liabilities. The resulting figure represents the net assets of the business. The capital of the business is shown at the bottom of the balance sheet.

Accounting conventions:

- Accounting conventions are the rules of accounting that have evolved to deal with practical problems experienced by those preparing financial statements.
- The main conventions relating to the balance sheet include business entity, money measurement, historic cost, going concern, dual aspect, prudence, stable monetary unit and objectivity.

Asset valuation:

- Property, plant and equipment are shown at historic cost less any amounts written off for depreciation. However, fair values may be used rather than depreciated cost.
- Where the amount that can be recovered from the tangible non-current assets is below the net book value, this lower amount should be reflected in the balance sheet.
- Intangible non-current assets broadly follow the same valuation rules as just described.
- Current assets are shown at the lower of cost or net realisable value.

→ **Key terms**

Further reading

If you would like to explore the topics covered in this chapter in more depth, we recommend the following books:

Alexander, D. and Nobes, C. *Financial Accounting: An International Introduction*, 2nd edn, Financial Times Prentice Hall, 2004, Chapters 8 and 9.

Elliott, B. and Elliott, J. *Financial Accounting and Reporting*, 9th edn, Prentice Hall, 2004, Chapters 16 and 18.

IASB *International Financial Reporting Standards (IFRSs) 2003, International Accounting Standards Board*, 2003, IAS 16, IAS 36 and IAS 38.

Sutton, T. *Corporate Financial Accounting and Reporting*, 2nd edn, Financial Times Prentice Hall, 2004, Chapters 2 and 8.

? Review questions

Answers to these questions can be found at the back of the book (pp. 487–8).

2.1 An accountant prepared a balance sheet for a business using the horizontal layout. In the balance sheet, the capital of the owner was shown next to the liabilities. This confused the owner, who argued: 'My capital is my major asset and so should be shown as an asset on the balance sheet.' How would you explain this misunderstanding to the owner?

2.2 'The balance sheet shows how much a business is worth.' Do you agree with this statement? Discuss.

2.3 What is meant by the balance sheet equation? How does the form of this equation differ between the horizontal and vertical balance sheet format?

2.4 In recent years there have been attempts to place a value on the 'human assets' of a business in order to derive a figure that can be included on the balance sheet. Do you think humans should be treated as assets? Would 'human assets' meet the conventional definition of an asset for inclusion on the balance sheet?

✳ Exercises

Exercise 2.5 is more advanced than 2.1 to 2.4. Those exercises with coloured numbers have answers at the back of the book (pp. 499–501).

> If you wish to try more exercises, visit the students' side of the companion website.

2.1 On the fourth day of his business venture, Paul, the street trader in wrapping paper (see earlier in the chapter), purchased more inventories (stock) for £53 cash. During the day he sold inventories that had cost £33 for a total of £47.

Required:
Draw up the three financial statements for day 4 of Paul's business venture.

2.2 Whilst on holiday in Bridlington, Helen had her credit cards and purse stolen from the beach while she was swimming. She was left with only £40, which she had kept in her hotel room, but she had three days of her holiday remaining. She was determined to continue her holiday and decided to make some money to enable her to do so. She decided to sell orange juice to holidaymakers using the local beach. On day 1 she bought 80 cartons of orange juice at £0.50 each for cash and sold 70 of these at £0.80 each. On the following day she purchased 60 cartons at £0.50 each for cash and sold 65 at £0.80 each. On the third and final day she purchased another 60 cartons at £0.50 each for cash. However, it rained and, as a result, business was poor. She managed to sell 20 at £0.80 each but sold off the rest of her inventories at £0.40 each.

Required:
Prepare an income statement and cash flow statement for each day's trading and prepare a balance sheet at the end of each day's trading.

2.3 On 1 March, Joe Conday started a new business. During March he carried out the following transactions:

1 March	Deposited £20,000 in a bank account
2 March	Purchased fixtures and fittings for £6,000 cash, and inventories £8,000 on credit
3 March	Borrowed £5,000 from a relative and deposited it in the bank
4 March	Purchased a motor car for £7,000 cash and withdrew £200 in cash for his own use
5 March	A further motor car costing £9,000 was purchased. The motor car purchased on 4 March was given in part exchange at a value of £6,500. The balance of purchase price for the new car was paid in cash
6 March	Conday won £2,000 in a lottery and paid the amount into the business bank account. He also repaid £1,000 of the loan

Required:
Draw up a balance sheet for the business at the end of each day.

→

2.4 The following is a list of the assets and claims of Crafty Engineering Ltd at 30 June last year:

	£000
Trade payables (creditors)	86
Motor vehicles	38
Loan from Industrial Finance Co. (long-term)	260
Machinery and tools	207
Bank overdraft	116
Inventories (stock)	153
Freehold premises	320
Trade receivables (debtors)	185

Required:

(a) Prepare the balance sheet of the business as at 30 June last year from the above information using the vertical format. (*Hint*: There is a missing item that needs to be deduced and inserted.)

(b) Discuss the significant features revealed by this financial statement.

2.5 The balance sheet of a business at the start of the week is as follows:

Assets	£	Claims	£
Freehold premises	145,000	Capital	203,000
Furniture and fittings	63,000	Bank overdraft	43,000
Inventories (stocks)	28,000	Trade payables (creditors)	23,000
Trade receivables (debtors)	33,000		
	269,000		269,000

During the week the following transactions take place:

(a) Inventories sold for £11,000 cash; these inventories had cost £8,000.

(b) Sold inventories for £23,000 on credit; these inventories had cost £17,000.

(c) Received cash from trade receivables totalling £18,000.

(d) The owners of the business introduced £100,000 of their own money, which was placed in the business bank account.

(e) The owners brought a motor van, valued at £10,000, into the business.

(f) Bought inventories on credit for £14,000.

(g) Paid trade payables £13,000.

Required:

Show the balance sheet after all of these transactions have been reflected.

Chapter 3

Measuring and reporting financial performance

Introduction

In this chapter, we shall continue our examination of the major financial statements by looking at the income statement (profit and loss account). This statement was briefly considered in Chapter 2 and we shall now examine it in some detail. We shall see how this statement is prepared and how it links with the balance sheet. We shall also consider some of the key measurement problems to be faced when preparing this statement.

Learning outcomes

When you have completed this chapter, you should be able to:

- discuss the nature and purpose of the income statement;
- prepare an income statement from relevant financial information;
- discuss the main recognition and measurement issues that must be considered when preparing the income statement;
- explain the main accounting conventions underpinning the income statement.

The income statement (profit and loss account)

The previous chapter examined the nature and purpose of the balance sheet. We saw that this statement is concerned with setting out the financial position of a business at a particular moment in time. However, it is not usually enough for users to have information relating only to the amount of wealth held by a business at one moment in time. Businesses exist for the primary purpose of generating wealth, or profit, and it is the profit generated *during a period* that is the main concern of many users of financial statements. Although the amount of profit generated is of particular interest to the owners of a business, other groups such as managers, employees and suppliers will also have an interest in the profit-making ability of the business. The purpose of the income statement – or profit and loss account, as it is sometimes called – is to measure and report how much profit (wealth) the business has generated over a period. As with the balance sheet that we examined in Chapter 2, the income statement is prepared following the same principles, irrespective of whether the business is a sole proprietorship or a limited company.

The measurement of profit requires that the total revenue of the business, generated during a particular period, be identified. Revenue is simply a measure of the inflow of economic benefits arising from the ordinary activities of a business. These benefits, which accrue to the owners, will result in either an increase in assets (such as cash or amounts owed to the business by its customers) or a decrease in liabilities. Different forms of business enterprise will generate different forms of revenue. Some examples of the different forms that revenue can take are as follows:

- sales of goods (for example, of a manufacturer);
- fees for services (for example, of a solicitor);
- subscriptions (for example, of a club);
- interest received (for example, of an investment fund).

Real World 3.1 below shows the various forms of revenue generated by a leading football club.

The total expenses relating to each accounting period must also be identified. Expense is really the opposite of revenue. It represents the outflow of economic benefits arising from the ordinary activities of a business. This loss of benefits will result in either a decrease in assets or an increase in liabilities. Expenses are incurred in the process of generating revenue, or attempting to generate it. The nature of the business will again determine the type of expenses that will be incurred. Examples of some of the more common types of expenses are:

- the cost of buying goods that are subsequently sold – known as *cost of sales* or *cost of goods sold*;
- salaries and wages;
- rent and rates;
- motor vehicle running expenses;
- insurances;

Real World 3.1

Away the lads!

Newcastle United is a well-known football club in the English Premiership. For the year to 31 July 2004, the club generated revenue totalling £90.2m. A breakdown of this amount is provided in Figure 3.1 below.

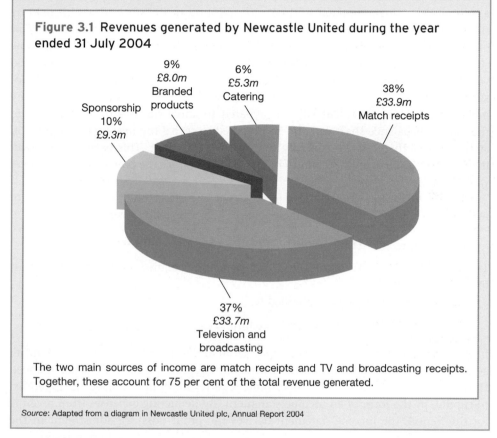

Figure 3.1 Revenues generated by Newcastle United during the year ended 31 July 2004

The two main sources of income are match receipts and TV and broadcasting receipts. Together, these account for 75 per cent of the total revenue generated.

Source: Adapted from a diagram in Newcastle United plc, Annual Report 2004

- printing and stationery;
- heat and light;
- telephone and postage, and so on.

The income statement for a particular period simply shows the total revenue generated during that period and deducts from this the total expenses incurred in generating that revenue. The difference between the total revenue and total expenses will represent either profit (if revenue exceeds expenses) or loss (if expenses exceed revenue). Thus, we have:

Profit (loss) for the period = Total revenue for the period *less* Total expenses incurred in generating the revenue

Relationship between the income statement and the balance sheet

The income statement and the balance sheet should not be viewed in any way as substitutes for one another. Rather they should be seen as performing different functions. The balance sheet is, as stated earlier, a statement of the financial position of a business at a single moment in time – a 'snapshot' of the stock of wealth held by the business. The income statement, on the other hand, is concerned with the *flow* of wealth over a period of time. The two statements are closely related. The income statement can be viewed as linking the balance sheet at the beginning of the period with the balance sheet at the end. Thus, at the start of a new business, a balance sheet will be produced to reveal the opening financial position. After an appropriate period, an income statement will be prepared to show the wealth generated over the period. A balance sheet will also be prepared to reveal the new financial position at the end of the period covered by the income statement. This balance sheet will incorporate the changes in wealth that have occurred since the previous balance sheet was drawn up.

We saw in the previous chapter (p. 38) that the effect on the balance sheet of making a profit (loss) means that the equation can be extended as follows:

$$\text{Assets} = \text{Capital} + \text{Profit (or} - \text{Loss)} + \text{Liabilities}$$

The amount of profit or loss for the period affects the balance sheet as an adjustment to capital.

The above equation can be extended to:

$$\text{Assets} = \text{Capital} + \text{(Sales revenue} - \text{Expenses)} + \text{Liabilities}$$

In theory, it would be possible to calculate profit and loss for the period by making all adjustments for revenue and expenses through the capital section of the balance sheet. However, this would be rather cumbersome. A better solution is to have an 'appendix' to capital, in the form of an income statement. By deducting expenses from revenue for the period, the income statement derives the profit (loss) for adjustment in the capital item in the balance sheet. This figure represents the net effect of trading for the period. Providing this 'appendix' means that a detailed and more informative view of performance is presented to users.

The format of the income statement

The format of the income statement will vary according to the type of business to which it relates. To illustrate an income statement, let us consider the case of a retail business (that is, a business that purchases goods in their completed state and resells them). This type of business usually has straightforward operations and, as a result, the income statement is relatively easy to understand.

Example 3.1 sets out a typical format for the income statement of a retail business.

Example 3.1

Better-Price Stores
Income statement for the year ended 31 October 2005

	£	£
Sales revenue		232,000
Less Cost of sales		154,000
Gross profit		78,000
Add Interest received from investments		2,000
		80,000
Less Salaries and wages	24,500	
Rent and rates	14,200	
Heat and light	7,500	
Telephone and postage	1,200	
Insurance	1,000	
Motor vehicle running expenses	3,400	
Loan interest	1,100	
Depreciation – fixtures and fittings	1,000	
Depreciation – motor van	600	
		54,500
Net profit		25,500

The first part of the statement is concerned with calculating the gross profit for the period. The trading revenue, which arises from selling the goods, is the first item that appears. Deducted from this item is the cost of sales, which is the cost of the goods sold during the period. The difference between the trading revenue and cost of sales is referred to as gross profit. This represents the profit from simply buying and selling goods without taking into account any other expenses or revenues associated with the business.

Having calculated the gross profit, any additional sources of revenue of the business are then added to this figure. In the above example, interest from investments represents an additional source of revenue. From this subtotal of gross profit and additional revenues, the other expenses (overheads) that have to be incurred in operating the business (salaries and wages, rent and rates and so on) are deducted. The final figure derived is the net profit for the period. This net profit figure represents the wealth generated during the period that is attributable to the owner(s) of the business and which will be added to their capital in the balance sheet. As can be seen, net profit is a residual – that is, the amount left over after deducting all expenses incurred in generating the sales revenue for the period.

The income statement – some further aspects

Having set out the main principles involved in preparing an income statement, we need to consider some further points.

Cost of sales

→ The cost of sales figure for a period can be identified in different ways. In some businesses, the cost of sales is identified at the time a sale has been made. Sales are closely matched with the cost of those sales and so identifying the cost of sales figure for inclusion in the income statement is not a problem. Many large retailers (for example, supermarkets) have point-of-sale (checkout) devices that not only record each sale but also simultaneously pick up the cost of the goods that are the subject of the particular sale. Other businesses that sell a relatively small number of high-value items (for example, an engineering business that produces custom-made equipment) also tend to match sales revenue with the cost of the goods sold at the time of the sale. However, some businesses (for example, small retailers) do not usually find it practical to match each sale to a particular cost of sales figure as the accounting period progresses. They find it easier to identify the cost of sales figure at the end of the accounting period.

To understand how this is done, it is important to recognise that the cost of sales figure represents the cost of goods that were *sold* during the period rather than the cost of goods that were *purchased* during the period. Part of the goods purchased during a particular period may remain in the business, as inventories, and not be sold until a later period. To derive the cost of sales for a period, it is necessary to know the amount of opening and closing inventories (stocks) for the period and the cost of goods purchased during the period. Example 3.2 below illustrates how the cost of sales is derived.

Example 3.2

Better-Price Stores, which we considered in Example 3.1 above, began the accounting year with unsold inventories of £40,000 and during that year purchased inventories at a cost of £189,000. At the end of the year, unsold inventories of £75,000 was still held by the business.

The opening inventories at the beginning of the year *plus* the goods purchased during the year will represent the total goods available for resale. Thus:

	£
Opening inventories	40,000
Plus Goods purchased	189,000
Goods available for resale	229,000

The closing inventories will represent that portion of the total goods available for resale that remains unsold at the end of the period. Thus, the cost of goods actually sold during the period must be the total goods available for resale *less* the inventories remaining at the end of the period. That is:

	£
Goods available for resale	229,000
Less Closing inventories	75,000
Cost of goods sold (or cost of sales)	154,000

These calculations are sometimes shown on the face of the income statement as in Example 3.3.

Example 3.3

	£	£
Sales revenue		232,000
Less Cost of sales		
Opening inventories	40,000	
Plus Goods purchased	189,000	
	229,000	
Less Closing inventories	75,000	154,000
Gross profit		78,000

The above is just an expanded version of the first section of the income statement for Better-Price Stores, as set out in Example 3.1. We have simply included the additional information concerning inventories balances and purchases for the year provided in Example 3.2.

Classification of expenses

The classifications for the revenue and expense items, as with the classifications of various assets and claims in the balance sheet, are often a matter of judgement by those who design the accounting system. In the income statement in Example 3.1, the insurance expense could have been included with telephone and postage under a single heading – say, general expenses. Such decisions are normally based on how useful a particular classification will be to users. This will usually mean, however, that expense items of material size will be shown separately. For businesses that trade as limited companies, there are rules that dictate the classification of various items appearing in the accounts for external reporting purposes. These rules will be discussed in Chapter 4.

Activity 3.1

The following information relates to the activities of H & S Retailers for the year ended 30 April 2006:

	£
Motor vehicle running expenses	1,200
Rent received from subletting	2,000
Closing inventories	3,000
Rent and rates payable	5,000
Motor vans	6,300
Annual depreciation – motor vans	1,500
Heat and light	900
Telephone and postage	450
Sales revenue	97,400
Goods purchased	68,350
Insurance	750
Loan interest payable	620
Balance at bank	4,780
Salaries and wages	10,400
Opening inventories	4,000

Prepare an income statement for the year ended 30 April 2006. (*Hint*: Not all items shown above should appear on this statement.)

Your answer to this activity should be as follows:

H & S Retailers
Income statement for the year ended 30 April 2006

	£	£
Sales revenue		97,400
Less Cost of sales		
Opening inventories	4,000	
Plus Purchases	68,350	
	72,350	
Less Closing inventories	3,000	69,350
Gross profit		28,050
Rent received		2,000
		30,050
Less Salaries and wages	10,400	
Rent and rates	5,000	
Heat and light	900	
Telephone and postage	450	
Insurance	750	
Motor vehicle running expenses	1,200	
Loan interest	620	
Depreciation – motor van	1,500	
		20,820
Net profit		9,230

In the case of the balance sheet, we saw that the information could be presented in either a horizontal format or a vertical format. This is also true of the income statement. Where a horizontal format is used, expenses are listed on the left-hand side and revenues on the right, the difference being either net profit or net loss. The vertical format has been used above as it is easier to understand and is now almost always used.

The reporting period

We have seen already that for reporting to those outside the business, a financial reporting cycle of one year is the norm, though some large businesses will produce a half-yearly, or interim, financial statement to provide more frequent feedback on progress. For those who manage a business, however, it is important to have much more frequent feedback on performance. Thus it is quite common for income statements to be prepared on a quarterly, monthly, weekly or even daily basis in order to show how things are progressing.

Profit measurement and the recognition of revenue

A key issue in the measurement of profit concerns the point at which revenue is recognised. Where there is a sale of goods or provision of services, the revenue arising from a particular sale could be recognised at various points. Where, for example, a firm of solicitors undertakes to handle a house purchase for a client for which it will charge a fixed fee, the firm could recognise the revenue:

- at the time of agreement to do the work;
- at the time of completing the work; or
- at the time the client pays.

This particular point chosen is not simply a matter of academic interest: it can have a profound impact on the total revenues, and therefore total profits, reported for a particular period. If the solicitors' case (above) straddled the end of an accounting period, the choice made between the three possible times for recognising the revenue could determine whether the revenue is included as revenue of an earlier accounting period or a later one.

When dealing with the sale of goods or the provision of services, the basic criteria that must be met before revenue is recognised are that:

- the amount of revenue can be measured reliably;
- it is probable that the economic benefits will be received.

However, there is an additional criterion to be applied where the revenue comes from the sale of goods, which is that:

- ownership and control of the items should pass to the buyer.

Activity 3.2 below provides an opportunity to apply these criteria to a practical problem.

Activity 3.2

A manufacturing business sells goods on credit (that is, the customer pays for the goods some time after they are received). Below are four points in the production/selling cycle at which revenue might be recognised by the business:

1 when the goods are produced;
2 when an order is received from a customer;
3 when the goods are delivered to, and accepted by, the customer;
4 when the cash is received from the customer.

A significant amount of time may elapse between these different points. At what point do you think the business should recognise revenue?

The criteria will usually be fulfilled at point 3; when the goods are passed to, and accepted by, the customer. By this point the buyer and seller will have agreed both the selling price and the settlement terms and both parties will have legally enforceable rights. As a result, the revenue can be reliably measured, it is probable that the amounts due will be paid and ownership and control will have passed to the buyer.

We can see that the effect of applying these criteria is that a sale on credit is usually recognised *before* the cash is received. Thus, the total sales revenue figure shown in the income statement may include sales transactions for which the cash has yet to be received. The total sales revenue figure in the income statement for a period will often, therefore, be different from the total cash received from sales during that period.

Where goods are sold for cash rather than on credit, the revenue will normally be recognised at the point of sale. It is at this point that all the criteria will usually be met. For cash sales, there will be no difference in timing between reporting sales revenue and cash received.

Long-term contracts

Some products (and services) have long production cycles. One example is a new building. A customer may enter a contract with a builder to build a new house, with all of the conditions regarding the work specified in the contract. The contract may also break the building work into a number of stages. Stage 1 might be clearing and levelling the land and putting in the foundations. Stage 2 might be building the walls. Stage 3 might be putting on the roof, and so on. Each stage would have a separate price, the total for all the stages equalling the contract total for building the house. As each stage is completed, the builder recognises the price for it as revenue and bills the customer. Were the builder to wait until the house is completed before recognising the revenue, all of the profit would be recognised in the accounting year in which the house was completed. If the building work was started in one accounting year and completed in the following one, none of the revenue and profit would be recognised in the earlier year, when perhaps nearly all of the work was done. This could provide misleading information in the income statement. Other business activities, like ship-building, where the time taken from the start of the work to completion is lengthy, adopt a similar approach to revenue recognition.

When a business provides an unspecified number of services over an agreed period of time, revenue may be recognised before the service is complete. For example, an Internet business may provide open access to the Internet for those who pay a subscription fee. In this case, it is usually assumed that the economic benefits flow evenly over time and so revenue would normally be recognised evenly over the subscription period.

Real World 3.2 provides some examples of how different kinds of businesses recognise revenue in practice.

Real World 3.2

Recognising revenue in practice

Large businesses often disclose the way in which revenue appearing in the income statement is recognised. Here are a few examples:

mmO$_2$, the mobile phone operator recognises:
- revenues from handsets and accessories sales – when the goods are delivered and accepted by the customer;
- revenues from customers for network usage – when the service is rendered;
- revenues from subscriptions fees – evenly over the period to which they relate.

Source: mmO$_2$, Annual Report 2005

Brandon Hire plc operates tool and equipment hire services and recognises revenues from hiring over the period of the hire contract.

Source: Brandon Hire plc, Annual Report and Accounts 2004

Hyder Consulting plc is an engineering design, planning and management consultancy business that generates revenue principally from long-term contracts. Revenue from contracts is recognised on the basis of the sales value of the work performed in relation to the total sales value of the contract and its stage of completion.

Source: Hyder Consulting plc, Annual Report 2004

Profit measurement and the recognition of expenses

Having decided on the point at which revenue is recognised, we can now turn to the issue of the recognition of expenses. The matching convention in accounting is designed to provide guidance concerning the recognition of expenses. This convention states that expenses should be matched to the revenue that they helped to generate. In other words, expenses must be taken into account in the same income statement in which the revenue from the associated sale is included in the total sales revenue figure. Applying this convention may mean that a particular expense reported in the income statement for a period may not be the same figure as the cash paid for that item during the period. The expense reported might be either more or less than the cash paid during the period. Let us consider two examples that illustrate this point.

When the expense for the period is more than the cash paid during the period

Example 3.4

Domestic Ltd retails household electrical appliances. It pays its sales staff a commission of 2 per cent of sales revenue generated, and total sales revenue for the year amounted to £300,000. This will mean that the commission to be paid in respect of the sales for the period will be £6,000. However, by the end of the period, the sales commission paid to staff was £5,000. If the business reported only the amount paid, it would mean that the income statement would not reflect the full expense for the year. This would contravene the *matching convention* because not all of the expenses associated with the revenue of the period would have been matched in the income statement. This will be remedied as follows:

- Sales commission expense in the income statement will include the amount paid plus the amount outstanding (that is, £6,000 = £5,000 + £1,000).
- The amount outstanding (£1,000) represents an outstanding liability at the balance sheet date and will be included under the heading accrued expenses, or 'accruals', in the balance sheet. As this item will have to be paid within 12 months of the balance sheet date, it will be treated as a current liability.
- The cash will already have been reduced to reflect the commission paid (£5,000) during the period.

These points are illustrated in Figure 3.2.

In principle, all expenses should be matched to the period in which the sales revenue to which they relate is reported. However, it is sometimes difficult to match closely certain expenses to sales revenue in the same precise way that we have matched sales commission to sales revenue. It is unlikely, for example, that electricity charges incurred can be linked directly to particular sales in this way. As a result, the electricity charges incurred by, say, a retailer would be matched to the *period* to which they relate. Example 3.5 illustrates this.

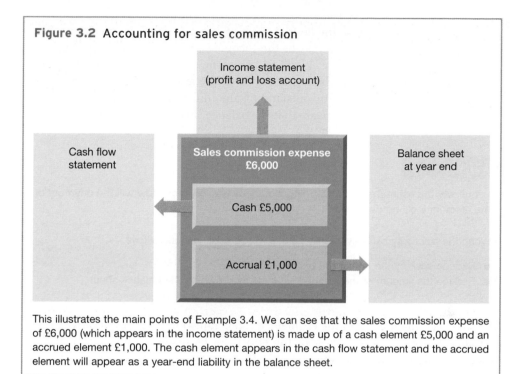

Figure 3.2 Accounting for sales commission

This illustrates the main points of Example 3.4. We can see that the sales commission expense of £6,000 (which appears in the income statement) is made up of a cash element £5,000 and an accrued element £1,000. The cash element appears in the cash flow statement and the accrued element will appear as a year-end liability in the balance sheet.

Example 3.5

Domestic Ltd has reached the end of its accounting year and has only been charged electricity for the first three quarters of the year (amounting to £1,900). This is simply because the electricity company has yet to send out bills for the quarter that ends on the same date as Domestic Ltd's year end. In this situation, an estimate should be made of the electricity expense outstanding (that is, the bill for the last three months of the year is estimated). This figure (let us say the estimate is £500) is dealt with as follows:

- Electricity expense in the income statement will include the amount paid, plus the amount of the estimate (that is, £1,900 + £500 = £2,400) in order to cover the whole year.
- The amount of the estimate (£500) represents an outstanding liability at the balance sheet date, and will be included under the heading 'accruals' or 'accrued expenses' in the balance sheet. As this item will have to be paid within 12 months of the balance sheet date, it will be treated as a current liability.
- The cash will already have been reduced to reflect the electricity paid (£1,900) during the period.

This treatment will have the desired effect of increasing the electricity expense to the 'correct' figure for the year in the income statement, presuming that the estimate is reasonably accurate. It will also have the effect of showing that, at the end of the accounting year, Domestic Ltd owed the amount of the last quarter's electricity bill. Dealing with the outstanding amount in this way reflects the dual aspect of the item, and will ensure that the balance sheet equation is maintained.

Activity 3.3

Let us say the estimate for outstanding electricity was correct. How will the payment of the electricity bill be dealt with?

When the electricity bill is eventually paid, it will be dealt with as follows:

- Reduce cash by the amount of the bill.
- Reduce the amount of the accrued expense as shown on the balance sheet.

If there is a slight error in the estimate, a small adjustment (either negative or positive depending on the direction of the error) can be made to the following year's expense. Dealing with the estimation error in this way is not strictly correct, but the amount is likely to be insignificant.

Activity 3.4

Can you think of other expenses of a retailer, apart from electricity charges, that cannot be linked directly to sales revenue and for which matching will therefore be done on a time basis?

You may have thought of the following examples:

- rent and rates;
- insurance;
- interest payments;
- licences.

This is not an exhaustive list. You may have thought of others.

When the amount paid during the year is more than the full expense for the period

It is not unusual for a business to be in a situation where it has paid more during the year than the full expense for that year. Example 3.6 below illustrates how we deal with this.

Example 3.6

Images Ltd, an advertising agency, normally pays rent for its premises quarterly in advance (on 1 January, 1 April, 1 July and 1 October). On the last day of the last accounting year (31 December), it paid the next quarter's rent (£4,000) to the following 31 March, which was a day earlier than required. This would mean that a total of five quarters' rent was paid during the year. If Images Ltd reports all of the cash paid as an expense in the income statement, this would be more than the full expense for the year. This would contravene the matching convention because a higher figure than the expenses associated with the revenue of the year would appear in the income statement.

The problem is overcome by dealing with the rental payment as follows:

- Show the rent for four quarters as the appropriate expense in the income statement (that is, 4 × £4,000 = £16,000).
- The cash (that is, 5 × £4,000 = £20,000) would already have been paid during the year.
- Show the quarter's rent paid in advance (£4,000) as a prepaid expense on the asset side of the balance sheet. (The prepaid expense will appear as a current asset in the balance sheet, under the heading prepaid expenses or 'prepayments'.)

In the next accounting period, this prepayment will cease to be an asset and will become an expense in the income statement of that period. This is because the rent prepaid relates to that period and will be 'used up' during that period.

These points are illustrated in Figure 3.3.

In practice, the treatment of accruals and prepayments will be subject to the materiality convention of accounting. This convention states that, where the amounts involved are immaterial, we should consider only what is expedient. This may mean that an item will be treated as an expense in the period in which it is paid, rather than being strictly matched to the revenue to which it relates. For example, a business may find that, at the end of an accounting period, there is a bill of £5 owing for stationery used during the year. For a business of any size, the time and effort involved in recording this as an accrual would not be justified by the little effect that this could have on the measurement of profit or financial position. It would, therefore, be ignored when preparing the income statement for the period. The bill would, presumably, be paid in the following period and therefore be treated as an expense of that period.

Profit, cash and accruals accounting

As we have just seen, revenue does not usually represent cash received and expenses are not the same as cash paid. As a result, the net profit figure (that is, total revenue minus total expenses) will not normally represent the net cash generated during a period. It is therefore important to distinguish between profit and liquidity. Profit is a

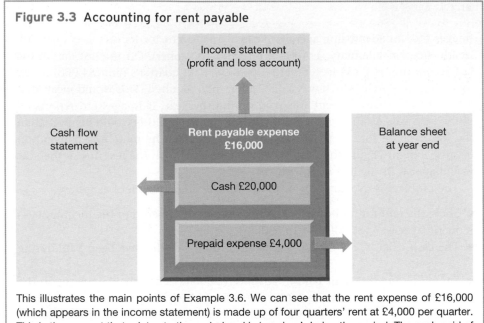

Figure 3.3 Accounting for rent payable

This illustrates the main points of Example 3.6. We can see that the rent expense of £16,000 (which appears in the income statement) is made up of four quarters' rent at £4,000 per quarter. This is the amount that relates to the period and is 'used up' during the period. The cash paid of £20,000 (which appears in the cash flow statement) is made up of the cash paid during the period, which is five quarters at £4,000 per quarter. Finally, the prepayment of £4,000 (which appears on the balance sheet) represents the payment made on 31 December and relates to the next financial year.

measure of achievement, or productive effort, rather than a measure of cash generated. Although making a profit will increase wealth, as we have already seen in Chapter 2, cash is only one form in which that wealth may be held. These points are summarised as the accruals convention of accounting. This asserts that profit is the excess of revenue over expenses for a period, not the excess of cash receipts over cash payments.

Leading on from this, the approach to accounting encompassed in the accruals convention is frequently referred to as accruals accounting. Thus the balance sheet and the income statement are both prepared on the basis of accruals accounting. On the other hand, the cash flow statement is not. It deals with cash receipts and payments.

Profit measurement and the calculation of depreciation

The expense of depreciation, which appeared in the income statement in Activity 3.1, requires further explanation. Non-current assets (with the exception of freehold land) do not usually have a perpetual existence. They are eventually used up in the process of generating revenue for the business. In essence, depreciation is an attempt to measure that portion of the cost (or fair value) of a non-current asset that has been used up in generating the revenue recognised during a particular period. The depreciation charge is considered to be an expense of the period to which it relates. Depreciation tends to be relevant both to property, plant and equipment (tangible non-current assets) and to intangible non-current assets.

To calculate a depreciation charge for a period, four factors have to be considered:

- the cost (or fair value) of the asset;
- the useful life of the asset;
- the residual value of the asset;
- the depreciation method.

The cost (or fair value) of the asset

The cost of an asset will include all costs incurred by the business to bring the asset to its required location and to make it ready for use. Thus, in addition to the costs of acquiring the asset, any delivery costs, installation costs (for example, setting up a new machine) and legal costs incurred in the transfer of legal title (for example, in the case of freehold property) will be included as part of the total cost of the asset. Similarly, any costs incurred in improving or altering an asset in order to make it suitable for its intended use within the business will also be included as part of the total cost.

Activity 3.5

Andrew Wu (Engineering) Ltd purchased a new motor car for its marketing director. The invoice received from the motor car supplier revealed the following:

	£	£
New BMW 325i		26,350
Delivery charge	80	
Alloy wheels	660	
Sun roof	200	
Petrol	30	
Number plates	130	
Road fund licence	160	1,260
		27,610
Part exchange – Reliant Robin		1,000
Amount outstanding		26,610

What is the total cost of the new car that will be treated as part of the business's property, plant and equipment?

The cost of the new car will be as follows:

	£	£
New BMW 325i		26,350
Delivery charge	80	
Alloy wheels	660	
Sun roof	200	
Number plates	130	1,070
		27,420

→

This cost includes delivery charges and number plates, as they are a necessary and integral part of the asset. Improvements (alloy wheels and sun roof) are also regarded as part of the total cost of the motor car. The petrol and road fund licence, however, represent costs of operating the asset rather than a part of the total cost of acquiring the asset and making it ready for use: hence these amounts will be charged as an expense in the period incurred (although part of the cost of the licence may be regarded as a prepaid expense in the period incurred).

The part-exchange figure shown is part payment of the total amount outstanding, and is not relevant to a consideration of the total cost.

The fair value of an asset was defined in Chapter 2 as the exchange value that could be obtained in an arm's-length transaction. For land and buildings, this is normally the market value, as determined by professionally qualified valuers. For other types of property, plant and equipment, such as a motor vehicle, market values may also be used. However, where the asset is very specialised and this value is difficult to determine, replacement cost may be used instead. The problems of using current values were discussed in Chapter 2.

The useful life of the asset

An asset has both a *physical life* and an *economic life*. The physical life of an asset will be exhausted through the effects of wear and tear and/or the passage of time. It is possible, however, for the physical life to be extended considerably through careful maintenance, improvements and so on. The economic life of an asset is decided by the effects of technological progress and by changes in demand. After a while, the benefits of using the asset may be less than the costs involved. This may be because the asset is unable to compete with newer assets, or because it is no longer relevant to the needs of the business. The economic life of an asset may be much shorter than its physical life. For example, a computer may have a physical life of eight years and an economic life of three years.

It is the economic life of an asset that will determine the expected useful life for the purpose of calculating depreciation. Forecasting the economic life of an asset, however, may be extremely difficult in practice: both the rate at which technology progresses and shifts in consumer tastes can be swift and unpredictable.

Residual value (disposal value)

When a business disposes of a non-current asset that may still be of value to others, some payment may be received. This payment will represent the residual value, or *disposal value*, of the asset. To calculate the total amount to be depreciated with regard to an asset, the residual value must be deducted from the cost of the asset. The likely amount to be received on disposal is, once again, often difficult to predict.

Depreciation method

Once the amount to be depreciated (that is, the cost, or fair value, of the asset less the residual value) has been estimated, the business must select a method of allocating this depreciable amount between the accounting periods covering the asset's useful life. Although there are various ways in which the total depreciation may be allocated and, from this, a depreciation charge for each period derived, there are really only two methods that are commonly used in practice.

→ The first of these is known as the straight-line method. This method simply allocates the amount to be depreciated evenly over the useful life of the asset. In other words, an equal amount of depreciation will be charged for each year the asset is held.

Example 3.7

To illustrate this method, consider the following information:

Cost of machine	£40,000
Estimated residual value at the end of its useful life	£1,024
Estimated useful life	4 years

To calculate the depreciation charge for each year, the total amount to be depreciated must be calculated. This will be the total cost less the estimated residual value: that is, £40,000 − £1,024 = £38,976. Having done this, the annual depreciation charge can be derived by dividing the amount to be depreciated by the estimated useful life of the asset of four years. The calculation is therefore:

$$\frac{£38,976}{4} = £9,744$$

Thus, the annual depreciation charge that appears in the income statement in relation to this asset will be £9,744 for each of the four years of the asset's life.

The amount of depreciation relating to the asset will be accumulated for as long as the asset continues to be owned by the business. This accumulated depreciation figure will increase each year as a result of the annual depreciation amount charged to the income statement. This accumulated amount will be deducted from the cost of the asset on the balance sheet. Thus, for example, at the end of the second year the accumulated depreciation will be £9,744 × 2 = £19,488, and the asset details will appear on the balance sheet as follows:

	£	£
Machine at cost	40,000	
Less Accumulated depreciation	19,488	
		20,512

→ The balance of £20,512 shown above is referred to as the written-down value, net book value or carrying amount of the asset. It represents that portion of the cost (or fair value) of the asset that has still to be written off (that is treated as an expense).

It must be emphasised that this figure does not represent the current market value, which may be quite different.

The straight-line method derives its name from the fact that the written-down value of the asset at the end of each year, when plotted against time, will result in a straight line, as shown in Figure 3.4.

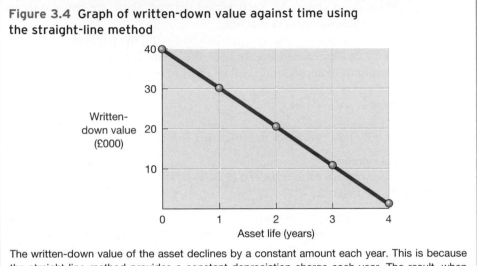

Figure 3.4 Graph of written-down value against time using the straight-line method

The written-down value of the asset declines by a constant amount each year. This is because the straight-line method provides a constant depreciation charge each year. The result, when plotted on a graph, is a straight line.

The second approach to calculating depreciation for a period, found in practice, is referred to as the reducing-balance method. This method applies a fixed percentage rate of depreciation to the written-down value of an asset each year. The effect of this will be high annual depreciation charges in the early years and lower charges in the later years. To illustrate this method, let us take the same information used in Example 3.7. It can be shown that using a fixed percentage of 60 per cent of the written-down value to determine the annual depreciation charge will have the effect of reducing the written-down value to £1,024 after four years.

The calculations will be as follows:

	£
Cost of machine	40,000
Year 1 Depreciation charge (60%* of cost)	(24,000)
Written-down value (WDV)	16,000
Year 2 Depreciation charge (60% WDV)	(9,600)
Written-down value	6,400
Year 3 Depreciation charge (60% WDV)	(3,840)
Written-down value	2,560
Year 4 Depreciation charge (60% WDV)	(1,536)
Residual value	1,024

* See box at the top of p. 81.

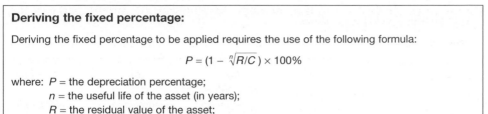

Deriving the fixed percentage:

Deriving the fixed percentage to be applied requires the use of the following formula:

$$P = (1 - \sqrt[n]{R/C}) \times 100\%$$

where: P = the depreciation percentage;
n = the useful life of the asset (in years);
R = the residual value of the asset;
C – the cost, or fair value, of the asset.

The fixed percentage rate will, however, be given in all examples used in this text.

We can see that the pattern of depreciation is quite different for the two methods. If we plot the written-down value of the asset, which has been derived using the reducing-balance method, against time, the result will be as shown in Figure 3.5.

Figure 3.5 Graph of written-down value against time using the reducing-balance method

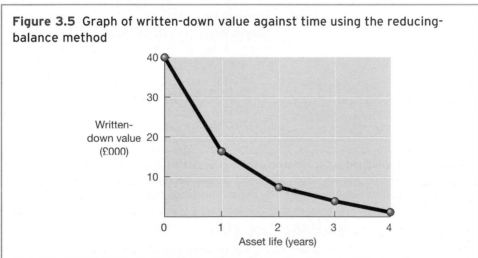

Under the reducing-balance method, the written-down value of an asset falls by a larger amount in the earlier years than in the later years. This is because the depreciation charge is based on a fixed-rate percentage of the written-down value.

Activity 3.6

Assume that the machine used in the example above was owned by a business that made a profit before depreciation of £20,000 for each of the four years in which the asset was held.

Calculate the net profit for the business for each year under each depreciation method, and comment on your findings.

→

Your answer should be as follows:

Straight-line method

	(a) Profit before depreciation	(b) Depreciation	(a – b) Net profit
	£	£	£
Year 1	20,000	9,744	10,256
Year 2	20,000	9,744	10,256
Year 3	20,000	9,744	10,256
Year 4	20,000	9,744	10,256

Reducing-balance method

	(a) Profit before depreciation	(b) Depreciation	(a – b) Net profit/ (loss)
	£	£	£
Year 1	20,000	24,000	(4,000)
Year 2	20,000	9,600	10,400
Year 3	20,000	3,840	16,160
Year 4	20,000	1,536	18,464

The straight-line method of depreciation results in a constant net profit figure over the four-year period. This is because both the profit before depreciation and the depreciation charge are constant over the period. The reducing-balance method, however, results in a changing profit figure over time, despite the fact that in this example the pre-depreciation profit is the same each year. In the first year a net loss is reported, and thereafter a rising net profit is reported.

Although the *pattern* of net profit over the four-year period will be quite different, depending on the depreciation method used, the *total* net profit for the period (£41,024) will remain the same. This is because both methods of depreciating will allocate the same amount of total depreciation (£38,976) over the four-year period. It is only the amount allocated *between years* that will differ.

In practice, the use of different depreciation methods may not have such a dramatic effect on profits as suggested in the activity above. Where a business replaces some of its assets each year, the total depreciation charge calculated under the reducing-balance method will reflect a range of charges (from high through to low), as assets will be at different points in the replacement cycle. This could mean that the total depreciation charge may not be significantly different from the total depreciation charge that would be derived under the straight-line method.

Selecting a depreciation method

How does a business choose which depreciation method to use for a particular asset? The most appropriate method should be the one that best matches the depreciation expense to the economic benefits that are consumed. The business may therefore decide to undertake an examination of the pattern of benefits consumed. Where the asset's benefits are likely to be consumed evenly over time (buildings, for example), the straight-line method may be considered appropriate. Where assets lose their efficiency and the benefits consumed decline over time as a result (for example, certain types of machinery), the reducing-balance method may be considered more appropriate. Where the pattern of economic benefits consumed is uncertain, the straight-line method is normally chosen.

There is an international accounting standard to deal with the problem of depreciation. As we shall see in Chapter 4, the purpose of accounting standards is to narrow areas of accounting difference and to ensure that information provided to users is transparent and comparable. The standard for handling depreciation endorses the view that the depreciation method chosen should reflect the pattern in which the asset's economic benefits are consumed. The standard also requires that businesses disclose a fair amount of detail concerning depreciation charges in their financial statements. Thus, information such as the methods of depreciation used, the accumulated amount of depreciation at the beginning and end of the financial period, and either the depreciation rates applied or the useful lives of the assets must be disclosed.

Real World 3.3 sets out the depreciation policies of Thorntons plc.

Real World 3.3

Depreciation policies in practice

Thorntons plc, the manufacturer and retailer of confectionery, uses the straight-line method to depreciate its non-current assets. In practice, this appears to be the most widely used method of depreciation. The financial statements for the year ended 30 June 2004 show the period over which different classes of tangible non-current assets are depreciated as follows:

In equal annual instalments

Factory freehold premises	50 years
Short leasehold land and buildings	Period of the lease
Retail fixtures and fittings	5 years
Retail equipment	4 to 5 years
Retail store improvements	10 years
Other equipment and vehicles	3 to 7 years
Manufacturing plant and machinery	12 to 15 years

We can see that there are wide variations in the expected useful lives of the various non-current assets held.

Source: Thorntons plc, Annual Report and Accounts 2004

Where the non-current asset is an intangible one, the approach taken for the depreciation (or *amortisation* as it is usually called with intangibles) is broadly the same as that of property, plant and equipment (tangible non-current assets). However, there is often much greater uncertainty surrounding the future economic benefits from intangible non-current assets. International accounting standards deal with this greater uncertainty by applying stricter rules. For example, there is a presumption that the depreciation (or amortisation) period for intangible assets is no more than 20 years. This presumption can only be rebutted if there is persuasive evidence to the contrary. International accounting standards also insist that a review of the depreciation period and depreciation method used must be carried out at least annually. For property, plant and equipment (tangible non-current assets), the review periods can be less frequent.

The approach taken to calculating depreciation is summarised in Figure 3.6.

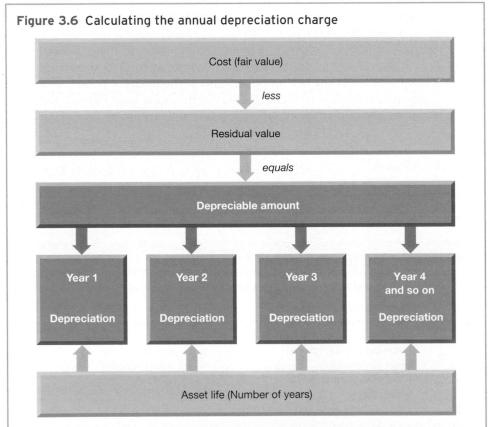

Figure 3.6 Calculating the annual depreciation charge

The cost (fair value) of an asset less the residual value will represent the amount to be depreciated. This amount is depreciated over the useful life (four years in this particular case) of the asset using an appropriate depreciation method.

Depreciation and the replacement of non-current assets

There seems to be a misunderstanding in the minds of some people that the purpose of depreciation is to provide the funds for the replacement of an asset when it reaches the end of its useful life. However, this is not the purpose of depreciation as conventionally defined. It was mentioned earlier that depreciation represents an attempt to allocate the cost, or fair value, (less any residual value) of an asset over its expected useful life. The resulting depreciation charge in each period represents an expense, which is then used in the calculation of net profit for the period. Calculating the depreciation charge for a period is therefore necessary for the proper measurement of financial performance, and must be done whether or not the business intends to replace the asset in the future. The principle is illustrated in Figure 3.6.

If there is an intention to replace the asset, the depreciation charge in the income statement will not ensure that liquid funds are set aside by the business specifically for this purpose. Although the effect of a depreciation charge is to reduce net profit, and therefore to reduce the amount available for withdrawal by the owners, the amounts retained within the business as a result may be invested in ways that are unrelated to the replacement of the specific asset.

Activity 3.7

Suppose that a business sets aside liquid funds, equivalent to the depreciation charge each year, with the intention of using these to replace the asset at the end of its useful life.

Will this ensure that there will be sufficient funds available for this purpose?

No. Even if funds are set aside each year that are equal to the depreciation charge for the year, the total amount accumulated at the end of the asset's useful life may be insufficient for replacement purposes. This may be because inflation or technological advances have resulted in an increase in the replacement cost.

Depreciation and judgement

When reading the above sections on depreciation, it may have struck you that accounting is not as precise and objective as is sometimes suggested. There are areas where subjective judgement is required, and depreciation provides a good illustration of this.

Activity 3.8

What kinds of judgements must be made to calculate a depreciation charge for a period?

In answering this activity, you may have thought of the following:

■ the expected residual or disposal value of the asset;
■ the expected useful life of the asset;
■ the choice of depreciation method.

Making different judgements on these matters would result in a different pattern of depreciation charges over the life of the asset, and therefore in a different pattern of reported profits. However, underestimations or overestimations that are made in relation to the above will be adjusted for in the final year of an asset's life, and so the total depreciation charge (and total profit) over the asset's life will not be affected by estimation errors.

Profit measurement and inventories (stock) costing methods

The way in which we measure the cost of inventories (or stock) is important, because the cost of the inventories sold during a period will affect the calculation of net profit, and the remaining inventories held at the end of the period will affect the portrayal of the financial position. In the previous chapter, we saw that historic cost is the basis for valuing assets, and so it is tempting to think that determining the cost of inventories held is not a difficult issue. However, in a period of *changing prices*, the costing of inventories can be a problem.

A business must determine the cost of the inventories sold during the period and the cost of the inventories remaining at the end of the period. To do this, both of these costs are calculated as if it had been physically handled in a particular assumed manner. The assumption made has nothing to do with how the inventories are *actually* handled; it is concerned only with which assumption is likely to lead to the most useful accounting information.

Two common assumptions used are:

- first in, first out (FIFO) – the earliest inventories held are the first to be sold;
- last in, first out (LIFO) – the latest inventories held are the first to be sold.

Another approach to deriving the cost of inventories is to assume that inventories entering the business lose their separate identity, and any issues of inventories reflect the average cost of the inventories that are held. This is the weighted average cost (AVCO) method, where the weights used in deriving the average cost figures are the quantities of each batch of inventories purchased. Example 3.8 below provides a simple illustration of the way in which each method is applied.

Example 3.8

A business commenced on 1 May to supply oil to factories. During this month, the following transactions took place:

	Tonnes	Cost per tonne
May 2 Purchased	10,000	£10
10 Purchased	20,000	£13
18 Sold	10,000	

Using the FIFO approach, it is the first 10,000 tonnes that are assumed to be sold first. The remainder, which are the later purchases, will comprise the closing inventories. Thus we have:

Cost of sales (10,000 @ £10 per tonne)	£100,000
Closing inventories (20,000 @ £13 per tonne)	£260,000

Using the LIFO approach, the later purchases are assumed to be the first to be sold and so the earlier purchases, plus any later purchases that remain unsold, will comprise the closing inventories. Thus we have:

Cost of sales (10,000 @ £13 per tonne)	£130,000
Closing inventories (10,000 @ £13 per tonne + 10,000 @ £10 per tonne)	£230,000

Using the AVCO approach, the weighted average of the inventories purchased during the period will be determined as follows:

Average cost = $[(10{,}000 \times £10) + (20{,}000 \times £13)]/(10{,}000 + 20{,}000) = £12$ per tonne

This cost per tonne will then be used to derive both the cost of goods sold and the cost of the remaining inventories. Thus we have:

Cost of sales (10,000 @ £12 per tonne)	£120,000
Closing inventories (20,000 @ £12 per tonne)	£240,000

Activity 3.9

What would be the effect on the business in Example 3.8 of adopting each inventory costing method in terms of:

(a) the size of the reported profit for the period, and
(b) the assets shown on the balance sheet at the end of the period?

Can you explain the effect of each method on reported profit and financial position?

The FIFO method gives the lowest cost of sales figure, which when deducted from sales will give the highest gross profit figure. This method gives the lowest cost of sales figure because it reflects the cost of the earlier (and cheaper) inventories. This method will also give the highest inventories figure in the balance sheet at the end of the period. This is because it is the later (and more expensive) inventories that are reflected in this figure.

The last in, first out approach gives the highest cost of sales figure and so will give the lowest gross profit figure. This approach gives the highest cost of sales figure because it reflects the cost of the later (and more expensive) inventories. This approach will also give the lowest inventories figure in the balance sheet at the end of the period. This is because it is the earlier (and cheaper) inventories that are reflected in this figure. The weighted average cost will provide a cost of sales figure and closing inventories figure that fall between the two extremes.

→

It is important to emphasise that differences in the cost of sales and closing inventories figures produced by the three inventory costing methods only arise during a period of changing prices. Where inventories prices are rising, the FIFO method will give the highest gross profit and LIFO will give the lowest gross profit, with the AVCO method providing a figure between these two extremes. During a period of falling prices, the position of FIFO and LIFO is reversed.

Different inventory costing methods will only have an effect on the reported profit from one year to the next. The figure derived for closing inventories will be carried forward and matched with sales revenue in a later period. Thus, if the cheaper purchases of inventories are matched to sales revenue in the current period, it will mean that the dearer purchases will be matched to sales revenue in a later period. Over the life of the business, therefore, the total profit will be the same whichever costing method has been used.

Inventories – some further issues

We saw in Chapter 2 that the closing inventories figure will appear as part of the current assets of the business and that the convention of prudence requires current assets to be valued at the lower of cost and net realisable value. (The net realisable value of inventories is the estimated selling price less any further costs that may be necessary to complete the goods and any costs involved in selling and distributing the goods.) This rule may mean that the valuation method applied to inventories (cost or net realisable value) will switch each year depending on which of cost and net realisable value is the lower. In practice, however, the cost of the inventories held is usually below the current net realisable value – particularly during a period of rising prices. It is, therefore, the cost figure that will normally appear in the balance sheet.

Activity 3.10

Can you think of any circumstances where the net realisable value will be lower than the cost of inventories held, even during a period of generally rising prices?

The net realisable value may be lower where:

- goods have deteriorated or become obsolete;
- there has been a fall in the market price of the goods;
- the goods are being used as a 'loss leader';
- bad purchasing decisions have been made.

There is an international accounting standard to deal with the issue of inventory costing and valuation. The 'benchmark treatment' is that the cost of inventories held should be determined using either FIFO or AVCO. The LIFO approach is not an acceptable method to use. The standard also supports the 'lower of cost or net realisable value' rule.

Real World 3.4 sets out the policies of two businesses with respect to their inventories holdings.

Inventory costing in practice

Some businesses indicate the basis for establishing the cost of inventories held. For example, Tate and Lyle plc, the sugar and other starch-based food processor, reveals that inventories are transferred to the income statement on a 'first in, first out' basis whereas Euro-Disney uses weighted average cost.

Sources: Tate and Lyle plc, Annual Report 2004; Euro-Disney S.C.A., Reference Document 2004

Inventory costing and depreciation provide two examples where the consistency convention must be applied. This convention holds that when a particular method of accounting is selected to deal with a transaction, this method should be applied consistently over time. Thus, it would not be acceptable to switch from, say, FIFO to AVCO between periods (unless there are exceptional circumstances that make this appropriate). The purpose of this convention is to try to ensure that users are able to make valid comparisons between periods.

Activity 3.11

Inventories valuation provides a further example of where subjective judgement is required to derive the figures for inclusion in the financial statements. For a retail business, what are the main areas where judgement is required?

The main areas are:

- the choice of cost method (FIFO, LIFO, AVCO);
- deriving the net realisable value figure for inventories held.

Profit measurement and the problem of bad and doubtful debts

Many businesses sell goods on credit. When credit sales are made, the revenue is usually recognised as soon as the goods are passed to, and accepted by, the customer. Recording the dual aspect of a credit sale will involve:

- increasing sales revenue;
- increasing receivables by the amount of the credit sale.

With this type of sale there is always the risk that the customer will not pay the amount due, however reliable they might have appeared to be at the time of the sale. When it becomes reasonably certain that the customer will never pay, the debt is considered to be 'bad' and this must be taken into account when preparing the financial statements.

Activity 3.12

When preparing the financial statements, what would be the effect on the income statement and on the balance sheet, of not taking into account the fact that a debt is bad?

The effect would be to overstate the assets (receivables) on the balance sheet and to overstate profit in the income statement, as the sale (which has been recognised) will not result in any future benefit arising.

To provide a more realistic picture of financial performance and position, the bad debt must be 'written off'. This will involve:

- reducing the receivables;
- increasing expenses (by creating an expense known as 'bad debts written off') by the amount of the bad debt.

The matching convention requires that the bad debt is written off in the same period as the sale that gave rise to the debt is recognised.

Note that, when a debt is bad, the accounting response is not simply to cancel the original sale. If this were done, the income statement would not be so informative. Reporting the bad debts as an expense can be extremely useful in the evaluation of management performance.

Activity 3.13

The treatment of bad debts represents a further area where judgement is required in deriving expenses figures for a particular period. What will be the effect of different judgements concerning the amount of bad debts on the profit for a particular period and on the total profit reported over the life of the business?

Judgement is often required in deriving a figure for bad debts incurred during a period. There may be situations where views will differ concerning whether or not a debt is irrecoverable. The decision concerning whether or not to write off a bad debt will have an effect on the expenses for the period and, hence, the reported profit. However, over the life of the business the total reported profit would not be affected, as incorrect judgements in one period will be adjusted for in a later period.

Suppose, for example, that a debt of £100 was written off in a period and that, in a later period, the amount owing was actually received. The increase in expenses of £100 in the period in which the bad debt was written off would be compensated for by an increase in revenue of £100 when the amount outstanding was finally received (bad debt recoverable). If, on the other hand, the amount owing of £100 was never written off in the first place, the profit for the two periods would not be affected by the bad debt adjustment and would, therefore, be different – but the total profit for the two periods would be the same.

Real World 3.5 shows the effect of bad debt provisions on the banking sector.

Household debt adds to rise in bank write-offs   FT

Banks were forced to write off record amounts of bad debts last year, Bank of England figures are expected to show this week. The figures, to be published on Thursday, are likely to increase concern about soaring levels of consumer debt and, in particular, the willingness of banks to offer large loans to poorer households.

The data are expected to show that write-offs in the fourth quarter of 2004 reached a record level of more than £6bn for the year as a whole. The previous record for bad debt write-offs occurred in the early 1990s when Britain was mired in a recession.

The banks' write-offs, which have risen sharply since 2001, are largely a result of consumer rather than corporate bad debts.

Credit card lending, in particular, has been a problem, with write-offs more than trebling since 1995 to more than 3 per cent by the end of 2003.

Simon Walker, head of retail banking at accountants KPMG, said most of the rise in write-offs could be attributed to the decision of banks to go 'more downmarket' as they expanded their credit card lending books.

Write-offs of lending to individuals because of increased write-offs of credit card debt have risen from £100m a decade ago to nearly £2bn now.

The increase has driven up the percentage of household write-offs accounted for by credit card debt from less than 20 per cent in 1993 to nearly 50 per cent now.

The boom in lending has generally been profitable for the banks despite sharp rises in bad debts.

Write-offs on mortgage debts have declined and remain at modest levels. Secured lending, such as mortgages, is less likely to be written off since banks can possess the property if the loan cannot be repaid.

Rising house prices have also reduced the amount of debt outstanding after a property is possessed and sold, thereby cutting the amounts a bank would need to write off.

Source: 'Household debt adds to rise in bank write-offs', Simon Briscoe, *Financial Times*, 28 March 2005, FT.com

Let us now try to bring together some of the points that we have raised in this chapter through a self-assessment question.

? Self-assessment question 3.1

TT and Co is a new business that started trading on 1 January 2005. The following is a summary of transactions that occurred during the first year of trading:

1 The owners introduced £50,000 of capital, which was paid into a bank account opened in the name of the business.
2 Premises were rented from 1 January 2005 at an annual rental of £20,000. During the year, rent of £25,000 was paid to the owner of the premises.
3 Rates (a tax on business premises) were paid during the year as follows:

→

For the period 1 January 2005 to 31 March 2005	£500
For the period 1 April 2005 to 31 March 2006	£1,200

4 A delivery van was bought on 1 January 2005 for £12,000. This is expected to be used in the business for four years and then to be sold for £2,000.

5 Wages totalling £33,500 were paid during the year. At the end of the year, the business owed £630 of wages for the last week of the year.

6 Electricity bills for the first three quarters of the year were paid totalling £1,650. After 31 December 2005, but before the financial statements had been finalised for the year, the bill for the last quarter arrived showing a charge of £620.

7 Inventories totalling £143,000 were bought on credit.

8 Inventories totalling £12,000 were bought for cash.

9 Sales revenue on credit totalled £152,000 (cost of sales £74,000).

10 Cash sales revenue totalled £35,000 (cost of sales £16,000).

11 Receipts from trade receivables totalled £132,000.

12 Payments to trade payables totalled £121,000.

13 Van running expenses paid totalled £9,400.

At the end of the year it was clear that a trade debtor who owed £400 would not be able to pay any part of the debt. The business uses the straight-line method for depreciating non-current assets.

Required:
Prepare a balance sheet as at 31 December 2005 and an income statement for the year to that date. (Use the outline financial statements produced below to help you.)

TT and Co
Balance sheet as at 31 December 2005

	£	£	£
Non-current assets			
Motor van			
Current assets			
Inventories			
Trade receivables			
Prepaid expenses	____		
Cash			
Less **Current liabilities**			
Trade payables	____	____	
Accrued expenses		____	
		____	
Capital			
Original			
Add Profit		____	
		____	

Income statement for the year ended 31 December 2005

	£	£
Sales revenue		
Less Cost of sales		
Gross profit		
Less Rent		
Rates		
Wages		
Electricity		
Bad debts		
Van expenses		
Van depreciation		
Net profit for the year		

Interpreting the income statement

When an income statement is presented to users it is sometimes the case that the only item that will concern them will be the final net profit figure, or *bottom line* as it is sometimes called. Although the net profit figure is a primary measure of performance, and its importance is difficult to overstate, the income statement contains other information that should also be of interest. To evaluate business performance effectively, it is important to find out how the final net profit figure was derived. Thus the level of sales revenue, the nature and amount of expenses incurred, and the profit in relation to sales revenue are important factors in understanding the performance of the business over a period. The analysis and interpretation of financial statements is considered in detail in Chapter 6.

Summary

The main points of this chapter may be summarised as follows:

The income statement (profit and loss account):

- Measures and reports how much profit (loss) has been generated over a period.
- Profit (loss) for the period is the difference between the total revenue and total expenses for the period.
- Links the balance sheets at the beginning and end of a financial period.
- The income statement of a retail business will first calculate gross profit, then add any additional revenue and then deduct any overheads for the period. The final figure derived is the net profit (loss) for the period.

- Gross profit represents the difference between the sales revenue for the period and the cost of sales.

Expenses and revenue:

- Cost of sales may be identified by either matching the cost of each sale to the particular sale or by adjusting the goods purchased during the period to take account of opening and closing inventories.
- The classification of expenses is often a matter of judgement, although there are statutory rules for businesses that trade as limited companies.
- Revenue is recognised when the amount of revenue can be measured reliably, it is probable that the economic benefits will be received.
- Where there is a sale of goods, there is an additional criterion that ownership and control must pass to the buyer before revenue can be recognised.
- Revenue can be recognised after partial completion provided a particular stage of completion can be measured reliably.
- The matching convention states that expenses should be matched to the revenue that they help generate.
- A particular expense reported in the income statement may not be the same as the cash paid. This will result in some adjustment for accruals or prepayments.
- The materiality convention states that where the amounts are immaterial, we should consider only what is expedient.
- 'Accruals accounting' is preparing the income statement and balance sheet following the accruals convention, which says that profit = revenue − expenses (not cash receipts − cash payments).

Depreciation of non-current assets:

- Depreciation requires a consideration of the cost (or fair value), useful life and residual value of an asset. It also requires a consideration of the method of depreciation.
- The straight-line method of depreciation allocates the amount to be depreciated evenly over the useful life of the asset.
- The reducing-balance method applies a fixed percentage rate of depreciation to the written-down value of an asset each year.
- The depreciation method chosen should reflect the pattern of benefits associated with the asset.
- Depreciation is an attempt to allocate the cost (or fair value), less the residual value, of an asset over its useful life. It does not provide funds for replacement of the asset.

Inventory (stock) costing methods:

- The way in which we derive the cost of inventories is important in the calculation of profit and the presentation of financial position.

- The first in, first out (FIFO) method approaches matters as if the earliest inventories held are the first to be used.

- The last in, first out (LIFO) method approaches matters as if the latest inventories are the first to be used.

- The weighted average cost (AVCO) method applies an average cost to all inventories used.

- When prices are rising, FIFO gives the lowest cost of sales and highest closing inventories figure and LIFO gives the highest cost of sales figure and the lowest closing inventories figure. AVCO gives a figure for cost of sales and closing inventories that lies between FIFO and LIFO.

- When prices are falling, the positions of FIFO and LIFO are reversed.

- Inventories are shown at the lower of cost and net realisable value.

- When a particular method of accounting, such as an inventory costing method, is selected, it should be applied consistently over time.

Bad debts:

- Where it is reasonably certain that a credit customer will not pay, the debt is regarded as 'bad' and written off.

→ Key terms

profit p. 62
revenue p. 62
expense p. 62
income statement p. 63
gross profit p. 65
net profit p. 65
cost of sales p. 66
matching convention p. 71
accrued expenses p. 72
prepaid expenses p. 75
materiality convention p. 75
accruals convention p. 76

accruals accounting p. 76
depreciation p. 76
residual value p. 78
straight-line method p. 79
written-down value p. 79
reducing-balance method p. 80
first in, first out (FIFO) p. 86
last in, first out (LIFO) p. 86
weighted average cost (AVCO) p. 86
consistency convention p. 89
bad debt p. 90

Further reading

If you would like to explore the topics covered in this chapter in more depth, we recommend the following books:

Alexander, D. and Nobes, C. *Financial Accounting: An International Introduction*, 2nd edn, Financial Times Prentice Hall, 2004, Chapters 8 and 10.

Elliott, B. and Elliott, J. *Financial Accounting and Reporting*, 9th edn, Financial Times Prentice Hall, 2004, Chapters 2, 16, 18 and 19.

IASB *International Financial Reporting Standards (IFRSs) 2003, International Accounting Standards Board*, 2003, IAS 16 and IAS 38.

Sutton, T. *Corporate Financial Accounting and Reporting*, 2nd edn, Financial Times Prentice Hall, 2004, Chapters 2, 8, 9 and 10.

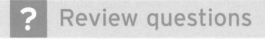 Review questions

Answers to these questions can be found at the back of the book (pp. 488-9).

3.1 'Although the income statement is a record of past achievement, the calculations required for certain expenses involve estimates of the future.' What is meant by this statement? Can you think of examples where estimates of the future are used?

3.2 'Depreciation is a process of allocation and not valuation.' What do you think is meant by this statement?

3.3 What is the convention of consistency? Does this convention help users in making a more valid comparison between businesses?

3.4 'An asset is similar to an expense.' Do you agree?

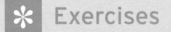 Exercises

Exercises 3.4 to 3.5 are more advanced than 3.1 to 3.3. Those with a coloured number have answers at the back of the book (pp. 502-5).

If you wish to try more exercises, visit the students' side of the companion website.

3.1 You have heard the following statements made. Comment critically on them.

(a) 'Capital only increases or decreases as a result of the owners putting more cash into the business or taking some out.'
(b) 'An accrued expense is one that relates to next year.'
(c) 'Unless we depreciate this asset we shall be unable to provide for its replacement.'
(d) 'There is no point in depreciating the factory building. It is appreciating in value each year.'

3.2 Singh Enterprises has an accounting year to 31 December and uses the straight-line method of depreciation. On 1 January 2003 the business purchased a machine for £10,000. The machine had an expected useful life of four years and an estimated residual value of £2,000. On 1 January 2004 the business purchased another machine for £15,000. This machine had an expected useful life of five years and an estimated residual value of £2,500. On 31 December 2005 the business sold the first machine purchased for £3,000.

Required:
Show the relevant income statement extracts and balance sheet extracts for the years 2003, 2004 and 2005.

3.3 The owner of a business is confused, and comes to you for help. The financial statements for his business, prepared by an accountant, for the last accounting period revealed an increase in profit of £50,000. However, during the accounting period the bank balance declined by £30,000. What reasons might explain this apparent discrepancy?

3.4 The following is the balance sheet of WW Company as at 31 December 2004:

Balance sheet as at 31 December 2004

	£	£	£
Non-current assets			
Machinery			25,300
Current assets			
Inventories	12,200		
Trade receivables	21,300		
Prepaid expenses (rates)	400		
Cash	8,300		
		42,200	
Less **Current liabilities**			
Trade payables	16,900		
Accrued expenses (wages)	1,700		
		18,600	
			23,600
			48,900
Capital			
Original			25,000
Retained profit			23,900
			48,900

During 2005 the following transactions took place:

1 The owners withdrew capital in the form of cash of £23,000.
2 Premises were rented at an annual rental of £20,000. During the year, rent of £25,000 was paid to the owner of the premises.
3 Rates on the premises were paid during the year for the period 1 April 2005 to 31 March 2006 and amounted to £2,000.
4 Some machinery (a non-current asset), which was bought on 1 January 2004 for £13,000, has proved to be unsatisfactory. It was part-exchanged for some new machinery on 1 January 2005, and WW Limited paid a cash amount of £6,000. The new machinery would have cost £15,000 had the business bought it without the trade-in.
5 Wages totalling £23,800 were paid during the year. At the end of the year, the business owed £860 of wages.
6 Electricity bills for the four quarters of the year were paid totalling £2,700.
7 Inventories totalling £143,000 were bought on credit.
8 Inventories totalling £12,000 were bought for cash.

→

9 Sales revenue on credit totalled £211,000 (cost £127,000).

10 Cash sales revenue totalled £42,000 (cost £25,000).

11 Receipts from trade receivables (debtors) totalled £198,000.

12 Payments to trade payables (creditors) totalled £156,000.

13 Van running expenses paid totalled £17,500.

The business uses the reducing-balance method of depreciation for non-current assets at the rate of 30 per cent each year.

Required:

Prepare a balance sheet as at 31 December 2005 and an income statement (profit and loss account) for the year to that date.

3.5 The following is the balance sheet of TT and Co at the end of its first year of trading (from Self-assessment question 3.1):

TT and Co

Balance sheet as at 31 December 2005

	£	£	£
Non-current assets			
Motor van: Cost			12,000
Depreciation			(2,500)
			9,500
Current assets			
Inventories	65,000		
Trade receivables	19,600		
Prepaid expenses*	5,300		
Cash	750		
		90,650	
Less **Current liabilities**			
Trade payables	22,000		
Accrued expenses†	1,250		
		23,250	
			67,400
			£76,900
Capital			
Original			50,000
Add Profit			26,900
			£76,900

* The prepaid expenses consisted of rates (£300) and rent (£5,000).

† The accrued expenses consisted of wages (£630) and electricity (£620).

During 2006, the following transactions took place:

1 The owners withdrew capital in the form of cash of £20,000.

2 Premises continued to be rented at an annual rental of £20,000. During the year, rent of £15,000 was paid to the owner of the premises.

3 Rates on the premises were paid during the year as follows: for the period 1 April 2006 to 31 March 2007 £1,300.

4 A second delivery van was bought on 1 January 2006 for £13,000. This is expected to be used in the business for four years and then to be sold for £3,000.

5 Wages totalling £36,700 were paid during the year. At the end of the year, the business owed £860 of wages for the last week of the year.

6 Electricity bills for the first three quarters of the year and £620 for the last quarter of the previous year were paid totalling £1,820. After 31 December 2006, but before the accounts had been finalised for the year, the bill for the last quarter arrived showing a charge of £690.

7 Inventories totalling £67,000 were bought on credit.

8 Inventories totalling £8,000 were bought for cash.

9 Sales revenue on credit totalled £179,000 (cost £89,000).

10 Cash sales revenue totalled £54,000 (cost £25,000).

11 Receipts from trade receivables totalled £178,000.

12 Payments to trade payables totalled £71,000.

13 Van running expenses paid totalled £16,200.

The business uses the straight-line method for depreciating non-current assets.

Required:
Prepare a balance sheet as at 31 December 2006 and an income statement for the year to that date.

Chapter 4

Accounting for limited companies

Introduction

In the UK, most businesses, except the very smallest, trade in the form of limited companies. There are currently about 1.5 million limited companies in the UK. It is estimated that in the UK, 80 per cent of business activity and 60 per cent of all employment occurs in limited companies. This is probably fairly representative of many of the world's developed countries.

In this chapter we shall examine the nature of limited companies to see how they differ in practical terms from sole proprietorship businesses. This involves considering the ways in which the owners provide finance as well as the rules governing the way in which companies must account to their owners and to other interested parties. It also requires an examination of the ways in which the financial statements, which we discussed in the previous two chapters, are prepared for this type of business enterprise.

Learning outcomes

When you have completed this chapter, you should be able to:

- discuss the nature of the limited company;
- describe the main features of the owners' claim in a limited company;
- discuss the framework of rules that surround accounting for limited companies;
- explain how the income statement and balance sheet of a limited company differ in detail from that of a sole proprietorship or a partnership business.

Generating wealth through limited companies

The nature of limited companies

Let us begin our examination of limited companies by discussing their legal nature. A limited company has been described as an artificial person that has been created by law. This means that a company has many of the rights and obligations that 'real' people have. For example, it can sue or be sued by others and can enter into contracts in its own name. This contrasts sharply with other types of businesses, such as sole proprietorships and partnerships (that is unincorporated businesses), where it is the owner(s) rather than the business that must sue, enter into contracts and so on, because the business has no separate legal identity.

With the rare exceptions of those that are created by Act of Parliament or by Royal Charter, all UK companies are created (or *incorporated*) by registration. To create a company the person or persons (usually known as *promoters*) wishing to create it, fill in a few simple forms and pay a modest registration fee. After having ensured that the necessary formalities have been met, the Registrar of Companies, a government official, enters the name of the new company on the Registry of Companies. Thus, in the UK, companies can be formed very easily and cheaply (for about £100).

Companies may be owned by just one person, but most have more than one owner and some have many owners. The owners are usually known as *members* or *shareholders*. The ownership of a company is normally divided into a number, frequently a large number, of shares, each of equal size. Each owner, or shareholder, owns one or more shares in the company. Large companies typically have a very large number of shareholders. For example at 31 March 2005, BT Group plc, the telecommunications business, had over 1.5 million different shareholders.

As a limited company has its own legal identity, it is regarded as being quite separate from those who own and manage it. This fact leads to two important features of the limited company: perpetual life and limited liability. These are now explained.

Perpetual life

A company is normally granted a perpetual existence and so will continue even where an owner of some, or even all, of the shares in the company dies. The shares of the deceased person will simply pass to the beneficiary of his or her estate. The granting of perpetual existence means that the life of a company is quite separate from the lives of those individuals who own or manage it. It is not, therefore, affected by changes in ownership that arise when individuals buy and sell shares in the company.

Though a company may be granted a perpetual existence when it is first formed, it is possible for either the shareholders or the courts to bring this existence to an end. When this is done, the assets of the company are sold off to meet outstanding liabilities. Any surplus arising from the sale will then be used to pay the shareholders. Shareholders may agree to end the life of a company where it has achieved the purpose for which it was formed or where they feel that the company has no real future. The courts may bring the life of a company to an end where creditors have applied to the courts for this to be done because they have not been paid amounts owing.

Where shareholders agree to end the life of a company, it is referred to as a 'voluntary liquidation'. Real World 4.1 describes the demise of one company by this method.

Real World 4.1

Monotub Industries in a spin as founder gets Titan for £1 FT

Monotub Industries, maker of the Titan washing machine, yesterday passed into corporate history with very little ceremony and with only a whimper of protest from minority shareholders.

At an extraordinary meeting held in a basement room of the group's West End headquarters, shareholders voted to put the company into voluntary liquidation and sell its assets and intellectual property to founder Martin Myerscough for £1. (The shares in the company were at one time worth 650p each.)

The only significant opposition came from Giuliano Gnagnatti who, along with other shareholders, has seen his investment shrink faster than a wool twin-set on a boil wash.

The not-so-proud owner of 100,000 Monotub shares, Mr Gnagnatti, the managing director of an online retailer . . . described the sale of Monotub as a 'free gift' to Mr Myerscough. This assessment was denied by Ian Green, the chairman of Monotub, who said the closest the beleaguered company had come to a sale was an offer for £60,000 that gave no guarantees against liabilities, which are thought to amount to £750,000.

The quiet passing of the washing machine, eventually dubbed the Titanic, was in strong contrast to its performance in many kitchens.

Originally touted as the 'great white goods hope' of the washing machine industry with its larger capacity and removable drum, the Titan ran into problems when it kept stopping during the spin cycle, causing it to emit a loud bang and leap into the air.

Summing up the demise of the Titan, Mr Green said: 'Clearly the machine had some revolutionary aspects, but you can't get away from the fact that the machine was faulty and should not have been launched with those defects.'

The usually vocal Mr Myerscough, who has promised to pump £250,000 into the company and give Monotub shareholders £4 for every machine sold, refused to comment on his plans for the Titan or reveal who his backers were. But . . . he did say that he intended to 'take the Titan forward'.

Source: 'Monotub Industries in a spin as founder gets Titan for £1', Lisa Urquhart, *Financial Times*, 23 January 2003, FT.com

Limited liability

Since the company is a legal person in its own right, it must take responsibility for its own debts and losses. This means that once the shareholders have paid what they have agreed to pay for the shares, their obligation to the company, and to the company's creditors, is satisfied. Thus shareholders can limit their losses to that which they have paid, or agreed to pay, for their shares. This is of great practical importance to potential shareholders, since they know that what they can lose, as part owners of the business, is limited.

Contrast this with the position of sole proprietors or partners. They cannot 'ring fence' assets that they do not want to put into the business. If a sole proprietary or partnership business finds itself in a position where liabilities exceed the business assets, the law gives unsatisfied creditors the right to demand payment out of what the sole proprietor or partner may have regarded as 'non-business' assets. Thus the sole proprietor or partner could lose everything – house, car, the lot. This is because the law sees Jill, the sole proprietor, as being the same as Jill the private individual. The shareholder, by contrast, can lose only the amount committed to that company. Legally, the business operating as a limited company, in which Jack owns shares, is not the same as Jack himself. This is true even if Jack were to own all of the shares in the company.

Real World 4.2 gives an example of a well-known case where the shareholders of a particular company were able to avoid any liability to those that had lost money as a result of dealing with the company.

Real World 4.2

Carlton and Granada 1 – Nationwide Football League 0

A recent example of shareholders taking advantage of limited liability status is that of two tele-vision companies, Carlton and Granada, which each owned 50 per cent of a separate company, ITV Digital (formerly ON Digital). ITV Digital signed a contract to pay the Nationwide Football League more than £89 million on both 1 August 2002 and 1 August 2003 for the rights to broad-cast football matches over three seasons. ITV Digital was unable to sell enough subscriptions for the broadcasts and collapsed because it was unable to meet its liabilities. The Nationwide Football League tried to force Carlton and Granada (ITV Digital's only shareholders) to meet the ITV Digital's contractual obligations. It was unable to do so because the shareholders could not be held legally liable for the amounts owing.

Carlton and Granada merged into one business in 2003, but at the time of ITV Digital were two independent companies.

Activity 4.1

We have just said that the fact that shareholders can limit their losses to that which they have paid, or have agreed to pay, for their shares is of great practical importance to potential shareholders.

Can you think of any practical benefit to a private-sector economy, in general, of this ability of shareholders to limit losses?

Business is a risky venture – in some cases very risky. People with money to invest will tend to be more content to do so where they know the limit of their liability. This means that more businesses will tend to be formed and existing ones will find it easier to raise additional finance from existing and/or additional part-owners. This is good for the private-sector economy, since businesses will tend to form and expand more readily. Thus, the wants of society are more likely to be met where limited liability exists.

→   Though limited liability has this advantage to the providers of capital (the share-holders), it is not necessarily to the advantage of all others who have a stake in the business, like the Nationwide Football League clubs (see Real World 4.2). Limited liability is attractive to shareholders because they can, in effect, walk away from the unpaid debts of the company if their contribution has not been sufficient to meet those debts. This is likely to make any individual, or another business, that is con-sidering entering into a contract, wary of dealing with the limited company. This can be a real problem for smaller, less established companies. For example, suppliers may insist on cash payment before delivery of goods or the rendering of a service. Alternatively, a supplier may require a personal guarantee from a major shareholder that the debt will be paid before allowing a company trade credit. In the latter case, the supplier will circumvent the company's limited liability status by establishing the personal liability of an individual. Larger, more established companies, on the other hand, tend to have built up the confidence of suppliers.

Legal safeguards

The fact that a company is limited must be indicated in the name of the company. This is mainly to warn individuals and other businesses contemplating dealing with a limited company that the liability of the owners (shareholders) is limited. As we shall see later in this chapter, there are other safeguards for those dealing with a limited company, in that the extent to which shareholders may withdraw their investment from the company is restricted.

Another important safeguard for those dealing with a limited company is that all limited companies must produce annual financial statements (income statement (profit and loss account), balance sheet and cash flow statement), and make these available to the public. Later in this chapter we shall consider the financial statements of limited companies in some detail. Just before we leave the topic of the legal separ-ateness of owners and the company, it is worth emphasising that this has no con-nection with the business entity convention of accounting, which we discussed in Chapter 2. This accounting convention applies equally well to all business types, including sole proprietorships and partnerships where there is certainly no legal distinction between the owner(s) and the business.

Public and private companies

When a company is registered with the Registrar of Companies, it must be registered either as a public or as a private company. The main practical difference between these
→   is that a public company can offer its shares for sale to the general public, but a
→   private company is restricted from doing so. A public limited company must signal its status to all interested parties by having the words 'public limited company', or its abbreviation 'plc' in its name. For a private limited company, the word 'limited' or 'Ltd' must appear as part of its name.

Private limited companies tend to be smaller businesses where the ownership is divided among relatively few shareholders who are usually fairly close to one another – for example, a family company. Numerically, there are vastly more private limited companies in the UK than there are public ones. Of the total of 1.5 million UK limited companies, about 99 per cent are private limited companies and just 1 per cent are public limited companies.

Since public companies tend to be individually larger, they are often economically important. In some industry sectors such as banking, insurance, oil refining and grocery retailing they are completely dominant. Whilst there are some large private limited companies, many are little more than the vehicle through which sole proprietorships operate. Real World 4.3 reveals the extent of market dominance of public limited companies in one particular business sector.

Real World 4.3

A big slice of the market

The grocery sector is dominated by four large players: Tesco, Sainsbury, Morrisons/ Safeway and Asda. The first three are public limited companies and the fourth, Asda, is owned by a large US public company (Wal-Mart). Figure 4.1 below shows the share of the grocery market enjoyed by each.

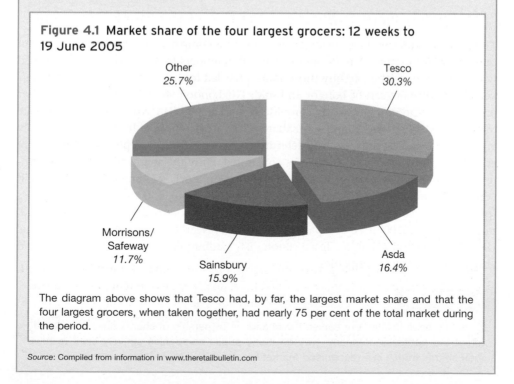

Figure 4.1 Market share of the four largest grocers: 12 weeks to 19 June 2005

Other 25.7%
Tesco 30.3%
Morrisons/ Safeway 11.7%
Sainsbury 15.9%
Asda 16.4%

The diagram above shows that Tesco had, by far, the largest market share and that the four largest grocers, when taken together, had nearly 75 per cent of the total market during the period.

Source: Compiled from information in www.theretailbulletin.com

Taxation

Another consequence of the legal separation of the limited company from its owners is that companies must be accountable to the Inland Revenue for tax on their profits and gains. This introduces the effects of tax into the accounting statements of limited companies. The charge for tax is shown in the income statement (profit and loss account). The tax charge for a particular year is based on that year's profit. Since only 50 per cent of a company's tax liability is due for payment during the year concerned, the other 50 per cent will appear on the end-of-year balance sheet as a short-term liability. This will be illustrated a little later in the chapter. The tax position of companies contrasts with that of sole proprietorships and partnerships, where tax is levied not on the business but on the owner(s). Thus tax does not impact on the financial statements of unincorporated businesses, but is an individual matter between the owner(s) and the Inland Revenue.

Companies are charged corporation tax on their profits and gains. The percentage rates of tax tend to vary from year to year, but have recently been in the low thirties for larger companies and in the low twenties for smaller companies. These rates of tax are levied on the company's taxable profit, which is not necessarily the same as the profit shown on the income statement (profit and loss account). This is because tax law does not, in every respect, follow the normal accounting rules. Generally, however, the taxable profit and the company's accounting profit are pretty close to one another.

Transferring share ownership – the role of the Stock Exchange

The point has already been made that shares in a company may be transferred from one owner to another. The desire of some shareholders to sell their shares, coupled with the desire of others to buy those shares, has led to the existence of a formal market in which shares can be bought and sold. The London Stock Exchange, and similar organisations around the world, provide a market place in which shares in public companies may be bought and sold. Share prices are determined by the laws of supply and demand, which are, in turn, determined by investors' perceptions of the future economic prospects of the companies concerned. Only the shares of certain companies (*listed* companies) may be traded on the London Stock Exchange. About 2,700 UK companies are listed. This represents only one in about 550 of all UK companies (public and private) and about one in six public limited companies. On the other hand, many of these 2,700 listed companies are massive. Nearly all of the 'household name' UK businesses (for example, Tesco, Boots, BT, Cadbury-Schweppes, JD Wetherspoon and so on) are listed companies.

Activity 4.2

If, as has been pointed out earlier, the change in ownership of shares does not directly affect the particular company, why do many public companies actively seek to have their shares traded in a recognised market?

The main reason is that investors are generally very reluctant to pledge their money unless they can see some way in which they can turn their investment back into cash. In theory, the shares of a particular company may be very valuable because it has bright prospects, However, unless this value is capable of being realised in cash, the benefit to the shareholders is dubious. After all, we cannot spend shares; we generally need cash.

This means that potential shareholders are much more likely to be prepared to buy new shares from the company (thereby providing the company with new finance) where they can see a way of liquidating their investment (turning it into cash), as and when they wish. Stock exchanges provide the means of liquidation.

Though the buying and selling of 'second-hand' shares does not provide the company with cash, the fact that the buying and selling facility exists will make it easier for the company to raise new share capital when it needs to do so.

Managing a company – corporate governance and the role of directors

A limited company may have legal personality, but it is not a human being capable of making decisions and plans about the business and exercising control over it. People must undertake these management tasks. The most senior level of management of a company is the board of directors.

The shareholders elect directors (by law there must be at least one director) to manage the company on a day-to-day basis on behalf of those shareholders. In a small company, the board may be the only level of management and consist of all of the shareholders. In larger companies, the board may consist of ten or so directors out of many thousands of shareholders. Indeed, directors are not even required to be shareholders. Below the board of directors of the typical large company could be several layers of management comprising thousands of people.

In recent years, the issue of corporate governance has generated much debate. The term is used to describe the ways in which companies are directed and controlled. The issue of corporate governance is important because, in companies of any size, those who own the company (that is, the shareholders) are usually divorced from the day-to-day control of the business. The shareholders employ the directors to manage the company for them. Given this position, it may seem reasonable to assume that the best interests of shareholders will guide the directors' decisions. However, in practice this does not always occur. The directors may be more concerned with pursuing their own interests, such as increasing their pay and 'perks' (such as expensive motor cars, overseas visits and so on) and improving their job security and status. As a result, a conflict can occur between the interests of shareholders and the interests of directors.

Where directors pursue their own interests at the expense of the shareholders, there is clearly a problem for the shareholders. However, it may also be a problem for society as a whole. If shareholders feel their funds are likely to be mismanaged, they will be reluctant to invest. A shortage of funds will mean fewer investments can be made and the costs of funds will increase as businesses compete for what funds are available. Thus, a lack of concern for shareholders can have a profound effect on the performance of the economy. To avoid these problems, most competitive market economies have a framework of rules to help monitor and control the behaviour of directors.

These rules are usually based around three guiding principles:

■ *Disclosure*. This lies at the heart of good corporate governance. An OECD report (see the reference at the end of chapter for details) summed up the benefits of disclosure as follows:

> Adequate and timely information about corporate performance enables investors to make informed buy-and-sell decisions and thereby helps the market reflect the value of a corporation under present management. If the market determines that present management is not performing, a decrease in stock [share] price will sanction management's failure and open the way to management change.   (OECD 1998)

■ *Accountability*. This involves defining the roles and duties of the directors and establishing an adequate monitoring process. In the UK, company law requires that the directors of a business act in the best interests of the shareholders. This means, among other things, that they must not try to use their position and knowledge to make gains at the expense of the shareholders. The law also requires larger companies to have their annual financial statements independently audited. The purpose of an independent audit is to lend credibility to the financial statements prepared by the directors.

■ *Fairness*. Directors should not be able to benefit from access to 'inside' information that is not available to shareholders. As a result, both the law and the Stock Exchange place restrictions on the ability of directors to buy and sell the shares of the business. One example of these restrictions is that the directors cannot buy or sell shares immediately before the announcement of the annual trading results of the business or before the announcement of a significant event such as a planned merger or the loss of the chief executive.

Strengthening the framework of rules

The number of rules designed to safeguard shareholders has increased considerably over the years. This has been in response to weaknesses in corporate governance procedures, which have been exposed through well-publicised business failures and frauds, excessive pay increases to directors and evidence that some financial reports were being 'massaged' so as to mislead shareholders. However, some believe that the shareholders must shoulder some of the blame for any weaknesses. Not all shareholders in large companies are private individuals owning just a few shares each. In fact, 80 per cent, by market value, of the shares listed on the London Stock Exchange are owned by the investing 'institutions'. These include insurance businesses, pension funds and so on. These are often massive operations, owning large quantities of the shares of the companies in which they invest. The institutional investors employ specialist staff to manage their portfolios of shares in various companies. It has been argued that these large institutional shareholders, despite their size and relative expertise, have not been very active in corporate governance matters. Thus there has been little monitoring of directors. However, things seem to be changing. There is increasing evidence that institutional investors are becoming more proactive in relation to the companies in which they hold shares.

The codes of practice

During the 1990s there was a real effort by the accountancy profession and the London Stock Exchange to address the problems mentioned above. A Code of Best Practice on Corporate Governance emerged in 1992. This was concerned with accountability and financial reporting. In 1995, a separate code of practice emerged. This dealt with directors' pay and conditions. These two codes were revised, 'fine tuned' and amalgamated to produce the Combined Code, which was issued in 1998.

The Combined Code was revised in 2003, following the recommendations of the Higgs Report. These recommendations were mainly concerned with the roles of the company chairman (senior director) and the other directors. It was particularly concerned with the role of 'non-executive' directors. Non-executive directors do not work full time in the company, but act solely in the role of director. This contrasts with 'executive' directors who are salaried employees. For example, the finance director of most large companies is a full-time employee. This person is a member of the board of directors and, as such, takes part in the key decision making at board level. At the same time, s/he is also responsible for managing the departments of the company that act on those board decisions as far as finance is concerned.

The view reflected in the 2003 Combined Code is that executive directors can become too embroiled in the day-to-day management of the company to be able to take a broad view. It also reflects the view that, for executive directors, conflicts can arise between their own interests and those of the shareholders. The advantage of non-executive directors can be that they are much more independent of the company than their executive colleagues. Non-executive directors are remunerated by the company for their work, but this would normally form only a small proportion of their total income. This gives them an independence that the executive directors may not have. Non-executive directors are often senior managers in other businesses or people who have had good experience of such roles.

Both the 1998 and 2003 Combined Codes received the backing of the London Stock Exchange. This means that companies listed on the London Stock Exchange are expected to comply with the requirements of the Code or must give their shareholders good reason why they do not. Failure to do one or other of these can lead to the company's shares being suspended from listing. This is an important sanction against non-compliant directors.

The Combined Code sets out a number of principles relating to such matters as the role of the directors, their relations with shareholders, and their accountability. Real World 4.4 outlines some of the more important of these.

Real World 4.4

The Combined Code

Some of the key elements of the Combined Code are as follows:

- Every listed company should have a board of directors to lead and control the company.
- There should be a clear division of responsibilities between the chairman and the chief executive officer of the company to ensure that a single person does not have unbridled power.
- There should be a balance between executive and non-executive (who are often part-time and independent) members of the board, to ensure that small groups of individuals cannot dominate proceedings.
- The board should receive timely information that is of sufficient quality to enable them to carry out their duties.
- Appointments to the board should be the subject of rigorous, formal and transparent procedures. All directors should submit themselves for re-election by the shareholders within a maximum period of three years.
- Boards should use the annual general meeting to communicate with private investors and encourage their participation.
- The board should publish a balanced and understandable assessment of the company's position and performance.
- Internal controls should be in place to protect the shareholders' wealth.
- The board should set up an audit committee of non-executive directors to oversee the internal controls and financial reporting principles that are being applied, and to liaise with the external auditors.

Strengthening the framework of rules has improved the quality of information available to shareholders, resulted in better checks on the powers of directors, and provided greater transparency in corporate affairs. However, rules can only be a partial answer. A balance must be struck between the need to protect shareholders and the need to encourage the entrepreneurial spirit of directors – which could be stifled under a welter of rules. This implies that rules should not be too tight and so unscrupulous directors may still find ways around them.

Financing limited companies

The owners' claim of limited companies

The owner's claim of a sole proprietorship is normally encompassed in one figure on the balance sheet, usually labelled 'capital'. With companies, this is usually a little more complicated, though in essence the same broad principles apply. With a company, the owners' claim is divided between shares – for example, the original investment – on the one hand and reserves – that is, profits and gains subsequently made – on the other. There is also the possibility that there will be more than one type of shares and of reserves. Thus, within the basic divisions of share capital and reserves, there might well be further subdivisions. This might seem quite complicated, but we shall shortly consider the reasons for these subdivisions and all should become clearer. The sum of share capital and reserves is commonly known as equity.

The basic division

When a company is first formed, those who take steps to form it (the promoters) will decide how much needs to be raised by the potential shareholders to set the company up with the necessary assets to operate. Example 4.1 acts as a basis for illustration.

Example 4.1

Let us imagine that several people get together and decide to form a company to operate a particular business. They estimate that the company will need £50,000 to obtain the necessary assets to operate. Between them, they raise the cash, which they use to buy shares in the company, on 31 March 2005, with a nominal (or par) value of £1 each.

At this point the balance sheet of the company would be:

Balance sheet as at 31 March 2005

	£
Net assets (all in cash)	50,000
Equity	
Share capital	
50,000 shares of £1 each	50,000

The company now buys the necessary non-current assets and inventories (stock) and starts to trade. During the first year, the company makes a profit of £10,000. This, by definition, means that the owners' claim expands by £10,000. During the year, the shareholders (owners) make no drawings of their claim, so at the end of the year the summarised balance sheet looks like this:

Balance sheet as at 31 March 2006

	£
Net assets (various assets less liabilities)	60,000
Equity	
Share capital	
50,000 shares of £1 each	50,000
Reserves (revenue reserve)	10,000
	60,000

The profit is shown in a reserve, known as a revenue reserve, because it arises from generating revenue (making sales). Note that we do not simply merge the profit with the share capital: we must keep the two amounts separate (to satisfy company law). The reason for this is that there is a legal restriction on the maximum drawings of the shareholders' claim (or payment of a dividend) that the owners can make. This is defined by the amount of revenue reserves, and so it is helpful to show these separately. We shall look at why there is this restriction, and how it works, a little later in the chapter.

Share capital

Shares represent the basic units of ownership of a business. All companies issue
ordinary shares. Ordinary shares are often known as *equities*. The nominal value of
such shares is at the discretion of the people that start up the company. For example,
if the initial capital is to be £50,000, this could be two shares of £25,000 each, 5 million shares of one penny each or any other combination that gives a total of £50,000.
Each share must have equal value.

Activity 4.3

The initial capital requirement for a new company is £50,000. There are to be two equal
shareholders. Would you advise them to issue two shares of £25,000 each? Why?

Such large denomination shares tend to be unwieldy. Suppose that one of the shareholders
wanted to sell his or her shares. S/he would have to find one buyer. If there were shares
of smaller denomination, it would be possible to sell part of the shareholding to various
potential buyers. Furthermore, it would be possible to sell just part of the holding and retain
a part.

In practice, £1 is the normal maximum nominal value for shares. Shares of 25 pence
each and 50 pence each are probably the most common.

Some companies also issue other classes of shares, preference shares being the most
common. Preference shares guarantee that *if a dividend is paid*, the preference shareholders will be entitled to the first part of it up to a maximum value. This maximum
is normally defined as a fixed percentage of the nominal value of the preference shares.
If, for example, a company issues 10,000 preference shares of £1 each with a dividend
rate of 6 per cent, this means that the preference shareholders are entitled to receive
the first £600 (that is, 6 per cent of £10,000) of any dividend that is paid by the company for a year. The excess over £600 goes to the ordinary shareholders. Normally, any
undistributed profits and gains also accrue to the ordinary shareholders.

The ordinary shareholders are the primary risk-takers as they are entitled to share
in the profits of the company only after other claims have been satisfied, and their
potential rewards reflect this risk. There are no upper limits, however, on the amount
by which they may benefit. The potential rewards available to ordinary shareholders
reflect the risks that they are prepared to take. Since ordinary shareholders take most
of the risks, power normally resides in their hands. Usually, only the ordinary shareholders are able to vote on issues that affect the company, such as who the directors
should be.

It is open to the company to issue shares of various classes – perhaps with some
having unusual and exotic conditions – but in practice it is rare to find other than
straightforward ordinary and preference shares. Though a company may have different classes of shares whose holders have different rights, within each class all shares
must be treated equally. The rights of the various classes of shareholders, as well as

other matters relating to a particular company, are contained in that company's set of rules, known as the 'articles and memorandum of association'. A copy of these rules must be lodged with the Registrar of Companies, who makes it available for inspection by the general public.

Reserves

Reserves are profits and gains that have been made by a company, which still form part of the shareholders' (owners') claim or equity because they have not been paid out to the shareholders. The shareholders' claim normally consists of share capital and reserves.

Activity 4.4

Are reserves amounts of cash? Can you think of a reason why this is an odd question?

To deal with the second point first, it is an odd question because reserves are a claim, or part of one, on the assets of the company, whereas cash is an asset. So reserves cannot be cash.

Reserves are classified as either revenue reserves or capital reserves. In Example 4.1 we came across one type of reserve, the revenue reserve. We should recall that this reserve represents the company's retained trading profits and gains on the disposal of non-current assets. It is worth mentioning that retained profits represent overwhelmingly the largest source of new finance for UK companies – amounting for most companies to more than share issues and borrowings combined.

Capital reserves arise for two main reasons:

- issuing shares at above their nominal value (for example, issuing £1 shares at £1.50);
- revaluing (upwards) non-current assets.

Where a company issues shares at above their nominal value, UK law requires that the excess of the issue price over the nominal value be shown separately.

Activity 4.5

Can you think why shares might be issued at above their nominal value? (*Hint*: This would not usually happen when a company is first formed and the initial shares are being issued.)

Once a company has traded and has been successful, the shares would normally be worth more than the nominal value at which they were issued. If additional shares are to be issued to new shareholders to raise finance for further expansion, unless they are issued at a value higher than the nominal value, the new shareholders will be gaining at the expense of the original ones.

Now let us consider another example.

Example 4.2

Based on future prospects, the net assets of a company are worth £1.5 million. There are currently 1m ordinary shares in the company, each with a face (nominal) value of £1. The company wishes to raise an additional £0.6 million of cash for expansion and has decided to raise it by issuing new shares. If the shares are issued for £1 each (that is 600,000 shares), the total number of shares will be:

$$1.0m + 0.6m = 1.6 \text{ million}$$

and their total value will be the value of the existing net assets plus the new injection of cash:

$$£1.5m + £0.6m = £2.1 \text{ million}$$

This means that the value of each share after the new issue will be:

$$£2.1m/1.6m = £1.3125$$

The current value of each share is:

$$£1.5m/1.0m = £1.50$$

So the original shareholders will lose:

$$£1.50 - £1.3125 = £0.1875 \text{ a share}$$

and the new shareholders will have gained

$$£1.3125 - £1.0 = £0.3125 \text{ a share}$$

The new shareholders will, no doubt, be delighted with this outcome; the original ones will not.

Things could be made fair between the two sets of shareholders described in Example 4.2 by issuing the new shares at £1.50 each. In this case it would be necessary to issue 400,000 shares to raise the necessary £0.6 million. £1 a share of the £1.50 is the nominal value and will be included with share capital in the balance sheet (£400,000 in total). The remaining £0.50 is a share premium, which will be shown as a capital reserve known as the share premium account (£200,000 in total).

It is not clear why UK company law insists on the distinction between nominal share values and the premium. Certainly, other countries (for example, the United States) with a similar set of laws governing the corporate sector do not see the necessity of distinguishing between share capital and share premium. Instead, the total value at which shares are issued is shown as one comprehensive figure on the company balance sheet. Real World 4.5 shows the shareholders' claim of one well-known business.

Real World 4.5

How Tesco is funded

Tesco plc, the UK and international supermarket business, had the following share capital and reserves as at 26 February 2005:

	£m
Share capital (5p ordinary shares)	389
Share premium account	3,704
Other reserves (capital)	40
Retained profit	4,873
	9,006

Note how the nominal share capital is tiny compared with the share premium account figure. This implies that Tesco has issued shares at much higher prices than the 5p per share nominal value. This reflects Tesco's trading success since the company was first formed. Note also how, at balance sheet values, retained profit makes up more than half of the total for share capital and reserves.

Source: Adapted from Tesco plc, Annual Report and Financial Statements 2005

Bonus shares

It is always open to a company to take reserves of any kind (irrespective of whether they are capital or revenue) and turn them into share capital. This will involve transferring the desired amount from the reserve concerned to share capital and then distributing the appropriate number of new shares to the existing shareholders. New shares arising from such a conversion are known as bonus shares. Issues of bonus shares are quite frequently encountered in practice. Example 4.3 illustrates this aspect of share issues.

Example 4.3

The summary balance sheet of a company is as follows:

Balance sheet as at 31 March 2006

	£
Net assets (various assets less liabilities)	128,000
Equity	
Share capital	
50,000 shares of £1 each	50,000
Reserves	78,000
	128,000

The company decides that it will issue to existing shareholders one new share for every share owned by each shareholder. The balance sheet immediately following this will appear as follows:

Balance sheet as at 31 March 2006

	£
Net assets (various assets less liabilities)	128,000
Equity	
Share capital	
100,000 shares of £1 each (50,000 + 50,000)	100,000
Reserves (78,000 − 50,000)	28,000
	128,000

We can see that the reserves have decreased by £50,000 and share capital has increased by the same amount. Share certificates for the 50,000 ordinary shares of £1 each that have been created from reserves will be issued to the existing shareholders to complete the transaction.

Activity 4.6

A shareholder of the company in Example 4.3 owned 100 shares before the bonus issue. How will things change for this shareholder as regards the number of shares owned and the value of the shareholding?

The answer should be that the number of shares will double, from 100 to 200. Now the shareholder owns one five-hundredth of the company (that is, 200/100,000). Before the bonus issue, the shareholder also owned one five-hundredth of the company (that is, 100/50,000). The company's assets and liabilities have not changed as a result of the bonus issue and so, logically, one five-hundredth of the value of the company should be identical to what it was before. Thus, each share is worth half as much.

A bonus issue simply takes one part of the owners' claim (part of a reserve) and puts it into another part of the owners' claim (share capital). The transaction has no effect on the company's assets or liabilities, so there is no effect on shareholders' wealth.

Activity 4.7

Can you think of any reasons why a company might want to make a bonus issue if it has no economic consequence?

We think that there are three possible reasons:

■ *Share price*. To lower the value of each share without reducing the shareholders' collective or individual wealth.
■ *Shareholder confidence*. To provide the shareholders with a 'feel-good factor'. It is believed that shareholders like bonus issues because it seems to make them better off, though in practice it should not affect their wealth.

- *Lender confidence.* Where reserves arising from operating profits and/or realised gains on the sale of non-current assets are used to make the bonus issue, it has the effect of taking part of that portion of the owners' claim that could be drawn by the shareholders, as drawings (or dividends), and locking it up. The amount transferred becomes part of the permanent capital base of the company. (We shall see, a little later in this chapter, that there are severe restrictions on the extent to which shareholders may make drawings from their claim.) An individual or organisation contemplating lending money to the company may insist that the dividend payment possibilities are restricted as a condition of making the loan. This point will be explained shortly.

Real World 4.6 is an example of a bonus share issue by a well-known UK retailer.

Real World 4.6

Bonus on the cards

In October 2003, Clinton Cards plc announced a one-for-two bonus issue. The company said that the objective of this was to increase the liquidity/marketability of the shares, by reducing the market price per share. This is the first of the three reasons mentioned above for making bonus issues. The company's share price had increased strongly on the back of strong past, and expected future, profit growth. Clinton Cards plc is the UK's largest specialist greetings card retailer.

Source: Based on information in 'FT Money – Markets week world: Clinton Cards', *Financial Times*, 4 October 2003, FT.com.

Share capital – some expressions used in company law

Before leaving our detailed discussion of share capital, it might be helpful to clarify some of the jargon relating to shares that is used in company financial statements.

When a company is first formed, the shareholders give the directors an upper limit on the amount of nominal value of the shares that can be issued. This is known as the authorised share capital. This value can easily be revised upwards, but only if the shareholders agree. That part of the authorised share capital that has been issued to shareholders is known as the issued (or allotted) share capital.

Raising share capital

Once the company has made its initial share issue to start business, usually soon after the company is first formed, it may decide to make further issues of new shares. These may be:

- Rights issues, that is issues made to existing shareholders, in proportion to their existing shareholding.
- Public issues, that is issues made to the general investing public.
- Private placings, that is issues made to selected individuals who are usually approached and asked if they would be interested in taking up new shares.

During its lifetime a company may use all three of these approaches to raising funds through issuing new shares (although only public companies can make appeals to the general public). These approaches will be discussed in detail in Chapter 12.

Loans and other sources of finance

Many companies borrow money to supplement that raised from share issues and ploughed-back profits. Company borrowing is often on a long-term basis, perhaps on a ten-year contract. Lenders may be banks and other professional providers of loan finance. Many companies raise loan finance in such a way that small investors, including private individuals, are able to lend small amounts. This is particularly the case with the larger, Stock Exchange listed, companies and involves their making a loan stock or debenture issue, which, though large in total, can be taken up in small slices by individual investors, both private individuals and investing institutions, such as pension funds and insurance companies. In some cases, these slices of loans can be bought and sold through the Stock Exchange. This means that investors do not have to wait the full term of the loan to obtain repayment, but can sell their slice of the loan to another would-be lender at intermediate points in the term of the loan.

Some of the features of loan-stock financing, particularly the possibility that the loan stocks may be traded on the Stock Exchange, can lead to a confusion that loan stock are shares by another name. We should be clear that this is not the case. It is the shareholders who own the company and, therefore, who share in its losses and profits. Loan stockholders lend money to the company under a legally binding contract that normally specifies the rate of interest, the interest payment dates and the date of repayment of the loan itself. Usually, long-term loans are secured on assets of the company.

Long-term financing of companies can be depicted as in Figure 4.2.

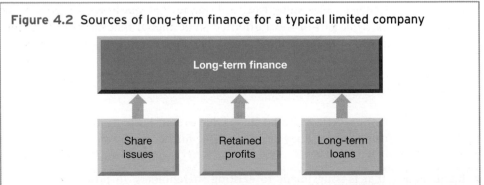

Figure 4.2 Sources of long-term finance for a typical limited company

Companies derive their long-term financing needs from three sources: new share issues, retained profit and long-term borrowings. For a typical company, the sum of the first two (jointly known as 'equity finance') exceeds the third. Retained profit usually exceeds either of the other two in terms of the amount of finance raised in most years.

It is important to the prosperity and stability of a company that it strikes a suitable balance between finance provided by the shareholders (equity) and loan financing. This topic will be explored in Chapter 6. Equity and loan finance are, of course, not the only forms of finance available to a company. In Chapter 12, we consider other sources of finance available to businesses, including companies.

Restriction on the right of shareholders to make drawings of their claim

Limited companies are required by law to distinguish between that part of their claim or equity that may be withdrawn by the shareholders and that part which may not. The withdrawable part is that which has arisen from trading profits and from realised profits on the disposal of non-current assets. This withdrawable element of the shareholders' claim is *revenue reserves*.

It is important to understand that the total revenue reserves, of a particular company at some point in time, is *not normally* the total of all trading profits and realised profits on disposals of non-current assets since the company was first formed. In fact this total will almost certainly have been reduced by at least one of the following three factors:

- corporation tax paid on those profits;
- any dividends paid;
- any trading losses and losses on disposals of non-current assets.

The non-withdrawable part normally consists of that which has arisen from funds injected by shareholders buying shares in the company and that which came from upward revaluations of company assets that still remain in the company – that is, *share capital and capital reserves*.

The law does not specify how large the non-withdrawable part of a particular company's shareholders' claim should be, but simply that anyone dealing with the company should be able to tell from looking at the company's balance sheet how large it is. In the light of this, a particular prospective lender, or supplier of goods or services on credit, can make a commercial judgement as to whether to deal with the company or not. The larger it is, however, the easier the company is likely to find it to persuade potential lenders to lend and suppliers to supply goods and services on credit.

Activity 4.8

Can you think of the reason why limited companies are required to distinguish different parts of their shareholders' claim, whereas sole proprietorship and partnership businesses are not required to do so?

The reason for this situation is the limited liability that company shareholders enjoy, but which owners of unincorporated businesses do not. If a sole proprietor or partner withdraws →

all of the owner's claim, or even an amount in excess of this, the position of the creditors of the business is not weakened since they can legally enforce their claims against the sole proprietor or partner as an individual. With a limited company, where the business and the owners are legally separated, such a legal right to enforce claims against individuals does not exist. To protect the company's creditors, however, the law insists that the shareholders cannot legally withdraw a specific part of their claim.

Let us now look at another example.

Example 4.4

The summary balance sheet of a company at a particular date is as follows:

Balance sheet

	£
Total assets *less* current liabilities	43,000
Equity	
Share capital	
20,000 shares of £1 each	20,000
Reserves (revenue)	23,000
	43,000

A bank has been asked to make a £25,000 long-term loan to the company. If the loan were to be made, the balance sheet immediately following would appear as follows:

Balance sheet (after the loan)

	£
Total assets *less* current liabilities (£43,000 + £25,000)	68,000
Less Non-current liability	
Long-term loan	25,000
	43,000
Equity	
Share capital	
20,000 shares of £1 each	20,000
Reserves (revenue)	23,000
	43,000

As things stand, there are total assets less current liabilities to a total balance sheet value of £68,000 to meet the bank's claim of £25,000. It would be possible and perfectly legal, however, for the company to pay a dividend (withdraw part of their claim) of £23,000. The balance sheet would then appear as follows:

Balance sheet

	£
Total assets *less* current liabilities (£68,000 – £23,000)	45,000
Less **Non-current liabilities**	
Long-term loan	25,000
	20,000
Equity	
Share capital	
20,000 shares of £1 each	20,000
Reserves (revenue (£23,000 – £23,000))	–
	20,000

This leaves the bank in a very much weaker position, in that there are now total assets less current liabilities with a balance sheet value of £45,000 to meet a claim of £25,000. Note that the difference between the amount of the bank loan and the total assets less current liabilities always equals the capital and reserves total. Thus, the capital and reserves represent a margin of safety for creditors. The larger the amount of the owners' claim withdrawable by the shareholders, the smaller is the potential margin of safety for creditors.

As we have already seen, company law says nothing about how large the margin of safety must be. It is up to the company concerned to do what is desirable.

Perhaps it is worth noting, as a practical footnote to Example 4.4, that most potential long-term lenders would seek to have the loan secured against a particular asset of the company, particularly an asset such as freehold property. This, as we have seen, would give the lender the right to seize the asset concerned, sell it and satisfy the repayment obligation, should the company default.

Activity 4.9

Would you expect a company to pay all of its revenue reserves as a dividend? What factors might be involved with a dividend decision?

It would be rare for a company to pay all of its revenue reserves as a dividend: a legal right to do so does not necessarily make it a good idea. Most companies see ploughed-back profits as a major – usually *the* major – source of new finance.

The factors that influence the dividend decision are likely to include:

- the availability of cash to pay a dividend; it would not be illegal to borrow to pay a dividend, but it would be unusual and, possibly, imprudent;
- the needs of the business for finance for new investment;
- the expectations of shareholders concerning the amount of dividends to be paid.

You may have thought of others.

The law is adamant, however, that it is illegal, under normal circumstances, for shareholders to withdraw that part of their claim that is represented by shares and capital reserves. This means that potential creditors of the company know the maximum amount of the shareholders' claim that can be drawn by the shareholders. Figure 4.3 shows the important division between that part of the shareholders' claim that can be withdrawn as a dividend and that part that cannot.

Figure 4.3 Availability for dividends of various parts of the shareholders' claim

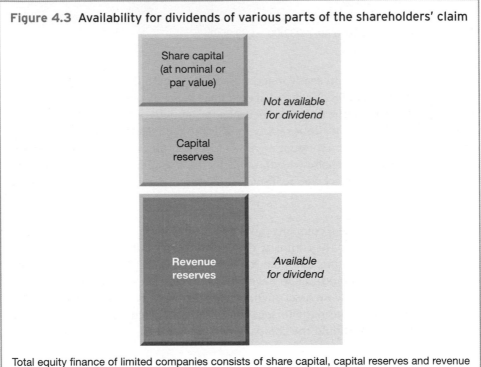

Total equity finance of limited companies consists of share capital, capital reserves and revenue reserves. Only the revenue reserves (which arise from realised profits and gains) can be used to fund a dividend. In other words, the maximum legal dividend is the amount of the revenue reserves.

Accounting for limited companies

The main financial statements

As we might expect, the financial statements of a limited company are, in essence, identical to those of a sole proprietor. There are, however, some differences of detail, and we shall now consider these. Example 4.5 sets out the income statement (profit and loss account) and balance sheet of a limited company:

Example 4.5

Da Silva plc
Income statement for the year ended 31 December 2005

	£m	£m
Revenue		840
Less Cost of sales		520
Gross profit		320
Less Operating expenses		
Wages and salaries	98	
Heat and light	18	
Rent and rates	24	
Motor-vehicle expenses	20	
Insurance	4	
Printing and stationery	12	
Depreciation	45	
Audit fee	4	
		225
Operating profit		95
Less Interest payable		10
Profit before tax		85
Less Tax on profit		24
Profit after tax		61
Less Transfer to general reserve	20	
Dividend paid	25	
		45
Retained (Unappropriated profit) carried forward		16

Balance sheet as at 31 December 2005

	£m	£m
Non-current assets		
Property, plant and equipment		303
Current assets		
Inventories (stock)	65	
Trade receivables (debtors)	112	
Cash	36	
	213	
Less Current liabilities		
Trade payables (creditors)	99	
Corporation tax	12	
	111	
Net current assets (working capital)		102
Total assets less current liabilities		405
Less Non-current liabilities		
10% debentures		100
Net assets		305
Equity		
Share capital		
Ordinary shares of £0.50 each		200
Reserves		
Share premium account	30	
General reserve	50	
Retained profit	25	
		105
		305

Perhaps the most striking thing about these statements is the extent to which they look exactly the same as those that we have been used to with sole proprietors. This is correct; the differences are small. Let us go through and pick up these differences.

The income statement (profit and loss account)

There are several features in the income statement that need consideration.

Profit

We can see that, following the calculation of gross profit, four further measures of profit are shown.

- The first of these is operating profit. This represents the profit achieved for the year before any financing expenses are taken into account. By excluding the financing expenses from the calculation of profit, a better idea of the operating performance for the year may be achieved.
- The second measure of profit is the net profit for the year (profit before tax). Interest charges are deducted from the operating profit to derive this figure. This measure is already familiar to us, and in the case of a sole proprietor business, the income statement (profit and loss account) would end here.
- The third measure of profit is the net profit after tax. As the company is a separate legal entity, it is liable to pay tax (known as corporation tax) on the profits generated. (This contrasts with the sole proprietor business where it is the owner rather than the business that is liable for the tax on profits, as we saw earlier in the chapter.) This measure of profit represents the amount that is available for the shareholders.
- The final measure of profit is the retained, or unappropriated, profit for the year. We can see that most of the net profit after tax is appropriated, or allocated, to pay a dividend and to transfer to a general reserve (see below). Once these appropriations have been made we are left with the fourth measure of profit, which represents the unallocated profits. It is probably worth pointing out that the last part of the income statement (profit and loss account) dealing with appropriations for taxation, dividends and transfers to reserves is known as the 'appropriation account'.

Audit fee

As we shall see later in this chapter, companies greater than a particular size are required to have their financial statements audited by an independent firm of auditors, for which a fee is charged. Though it is also open to sole proprietors and partnerships to have their financial statements audited, very few do, so this is an expense that will normally be present in the income statement of a company but not that of a sole proprietor or partnership.

Dividend

This represents the drawings of part of their claim by the shareholders of the company. Only those dividends paid during the year and those approved by the shareholders before the year end, whether paid or not, appear in the income statement. Sometimes shareholders receive a dividend before the end of the year. Companies may pay their shareholders an 'interim' dividend, part way through the year, and a 'final' dividend shortly after the year end. Had a dividend been approved before the year end, but was not yet paid at the year end, it would appear on the balance sheet as a current liability. Where a dividend has been recommended by the directors, but not approved by the shareholders, it should be mentioned in a note to the financial statements.

Transfer to general reserve

After dividends have been deducted from the net profit after tax figure, the remaining profit is normally reinvested ('ploughed back') into the operations of the company. For this company, the amount reinvested is £36 million (that is, £61 million less £25 million). This amount could all have been unallocated and simply gone to increase the retained, or unappropriated, profit figure. We can see, however, that an amount (£20 million for this company) has been transferred to a separate general reserve, which is quite common in practice.

It is not entirely clear why directors decide to make transfers to general reserves, since the funds concerned remain part of the revenue reserves, and are, therefore, still available for dividend. The most plausible explanation seems to be that directors feel that taking amounts out of the income statement and placing them in a 'reserve' indicates an intention to retain the funds permanently in the company and not to use them to pay a dividend. Of course, the retained profit is also a reserve, but that fact is not indicated in its title.

The balance sheet

The main points for consideration in the balance sheet are:

- *Corporation tax*. The amount that appears as part of the short-term liabilities represents 50 per cent of the tax on the profit for the year 2005. It is, therefore, 50 per cent (£12m) of the charge that appears in the income statement (£24m); the other 50 per cent (£12m) will already have been paid. The unpaid 50 per cent will be paid shortly after the balance sheet date. These payment dates are set down by law.
- *Equity*. We have already discussed this area earlier in the chapter. The general reserve balance must have stood at £30 million before the year end as it was increased to its final level of £50 million by the transfer of £20 million of the year 2005 profit. Similarly, the retained profit balance must have been £9 million, just before the year end. As was mentioned above, the legal status of the general reserve and the retained profit balances are identical in all respects; they both arise from retained profits, and are both available for dividend.

The directors' duty to account

It is not usually possible for all of the shareholders to be involved in the general management of the company, nor do most of them wish to be involved. Instead, they elect directors to act on their behalf. It is both logical, and required by UK company law, that directors are accountable for their actions in respect of their stewardship (management) of the company's assets. In this context, directors are required by law to:

- maintain appropriate accounting records;
- prepare annual financial statements and a directors' report, and to make these available to all shareholders and to the public at large.

The financial statements are made available to the general public by the company submitting a copy to the Companies Registry (Department of Trade and Industry), which allows any one who wishes to do so to inspect these financial statements.

The need for accounting rules

If we accept the need for directors of limited companies to prepare and publish financial statements, we must also accept the need for a framework of rules concerning how these statements are prepared and presented. A lack of regulation increases the risk that unscrupulous directors will use 'unacceptable' accounting practices when preparing the financial statements in an attempt to portray an unfair view of company performance. It also increases the risk that the financial statements of different companies will not be comparable, thereby making investment decisions difficult. Both of these risks can damage the credibility of the financial statements in the eyes of users.

Users must, however, be realistic about what can be achieved through regulation. Problems of manipulation and concealment can still occur within a highly regulated environment, although the scale of these problems should be reduced. Problems in achieving comparability can also still occur. Accounting is not a precise science: judgements and estimates must be made when preparing financial statements, which may hinder comparisons. Moreover, no two companies are exactly the same and different companies may adopt different accounting methods for valid reasons.

The main sources of accounting rules

In recent years we have seen a trend towards the internationalisation of business, which seems set to continue. This has led to calls for the international harmonisation of accounting rules to help both users of accounting information and companies. Harmonisation should help investors and other users of financial statements by making it easier to compare the performance and position of different companies operating in different countries. It should help companies with international operations by reducing the time and cost of producing financial statements: different sets of financial statements would no longer have to be prepared to comply with the rules of different countries.

The International Accounting Standards Board (IASB) is an independent body funded by voluntary contributions that is committed to developing and promoting international accounting rules (known as International Financial Reporting Standards). The overriding requirement for financial statements prepared according to IASB standards is to provide a fair representation of the company's financial position, financial performance and cash flows, and there is a presumption that this will be achieved where the financial statements are drawn up in accordance with the various IASB standards that have been issued.

The authority of the IASB was given a huge boost when the European Commission adopted a regulation requiring Stock Exchange listed companies of EU member states to prepare their financial statements according to IASB standards for accounting periods commencing on or after 1 January 2005. Although non-listed UK companies are not currently required to adopt IASB standards, they have the option to do so. Many informed observers believe, however, that IASB standards will soon become a requirement for all UK companies.

The EU regulation overrides any laws in force in member states that could either hinder or restrict compliance with IASB standards. The ultimate aim is to achieve a single framework of accounting rules for companies from all member states. The EU recognises that this will only be achieved if individual governments do not add to the requirements imposed by the various IASB standards. Thus, it seems that accounting rules developed within individual EU member countries will eventually disappear. For the time being, however, the EU accepts that the governments of member states may need to impose additional disclosures for some corporate governance matters and regulatory requirements. In the UK, company law requires disclosure relating to various corporate governance issues. There is, for example, a requirement to disclose details of directors' remuneration in the published financial statements, which goes beyond anything required by IASB standards. Furthermore, the Financial Services Authority (FSA), in its role as the UK (Stock Exchange) listing authority, imposes rules on Stock Exchange listed companies. These include the publication of summarised interim (half-year) financial statements in addition to the annual financial statements.

Figure 4.4 sets out the main sources of accounting rules for Stock Exchange listed companies discussed above. Whilst company law and the FSA still play an important role, in the longer term, IASB standards seem set to become the sole source of company accounting rules.

Directors' report

In addition to preparing the financial statements discussed above, the law requires the directors to prepare an annual report to shareholders and other interested parties. This report contains information of both a financial and a non-financial nature and goes beyond that which is contained in the financial statements. The information disclosed

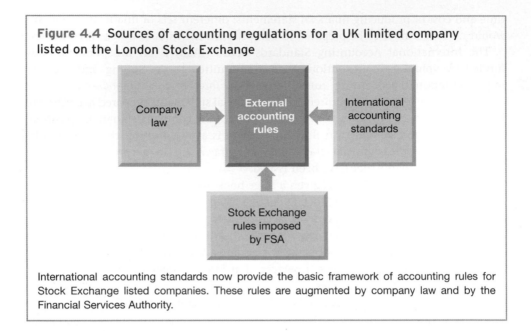

Figure 4.4 Sources of accounting regulations for a UK limited company listed on the London Stock Exchange

International accounting standards now provide the basic framework of accounting rules for Stock Exchange listed companies. These rules are augmented by company law and by the Financial Services Authority.

covers a variety of topics including details of share ownership, details of directors and their financial interests in the company, employment policies, and charitable and political donations. The auditors do not carry out an audit of the directors' report. However, they will check to see that the information in the report is consistent with that contained within the audited financial statements.

Auditors

Shareholders are required to elect a qualified and independent person or, more usually, a firm to act as auditors. The auditors' main duty is to make a report as to whether, in their opinion, the financial statements do what they are supposed to do, namely show a fair view of the financial performance, position and cash flows of the company by complying with the relevant accounting rules. To be in a position to form such an opinion, auditors must scrutinise both the annual financial statements (prepared by the directors) and the evidence on which they are based. The auditors' opinion must be included with the accounting statements that are sent to the shareholders and to the Registrar of Companies.

The relationship between the shareholders, the directors and the auditors is illustrated in Figure 4.5. This shows that the shareholders elect the directors to act on their behalf, in the day-to-day running of the company. The directors are required to 'account' to the shareholders on the performance, position and cash flows of the company, on an annual basis. The shareholders also elect auditors, whose role it is to give the shareholders an impression of the extent to which the accounting statements (prepared by the directors) can be regarded as reliable.

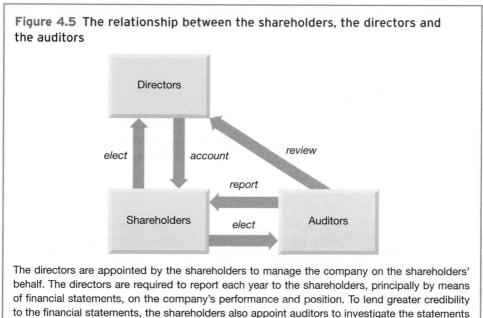

Figure 4.5 The relationship between the shareholders, the directors and the auditors

The directors are appointed by the shareholders to manage the company on the shareholders' behalf. The directors are required to report each year to the shareholders, principally by means of financial statements, on the company's performance and position. To lend greater credibility to the financial statements, the shareholders also appoint auditors to investigate the statements and to express an opinion on their reliability.

Accounting rules and the quality of financial statements

Despite the proliferation of accounting rules and the independent checks that are imposed, concerns about the quality of company financial statements surface from time to time. Over the years, directors of some companies have employed particular accounting policies or structured particular transactions in such a way that portrays a picture of financial health that is in line with what they would like users to see rather than what is a fair view of financial position and performance. This practice is referred to as creative accounting and it poses a major problem for accounting rule-makers and for society generally.

Activity 4.10

Why might the directors of a company engage in creative accounting?

There are many reasons and these include:

- to get around restrictions (for example, to report sufficient profit to pay a dividend);
- to avoid government action (for example, the taxation of excessive profits);
- to hide poor management decisions;
- to achieve sales or profit targets, thereby ensuring that performance bonuses are paid to the directors;
- to attract new share capital or loan capital by showing a healthy financial position;
- to satisfy the demands of major investors concerning levels of return.

The ways in which unscrupulous directors can manipulate the financial statements are many and varied. Real World 4.7 below, which is an extract from an article that appeared in *The Times*, identifies some of the more popular methods.

Real World 4.7

Dirty laundry: how companies fudge the numbers

Hollow swaps: telecoms companies sell useless fibre optic capacity to each other in order to generate revenues on their income statements. Example: Global Crossing.

Channel stuffing: a company floods the market with more products than its distributors can sell, artificially boosting its sales. SSL, the condom maker, shifted £60 million in excess inventories on to trade customers. Also known as 'trade loading'.

Round tripping: also known as 'in-and-out trading'. Used to notorious effect by Enron. Two or more traders buy and sell energy among themselves for the same price and at the same time. Inflates trading volumes and makes participants appear to be doing more business than they really are.

Pre-dispatching: goods such as carpets are marked as 'sold' as soon as an order is placed . . . This inflates sales and profits.

Off-balance sheet activities: companies use special purpose entities and other devices such as leasing . . . to push assets and liabilities off their balance sheets . . .

Source: 'Dirty laundry: How companies fudge the numbers', *The Times* Business, 22 September 2002

A few years ago there was a wave of creative accounting scandals, particularly in the USA, but also in the UK; however, it seems that this wave has now subsided. The quality of financial statements is improving and, it is to be hoped, trust among investors and others is being restored. Nevertheless, such scandals may re-emerge in the future. The recent wave of scandals coincided with a period of strong economic growth in both the USA and the UK. It has been argued that during good economic times, investors and auditors become less vigilant and so the opportunity to manipulate the figures becomes easier. Thus, we must not become too complacent. Things may change again when we next experience a period of strong growth.

? Self-assessment question 4.1

This question requires you to correct some figures on a set of company financial statements. It should prove useful practice for the material that you covered in Chapters 2 and 3, as well as helping you to become familiar with the financial statements of a company.

Presented below is a draft set of simplified financial statements for Pear Limited for the year ended 30 September 2006.

Pear Limited
Income statement (profit and loss account) for the year ended 30 September 2006

	£000	£000
Revenue		1,456
Costs of sales		(768)
Gross profit		688
Less Expenses		
Salaries	220	
Depreciation	249	
Other operating costs	131	(600)
Operating profit		88
Interest payable		(15)
Profit before taxation		73
Taxation at 30%		(22)
Profit after taxation		51

Balance sheet as at 30 September 2006

	£000	£000
Non-current assets		
Property, plant and equipment		
Cost	1,570	
Depreciation	(690)	880
Current assets		
Inventories (stock)	207	
Trade receivables (debtors)	182	
Cash at bank	21	
	410	
Less **Current liabilities**		
Trade payables (creditors)	88	
Other payables (creditors)	20	
Taxation	22	
Bank overdraft	105	
	235	
Net current assets		175
Less **Non-current liabilities**		
10% debenture – repayable 2013		(300)
		755
Equity		
Share capital		300
Share premium account	300	
Retained profit at beginning of year	104	
Profit for year	51	455
		755

→

The following information is available:

1 Depreciation has not been charged on office equipment with a written-down value of £100,000. This class of assets is depreciated at 12 per cent a year using the reducing-balance method.

2 A new machine was purchased, on credit, for £30,000 and delivered on 29 September 2006 but has not been included in the financial statements. (Ignore depreciation.)

3 A sales invoice to the value of £18,000 for September 2006 has been omitted from the financial statements. (The cost of sales figure is stated correctly.)

4 A dividend of £25,000 had been approved by the shareholders before 30 September 2006, but was unpaid at that date. This is not reflected in the financial statements.

5 The interest payable on the debenture for the second half-year was not paid until 1 October 2006 and has not been included in the financial statements.

6 An invoice for electricity to the value of £2,000 for the quarter ended 30 September 2006 arrived on 4 October and has not been included in the financial statements.

7 The charge for taxation will have to be amended to take account of the above information. Make the simplifying assumption that tax is payable shortly after the end of the year, at the rate of 30 per cent of the profit before tax.

Required:
Prepare a revised set of financial statements for the year ended 30 September 2006 incorporating the additional information in 1–7 above. Note: Work to the nearest £1,000.

Summary

The main points of this chapter may be summarised as follows:

The main features of a limited company:

- It is an artificial person that has been created by law.

- It has a separate life to its owners and is granted a perpetual existence.

- It must take responsibility for its own debts and losses but its owners are granted limited liability.

- A public company can offer its shares for sale to the public; a private company cannot.

- It is governed by a board of directors, which is elected by the shareholders.

- Corporate governance is a major issue, various scandals have led to the emergence of the Combined Code.

Financing the limited company:

- The share capital of a company can be of two main types – ordinary shares and preference shares.

- Ordinary shares (equities) are the main risk-takers and are given voting rights; they form the backbone of the company.
- Preference shares are given a right to a fixed dividend before ordinary shareholders receive a dividend.
- Reserves are profits and gains made by the company and form part of the ordinary shareholders' claim.
- Loan capital provides another major source of finance.

Share issues:

- Bonus shares are issued to existing shareholders when part of the reserves of the company is converted into share capital.
- Rights shares give existing shareholders the right to buy new shares in proportion to their existing holding.
- Public issues are made direct to the investing public generally.
- Private placings are share issues to particular investors.
- The shares of public companies may be bought and sold on a recognised Stock Exchange.

Reserves:

- Reserves are of two types – revenue reserves and capital reserves.
- Revenue reserves arise from trading profits and from realised profits on the sale of non-current assets.
- Capital reserves arise from the issue of shares above their nominal value or from the upward revaluation of non-current assets.
- Revenue reserves can be withdrawn as dividends by the shareholders whereas capital reserves cannot.

Financial statements of limited companies:

- The financial statements of limited companies are based on the same principles as those of sole proprietorship and partnership businesses. However, there are some differences in detail.
- The income statement has four measures of profit displayed after the gross profit figure: operating profit, net profit for the year (profit before tax), net profit after tax and retained (unappropriated) profit.
- The income statement also shows audit fees, transfers to reserves, corporation tax on profits for the year and dividends for the year.
- Any unpaid tax and unpaid, but authorised, dividends will appear in the balance sheet as current liabilities.
- The share capital plus the reserves will be shown as 'equity'.

Rules surrounding limited companies:

- The directors are legally obliged to keep proper accounting records and to prepare the financial statements.

→

- IASB rules require that the financial statements show a fair view and prescribe much of the form and content of the financial statements.
- Auditors are appointed to provide an independent opinion as to whether the financial statements show a fair view.
- Despite the accounting rules that are in place, there have been examples of creative accounting by directors of companies.

→ Key terms

limited company p. 101	preference shares p. 112
shares p. 101	capital reserves p. 113
limited liability p. 104	share premium account p. 114
public company p. 104	bonus shares p. 115
private company p. 104	authorised share capital p. 117
corporation tax p. 106	issued share capital p. 117
director p. 107	loan stock/debenture p. 118
corporate governance p. 107	margin of safety p. 121
Combined Code p. 109	operating profit p. 124
reserves p. 110	International Financial Reporting
equity p. 111	Standards p. 127
nominal value p. 111	directors' report p. 128
revenue reserve p. 111	auditors p. 128
dividend p. 111	creative accounting p. 129
ordinary shares p. 112	

Further reading

If you would like to explore the topics covered in this chapter in more depth, we recommend the following books:

Elliott, B. and Elliott, J. *Financial Accounting and Reporting*, 9th edn, Financial Times Prentice Hall, 2004, Chapters 5 and 6.

McLaney, E. and Atrill, P. *Accounting: An Introduction*, 3rd edn, Financial Times Prentice Hall, 2005, Chapters 4 and 5.

IASB *International Financial Reporting Standards (IFRSs) 2003, International Accounting Standards Board*, 2003, IAS 1.

Sutton, T. *Corporate Financial Accounting and Reporting*, 2nd edn, Financial Times Prentice Hall, 2004, Chapters 6 and 12.

Reference

OECD, *Corporate Governance: Improving Competitiveness and Access to Capital in Global Markets*, report by Business Sector Advisory Group on Corporate Governance, Organisation for Economic Co-operation and Development (OECD), 1998, p. 14.

Review questions

Answers to these questions can be found at the back of the book (pp. 489-90).

4.1 How does the liability of a limited company differ from the liability of a real person, in respect of amounts owed to others?

4.2 Some people are about to form a company, as a vehicle through which to run a new business. What are the advantages to them of forming a private limited company rather than a public one?

4.3 What is a reserve? Distinguish between a revenue reserve and a capital reserve.

4.4 What is a preference share? Compare the main features of a preference share with those of
(a) an ordinary share, and
(b) a debenture.

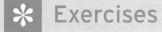

Exercises

Exercises 4.4 and 4.5 are more advanced than 4.1 to 4.3. Those with coloured numbers have answers at the back of the book (pp. 504-5).

If you wish to try more exercises, visit the students' side of the companion website.

4.1 Comment on the following quote:

> Limited companies can set a limit on the amount of debts that they will meet. They tend to have reserves of cash, as well as share capital and they can use these reserves to pay dividends to the shareholders. Many companies have preference as well as ordinary shares. The preference shares give a guaranteed dividend. The shares of many companies can be bought and sold on the Stock Exchange, and shareholders selling their shares can represent a useful source of new capital to the company.

4.2 Comment on the following quotes:

(a) 'Bonus shares increase the shareholders' wealth because, after the issue, they have more shares, but each one of the same nominal value as they had before.
(b) 'By law, once shares have been issued at a particular nominal value, they must always be issued at that value in any future share issues.'

(c) 'By law, companies can pay as much as they like by way of dividends on their shares, provided that they have sufficient cash to do so.'

(d) 'Companies do not have to pay tax on their profits because the shareholders have to pay tax on their dividends.'

4.3 Briefly explain each of the following expressions that you have seen in the financial statements of a limited company:

(a) dividend;

(b) debenture;

(c) share premium account.

4.4 Presented below is a draft set of financial statements for Chips Limited.

Chips Limited

Income statement (profit and loss account) for the year ended 30 June 2006

	£000	£000
Revenue		1,850
Cost of sales		(1,040)
Gross profit		810
Less Depreciation	(220)	
Other operating costs	(375)	(595)
Operating profit		215
Interest payable		(35)
Profit before taxation		180
Taxation		(60)
Profit after taxation		120

Balance sheet as at 30 June 2006

	Cost £000	Depreciation £000	£000
Non-current assets			
Property, plant and equipment			
Buildings	800	(112)	688
Plant and equipment	650	(367)	283
Motor vehicles	102	(53)	49
	1,552	(532)	1,020
Current assets			
Inventories (stock)		950	
Trade receivables (debtors)		420	
Cash at bank		16	
		1,386	
Less **Current liabilities**			
Trade payables (creditors)		(361)	
Other payables (creditors)		(117)	
Taxation		(60)	
		(538)	
Net current assets			848
Less **Non-current liabilities**			
Secured 10% loan			(700)
			1,168

Equity

Ordinary shares of £1, fully paid		800
Reserves at 1 July 2005	248	
Profit for the year	120	368
		1,168

The following additional information is available:

1 Purchase invoices for goods received on 29 June 2006 amounting to £23,000 have not been included. This means that the cost of sales figure in the income statement has been understated.

2 A motor vehicle costing £8,000 with depreciation amounting to £5,000 was sold on 30 June 2006 for £2,100, paid by cheque. This transaction has not been included in the company's records.

3 No depreciation on motor vehicles has been charged. The annual rate is 20 per cent of cost at the year end.

4 A sale on credit for £16,000 made on 1 July 2006 has been included in the financial statements in error. The cost of sales figure is correct in respect of this item.

5 A half-yearly payment of interest on the secured loan due on 30 June 2006 has not been paid.

6 The tax charge should be 30 per cent of the reported profit before taxation. Assume that it is payable, in full, shortly after the year-end.

Required:
Prepare a revised set of financial statements incorporating the additional information in 1–6 above. Note: Work to the nearest £1,000.

4.5 Rose Limited operates a small chain of retail shops that sell high-quality teas and coffees. Approximately half of sales are on credit. Abbreviated and unaudited financial statements are given below:

Rose Limited
Income statement (profit and loss account) for the year ended 31 March 2006

	£000	£000
Revenue		12,080
Cost of sales		(6,282)
Gross profit		5,798
Labour costs	(2,658)	
Depreciation	(625)	
Other operating costs	(1,003)	
		(4,286)
Net profit before interest		1,512
Interest payable		(66)
Net profit before tax		1,446
Tax payable		(434)
Net profit after tax		1,012
Dividend paid		(300)
Retained profit for year		712
Retained profit brought forward		756
Retained profit carried forward		1,468

Balance sheet as at 31 March 2006

	£000	£000
Non-current assets		2,728
Current assets		
Inventories (stock)	1,583	
Receivables (debtors)	996	
Cash	26	
	2,605	
Current liabilities		
Trade payables (creditors)	(1,118)	
Other payables (creditors)	(417)	
Tax	(434)	
Overdraft	(596)	
	(2,565)	
Net current assets		40
Non-current liabilities		
Secured loan (2011)		(300)
		2,468
Equity		
Share capital (50p shares, fully paid)		750
Share premium		250
Retained profit		1,468
		2,468

Since the unaudited financial statements for Rose Limited were prepared, the following information has become available:

1 An additional £74,000 of depreciation should have been charged on fixtures and fittings.
2 Invoices for credit sales on 31 March 2006 amounting to £34,000 have not been included; cost of sales is not affected.
3 Bad debts should be provided at a level of 2 per cent of receivables at the year end.
4 Inventories, which had been purchased for £2,000, have been damaged and are unsaleable. This is not reflected in the financial statements.
5 Fixtures and fittings to the value of £16,000 were delivered just before 31 March 2006, but these assets were not included in the financial statements and the purchase invoice had not been processed.
6 Wages for Saturday-only staff, amounting to £1,000, have not been paid for the final Saturday of the year. This is not reflected in the financial statements.
7 Tax is payable at 30 per cent of net profit after tax. Assume that it is payable shortly after the year-end.

Required:
Prepare revised financial statements for Rose Limited for the year ended 31 March 2006, incorporating the information in 1–7 above. Note: Work to the nearest £1,000.

Chapter 5

Measuring and reporting cash flows

Introduction

This chapter is devoted to the third major financial statement identified in Chapter 2 – the cash flow statement. This statement reveals the movements of cash over a period and the effect of these movements on the cash position of the business. It is an important financial statement because cash is important to the survival of a business. Without cash, no business can operate.

In this chapter, we shall see how the cash flow statement is prepared and how the information that it contains may be interpreted. We shall also see why the deficiencies of the income statement (profit and loss account) in revealing cash flows over time make a separate cash flow statement necessary.

The cash flow statement is being considered after the chapter on limited companies because the format of the statement requires an understanding of this type of business. Limited companies are required to provide a cash flow statement, as well as the more traditional income statement and balance sheet, for shareholders and other interested parties.

Learning outcomes

When you have completed this chapter, you should be able to:

- discuss the crucial importance of cash to a business;
- explain the nature of the cash flow statement and discuss how it can be helpful in identifying cash flow problems;
- prepare a cash flow statement;
- interpret a cash flow statement.

The cash flow statement

The cash flow statement is a fairly recent addition to the set of financial statements sent to shareholders and to others. There used to be no regulation requiring companies to produce more than an income statement and balance sheet. The prevailing view seemed to have been that any financial information required would be contained within these two statements. This view may have been based partly on the assumption that if a business were profitable, it would also have plenty of cash. Though in the very long run this is likely to be true, it is not necessarily true in the short to medium term.

We have already seen in Chapter 3 that the income statement sets out the revenue and expenses, rather than the cash receipts and cash payments, for the period. Thus, profit (loss), which represents the difference between the revenue and expenses for the period, may have little or no relation to the cash generated for the period. To illustrate this point, let us take the example of a business making a sale (a revenue). This may well lead to an increase in wealth and will be reflected in the income statement. However, if the sale is made on credit, no cash changes hands – not at the time of sale at least. Instead, the increase in wealth is reflected in another asset – an increase in trade receivables (debtors). Furthermore, if an item of inventories (stock) is the subject of the sale, wealth is lost to the business through the reduction in the inventories. This means an expense is incurred in making the sale, which will be shown in the income statement. Once again, however, no cash has changed hands at the time of sale. For such reasons, the profit and the cash generated for a period will rarely go hand in hand.

The following activity helps to underline how profit and cash for a period may be affected differently by particular transactions or events.

Activity 5.1

The following is a list of business/accounting events. In each case, state the effect (increase, decrease or no effect) on both cash and profit:

	Effect	
	on profit	*on cash*
1 Repayment of a loan	_____	_____
2 Making a sale on credit	_____	_____
3 Buying a non-current asset for cash	_____	_____
4 Receiving cash from a trade receivable (debtor)	_____	_____
5 Depreciating a non-current asset	_____	_____
6 Buying some inventories for cash	_____	_____
7 Making a share issue for cash	_____	_____

You should have come up with the following:

		Effect	
		On profit	*on cash*
1	Repayment of a loan	none	decrease
2	Making a sale on credit	increase	none
3	Buying a non-current asset for cash	none	decrease
4	Receiving cash from a trade receivable (debtor)	none	increase
5	Depreciating a non-current asset	decrease	none
6	Buying some inventories for cash	none	decrease
7	Making a share issue for cash	none	increase

The reasons for these answers are as follows:

1 Repaying the loan requires that cash be paid to the lender. Thus two figures in the balance sheet will be affected, but not the income statement.

2 Making a sale on credit will increase the sales revenue figure (and a profit or a loss – unless the sale was made for a price that precisely equalled the expenses involved). No cash will change hands at this point, however.

3 Buying a non-current asset for cash obviously reduces the cash balance of the business, but the profit figure is not affected.

4 Receiving cash from a receivable (debtor) increases the cash balance and reduces the receivable's balance. Both of these figures are on the balance sheet. The income statement is unaffected.

5 Depreciating a non-current asset means that an expense is recognised. This causes the value of the asset, as it is recorded on the balance sheet, to fall by an amount equal to the amount of the expense. No cash is paid or received.

6 Buying some inventories for cash means that the value of the Inventories will increase and the cash balance will decrease by a similar amount. Profit is not affected.

7 Making a share issue for cash increases the owners' claim and increases the cash balance; profit is unaffected.

It is clear from the above that if we are to gain an insight to cash movements over time, the income statement is not the answer. Instead we need a separate financial statement. This fact has become widely recognised in recent years and in 1991 a UK financial reporting standard, FRS 1, emerged that requires all but the smallest companies to produce and publish a cash flow statement. This standard has been superseded for many companies from 2005 by the international accounting standard IAS 7. The two standards have broadly similar requirements. This chapter follows the provisions of IAS 7.

Why is cash so important?

It is worth asking why is cash so important? After all, cash is just an asset that a business needs to help it to function. In that sense, it is no different from inventories or non-current assets.

The reason for the importance of cash is that people and organisations will not normally accept other than cash in settlement of their claims against the business. If a business wants to employ people it must pay them in cash. If it wants to buy a new non-current asset to exploit a business opportunity, the seller of the asset will normally insist on being paid in cash, probably after a short period of credit. When businesses fail, it is their inability to find the cash to pay the amounts owed that really pushes them under.

These factors lead to cash being the pre-eminent business asset. It is the one that analysts tend to watch most carefully when trying to assess the ability of businesses to survive and/or to take advantage of commercial opportunities as they arise. The fact that cash and profits do not always go hand in hand is illustrated in Real World 5.1. This explains how Eurotunnel, the cross-channel business between England and France continues to struggle to achieve profit, yet generates positive cash flows.

Real World 5.1

Cash flows under the channel   **FT**

Richard Shirrefs [Eurotunnel's chief executive] called for a shift from 'a stable equilibrium of failure to a stable equilibrium of success'.

The company, which last restructured its long term debt in 2003, proposes to shift to a lower price, higher volume model for tunnel usage. Access rates for train operators would be reduced to entice them to introduce more services to more destinations, such as Amsterdam, and to encourage greater freight traffic.

Eurotunnel progressed its own plans for freight on Monday, announcing it expected to start a traction business in 2005 and that a platform designed to accept continental gauge freight trains would begin operations at Folkestone at the same time.

Mr Shirrefs said taxpayers had invested £10bn and industry £15bn in the tunnel and associated infrastructure and: 'We need to get all that infrastructure working . . . neither investor nor taxpayer is getting value'.

Last year was a difficult one for Eurotunnel with reduced cross channel passenger flows bringing fare competition from ferry operators.

The company's operating revenue was down 5 per cent at £566m and its operating profit down 18 per cent at £170m. With interest payments of £318m, the underlying loss was up 40 per cent at £148m. However, it maintained a positive cash flow of £290m, down from £307m in 2002.

Source: Extracts from 'Eurotunnel takes £1.3bn impairment charge', Toby Shelley, *FT.com*, 9 February 2004

The main features of the cash flow statement

The cash flow statement is, in essence, a summary of the cash receipts and payments over the period concerned. All payments of a particular type, for example cash payments to acquire additional non-current assets or other investments, are added together to give just one figure that appears in the statement. The net total of the statement is the net increase or decrease of the cash (and cash equivalents) of the business over the period. The statement is basically an analysis of the business's cash (and cash equivalents) movements for the period.

A definition of cash and cash equivalents

IAS 7 defines cash as notes and coins in hand and deposits in banks and similar institutions that are accessible to the business on demand. Cash equivalents are short-term, highly liquid investments that are readily convertible to known amounts of cash and which are subject to an insignificant risk of changes of value. Cash equivalents are held for the purpose of meeting short-term cash commitments rather than for investment or other purposes.

Activity 5.2 should clarify the types of items that fall within the definition of 'cash equivalents'.

Activity 5.2

At the end of its accounting period, Zeneb plc's balance sheet included the following items:

1 *A bank deposit account where one month's notice of withdrawal is required.* This deposit was made because the business has a temporary cash surplus that it will need to use in the short term for operating purposes;

2 *Ordinary shares in Jones plc (a Stock Exchange listed business).* These were acquired because the business has a temporary cash surplus and Zeneb plc's directors believed that the share represented a good short-term investment. The funds invested will need to be used in the short term for operating purposes.

3 *A bank deposit account that is withdrawable instantly.* This represents an investment of surplus funds that are not seen as being needed in the short term.

4 *An overdraft on the business's bank current account.*

Which (if any) of these four items would be included in the figure for cash and cash equivalents?

Your response should have been as follows:

1 A cash equivalent, because the deposit is part of the business's normal cash management activities and there is little doubt about how much cash will be obtained when the deposit is withdrawn.

2 Not a cash equivalent. Although the investment was made as part of normal cash management, there is a significant risk that the amount expected (hoped for!) when the shares are sold may not actually be forthcoming.

3 Not a cash equivalent, because this represents an investment, rather than a short-term surplus amount of cash.

4 This is cash itself, though a negative amount of it. The only exception to this classification would be where the business is financed in the longer term by an overdraft, when it would be part of the financing of the business.

As can be seen from the responses to Activity 5.2, whether a particular item falls within the definition of cash and cash equivalent depends on two factors:

- the nature of the item;
- why it has arisen.

In practice, it is not usually difficult to decide whether an item is a cash equivalent.

The cash flow statement, the income statement and the balance sheet

The cash flow statement is now accepted, along with the income statement and balance sheet, as a primary financial statement. The relationship between the three statements is shown in Figure 5.1. The balance sheet reflects the combination of assets (including cash) and claims (including the owners' claim) of the business *at a particular point in time*. Both the cash flow statement and the income statement explain the *changes over a period* to two of the items in the balance sheet, namely cash and owners' claim respectively. In practice, this period is typically the business's accounting year.

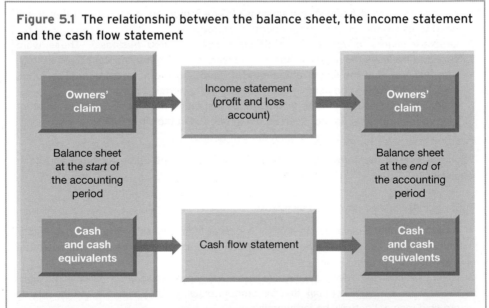

Figure 5.1 The relationship between the balance sheet, the income statement and the cash flow statement

The balance sheet shows the position, at a particular point in time, of the business's assets and claims. The income statement explains how, over a period between two balance sheets, the owners' claim figure in the first balance sheet has altered as a result of trading operations to become the figure in the second balance sheet. The cash flow statement also looks at changes over the accounting period, but this statement explains the alteration in the cash (and cash equivalent) balances shown in the two consecutive balance sheets.

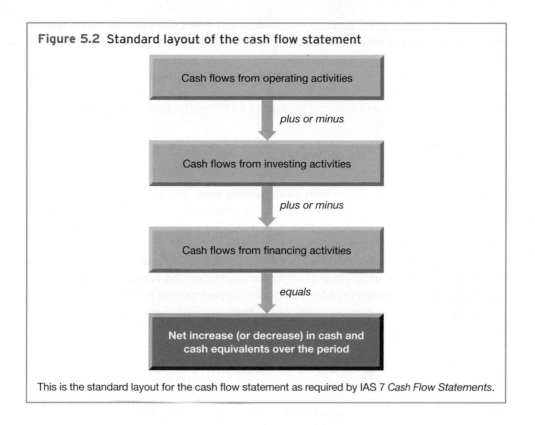

Figure 5.2 Standard layout of the cash flow statement

Cash flows from operating activities

plus or minus

Cash flows from investing activities

plus or minus

Cash flows from financing activities

equals

Net increase (or decrease) in cash and cash equivalents over the period

This is the standard layout for the cash flow statement as required by IAS 7 *Cash Flow Statements*.

The form of the cash flow statement

The standard layout of the cash flow statement is summarised in Figure 5.2. Explanations of the terms used in the cash flow statement are given below.

Cash flows from operating activities

This is the net inflow or outflow from trading operations, after tax and financing costs. It is equal to the sum of cash receipts from trade receivables, and cash receipts from cash sales where relevant, less the sums paid to buy inventories, to pay rent, to pay wages and so on. From this are also deducted payments for interest on the business's borrowings, corporation tax and dividends paid.

Note that it is the amounts of cash received and paid during the period that feature in the cash flow statement, not the revenue and expense for that period. It is, of course, the income statement that deals with the revenue and expenses. Similarly the tax and dividend payments that appear in the cash flow statement are those made in the period of the statement. Companies normally pay tax on their profits in four equal instalments. Two of these are during the year concerned, and the other two are during the following year. Thus by the end of each accounting year, one half of the tax will have been paid and the remainder will be a current liability at the end of the year, to be paid off during the following year. During any particular year, therefore, the tax payment would normally equal 50 per cent of the previous year's tax charge and 50 per cent of that of the current year.

The net figure for this section is intended to indicate the net cash flows for the period that arose from normal day-to-day trading activities after taking account of the tax that has to be paid on them and the cost of servicing the finance (equity and loans) needed to support them.

Cash flows from investing activities

This section of the statement is concerned with cash payments made to acquire additional non-current assets and with cash receipts from the disposal of non-current assets. These non-current assets will tend to be the usual non-current assets such as buildings, machinery and so on. They might also be loans made by the business or shares in another business bought by the business.

This section also includes receipts from investments (loans and equity investments) made outside the business. These receipts are interest on loans made by the business and dividends from shares in other businesses that are owned by the business.

This section shows the net cash flows from making new investments and/or disposing of existing ones.

Cash flows from financing activities

This part of the statement is concerned with the long-term financing of the business. So we are considering borrowings (other than very short term) and finance from share issues. This category is concerned with repayment/redemption of finance as well as with the raising of it. It is permissible under IAS 7 to include dividend payments made by the business here, as an alternative to including them in 'Cash flows from operating activities' (above).

This section shows the net cash flows from raising and/or paying back long-term finance.

Net increase or decrease in cash and cash equivalents

The total of the statement must, of course, be the net increase or decrease in cash and cash equivalents over the period covered by the statement.

The effect on a business's cash and cash equivalents of its various activities is shown in Figure 5.3. The activities that affect cash are analysed in the same way as is required by IAS 7. As explained below, the arrows in the figure show the *normal* direction of cash flow for the typical healthy, profitable business in a typical year.

The normal direction of cash flows

Normally 'operating activities' provide positive cash flows: that is, they help to increase the business's cash resources. In fact, for UK businesses, cash generated from day-to-day trading, even after deducting tax, interest and dividends, is overwhelmingly the most important source of new finance for most businesses in most time periods.

Figure 5.3 Diagrammatical representation of the cash flow statement

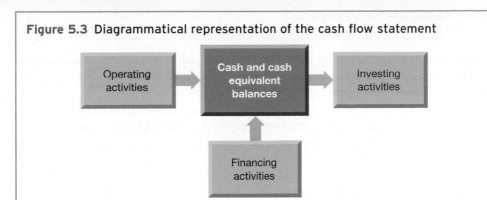

Various activities of the business each have their own effect on its cash and cash equivalent balances, either positive (increasing them) or negative (reducing them). The net increase or decrease in the cash and cash equivalent balances over a period will be the sum of these individual effects, taking account of the direction (cash in or cash out) of each activity.

Note that the direction of the arrow shows the *normal* direction of the cash flow in respect of each activity. In certain circumstances, each of these arrows could be reversed in direction.

Activity 5.3

Last year's cash flow statement for Angus plc showed a negative cash flow from operating activities. What could be the reason for this, and should the business's management be alarmed by it? (*Hint*: We think that there are two broad possible reasons for a negative cash flow.)

The two reasons are:

■ The business is unprofitable. This leads to more cash being paid out to employees, suppliers of goods and services, interest and so on, than is received from receivables in respect of sales. This would be particularly alarming, because a major expense for most businesses is depreciation of non-current assets. Since depreciation does not lead to a cash flow, it is not considered in 'net cash inflows from operating activities'. Thus, a negative operating cash flow might well indicate a very much larger trading loss – in other words, a significant loss of the business's wealth; something to concern management.

■ The other reason might be less alarming. A business that is expanding its activities (level of sales revenue) would tend to spend quite a lot of cash, relative to the amount of cash coming in from sales. This is because it will probably be expanding its assets (non-current and current) to accommodate the increased demand. For example, a business may well have to have inventories in place before additional sales can be made. Even when the additional sales are made, they would normally be made on credit, with the cash inflow lagging behind the sale. All of this means that in the first instance, in cash flow terms, the business would not necessarily benefit from the additional sales revenue. This would be particularly likely to be true of a new business, which would be expanding inventories and other assets from zero. Expansion typically causes cash flow strains for the reasons just explained. This can be a particular problem because the business's increased profitability might encourage a feeling of optimism, which could lead to lack of attention being paid to the cash flow problem.

Investing activities typically cause net negative cash flows. This is because most types of non-current asset wear out, and because businesses tend to seek to expand their asset base. When a business sells some non-current assets, this will give rise to positive cash flows, but in net terms the cash flows are normally negative with cash spent on new assets outweighing that received from disposal of old ones.

Financing can go in either direction, depending on the financing strategy at the time. Since businesses seek to expand, there is a general tendency for this area to lead to cash coming into the business rather than leaving it.

Real World 5.2 shows the summarised cash flow statement of Rolls-Royce plc, a major aerospace business, for the six month period to 30 June 2005.

Real World 5.2

Cash out of thin air

The published, summarised cash flow statement for Rolls-Royce plc for the six months to 30 June 2005, shows the cash flows of the business under each of the headings described above.

Summarised cash flow statement for the half year to 30 June 2005

	£m
Net cash inflow from operating activities	340
Net cash outflow from investing activities	(118)
Net cash (outflow)/inflow from financing activities	(63)
Increase in cash and cash equivalents	159
Cash and cash equivalents at 1 January	1,391
Exchange and other non-cash adjustments*	11
Cash and cash equivalents at period end	1,561

* This adjustment is required because transactions are undertaken by the company in different currencies and movements in exchange rates can lead to gains or losses.

Source: Rolls-Royce plc Interim results 2005. Published in *Financial Times*, 29 July 2005, p. 25

As we shall see below, more detailed information under each of the main headings is provided when a cash flow statement for a full year is prepared.

Preparing the cash flow statement

Deducing net cash flows from operating activities

The first section of the cash flow statement, and the one that is typically the most important for most businesses, is the 'cash flows from operating activities'. There are two methods that can be used to derive this figure: the direct method and the indirect method.

The direct method

→ The direct method involves an analysis of the cash records of the business for the period, picking out all payments and receipts relating to operating activities. These are summarised to give the total figures for inclusion in the cash flow statement. This could be a time-consuming and laborious activity, though a computer could do it. Not many businesses adopt this approach.

The indirect method

→ The indirect method is the more popular method. It relies on the fact that, broadly, sales revenue gives rise to cash inflows, and expenses give rise to outflows. Broadly, therefore, the net profit figure will be closely linked to the net cash inflows from operating activities. Since businesses have to produce an income statement in any case, information from it can be used as a starting point to deduce the cash flows from operating activities.

Of course, within a particular accounting period, net profit will not normally equal the net cash inflows from operating activities. We saw in Chapter 3 that, when sales are made on credit, the cash receipt occurs some time after the sale. This means that sales revenue made towards the end of an accounting year will be included in that year's income statement, but most of the cash from those sales will flow into the business, and should be included in the cash flow statement, in the following year. Fortunately it is easy to deduce the cash received from sales if we have the relevant income statement and balance sheets, as we shall see in Activity 5.4.

Activity 5.4

How can we deduce the cash inflows from sales using the income statement and balance sheet for the business?

The balance sheet will tell us how much was owed in respect of credit sales at the beginning and end of the year (trade receivables). The income statement tells us the sales revenue figure. If we adjust the sales revenue figure by the increase or decrease in trade receivables over the year, we deduce the cash from sales for the year.

Example 5.1

The sales revenue figure for a business for the year was £34m. The trade receivables were £4m at the beginning of the year, but had increased to £5m by the end of the year.

Basically, the receivables figure is affected by sales revenue and cash receipts. It is increased when a sale is made and decreased when cash is received from a receivable (debtor). If, over the year, the sales revenue and the cash receipts had been equal, the beginning-of-year and end-of-year receivables figures would have been equal. Since the receivables figure increased, it must mean that less cash was received than sales revenues were made. Thus the cash receipts from sales must be £33m (34 − (5 − 4)).

Put slightly differently, we can say that as a result of sales, assets of £34m flowed into the business during the year. If £1m of this went to increasing the asset of trade receivables, this leaves only £33m that went to increase cash.

The same general point is true in respect of nearly all of the other items that are taken into account in deducing the operating profit figure. The exception is depreciation. This is not necessarily associated with any movement in cash during the accounting period.

All of this means that we can take the operating profit (that is, the profit after interest but before tax) for the year, add back the depreciation and interest expense charged in arriving at that profit, and adjust this total by movements in inventories, trade receivables and payables (creditors). If we then go on to deduct payments made during the accounting period for corporation tax, loan interest and dividends, we have the net cash from operating activities.

Example 5.2

The relevant information from the financial statements of Dido plc for last year is as follows:

	£m
Net profit, after interest, before taxation	122
Depreciation charged in arriving at net profit	34
Interest expense	6
At the beginning of the year	
Inventories	15
Trade receivables	24
Trade payables	18
At the end of the year	
Inventories	17
Trade receivables	21
Trade payables	19

The following further information is available about payments during last year:

	£m
Corporation tax paid	32
Interest paid	5
Dividends paid	9

The cash flow from operating activities is derived as follows:

	£m	£m
Net profit, after interest, before taxation		122
Add Depreciation	34	
Interest expense	6	40
		162
Less Increase in inventories (17 – 15)		(2)
Add Decrease in trade receivables (21 – 24)	3	
Increase in trade payables (19 – 18)	1	4
Cash generated from operations		164
Less Interest paid	5	
Corporation tax paid	32	
Dividends paid	9	46
Net cash from operating activities		118

Thus, the net increase in working capital, as a result of trading, was £162 million. Of this, £2 million went into increased inventories. More cash was received from trade receivables than sales revenues were made, and less cash was paid to trade payables than purchases of goods and services on credit. Both of these had a favourable effect on cash, which increased by £164 million. When account was taken of the payments for interest, tax and dividends, the net cash flow from operating activities was £118 million (inflow).

Note that we needed to adjust the net profit, after interest, before taxation by the depreciation and interest expenses to derive the profit before depreciation, interest and taxation.

The indirect method of deducing the net cash flow from operating activities is summarised in Figure 5.4.

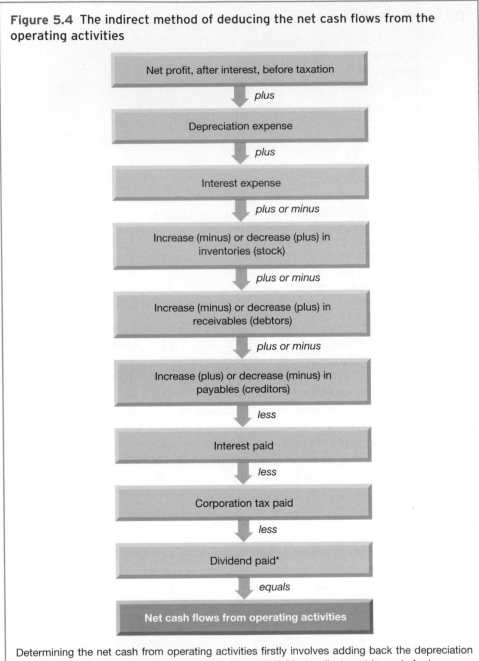

Figure 5.4 The indirect method of deducing the net cash flows from the operating activities

Net profit, after interest, before taxation

plus

Depreciation expense

plus

Interest expense

plus or minus

Increase (minus) or decrease (plus) in inventories (stock)

plus or minus

Increase (minus) or decrease (plus) in receivables (debtors)

plus or minus

Increase (plus) or decrease (minus) in payables (creditors)

less

Interest paid

less

Corporation tax paid

less

Dividend paid*

equals

Net cash flows from operating activities

Determining the net cash from operating activities firstly involves adding back the depreciation and the interest expense to the net profit for the period. Next, adjustment is made for increases or decreases in inventories, receivables and payables. Lastly, cash paid for interest, tax and dividends is deducted.

* Note that dividends could alternatively be included under the heading 'Cash flows from financing activities'.

Activity 5.5

The relevant information from the financial statements of Pluto plc for last year is as follows:

	£m
Net profit, after interest, before tax	165
Depreciation charged in arriving at net operating profit	41
Interest expense	21
At the beginning of the year:	
Inventories	22
Trade receivables	18
Trade payables	15
At the end of the year:	
Inventories	23
Trade receivables	21
Trade payables	17

The following further information is available about payments during last year:

	£m
Corporation tax paid	49
Interest paid	25
Dividends paid	28

What figure should appear in the cash flow statement for 'Cash flows from operating activities'?

Net cash inflows from operating activities:

	£m	£m
Net profit (after interest, before tax)		165
Add Depreciation	41	
Interest expense	21	62
		227
Less Increase in inventories (23 – 22)	1	
Increase in trade receivables (21 – 18)	3	(4)
Add Increase in trade payables (17 – 15)		2
Cash generated from operations		225
Less Interest paid	25	
Corporation tax paid	49	
Dividends paid	28	(102)
Net cash from operating activities		123

Figure 5.4 shows how the net cash flow from operating activities is derived. We can now go on to take a look at the preparation of a complete cash flow statement (see Example 5.3).

Example 5.3

Torbryan plc's income statement for the year ended 31 December 2006 and the balance sheets as at 31 December 2005 and 2006 are as follows:

Income statement for the year ended 31 December 2006

	£m	£m
Revenue		576
Less Cost of sales		307
Gross profit		269
Less Distribution costs	65	
Administrative expenses	26	91
		178
Other operating income		21
Operating profit		199
Interest receivable		17
		216
Less Interest payable		23
Profit on ordinary activities before taxation		193
Less Tax on profit (or loss) on ordinary activities		46
Profit on ordinary activities after taxation		147
Retained profit brought forward from last year		26
		173
Less Dividend paid on ordinary shares		50
Retained profit carried forward		123

Balance sheets as at 31 December 2005 and 2006

	2005 £m	*2006* £m
Non-current assets		
Property, plant and equipment		
Land and buildings	241	241
Plant and machinery	309	325
	550	566
Current assets		
Inventories	44	41
Trade receivables	121	139
	165	180
Less **Current liabilities**		
Bank overdraft	68	56
Trade payables	55	54
Corporation tax	16	23
	139	133
Net current assets	26	47
Total assets *less* current liabilities	576	613
Less **Non-current liabilities**		
Debenture loans	400	250
	176	363

Equity		
Called-up ordinary share capital	150	200
Share premium account	–	40
Retained earnings	26	123
	176	363

During 2006, the business spent £95 million on additional plant and machinery. There were no other non-current-asset acquisitions or disposals. The interest receivable revenue and the interest payable expenses for the year were equal to the cash inflow and outflow respectively.

The cash flow statement would be as follows:

Torbryan plc
Cash flow statement for the year ended 31 December 2006

	£m	£m
Cash flows from operating activities		
Net profit, after interest, before taxation (see Note 1 below)		193
Adjustments for:		
Depreciation (Note 2)		79
Investment income (Note 3)		(17)
Interest expense (Note 4)		23
		278
Increase in trade receivables (139 – 121)		(18)
Decrease in trade payables (55 – 54)		(1)
Decrease in inventories (44 – 41)		3
Cash generated from operations		262
Interest paid		(23)
Corporation tax paid (Note 5)		(39)
Dividend paid		(50)
Net cash from operating activities		150
Cash flows from investing activities		
Payments to acquire tangible non-current assets	(95)	
Interest received (Note 3)	17	
Net cash used in investing activities		(78)
Cash flows from financing activities		
Repayments of debenture stock (Note 6)	(150)	
Issue of ordinary shares (Note 7)	90	
Net cash used in financing activities		(60)
Net increase in cash and cash equivalents		12
Cash and cash equivalents at 1 January 2006 (Note 8)		(68)
Cash and cash equivalents at 31 December 2006		(56)

To see how this relates to the cash of the business at the beginning and end of the year it can be useful to provide a reconciliation as follows:

Analysis of cash and cash equivalents during the year ended 31 December 2006

	£m
Overdraft balance at 1 January 2006	(68)
Net cash inflow	12
Overdraft balance at 31 December 2006	(56)

→

Notes

1 This is simply taken from the income statement for the year.

2 Since there were no disposals, the depreciation charges must be the difference between the start and end of the year's plant and machinery (non-current assets) values, adjusted by the cost of any additions.

	£m
Book value, at 1 January 2006	309
Add Additions	95
	404
Less Depreciation (balancing figure)	79
Book value, at 31 December 2006	325

3 Investment income (interest receivable) must be taken away to work towards the profit before crediting it, because it is not part of operations, but of investing activities. The cash inflow from this source appears under the 'Cash flows from investing activities' heading.

4 Interest payable expense must be taken out, by adding it back to the profit figure. We subsequently deduct the cash paid for interest payable during the year. In this case the two figures are identical.

5 Tax is paid by companies 50 per cent during their accounting year and the other 50 per cent in the following year. Thus the 2006 payment would have been half the tax on the 2005 profit (that is, the figure that would have appeared in the current liabilities at the end of 2005), plus half of the 2006 tax charge (that is, $16 + (1/2 \times 46) = 39$). Probably the easiest way to deduce the amount paid during the year to 31 December 2006 is by following this approach:

	£m
Tax owed at start of the year (from the balance sheet as at 31 December 2005)	16
Add Tax charge for the year (from the income statement)	46
	62
Less Tax owed at the end of the year (from the balance sheet as at 31 December 2006)	23
Tax paid during the year	39

This follows the logic that if we start with what the business owed at the beginning of the year, add on the increase in what was owed as a result of the current year's tax and then deduct what was owed at the end, the resulting figure must be what was paid during the year.

6 It has been assumed that the debentures were redeemed for their balance sheet value. This is not, however, always the case.

7 The share issue raised £90 million, of which £50 million went into the share capital total on the balance sheet and £40 million into share premium.

8 There were no 'cash equivalents', just cash (though negative).

What does the cash flow statement tell us?

The cash flow statement tells us how the business has generated cash during the period and where that cash has gone. Since cash is properly regarded as the lifeblood of just about any business, this is potentially very useful information.

Tracking the sources and uses of cash over several years could show financing trends that a reader of the statements could use to help to make predictions about the likely future behaviour of the company.

Looking specifically at the cash flow statement for Torbryan plc, in Example 5.3, we can see the following:

- Net cash flow from operations was strong, much larger than the profit figure, after taking account of the dividend paid. This would be expected because depreciation is deducted in arriving at profit. There was a general tendency for working capital to absorb some cash. This would not be surprising had there been an expansion of activity (sales output) over the year. From the information supplied, we do not know whether there was an expansion or not. (We have only one year's income statement.)
- There were net outflows of cash for investing activities, but this would not be unusual. Many items of property, plant and equipment have limited lives and need to be replaced with new ones. The expenditure during the year was not out of line with the depreciation expense for the year, which is what we might expect.
- There was a fairly major outflow of cash to redeem some debt finance, partly offset by the proceeds of a share issue. This presumably represents a change of financing strategy. Together with the ploughed-back profit from trading, there has been a significant shift in the equity/debt balance.

Real World 5.3 below indicates the importance of the cash flow statement in analysing the health of one well-known business.

Real World 5.3

Watching the cash flows   **FT**

When WaterfordWedgwood reports its annual results today, brokers will be focused not just on the income statement of the crystal and porcelain manufacturer, or the balance sheet – the traditional windows on the health of a company – but on the cash flow statement.

Brokers, in particular, are looking for signs of improvement in the working capital position – the company's ability to squeeze more cash from suppliers, to get paid earlier by its customers and reduce the amount of costly product held in its warehouses or elsewhere in the supply chain.

The signs are mixed. The company this month warned that profits for the period to March 31 would be €12m (£8m) or 15 per cent shy of what it had been predicting in January.

It cited difficulties at its German porcelain subsidiary. It was also hit when US stores did not restock after the Christmas sales.

The poorer trading means inventories levels should be lower. On the other hand, there is less cash generated to pay down the debt . . .

Going forward, the big challenge is to extract more cash from the businesses. Accenture, the consultant, has been asked to look at the issue.

John Sheehan, at NCB stockbrokers, anticipates big inventories write-offs. 'The real issue is can they do this without saturating the market and hurting the brand?' he asks.

On the manufacturing side, the company is adopting a twin approach, outsourcing the manufacturing to cheaper locations while harnessing big-name designers to appeal to a younger consumer.

Source: 'WaterfordWedgwood face some intense questions over its cash flow', *Financial Times*, 17 June 2004, FT.com

Touchstone plc's income statements for the years ended 31 December 2005 and 2006 and the balance sheets as at 31 December 2005 and 2006 are as follows:

Income statements for the years ended 2005 and 2006

	2005 £m	2006 £m
Revenue	173	207
Cost of sales	(96)	(101)
Gross profit	77	106
Distribution costs	(18)	(20)
Administrative expenses	(24)	(26)
	35	60
Other operating income	3	4
Operating profit	38	64
Interest payable	(2)	(4)
Profit on ordinary activities before taxation	36	60
Tax on profit on ordinary activities	(8)	(16)
Profit on ordinary activities after taxation	28	44
Retained profit brought forward from last year	16	30
	44	74
Less Dividend paid on ordinary shares	14	18
Retained profit carried forward	30	56

Balance sheets as at 31 December 2005 and 2006

	2005 £m	2006 £m
Non-current assets		
Property, plant and equipment		
Land and buildings	94	110
Plant and machinery	53	62
	147	172
Current assets		
Inventories	25	24
Treasury bills (short-term investments)	–	15
Trade receivables	16	26
Cash at bank and in hand	4	4
	45	69
Less **Current liabilities**		
Trade payables	38	37
Corporation tax	4	8
	42	45
Net current assets	3	24
Total assets less current liabilities	150	196
Less **Non-current liabilities**		
Debenture loans (10%)	20	40
	130	156

Equity

Called-up ordinary share capital		100	100
Retained earnings		30	56
		130	156

Included in 'cost of sales', 'distribution costs' and 'administration expenses', depreciation was as follows:

	2005	2006
	£m	£m
Land and buildings	5	6
Plant and machinery	6	10

There were no non-current asset disposals in either year.

The interest payable expense equalled the cash payment made during the year.

The Treasury bills represent a short-term investment of funds that will be used shortly in operations. There is insignificant risk that this investment will lose value.

Required:

Prepare a cash flow statement for the business for 2006.

Summary

The main points of this chapter may be summarised as follows:

The need for a cash flow statement:

- Cash is important because no business can operate without it.
- The cash flow statement is specifically designed to reveal movements in cash over a period.
- Cash movements cannot be readily detected from the income statement, which focuses on revenue and expenses rather than on cash receipts and cash payments.
- Profit (loss) and cash generated for the period are rarely equal.
- The cash flow statement is a primary financial statement, along with the income statement and the balance sheet.

Preparing the cash flow statement:

- The layout of the statement contains three categories of cash movement:
  - cash flows from operating activities;
  - cash flows from investing activities;
  - cash flows from financing activities.
- The total of the cash movements under these three categories will provide the net increase or decrease in cash and cash equivalents for the period.

→

- A reconciliation can be undertaken to check that the opening balance of cash and cash equivalents plus the net increase (decrease) for the period equals the closing balance.

Calculating the cash generated from operations:

- The net cash flows from operating activities can be derived by either the direct method or the indirect method.

- The direct method is based on an analysis of the cash records for the period, whereas the indirect method uses information contained within the income statement and balance sheets of the business.

- The indirect method takes the net operating profit for the period, adds back any depreciation charge and then adjusts for changes in inventories, receivables and payables during the period.

Interpreting the cash flow statement:

- The cash flow statement shows the main sources and uses of cash.

- Tracking the cash movements over several periods may reveal financing and investing patterns and may help predict future management action.

→ Key terms

direct method p. 149
indirect method p. 149

Further reading

If you would like to explore the topics covered in this chapter in more depth, we recommend the following books:

Elliott, B. and Elliott, J. *Financial Accounting and Reporting*, 9th edn, Financial Times Prentice Hall, 2004, Chapter 13.

IASB, *International Accounting Standard (IAS)7*, International Accounting Standards Board, 1993.

McLaney, E. and Atrill, P. *Accounting: An Introduction*, 3rd edn, Financial Times Prentice Hall, 2005, Chapter 6.

Sutton, T. *Corporate Financial Accounting and Reporting*, 2nd edn, Financial Times Prentice Hall, 2004, Chapter 18.

? Review questions

Answers to these questions can be found at the back of the book (pp. 490–1).

5.1 The typical business outside the service sector has about 50 per cent more of its resources tied up in inventories than in cash, yet there is no call for a 'inventories flow statement' to be prepared. Why is cash regarded as more important than inventories?

5.2 What is the difference between the direct and indirect methods of deducing cash generated from operations?

5.3 Taking each of the categories of the cash flow statement in turn, in which direction would you normally expect the cash flow to be? Explain your answer.
(a) Cash flows from operating activities.
(b) Cash flows from investing activities.
(c) Cash flows from financing activities.

5.4 What causes the net profit for the year not to equal the net cash inflow?

✳ Exercises

Exercises 5.3 to 5.5 are more advanced than 5.1 and 5.2. Those with coloured numbers have answers at the back of the book (pp. 506–8).

If you wish to try more exercises, visit the students' side of the companion website.

5.1 How will each of the following events ultimately affect the amount of cash?
(a) An increase in the level of inventories.
(b) A rights issue of ordinary shares.
(c) A bonus issue of ordinary shares.
(d) Writing off part of the value of some inventories.
(e) The disposal of a large number of the business's shares by a major shareholder.
(f) Depreciating a non-current asset.

5.2 The following information has been taken from the financial statements of Juno plc for last year and the year before last:

	Year before last	Last year
	£m	£m
Net operating profit	156	187
Depreciation charged in arriving at net operating profit	47	55
Inventories held at the end of:	27	31
Receivables at the end of:	24	23
Payables at the end of:	15	17

Required:
What is the cash generated from operations figure for Juno plc for last year?

→

5.3 Torrent plc's income statement for the year ended 31 December 2006 and the balance sheets as at 31 December 2005 and 2006 are as follows:

Income statement

	£m	£m
Revenue		623
Less Cost of sales		353
Gross profit		270
Less Distribution costs	71	
Administrative expenses	30	101
		169
Rental income		27
Operating profit		196
Less Interest payable		26
Profit on ordinary activities before taxation		170
Less Tax on profit on ordinary activities		36
Profit on ordinary activities after taxation		134
Retained profit brought forward from last year		123
		257
Less Dividend paid on ordinary shares		60
Retained profit carried forward		197

Balance sheets as at 31 December 2005 and 2006

	2005 £m	2006 £m
Non-current assets		
Property, plant and equipment		
Land and buildings	310	310
Plant and machinery	325	314
	635	624
Current assets		
Inventories	41	35
Trade receivables	139	145
	180	180
Current liabilities		
Bank overdraft	56	89
Trade payables	54	41
Corporation tax	23	18
	133	148
Net current assets	47	32
Total assets less current liabilities	682	656
Less **Non-current liabilities**		
Debenture loans	250	150
	432	506
Equity		
Called-up ordinary share capital	200	300
Share premium account	40	–
Revaluation reserve	69	9
Retained earnings	123	197
	432	506

During 2006, the business spent £67 million on additional plant and machinery. There were no other non-current asset acquisitions or disposals.

There was no share issue for cash during the year. The interest payable expense was equal in amount to the cash outflow.

Required:

Prepare the cash flow statement for Torrent plc for the year ended 31 December 2006.

5.4 Chen plc's income statements for the years ended 31 December 2005 and 2006 and the balance sheets as at 31 December 2005 and 2006 are as follows:

Income statement

	2005 £m	2006 £m
Revenue	207	153
Cost of sales	(101)	(76)
Gross profit	106	77
Distribution costs	(22)	(20)
Administrative expenses	(20)	(28)
Operating profit	64	29
Interest payable	(4)	(4)
Profit on ordinary activities before taxation	60	25
Tax on profit (or loss) on ordinary activities	(16)	(6)
Profit on ordinary activities after taxation	44	19
Retained profit brought forward from last year	30	56
	74	75
Dividends paid on ordinary shares	(18)	(18)
Retained profit carried forward	56	57

Balance sheets as at 31 December 2005 and 2006

	2005 £m	2006 £m
Non-current assets		
Property, plant and equipment		
Land and buildings	110	130
Plant and machinery	62	56
	172	186
Current assets		
Inventories	24	25
Trade receivables	26	25
Cash at bank and in hand	19	–
	69	50
Less **Current liabilities**		
Bank overdraft	–	2
Trade payables	37	34
Corporation tax	8	3
	45	39
Net current assets	24	11
Total assets less current liabilities	196	197
Less **Non-current liabilities**		
Debenture loans (10%)	40	40
	156	157

→

Equity

Called-up ordinary share capital	100	100
Retained earnings	56	57
	156	157

Included in 'cost of sales', 'distribution costs' and 'administrative expenses', depreciation was as follows:

	2005	2006
	£m	£m
Land and buildings	6	10
Plant and machinery	10	12

There were no non-current asset disposals in either year. The amount of cash paid for interest equalled the expense in both years.

Required:

Prepare a cash flow statement for the business for 2006.

5.5 The following financial statements for Blackstone plc are a slightly simplified set of published accounts. Blackstone plc is an engineering business that developed a new range of products in 2004; these now account for 60 per cent of its turnover.

Income statement for the years ended 31 March

	Notes	2005 £m	2006 £m
Revenue		7,003	11,205
Cost of sales		(3,748)	(5,809)
Gross profit		3,255	5,396
Operating costs		(2,205)	(3,087)
Operating profit		1,050	2,309
Interest payable	1	(216)	(456)
Profit before taxation		834	1,853
Taxation		(210)	(390)
Profit after taxation		624	1,463
Dividend paid		(300)	(400)
Retained profit for the year		324	1,063
Retained profit brought forward		361	685
Retained profit carried forward		685	1,748

Balance sheets as at 31 March

	Notes	2005 £m	2005 £m	2006 £m	2006 £m
Non-current assets					
Intangible assets	2		–		700
Property, plant and equipment	3		4,300		7,535
			4,300		8,235
Current assets					
Inventories		1,209		2,410	
Trade receivables		641		1,173	
Cash at bank		123		–	
		1,973		3,583	
Current liabilities					
Trade payables		(931)		(1,507)	
Taxation		(105)		(195)	
Bank overdraft		–		(1,816)	
		(1,036)		(3,518)	
Net current assets			937		65
Non-current liabilities					
Bank loan (repayable 2010)			(1,800)		(3,800)
			3,437		4,500
Equity					
Share capital			1,800		1,800
Share premium			600		600
Capital reserves			352		352
Retained profits			685		1,748
			3,437		4,500

Notes

1 The expense and the cash outflow for interest payable are equal.
2 Intangible assets represent the amounts paid for the goodwill of another engineering business acquired during the year.
3 The movements in property, plant and equipment during the year are set out below.

	Land and buildings £m	Plant and machinery £m	Fixtures and fittings £m	Total £m
Cost				
At 1 April 2005	4,500	3,850	2,120	10,470
Additions	–	2,970	1,608	4,578
Disposals	–	(365)	(216)	(581)
At 31 March 2006	4,500	6,455	3,512	14,467
Depreciation				
At 1 April 2005	1,275	3,080	1,815	6,170
Charge for year	225	745	281	1,251
Disposals	–	(305)	(184)	(489)
At 31 March 2006	1,500	3,520	1,912	6,932
Net book value				
At 31 March 2006	3,000	2,935	1,600	7,535

Proceeds from the sale of non-current assets in the year ended 31 March 2006 amounted to £54 million.

Required:

Prepare a cash flow statement for Blackstone plc for the year ended 31 March 2006. (*Hint*: A loss (deficit) on disposal of non-current assets is simply an additional amount of depreciation and should be dealt with as such in preparing the cash flow statement.)

Chapter 6

Analysing and interpreting financial statements

Introduction

In this chapter we shall consider the analysis and interpretation of the financial statements discussed in Chapters 2 and 3. We shall see how financial (or accounting) ratios can help in assessing the financial health of a business. We shall also consider the problems that are encountered when applying this technique.

Financial ratios can be used to examine various aspects of financial position and performance and are widely used for planning and control purposes. As we shall see in later chapters, they can be very helpful to managers in a wide variety of decision areas, such as working-capital management and financial structure.

Learning outcomes

When you have completed this chapter, you should be able to:

- identify the major categories of ratios that can be used for analysis purposes;
- calculate important ratios for assessing the financial performance and position of a business;
- explain the significance of the ratios calculated;
- discuss the limitations of ratios as a tool of financial analysis.

Financial ratios

Financial ratios provide a quick and relatively simple means of assessing the financial health of a business. A ratio simply relates one figure appearing in the financial statements to some other figure appearing there (for example, net profit in relation to capital employed) or, perhaps, to some resource of the business (for example, net profit per employee, sales revenue per square metre of counter space and so on).

Ratios can be very helpful when comparing the financial health of different businesses. Differences may exist between businesses in the scale of operations, and so a direct comparison of, say, the profits generated by each business may be misleading. By expressing profit in relation to some other measure (for example, capital (or funds) employed), the problem of scale is eliminated. A business with a profit of, say, £10,000 and capital employed of £100,000 can be compared with a much larger business with a profit of, say, £80,000 and sales revenue of £1,000,000 by the use of a simple ratio. The net profit to capital employed ratio for the smaller business is 10 per cent ([10,000/100,000] × 100%) and the same ratio for the larger business is 8 per cent ([80,000/1,000,000] × 100%). These ratios can be directly compared whereas comparison of the absolute profit figures would be less meaningful. The need to eliminate differences in scale through the use of ratios can also apply when comparing the performance of the same business over time.

By calculating a relatively small number of ratios, it is often possible to build up a good picture of the position and performance of a business. Thus, it is not surprising that ratios are widely used by those who have an interest in businesses and business performance. Though ratios are not difficult to calculate, they can be difficult to interpret and so it is important to appreciate that they are really only the starting point for further analysis.

Ratios help to highlight the financial strengths and weaknesses of a business, but they cannot, by themselves, explain why certain strengths or weaknesses exist, or why certain changes have occurred. Only a detailed investigation will reveal these underlying reasons.

Ratios can be expressed in various forms, for example as a percentage or as a proportion. The way that a particular ratio is presented will depend on the needs of those who will use the information. Although it is possible to calculate a large number of ratios, only a relatively few based on key relationships tend to be helpful to a particular user. Many ratios that could be calculated from the financial statements (for example, rent payable in relation to current assets) may not be considered because there is no clear or meaningful relationship between the two items.

There is no generally accepted list of ratios that can be applied to the financial statements, nor is there a standard method of calculating many ratios. Variations in both the choice of ratios and their calculation will be found in practice. However, it is important to be consistent in the way in which ratios are calculated for comparison purposes. The ratios that we shall now go on to discuss are those that are widely used.

They are popular because many consider them to be among the more important for decision-making purposes.

Financial ratio classifications

Ratios can be grouped into categories, each of which relates to a particular aspect of financial performance or position. The following broad categories provide a useful basis for explaining the nature of the financial ratios to be dealt with. There are five of them:

- *Profitability*. Businesses generally exist with the primary purpose of creating wealth for their owners. Profitability ratios provide an insight to the degree of success in achieving this purpose. They express the profits made (or figures bearing on profit, such as overheads) in relation to other key figures in the financial statements or to some business resource.
- *Efficiency*. Ratios may be used to measure the efficiency with which particular resources have been used within the business. These ratios are also referred to as *activity* ratios.
- *Liquidity*. It is vital to the survival of a business for there to be sufficient liquid resources available to meet maturing obligations (that is, debts that must be paid in the relatively near future). Some liquidity ratios examine the relationship between liquid resources held and payables (creditors) due for payment in the near future.
- *Financial gearing*. This is the relationship between the contribution to financing the business made by the owners of the business and the amount contributed by others, in the form of loans. The level of gearing has an important effect on the degree of risk associated with a business, as we shall see. Gearing is, therefore, something that managers must consider when making financing decisions. Gearing ratios tend to highlight the extent to which the business uses loan finance.
- *Investment*. Certain ratios are concerned with assessing the returns and performance of shares held in a particular business from the perspective of shareholders who are not involved with the management of the business.

The analyst must be clear *who* the target users are and *why* they need the information.

Different users of financial information are likely to have different information needs, which will in turn determine the ratios that they find useful. For example, shareholders are likely to be interested in their returns in relation to the level of risk associated with their investment. Thus profitability, investment and gearing ratios will be of particular interest. Long-term lenders are concerned with the long-term viability of the business and to help them to assess this, the profitability and gearing ratios of the business are also likely to be of particular interest. Short-term lenders, such as suppliers of goods and services on credit, may be interested in the ability of the business to repay the amounts owing in the short term. As a result, the liquidity ratios should be of interest.

We shall consider ratios falling into each of the five categories (profitability, efficiency, liquidity, gearing and investment) a little later in the chapter.

The need for comparison

Merely calculating a ratio will not tell us very much about the position or performance of a business. For example, if a ratio revealed that the business was generating £100 in sales revenue per square metre of counter space, it would not be possible to deduce from this information alone whether this particular level of performance was good, bad or indifferent. It is only when we compare this ratio with some 'benchmark' that the information can be interpreted and evaluated.

Activity 6.1

Can you think of any bases that could be used to compare a ratio you have calculated from the financial statements of a particular period?
   We feel that there are three sensible possibilities.

You may have thought of the following bases:

- past periods for the same business;
- similar businesses for the same or past periods;
- planned performance for the business.

We shall now take a closer look at these three in turn.

Past periods

By comparing the ratio we have calculated with the same ratio, but for a previous period, it is possible to detect whether there has been an improvement or deterioration in performance. Indeed, it is often useful to track particular ratios over time (say, five or ten years) to see whether it is possible to detect trends. The comparison of ratios from different time periods brings certain problems, however. In particular, there is always the possibility that trading conditions may have been quite different in the periods being compared. There is the further problem that, when comparing the performance of a single business over time, operating inefficiencies may not be clearly exposed. For example, the fact that sales revenue per employee has risen by 10 per cent over the previous period may at first sight appear to be satisfactory. This may not be the case, however, if similar businesses have shown an improvement of 50 per cent for the same period. Finally, there is the problem that inflation may have distorted the figures on which the ratios are based. Inflation can lead to an overstatement of profit and an understatement of asset values.

Similar businesses

In a competitive environment, a business must consider its performance in relation to that of other businesses operating in the same industry. Survival may depend on the ability to achieve comparable levels of performance. Thus a very useful basis for comparing a particular ratio is the ratio achieved by similar businesses during the same period. This basis is not, however, without its problems. Competitors may have different year ends, and therefore trading conditions may not be identical. They may also have different accounting policies, which can have a significant effect on reported profits and asset values (for example, different methods of calculating depreciation or valuing inventories (stock)). Finally, it may be difficult to obtain the financial statements of competitor businesses. Sole proprietorships and partnerships, for example, are not obliged to make their financial statements available to the public. In the case of limited companies, there is a legal obligation to do so. However, a diversified business may not provide a breakdown of activities that is sufficiently detailed to enable analysts to compare the activities with those of other businesses.

Planned performance

Ratios may be compared with the targets that management developed before the start of the period under review. The comparison of planned performance with actual performance may therefore be a useful way of revealing the level of achievement attained. However, the planned levels of performance must be based on realistic assumptions if they are to be useful for comparison purposes.

Planned performance is likely to be the most valuable benchmark for the managers to assess their own business. Businesses tend to develop planned ratios for each aspect of their activities. When formulating its plans, a business may usefully take account of its own past performance and that of other businesses. There is no reason, however, why a particular business should seek to achieve either its own previous performance or that of other businesses. Neither of these may be seen as an appropriate target.

Analysts outside the business do not normally have access to the business's plans. For these people, past performance and the performances of other, similar, businesses may be the only practical benchmarks.

Calculating the ratios

Probably the best way to explain financial ratios is through an example. Example 6.1 provides a set of financial statements from which we can calculate important ratios.

Example 6.1

The following financial statements relate to Alexis plc, which operates a wholesale carpet business:

Balance sheets as at 31 March

	2005 £m	2005 £m	2006 £m	2006 £m
Non-current assets				
Property, plant and equipment (at cost less depreciation)				
Freehold land and buildings	381		427	
Fixtures and fittings	129		160	
		510		587
Current assets				
Inventories at cost	300		406	
Trade receivables	240		273	
Bank	4		–	
	544		679	
Current liabilities				
Trade payables	(221)		(314)	
Dividends approved, but unpaid	(40)		(40)	
Corporation tax due	(30)		(2)	
Bank overdraft	–		(76)	
	(291)	253	(432)	247
		763		834
Non-current liabilities				
9% debentures (secured)		(200)		(300)
		563		534
Equity				
£0.50 ordinary shares (Note 1)		300		300
Retained profit		263		234
		563		534

Income statements (profit and loss accounts) for the year ended 31 March

	2005 £m	2006 £m
Revenue (Note 2)	2,240	2,681
Less Cost of sales (Note 3)	1,745	2,272
Gross profit	495	409
Less Operating costs	252	362
Net profit before interest and tax	243	47
Less Interest payable	18	32
Net profit before tax	225	15
Less Corporation tax	60	4
Net profit after tax	165	11
Add Retained profit brought forward	138	263
	303	274
Less Dividends approved, but unpaid (Note 4)	40	40
Retained profit carried forward	263	234

Notes

1 The market value of the shares of the business at the end of the year was £2.50 for 2005 and £1.50 for 2006.
2 All sales and purchases are made on credit.
3 The cost of sales figure can be analysed as follows:

	2005 £m	2006 £m
Opening inventories	241	300
Purchases (Note 2)	1,804	2,378
	1,045	2,678
Less Closing inventories	300	406
Cost of sales	1,745	2,272

4 The dividend had been approved by the shareholders before the end of the accounting year (in both years), but not paid until after then.
5 The business employed 13,995 staff at 31 March 2005 and 18,623 at 31 March 2006.
6 The business expanded its capacity during 2006 by setting up a new warehouse and distribution centre in the north of England.
7 At 1 April 2004, the total of equity stood at £438 million and the total of equity and non-current liabilities stood at £638 million.

A brief overview

Before we start our detailed look at the ratios for Alexis plc (in Example 6.1), it is helpful to take a quick look at what information is obvious from the financial statements. This will usually pick up some issues that the ratios may not be able to identify. It may also highlight some points that could help us in our interpretation of the ratios. Starting at the top of the balance sheet, the following points can be noted:

- *Expansion of non-current assets.* These have increased by about 15 per cent (from £510 million to £587 million). Note 5 mentions a new warehouse and distribution centre, which may account for much of the additional investment in non-current assets. We are not told when this new facility was established, but it is quite possible that it was well into the year. This could mean that not much benefit was reflected in terms of additional sales revenue or cost saving during 2006. Sales revenue, in fact, expanded by about 20 per cent (from £2,240 million to £2,681 million), greater than the expansion in non-current assets.
- *Major expansion in the elements of working capital.* Inventories (stock) increased by about 35 per cent, trade receivables (debtors) by about 14 per cent and trade payables (creditors) by about 42 per cent between 2005 and 2006. These are major increases, particularly in inventories and payables (which are linked because the inventories are all bought on credit – see Note 2).
- *Reduction in the cash balance.* The cash balance fell from £4 million (in funds) to a £76 million overdraft, between 2005 and 2006. The bank may be putting the business under pressure to reverse this, which could raise difficulties.

- *Apparent debt capacity.* Comparing either the non-current assets or the net assets with the long-term borrowings implies that the business may well be able to offer security on further borrowing. This is because potential lenders usually look at the value of assets that can be offered as security when assessing loan requests. Lenders seem particularly attracted to freeholds as security. For example, at 31 March 2006, non-current assets had a balance sheet value of £587 million, but long-term borrowing was only £300 million (though there was also an overdraft of £74 million). Balance sheet values are not normally, of course, market values. On the other hand, freeholds tend to have a market value higher than their balance sheet value due to inflation in land values.
- *Lower profit.* Though sales revenue expanded by 20 per cent between 2005 and 2006, both cost of sales and operating costs rose by a greater percentage, leaving both gross profit and, particularly, net profit massively reduced. The level of staffing, which increased by about 33 per cent (from 13,995 to 18,623), may have greatly affected the operating costs. (Without knowing when the additional employees were recruited during 2006, we cannot be sure of the effect on operating costs.) Increasing staffing by 33 per cent must put an enormous strain on management, at least in the short term. It is not surprising, therefore that 2006 was not successful for the business.

Having had a quick look at what is fairly obvious without calculating the normal ratios, we shall now go on to do so.

Profitability

The following ratios may be used to evaluate the profitability of the business:

- return on ordinary shareholders' funds;
- return on capital employed;
- net profit margin; and
- gross profit margin.

We shall now look at each of these in turn.

Return on ordinary shareholders' funds (ROSF)

The return on ordinary shareholders' funds compares the amount of profit for the period available to the owners, with the owners' average stake in the business during that same period. The ratio (which is normally expressed in percentage terms) is as follows:

$$\text{ROSF} = \frac{\text{Net profit after taxation and preference dividend (if any)}}{\text{Ordinary share capital plus reserves}} \times 100$$

The net profit after taxation and any preference dividend is used in calculating the ratio, as this figure represents the amount of profit that is left for the owners.

In the case of Alexis plc, the ratio for the year ended 31 March 2005 is:

$$\text{ROSF} = \frac{165}{(438 + 563)/2} \times 100 = 33.0\%$$

Note that, when calculating the ROSF, the average of the figures for ordinary shareholders' funds as at the beginning and at the end of the year has been used. It is preferable to use an average figure, as this might be more representative. This is because the shareholders' funds did not have the same total throughout the year, yet we want to compare it with the profit earned during the whole period. We know, from Note 7, that the total of the shareholders' funds at 1 April 2004 was £438 million. By a year later, however, it had risen to £563 million, according to the balance sheet as at 31 March 2005.

The easiest approach to calculating the average amount of shareholders' funds is to take a simple average based on the opening and closing figures for the year. This is often the only information available, as is the case with Example 6.1. Where not even the beginning-of-year figure is available, it is usually acceptable to use just the year-end figure, provided that this approach is consistently adopted. This is generally valid for all ratios that combine a figure for a period (such as net profit) with one taken at a point in time (such as shareholders' funds).

Activity 6.2

Calculate the ROSF for Alexis plc for the year to 31 March 2006.

The ROSF for 2006 is:

$$\text{ROSF} = \frac{11}{(563 + 534)/2} \times 100 = 2.0\%$$

Broadly, businesses seek to generate as high a value as possible for this ratio, provided that it is not achieved at the expense of potential future returns by, for example, taking on more risky activities. In view of this, the 2006 ratio is very poor by any standards; a bank deposit account will yield a better return than this. We need to try to find out why things went so badly wrong in 2006. As we look at other ratios, we should find some clues.

Return on capital employed (ROCE)

The return on capital employed is a fundamental measure of business performance. This ratio expresses the relationship between the net profit generated during a period and the average long-term capital invested in the business during that period.

The ratio is expressed in percentage terms and is as follows:

$$\text{ROCE} = \frac{\textbf{Net profit before interest and taxation}}{\textbf{Share capital + Long term loans}} \times 100$$

Note, in this case, that the profit figure used is the net profit *before* interest and taxation, because the ratio attempts to measure the returns to all suppliers of long-term finance before any deductions for interest payable to lenders, or payments of dividends to shareholders, are made.

For the year to 31 March 2005, the ratio for Alexis plc is:

$$\text{ROCE} = \frac{243}{(638 + 763)/2} \times 100 = 34.7\%$$

ROCE is considered by many to be a primary measure of profitability. It compares inputs (capital invested) with outputs (profit). This comparison is vital in assessing the effectiveness with which funds have been deployed. Once again, an average figure for capital employed may be used where the information is available.

Activity 6.3

Calculate the ROCE for Alexis plc for the year to 31 March 2006.

For 2006, the ratio is:

$$\text{ROCE} = \frac{47}{(763 + 834)/2} \times 100 = 5.9\%$$

This ratio tells much the same story as ROSF; namely a poor performance, with the return on the assets being less than the rate that the business has to pay for most of its borrowed funds (that is, 9 per cent for the debentures). See Real World 6.4 (p. 194) for how Tesco plc, the well-known supermarket chain has been able to use loan financing to increase its ROSF ratios, despite a decline in ROCE.

Real World 6.1 shows how financial ratios are used by businesses as a basis for setting profitability targets.

Real World 6.1

Setting profitability targets

The ROSF and ROCE ratios are widely used by businesses when establishing targets for profitability. These targets are sometimes made public and here are some examples:

Volkswagen, Europe's largest car maker, announced in 2003 that it aims to achieve a 9 per cent return on ordinary shareholders funds by 2006.

Deutsche Bank, one of Europe's largest banks, announced in 2004 that it aims to increase its pretax return on ordinary shareholders funds from 13 per cent to 25 per cent in the following two years.

Imperial Chemical Industries plc, a major UK chemical company, announced in 2003 that it aimed to increase ROCE to 10 per cent from between 7.0 and 7.8 per cent, which had been achieved over the previous five years.

Sources: 'VW's Poetsch sees 9pct return on equity by 2006', *AFX UK (Focus)*, 2 December 2003; 'Deutsche Bank aims for 25pct pretax return on equity in next two years', *AFX UK (Focus)*, 25 March 2004; 'Ambitions go hand in hand with targets at ICI. A positive chemical reaction', *FT.com*, 31 October 2003

Net profit margin

The net profit margin ratio relates the net profit for the period to the sales revenue during that period. The ratio is expressed as follows:

$$\text{Net profit margin} = \frac{\text{Net profit before interest and taxation}}{\text{Sales revenue}} \times 100$$

The net profit before interest and taxation is used in this ratio as it represents the profit from trading operations before the interest costs are taken into account. This is often regarded as the most appropriate measure of operational performance, when used as a basis of comparison, because differences arising from the way in which the business is financed will not influence the measure.

For the year ended 31 March 2005, Alexis plc's net profit margin ratio is:

$$\text{Net profit margin} = \frac{243}{2{,}240} \times 100 = 10.8\%$$

This ratio compares one output of the business (profit) with another output (sales revenue). The ratio can vary considerably between types of business. For example, supermarkets tend to operate on low prices and, therefore, low profit margins to stimulate sales and thereby increase the total amount of profit generated. Jewellers, on the other hand, tend to have high net profit margins, but have much lower levels of sales volume. Factors such as the degree of competition, the type of customer, the economic climate and industry characteristics (such as the level of risk) will influence the net profit margin of a business. This point is picked up again later in the chapter.

Activity 6.4

Calculate the net profit margin for Alexis plc for the year to 31 March 2006.

The net profit margin for 2006 is:

$$\text{Net profit margin} = \frac{47}{2{,}681} \times 100 = 1.8\%$$

Once again a very weak performance compared with that of 2005. Whereas in 2005 for every £1 of sales revenue an average of 10.8p (that is, 10.8 per cent) was left as profit, after paying the cost of the carpets sold and other expenses of operating the business, for 2006 this had fallen to only 1.8p for every £1. Thus the reason for the poor ROSF and ROCE ratios was partially, perhaps wholly, a high level of expenses relative to sales revenue. The next ratio should provide us with a clue as to how the sharp decline in this ratio occurred.

Real World 6.2 describes how one well-known business intends to increase its net profit margin over time.

Real World 6.2

Increasing the net profit margin

Sony has vowed to increase net profit margins from 2.5 per cent in 2002 to 10 per cent in three years. This is expected to be achieved by cutting costs and increasing competitiveness. As part of its strategy, Sony plans to reduce the number of parts it uses in its consumer electronics division from 840,000 to 100,000 by the end of 2005. A Sony representative explained that 'In order to differentiate our products and raise their competitiveness, it is becoming necessary to even differentiate the parts that go into those products'. By reducing the number of parts it uses, Sony hopes also to free up product developers' time, so that they can concentrate more on the design of the product itself. The reduction in parts is expected to affect Sony's 4,700 parts suppliers, whose number Sony wants to reduce to 1,000. In a further effort to cut costs and increase competitiveness, Sony decided to broaden its voluntary redundancy programme for staff.

Source: Adapted from 'Sony sets more steps to raise profit margins', *FT.com*, 6 October 2003

Gross profit margin

The gross profit margin ratio relates the gross profit of the business to the sales revenue generated for the same period. Gross profit represents the difference between sales revenue and the cost of sales. The ratio is therefore a measure of profitability in buying (or producing) and selling goods before any other expenses are taken into account. As cost of sales represents a major expense for many businesses, a change in this ratio can have a significant effect on the 'bottom line' (that is, the net profit for the year). The gross profit margin ratio is calculated as follows:

$$\text{Gross profit margin} = \frac{\text{Gross profit}}{\text{Sales revenue}} \times 100$$

For the year to 31 March 2005, the ratio for Alexis plc is:

$$\text{Gross profit margin} = \frac{495}{2,240} \times 100 = 22.1\%$$

Activity 6.5

Calculate the gross profit margin for Alexis plc for the year to 31 March 2006.

The gross profit margin for 2006 is:

$$\text{Gross profit margin} = \frac{409}{2,681} \times 100 = 15.3\%$$

The decline in this ratio means that gross profit was lower *relative* to sales revenue in 2006 than it had been in 2005. Bearing in mind that:

Gross profit = Sales revenue − Cost of sales (or cost of goods sold)

this means that cost of sales was higher *relative* to sales revenue in 2006, than in 2005. This could mean that sales prices were lower and/or that the purchase cost of goods sold had increased. It is possible that both sales prices and goods sold prices had reduced, but the former at a greater rate than the latter. Similarly they may both have increased, but with sales prices having increased at a lesser rate than costs of the goods sold.

Clearly, part of the decline in the net profit margin ratio is linked to the dramatic decline in the gross profit margin ratio. Whereas, after paying for the carpets sold, for each £1 of sales revenue 22.1p was left to cover other operating expenses and leave a profit in 2005, this was only 15.3p in 2006.

The profitability ratios for the business over the two years can be set out as follows:

	2005	2006
	%	%
ROSF	33.0	2.0
ROCE	34.7	5.9
Net profit margin	10.8	1.8
Gross profit margin	22.1	15.3

Activity 6.6

What do you deduce from a comparison of the declines in the net profit and gross profit margin ratios?

It occurs to us that the decline in the net profit margin was 9 per cent (that is, 10.8 per cent to 1.8 per cent), whereas that of the gross profit margin was only 6.8 per cent (that is, from 22.1 per cent to 15.3 per cent). This can only mean that operating expenses were greater, compared with sales revenue in 2006, than they had been in 2005. Thus, the declines in both ROSF and ROCE were caused partly by the business incurring higher inventories purchasing costs relative to sales revenue and partly through higher operating expenses to sales revenue. We would need to compare these ratios with the planned levels for them before we could usefully assess the business's success.

The analyst must now carry out some investigation to discover what caused the increases in both cost of sales and operating costs, relative to sales revenue, from 2005 to 2006. This will involve checking on what has happened with sales and inventory prices over the two years. Similarly, it will involve looking at each of the individual expenses that make up operating costs to discover which ones were responsible for the increase, relative to sales revenue. Here further ratios, for example, staff costs (wages and salaries) to sales revenue, could be calculated in an attempt to isolate the cause of the change from 2005 to 2006. In fact, as we discussed when we took an overview of the financial statements, the increase in staffing may well account for most of the increase in operating costs.

Real World 6.3 shows how one well-known international business is seeking to improve its ROCE.

Real World 6.3

Lazy assets raise the ROCE at Shell

During 2003 Shell, the oil business (The 'Shell' Transport and Trading Company plc) disposed of $4 billion of what it called 'lazy assets'. These are assets that the business felt were not earning their keep and were holding the ROCE below the target range of 13 to 15 per cent. The business had also identified a further $3 billion of assets that could be 'improved', so that they could also boost the business's ROCE.

Source: Based on information in 'Shell disposals of $4 billion double initial estimate', Toby Shelley, *FT.com*, 22 December 2003

Efficiency

Efficiency ratios examine the ways in which various resources of the business are managed. The following ratios consider some of the more important aspects of resource management:

- average inventories turnover period;
- average settlement period for receivables;
- average settlement period for payables;
- sales revenue to capital employed;
- sales revenue per employee.

We shall now look at each of these in turn.

Average inventories (stock) turnover period

Inventories often represent a significant investment for a business. For some types of business (for example, manufacturers), inventories may account for a substantial proportion of the total assets held (see Real World 11.1, p. 370). The average inventories turnover period measures the average period for which inventories are being held. The ratio is calculated as follows:

$$\text{Average inventories turnover period} = \frac{\text{Average inventories held}}{\text{Cost of sales}} \times 365$$

The average inventories for the period can be calculated as a simple average of the opening and closing inventories levels for the year. However, in the case of a highly seasonal business, where inventories levels may vary considerably over the year, a monthly average may be more appropriate.

In the case of Alexis plc, the inventories turnover period for the year ended 31 March 2005 is:

$$\text{Average inventories turnover period} = \frac{(241 + 300)/2}{1,745} \times 365 = 56.6 \text{ days}$$

This means that, on average, the inventories held are being 'turned over' every 56.6 days. So, a carpet bought by the business on a particular day would, on average, have been sold about eight weeks later. A business will normally prefer a short inventories turnover period to a long one, as funds tied up in inventories cannot be used for other purposes. When judging the amount of inventories to carry, the business must consider such things as the likely demand for the inventories, the possibility of supply shortages, the likelihood of price rises, the amount of storage space available and the perishability of the inventories. The management of inventories will be considered in more detail in Chapter 11.

This ratio is sometimes expressed in terms of months rather than days. Multiplying by 12 rather than 365 will achieve this.

Activity 6.7

Calculate the average inventories turnover period for Alexis plc for the year ended 31 March 2006.

The inventories turnover period for 2006 is:

$$\text{Average inventories turnover period} = \frac{(300 + 406)/2}{2{,}272} \times 365 = 56.7 \text{ days}$$

Thus the inventories turnover period is virtually the same in both years.

Average settlement period for receivables

A business will usually be concerned with how long it takes for customers to pay the amounts owing. The speed of payment can have a significant effect on the business's cash flow. The average settlement period for receivables calculates how long, on average, credit customers take to pay the amounts that they owe to the business. The ratio is as follows:

$$\text{Average settlement period of receivables} = \frac{\text{Trade receivables}}{\text{Credit sales revenue}} \times 365$$

A business will normally prefer a shorter average settlement period to a longer one as, once again, funds are being tied up that may be used for more profitable purposes. Though this ratio can be useful, it is important to remember that it produces an *average* figure for the number of days for which debts are outstanding. This average may be badly distorted by, for example, a few large customers who are very slow or very fast payers.

Since all sales made by Alexis plc are on credit, the average settlement period for receivables for the year ended 31 March 2005 is:

$$\text{Average settlement period for receivables} = \frac{240}{2{,}240} \times 365 = 39.1 \text{ days}$$

As no figures for opening receivables are available, the year-end receivables figure only is used. This is common practice for calculating any ratio where averaging would be desirable, but impossible through lack of the opening value.

Activity 6.8

Calculate the average settlement period for Alexis plc's receivables for the year ended 31 March 2006. (In the interests of consistency, use the year-end receivables figure rather than an average figure.)

The average settlement period for 2006 is:

$$\text{Average settlement period for receivables} = \frac{273}{2,681} \times 365 = 37.2 \text{ days}$$

On the face of it, this reduction in the settlement period is welcome. It means that less cash was tied up in receivables for each £1 of sales revenue in 2006 than in 2005. Only if the reduction were achieved at the expense of customer goodwill or a high direct financial cost, might the desirability of the reduction be questioned. For example, the reduction may have been due to chasing customers too vigorously or as a result of incurring higher costs, such as discounts allowed to customers who pay quickly.

Average settlement period for payables (creditors)

The average settlement period for payables measures how long, on average, the business takes to pay its trade payables. The ratio is calculated as follows:

$$\text{Average settlement period for payables} = \frac{\text{Trade payables}}{\text{Credit purchases}} \times 365$$

This ratio provides an average figure, which, like the average settlement period for receivables ratio, can be distorted by the payment period for one or two large suppliers.

As trade payables provide a free source of finance for the business, it is perhaps not surprising that some businesses attempt to increase their average settlement period for trade payables. However, such a policy can be taken too far and result in a loss of goodwill of suppliers. We shall return to the issues concerning the management of trade receivables and trade payables in Chapter 11.

For the year ended 31 March 2005, Alexis plc's average settlement period for payables is:

$$\text{Average settlement period for payables} = \frac{221}{1,804} \times 365 = 44.7 \text{ days}$$

Once again, the year-end figure rather than an average figure for payables has been used in the calculations.

Activity 6.9

Calculate the average settlement period for payables for Alexis plc for the year ended 31 March 2006. (For the sake of consistency, use a year-end figure for payables.)

The average settlement period for payables for 2006 is:

$$\text{Average settlement period for payables} = \frac{314}{2,378} \times 365 = 48.2 \text{ days}$$

There was an increase, between 2005 and 2006, in the average length of time that elapsed between buying inventories and paying for them. On the face of it, this is beneficial because the business is using free finance provided by suppliers. If, however, this is leading to a loss of supplier goodwill that could have adverse consequences for Alexis plc, it is not necessarily advantageous.

Sales revenue to capital employed

The sales revenue to capital employed ratio (or asset turnover ratio) examines how effectively the assets of the business are being used to generate sales revenue. It is calculated as follows:

$$\frac{\textbf{Sales revenue to}}{\textbf{capital employed ratio}} = \frac{\textbf{Sales revenue}}{\textbf{Share capital + Reserves + Non-current liabilities}}$$

Generally speaking, a higher asset turnover ratio is preferred to a lower one. A higher ratio will normally suggest that assets are being used more productively in the generation of revenue. However, a very high ratio may suggest that the business is 'overtrading on its assets', that is, it has insufficient assets to sustain the level of sales revenue achieved. (Overtrading will be discussed in more detail later in the chapter.) When comparing this ratio for different businesses, factors such as the age and condition of assets held, the valuation bases for assets and whether assets are rented or purchased outright can complicate interpretation.

A variation of this formula is to use the total assets less current liabilities (which is equivalent to long-term capital employed) in the denominator (lower part of the fraction) – the identical result is obtained.

For the year ended 31 March 2005 this ratio for Alexis plc is as follows:

$$\text{Sales revenue to capital employed} = \frac{2,240}{(638 + 763)/2} = 3.19 \text{ times}$$

Activity 6.10

Calculate the sales revenue to capital employed ratio for Alexis plc for the year ended 31 March 2006.

The sales revenue to capital employed ratio for the 2006 is:

$$\text{Sales revenue to capital employed} = \frac{2,681}{(763 + 834)/2} = 3.36 \text{ times}$$

This seems to be an improvement, since in 2006 more sales revenue was being generated for each £1 of capital employed (£3.36) than was the case in 2005 (£3.19). Provided that overtrading is not an issue, this is to be welcomed.

Sales revenue per employee

→ The sales revenue per employee ratio relates sales revenue generated to a particular business resource, that is, labour. It provides a measure of the productivity of the workforce. The ratio is:

$$\textbf{Sales revenue per employee} = \frac{\textbf{Sales revenue}}{\textbf{Number of employees}}$$

Generally, businesses would prefer to have a high value for this ratio, implying that they are using their staff efficiently.

For the year ended 31 March 2005, the ratio for Alexis plc is:

$$\text{Sales revenue per employee} = \frac{£2,240m}{13,995} = £160,057$$

Activity 6.11

Calculate the sales revenue per employee for Alexis plc for the year ended 31 March 2006.

The ratio for 2006 is:

$$\text{Sales revenue per employee} = \frac{£2,681m}{18,623} = £143,962$$

This represents a fairly significant decline and probably one that merits further investigation. As we discussed previously, the number of employees had increased quite notably (by about 33 per cent) during 2006 and the analyst will probably try to discover why this had not generated sufficient additional sales revenue to maintain the ratio at its 2005 level. It could be that the additional employees were not appointed until late in the year ended 31 March 2006.

The efficiency, or activity, ratios may be summarised as follows:

	2005	2006
Average inventories turnover period	56.6 days	56.7 days
Average settlement period for receivables	39.1 days	37.2 days
Average settlement period for payables	44.7 days	48.2 days
Sales revenue to capital employed (asset turnover)	3.19 times	3.36 times
Sales revenue per employee	£160,057	£143,962

Activity 6.12

What do you deduce from a comparison of the efficiency ratios over the two years?

We feel that maintaining the inventories turnover period at the 2005 level seems reasonable, though whether this represents a satisfactory period can probably only be assessed by looking at the business's planned inventories period. The inventories holding period for other businesses operating in carpet retailing, particularly those regarded as the market leaders, may have been helpful in formulating the plans. On the face of things, a shorter receivables collection period and a longer payables payment period are both desirable. On the other hand, these may have been achieved at the cost of a loss of the goodwill of customers and suppliers, respectively. The increased asset turnover ratio seems beneficial, provided that the business can manage this increase. The decline in the sales revenue per employee ratio is undesirable but, as we have already seen, is probably related to the dramatic increase in the level of staffing. As with the inventories turnover period, these other ratios need to be compared with the planned standard of efficiency.

The relationship between profitability and efficiency

In our earlier discussions concerning profitability ratios on page 176, we saw that return on capital employed (ROCE) is regarded as a key ratio by many businesses. The ratio is:

$$\text{ROCE} = \frac{\text{Net profit before interest and taxation}}{\text{Long-term capital employed}} \times 100$$

(where long-term capital comprises share capital plus reserves plus long-term loans). This ratio can be broken down into two elements, as shown in Figure 6.1. The first ratio is the net profit margin ratio, and the second is the sales revenue to capital employed (asset turnover) ratio, which we discussed earlier.

By breaking down the ROCE ratio in this manner, we highlight the fact that the overall return on funds employed within the business will be determined both by the profitability of sales and by efficiency in the use of capital.

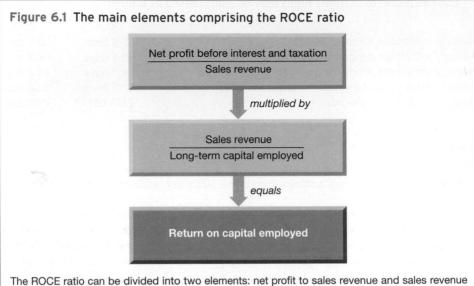

Figure 6.1 The main elements comprising the ROCE ratio

The ROCE ratio can be divided into two elements: net profit to sales revenue and sales revenue to capital employed. By analysing ROCE in this way, we can see the influence of both profitability and efficiency on this important ratio.

Example 6.2

Consider the following information concerning two different businesses operating in the same industry:

	Antler plc	Baker plc
Profit before interest and tax	£20m	£15m
Long-term capital employed	£100m	£75m
Sales revenue	£200m	£300m

The ROCE for each business is identical (20 per cent). However, the manner in which the return was achieved by each business was quite different. In the case of Antler plc, the net profit margin is 10 per cent and the sales revenue to capital employed ratio is 2 times (so, ROCE = 10% × 2 = 20%). In the case of Baker plc, the net profit margin is 5 per cent and the sales revenue to capital employed ratio is 4 times (and so, ROCE = 5% × 4 = 20%).

Example 6.2 demonstrates that a relatively low net profit margin can be compensated for by a relatively high sales revenue to capital employed ratio, and a relatively low sales revenue to capital employed ratio can be compensated for by a relatively high net profit margin. In many areas of retail and distribution (for example, supermarkets and delivery services) the net profit margins are quite low but the ROCE can be high, provided that the assets are used productively (that is, low margin, high turnover).

Activity 6.13

Show how the ROCE ratio for Alexis plc can be analysed into the two elements for each of the years 2005 and 2006.

What conclusions can we draw from your figures?

	ROCE	=	Net profit margin	×	Sales revenue to capital employed
2005	34.7%		10.8%		3.19
2006	5.9%		1.8%		3.36

Thus the relationship between the three ratios holds for Alexis plc, for both years. The small apparent differences arise because the three ratios are stated above only to one or two decimal places.

Though the business was more effective at generating sales (sales revenue to capital employed ratio increased) from 2005 to 2006, it fell well below the level necessary to compensate for the sharp decline in the effectiveness of each sale (net profit margin). As a result, the 2006 ROCE was well below the 2005 value.

Liquidity

Liquidity ratios are concerned with the ability of the business to meet its short-term financial obligations. The following ratios are widely used:

- current ratio;
- acid test ratio.

These two will now be considered.

Current ratio

The current ratio compares the 'liquid' assets (that is, cash and those assets held that will soon be turned into cash) of the business with the current liabilities. The ratio is calculated as follows:

$$\text{Current ratio} = \frac{\text{Current assets}}{\text{Current liabilities}}$$

Some people seem to believe that there is an 'ideal' current ratio (usually 2 times or 2:1) for all businesses. However, this fails to take into account the fact that different types of business require different current ratios. For example, a manufacturing business will often have a relatively high current ratio because it is necessary to hold inventories of finished goods, raw materials and work in progress. It will also normally sell goods on credit, thereby giving rise to receivables. A supermarket chain, on the other hand, will have a relatively low ratio, as it will hold only fast-moving inventories of finished goods and all of its sales will be made for cash (no credit sales). (See Real World 11.1 on p. 370.)

The higher the ratio, the more liquid the business is considered to be. As liquidity is vital to the survival of a business, a higher current ratio might be thought to be preferable to a lower one. If a business has a very high ratio, however, it may be that funds are tied up in cash or other liquid assets and are not, therefore, being used as productively as they might otherwise be.

As at 31 March 2005, the current ratio of Alexis plc is:

$$\text{Current ratio} = \frac{544}{291} = 1.9 \text{ times (or 1.9:1)}$$

Activity 6.14

Calculate the current ratio for Alexis plc as at 31 March 2006.

The current ratio as at 31 March 2006 is:

$$\text{Current ratio} = \frac{679}{432} = 1.6 \text{ times (or 1.6:1)}$$

Though this is a decline from 2005 to 2006, it is not necessarily a matter of concern. The next ratio may provide a clue as to whether there seems to be a problem.

Acid test ratio

The acid test ratio is very similar to the current ratio, but it represents a more stringent test of liquidity. It can be argued that, for many businesses, inventories cannot be converted into cash quickly. (Note that, in the case of Alexis plc, the inventories turnover period was about 57 days in both years (see pp. 180–1).) As a result, it may be better to exclude this particular asset from any measure of liquidity. The acid test ratio is a variation of the current ratio, but excluding inventories.

The minimum level for this ratio is often stated as 1.0 times (or 1:1 – that is, current assets (excluding inventories) equals current liabilities). In many highly successful businesses that are regarded as having adequate liquidity, however, it is not unusual for the acid test ratio to be below 1.0 without causing particular liquidity problems. (See Real World 11.1 on p. 370.)

The acid test ratio is calculated as follows:

$$\text{Acid test ratio} = \frac{\text{Current assets (excluding inventories)}}{\text{Current liabilities}}$$

The acid test ratio for Alexis plc as at 31 March 2005 is:

$$\text{Acid test ratio} = \frac{544 - 300}{291} = 0.8 \text{ times (or 0.8:1)}$$

We can see that the 'liquid' current assets do not quite cover the current liabilities, so the business may be experiencing some liquidity problems.

Activity 6.15

Calculate the acid test ratio for Alexis plc as at 31 March 2006.

Acid test ratio as at 31 March 2005 is:

$$\text{Acid test ratio} = \frac{679 - 406}{432} = 0.6 \text{ times}$$

The 2006 ratio is significantly below that for 2005. The 2006 level may well be a cause for concern. The rapid decline in this ratio should lead to steps being taken, at least, to stop further decline.

The liquidity ratios for the two-year period may be summarised as follows:

	2005	2006
Current ratio	1.9	1.6
Acid test ratio	0.8	0.6

Activity 6.16

What do you deduce from the liquidity ratios set out above?

Though it is probably not really possible to make a totally valid judgement without knowing the planned ratios, there appears to have been a decline in liquidity. This, however, may be planned, short term and linked to the expansion in non-current assets and staffing. It may be that when the benefits of the expansion come on stream, liquidity will improve. On the other hand, short-term payables may become anxious when they see signs of weak liquidity. This anxiety could lead to steps being taken to press for payment and this could cause problems for Alexis plc.

Financial gearing

→ Financial gearing occurs when a business is financed, at least in part, by borrowing, instead of by finance provided by the owners (the shareholders). A business's level of gearing (that is, the extent to which it is financed from sources that require a fixed return) is an important factor in assessing risk. Where a business borrows, it takes on a commitment to pay interest charges and make capital repayments. Where the borrowing is heavy, this can be a significant financial burden; it can increase the risk of the business becoming insolvent. Nevertheless, most businesses are geared to some extent.

Given the risks involved, we may wonder why a business would want to take on gearing (that is, to borrow). One reason may be that the owners have insufficient funds, so the only way to finance the business adequately is to borrow from others. Another reason is that gearing can be used to increase the returns to owners. This is possible provided the returns generated from borrowed funds exceed the cost of paying interest. Example 6.3 illustrates this point.

Example 6.3

The long-term capital structures of two new businesses, Lee Ltd and Nova Ltd, are as follows:

	Lee Ltd	Nova Ltd
	£	£
£1 ordinary shares	100,000	200,000
10% loan	200,000	100,000
	300,000	300,000

In their first year of operations, they each make a profit before interest and taxation of £50,000. The tax rate is 30 per cent of the net profit after interest.

Lee Ltd would probably be considered relatively highly geared, as it has a high proportion of borrowed funds in its long-term capital structure. Nova Ltd is much lower geared. The profit available to the shareholders of each business in the first year of operations will be:

	Lee Ltd	Nova Ltd
	£	£
Profit before interest and taxation	50,000	50,000
Interest payable	(20,000)	(10,000)
Profit before taxation	30,000	40,000
Taxation (30%)	(9,000)	(12,000)
Profit available to ordinary shareholders	21,000	28,000

The return on ordinary shareholders' funds (ROSF) for each business will be:

Lee Ltd   Nova Ltd

$$\frac{21,000}{100,000} \times 100 = 21\% \qquad \frac{28,000}{200,000} \times 100 = 14\%$$

We can see that Lee Ltd, the more highly geared business, has generated a better ROSF than Nova Ltd. This is despite the fact that the ROCE (return on capital employed) is identical for both businesses (that is (£50,000/£300,000) × 100 = 16.7%).

Note that at the £50,000 level of profit, the shareholders of both Lee Ltd and Nova Ltd benefit from gearing. Were the two businesses totally reliant on equity financing, the after tax profit would be £35,000 (that is, £50,000 less 30 per cent tax), giving a ROSF of 11.7 per cent (that is £35,000/£300,000). Both businesses generate higher ROSFs than this as a result of financial gearing.

An effect of gearing is that returns to shareholders become more sensitive to changes in profits. For a highly geared business, a change in profits can lead to a proportionately greater change in the ROSF ratio.

Activity 6.17

Assume that the profit before interest and tax was 20 per cent higher for each business than stated above (that is, a profit of £60,000). What would be the effect of this on ROSF?

The revised profit available to the shareholders of each business in the first year of operations will be:

	Lee Ltd	Nova Ltd
	£	£
Profit before interest and taxation	60,000	60,000
Interest payable	(20,000)	(10,000)
Profit before taxation	40,000	50,000
Taxation (30%)	(12,000)	(15,000)
Profit available to ordinary shareholders	28,000	35,000

The ROSF for each business will now be:

Lee Ltd

$$\frac{28,000}{100,000} \times 100 = 28\%$$

Nova Ltd

$$\frac{35,000}{200,000} \times 100 = 17.5\%$$

We can see that for Lee Ltd, the higher-geared business, the returns to shareholders have increased by a third (from 21 per cent to 28 per cent), whereas for the lower-geared business, Nova Ltd, the benefits of gearing are less pronounced, increasing by only a quarter (from 14 per cent to 17.5 per cent). The effect of gearing, of course, can work in both directions. Thus, for a highly geared business, a small decline in profits may bring about a much greater decline in the returns to shareholders.

The reason that gearing tends to be beneficial to shareholders is that loan interest rates are relatively low, compared with the returns that the typical business can earn. On top of this, interest costs are tax deductible, in the way shown in Example 6.3 and Activity 6.17, making the effective cost of borrowing quite cheap. It is debatable whether the apparent low interest rates really are beneficial to the shareholders. Some argue that since borrowing increases the risk to shareholders, there is a hidden cost of borrowing. What are not illusory, however, are the benefits to the shareholders of the tax deductibility of loan interest.

The effect of gearing is like that of two intermeshing cogwheels of unequal size (see Figure 6.2). The movement in the larger cog (profit before interest and tax) causes a more than proportionate movement in the smaller cog (returns to ordinary shareholders). The subject of gearing is discussed further in Chapter 12.

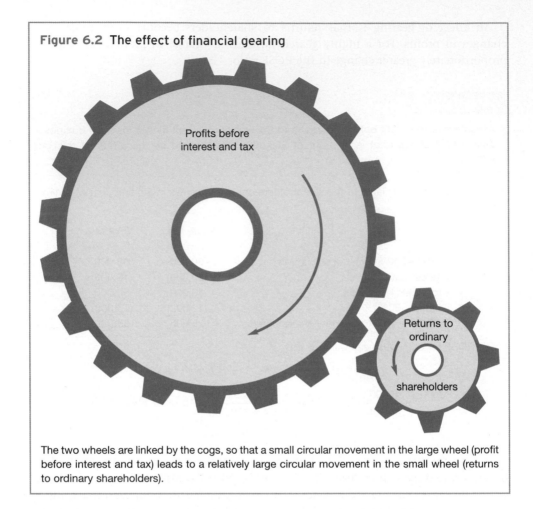

Figure 6.2 The effect of financial gearing

Profits before interest and tax

Returns to ordinary

shareholders

The two wheels are linked by the cogs, so that a small circular movement in the large wheel (profit before interest and tax) leads to a relatively large circular movement in the small wheel (returns to ordinary shareholders).

Real World 6.4, which appears later in this section on gearing ratios, provides an example of the effective use of gearing by a well-known business (Tesco plc).

Two ratios are widely used to assess gearing:

■ gearing ratio;
■ interest cover ratio.

Gearing ratio

The gearing ratio measures the contribution of long-term lenders to the long-term capital structure of a business:

$$\text{Gearing ratio} = \frac{\text{Long-term (non-current) liabilities}}{\text{Share capital} + \text{Reserves} + \text{Long-term (non-current) liabilities}} \times 100$$

The gearing ratio for Alexis plc, as at 31 March 2005, is:

$$\text{Gearing ratio} = \frac{200}{(563 + 200)} \times 100 = 26.2\%$$

This ratio reveals a level of gearing that would not normally be considered to be very high.

Activity 6.18

Calculate the gearing ratio of Alexis plc as at 31 March 2006.

The gearing ratio as at 31 March 2006 will be:

$$\text{Gearing ratio} = \frac{300}{(534 + 300)} \times 100 = 36.0\%$$

This ratio reveals a substantial increase in the level of gearing over the year.

Interest cover ratio

The interest cover ratio measures the amount of profit available to cover interest payable. The ratio may be calculated as follows:

$$\text{Interest cover ratio} = \frac{\textbf{Profit before interest and taxation}}{\textbf{Interest payable}}$$

The ratio for Alexis plc for the year ended 31 March 2005 is:

$$\text{Interest cover ratio} = \frac{243}{18} = 13.5 \text{ times}$$

This ratio shows that the level of profit is considerably higher than the level of interest payable. Thus a significant fall in profits could occur before profit levels failed to cover interest payable. The lower the level of profit coverage, the greater the risk to lenders that interest payments will not be met, and the greater the risk to the shareholders that the lenders will take action against the business to recover the interest due.

Activity 6.19

Calculate the interest cover ratio of Alexis plc for the year ended 31 March 2006.

The interest cover ratio for the year ended 31 March 2006 will be:

$$\text{Interest cover ratio} = \frac{47}{32} = 1.5 \text{ times}$$

Real World 6.4 shows how Tesco plc, the UK and, increasingly, international supermarket chain has been able to use increasing loan financing to boost ROSF in the early 2000s.

Tesco gears up for shareholders' returns

The following information relates to Tesco plc for its accounting years to the end of February 1999 to 2003:

	1999	2000	2001	2002	2003
ROCE (%)	17.2	16.1	16.6	16.1	15.3
Interest cover (times)	10.7	10.5	9.4	8.7	8.4
ROSF (%)	21.3	20.9	22.7	23.2	23.3

Over the five years, there was a decline in ROCE, but a steady increase in gearing (as measured by a decline in the interest cover ratio) had the effect of broadly increasing ROSF. The business must have been able to borrow at a lower rate of interest rate than its rate of ROCE. This boosted the returns to shareholders.

There is absolutely no suggestion here that Tesco's increased gearing was unwise. This is an extremely well-managed and successful business.

Source: Tesco plc, Annual Report and Financial Statements 2003

Alexis plc's gearing ratios are:

	2005	2006
Gearing ratio	26.2%	36.0%
Interest cover ratio	13.5 times	1.5 times

Activity 6.20

What do you deduce from a comparison of Alexis plc's gearing ratios over the two years?

The gearing ratio altered significantly. This is mainly due to the substantial increase in the long-term loan during 2006, which has had the effect of increasing the relative contribution of long-term lenders to the financing of the business.

The interest cover ratio has declined dramatically from a position where profit covered interest 13.5 times in 2005, to one where profit covered interest only 1.5 times in 2006. This was partly caused by the increase in borrowings in 2006, but mainly caused by the dramatic decline in profitability in that year. The later situation looks hazardous; only a small decline in future profitability in 2006 would leave the business with insufficient profit to cover the interest payments. The gearing ratio at 31 March 2006 would not necessarily be considered to be very high for a business that was trading successfully. It is the low profitability that is the problem.

Without knowing what the business planned these ratios to be, it is not possible to reach a totally valid conclusion on Alexis plc's gearing.

Real World 6.5 below provides some evidence concerning the gearing of listed businesses.

Real World 6.5

The gearing of listed businesses

Larger listed businesses tend to have higher levels of gearing than smaller ones. A Bank of England report on the financing of small businesses found that the average level of gearing among smaller listed businesses was 27 per cent compared with 37 per cent for the top 350 listed businesses. Over recent years the level of borrowing by larger listed businesses has risen steadily [Tesco – see Real World 6.4 – provides an example of this] whereas the level of borrowing for smaller listed businesses has remained fairly stable. This difference in gearing levels between larger and smaller businesses flies in the face of conventional wisdom.

Recent government investigations have found that smaller listed businesses often find it hard to attract investors. Many large institutional investors, who dominate the stock market, are not interested in the shares of smaller listed businesses because the amount of investment required is too small. As a result, shares in smaller businesses are less marketable. In such circumstances, it may be imagined that smaller businesses would become more reliant on loan financing and so would have higher levels of gearing than larger businesses. However, this is clearly not the case.

Although smaller businesses increase the level of shareholder funds by paying relatively low dividends and retaining more profits, they tend to be less profitable than larger businesses. Thus, higher retained profits do not seem to explain satisfactorily this phenomenon.

The only obvious factors that could explain this difference between smaller and larger businesses are the level of tax relief on loan interest and borrowing capacity. Broadly, larger businesses pay tax at a higher rate than their smaller counterparts. This means that the tax benefits of borrowing tend to be greater per £ of interest paid for larger businesses than for smaller ones. It may well be that larger businesses can borrow at lower interest rates than smaller ones, if only because they tend to borrow larger sums and so the economies of scale may apply. Also larger businesses tend to be less likely to get into financial difficulties than smaller ones, so they may be able to borrow at lower interest rates.

Source: Adapted from 'Small companies surprise on lending', *Financial Times*, 25 April 2003

Investment ratios

There are various ratios available that are designed to help investors assess the returns on their investment. The following are widely used:

- dividend payout ratio;
- dividend yield ratio;
- earnings per share;
- price/earnings ratio.

Dividend payout ratio

The dividend payout ratio measures the proportion of earnings that a business pays out to shareholders in the form of dividends. The ratio is calculated as follows:

$$\text{Dividend payout ratio} = \frac{\text{Dividends announced for the year}}{\text{Earnings for the year available for dividends}} \times 100$$

In the case of ordinary shares, the earnings available for dividend will normally be the net profit after taxation and after any preference dividends relating to the period. This ratio is normally expressed as a percentage.

The dividend payout ratio for Alexis plc for the year ended 31 March 2005 is:

$$\text{Dividend payout ratio} = \frac{40}{165} \times 100 = 24.2\%$$

The information provided by this ratio is often expressed slightly differently as the dividend cover ratio. Here the calculation is:

$$\text{Dividend cover ratio} = \frac{\textbf{Earnings for the year available for dividend}}{\textbf{Dividend announced for the year}}$$

In the case of Alexis plc, (for 2005) it would be 165/40 = 4.1 times. That is to say, the earnings available for dividend cover the actual dividend by just over four times.

Activity 6.21

Calculate the dividend payout ratio of Alexis plc for the year ended 31 March 2006.

The ratio for 2006 is:

$$\text{Dividend payout ratio} = \frac{40}{11} \times 100 = 363.6\%$$

This would normally be considered to be a very alarming decline in the ratio over the two years. Paying a dividend of £40m in 2006 would probably be regarded as very imprudent.

Dividend yield ratio

The dividend yield ratio relates the cash return from a share to its current market value. This can help investors to assess the cash return on their investment in the business. The ratio, expressed as a percentage is:

$$\text{Dividend yield} = \frac{\textbf{Dividend per share}/(1 - t)}{\textbf{Market value per share}} \times 100$$

where t is the 'lower' rate of income tax. This requires some explanation. In the UK, investors who receive a dividend from a business also receive a tax credit. This tax credit is equal to the amount of tax that would be payable on the dividends received by a lower-rate taxpayer. As this tax credit can be offset against any tax liability arising from the dividends received, the dividends are effectively issued net of tax to lower-rate income taxpayers.

Investors may wish to compare the returns from shares with the returns from other forms of investment. As these other forms of investment are often quoted on a 'gross' (that is, pre-tax) basis it is useful to 'gross up' the dividend to make comparison easier.

→ We can achieve this by dividing the dividend per share by $(1 - t)$, where t is the 'lower' rate of income tax.

Assuming a lower rate of income tax of 10 per cent, the dividend yield for Alexis plc for the year ended 31 March 2005 is:

$$\text{Dividend yield} = \frac{0.067^*/(1 - 0.10)}{2.50} \times 100 = 3.0\%$$

* Dividend proposed/number of shares = 40/(300 × 2) = £0.067 dividend per share (the 300 is multiplied by 2 because they are £0.50 shares).

Activity 6.22

Calculate the dividend yield for Alexis plc for the year ended 31 March 2006.

The dividend yield ratio for 2006 is:

$$\text{Dividend yield} = \frac{0.067^*/(1 - 0.10)}{1.50} \times 100 = 4.9\%$$

* 40/(300 × 2) = £0.067

Earnings per share

→ The earnings per share (EPS) ratio relates the earnings generated by the business, and available to shareholders, during a period to the number of shares in issue. For equity (ordinary) shareholders, the amount available will be represented by the net profit after tax (less any preference dividend, where applicable). The ratio for equity shareholders is calculated as follows:

$$\text{Earnings per share} = \frac{\text{Earnings available to ordinary shareholders}}{\text{Number of ordinary shares in issue}}$$

In the case of Alexis plc, the earnings per share for the year ended 31 March 2005 is as follows:

$$\text{EPS} = \frac{£165m}{600m} = 27.5p$$

Many investment analysts regard the EPS ratio as a fundamental measure of share performance. The trend in earnings per share over time is used to help assess the investment potential of a business's shares. Though it is possible to make total profits rise through ordinary shareholders investing more in the business, this will not necessarily mean that the profitability *per share* will rise as a result.

It is not usually very helpful to compare the earnings per share of one business with those of another. Differences in capital structure (for example, in the nominal value of shares issued) can render any such comparison meaningless. However, it can be very useful to monitor the changes that occur in this ratio for a particular business over time.

Activity 6.23

Calculate the earnings per share of Alexis plc for the year ended 31 March 2006.

The earnings per share for 2006 is:

$$\text{EPS} - \frac{£11\text{m}}{600\text{m}} = 1.8\text{p}$$

Price/earnings (P/E) ratio

The price/earnings ratio relates the market value of a share to the earnings per share. This ratio can be calculated as follows:

$$\text{P/E ratio} = \frac{\textbf{Market value per share}}{\textbf{Earnings per share}}$$

The P/E ratio for Alexis plc as at 31 March 2005 is:

$$\text{P/E ratio} = \frac{£2.50}{27.5\text{p*}} = 9.1 \text{ times}$$

* The EPS figure (27.5p) was calculated on p. 197.

This ratio reveals that the capital value of the share is 9.1 times higher than its current level of earnings. The ratio is a measure of market confidence in the future of a business. The higher the P/E ratio, the greater the confidence in the future earning power of the business and, consequently, the more investors are prepared to pay in relation to the earnings stream of the business.

P/E ratios provide a useful guide to market confidence concerning the future and they can, therefore, be helpful when comparing different businesses. However, differences in accounting policies between businesses can lead to different profit and earnings per share figures, and this can distort comparisons.

Activity 6.24

Calculate the P/E ratio of Alexis plc as at 31 March 2006.

The price earnings ratio for 2006 is:

$$\text{P/E ratio} = \frac{£1.50}{1.8\text{p}} = 83.3 \text{ times}$$

The investment ratios for Alexis plc over the two-year period are as follows:

	2005	2006
Dividend payout ratio	24.2%	363.6%
Dividend yield ratio	3.0%	4.9%
Earnings per share	27.5p	1.8p
P/E ratio	9.1 times	83.3 times

Activity 6.25

What do you deduce from the investment ratios set out above?

Can you offer an explanation why the share price has not fallen as much as it might have done, bearing in mind the very poor (relative to 2005) trading performance in 2006?

We thought that, though the EPS has fallen dramatically and the dividend payment for 2006 seems very imprudent, the share price seems to have held up remarkably well (fallen from £2.50 to £1.50, see p. 173). This means that dividend yield and P/E value for 2006 look better than those for 2005. This is an anomaly of these two ratios, which stems from using a forward-looking value (the share price) in conjunction with historic data (dividends and earnings). Share prices are based on investors' assessments of the business's future. It seems with Alexis plc that, at the end of 2006, the 'market' was not happy with the business, relative to 2005. This is evidenced by the fact that the share price had fallen by £1 a share. On the other hand, the share price has not fallen as much as profits. It appears that investors believe that the business will perform better in the future than it did in 2006. This may well be because they believe that the large expansion in assets and employee numbers that occurred in 2006 will yield benefits in the future; benefits that the business was not able to generate during 2006.

Real World 6.6 gives some information about the shares of several large, well-known UK businesses. This type of information is provided on a daily basis by several newspapers, notably the *Financial Times*.

Real World 6.6

Market statistics for some well-known businesses

The following shares were extracted from the *Financial Times* on 23 July 2005, relating to the previous day's trading of the shares of some well-known businesses on the London Stock Exchange:

Share	Price	Chng	2005		Y'ld	P/E	Volume
			High	Low			000s
BP	626	+7$\frac{1}{2}$	641$\frac{1}{2}$	504	2.7	14.2	53,015
JD Wetherspoon	276	+3	287	243	1.5	16.4	4,834
BSkyB	523$\frac{1}{2}$	+1$\frac{1}{2}$	595	509	1.4	20.3	6,284
Marks and Spencer	359	+$\frac{1}{2}$	374	319$\frac{1}{4}$	3.4	16.5	8,025
Rolls-Royce	310$\frac{3}{4}$	−$\frac{1}{2}$	311$\frac{1}{4}$	236	2.6	21.4	12,759
Vodafone	143$\frac{1}{2}$	+1$\frac{1}{4}$	146$\frac{1}{2}$	133$\frac{1}{2}$	2.8	13.6	250,852

The column headings are as follows:

Price   Mid-market price in pence (that is, the price midway between buying and selling price) of the shares at the end of 22 July 2005.

Chng	Gain or loss from the previous day's mid-market price.
High/Low	Highest and lowest prices reached by the share during the year.
Y'ld	Gross dividend yield, based on the most recent year's dividend and the current share price.
P/E	Price/earnings ratio, based on the most recent year's after-tax profit and the current share price.
Volume	The number of shares (in thousands) that were bought and sold on 22 July 2005.

Real World 6.7 shows how investment ratios can vary between different industry sectors.

Real World 6.7

How investment ratios vary between industries

Investment ratios can vary significantly between businesses and between industries. To give some indication of the range of variations that occur, the average dividend yield ratios and average P/E ratios for listed businesses in 12 different industries are shown in Figures 6.3 and 6.4 respectively.

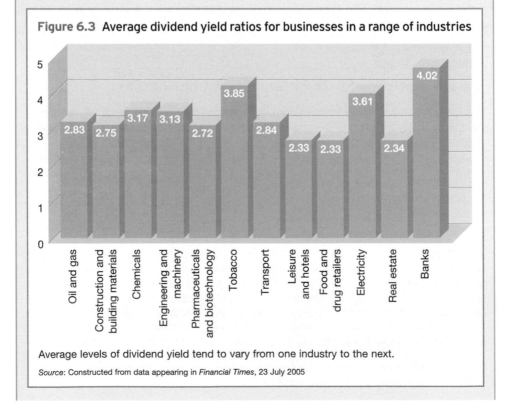

Figure 6.3 Average dividend yield ratios for businesses in a range of industries

Oil and gas: 2.83; Construction and building materials: 2.75; Chemicals: 3.17; Engineering and machinery: 3.13; Pharmaceuticals and biotechnology: 2.72; Tobacco: 3.85; Transport: 2.84; Leisure and hotels: 2.33; Food and drug retailers: 2.33; Electricity: 3.61; Real estate: 2.34; Banks: 4.02

Average levels of dividend yield tend to vary from one industry to the next.

Source: Constructed from data appearing in *Financial Times*, 23 July 2005

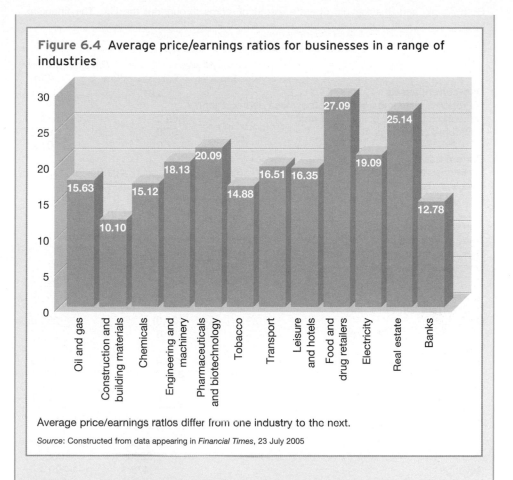

Figure 6.4 Average price/earnings ratios for businesses in a range of industries

Average price/earnings ratios differ from one industry to the next.

Source: Constructed from data appearing in *Financial Times*, 23 July 2005

These ratios are calculated from the current market value of the shares and the most recent year's dividend paid (dividend yield) or earnings per share (P/E).

Some industries tend to pay out lower dividends than others, leading to lower dividend yield ratios. Pharmaceutical businesses tend to invest heavily in developing new drugs, hence their tendency to pay low dividends compared with their share prices. Electricity businesses probably tend to invest less heavily than pharmaceuticals, hence their rather higher level of dividend yields. Some of the inter-industry differences in the dividend yield ratio can be explained by the nature of the calculation of the ratio. The prices of shares at any given moment are based on expectations of their economic futures; dividends are actual past events. A business that had a good trading year recently may have paid a dividend that, in the light of investors' assessment on the business's economic future, may be high (a high dividend yield).

Businesses that have a high share price relative to their recent historic earnings have high P/E ratios. This may be because their future is regarded as economically bright, which may be the result of investing heavily in the future at the expense of current profits (earnings). On the other hand, high P/Es also arise where businesses have recent low earnings, but investors believe that their future is brighter.

Both Ali plc and Bhaskar plc operate electrical stores throughout the UK. The financial statements of each business for the year ended 30 June 2006 are as follows:

Balance sheets as at 30 June 2006

	Ali plc		Bhaskar plc	
	£m	£m	£m	£m
Non-current assets				
Property, plant and equipment (cost less depreciation)				
Freehold land and buildings at cost		360.0		510.0
Fixtures and fittings at cost		87.0		91.2
		447.0		601.2
Current assets				
Inventories at cost	592.0		403.0	
Receivables	176.4		321.9	
Cash at bank	84.6		91.6	
	853.0		816.5	
Current liabilities				
Trade payables	(271.4)		(180.7)	
Dividends (approved, but unpaid)	(135.0)		(95.0)	
Corporation tax	(16.0)		(17.4)	
	(422.4)	430.6	(293.1)	523.4
		877.6		1,124.6
Non-current liabilities				
Debentures		(190.0)		(250.0)
		687.6		874.6
Equity				
£1 ordinary shares		320.0		250.0
General reserves		355.9		289.4
Retained profit		11.7		335.2
		687.6		874.6

Income statements for the year ended 30 June 2006

	Ali plc	Bhaskar plc
	£000	£000
Revenue	1,478.1	1,790.4
Less Cost of sales	1,018.3	1,214.9
Gross profit	459.8	575.5
Less Operating expenses	308.5	408.6
Net profit before interest and tax	151.3	166.9
Less Interest payable	19.4	27.5
Net profit before tax	131.9	139.4
Less Corporation tax	32.0	34.8
Net profit after taxation	99.9	104.6
Add Retained profit brought forward	46.8	325.6
	146.7	430.2
Less Dividends approved, but unpaid	135.0	95.0
Retained profit carried forward	11.7	335.2

All purchases and sales were on credit. The dividends for both years had been approved by the shareholders before the respective year ends, but were paid after those times. The market values of a share in each business at the end of the year were £6.50 and £8.20 respectively.

Required:
For each business, calculate two ratios that are concerned with liquidity, gearing and investment (six ratios in total). What can you conclude from the ratios that you have calculated?

Trend analysis

It is often helpful to see whether ratios are indicating trends. Key ratios can be plotted on a graph to provide a simple visual display of changes occurring over time. The trends occurring within a business may, for example, be plotted against trends for rival businesses or for the industry as a whole for comparison purposes. An example of trend analysis is shown in Real World 6.8.

Real World 6.8

Trend setting

In Figure 6.5 below the current ratio of Tesco plc is plotted against the same ratio for two other businesses within the same industry – J. Sainsbury plc and Wm Morrison plc – over a six-year period. We can see that the current ratio of Tesco plc has risen slightly over the period but it is, nevertheless, consistently lower than that of its main rivals, until 2005.

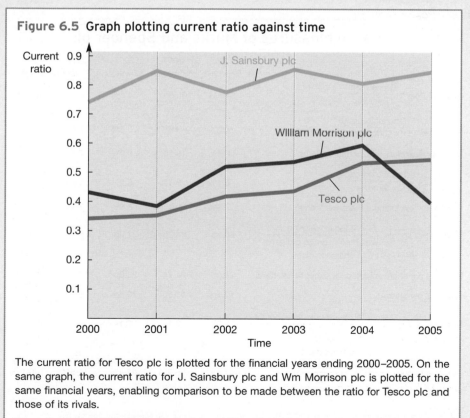

Figure 6.5 Graph plotting current ratio against time

The current ratio for Tesco plc is plotted for the financial years ending 2000–2005. On the same graph, the current ratio for J. Sainsbury plc and Wm Morrison plc is plotted for the same financial years, enabling comparison to be made between the ratio for Tesco plc and those of its rivals.

Source: Complied using information in the annual reports of Tesco plc, J. Sainsbury plc and Wm Morrison plc

Many larger businesses publish certain key financial ratios as part of their annual reports to help users identify significant trends. These ratios typically cover several years' activities. Real World 6.9 shows part of the table of 'key performance measures' of Marks and Spencer plc (M&S), the well-known UK high street store. After many years of profitable growth, M&S suffered a decline in its fortunes during the late 1990s. This was seen by the directors, and by many independent commentators, as arising from the business allowing itself to be drawn away from its traditional areas of strength. Steps were taken to deal with the problem and the business seemed to have 'turned the corner'. M&S seemed to have reached its low point in the year ended March 2001 when it incurred a significant overall loss, with a trading profit well below that achieved in 1998. The income statements reveal that turnover was down in 2001 and expenses were up relative to 2000. The improvements in 2002, 2003 and 2004 are very clear. The return on equity (return on ordinary shareholders funds) in 2005 is significantly better than for any others of the five years, though in 2005, both the gross (profit) and net (profit) margins are lower than in 2004. The return on equity was

Real World 6.9

Key performance measures of Marks and Spencer plc

		2005 52 weeks	2004 53 weeks	2003 52 weeks	2002 52 weeks	2001 52 weeks
Gross margin	$\dfrac{\text{Gross profit}}{\text{Turnover}}$	34.8%	35.3%	34.8%	34.4%	32.6%
Net margin	$\dfrac{\text{Operating profit}}{\text{Turnover}}$	7.6%	9.6%	8.4%	7.5%	5.1%
Net margin excluding exceptional items		8.8%	10.2%	8.9%	7.5%	5.5%
Profitability	$\dfrac{\text{Profit before tax}}{\text{Turnover}}$	6.4%	9.1%	8.2%	8.3%	4.1%
Profitability excluding exceptional items		7.6%	9.4%	8.8%	7.7%	5.7%
Earning per share	$\dfrac{\text{Standard earning}}{\text{Weighted average ordinary shares in issue}}$	29.1p	24.2p	21.8p	5.4p	(0.2)p
Earnings per share adjusted for exceptional items		21.9p	24.7p	23.3p	16.3p	11.2p
Dividend per share		12.1p	11.5p	10.5p	9.5p	9.0p
Dividend cover	$\dfrac{\text{Profit attributable to shareholders}}{\text{Dividends}}$	2.9x	2.1x	2.1x	2.2x	n/a
Return on equity	$\dfrac{\text{Profit attributable to equity shareholders}}{\text{Average equity shareholders' funds}}$	41.4%	25.2%	22.4%	11.5%	(0.1)%

Source: Marks and Spencer plc Annual Report 2005. Reproduced by kind permission of Marks and Spencer plc
The results for 2001 and 2002 have not been restated following the adoption of a number of accounting standards in 2004. This means that the results over the five years are not readily comparable.

boosted in 2005 by the profit on disposal of the business's financial services division and a lower equity base due to Marks and Spencer buying and concelling some of its own shares.

Ratios and prediction models

Financial ratios, based on current or past performance, are often used to help predict the future, though both the choice of ratios and the interpretation of results are normally dependent on the judgement of the analyst. Attempts have been made, however, to develop a more rigorous and systematic approach to the use of ratios for prediction purposes. In particular, researchers have shown an interest in the use of ratios to predict financial distress in a business. Several methods and models using ratios have been developed that are claimed to predict future financial distress. Researchers have also developed ratio-based models with which to assess the supposed vulnerability of a business to takeover by another business. These areas, of course, are of interest to all those connected with the business. In the future, it is likely that further ratio-based models will be developed that predict other aspects of future performance.

Limitations of ratio analysis

Though ratios offer a quick and useful method of analysing the position and performance of a business, they are not without their problems and limitations. Some of the more important limitations are as follows:

- *Quality of financial statements*. It must always be remembered that ratios are based on financial statements, and the results of ratio analysis are dependent on the quality of these underlying statements. Ratios will inherit the limitations of the financial statements on which they are based. A significant example of this arises from the application of the prudence convention to internally generated intangible non-current assets (as compared with purchased ones). This convention tends to lead to assets of considerable value, like goodwill and brand names, being excluded from the balance sheet. This can mean that ratios, like ROSF, ROCE and the gearing ratio, fail to take account of these assets.

  There is also the problem of deliberate attempts to make the financial statements misleading. We discussed this problem of *creative accounting* in Chapter 4.
- *The restricted vision of ratios*. It is important not to rely exclusively on ratios, thereby losing sight of information contained in the underlying financial statements. As we saw earlier in the chapter, some items reported in these statements can be vital in assessing position and performance. For example, the total sales revenue, capital employed and profit figures may be useful in assessing changes in absolute size that occur over time, or differences in scale between businesses. Ratios do not provide such information. When comparing one figure with another, ratios measure *relative* performance and position, and therefore provide only part of the picture. Thus,

when comparing two businesses, it will often be useful to assess the absolute size of profits, as well as the relative profitability of each business. For example, Business A may generate £1m profit and have a ROCE of 15 per cent, and Business B may generate £100,000 profit and have a ROCE of 20 per cent. Although Business B has a higher level of *profitability*, as measured by ROCE, it generates lower total profits.

- *The basis for comparison.* We saw earlier that for ratios to be useful they require a basis for comparison. Moreover, it is important that the analyst compares like with like. When comparing businesses, however, no two businesses will be identical, and the greater the differences between the businesses being compared, the greater the limitations of ratio analysis. Also, when comparing businesses, differences in such matters as accounting policies, financing methods (gearing levels) and financial year ends will add to the problems of evaluation.

- *Balance sheet ratios.* Because the balance sheet is only a 'snapshot' of the business at a particular moment in time, any ratios based on balance sheet figures, such as the liquidity ratios above, may not be representative of the financial position of the business for the year as a whole. For example, it is common for a seasonal business to have a financial year end that coincides with a low point in business activity. Thus inventories and receivables may be low at the balance sheet date, and the liquidity ratios may also be low as a result. A more representative picture of liquidity can only really be gained by taking additional measurements at other points in the year.

Real World 6.10 points out another way in which ratios are limited.

Real World 6.10

Remember, it's people that really count . . .

Lord Weinstock (1924–2002) was an influential industrialist whose management style and philosophy helped to shape management practice in many UK businesses. During his long and successful reign at GEC plc, a major engineering business, Lord Weinstock relied heavily on financial ratios to assess performance and to exercise control. In particular, he relied on ratios relating to sales revenue, costs, receivables, profit margins and inventories turnover. However, he was keenly aware of the limitations of ratios and recognised that, ultimately, people produce profits.

In a memo written to GEC managers he pointed out that ratios are an aid to good management, rather than a substitute for it. He wrote:

> The operating ratios are of great value as measures of efficiency but they are only the measures and not efficiency itself. Statistics will not design a product better, make it for a lower cost or increase sales. If ill-used, they may so guide action as to diminish resources for the sake of apparent but false signs of improvement.
>
> Management remains a matter of judgement, of knowledge of products and processes and of understanding and skill in dealing with people. The ratios will indicate how well all these things are being done and will show comparison with how they are done elsewhere. But they will tell us nothing about how to do them. That is what you are meant to do.

Source: Extract from *Arnold Weinstock and the Making of GEC*, by S. Aris (Aurum Press, 1998), published in *The Sunday Times*, 22 February 1998, p. 3

Summary

The main points of this chapter may be summarised as follows:

Ratio analysis:

- Compares two related figures, usually both from the same set of financial statements.
- Is an aid to understanding what the financial statements portray.
- Is an inexact science so results must be interpreted cautiously.
- Past periods, the performance of similar businesses and planned performance are often used to provide benchmark ratios.
- A brief overview of the financial statements can often provide insights that may not be revealed by ratios and/or may help in the interpretation of them.

Profitability ratios – concerned with effectiveness at generating profit:

- Return on ordinary shareholders' funds (ROSF).
- Return on capital employed (ROCE).
- Net profit margin.
- Gross profit margin.

Efficiency ratios – concerned with efficiency of using assets/resources:

- Average inventories turnover period.
- Average settlement period for receivables.
- Average settlement period for payables.
- Sales revenue to capital employed.
- Sales revenue per employee.

Liquidity ratios – concerned with the ability to meet short-term obligations:

- Current ratio.
- Acid test ratio.

Gearing ratios – concerned with relationship between equity and debt financing:

- Gearing ratio.
- Interest cover ratio.

Investment ratios – concerned with returns to shareholders:

- Dividend payout ratio.
- Dividend yield ratio.
- Earnings per share.
- Price/earnings ratio.

→

Individual ratios can be tracked (for example, plotted on a graph) to detect trends.

Ratios can be used to predict financial failure.

Limitations of ratio analysis:

■ Ratios are only as reliable as the financial statements from which they derive.

■ Ratios have restricted vision.

■ It can be difficult to find a suitable benchmark (for example, another business) to compare with.

■ Some ratios could mislead due to the 'snapshot' nature of the balance sheet.

→ Key terms

return on ordinary shareholders' funds (ROSF) p. 174

return on capital employed (ROCE) p. 175

net profit margin ratio p. 177

gross profit margin ratio p. 178

average inventories turnover period p. 180

average settlement period for receivables p. 181

average settlement period for payables p. 182

sales revenue to capital employed ratio p. 183

sales revenue per employee ratio p. 184

current ratio p. 187

acid test ratio p. 188

financial gearing p. 189

gearing ratio p. 192

interest cover ratio p. 193

dividend payout ratio p. 195

dividend cover ratio p. 196

dividend yield ratio p. 196

dividend per share p. 197

earnings per share p. 197

price/earnings ratio p. 198

Further reading

If you would like to explore the topics covered in this chapter in more depth, we recommend the following books:

Elliott, B. and Elliott, J. *Financial Accounting and Reporting*, 9th edn, Financial Times Prentice Hall, 2004, Chapters 28 and 29.

Revsine, L., Collins, D. and Bruce Johnson, W. *Financial Reporting and Analysis*, 3rd edn, Prentice Hall, 2004, Chapter 5.

Sutton, T. *Corporate Financial Accounting and Reporting*, 2nd edn, Financial Times Prentice Hall, 2004, Chapter 19.

Wild, J., Subramanyam, K. and Halsey, R. *Financial Statement Analysis*, 8th edn, McGraw Hill, 2003, Chapters 8, 9 and 11.

? Review questions

Answers to these questions can be found at the back of the book (p. 491).

6.1 Some businesses operate on a low net profit margin (for example, a supermarket chain). Does this mean that the return on capital employed from the business will also be low?

6.2 What potential problems arise for the external analyst from the use of balance sheet figures in the calculation of financial ratios?

6.3 Two businesses operate in the same industry. One has an inventories turnover period that is higher than the industry average. The other has an inventories turnover period that is lower than the industry average. Give three possible explanations for each business's inventories turnover period ratio.

6.4 Identify and discuss three reasons why the P/E ratio of two businesses operating within the same industry may differ.

* Exercises

Exercises 6.4 and 6.5 are more advanced than 6.1 to 6.3. Those with a coloured number have an answer at the back of the book (pp. 508–10).

> If you wish to try more exercises, visit the students' side of the companion website

6.1 Jiang Ltd has recently produced its financial statements for the current year. The directors are concerned that the return on capital employed (ROCE) had decreased from 14 per cent last year to 12 per cent for the current year.

The following reasons were suggested as to why this reduction in ROCE had occurred:

(i) an increase in the gross profit margin;
(ii) a reduction in sales revenue;
(iii) an increase in overhead expenses;
(iv) an increase in amount of inventories held;
(v) the repayment of a loan at the year end; and
(vi) an increase in the time taken for credit customers (trade receivables) to pay.

Required:
Taking each of these six suggested reasons in turn, state, with reasons, whether each of them could lead to a reduction in ROCE.

6.2 Amsterdam Ltd and Berlin Ltd are both engaged in retailing, but they seem to take a different approach to it according to the following information:

Ratio	Amsterdam Ltd	Berlin Ltd
Return on capital employed (ROCE)	20%	17%
Return on ordinary shareholders' funds (ROSF)	30%	18%
Average settlement period for receivables	63 days	21 days
Average settlement period for payables	50 days	45 days
Gross profit margin	40%	15%
Net profit margin	10%	10%
Inventories turnover period	52 days	25 days

Required:

Describe what this information indicates about the differences in approach between the two businesses. If one of them prides itself on personal service and one of them on competitive prices, which do you think is which and why?

6.3 Conday and Co. Ltd has been in operation for three years and produces antique reproduction furniture for the export market. The most recent set of financial statements for the business is set out as follows:

Balance sheet as at 30 November

	£000	£000	£000
Non-current assets			
Property, plant and equipment			
Freehold land and buildings at cost			228
Plant and machinery at cost		942	
Less Accumulated depreciation		180	762
			990
Current assets			
Inventories		600	
Trade receivables		820	
		1,420	
Less **Current liabilities**			
Trade payables	665		
Taxation	48		
Bank overdraft	432	1,145	275
			1,265
Less **Non-current liabilities**			
9% debentures (Note 1)			200
			1,065
Equity			
Ordinary shares of £1 each			700
Retained profit			365
			1,065

Income statement for the year ended 30 November

	£000	£000
Revenue		2,600
Less Cost of sales		1,620
Gross profit		980
Less Selling and distribution expenses (Note 2)	408	
Administration expenses	194	
Finance expenses	58	660
Net profit before taxation		320
Less Corporation tax		95
Net profit after taxation		225
Less Dividend paid		160
Retained profit for the year		65

Notes:
1 The debentures are secured on the freehold land and buildings.
2 Selling and distribution expenses include £170,000 in respect of bad debts.

The directors have invited an investor to take up a new issue of ordinary shares in the business at £6.40 each making a total investment of £200,000. The directors wish to use the funds to finance a programme of further expansion.

Required:
(a) Analyse the financial position and performance of the business and comment on any features that you consider to be significant.
(b) State, with reasons, whether or not the investor should invest in the business on the terms outlined.

6.4 Threads Limited manufactures nuts and bolts, which are sold to industrial users. The abbreviated financial statements for 2005 and 2006 are as follows:

Income statements for the year ended 30 June

	2005		2006	
	£000	£000	£000	£000
Revenue		1,180		1,200
Cost of sales		(680)		(750)
Gross profit		500		450
Operating expenses	(200)		(208)	
Depreciation	(66)		(75)	
Interest	(–)		(8)	
		(266)		(291)
Profit before tax		234		159
Tax		(80)		(48)
Profit after tax		154		111
Dividend – paid		(70)		(72)
Retained profit for year		84		39

Balance sheets as at 30 June

	2005		2006	
	£000	£000	£000	£000
Non-current assets		702		687
Current assets				
Inventories	148		236	
Receivables	102		156	
Cash	3		4	
	253		396	
Current liabilities				
Trade payables	(60)		(76)	
Other payables and accruals	(18)		(16)	
Tax	(40)		(24)	
Bank overdraft	(81)		(122)	
	(199)		(238)	
Net current assets		54		158
Non-current liabilities				
Bank loan		–		(50)
		756		795
Equity				
Ordinary share capital of £1 (fully paid)		500		500
Retained profits		256		295
		756		795

Required:

(a) Calculate the following financial ratios for *both* 2005 and 2006 (using year-end figures for balance sheet items):

    (i)   return on capital employed;

    (ii) net profit margin;

    (iii) gross profit margin;

    (iv) current ratio;

    (v) acid test ratio;

    (vi) settlement period for receivables;

    (vii) settlement period for payables; and

    (viii) inventories turnover period.

(b) Comment on the performance of Threads Limited from the viewpoint of a business considering supplying a substantial amount of goods to Threads Limited on usual trade credit terms.

6.5 Bradbury Ltd is a family-owned clothes manufacturer based in the southwest of England. For a number of years the chairman and managing director was David Bradbury. During his period of office, sales revenue had grown steadily at a rate of 2 to 3 per cent each year. David Bradbury retired on 30 November 2005 and was succeeded by his son Simon. Soon after taking office, Simon decided to expand the business. Within weeks he had successfully negotiated a five-year contract with a large clothes retailer to make a range of sports and leisurewear items. The contract will result in an additional £2 million in sales revenue during each year of the contract. To fulfil the contract, Bradbury Ltd acquired new equipment and premises.

Financial information concerning the business is given below:

Income statements for the year ended 30 November

	2005	2006
	£000	£000
Turnover	9,482	11,365
Profit before interest and tax	914	1,042
Interest charges	(22)	(81)
Profit before tax	892	961
Taxation	(358)	(386)
Profit after tax	534	575
Dividend paid	(120)	(120)
Retained profit	414	455

Balance sheets as at 30 November

	2005		2006	
	£000	£000	£000	£000
Non-current assets				
Property, plant and equipment				
Freehold premises at cost		5,240		7,360
Plant and equipment (net)		2,375		4,057
		7,615		11,417
Current assets				
Inventories	2,386		3,420	
Trade receivables	2,540		4,280	
	4,926		7,700	
Current liabilities				
Trade payables	(1,157)		(2,245)	
Taxation	(179)		(193)	
Bank overdraft	(172)		(2,736)	
	(1,508)		(5,174)	
Net current assets		3,418		2,526
		11,033		13,943
Non-current liabilities				
Loans		(1,220)		(3,675)
Total net assets		9,813		10,268
Equity				
Share capital		2,000		2,000
Reserves		7,813		8,268
		9,813		10,268

→

Required:

(a) Calculate, for each year (using year-end figures for balance sheet items), the following ratios:

   (i)   net profit margin;

   (ii)   return on capital employed;

   (iii) current ratio;

   (iv) gearing ratio;

   (v)   days receivables (settlement period); and

   (vi) sales revenue to capital employed.

(b) Using the above ratios, and any other ratios or information you consider relevant, comment on the results of the expansion programme.

Part 2

MANAGEMENT ACCOUNTING

Chapter 7

Cost-volume-profit analysis

Introduction

This chapter is concerned with the relationship between volume of activity, costs and profit. By volume of activity we mean the quantity of a particular service rendered or the number of units of a particular product made or how many times a particular process is undertaken and so on. Broadly, costs can be analysed between those that are fixed, relative to the volume of activity, and those that vary with the volume of activity. We shall consider how we can use knowledge of this relationship to make decisions and to assess risk, particularly in the context of short-term decisions. Though the distinction between financial and management accounting is rather blurred, and much relating to the financial statements that we have discussed so far in the book relates to providing information to managers, this chapter is the first one that is clearly in the area of management accounting.

Learning outcomes

When you have completed this chapter, you should be able to:

- distinguish between fixed costs and variable costs and use this distinction to explain the relationship between costs, volume and profit;

- prepare a break-even chart and deduce the break-even point for some activity;

- discuss the weaknesses of break-even analysis;

- demonstrate the way in which marginal analysis can be used when making short-term decisions.

The behaviour of costs

Costs represent the resources that have to be sacrificed to achieve a business objective. The objective may be to make a particular product, to provide a particular service and so on. The costs incurred by a business may be classified in various ways and one important way is according to how they behave in relation to changes in the volume of activity. There are:

- those that are fixed (stay the same) when changes occur to the volume of activity; and
- those that vary according to the volume of activity.

→ These are known as fixed costs and variable costs respectively. For some particular activity:

Total cost = fixed costs + variable costs

A restaurant manager's salary would normally provide an example of a fixed cost of operating the restaurant. The manager's salary would probably be identical irrespective of how many meals were served – in the short term, at least. The cost to the restaurant of buying the raw food would be a typical variable cost of operating the restaurant.

We shall see in this chapter that knowledge of how much of each type of cost is associated with some particular activity can be of great value to the decision maker.

Fixed costs

The way in which fixed costs behave can be shown graphically, as in Figure 7.1. The distance 0F represents the amount of fixed costs, and this stays the same irrespective of the volume of activity.

Activity 7.1

A business operates a small chain of hairdressing salons. Can you give some examples of costs that are likely to be fixed for this business?

We came up with the following:

- rent;
- insurance;
- cleaning costs;
- staff salaries.

These costs seem likely to be the same irrespective of the number of customers having their hair cut or styled.

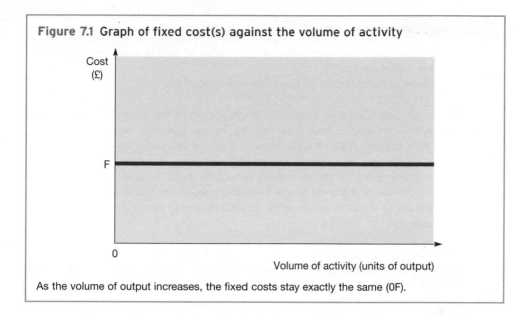

Figure 7.1 Graph of fixed cost(s) against the volume of activity

Cost (£)

F

0

Volume of activity (units of output)

As the volume of output increases, the fixed costs stay exactly the same (0F).

Staff salaries and wages are sometimes automatically assumed always to be variable costs. In practice, they tend to be fixed. People are generally not paid according to the volume of activity, and it is not normal to dismiss staff when there is a short-term downturn in activity. If there is a long-term decline, or at least if it looks that way to management, redundancies may occur, with fixed-cost savings. This, however, is true of all costs. If there is seen to be a likely reduction in demand, the business may, for example, decide to move to smaller premises and make rental cost savings. Thus 'fixed' does not mean set in stone for all time; it usually means fixed over the short to medium term.

Nevertheless, in some circumstances, labour costs are variable (for example, where employees are paid according to how much output they produce), but this is unusual.

It is important to be clear that 'fixed', in this context, means only that the cost is not altered by changes in the volume of activity. Fixed costs are likely to be affected by inflation. If rent (a typical fixed cost) goes up because of inflation, a fixed cost will have increased, but not because of a change in the volume of activity.

The level of fixed costs does not stay the same, irrespective of the time period involved. Fixed costs are almost always *time-based*: that is, they vary with the length of time concerned. The rental charge for two months is normally twice that for one month. Thus fixed costs normally vary with time, but (of course) not with the volume of activity. We should note that when we talk of fixed costs being, say, £1,000, we must add the period concerned, say, £1,000 a month.

Activity 7.2

Do fixed costs stay the same irrespective of the volume of activity, even where there is a massive rise in that volume?
   Think in terms of the rent cost for the hairdressing business.

In fact, the rent is only fixed over a particular range (known as the 'relevant' range). If the number of people wanting to have their hair cut by the business increased, and the business wished to meet this increased demand, it would eventually have to expand its physical size. This might be achieved by opening additional branches, or perhaps by moving existing branches to larger premises in the vicinity. It may be possible to cope with relatively minor increases in activity by using existing space more efficiently, or by having longer opening hours. If activity continued to expand, increased rent charges would seem inevitable, however.

In practice, the situation described in Activity 7.2 would look something like Figure 7.2.

At lower volumes of activity, the rent cost shown in Figure 7.2 would be 0R. As the volume of activity expands, the accommodation becomes inadequate and further expansion requires an increase in premises and, therefore, cost. This higher level of accommodation provision will enable further expansion to take place. Eventually, additional costs will need to be incurred if further expansion is to occur. Fixed costs that behave like this are often referred to as stepped fixed costs.

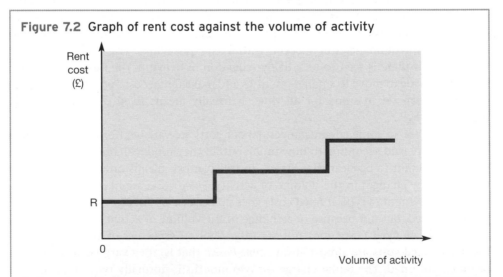

Figure 7.2 Graph of rent cost against the volume of activity

As the volume of activity increases from zero, the rent (a fixed cost) is unaffected. At a particular point, the volume of activity cannot increase further without additional space being rented. The cost of renting the additional space will cause a 'step' in the rent cost. The higher rent cost will continue unaffected if volume rises further until eventually another step point is reached.

Variable costs

We saw earlier that variable costs are costs that vary with the volume of activity. In a manufacturing business, for example, this would include raw materials used.

Variable costs can be represented graphically as in Figure 7.3. At zero volume of activity the variable cost is zero. The cost increases in a straight line as activity increases. The fact that the line for variable cost on this graph is straight implies that the variable cost will normally be the same per unit of activity, irrespective of the volume of activity concerned. We shall consider the practicality of this assumption a little later in this chapter.

Figure 7.3 Graph of variable costs against the volume of activity

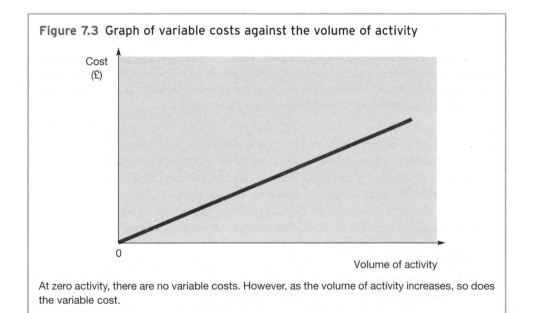

At zero activity, there are no variable costs. However, as the volume of activity increases, so does the variable cost.

Activity 7.3

Can you think of some examples of variable costs in the hairdressing business?

We can think of a couple:

■ lotions and other materials used;
■ laundry costs to wash towels used to dry customers' hair.

As with many types of business activity, variable costs of hairdressers tend to be relatively light in comparison with fixed costs: that is, fixed costs tend to make up the bulk of total costs.

Semi-fixed (semi-variable) costs

In some cases, particular costs have an element of both fixed and variable cost. These can be described as semi-fixed (semi-variable) costs. An example might be the electricity cost for the hairdressing business. Some of this will be for heating and lighting, and this part is probably fixed, at least until the volume of activity expands to a point where longer opening hours or larger premises are necessary. The other part of the cost will vary with the volume of activity. Here we are talking about such things as power for hairdryers and so on.

Activity 7.4

Can you suggest another cost for a hairdressing business that is likely to be semi-fixed (semi-variable)?

We thought of telephone charges for landlines. These tend to have a rental element, which is fixed, and there may also be certain calls that have to be made irrespective of the volume of activity involved. However, increased business would be likely to lead to the need to make more telephone calls and hence increased call charges.

Usually, it is not obvious how much of each element a particular cost contains. It is normally necessary to look at past experience. If we have data on what the electricity cost has been for various volumes of activity, say the relevant data over several three-month periods (electricity is usually billed by the quarter), we can estimate the fixed and variable portions. This may be done graphically, as shown in Figure 7.4. We tend to use past data here purely because they provide us with an estimate of future costs; past costs are not, of course, relevant for their own sake.

Each of the dots in Figure 7.4 is the electricity charge for a particular quarter plotted against the volume of activity (probably measured in terms of sales revenue) for the same quarter. The diagonal line on the graph is the *line of best fit*. This means that this was the line that best seemed (to us, at least) to represent the data. A better estimate can usually be made using a statistical technique (*least squares regression*), which does not involve drawing graphs and making estimates. In practice though, it probably makes little difference which approach is taken.

From the graph we can say that the fixed element of the electricity cost is the amount represented by the vertical distance from the origin at zero (bottom left-hand corner) to the point where the line of best fit crosses the vertical axis of the graph. The variable cost per unit is the amount that the graph rises for each increase in the volume of activity.

By breaking down semi-fixed costs in this way into their fixed and variable elements, we are left with just two aspects of total cost for the activity: fixed costs and variable costs.

Now that we have considered the nature of fixed and variable costs, we can go on to do something useful with that knowledge – carry out a break-even analysis.

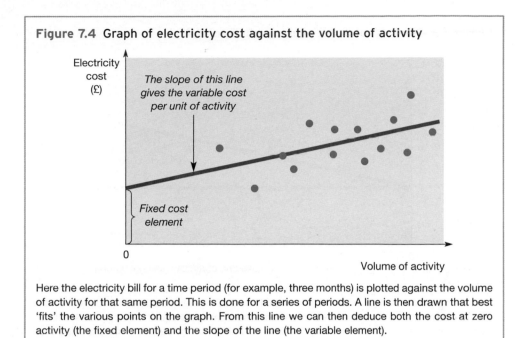

Figure 7.4 Graph of electricity cost against the volume of activity

Electricity cost (£)

The slope of this line gives the variable cost per unit of activity

Fixed cost element

0

Volume of activity

Here the electricity bill for a time period (for example, three months) is plotted against the volume of activity for that same period. This is done for a series of periods. A line is then drawn that best 'fits' the various points on the graph. From this line we can then deduce both the cost at zero activity (the fixed element) and the slope of the line (the variable element).

Break-even analysis

If, in respect of a particular activity, we know the total fixed costs for a period and the total variable cost per unit, we can produce a graph like the one shown in Figure 7.5.

The bottom part of Figure 7.5 shows the fixed cost area. Added to this is the variable cost, the wedge-shaped portion at the top of the graph. The uppermost line represents the total cost at any particular volume of activity. This total is the vertical distance between the graph's horizontal axis and the uppermost line for the particular volume of activity concerned. Logically enough, the total cost at zero activity is the amount of the fixed costs. This is because, even where there is nothing going on, the business will still be paying rent, salaries and so on, at least in the short term. The total cost increases by the amount of the relevant variable costs, as the volume of activity increases.

If we take this total cost graph in Figure 7.5, and superimpose on it a line representing total revenue for each volume of activity, we obtain the break-even chart. This is shown in Figure 7.6. Note in Figure 7.6 that, at zero volume of activity (zero sales), there is zero sales revenue. The profit (loss), which is the difference between total sales revenue and total cost, for a particular volume of activity is the vertical distance between the total sales revenue line and the total cost line at that volume of activity. Where the volume of activity is at break-even point (BEP), there is no vertical distance between these two lines (total sales revenue equals total costs) and so there is no profit or loss; that is, the activity breaks even. Where the volume of activity is below BEP, a

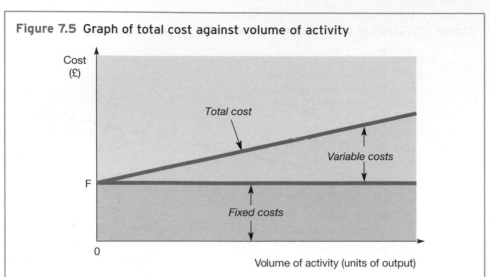

Figure 7.5 Graph of total cost against volume of activity

The bottom part of the graph represents the fixed cost element. To this is added the wedge-shaped top portion, which represents the variable costs. The two parts together represent total cost. At zero activity, the variable costs are zero, so total costs equal fixed costs. As activity increases so does total cost, but only because variable costs increase. We are assuming that there are no steps in the fixed costs.

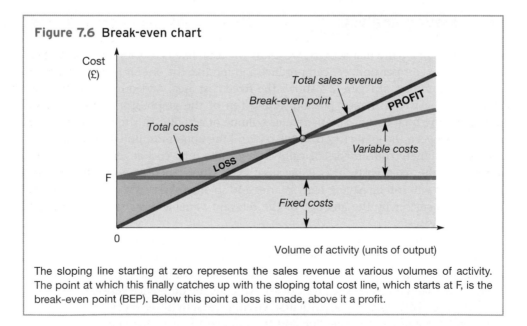

Figure 7.6 Break-even chart

The sloping line starting at zero represents the sales revenue at various volumes of activity. The point at which this finally catches up with the sloping total cost line, which starts at F, is the break-even point (BEP). Below this point a loss is made, above it a profit.

loss will be incurred because total costs exceed total sales revenue. Where the business operates at a volume of activity above BEP, there will be a profit because total sales revenue will exceed total costs. The further below BEP, the higher the loss: the further above BEP, the higher the profit.

As may be imagined, deducing BEPs by drawing graphs is a laborious business. However, since the relationships in the graph are all linear (that is, the lines are all straight), it is easy to calculate the BEP.

We know that at BEP (but not at any other point):

Total sales revenue = Total costs

(At all other points except the BEP, either total sales revenue will exceed total cost or the other way round. Only at BEP are they equal.) That is,

Total sales revenue = Fixed costs + Total variable costs

If we call the number of units of output at BEP b, then

$b \times$ Sales revenue per unit = Fixed costs + ($b \times$ Variable costs per unit)

Thus:

($b \times$ Sales revenue per unit) − ($b \times$ Variable costs per unit) = Fixed costs

and:

$b \times$ (Sales revenue per unit − Variable costs per unit) = Fixed costs

giving:

$$b = \frac{\text{Fixed costs}}{\text{Sales revenue per unit} - \text{Variable costs per unit}}$$

If we look back at the break-even chart in Figure 7.6, this seems logical. The total cost line starts off at point F, higher than the starting point for the total sales revenues line (zero) by amount F (the amount of the fixed costs). Because the sales revenue per unit is greater than the variable cost per unit, the sales revenue line will gradually catch up with the total cost line. The rate at which it will catch up is dependent on the relative steepness of the two lines and the amount that it has to catch up (the fixed costs). Bearing in mind that the slopes of the two lines are the variable cost per unit and the selling price per unit, the above equation for calculating b looks perfectly logical.

Though the BEP can be calculated quickly and simply, as shown, it does not mean that the graphical approach of the break-even chart is without value. The chart shows the relationship between cost, volume and profit over a range of activity and in a form that can easily be understood by non-financial managers. The break-even chart can therefore be a useful device for explaining this relationship.

Example 7.1

Cottage Industries Ltd makes baskets. The fixed costs of operating the workshop for a month total £500. Each basket requires materials that cost £2. Each basket takes one hour to make, and the business pays the basket makers £10 an hour. The basket makers are all on contracts such that if they do not work for any reason, they are not paid. The baskets are sold to a wholesaler for £14 each.

What is the BEP for basket making for the business?

→

The BEP (in number of baskets):

$$= \frac{\text{Fixed costs}}{\text{(Sales revenue per unit – Variable costs per unit)}}$$

$$= \frac{£500}{£14 - (£2 + £10)} = 250 \text{ baskets a month}$$

Note that the BEP must be expressed with respect to a period of time (a month in this case).

Real World 7.1 shows information on the BEPs of three well-known businesses.

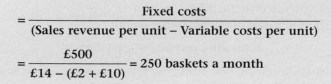

BEP at BA, Ryanair and EasyJet

Commercial airlines seem to pay a lot of attention to their BEPs and their 'load factors', that is, their actual level of activity. Figure 7.7 shows the BEP and load factor for three well-known airlines operating from the UK. British Airways (BA) is a traditional airline. Ryanair and Easyjet are 'no frills' carriers, which means that passengers receive lower levels of service in return for lower fares. All three operate flights within the UK and from the UK to other European countries. Only BA operates flights beyond Europe. We can see that all three airlines are making operating profits as each has a load factor greater than its BEP.

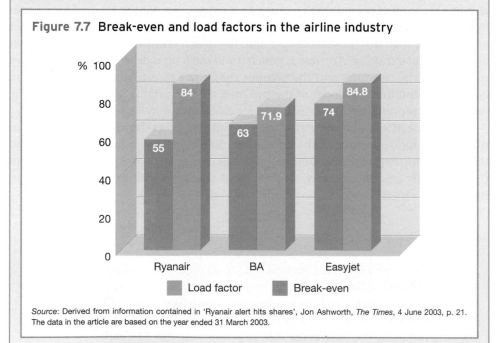

Figure 7.7 Break-even and load factors in the airline industry

Source: Derived from information contained in 'Ryanair alert hits shares', Jon Ashworth, *The Times*, 4 June 2003, p. 21. The data in the article are based on the year ended 31 March 2003.

Activity 7.5

Can you think of reasons why the managers of a business might find it useful to know the BEP of some activity that they are planning to undertake?

The usefulness of being able to deduce the BEP is that it makes it possible to compare the planned or expected volume of activity with the BEP and so make a judgement about risk. Planning to operate only just above the volume of activity needed to break even may indicate that it is a risky venture, since only a small fall from the planned volume of activity could lead to a loss. Real World 7.1 above reveals that Ryanair's operations look rather less risky than those of the other two airlines in that the difference between its load factor and its BEP is largest.

Activity 7.6

Cottage Industries Ltd (see Example 7.1) expects to sell 500 baskets a month. The business has the opportunity to rent a basket-making machine. Doing so would increase the total fixed costs of operating the workshop for a month to £3,000. Using the machine would reduce the labour time to half an hour per basket. The basket makers would still be paid £10 an hour.

(a) How much profit would the business make each month from selling baskets (i) assuming that the basket-making machine is not rented, and (ii) assuming that it is rented?
(b) What is the BEP if the machine is rented?
(c) What do you notice about the figures that you calculate?

(a) Estimated monthly profit from basket making:

	Without the machine		With the machine	
	£	£	£	£
Sales (500 × £14)		7,000		7,000
Less Materials (500 × £2)	1,000		1,000	
Labour (500 × 1 × £10)	5,000			
(500 × ½ × £10)			2,500	
Fixed costs	500		3,000	
		6,500		6,500
Profit		500		500

(b) The BEP (in number of baskets) with the machine:

$$= \frac{\text{Fixed costs}}{\text{Sales revenue per unit} - \text{Variable costs per unit}}$$

$$= \frac{£3,000}{£14 - (£2 + £5)} = 429 \text{ baskets a month}$$

The BEP without the machine is 250 baskets a month (see Example 7.1).

→

(c) There seems to be nothing to choose between the two manufacturing strategies regarding profit, at the estimated sales volume. There is, however, a distinct difference between the two strategies regarding the BEP. Without the machine, the actual volume of sales could fall by a half of that which is expected (from 500 to 250) before the business would fail to make a profit. With the machine, however, a 14 per cent fall (from 500 to 429) would be enough to cause the business to fail to make a profit. On the other hand, for each additional basket sold above the estimated 500, an additional profit of only £2 (that is, £14 – (£2 + £10)) would be made without the machine, whereas £7 (that is, £14 – (£2 + £5)) would be made with the machine. (Note that knowledge of the BEP and the planned volume of activity gives some basis for assessing the riskiness of the activity.)

We shall take a closer look at the relationship between fixed costs, variable costs and break-even together with any advice that we might give the management of Cottage Industries Ltd after we have briefly considered the notion of contribution.

Contribution

The bottom part of the break-even formula (sales revenue per unit less variable costs per unit) is known as the contribution per unit. Thus for the basket-making activity, without the machine the contribution per unit is £2, and with the machine it is £7. This can be quite a useful figure to know in a decision-making context. It is called 'contribution' because it contributes to meeting the fixed costs and, if there is any excess, it also contributes to profit.

We shall see, a little later in this chapter, how knowing the amount of the contribution generated by a particular activity can be valuable in making short-term decisions of various types, as well as being useful in the BEP calculation.

Margin of safety and operating gearing

The margin of safety is the extent to which the planned volume of activity or sales lies above the BEP. Going back to Activity 7.6, we saw that the following situation exists:

	Without the machine	With the machine
Expected volume of sales (baskets)	500	500
BEP (baskets)	250	429
Difference (margin of safety):		
Number of baskets	250	71
Percentage of estimated volume of sales	50%	14%

Activity 7.7

What advice would you give Cottage Industries Ltd about renting the machine, on the basis of the values for margin of safety?

It is a matter of personal judgement, which in turn is related to individual attitudes to risk, as to which strategy to adopt. Most people, however, would prefer the strategy of not renting the machine, since the margin of safety between the expected volume of activity and the BEP is much greater. Thus, for the same level of return, the risk will be lower without renting the machine.

The relative margins of safety are directly linked to the relationship between the selling price per basket, the variable costs per basket, and the fixed costs per month. Without the machine, the contribution (selling price less variable costs) per basket is £2; with the machine it is £7. On the other hand, without the machine the fixed costs are £500 a month; with the machine they are £3,000. This means that, with the machine, the contributions have more fixed costs to 'overcome' before the activity becomes profitable. However, the rate at which the contributions can overcome fixed costs is higher with the machine, because variable costs are lower. This means that one more, or one less, basket sold has a greater impact on profit than it does if the machine is not rented. The contrast between the two scenarios is shown graphically in Figures 7.8(a) and 7.8(b).

→ The relationship between contribution and fixed costs is known as operating gearing. An activity with relatively high fixed costs compared with its variable costs is said to have high operating gearing. Thus, Cottage Industries Ltd has higher operating gearing using the machine than not using it. Renting the machine increases the level of operating gearing quite dramatically because it causes an increase in fixed costs, but at the same time it leads to a reduction in variable costs per basket.

The word 'gearing' is used in this context because, as with intermeshing gear wheels of different circumferences, a movement in one of the factors (volume of activity) causes a more-than-proportionate movement in the other (profit) as illustrated by Figure 7.9.

Increasing the level of operating gearing tends to make profits more sensitive to changes in the volume of activity. We can demonstrate operating gearing with Cottage Industries Ltd's basket-making activities as follows:

	Without the machine			With the machine		
Volume (baskets)	500	1,000	1,500	500	1,000	1,500
	£	£	£	£	£	£
Contributions*	1,000	2,000	3,000	3,500	7,000	10,500
Less Fixed costs	500	500	500	3,000	3,000	3,000
Profit	500	1,500	2,500	500	4,000	7,500

* £2 per basket without the machine and £7 per basket with it.

Note that, without the machine (low operating gearing), a doubling of the output from 500 to 1,000 baskets brings a trebling of the profit. With the machine (high

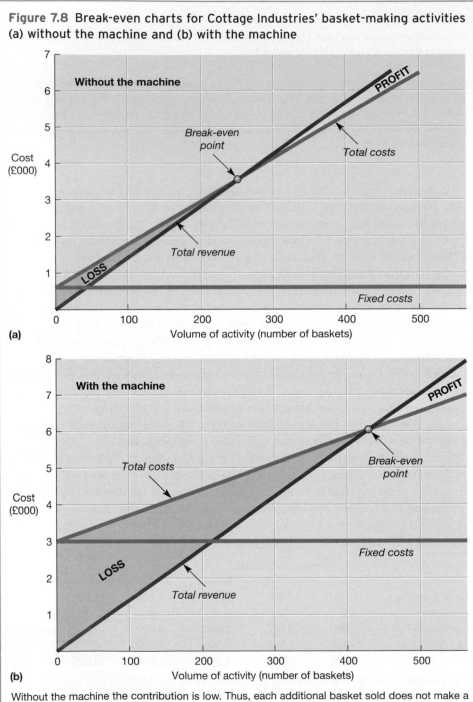

Figure 7.8 Break-even charts for Cottage Industries' basket-making activities (a) without the machine and (b) with the machine

Without the machine the contribution is low. Thus, each additional basket sold does not make a dramatic difference to the profit or loss. With the machine, however, the opposite is true, and small increases or decreases in the sales volume will have a marked effect on the profit or loss.

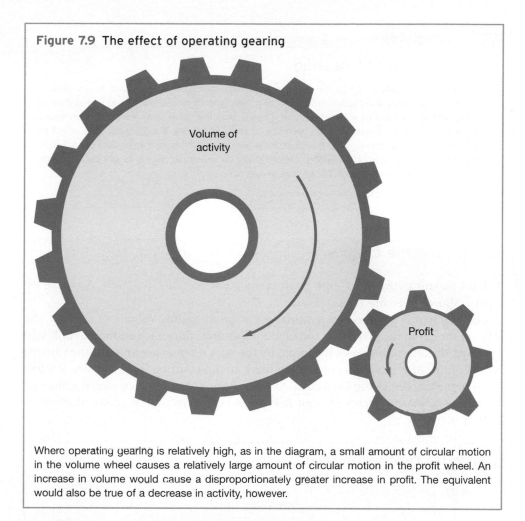

Figure 7.9 The effect of operating gearing

Where operating gearing is relatively high, as in the diagram, a small amount of circular motion in the volume wheel causes a relatively large amount of circular motion in the profit wheel. An increase in volume would cause a disproportionately greater increase in profit. The equivalent would also be true of a decrease in activity, however.

operating gearing), doubling output causes profit to rise by eight times. At the same time, reductions in the volume of activity tend to have a more damaging effect on profit where the operating gearing is higher.

Operating gearing is quite similar in nature and effect to financial gearing that we met in Chapter 6.

Activity 7.8

In general terms, what types of business activity tend to have the highest operating gearing? (*Hint*: Cottage Industries Ltd might give you some idea.)

In general, activities that are capital intensive tend to have high operating gearing. This is because renting or owning capital equipment gives rise to additional fixed costs, but it can also give rise to lower variable costs. Real World 7.2 shows how a very well-known business has benefited from high operating gearing.

Sky-high operating gearing

British Sky Broadcasting Group plc (Sky), the satellite television broadcaster, is an obvious example of a business with high operating gearing. Nearly all of its costs are fixed in that they do not vary with the number of subscribers that it has or with the value of its advertising revenues. This means that any increase in total revenues is likely to have a strong favourable effect on profit. The business acknowledged this in its 2003 annual report where it said, 'Sky continues to benefit from strong operational gearing', before going on to explain how a 15 per cent increase in revenues led to an increase of 94 per cent in operating profit.

Source: British Sky Broadcasting Group plc Annual Report 2003

Profit-volume charts

A slight variant of the break-even chart is the profit-volume (PV) chart. A typical PV chart is shown in Figure 7.10.

The PV chart is obtained by plotting loss or profit against volume of activity. The slope of the graph is equal to the contribution per unit, since each additional unit sold decreases the loss, or increases the profit, by the sales revenue per unit less the variable cost per unit. At zero volume of activity there are no contributions, so there is a loss equal to the amount of the fixed costs. As the volume of activity increases, the amount of the loss gradually decreases until BEP is reached. Beyond BEP, profits increase as activity increases.

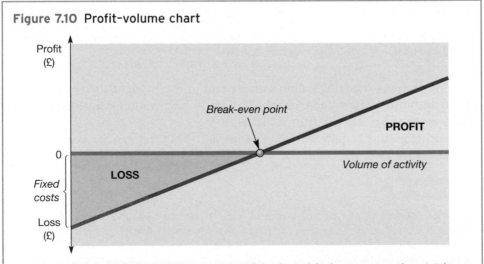

Figure 7.10 Profit-volume chart

The sloping line is profit (loss) plotted against activity. As activity increases, so does total contribution (sales revenue less variable costs). At zero activity there are no contributions, so there will be a loss equal in amount to the total fixed costs.

As we can see, the PV chart does not tell us anything not shown by the break-even chart. On the other hand, information is perhaps more easily absorbed from the PV chart. This is particularly true of the profit (loss) at any volume of activity. The break-even chart shows this as the vertical distance between the total cost and total sales revenue lines. The PV chart, in effect, combines the total sales revenue and total variable cost lines, which means that profit (or loss) is plotted directly.

Failing to break even

Where a business fails to reach its BEP, steps must be taken to remedy the problem: there must be an increase in sales revenue or a reduction in costs, or both of these. Real World 7.3 reveals how one well-known business is striving to reach to achieve its BEP.

Real World 7.3

Trying to keep on the road   FT

Jaguar, Ford's heavily loss-making luxury cars division, is facing a tougher climate than expected in trying to reach break-even by 2007.

But it will keep to its restructuring plans announced last year, according to Joe Greenwell, chairman and chief executive, who also confirmed yesterday that Jaguar is to diversify into 'crossover' vehicles, which combine the characteristics of sports-utility vehicles and conventional cars.

Jaguar, which has all its production in the UK, is closing its Browns Lane factory in Coventry with the loss of 1,150 jobs and closing a UK plant as part of efforts to stem losses which reached several hundred million pounds last year.

Speaking at a Barcelona conference, Mr Greenwell blamed a weak dollar, increased taxes and increasingly stringent regulatory requirements for the company's problems.

Source: 'Jaguar struggles over break even', *Financial Times*, 6 May 2005, FT.com

Weaknesses of break-even analysis

As we have seen, break-even analysis can provide some useful insights to the important relationship between fixed costs, variable costs and the volume of activity. It does, however, have its weaknesses. There are three general problems:

■ *Non-straight-line relationships*. The normal approach to break-even analysis assumes that the relationships between sales revenues, variable costs and volume are strictly straight-line (linear) ones. In real life this is unlikely to be so and we shall look at the reasons for this in Activity 7.9, below. Non-straight line relationships are probably not a major problem, since:
 – break-even analysis is normally conducted in advance of the activity actually taking place. Our ability to predict future costs, revenues and so on is somewhat

limited: hence what are probably minor variations from strict linearity are unlikely to be significant, compared with other forecasting errors;

– most businesses operate within a narrow range of volume of activity. Over short ranges, curved lines tend to be relatively straight.

■ *Stepped fixed costs*. Most fixed costs are not fixed over all volumes of activity. They tend to be 'stepped' in the way shown in Figure 7.2. This means that, in practice, great care must be taken in making assumptions about fixed costs. The problem is particularly heightened because most activities will probably involve fixed costs of various types (rent, supervisory salaries, administration costs), all of which are likely to have steps at different points.

■ *Multi-product businesses*. Most businesses do not offer just one product or service. This is a problem for break-even analysis since it raises the question of the effect of additional sales of one product or service on sales of another of the business's products or services. There is also the problem of identifying the fixed costs of one particular activity. Fixed costs tend to relate to more than one activity – for example, two activities may be carried out in the same rented premises. There are ways of dividing fixed costs between activities, but these tend to be arbitrary, which calls into question the value of the break-even analysis and the validity of the conclusion reached.

Activity 7.9

We saw above that, in practice, relationships between costs, revenues and volumes of activity are not necessarily straight-line ones.
   Can you think of any reasons for this and examples of it?

We thought of the following:

■ *Economies of scale with labour.* A business may do things more economically where there is a higher volume of activity than are possible at lower levels of activity. It may, for example, be possible for employees to specialise.

■ *Economies of scale with buying goods or services.* A business may find it cheaper to buy in goods and services if it buys in bulk.

■ *Diseconomies of scale.* This may mean that the per-unit cost of output is higher at higher levels of activity. For example, it may be necessary to pay higher rates of pay to workers to recruit the additional staff needed at higher volumes of activity.

■ *Lower sales prices at high levels of activity.* It may not be possible to achieve high levels of sales activity without lowering the selling price.

The popularity of break-even analysis

Despite some problems, the notions of break-even analysis and BEP seem to be widely used. The media frequently refer to the BEP for businesses and activities. For example, there was much discussion at the turn of this century about the BEP, in terms of the number of visitors, for the London Millennium Dome. Eurotunnel's BEP, and whether it will be reached, also seems to be a much-reported topic. Similarly, the number of people regularly needed to pay to watch a football team so that the club breaks even often seems to be referred to. Real World 7.4 provides an insight to the extent that break-even analysis is used by managers in practice.

Real World 7.4

Break-even analysis in practice

A survey of management accounting practice in the United States was conducted in 2003. Nearly 2,000 businesses replied to the survey. These tended to be larger businesses, of which about 40 per cent were manufacturers and about 16 per cent financial services; the remainder were across a range of other industries.

The survey revealed that 62 per cent use break-even analysis extensively, with a further 22 per cent considering using the technique in the future.

Though the survey relates to the USA, in the absence of UK evidence, it provides some insight to what is likely also to be practice in the UK and elsewhere in the developed world.

Source: Taken from the *2003 Survey of Management Accounting* by Ernst and Young, 2003

Marginal analysis

When we are trying to decide between two or more possible courses of action, and where economic costs and benefits are the decision-making criteria, *only costs that vary with the decision should be included in the decision analysis.*

Example 7.2

A householder wants a house decorated. Two decorators have been asked to price the job. One of them will do the work for £250, the other one wants £300, in both cases on the basis that the householder will supply the materials. It is believed that the two decorators will do an equally good job. The materials will cost £200 irrespective of which decorator does the work. Assuming that the householder wants the house decorated at the lower cost, which decorator should be asked to do the work? Is the cost of the materials relevant to the decision?

Clearly the first of the two decorators should be selected. The cost of the materials is irrelevant because it will be the same in each case. It is only possible to distinguish rationally between courses of action on the basis of differences between them.

In Example 7.2 a distinction is made between relevant and irrelevant costs. For many decisions that involve relatively small variations from existing practice and/or relatively limited periods of time, all fixed costs are irrelevant to the decision, because they will be the same irrespective of the decision made. This is because either:

- fixed costs tend to be impossible to alter in the short term; or
- managers are reluctant to alter them in the short term.

Activity 7.10

Ali plc owns the premises that it uses to provide a service. There is a downturn in demand for the service, and it would be possible for Ali plc to carry on the business from smaller, cheaper premises.

Can you think of any reasons why the business might not immediately move to smaller, cheaper premises?

We thought of broadly three reasons:

1 It is not usually possible to find a buyer for premises at very short notice.
2 It may be difficult to move premises quickly where there is, say, delicate equipment to be moved.
3 Management may feel that the downturn might not be permanent, and would thus be reluctant to take such a dramatic step and deny itself the opportunity to benefit from a possible revival of trade.

The business's premises in Activity 7.10 may provide an example of one of the more inflexible types of cost, but most fixed costs tend to be broadly similar in this context.

We shall now consider some types of decisions where fixed costs can be regarded as irrelevant. In making these decisions, we should have as our key strategic objective the maximisation of owners' (shareholders') wealth. Since these decisions are short-term in nature, this means that wealth will normally be maximised by trying to generate as much net cash inflow as possible.

In marginal analysis we concern ourselves just with costs and revenues that vary with the decision and so this usually means that fixed costs are ignored. Marginal analysis tends to assume that the variable cost per unit will be equal to the marginal cost, which is the additional cost of producing one more unit of output. Although this is normally the case, there may be times when producing one more unit will involve a step in the fixed costs. If this occurs, the marginal cost is not just the variable cost, but will include the increment, or step, in the fixed costs as well.

Marginal analysis may be used in four key areas of decision making:

- accepting/rejecting special contracts;
- determining the most efficient use of scarce resources;
- make-or-buy decisions;
- closing or continuation decisions.

We shall now consider each of these areas in turn.

Accepting/rejecting special contracts

To understand how marginal analysis may be used in decisions as to whether to accept or reject special contracts, let us consider the following activity.

Activity 7.11

Cottage Industries Ltd (see Example 7.1) has spare capacity in that its basket makers have some spare time. An overseas retail chain has offered the business an order for 300 baskets at a price of £13 each.

Without considering any wider issues, should the business accept the order? (Assume that the business does not rent the machine.)

Since the fixed costs will be incurred in any case, they are not relevant to this decision. All we need to do is see whether the price offered will yield a contribution. If it will, the business will be better off by accepting the contract than by refusing it.

	£
Additional revenue per unit	13
Less Marginal (variable) cost per unit	12
Additional contribution per unit	1

For 300 units, the additional contribution will be £300 (that is, 300 × £1). Since no fixed cost increase is involved, irrespective of what else is happening to the business, it will be £300 better off by taking this contract than by refusing it.

As ever with decision making, there are other factors that are either difficult or impossible to quantify. These should be taken into account before reaching a final decision. In the case of Cottage Industries Ltd's decision on the overseas customer, these could include the following:

- The possibility that spare capacity will have been 'sold off' cheaply when there might be another potential customer who will offer a higher price, but, by which time, the capacity will be fully committed. It is a matter of commercial judgement as to how likely this will be.
- Selling the same product, but at different prices, could lead to a loss of customer goodwill. The fact that a different price will be set for customers in different countries (that is, in different markets) may be sufficient to avoid this potential problem.
- If the business is going to suffer continually from being unable to sell its full production potential at the 'regular' price, it might be better, in the long run, to reduce capacity and make fixed cost savings. Using the spare capacity to produce marginal benefits may lead to the business failing to address this issue.
- On a more positive note, the business may see this as a way of breaking into the overseas market. This is something that might be impossible to achieve if the business charges its regular price.

The most efficient use of scarce resources

We tend to think in terms of the size of the market being the brake on output. This is to say that the ability of a business to sell will limit production, rather than the ability to produce will limit sales. In some cases, however, it is a limit on what can be produced that limits sales. Limited production might stem from a shortage of any factor of production – labour, raw materials, space, machinery and so on. Such scarce factors are often known as *key* or *limiting* factors.

The most profitable combination of products will occur where the *contribution per unit of the scarce factor* is maximised. Example 7.3 should illustrate this point.

Example 7.3

A business provides three different services, the details of which are as follows:

Service (code name)	AX107	AX109	AX220
	£	£	£
Selling price per unit	50	40	65
Variable cost per unit	(25)	(20)	(35)
Contribution per unit	25	20	30
Labour time per unit	5 hours	3 hours	6 hours

Within reason, the market will take as many units of each service as can be provided, but the ability to provide the service is limited by the availability of labour, all of which needs to be skilled. Fixed costs are not affected by the choice of service provided because all three services use the same facilities.

The most profitable service is AX109 because it generates a contribution of £6.67 (£20/3) an hour. The other two generate only £5.00 each an hour (£25/5 and £30/6). So, to maximise profit, priority should be given to the production that maximises the contribution per unit of limiting factor.

Our first reaction may have been that the business should provide only service AX220, because this is the one that yields the highest contribution per unit sold. If so, we should have been making the mistake of thinking that it is the ability to sell that is the limiting factor. If the above analysis is not convincing, we can take an imaginary number of available labour hours and ask ourselves what is the maximum contribution (and, therefore, profit) that could be made by providing each service exclusively. Bear in mind that there is no shortage of anything else, including market demand, just a shortage of labour.

Let us assume, for example, that the business has just 30 hours of labour time available. This would enable it to make six AX107s (total contribution £150) or ten AX109s (total contribution £200) or five AX220s (total contribution £150). Thus we find exactly the same desirability of the AX109s relative to the other two products, as we found in Example 7.3.

Activity 7.12

A business makes three different products, the details of which are as follows:

Product (code name)	B14	B17	B22
Selling price per unit (£)	25	20	23
Variable cost per unit (£)	10	8	12
Weekly demand (units)	25	20	30
Machine time per unit (hours)	4	3	4

Fixed costs are not affected by the choice of product because all three products use the same machine. Machine time is limited to 148 hours a week.

Which combination of products should be manufactured if the business is to produce the highest profit?

Product (code name)	B14	B17	B22
	£	£	£
Selling price per unit	25	20	23
Variable cost per unit	(10)	(8)	(12)
Contribution per unit	15	12	11
Machine time per unit	4 hours	3 hours	4 hours
Contribution per machine hour	£3.75	£4.00	£2.75
Order of priority	2nd	1st	3rd

Therefore:

Produce	20 units (maximum demand) of product B17 using	60 hours
	22 units of product B14 using (remaining machine hours)	88 hours
		148 hours

This leaves unsatisfied the market demand for a further three units of product B14 and 30 units of product B22.

Activity 7.13

What steps could be contemplated that could lead to a higher level of contribution for the business in Activity 7.12?

The possibilities for improving matters that occurred to us are as follows:

■ Consider obtaining additional machine time. This could mean buying or hiring a new machine, subcontracting the machining to another business, or perhaps squeezing a few more hours a week out of the business's existing machine. Perhaps a combination of two or more of these is a possibility.
■ Redesign the products in a way that requires less time per unit on the machine.
■ Increase the price per unit of the three products. This might well have the effect of dampening demand, but the existing demand cannot be met at present, and it may be more profitable in the long run to make a greater contribution on each unit sold than to take one of the other courses of action to overcome the problem.

Activity 7.14

Going back to Activity 7.12, what is the maximum price that the business concerned would logically be prepared to pay to have the remaining B14s machined by a sub-contractor, assuming that no fixed or variable costs would be saved as a result of not doing the machining in-house?

Would there be a different maximum if we were considering the B22s?

If the remaining three B14s were subcontracted at no cost, the business would be able to earn a contribution of £15 a unit, which it would not otherwise be able to gain. Therefore, any price up to £15 a unit would be worth paying to a subcontractor to undertake the machining. Naturally, the business would prefer to pay as little as possible, but anything up to £15 would still make it worthwhile subcontracting the machining.

This would not be true of the B22s because they have a different contribution per unit; £11 would be the relevant figure in their case.

Make-or-buy decisions

Businesses are frequently confronted by the need to decide whether to produce the product or service that they sell themselves, or to buy it in from some other business. Thus, a producer of electrical appliances might decide to subcontract the manufacture of one of its products to another business, perhaps because there is a shortage of production capacity in the producer's own factory, or because it believes it to be cheaper to subcontract than to make the appliance itself.

It might just be part of a product or service that is subcontracted. For example, the producer may have a component for the appliance made by another manufacturer. In principle, there is hardly any limit to the scope of make-or-buy decisions. Virtually any part, component or service that is required in production of the main product or service, or the main product or service itself, could be the subject of a make-or-buy decision. So, for example, the personnel function of a business, which is normally performed in-house, could be subcontracted. At the same time, electrical power, which is typically provided by an outside electrical utility business, could be generated in-house. Obtaining services or products from a subcontractor is often called outsourcing.

Real World 7.5 provides an example of outsourcing by a well-known UK business.

Real World 7.5

Outsourcing at Boots

During 2002, Boots Company plc, the UK health-care manufacturer and retailer, decided to subcontract or 'outsource' its IT activities. Now, instead of employing its own IT staff, it has a contract for another business to run Boots' IT facility. Boots estimates that this will save it £100 million over a ten-year period. Outsourcing this type of activity is becoming very common in the UK and elsewhere.

Source: Boots Company plc Annual Report 2003

Example 7.4

Shah Ltd needs a component for one of its products. It can subcontract production of the component to a subcontractor who will provide the components for £20 each. The business can produce the components internally for total variable costs of £15 per component. Shah Ltd has spare capacity.

Should the component be subcontracted or produced internally?

The answer is that Shah Ltd should produce the component internally, since the variable cost of subcontracting is greater by £5 than the variable cost of internal manufacture.

Activity 7.15

Now assume that Shah Ltd (Example 7.4) has no spare capacity, so it can only produce the component internally by reducing its output of another of its products. While it is making each component, it will lose contributions of £12 from the other product.

Should the component be subcontracted or produced internally?

The answer is to subcontract.

The relevant cost of internal production of each component is:

	£
Variable cost of production of the component	15
Opportunity cost of lost production of the other product	12
	27

This is obviously more costly than the £20 per component that will have to be paid to the subcontractor.

Activity 7.16

What factors, other than the immediately financially quantifiable, would you consider when making a make-or-buy decision?

We feel that there are two major factors:

1 The general problems of subcontracting:
   (a) loss of control of quality;
   (b) potential unreliability of supply.
2 Expertise and specialisation. It is possible for most businesses, with sufficient determination, to do virtually everything in-house. This may, however, require a level of skill and facilities that most businesses neither have nor feel inclined to acquire. For example, though it is true that most businesses could generate their own electricity, their managements tend to take the view that this is better done by a specialist generator business. Specialists can often do things more cheaply, with less risk of things going wrong.

Closing or continuation decisions

It is quite common for businesses to produce separate financial statements for each department or section, to try to assess the relative effectiveness of each one.

Example 7.5

Goodsports Ltd is a retail shop that operates through three departments, all in the same premises. The three departments occupy roughly equal-sized areas of the premises. The trading results for the year just finished showed the following:

	Total £000	Sports equipment £000	Sports clothes £000	General clothes £000
Sales	534	254	183	97
Costs	(482)	(213)	(163)	(106)
Profit/(loss)	52	41	20	(9)

It would appear that if the general clothes department were to close, the business would be more profitable, by £9,000 a year, assuming last year's performance to be a reasonable indication of future performance.

When the costs are analysed between those that are variable and those that are fixed, however, the contribution of each department can be deduced and the following results obtained:

	Total £000	Sports equipment £000	Sports clothes £000	General clothes £000
Sales	534	254	183	97
Variable costs	(344)	(167)	(117)	(60)
Contribution	190	87	66	37
Fixed costs (rent, and so on)	(138)	(46)	(46)	(46)
Profit/(loss)	52	41	20	(9)

Now it is obvious that closing the general clothes department, without any other developments, would make the business worse off by £37,000 (the department's contribution). The department should not be closed, because it makes a positive contribution. The fixed costs would continue whether the department were closed or not. As can be seen from the above analysis, distinguishing between variable and fixed costs, and deducing the contribution, can make the picture a great deal clearer.

Activity 7.17

In considering Goodsports Ltd (in Example 7.5), we saw that the general clothes department should not be closed 'without any other developments'.

What 'other developments' could affect this decision, making continuation either more attractive or less attractive?

The things that we could think of are as follows:

■ Expansion of the other departments or replacing the general clothes department with a completely new activity. This would make sense only if the space currently occupied by the general clothes department could generate contributions totalling at least £37,000 a year.

■ Subletting the space occupied by the general clothes department. Once again, this would need to generate a net rent greater than £37,000 a year to make it more financially beneficial than keeping the department open.

■ Keeping the department open, even if it generated no contribution whatsoever (assuming that there is no other use for the space), may still be beneficial. If customers are attracted into the shop because it has general clothing, they may then buy something from one of the other departments. In the same way, the activity of a sub-tenant might attract customers into the shop. (On the other hand, it might drive them away!)

? Self-assessment question 7.1

Khan Ltd can render three different types of service (Alpha, Beta and Gamma) using the same staff. Various estimates for next year have been made as follows:

Service	Alpha £/unit	Beta £/unit	Gamma £/unit
Selling price	30	39	20
Variable material cost	15	18	10
Other variable costs	6	10	5
Share of fixed costs	8	12	4
Staff time required (hours)	2	3	1

Fixed costs for next year are expected to total £40,000.

Required:
(a) If the business were to render only service Alpha next year, how many units of the service would it need to provide in order to break even? (Assume for this part of the question that there is no effective limit to market size and staffing level.)
(b) If the business has a maximum of 10,000 staff hours next year, in which order of preference would the three services come?
(c) If the maximum market for next year for the three services is as follows:

Alpha	3,000 units
Beta	2,000 units
Gamma	5,000 units

what quantities of which service should the business provide next year and how much profit would this be expected to yield?

243

Summary

The main points in this chapter may be summarised as follows:

Behaviour of costs:

- Fixed costs are those that are independent of the level of activity (for example, rent).
- Variable costs are those that vary with the level of activity (for example, raw materials).
- Semi-fixed (semi-variable) costs are a mixture of the two (for example, electricity).

Break-even analysis:

- The break-even point (BEP) is the level of activity (in units of output or sales revenue) at which total costs (fixed + variable) = total sales revenue.
- Calculation of BEP is as follows:

$$\text{BEP (in units of output)} = \frac{\text{Fixed costs for the period}}{\text{Contribution per unit}}$$

- Knowledge of BEP for a particular activity can be used as a basis for risk assessment.
- Contribution per unit = sales revenue per unit less variable cost per unit.
- Margin of safety = excess of planned volume of activity over BEP.
- Operating gearing = the extent to which the total costs of some activity are fixed rather than variable.
- Profit–volume (PV) chart is an alternative approach to the BE chart.

Weaknesses of BE analysis:

- Non-linear relationships.
- Stepped fixed costs.
- Multi-product businesses.

Marginal analysis (ignores fixed costs where these are not affected by the decision):

- Accepting/rejecting special contracts – consider only the effect on contributions.
- Using scarce resources – the limiting factor is most effectively used by maximising its contribution per unit.
- Make-or-buy decisions – take the action that leads to the highest total contributions.
- Closing/continuing an activity – should be assessed by net effect on total contributions.

→ **Key terms**

fixed costs p. 218	contribution p. 228
variable costs p. 218	margin of safety p. 228
stepped fixed costs p. 220	operating gearing p. 229
semi-fixed (semi-variable) costs p. 222	profit–volume (PV) chart p. 232
break-even analysis p. 222	marginal analysis p. 236
break-even chart p. 223	marginal cost p. 236
break-even point (BEP) p. 223	outsourcing p. 240

Further reading

If you would like to explore the topics covered in this chapter in more depth, we recommend the following books:

Atkinson, A., Kaplan, R. and Young, M. *Management Accounting*, 4th edn, Prentice Hall, 2004, Chapter 2.

Drury, C. *Management and Cost Accounting*, 6th edn, Thomson Learning, 2004, Chapter 8.

Horngren, C., Datar, S. and Foster, G. *Cost Accounting: A Managerial Emphasis*, 12th edn, Prentice Hall International, 2005, Chapter 3.

Upchurch, A. *Management Accounting: Principles and Practice*, Financial Times/Pitman Publishing, 1998, Chapter 6.

? Review questions

Answers to these questions can be found at the back of the book (pp. 492–3).

7.1 Define the terms *fixed cost* and *variable cost*. Explain how an understanding of the distinction between fixed costs and variable costs can be useful to managers.

7.2 What is meant by the *BEP* for an activity? How is the BEP calculated? Why is it useful to know the BEP?

7.3 When we say that some business activity has *high operating gearing*, what do we mean? What are the implications for the business of high operating gearing?

7.4 If there is a scarce resource that is restricting sales, how will the business maximise its profit? Explain the logic of the approach that you have identified for maximising profit.

✳ Exercises

Exercises 7.3 to 7.5 are more advanced than 7.1 and 7.2. Those with a coloured number have answers at the back of the book (pp. 510–11).

> If you wish to try more exercises, visit the students' side of the companion website.

7.1 The management of a business is concerned about its inability to obtain enough fully trained labour to enable it to meet its present budget projection.

Service	Alpha	Beta	Gamma	Total
	£000	£000	£000	£000
Variable costs				
Materials	6	4	5	15
Labour	9	6	12	27
Expenses	3	2	2	7
Allocated fixed costs	6	15	12	33
Total cost	24	27	31	82
Profit	15	2	2	19
Sales revenue	39	29	33	101

The amount of labour likely to be available amounts to £20,000. All of the variable labour is paid at the same hourly rate. You have been asked to prepare a statement of plans ensuring that at least 50 per cent of the budget sales are achieved for each service, and the balance of labour is used to produce the greatest profit.

Required:
(a) Prepare a statement, with explanations, showing the greatest profit available from the limited amount of skilled labour available, within the constraint stated. *Hint*: Remember that all labour is paid at the same rate.
(b) What steps could the business take in an attempt to improve profitability, in the light of the labour shortage?

7.2 A hotel group prepares financial statements on a quarterly basis. The senior management is reviewing the performance of one hotel and making plans for next year.

The managers have in front of them the results for this year (based on some actual results and some forecasts to the end of this year):

Quarter	Sales	Profit/(loss)
	£000	£000
1	400	(280)
2	1,200	360
3	1,600	680
4	800	40
Total	4,000	800

The total estimated number of visitors (guest nights) for this year is 50,000. The results follow a regular pattern; there are no unexpected cost fluctuations beyond the seasonal trading pattern shown above. The management intends to incorporate into its plans for next year an anticipated increase in unit variable costs of 10 per cent and a profit target for the hotel of £1 million.

Required:

(a) Calculate the total variable and total fixed costs of the hotel for this year. Show the provisional annual results for this year in total, showing variable and fixed costs separately. Show also the revenue and costs per visitor.

(b) (i) If there is no increase in visitors for next year, what will be the required revenue rate per hotel visitor to meet the profit target?

(ii) If the required revenue rate per visitor is not raised above this year's level, how many visitors will be required to meet the profit target?

(c) Outline and briefly discuss the assumptions that are made in typical PV or break-even analysis, and assess whether they limit its usefulness.

7.3 A business makes three products, A, B and C. All three products require the use of two types of machine: cutting machines and assembling machines. Estimates for next year include the following:

Product	A	B	C
Selling price (£ per unit)	25	30	18
Sales demand (units)	2,500	3,400	5,100
Material cost (£ per unit)	12	13	10
Variable production cost (£ per unit)	7	4	3
Time required per unit on cutting machines (hours)	1.0	1.0	0.5
Time required per unit on assembling machines (hours)	0.5	1.0	0.5

Fixed costs for next year are expected to total £42,000. It is the business's policy for each unit of production to absorb these in proportion to its total variable costs.

The business has cutting machine capacity of 5,000 hours a year and assembling machine capacity of 8,000 hours a year.

Required:

(a) State, with supporting workings, which products in which quantities the business should plan to make next year on the basis of the above information. (*Hint:* First determine which machines will be a limiting factor (scarce resource).)

(b) State the maximum price per product that it would be worth the business paying to a subcontractor to carry out that part of the work that could not be done internally.

7.4 Darmor Ltd has three products, which require the same production facilities. Information about the production costs for one unit of its products is as follows:

Product	X	Y	Z
	£	£	£
Labour: Skilled	6	9	3
Unskilled	2	4	10
Materials	12	25	14
Other variable costs	3	7	7
Fixed costs	5	10	10

All labour and materials costs are variable. Skilled labour is paid £12 an hour, and unskilled labour is paid £10 an hour. All references to labour costs above, are based on basic rates →

of pay. Skilled labour is scarce, which means that the business could sell more than the maximum that it is able to make of any of the three products.

Product X is sold in a regulated market, and the regulators have set a price of £30 per unit for it.

Required:

(a) State, with supporting workings, the price that must be charged for products Y and Z, such that the business would find it equally profitable to make and sell any of the three products.

(b) State, with supporting workings, the maximum rate of overtime premium that the business would logically be prepared to pay its skilled workers to work beyond the basic time.

7.5 Gandhi Ltd renders a promotional service to small retailing businesses. There are three levels of service: the 'basic', the 'standard' and the 'comprehensive'. On the basis of past experience, the business plans next year to work at absolute full capacity as follows:

Service	Number of units of the service	Selling price	Variable cost per unit
		£	£
Basic	11,000	50	25
Standard	6,000	80	65
Comprehensive	16,000	120	90

The business's fixed costs total £660,000 a year. Each service takes about the same length of time, irrespective of the level.

One of the accounts staff has just produced a report that seems to show that the standard service is unprofitable. The relevant extract from the report is as follows:

Standard service cost analysis

	£	
Selling price per unit	80	
Variable cost per unit	(65)	
Fixed cost per unit	(20)	(£660,000/(11,000 + 6,000 + 16,000))
Net loss	(5)	

The producer of the report suggests that the business should not offer the standard service next year.

Required:

(a) Should the standard service be offered next year, assuming that the quantity of the other services could not be expanded to use the spare capacity?

(b) Should the standard service be offered next year, assuming that the released capacity could be used to render a new service, the 'nova', for which customers would be charged £75, and which would have variable costs of £50 and take twice as long as the other three services?

(c) What is the minimum price that could be accepted for one unit of the basic service, assuming that the necessary capacity to expand it will come only from not offering the standard service?

Chapter 8

Full costing

Introduction

In this chapter we continue our consideration of management accounting by looking at an approach to deducing the cost of a unit of output that takes account of all of the costs. This contrasts with the approach that we looked at in Chapter 7, where we concentrated just on the variable costs. This full-costing approach, as it is called, is very widely used in practice. Many businesses base their selling prices on the full cost. Also, in deriving a business's profit for a period, we need (as we saw in Chapter 3) to know the cost of the goods or service sold. We shall look at the traditional approach to full costing and at activity-based costing which represents an alternative approach. Finally, having considered how full costing is achieved, we shall consider its usefulness for management purposes.

Learning outcomes

When you have completed this chapter, you should be able to:

- deduce the full cost of a unit of output in a single-product environment;
- distinguish between direct and indirect costs and use this distinction to deduce the full cost of a job in a multi-product environment;
- discuss the problem of charging overheads to jobs in a multi-product environment;
- explain the role and nature of activity-based costing.

The nature of full costing

→ With full costing we are concerned with all costs involved with achieving some object-ive, such as providing a particular service. The logic of full costing is that all of the costs of running a particular facility, say an office, are part of the cost of the output of that office. For example, the rent may be a cost that will not alter merely because we provide one more unit of the service, but if the office were not rented there would be nowhere for providing the service to take place, so rent is an important element of the cost of each unit of output.

→ Full cost is the total amount of resources, usually measured in monetary terms, sacrificed to achieve a particular objective. It takes account of all resources sacrificed to achieve the objective. Thus, if the objective were to supply a customer with a prod-uct or service, all costs relating to the production of the product or provision of the service would be included as part of the full cost. To derive the full cost figure, we must accumulate the costs incurred and then assign them to the particular product or ser-vice. In the sections that follow we shall first see how this is done for a single-product operation and then see how it is done for a multi-product operation.

Deriving full costs in a single-product operation

The simplest case for which to deduce the full cost per unit is where the business has only one product line, that is, each unit of its product is identical. Here it is simply a question of adding up all the costs of production incurred in the period (materials, labour, rent, fuel, power and so on) and dividing this total by the total number of units of output for the period.

Activity 8.1

Fruitjuice Ltd has just one product, a sparkling orange drink that is marketed as 'Orange Fizz'. During last month the business produced 7,300 litres of the drink. The costs incurred were as follows:

	£
Ingredients (oranges and so on)	390
Fuel	85
Rent of premises	350
Depreciation of equipment	75
Labour	880

What is the full cost per litre of producing 'Orange Fizz'?

This figure is found by simply adding together all of the costs incurred and then dividing by the number of litres produced:

$$£(390 + 85 + 350 + 75 + 880)/7{,}300 = £0.24 \text{ per litre}$$

There can be problems in deciding exactly how much cost was incurred. In the case of Fruitjuice Ltd, for example, how is the cost of depreciation deduced? It is certainly an estimate, and so its reliability is open to question. The cost of raw materials may also be a problem. Should we use the 'relevant' cost of the raw materials (almost certainly the replacement cost), or the actual price (historic cost) paid for the inventories used? If it is worth calculating the cost per litre, it must be because this information will be used for some decision-making purpose, so the replacement cost is probably more logical. In practice, however, it seems that historic costs are more often used to deduce full costs.

There can also be problems in deciding precisely how many units of output there were. If making Orange Fizz is not a very fast process, some of the drink will be in the process of being made at any given moment. This, in turn, means that some of the costs incurred last month were for some Orange Fizz that was work in progress at the end of the month, so is not included in last month's output quantity of 7,300 litres. Similarly, part of the 7,300 litres was started and incurred costs in the previous month, yet all of those litres were included in the 7,300 litres that we used in our calculation of the cost per litre. Work in progress is not a serious problem, but some adjustment for opening and closing work in progress for a period needs to be made if reliable full cost information is to be obtained.

This approach to full costing, which can be taken with identical, or near identical units of output, is often referred to as process costing.

Deriving full costs in multi-product operations

Most businesses produce more than one type of product or service. In this situation, the units of output of the product, or service, will not be identical and so the approach that we used with litres of 'Orange Fizz' in Activity 8.1 cannot be used. Though it is reasonable to assign an identical cost to units of output that are identical, it is not reasonable to do this where the units of output are obviously different. It would not be reasonable, for example, to assign the same costs to each car repair carried out by a garage, irrespective of the complexity and size of the repair.

Direct and indirect costs

To provide full cost information, we need to have a systematic approach to accumulating costs and then assigning these costs to particular units of product or service on some reasonable basis. Where units of output are not identical, the starting point is to separate costs into two categories: direct costs and indirect costs.

- Direct costs. These are costs that can be identified with specific cost units. That is to say, the effect of the cost can be measured in respect of each particular unit of output. The main examples of these are direct materials and direct labour. Thus, in costing a motor car repair by a garage, both the cost of spare parts used in the repair and the cost of the mechanic's time would be direct costs. Collecting direct costs is a simple matter of having a cost-recording system that is capable of capturing the cost of direct materials used on each job and the cost, based on the hours worked and the rate of pay, of direct workers.

→ ■ Indirect costs (or overheads). These are all other costs, that is, those that cannot be directly measured in respect of each particular unit of output. Thus the rent of the garage premises would be an indirect cost of a motor car repair.

→ We shall use the terms 'indirect costs' and 'overheads' interchangeably for the remainder of this book. Overheads are also sometimes known as common costs because they are common to all outputs of the production unit (for example, factory or department) for the period.

Real World 8.1 provides some insight to the direct/indirect cost balance in practice.

Real World 8.1

Direct and indirect costs in practice

A survey of 176 fairly large UK businesses, conducted during 1999, revealed that, on average, total costs of businesses are in the following proportions:

Direct costs   70%
Indirect costs   30%

Perhaps surprisingly, these proportions did not vary greatly among manufacturers, retailers and service businesses. The only significant variation from the 70/30 proportions was with financial and commercial businesses, which had an average 52/48 split.

Source: Based on information taken from Drury and Tayles (see References section at the end of the chapter)

A more extensive (nearly 2,000 responses) and more recent (2003) survey of management accounting practice in the USA showed similar results. Like the 1999 UK survey, this tended to relate to larger businesses. About 40% were manufacturers and about 16% financial services; the remainder were from a range of other industries.

This survey revealed that, of total costs, indirect costs accounted for between:

34%   for retailers (lowest) and
42%   for manufacturers (highest),

with other industries' proportion of indirect costs falling within the 34% to 42% range. Financial and commercial businesses showed an indirect cost percentage of 38%.

Source: Ernst and Young (see References section at the end of the chapter)

The differences between the UK and the USA could be accounted for by a higher level of capital intensity in US industry, which would tend to increase indirect costs relative to direct ones. The fact that the US survey is more recent may have some influence on the results.

Job costing

→ The term job costing is used to describe the way in which we identify the full cost per unit of output (job) where the units of output differ. To cost (that is, deduce the full cost of) a particular unit of output (job), we first identify the direct costs of the job,

Figure 8.1 The relationship between direct costs and indirect costs

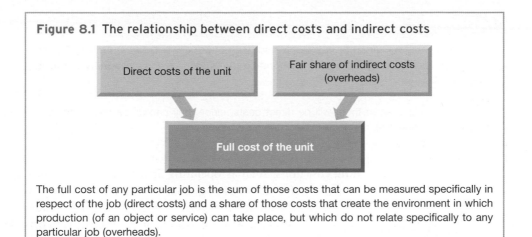

The full cost of any particular job is the sum of those costs that can be measured specifically in respect of the job (direct costs) and a share of those costs that create the environment in which production (of an object or service) can take place, but which do not relate specifically to any particular job (overheads).

which, by the definition of direct costs, is fairly straightforward. We then seek to 'charge' each unit of output with a fair share of indirect costs. This is shown graphically in Figure 8.1.

Activity 8.2

Sparky Ltd is a business that employs a number of electricians. The business undertakes a range of work for its customers, from replacing fuses to installing complete wiring systems in new houses.

In respect of a particular job done by Sparky Ltd, into which category (direct or indirect) would each of the following costs fall?

- The wages of the electrician who did the job.
- Depreciation of the tools used by the electrician.
- The salary of Sparky Ltd's accountant.
- The cost of cable and other materials used on the job.
- Rent of the premises where Sparky Ltd stores its inventories of cable and other materials.

Only the electrician's wages earned while working on the particular job and the cost of the materials used on the job are direct costs. This is because it is possible to measure how much time (and therefore the labour cost) was spent on the particular job and the amount of materials used in the job.

All of the other costs are general costs of running the business and, as such, must form part of the full cost of doing the job, but they cannot be directly measured in respect of the particular job.

It is important to note that whether a cost is direct or indirect depends on the item being costed – the cost objective. People tend to refer to overheads without stating what the cost objective is; this is incorrect.

Activity 8.3

Into which category, direct or indirect, would each of the costs listed in Activity 8.2 fall if we were seeking to find the cost of operating the entire business of Sparky Ltd for a month?

The answer is that all of them will be direct costs, since they can all be related to, and measured in respect of, running the business for a month.

Naturally, broader-reaching cost units, such as operating Sparky Ltd for a month, tend to include a higher proportion of direct costs than do more limited ones, such as a particular job done by Sparky Ltd. As we shall see shortly, this makes costing broader cost units rather more straightforward than costing narrower ones, since direct costs are easier to deal with than indirect ones.

Full costing and the behaviour of costs

We saw in Chapter 7 that the full cost of doing something (or total cost, as it is usually known in the context of marginal analysis) can be analysed between the fixed and the variable elements. This is illustrated in Figure 8.2.

The similarity of what is shown in Figure 8.2 to that depicted in Figure 8.1 seems to lead some people to believe, mistakenly, that variable costs and direct costs are the same and that fixed costs and overheads are the same. This is incorrect.

The notions of fixed and variable are concerned entirely with cost behaviour in the face of changes to the volume of activity. Directness of costs, on the other hand, is entirely concerned with collecting together the elements that make up full cost, that is, with the extent to which costs can be measured directly in respect of particular units of output or jobs. These are two entirely different concepts. Though it may be true that there is a tendency for fixed costs to be indirect costs (overheads) and for

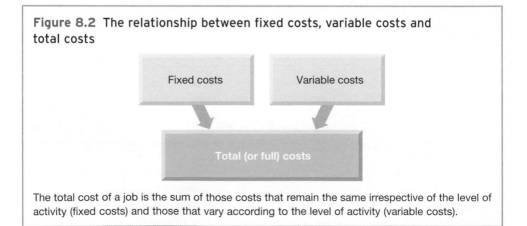

Figure 8.2 The relationship between fixed costs, variable costs and total costs

Fixed costs

Variable costs

Total (or full) costs

The total cost of a job is the sum of those costs that remain the same irrespective of the level of activity (fixed costs) and those that vary according to the level of activity (variable costs).

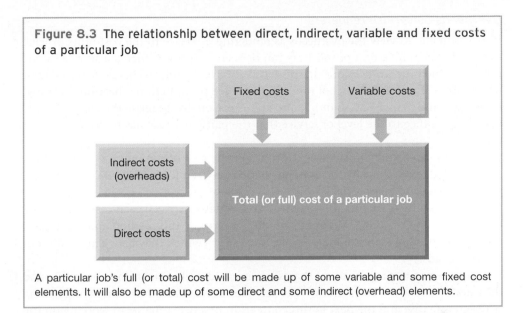

Figure 8.3 The relationship between direct, indirect, variable and fixed costs of a particular job

A particular job's full (or total) cost will be made up of some variable and some fixed cost elements. It will also be made up of some direct and some indirect (overhead) elements.

variable costs to be direct costs, there is no link, and there are many exceptions to this tendency. For example, most activities have variable overheads. Labour is a major element of direct cost in most types of business activity but is usually a fixed cost, at least over the short term.

The relationship between the reaction of costs to volume changes (cost behaviour), on the one hand, and how costs need to be gathered to deduce the full cost (cost collection), on the other, in respect of a particular job is shown in Figure 8.3.

Total cost is the sum of direct and indirect costs. It is also the sum of fixed and variable costs. These two facts are independent of one another. Thus a particular cost may, for example, be fixed relative to the level of output on the one hand, and be either direct or indirect on the other.

The problem of indirect costs

Distinguishing between direct and indirect costs is related only to deducing full cost in a job-costing environment, that is, where units of output differ. When we were considering costing a litre of 'Orange Fizz' drink in Activity 8.1, whether particular elements of cost were direct or indirect was of absolutely no consequence, because all costs were shared equally between the litres of 'Orange Fizz'. However, where we have units of output that are not identical, we have to look more closely at the make-up of the costs to achieve a fair measure of the full cost of a particular job.

Indirect costs of any activity must form part of the cost of each unit of output. By definition, however, they cannot be directly related to individual cost units. This raises a major practical issue: how are indirect costs to be apportioned to individual cost units?

Overheads as service renderers

It is reasonable to view the overheads as rendering a service to the cost units. A legal case undertaken by a firm of solicitors can be seen as being rendered a service by the office in which the work is done. In this sense, it is reasonable to charge each case (cost unit) with a share of the costs of running the office (rent, lighting, heating, cleaning, building maintenance and so on). It also seems reasonable to relate the charge for the 'use' of the office to the level of service that the particular case has received from the office.

The next step is the difficult one. How might the cost of running the office, which is a cost of all work done by the firm, be divided between individual cases that are not similar in size and complexity?

One possibility is sharing this overhead cost equally between each case handled by the firm within the period. Most of us would not propose this method unless the cases were close to being identical in terms of the extent to which they had 'benefited' from the overheads.

If we are not to propose equal shares, we must identify something observable and measurable about the cases that we feel provides a reasonable basis for distinguishing between one case and the next in this context. In practice, time spent working on the cost unit by direct labour is the basis that is most popular. It must be stressed that this is not the 'correct' way, and it certainly is not the only way.

Job costing: a worked example

To see how job costing (as it is usually called) works, let us consider Example 8.1.

Example 8.1

Johnson Ltd, a business that provides a television repair service to its customers, has overheads of £10,000 each month. Each month 1,000 direct labour hours are worked and charged to units of output (repairs carried out by the business). A particular repair undertaken by the business used direct materials costing £15. Direct labour worked on the repair was 3 hours and the wage rate is £8 an hour. Overheads are charged to jobs on a direct labour hour basis. What is the full cost of the repair?

First, let us establish the overhead absorption (recovery) rate, that is, the rate at which individual repairs will be charged with overheads. This is £10 (that is, £10,000/1,000) per direct labour hour.

Thus, the full cost of the repair is:

	£
Direct materials	15
Direct labour (3 × £8)	24
	39
Overheads (3 × £10)	30
Full cost of the job	69

Note, in Example 8.1, that the number of labour hours (3 hours) appears twice in deducing the full cost: once to deduce the direct labour cost and a second time to deduce the overheads to be charged to the repair. These are really two separate issues, though they are both based on the same number of labour hours.

Note also that if all of the repair jobs that are undertaken during the month are assigned overheads in a similar manner, all £10,000 of overheads will be charged to the jobs between them. Jobs that involve a lot of direct labour will be assigned a large share of overheads, and those that involve little direct labour will be assigned a small share of overheads.

Activity 8.4

Can you think of reasons why direct labour hours is regarded as the most logical basis for sharing overheads between cost units?

The reasons that occurred to us are as follows:

- Large jobs should logically attract large amounts of overheads because they are likely to have been rendered more 'service' by the overheads than small ones. The length of time that they are worked on by direct labour may be seen as a rough and ready way of measuring relative size, though other means of doing this may be found – for example, relative physical size, where the cost unit is a physical object, like a manufactured product.
- Most overheads are related to time. Rent, heating, lighting, non-current (fixed) asset depreciation, supervisors' and managers' salaries and loan interest, which are all typical overheads, are all more or less time based. That is to say that the overhead cost for one week tends to be about half of that for a similar two-week period. Thus, a basis of assigning overheads to jobs that takes account of the length of time that the units of output benefited from the 'service' rendered by the overheads seems logical.
- Direct labour hours are capable of being measured for each job. They will normally be measured to deduce the direct labour element of cost in any case. Thus, a direct labour hour basis of dealing with overheads is practical to apply in the real world.

It cannot be emphasised enough that there is no 'correct' way to assign overheads to jobs. Overheads (indirect costs), by definition, do not naturally relate to individual jobs. If, nevertheless, we wish to take account of the fact that overheads are part of the cost of all jobs, we must find some acceptable way of including a share of the total overheads in each job. If a particular means of doing this is accepted by those who use the full cost deduced, then the method is as good as any other method. Accounting is concerned only with providing useful information to decision makers. In practice, the method that seems to be regarded as being the most useful is the direct labour hour method. Real World 8.2, which we shall consider later in the chapter, provides some evidence of this.

Activity 8.5

Marine Suppliers Ltd undertakes a range of work, including making sails for small sailing boats on a made-to-measure basis.

The business expects to incur the following costs during the next month:

Direct labour costs	£60,000
Direct labour time	6,000 hours
Indirect labour cost	£9,000
Depreciation of machinery	£3,000
Rent and rates	£5,000
Heating, lighting and power	£2,000
Machine time	2,000 hours
Indirect materials	£500
Other miscellaneous indirect costs	£200
Direct materials cost	£3,000

The business has received an enquiry about a sail, and it is estimated that the sail will take 12 direct labour hours to make and will require 20 square metres of sailcloth, which costs £2 per square metre.

The business normally uses a direct labour hour basis of charging overheads to individual jobs.

What is the full cost of making the sail?

The direct costs of making the sail can be identified as follows:

	£
Direct materials (20 × £2)	40.00
Direct labour (12 × (£60,000/6,000))	120.00
	160.00

To deduce the indirect cost element that must be added to derive the full cost of the sail, we first need to total these costs as follows:

	£
Indirect labour	9,000
Depreciation	3,000
Rent and rates	5,000
Heating, lighting and power	2,000
Indirect materials	500
Other miscellaneous indirect costs	200
Total indirect costs	19,700

Since the business uses a direct labour hour basis of charging overheads to jobs, we need to deduce the indirect cost (or overhead) recovery rate per direct labour hour. This is simply:

£19,700/6,000 = £3.28 per direct labour hour

Thus, the full cost of the sail would be expected to be:

	£
Direct materials (20 × £2)	40.00
Direct labour (12 × (£60,000/6,000))	120.00
Indirect costs (12 × £3.28)	39.36
Full cost	199.36

Activity 8.6

Suppose that Marine Suppliers Ltd (see Activity 8.5) used a machine hour basis of charging overheads to jobs. What would be the cost of the job detailed if it was expected to take 5 machine hours (as well as 12 direct labour hours)?

The total overheads of the business will of course be the same irrespective of the method of charging them to jobs. Thus, the overhead recovery rate, on a machine hour basis, will be:

£19,700/2,000 = £9.85 per machine hour

Thus, the full cost of the sail would be expected to be:

	£
Direct materials (20 × £2)	40.00
Direct labour (12 × (£60,000/6,000))	120.00
Indirect costs (5 × £9.85)	49.25
Full cost	209.25

Selecting a basis for charging overheads

A question now presents itself as to which of the two costs for this sail is the correct one, or simply the better one. The answer is that neither is correct, as was pointed out earlier. Which is the better one is a matter of judgement. This judgement is concerned entirely with usefulness of information. Usefulness, however, is a concept that is difficult to assess.

Most people would probably feel that the nature of the overheads should influence the choice of the basis of charging the overheads to jobs. Where the operation is capital-intensive and overheads are primarily machine-based (such as depreciation, machine maintenance, power and so on), machine hours might be favoured. Otherwise direct labour hours might be preferred.

It could appear that one of these bases might be preferred to the other one simply because it apportions either a higher or a lower amount of overheads to a particular job. This would probably be irrational, however. Since the total overheads are the same irrespective of the method of dividing that total between individual jobs, a method that gives a higher share of overheads to one particular job must give a lower share to the remaining jobs. There is one cake of fixed size. If one person is to be given a relatively large slice, the other people, between them, must receive relatively small slices. To illustrate further this issue of apportioning overheads, consider Example 8.2.

Example 8.2

A business that provides a service expects to incur overheads totalling £20,000 next month. The total direct labour time worked is expected to be 1,600 hours and machines are expected to operate for a total of 1,000 hours.

During the next month, the business expects to do just two large jobs. Information concerning each job is as follows:

	Job 1	Job 2
Direct labour hours	800	800
Machine hours	700	300

How much of the total overheads will be charged to each job if overheads are to be charged on:

(a) a direct labour hour basis; and
(b) a machine hour basis?

What do you notice about the two sets of figures that you calculate?

(a) Direct labour hour basis

Overhead recovery rate = £20,000/1,600 = £12.50 per direct labour hour.

Job 1	£12.50 × 800 = £10,000
Job 2	£12.50 × 800 = £10,000

(b) Machine hour basis

Overhead recovery rate = £20,000/1,000 = £20.00 per machine hour.

Job 1	£20.00 × 700 = £14,000
Job 2	£20.00 × 300 = £6,000

It is clear from these calculations that the total of the overheads charged to jobs is the same (that is, £20,000) whichever method is used. So, whereas the machine hour basis gives Job 1 a higher share than does the direct labour hour method, the opposite is true for Job 2.

It is not practical to charge overheads on one basis to one job and on the other basis to the other job. This is because either total overheads will not be fully charged to the jobs, or the jobs will be overcharged with overheads. For example, using the direct labour hour method for Job 1 (£10,000) and the machine hour basis for Job 2 (£6,000) will mean that only £16,000 of a total £20,000 of overheads will be charged to jobs. As a result, the objective of full costing, which is to charge all overheads to jobs done, will not be achieved. In this particular case, if selling prices are based on full costs, the business may not charge high enough prices to cover all of its costs.

Activity 8.7

The point was made above that it would normally be irrational to prefer one basis of charging overheads to jobs simply because it apportions either a higher or a lower amount of overheads to a particular job. This is because the total overheads are the same irrespective of the method of charging the total to individual jobs. Can you think of any circumstances where it would not necessarily be so irrational?

This might apply where, for a particular job, a customer has agreed to pay a price based on full cost plus an agreed fixed percentage for profit. Here it would be beneficial to the producer for the total cost of the job to be as high as possible. This would be relatively unusual, but sometimes public sector organisations, particularly central and local government departments, have entered into contracts to have work done, with the price to be deduced, after the work has been completed, on a cost-plus basis. Such contracts are pretty rare these days, probably because they are open to abuse in the way described. Usually, contract prices are agreed in advance, typically in conjunction with competitive tendering.

Real World 8.2 provides some insight to the basis of overhead recovery in practice.

Real World 8.2

Overhead recovery rates in practice

A survey of 303 UK manufacturing businesses, published in 1993, showed that the direct labour hour basis of charging overheads to cost units was overwhelmingly the most popular, used by 73 per cent of the respondents to the survey. Where the work has a strong labour element this seems reasonable, but the survey also showed that 68 per cent of businesses used this basis for automated activities. It is surprising that direct labour hours should have been used as the basis of charging overheads in an environment dominated by machines and machine-related costs.

Though this survey is not very recent and applied only to manufacturing businesses, in the absence of other information it provides some impression of what happens in practice. There is no reason to believe that current practice is very different from that which applied at the beginning of the 1990s.

Source: Based on information taken from Drury, Braund, Osborne and Tayles (see References section at the end of the chapter)

Segmenting the overheads

As we have just seen, charging the same overheads to different jobs on different bases is not possible. It is possible, however, to charge one segment of the total overheads on one basis and another segment, or other segments, on another basis.

Activity 8.8

Taking the same business as in Example 8.2, on closer analysis we find that of the overheads totalling £20,000 next month, £8,000 relate to machines (depreciation, maintenance, rent of the space occupied by the machines and so on) and the remaining £12,000 to more general overheads. The other information about the business is exactly as it was before.

How much of the total overheads will be charged to each job if the machine-related overheads are to be charged on a machine hour basis and the remaining overheads are charged on a direct labour hour basis?

→

Direct labour hour basis

    Overhead recovery rate = £12,000/1,600 = £7.50 per direct labour hour

Machine hour basis

    Overhead recovery rate = £8,000/1,000 = £8.00 per machine hour

Overheads charged to jobs

	Job 1 £	Job 2 £
Direct labour hour basis		
£7.50 × 800	6,000	
£7.50 × 800		6,000
Machine hour basis		
£8.00 × 700	5,600	
£8.00 × 300		2,400
Total	11,600	8,400

We can see from this that the expected overheads of £20,000 are charged in total (that is, 11,600 + 8,400).

Segmenting the overheads in this way may well be seen as providing a better basis of charging overheads to jobs. This is quite often found in practice, usually by dividing a business into separate 'areas' for costing purposes, charging overheads differently from one area to the next.

Remember that there is no correct basis of charging overheads to jobs, so our frequent reference to the direct labour and machine hour bases should not be taken to imply that these are the correct methods. However, it should be said that these two methods do have something to commend them and are popular in practice. As we have already discussed, a sensible method does need to identify something about each job that can be measured and which distinguishes it from other jobs. There is also a lot to be said for methods that are concerned with time, because most overheads are time related.

Dealing with overheads on a departmental basis

In general, all but the smallest businesses are divided into departments. Normally, each department deals with a separate activity. The reasons for dividing a business into departments include the following:

- Many businesses are too large and complex to be managed as a single unit. It is usually more practical to operate each business as a series of relatively independent units (departments) with each one having its own manager.
- Each department normally has its own area of specialism and is managed by a specialist.

■ Each department can have its own accounting records that enable its performance to be assessed. This can lead to greater management control and motivation among the staff.

Very many businesses deal with charging overheads to cost units on a department-by-department basis. They do this in the expectation that it will give rise to a more useful way of charging overheads. It is probably often the case that it does not lead to any great improvement in the usefulness of the resulting full costs. Though it may not be of enormous benefit in many cases, it is probably not an expensive exercise to apply overheads on a departmental basis. Since costs are collected department by department for other purposes (particularly control), to apply overheads on a department-by-department basis is a relatively simple matter.

We shall now take a look at how the departmental approach to deriving full costs works, in a service-industry context, through Example 8.3.

Example 8.3

Autosparkle Ltd offers a motor vehicle paint-respray service. The jobs that it undertakes range from painting a small part of a saloon car, usually following a minor accident, to a complete respray of a double-decker bus.

Each job starts life in the Preparation Department, where it is prepared for the Paintshop. In the Preparation Department the job is worked on by direct workers, in most cases taking some direct materials from the stores with which to treat the old paintwork to render the vehicle ready for respraying. Thus the job will be charged with direct materials, direct labour and with a share of the Preparation Department's overheads. The job then passes into the Paintshop Department, already valued at the costs that it picked up in the Preparation Department.

In the Paintshop, the staff draw direct materials from the stores and direct workers spend time respraying the job, using sophisticated spraying apparatus as well as working by hand. So, in the Paintshop, the job is charged with direct materials, direct labour plus a share of that department's overheads. The job now passes into the Finishing Department, valued at the cost of the materials, labour and overheads that it accumulated in the first two departments.

In the Finishing Department, jobs are cleaned and polished ready to go back to the customers. Further direct labour and, in some cases, materials are added. All jobs also pick up a share of that department's overheads. The job, now complete, passes back to the customer.

Figure 8.4 shows how this works for a particular job.

The basis of charging overheads to jobs (for example, direct labour hours) might be the same for all three departments, or it might be different from one department to another. It is possible that spraying apparatus costs dominate the Paintshop costs, so overheads might well be charged to jobs on a machine hour basis. The other two departments are probably labour intensive, so that direct labour hours may be seen as being appropriate there.

→

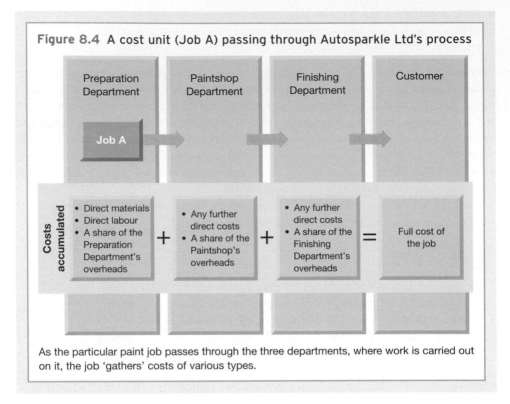

Figure 8.4 A cost unit (Job A) passing through Autosparkle Ltd's process

As the particular paint job passes through the three departments, where work is carried out on it, the job 'gathers' costs of various types.

The passage of the job through the departments can be compared to a snowball being rolled across snow: as it rolls, it picks up more and more snow.

Where costs are dealt with departmentally, each department is known as a cost centre. This can be defined as some physical area or some activity or function for which costs are separately identified. Charging direct costs to jobs, in a departmental system, is exactly the same as where the whole business is one single cost centre. It is simply a matter of keeping a record of:

- the number of hours of direct labour worked on the particular job and the grade of labour, assuming that there are different grades with different rates of pay;
- the cost of the direct materials taken from stores and applied to the job;
- any other direct costs, for example some subcontracted work, associated with the job.

This record keeping will normally be done departmentally in a departmental system.

It is obviously necessary to break down the production overheads of the entire business on a departmental basis. This means that the total overheads of the business must be divided between the departments, such that the sum of the departmental overheads equals the overheads for the entire business. By charging all of their overheads to jobs, the departments will, between them, charge all of the overheads of the business to jobs. Real World 8.3 provides an indication of the number of different cost centres that businesses tend to use in practice.

Cost centres in practice

It is not unusual for a large business to have several cost centres. The survey of large UK businesses by Drury and Tayles referred to earlier (see Real World 8.2), revealed the following:

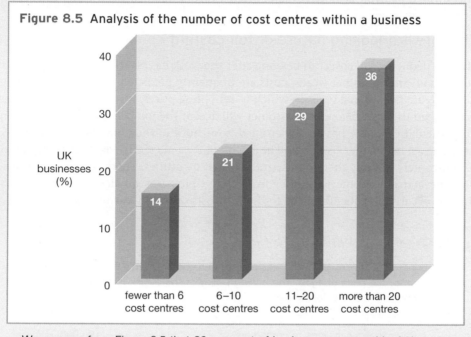

Figure 8.5 Analysis of the number of cost centres within a business

We can see from Figure 8.5 that 86 per cent of businesses surveyed had six or more cost centres and that 36 per cent of businesses had more than 20 cost centres. Though not shown on the diagram, 3 per cent of businesses surveyed had a single cost centre (that is, there was a single, business-wide (or overall) overhead rate).

Source: Based on information taken from Drury and Tayles (see References section at the end of the chapter)

Batch costing

The production of many types of goods and services (particularly goods) involves producing in a batch of identical, or nearly identical, units of output, but where each batch is distinctly different from other batches. For example, a theatre may put on a production whose nature (and therefore costs) is very different from that of other productions. On the other hand, ignoring differences in the desirability of the various types of seating, all of the individual units of output (tickets to see the production) are identical.

In these circumstances, we should normally deduce the cost per ticket by using a job costing approach (taking account of direct and indirect costs and so on) to find the cost of mounting the production and then we should simply divide this by the expected number of tickets to be sold to find the cost per ticket. This is known as batch costing.

Full cost as the break-even price

We should recognise that if all goes according to plan (so that direct costs, overheads and the basis of charging overheads, for example direct labour hours, prove to be as expected), then selling the output for its full cost should cause the business to break even exactly. Therefore, whatever profit (in total) is loaded onto full cost to set actual selling prices will, if plans are achieved, result in that level of profit being earned for the period.

The forward-looking nature of full costing

Though deducing full costs can be done after the work has been completed, it is often done in advance. In other words, costs are frequently predicted. Where, for example, full costs are needed as a basis on which to set selling prices, it is usually the case that prices need to be set before the customer will accept the job being done. Even where no particular customer has been identified, some idea of the ultimate price will need to be known before the business will be able to make a judgement as to whether potential customers will buy the product, and in what quantities. There is a risk, of course, that the actual outcome will differ from that which was predicted. If this occurs, corrections are subsequently made to the full costs originally calculated.

? Self-assessment question 8.1

Promptprint Ltd, a printing business, has received an enquiry from a potential customer for a quotation for the price of a job. The pricing policy of the business will be based on the plans for the next financial year shown below:

	£
Sales revenue (billings to customers)	196,000
Materials (direct)	(38,000)
Labour (direct)	(32,000)
Variable overheads	(2,400)
Advertising (for business)	(3,000)
Depreciation	(27,600)
Administration	(36,000)
Interest	(8,000)
Profit (before tax)	49,000

An estimate of the direct costs for the particular job is:

	£
Direct materials	4,000
Direct labour	3,600

Required:
(a) Prepare a recommended price for the job based on the plans, commenting on your method.
(b) Comment on the validity of using financial plans in pricing and recommend any improvements you would consider desirable for the business's pricing policy used in (a).

Activity-based costing (ABC)

What we have considered so far in this chapter is the traditional, and still very widely used, approach to job costing (deriving the full cost of output where one unit of output differs from another). This approach is to collect for each job those costs that can be unequivocally linked to, and measured in respect of, the particular job (direct costs). All other costs (overheads) are thrown into a pool of costs and charged to individual jobs according to some formula. Traditionally, this formula has been on the basis of the number of direct labour hours worked on each individual job.

The background to traditional full costing

The traditional approach to job costing developed when the notion of trying to cost industrial production first emerged, probably around the time of the Industrial Revolution. At that time, manufacturing industry was characterised by the following features:

■ *Direct labour-intensive and direct labour-paced production.* Labour was at the heart of production. To the extent that machinery was used, it was to support the efforts of direct labour, and the speed of production was dictated by direct labour.
■ *A low level of overheads relative to direct costs.* Little was spent on power, personnel services, machinery (therefore, low depreciation charges) and other areas typical of the overheads of modern businesses.
■ *A relatively uncompetitive market.* Transport difficulties, limited industrial production worldwide and lack of knowledge among customers of competitors' prices meant that businesses could prosper without being too scientific in costing and pricing their output.

Since overheads at that time represented a pretty small element of total costs, it was acceptable and practical to deal with overheads in a fairly arbitrary manner. Not too much effort was devoted to trying to control the cost of overheads because the rewards of better control were relatively small, certainly when compared with the potential rewards from firmer control of direct labour and material costs. It was also reasonable to charge overheads to individual jobs on a direct labour hour basis. Most of the overheads were incurred directly in support of direct labour: providing direct workers with a place to work, heating and lighting that workplace, employing people to supervise the direct workers and so on. Direct workers, perhaps aided by machinery, carried out all production.

At that time, service industries were a relatively unimportant part of the economy and would have largely consisted of self-employed individuals. These individuals would probably have been uninterested in trying to do more than work out a rough hourly/daily rate for their time and to try to base prices on this.

The current full costing environment

In more recent years, the world of industrial production has fundamentally altered. Most of it is now characterised by:

- *Capital-intensive and machine-paced production.* Machines are now at the heart of production, including service provision. Most labour supports the efforts of machines, for example technically maintaining them, and machines dictate the pace of production.
- *A high level of overheads relative to direct costs.* Modern businesses tend to have very high depreciation, servicing and power costs. There are also high costs of a nature scarcely envisaged in the early days of industrial production, such as personnel and staff welfare costs. At the same time, there are very low (sometimes no) direct labour costs. Though direct material cost often remains an important element of total cost, more efficient production methods lead to less waste and, therefore, less total material cost, again tending to make overheads more dominant.
- *A highly competitive international market.* Production, much of it highly sophisticated, is carried out worldwide. Transport, including fast airfreight, is relatively cheap. Fax, telephone and the Internet ensure that potential customers can quickly and cheaply find the prices of a range of suppliers. So the market is likely to be highly competitive. This means that businesses need to know their costs with a greater degree of accuracy than historically has been the case. Businesses also need to take a considered and informed approach to pricing their output.

In the UK, as in many developed countries, service industries now dominate the economy, employing the great majority of the workforce and producing most of the value of productive output. Though there are many self-employed individuals supplying services, many service providers are vast businesses such as banks, insurance companies and cinema operators. For most of these larger service providers, the activities very closely resemble modern manufacturing activity. They too are characterised by high capital intensity, overheads dominating direct costs and a competitive international market.

In the past, overhead recovery rates (that is, the rate at which overheads are absorbed by jobs) were typically much less per direct labour hour than the actual rate paid to direct workers. It is now, however, becoming increasingly common for overhead recovery rates to be between five and ten times the hourly rate of pay, because overheads are much more significant. When production is dominated by direct labour paid, say, £8 an hour, it might be reasonable to have a recovery rate of, say, £1 an hour. When, however, direct labour plays a relatively small part in production, to have overhead recovery rates of, say, £50 per direct labour hour is likely to lead to very arbitrary costing. Even a small change in the amount of direct labour worked on a job could massively affect the cost deduced. This is not because the direct worker is very highly paid, but because of the effect of the direct labour change on the overhead loading. Overheads are often charged on a direct labour hour basis, even though those overheads may not be particularly related to direct labour.

An alternative approach to full costing

As a result of changes in the business environment, the whole question of overheads, what causes them and how they are charged to jobs, has recently been receiving closer attention. Historically, businesses have been content to accept that overheads exist and, therefore, for costing purposes they must be dealt with, in as practical a way as possible. In recent years, however, there has been a growing realisation that overheads do not just happen; they must be caused by something. To illustrate this point, consider Example 8.4.

Example 8.4

Modern Producers Ltd has, like virtually all manufacturers, a storage area that is set aside for finished goods. The costs of running the stores include a share of the factory rent and other establishment costs, such as heating and lighting. These costs also include the salaries of staff employed to look after the inventories, and the cost of financing the inventories held in the stores.

The business has two product lines, Product A and Product B. Product A tends to be made in small batches and so low levels of finished goods inventories are held. The business prides itself on its ability to supply Product B in relatively large quantities instantly. As a consequence, much of the finished goods stores is filled with finished inventories of Product B ready to be dispatched as an order is received.

Traditionally, the whole cost of operating the stores would have been treated as a general overhead and included in the total of overheads charged to jobs, on a direct labour hour basis. This means that, when assessing the cost of Products A and B, the cost of operating the stores has fallen on them according to the number of direct labour hours worked on each one. In fact, most of the stores cost should be charged to Product B, since this product causes (and benefits from) the stores cost much more than is true of Product A. Failure to account more precisely for the costs of running the stores is masking the fact that Product B is not as profitable as it seems to be. It may even be leading to losses as a result of the relatively high stores operating cost that it causes. So far, much of this cost has been charged to Product A, without regard to the fact that Product A causes little of the it. The products absorb the stores cost (in their production cost) in proportion to the direct labour hour content; a factor that has nothing to do with storage.

Cost drivers

Realisation that overheads do not just occur, but that they are caused by activities, such as holding products in stores, that 'drive' the costs, is at the heart of activity-based costing (ABC). The traditional approach is that direct labour hours are a cost driver, which probably used to be true. It is now recognised to be no longer the case.

There is a basic philosophical difference between the traditional and ABC approaches. Traditionally, we tend to think of overheads as rendering a service to cost units, the cost of which must be charged to those units. ABC sees overheads as being *caused* by cost units, and those cost units must be charged with the costs that they cause.

Example 8.5

The accountant at Modern Producers Ltd (see Example 8.4) has estimated that the costs of running the finished goods stores for next year will be £90,000. (In the jargon of ABC, this £90,000 is known as the finished goods stores cost pool, that is the total of all of the costs relating to running that stores.) It is also estimated that each unit of Product A will spend an average of one week in the stores before being sold. With Product B, the equivalent period is four weeks. Both products are of roughly similar size and have very similar storage needs. It is felt, therefore, that the quantity of each product and the period spent in the stores are the cost drivers.

It is estimated that next year 50,000 units of Product A and 25,000 units of Product B will pass through the stores. The total number of 'product weeks' in the stores will therefore be:

$$
\begin{array}{lll}
\text{Product A} & 50{,}000 \times 1 \text{ week} = & 50{,}000 \\
\text{Product B} & 25{,}000 \times 4 \text{ weeks} = & \underline{100{,}000} \\
& & \underline{150{,}000}
\end{array}
$$

The stores cost per 'product week' is given by

$$\pounds 90{,}000/150{,}000 = \pounds 0.60$$

Therefore each unit of Product A will be charged with £0.60 for finished stores costs and each unit of Product B with £2.40 (that is, £0.60 × 4).

Activity 8.9

Can you think of any other purpose that identification of the cost drivers serves, apart from deriving more accurate costs?

Identification of the activities that cause costs puts management in a position where it may well be able to control them more effectively.

The opaque nature of overheads has traditionally rendered them difficult to control, relative to the much more obvious direct labour and material costs. If, however, analysis of overheads can identify the cost drivers, questions can be asked about whether the activity that is driving certain costs is necessary at all, and whether the cost justifies the benefit. In Examples 8.4 and 8.5, it may be a good marketing strategy that Product B can be supplied immediately from inventories, but there is an associated cost, and that cost should be recognised and assessed against the benefit.

Advocates of activity-based costing argue that most overheads can be analysed and cost drivers identified. If this is true, it means that it is possible to gain much clearer insights into the costs that are caused activity by activity. As a result, fairer and more accurate product costs can be identified, and costs can be controlled more effectively.

ABC and service industries

Much of the discussion of ABC so far in this chapter has concentrated on manufacturing industry, perhaps because early users of ABC were manufacturing businesses. In fact, ABC is possibly even more relevant to service industries because, in the absence of a direct materials element, its total costs are likely to be particularly heavily affected by overheads. There is certainly evidence that ABC has been adopted by many businesses that sell services rather than goods (see Real World 8.4 below).

Activity 8.10

What is the difference in the way in which direct costs are accounted for when using ABC, relative to their treatment taking a traditional approach to full costing?

The answer is no difference at all. ABC is concerned only with the way in which overheads are charged to jobs to derive the full cost.

Criticisms of ABC

Critics of ABC argue that analysis of overheads in order to identify cost drivers is very time consuming and costly, and that the benefit of doing so, in terms of more accurate costing and the potential for cost control, does not justify the cost of carrying out the analysis.

ABC is also criticised for the same reason that full costing generally is criticised. This is that it does not provide very relevant information for decision making. This point will be addressed shortly.

Despite the criticisms of ABC it has gained some popularity in practice, though it has not made the progress in popularity that its advocates might have expected. This is shown in Real World 8.4.

Real World 8.4

ABC in practice

A survey of large UK businesses in 1999 revealed that, on average, 15 per cent of businesses fully use an ABC approach to dealing with full costing. A further 8 per cent use it partially. The remaining 77 per cent do not use ABC at all. Even so, there was a surprising range in the level of usage of ABC from industry to industry (see Figure 8.6). It is particularly surprising that so few manufacturing businesses use ABC. The survey showed that it tends to be larger businesses that adopt ABC.

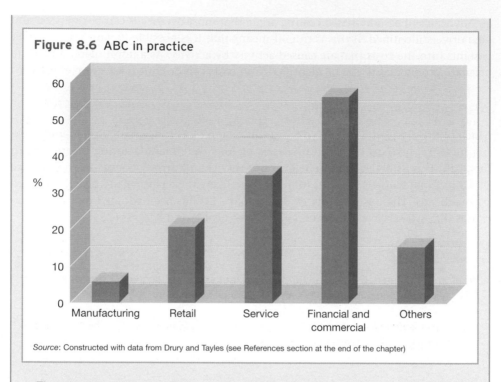

Figure 8.6 ABC in practice

Source: Constructed with data from Drury and Tayles (see References section at the end of the chapter)

There is some evidence of a decrease in the use of ABC over recent years. A different survey of large UK businesses (conducted by Innes, Mitchell and Sinclair) in 1999, replicated a 1994 survey conducted by the same researchers. They found the following:

	1994 %	1999 %
Currently using ABC	21.0	17.5
Currently considering using ABC	29.6	20.3
Rejected using ABC after assessing it	13.3	15.3

Thus, it seems that with regard to both current and potential usage of ABC, it was less popular in 1999 than it had been five years previously.

Source: Innes, Mitchell and Sinclair (see References section at the end of the chapter)

Uses of full-cost information

Why do we need to deduce full-cost information? There are probably two main reasons:

- *For pricing purposes*. In some industries and circumstances, full costs are used as the basis of pricing. Here, the full cost is deduced and a percentage is added for profit. This is known as cost-plus pricing. Garages, carrying out vehicle repairs, typically operate in this way. Solicitors and accountants doing work for clients often use this approach as well.

In many circumstances, suppliers are not in a position to deduce prices on a cost-plus basis, however. Where there is a competitive market, a supplier will usually have to accept the price that the market offers: that is, most suppliers are *price takers* not *price makers*.

■ *For income measurement purposes*. As we saw in Chapter 3, to provide a valid means of measuring a business's income it is necessary to match expenses with the revenues realised in the same accounting period. Where a service is partially rendered in one accounting period but the revenue is realised in the next, or where manufactured inventories are made or partially made in one period but sold in the next, the full cost (including an appropriate share of overheads) must be carried from the first accounting period to the second one. Unless we are able to identify the full cost of work done in one period that is the subject of a sale in the next, the profit figures of the periods concerned will become meaningless. This will mean that users of accounting information will not have a reliable means of assessing the effectiveness of the business as a whole, or the effectiveness of individual parts of it. This second reason for needing full cost information can be illustrated by Example 8.6.

Example 8.6

During the accounting year that ended on 31 December last year, Engineers Ltd made a special machine for a customer. At the beginning of this year, after having a series of tests successfully completed by a subcontractor, the machine was delivered to the customer. The business's normal practice (typical of most businesses and following the realisation convention) is to take account of sales when the product passes to the customer. The sale price of the machine was £25,000.

During last year, materials costing £3,500 were used on making the machine and 1,200 hours of direct labour, costing £9,300, were worked on the machine. The business uses a direct labour hour basis of charging overheads to jobs, which is believed to be fair because most of its work is labour intensive. The total manufacturing overheads for the business for last year were £77,000, and the total direct labour hours worked were 22,000. Testing the machine cost £1,000.

How much profit or loss did the business make on the machine during last year? How much profit or loss did the business make on the machine during this year? At what value should the business have included the machine on its balance sheet at the end of last year so that the correct profit will be recorded for each of the two years?

No profit or loss was made during last year, following the business's (and the generally accepted) approach to recognising revenues (sales). If the sale were not to be recognised until this year it would be illogical (and in contravention of the matching convention) to treat the costs of making the machine as expenses until that time.

During this year, the sale would be recognised and all of the costs, including a reasonable share of overheads, would be set against it in this year's income statement as follows:

→

	£	£
Sales price		25,000
Costs:		
Direct labour	(9,300)	
Direct materials	(3,500)	
Overheads (1,200 × (£77,000/22,000))	(4,200)	
Total incurred last year	(17,000)	
Testing cost	(1,000)	
Total cost		(18,000)
This year's profit from the machine		7,000

The machine needs to be shown as an asset of the business (valued at £17,000) in the balance sheet as at 31 December last year.

Unless all production costs are charged in the same accounting period as that in which the sale is recognised in the income statement (profit and loss account), distortions will occur that will render the income statement much less useful. Thus it is necessary to deduce the full cost of any production undertaken completely or partially in one accounting period, but sold in a subsequent one.

Criticisms of full costing

Full costing has been criticised because, in practice, it tends to use past costs and to restrict its consideration of future costs to outlay costs. It can be argued that past costs are irrelevant, irrespective of the purpose for which the information is to be used. This is basically because it is not possible to make decisions about the past, only about the future. Advocates of full costing would argue that it provides an informative long-run average cost.

Despite the criticisms that are made of full costing, it is, according to research evidence, very widely practised.

Summary

The main points in this chapter may be summarised as follows:

Full cost = the total amount of resources sacrificed to achieve a particular objective.

Single-product operations:

■ Where all the units of output are identical, the full cost can be calculated as follows:

$$\text{Cost per unit} = \frac{\text{Total cost of output}}{\text{Number of units produced}}$$

Multi-product operations – job costing:

■ Where units of output are not identical, it is necessary to divide the costs into two categories: direct costs and indirect costs.

■ Direct costs = costs that can be identified with specific cost units (for example, labour of a garage mechanic in relation to a particular car repair).

■ Indirect costs (overheads) = costs that cannot be directly measured in respect of a particular job (for cxample, the rent of a garage).

■ Full cost = direct cost + indirect cost.

■ Direct/indirect is not linked to variable/fixed.

■ Indirect costs are difficult to relate to individual cost units – arbitrary bases are used and there is no single correct method.

■ Traditionally, indirect costs are seen as the costs of providing a 'service' to cost units.

■ Direct labour hour basis of applying indirect costs to cost units is the most popular in practice.

Dealing with overheads on a departmental basis:

■ Indirect costs can be segmented – usually on a departmental basis – each department has its own overhead recovery rate.

■ Each department is a separate cost centre – that is an area, activity or function for which costs are separately collected.

Batch costing:

■ A variation of job costing where each job consists of a number of identical (or near identical) cost units:

$$\text{Cost per unit} = \frac{\text{Cost of the batch (direct + indirect)}}{\text{Number of units in the batch}}$$

If the full cost is charged as the sales price and things go according to plan, the business will break even.

Activity-based costing is an approach to dealing with overheads (in full costing) that treats all costs as being caused or 'driven' by activities. Advocates argue that it is more relevant to the modern commercial environment than is the traditional approach.

■ Identification of the cost drivers can lead to more relevant indirect cost treatment in full costing.

■ Identification of the cost drivers can lead to better control of overheads.

■ Critics argue that ABC is time-consuming and expensive to apply – not justified by the possible improvement in the quality of information.

→

Uses of full cost information:

■ Pricing (full cost) on a cost-plus basis.

■ Income measurement.

Full cost information is seen by some as not very useful because it can be backward looking: it includes information irrelevant to decision making, but excludes some relevant information.

→ **Key terms**

full costing p. 250
full cost p. 250
process costing p. 251
direct costs p. 251
indirect costs p. 252
overheads p. 252
common costs p. 252
job costing p. 252
cost behaviour p. 254
total cost p. 255

cost unit p. 255
overhead absorption (recovery) rate p. 256
cost centre p. 264
batch costing p. 265
activity-based costing (ABC) p. 269
cost driver p. 269
cost pool p. 270
cost-plus pricing p. 272

Further reading

If you would like to explore the topics covered in this chapter in more depth, we recommend the following books:

Atkinson, R., Kaplan, R. and Young, S.M. *Management Accounting*, 4th edn, Prentice Hall, 2004, Chapters 3 and 4.

Drury, C. *Management and Cost Accounting*, 6th edn, Thomson Learning, 2004, Chapter 8.

Horngren, C., Datar, S. and Foster, G. *Cost Accounting: A Managerial Emphasis*, 12th edn, Prentice Hall International, 2005, Chapters 3 and 10.

Upchurch, A. *Management Accounting: Principles and Practice*, Financial Times/Pitman Publishing, 1998, Chapter 4.

References

Drury, C., Braund, S., Osborne, P. and Tayles, M. *A Survey of Management Accounting Practices in UK Manufacturing Companies*, Chartered Association of Certified Accountants, 1993.

Drury, C. and Tayles, M. *Cost Systems Design and Profitability Analysis in UK Manufacturing Companies*, CIMA Publishing, 2000.

Ernst and Young *2003 Survey of Management Accounting*, Ernst and Young, 2003.
Innes, J., Mitchell, F. and Sinclair, D. 'Activity-based costing in the UK's largest companies', *Management Accounting Research*, Vol 11, No 3, 2000.

? Review questions

Answers to these questions can be found at the back of the book (pp. 493-4).

8.1 What problem does the existence of work in progress cause in process costing?

8.2 What is the point of distinguishing direct costs from indirect ones? Why is this not necessary in process costing environments?

8.3 Are direct costs and variable costs the same thing? Explain your answer.

8.4 It is sometimes claimed that the full cost of pursuing some objective represents the long-run break-even selling price. Why is this said, and what does it mean?

* Exercises

Exercises 8.4 and 8.5 are more advanced than 8.1 to 8.3. Those with a **coloured number** have answers at the back of the book (pp. 511-14).

If you wish to try more exercises, visit the students' side of the companion website.

8.1 Distinguish between:

- job costing;
- process costing;
- batch costing.

What tend to be the problems specifically associated with each of these?

8.2 Pieman Products Ltd makes road trailers to the precise specifications of individual customers. The following are predicted to occur during the forthcoming year, which is about to start:

Direct materials cost	£50,000
Direct labour costs	£160,000
Direct labour time	16,000 hours
Indirect labour cost	£25,000
Depreciation of machine	£8,000
Rent and rates	£10,000
Heating, lighting and power	£5,000
Indirect materials	£2,000
Other indirect costs	£1,000
Machine time	3,000 hours

→

All direct labour is paid at the same hourly rate.

A customer has asked the business to build a trailer for transporting a racing motor-cycle to races. It is estimated that this will require materials and components that will cost £1,150. It will take 250 direct labour hours to do the job, of which 50 will involve the use of machinery.

Required:

Deduce a logical cost for the job, and explain the basis of dealing with overheads that you propose.

8.3 Athena Ltd is an engineering business doing work for its customers to their particular requirements and specifications. It determines the full cost of each job taking a 'job cost-ing' approach, accounting for overheads on a departmental basis. It bases its prices to customers on this full cost figure. The business has two departments: a Machining Department, where each job starts, and a Fitting Department, which completes all of the jobs. Machining Department overheads are charged to jobs on a machine hour basis and those of the Fitting Department on a direct labour hour basis. The budgeted information for next year is as follows:

Heating and lighting	£25,000	(allocated equally between the two departments)
Machine power	£10,000	(all allocated to the Machining Department)
Direct labour	£200,000	(£150,000 allocated to the Fitting Department and £50,000 to the Machining Department. All direct workers are paid £10 an hour)
Indirect labour	£50,000	(apportioned to the departments in proportion to the direct labour cost)
Direct materials	£120,000	(all applied to jobs in the Machining Department)
Depreciation	£30,000	(all relates to the Machining Department)
Machine time	20,000 hours	(all worked in the Machining Department)

Required:

(a) Prepare a statement showing the budgeted overheads for next year, analysed between the two departments. This should be in the form of three columns: one for the total figure for each type of overhead and one column each for the two depart-ments, where each type of overhead is analysed between the two departments. Each column should also show the total of overheads for the year.

(b) Derive the appropriate rate for charging the overheads of each department to jobs (that is, a separate rate for each department).

(c) Athena Ltd has been asked by a customer to specify the price that it will charge for a particular job that will, if the job goes ahead, be undertaken early next year. The job is expected to use direct materials costing Athena Ltd £1,200, to need 50 hours of machining time, 10 hours of Machine Department direct labour and 40 hours of Fitting Department direct labour. Athena Ltd charges a profit loading of 20% to the full cost of jobs to determine the selling price.

Show workings to derive the proposed selling price for this job.

8.4 Kaplan plc makes a range of suitcases of various sizes and shapes. There are ten different models of suitcase produced by the business. In order to keep inventories of finished suitcases to a minimum, each model is made in a small batch. Each batch is costed as a separate job and the cost for each suitcase deduced by dividing the batch cost by the number of suitcases in the batch.

At present, the business derives the cost of each batch using a traditional job-costing approach. Recently, however, a new management accountant was appointed, who is advocating the use of activity-based costing (ABC) to deduce the cost of the batches. The management accountant claims that ABC leads to much more reliable and relevant costs and that it has other benefits.

Required:
(a) Explain how the business deduces the cost of each suitcase at present.
(b) Discuss the purposes to which the knowledge of the cost for each suitcase, deduced on a traditional basis, can be put and how valid the cost is for the purpose concerned.
(c) Explain how ABC could be applied to costing the suitcases, highlighting the differences between ABC and the traditional approach.
(d) Explain what advantages the new management accountant probably believes ABC to have over the traditional approach.

8.5 'In a job costing system, it is necessary to divide up the business into departments. Fixed costs (or overheads) will be collected for each department. Where a particular fixed cost relates to the business as a whole, it must be divided between the departments. Usually this is done on the basis of area of floor space occupied by each department relative to the entire business. When the total fixed costs for each department have been identified, this will be divided by the number of hours that were worked in each department to deduce an overhead recovery rate. Each job that was worked on in a department will have a share of fixed costs allotted to it according to how long it was worked on. The total cost for each job will therefore be the sum of the variable costs of the job and its share of the fixed costs. It is essential that this approach is taken in order to deduce a selling price for the business's output.'

Required:
Prepare a table of two columns. In the first column you should show any phrases or sentences in the above statement with which you do not agree, and in the second column you should show your reason for disagreeing with each one.

Chapter 9

Budgeting

Introduction

This chapter is concerned with budgets. Budgeting is an activity that most business managers see as one of the most crucial in which they are engaged. We shall consider the purpose of budgets and how they fit into the decision-making and planning process. We shall also consider how budgets are prepared. Preparing budgets relies on knowledge of the financial statements (balance sheet and income statement (profit and loss account)) that we considered in Chapters 2 and 3. It also picks up many of the issues relating to the behaviour of costs and full costing, topics that we explored in Chapters 7 and 8, respectively. Lastly, we shall take a look at how budgets are used to help exercise control over the business to try to ensure that its objectives are achieved.

Learning outcomes

When you have completed this chapter, you should be able to:

- define a budget and show how budgets, corporate objectives and long-term plans are related;
- explain the interlinking of the various budgets within the business;
- indicate the uses of budgeting, and construct various budgets, including the cash budget, from relevant data;
- use a budget to provide a means of exercising control over the business.

Budgets, long-term plans and corporate objectives

We saw in Chapter 1 that it is vital that businesses develop plans for the future. Whatever a business is trying to achieve, it is unlikely to be successful unless its managers have clear in their minds what the future direction of the business is going to be. Thus the starting point is to identify, as precisely as possible, the long-term objectives to be pursued. Once this has been done, the various options available to fulfil these objectives should be evaluated. The most appropriate option(s) should be selected and plans developed on the basis of this selection.

Businesses typically produce a long-term plan, perhaps going five years into the future, and a short-term plan normally looking at the following 12 months.

The planning sequence can be shown graphically, as in Figure 9.1. We can see that the overall objectives are first defined; they are then translated into long-term plans of action. These objectives are achieved by successfully working towards short-term plans or budgets.

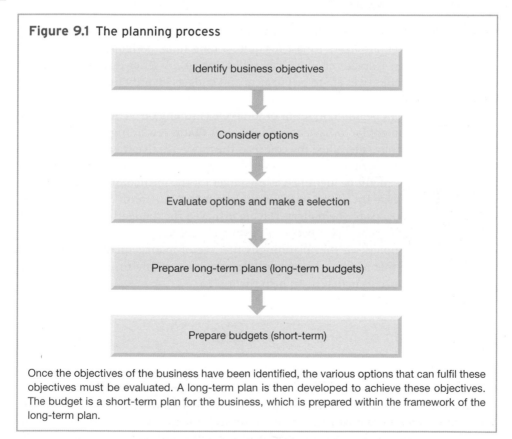

Figure 9.1 The planning process

Identify business objectives

Consider options

Evaluate options and make a selection

Prepare long-term plans (long-term budgets)

Prepare budgets (short-term)

Once the objectives of the business have been identified, the various options that can fulfil these objectives must be evaluated. A long-term plan is then developed to achieve these objectives. The budget is a short-term plan for the business, which is prepared within the framework of the long-term plan.

The long-term plan would define the general direction of the business over the next five or so years and would deal, in broad terms, with such matters as:

- the market that the business will seek to serve;
- production/service rendering methods;
- what the business will offer to its customers;
- target levels of profit and returns to shareholders;
- financial requirements and financing methods;
- personnel requirements;
- bought-in goods and services requirements and sources.

The budget is essentially a business plan for the short term. It is likely to be expressed mainly in financial terms, and is designed to convert the long-term plan into an actionable blueprint for the future. The budget will define precise targets for:

- sales revenues and expenses;
- cash receipts and payments;
- short-term credit to be given or taken;
- inventories (stock) requirements;
- personnel requirements.

Clearly, the relationship between objectives, long-term plans and budgets is that the objectives, once set, are likely to last for quite a long time, perhaps throughout the life of the business (though changes can and do occur). A series of long-term plans identify how the objectives are to be pursued, and budgets identify how the long-term plan is to be fulfilled.

An analogy might be found in terms of someone enrolling on a course of study. His, or her, objective might be to have a working career that is rewarding in various ways. The person might have identified the course as the most effective way to work towards this objective. In working towards achievement of the objective, passing a particular stage of the course might be identified as the target for the forthcoming year. Here the intention to complete the entire course is analogous to a long-term plan, and passing each stage is analogous to the budget. Having achieved the 'budget' for the first year, the 'budget' for the second year becomes passing the second stage.

It should be emphasised that planning is the role of management rather than of accountants. The role of the management accountant is simply to provide technical advice and assistance to managers to help them plan.

Time horizon of plans and budgets

It need not necessarily be the case that long-term plans are set for five years and that budgets are set for 12 months – it is up to the management of the business concerned – though these are very typical of the time periods found in practice. Businesses involved in certain industries, say, information technology, may feel that five years is too long a planning period since new developments can, and do, occur virtually overnight. Nor need it be the case that a budget is set for one year. However, this appears to be a widely used time horizon.

Activity 9.1

Can you think of any reason why most businesses prepare detailed budgets for the forthcoming year, rather than for a shorter or longer period?

The reason is probably that a year represents a long enough period for the budget preparation exercise to be worthwhile, yet short enough into the future for detailed plans to be made. As we shall see later in this chapter, the process of formulating budgets can be time consuming, but there are economies of scale: for example, preparing the budget for the next 12 months would not normally take twice as much time and effort as preparing the budget for the next six months.

The annual budget sets targets for the forthcoming year for all levels of the business. It is usually broken down into monthly budgets that define monthly targets. In many cases the annual budget will, in any case, be built up from monthly figures. For example, the sales staff will be required to make sales targets for each month of the budget period.

There will always be some aspect of the business that will stop it achieving its objectives to the maximum extent. This is often a limited ability of the business to sell its products. Sometimes, it is some production shortage (such as labour, materials or plant) that is the limiting factor, or, linked to these, a shortage of funds. Often, production shortages can be overcome by an increase in funds – for example, more plant can be bought or leased. This is not always a practical solution, because no amount of money will buy certain labour skills or increase the world supply of some raw material.

It is sometimes possible to ease an initial limiting factor – for example, subcontracting can eliminate a plant capacity problem. This means that some other factor, perhaps sales, will replace the production problem, though at a higher level of output. Ultimately, however, the business will hit a ceiling; some limiting factor will prove impossible to ease.

It is important that the limiting factor is identified. Ultimately, most, if not all, budgets will be affected by the limiting factor. If it can be identified at the outset, all managers can be informed of the restriction early in the process, so they can take account of it when preparing their budgets.

Budgets and forecasts

We saw earlier that a budget is a business plan for a future period of time. Note particularly that a budget is a plan, not a forecast. To talk of a plan suggests an intention or determination to achieve the targets. Forecasts tend to be predictions of the future state of the environment.

Clearly forecasts are very helpful to the planner/budget setter. If a reputable forecaster has forecast the particular number of new cars to be purchased in the UK during next year, it will be valuable for a manager in a car manufacturing business to obtain and take account of this forecast figure when setting sales budgets. However, a forecast and a budget are distinctly different.

The interrelationship of various budgets

For a particular business for a particular period, there is more than one budget. Each one will relate to a specific aspect of the business. It is generally considered that the ideal situation is that there should be a separate budget for each person who is in a managerial position, no matter how junior. The contents of all of the individual budgets will be summarised in master budgets consisting usually of a budgeted income statement (profit and loss account) and balance sheet. The cash flow statement (in summarised form) is considered by some to be a third master budget.

Figure 9.2 illustrates the interrelationship and interlinking of individual budgets, in this particular case using a manufacturing business as an example. The sales budget (at the left of Figure 9.2) is usually the first budget to be prepared, as this tends to determine the overall level of activity for the forthcoming period. This is because sales demand is probably the most common limiting factor. The level of sales would tend to dictate the finished inventories requirement, though it would also be dictated

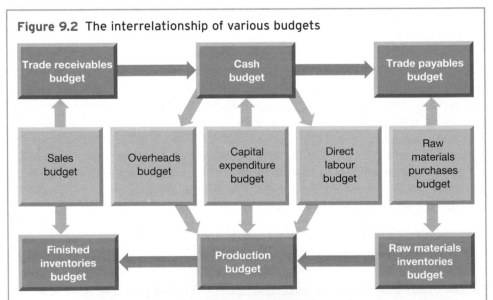

Figure 9.2 The interrelationship of various budgets

This shows the interrelationship of budgets for a manufacturing business. The starting point is usually the sales budget. The expected level of sales normally defines the overall level of activity for the business, and the other budgets will be drawn up in accordance with this. Thus, the sales budget will largely define the finished inventories requirements, and from this we can define the production requirements and so on.

by the policy of the business on finished inventories holding. The requirement for finished inventories would define the required production levels, which would, in turn, dictate the requirements of the individual production departments or sections. The demands of manufacturing, in conjunction with the business's policy on raw materials inventories, define the raw materials inventories budget. The purchases budget will be dictated by the materials inventories budget, which will, in conjunction with the policy of the business on payables payment, dictate the trade payables (creditors) budget. One of the determinants of the cash budget will be the trade payables budget; another will be the trade receivables (debtors) budget, which itself derives, through the receivables collection policy of the business, from the sales budget. Cash will also be affected by overheads and direct labour costs (themselves linked to production) and by capital expenditure. The factors that affect policies on matters such as inventories holding and receivables collection and payables payment periods will be discussed in some detail in Chapter 11.

It may actually prove to be the case that it is not sales demand that limits activities. Assuming that the budgeting process takes the order just described, it might be found in practice that there is some limiting factor other than sales. For example, the production capacity of the business may be incapable of meeting the necessary levels of output to match the sales budget for one or more months. As we saw earlier, it might be reasonable to look at the ways of overcoming the problem. As a last resort, it might be necessary to revise the sales budget to a lower level to enable production to meet the target.

Activity 9.2

Can you think of any ways in which a short-term shortage of production facilities of a manufacturer might be overcome?

We thought of the following:

- Higher production in previous months and stockpiling to meet periods of higher demand.
- Increasing production capacity, perhaps by working overtime and/or acquiring (buying or leasing) additional plant.
- Subcontracting some production.
- Encouraging potential customers to change the timing of their buying by offering discounts or other special terms during the months that have been identified as quiet.

You may well have thought of other approaches.

There will be the horizontal relationships between budgets, which we have just looked at, but there will usually be vertical ones as well. For example, the sales budget may be broken down into a number of subsidiary budgets, perhaps one for each regional sales manager. The overall sales budget will be a summary of the subsidiary ones. The same may be true of virtually all of the other budgets, most particularly the production budget.

Figure 9.2, which we just considered, gives a very simplified outline of the budgetary framework of a typical manufacturing business. We have looked at the interlinking of budgets in the context of a manufacturing business, purely because they have all of the types of budget that we tend to find in practice. A service supplier, for example, would have a similar set of budgets, but without some or all of those relating to inventories. The issues relating to budgets apply equally well to all types of business.

All of the operating budgets that we have just reviewed have to be consistent with the overall short-term plans laid out in the master budget, that is, the budgeted income statement and balance sheet.

The uses of budgets

Budgets are generally regarded as having five areas of usefulness. These are:

1 *Budgets tend to promote forward thinking and the possible identification of short-term problems.* We have just seen above that a shortage of production capacity might be identified during the budgeting process. Making this discovery in good time could leave a number of means of overcoming the problem open to exploration. If the potential production problem is picked up early enough, all of the suggestions in the answer to Activity 9.2 and, possibly, other ways of overcoming the problem can be explored. Early identification of the potential problem gives managers time for calm and rational consideration of the best way of overcoming it. The best solution to the potential problem may only be feasible if action can be taken well in advance. This would be true of all of the suggestions made in the answer to Activity 9.2.

2 *Budgets can be used to help co-ordination between the various sections of the business.* It is crucially important that the activities of the various departments and sections of the business are linked so that the activities of one are complementary to those of another. For example, the activities of the purchasing/procurement department of a manufacturing business should dovetail with the raw materials needs of the production departments. If this is not the case, production could run out of inventories, leading to expensive production stoppages. Possibly, and just as undesirable, excessive inventories could be bought, leading to large and unnecessary inventories holding costs. We shall see how this co-ordination tends to work in practice later in this chapter.

3 *Budgets can motivate managers to better performance.* Having a stated task can motivate managers and staff in their performance. It is a well-established view that to tell a manager to do his or her best is not very motivating, but to define a required level of achievement is more likely to be so. It is felt that managers will be better motivated by being able to relate their particular role in the business to its overall objectives. Since budgets are directly derived from corporate objectives, budgeting makes this possible. It is clearly not possible to allow managers to operate in an unconstrained environment. Having to operate in a way that matches the goals of the business

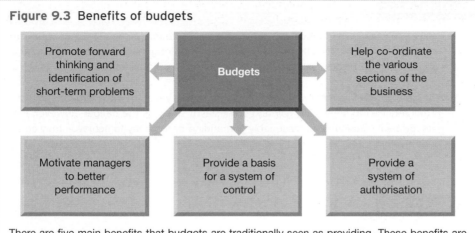

Figure 9.3 Benefits of budgets

| Promote forward thinking and identification of short-term problems | **Budgets** | Help co-ordinate the various sections of the business |

| Motivate managers to better performance | Provide a basis for a system of control | Provide a system of authorisation |

There are five main benefits that budgets are traditionally seen as providing. These benefits are discussed in the chapter.

is a price of working in an effective business. We shall consider the role of budgets as motivators later in the chapter.

4 *Budgets can provide a basis for a system of control.* Control is concerned with ensuring that events conform to plans. If senior management wishes to control and to monitor the performance of more junior staff, it needs some yardstick against which the performance can be measured and assessed. It is possible to compare current performance with past performance or perhaps with what happens in another business. However, the most logical yardstick is usually planned performance. If there is information available concerning the actual performance for a period, and this can be compared with the planned performance, then a basis for control will have been established. Such a basis will enable the use of management by exception, a technique where senior managers can spend most of their time dealing with those staff or activities that have failed to achieve the budget (the exceptions). This means that the senior managers do not have to spend too much time on those that are performing well. It also allows junior managers to exercise self-control. By knowing what is expected of them and what they have actually achieved, they can assess how well they are performing and take steps to correct matters where they are failing to achieve. We shall consider the effect of making plans and being held accountable for their achievement later in the chapter.

5 *Budgets can provide a system of authorisation* for managers to spend up to a particular limit. A good example of this is where there are certain activities (for example, staff development and research expenditure) that are allocated a fixed amount of funds at the discretion of senior management.

Figure 9.3 shows the benefits of budgets in diagrammatic form.

The following two activities pick up issues that relate to some of the uses of budgets.

Activity 9.3

The third on the above list of the uses of budgets (motivation), implies that managers are set stated tasks. Do you think there is a danger that requiring managers to work towards such predetermined targets will stifle their skill, flair and enthusiasm?

If the budgets are set in such a way as to offer challenging yet achievable targets, the manager is still required to show skill, flair and enthusiasm. There is the danger, however, that if targets are badly set (either unreasonably demanding or too easy to achieve), they could be a demotivating force. This could well stifle managers' skill, flair and enthusiasm.

Activity 9.4

The fourth on the above list of the uses of budgets (control), implies that current management performance is compared with some yardstick. What is wrong with comparing actual performance with past performance, or the performance of others, in an effort to exercise control?

There is no automatic reason to believe that what happened in the past, or is happening elsewhere, represents a sensible target for this year in this business. Considering what happened last year, and in other businesses, may help in the formulation of plans, but past events and the performance of others should not automatically be seen as the target.

The extent to which budgets are prepared

There is recent survey evidence that reveals the extent to which budgeting is used by larger US businesses. It shows that most of them prepare and use budgets (see Real World 9.1).

Real World 9.1

Budgeting in practice

A survey of management accounting practice in the US was conducted in 2003. Nearly 2,000 businesses replied to the survey. These tended to be larger businesses, of which about 40 per cent were manufacturers and about 16 per cent financial services; the remainder were across a range of other industries.

The survey revealed that 75 per cent extensively use operational budgeting, with a further 16 per cent considering using the technique in the future.

Though the survey relates to the US, in the absence of UK evidence, it provides some insight to what is likely also to be practice in the UK and elsewhere in the developed world.

Source: Ernst and Young (see References section at the end of the chapter)

A fairly recent survey of budgeting practice in small and medium-sized enterprises (SMEs) (see Real World 9.2) revealed that not all such businesses fully use budgeting. It seems that some smaller businesses prepare budgets only for what they see as key areas. The budget that is most frequently prepared by such businesses is the sales budget, followed by the budgeted income statement and the overheads budget. Perhaps surprisingly, the cash budget is prepared by less than two-thirds of the small businesses surveyed.

Real World 9.2

Preparation of budgets in SMEs

A study of budgeting practice in small and medium-sized enterprises (SMEs) revealed that the most frequently prepared budget is the sales budget, followed by the budgeted income statement and the overheads budget (see Figure 9.4).

Figure 9.4

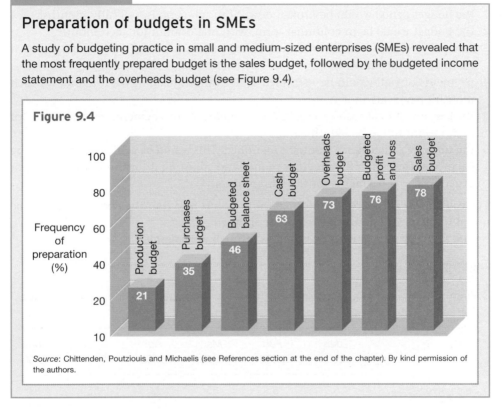

Source: Chittenden, Poutziouis and Michaelis (see References section at the end of the chapter). By kind permission of the authors.

Preparing the cash budget

We shall now look in some detail at how the various budgets used by the typical business are prepared, starting with the cash budget and then looking at the others. It is helpful for us to start with the cash budget because:

- it is a key budget; most economic aspects of a business are reflected in cash sooner or later, so that for a typical business the cash budget reflects the whole business more than any other single budget;

■ very small, unsophisticated businesses (for example, a corner shop) may feel that full-scale budgeting is not appropriate to their needs, but almost certainly they should prepare a cash budget as a minimum (despite the survey evidence mentioned in Real World 9.2 above).

Since budgets are documents that are to be used only internally by a business, their style is a question of management choice and will vary from one business to the next. However, since managers, irrespective of the business, are likely to be using budgets for similar purposes, some consistency of approach tends to be found. In most businesses the cash budget will probably possess the following features:

1 the budget period would be broken down into sub-periods, typically months;
2 the budget would be in columnar form, with one column for each month;
3 receipts of cash would be identified under various headings and a total for each month's receipts shown;
4 payments of cash would be identified under various headings and a total for each month's payments shown;
5 the surplus of total cash receipts over payments, or of payments over receipts, for each month would be identified;
6 the running cash balance would be identified. This would be achieved by taking the balance at the end of the previous month and adjusting it for the surplus or deficit of receipts over payments for the current month.

Typically, all of the pieces of information in points 3 to 6 in the above list would be useful to management for one reason or another.

The best way to deal with this topic is through an example.

Example 9.1

Vierra Popova Ltd is a wholesale business. The budgeted income statements for each of the next six months are as follows:

	Jan £000	Feb £000	Mar £000	Apr £000	May £000	June £000
Sales revenue	52	55	55	60	55	53
Cost of goods sold	30	31	31	35	31	32
Salaries and wages	10	10	10	10	10	10
Electricity	5	5	4	3	3	3
Depreciation	3	3	3	3	3	3
Other overheads	2	2	2	2	2	2
Total expenses	50	51	50	53	49	50
Net profit	2	4	5	7	6	3

The business allows all of its customers one month's credit (this means, for example, that cash from January sales will be received in February). Sales revenue during December totalled £60,000.

The business plans to maintain inventories at their existing level until some time in March, when they are to be reduced by £5,000. Inventories will remain at this lower level indefinitely. Inventories purchases are made on one month's credit. December purchases totalled £30,000. Salaries, wages and 'other overheads' are paid in the month concerned. Electricity is paid quarterly in arrears in March and June. The business plans to buy and pay for a new delivery van in March. This will cost a total of £15,000, but an existing van will be traded in for £4,000 as part of the deal.

The business expects to have £12,000 in cash at the beginning of January.

Solution

The cash budget for the six months ending in June will look as follows:

	Jan £000	Feb £000	Mar £000	Apr £000	May £000	June £000
Receipts						
Receivables (Note 1)	60	52	55	55	60	55
Payments						
Payables (Note 2)	30	30	31	26	35	31
Salaries and wages	10	10	10	10	10	10
Electricity	–	–	14	–	–	9
Other overheads	2	2	2	2	2	2
Van purchase	–	–	11	–	–	–
Total payments	42	42	68	38	47	52
Cash surplus	18	10	(13)	17	13	3
Opening balance (Note 3)	12	30	40	27	44	57
Closing balance	30	40	27	44	57	60

Notes:
1. The cash receipts from trade receivables lag a month behind sales because customers are given a month in which to pay for their purchases. So, December sales will be paid for in January and so on.
2. In most months, the purchases of inventories will equal the cost of goods sold. This is because the business maintains a constant level of inventories. For inventories to remain constant at the end of each month, the business must replace exactly the amount that has been used. During March, however, the business plans to reduce its inventories by £5,000. This means that inventories purchases will be lower than inventories usage in that month. The payments for inventories purchases lag a month behind purchases because the business expects to be allowed a month to pay for what it buys.
3. Each month's cash balance is the previous month's figure plus the cash surplus (or minus the cash deficit) for the current month. The balance at the start of January is £12,000 according to the information provided earlier.
4. Depreciation does not give rise to a cash payment. In the context of profit measurement (in the income statement), depreciation is a very important aspect. Here, however, we are interested only in cash.

Activity 9.5

Looking at the cash budget of Vierra Popova Ltd (above), what conclusions do you draw and what possible course of action do you recommend regarding the cash balance over the period concerned?

There appears to be a fairly large cash balance, given the size of the business, and it seems to be increasing. Management might give consideration to putting some of the cash into an income-yielding deposit. Alternatively, it could be used to expand the trading activities of the business by, for example, increasing the investment in non-current (fixed) assets.

Activity 9.6

Vierra Popova Ltd (see Example 9.1) now wishes to prepare its cash budget for the second six months of the year. The budgeted income statements for each month of the second half of the year are as follows:

	July £000	Aug £000	Sept £000	Oct £000	Nov £000	Dec £000
Sales revenue	57	59	62	57	53	51
Cost of goods sold	32	33	35	32	30	29
Salaries and wages	10	10	10	10	10	10
Electricity	3	3	4	5	6	6
Depreciation	3	3	3	3	3	3
Other overheads	2	2	2	2	2	2
Total expenses	50	51	54	52	51	50
Net profit	7	8	8	5	2	1

The business will continue to allow all of its customers one month's credit.

It plans to increase inventories from the 30 June level by £1,000 each month until, and including, September. During the following three months, inventories levels will be decreased by £1,000 each month.

Inventories purchases, which had been made on one month's credit until the June payment, will, starting with the purchases made in June, be made on two months' credit.

Salaries, wages and 'other overheads' will continue to be paid in the month concerned. Electricity is paid quarterly in arrears in September and December.

At the end of December the business intends to pay off part of a loan. This payment is to be such that it will leave the business with a cash balance of £5,000 with which to start next year.

Required:
Prepare the cash budget for the six months ending in December. (Remember that any information you need that relates to the first six months of the year, including the cash balance that is expected to be brought forward on 1 July, is given in Example 9.1.)

The cash budget for the six months ended 31 December is:

	July £000	Aug £000	Sept £000	Oct £000	Nov £000	Dec £000
Receipts						
Receivables	53	57	59	62	57	53
Payments						
Payables (Note 1)	–	32	33	34	36	31
Salaries and wages	10	10	10	10	10	10
Electricity	–	–	10	–	–	17
Other overheads	2	2	2	2	2	2
Loan repayment (Note 2)	–	–	–	–	–	131
Total payments	12	44	55	46	48	191
Cash surplus	41	13	4	16	9	(138)
Opening balance	60	101	114	118	134	143
Closing balance	101	114	118	134	143	5

Notes:

1 There will be no payment to payables in July because the June purchases will be made on two months' credit and will therefore be paid in August. The July purchases, which will equal the July cost of sales figure plus the increase in inventories made in July, will be paid for in September, and so on.

2 The repayment is simply the amount that will cause the balance at 31 December to be £5,000.

Preparing other budgets

Though each one will have its own particular features, other budgets will tend to follow the same sort of pattern as the cash budget, that is, they will show inflows and outflows during each month and the opening and closing balances in each month.

Example 9.2

To illustrate some of the other budgets, we shall continue to use the example of Vierra Popova Ltd that we considered in Example 9.1, on page 290. To the information given there, we need to add the fact that the inventories balance at 1 January was £30,000.

Show the trade receivables, trade payables and inventories budgets for the six months.

→

Solution

Trade receivables budget

This would normally show the planned amount owing from credit sales to the business at the beginning and at the end of each month, the planned total sales revenue for each month, and the planned total cash receipts from receivables. The layout would be something like the following:

	Jan £000	Feb £000	Mar £000	Apr £000	May £000	June £000
Opening balance	60	52	55	55	60	55
Add Sales revenue	52	55	55	60	55	53
	112	107	110	115	115	108
Less Cash receipts	60	52	55	55	60	55
Closing balance	52	55	55	60	55	53

The opening and closing balances represent the amount that the business plans to be owed (in total) by receivables at the beginning and end of each month, respectively.

Trade payables budget

Typically this shows the planned amount owed to suppliers by the business at the beginning and at the end of each month, the planned purchases for each month, and the planned total cash payments to payables. The layout would be something like the following:

	Jan £000	Feb £000	Mar £000	Apr £000	May £000	June £000
Opening balance	30	30	31	26	35	31
Add Purchases	30	31	26	35	31	32
	60	61	57	61	66	63
Less Cash payment	30	30	31	26	35	31
Closing balance	30	31	26	35	31	32

The opening and closing balances represent the amount planned to be owed (in total) by the business to payables, at the beginning and end of each month respectively.

Inventories budget

This would normally show the planned amount of inventories to be held by the business at the beginning and at the end of each month, the planned total inventories purchases for each month, and the planned total monthly inventories usage. The layout would be something like the following:

	Jan £000	Feb £000	Mar £000	Apr £000	May £000	June £000
Opening balance	30	30	30	25	25	25
Add Purchases	30	31	26	35	31	32
	60	61	56	60	56	57
Less Inventories used	30	31	31	35	31	32
Closing balance	30	30	25	25	25	25

The opening and closing balances represent the amount of inventories, at cost, planned to be held by the business at the beginning and end of each month respectively.

A *raw materials inventories budget*, for a manufacturing business, would follow a similar pattern, with the 'inventories usage' being the cost of the inventories put into production. A *finished inventories budget* for a manufacturer would also be similar to the above, except that 'inventories manufactured' would replace 'purchases'. A manufacturing business would normally prepare both a raw materials inventories budget and a finished inventories budget.

The inventories budget will normally be expressed in financial terms, but may also be expressed in physical terms (for example, kg or metres) for individual inventory items.

Note how the trade receivables, trade payables and inventories budgets in Example 9.2 link to one another, and to the cash budget for the same business in Example 9.1. Note particularly that:

- the rows of purchases figures in both the payables budget and the inventories budget are identical;
- the rows of cash payments figures in both the payables budget and the cash budget are identical;
- the rows of cash receipts figures in both the receivables budget and the cash budget are identical.

Other values would link with other budgets in a similar way. For example the row of sales figures in the receivables budget would be identical to figures that will be found in the sales budget.

This is how the linking (co-ordination), which was discussed earlier in this chapter, is achieved.

Activity 9.7

Have a go at preparing the trade receivables budget for Vierra Popova Ltd for the six months from July to December (see Activity 9.6).

The trade receivables budget for the six months ended 31 December is:

	July £000	Aug £000	Sept £000	Oct £000	Nov £000	Dec £000
Opening balance (Note 1)	53	57	59	62	57	53
Add Sales revenue (Note 2)	57	59	62	57	53	51
	110	116	121	119	110	104
Less Cash receipts (Note 3)	53	57	59	62	57	53
Closing balance (Note 4)	57	59	62	57	53	51

Notes:
1 The opening receivables figure is the previous month's sales revenue figure (sales are on one month's credit).
2 The sales revenues are the current month's figure.
3 The cash received each month is equal to the previous month's sales revenue figure.
4 The closing balance is equal to the current month's sales revenue figure.
Note that if we knew three of the four figures each month, we could deduce the fourth.

This budget could, of course, be set out in any manner that would have given the sort of information that management would require in respect of planned levels of receivables and associated transactions.

Activity 9.8

Have a go at preparing the payables budget for Vierra Popova Ltd for the six months from July to December (see Activity 9.6). (*Hint*: Remember that the payables' payment period alters from the June purchases onwards.)

The payables budget for the six months ended 31 December is:

	July £000	Aug £000	Sept £000	Oct £000	Nov £000	Dec £000
Opening balance	32	65	67	70	67	60
Add Purchases	33	34	36	31	29	28
	65	99	103	101	96	88
Less Cash payments	–	32	33	34	36	31
Closing balance	65	67	70	67	60	57

This, again, could be set out in any manner that would have given the sort of information that management would require in respect of planned levels of payables and associated transactions.

? Self-assessment question 9.1

Antonio Ltd has planned production and sales for the next nine months as follows:

	Production (units)	Sales (units)
May	350	350
June	400	400
July	500	400
August	600	500
September	600	600
October	700	650
November	750	700
December	750	800
January	750	750

During the period, the business plans to advertise so as to generate these increases in sales. Payments for advertising of £1,000 and £1,500 will be made in July and October respectively.

The selling price will be £20 a unit throughout the period. Forty per cent of sales are normally made on two months' credit. The other 60 per cent are settled within the month of the sale.

Raw material will be held in inventories for one month before it is taken into production. Purchases of raw materials will be on one month's credit (buy one month, pay the next). The cost of raw material is £8 a unit of production.

Other direct production expenses, including labour, are planned to be £6 a unit of production. These will be paid in the month concerned.

Various production overheads, which during the period to 30 June had run at £1,800 a month, are expected to rise to £2,000 each month from 1 July to 31 October. These are expected to rise again from 1 November to £2,400 a month and to remain at that level for the foreseeable future. These overheads include a steady £400 each month for depreciation. Overheads are planned to be paid 80 per cent in the month of production and 20 per cent in the following month.

To help to meet the planned increased production, a new item of plant will be bought and will be delivered in August. The cost of this item is £6,600; the contract with the supplier will specify that this will be paid in three equal amounts in September, October and November.

Raw material inventories are planned to be 500 units on 1 July. The balance at the bank on the same day is planned to be £7,500.

Required:
(a) Draw up the following, for the six months ending 31 December:
   (i)   a raw materials budget, showing both physical quantities and financial values;
   (ii) a payables budget;
   (iii) a cash budget.
(b) The cash budget reveals a potential cash deficiency during October and November. Can you suggest any ways in which a modification of plans could overcome this problem?

Using budgets for control

Earlier in this chapter, we saw that budgets can provide a useful basis for exercising control over the business, because control is usually seen as making events conform to a plan. Since the budget represents the plan, making events conform to it is the obvious way to try to control the business. Using budgets in this way is popular in practice, as we shall see in Real World 9.4.

For most businesses the routine is as shown in Figure 9.5. These steps in the control process are fairly easy to understand. The point is that, if plans are drawn up sensibly, we have a basis for exercising control over the business. It also requires us to have the means of measuring actual performance in the same terms as those in which the budget is stated. If they are not in the same terms, comparison will not usually be possible.

Taking steps to exercise control means finding out where and why things did not go according to plan and seeking ways to put things right for the future. One of the reasons why things may have gone wrong is that the plans may, in reality, prove to be unachievable. In this case, if budgets are to be a useful basis for exercising control in the future, it may be necessary to revise the budgets for future periods to bring targets into the realms of achievability.

This last point should not be taken to mean that budget targets can simply be ignored if the going gets tough. However, budgets may prove to be totally unrealistic. This could be for a variety of reasons, including unexpected changes in the commercial environment (for example, an unexpected collapse in demand for services of the type that the business provides). In this case, nothing whatsoever will be achieved by pretending that the targets can be met.

Real World 9.3 provides an example of where a budget of one well-known business proved to be spectacularly wrong and had to be revised.

Real World 9.3

If you're going to get it wrong, do it properly! **FT**

Royal Dutch/Shell, the Anglo-Dutch energy giant, yesterday said its flagship Russian gas project would be delayed by at least eight months and cost $20bn (£11.4bn) – twice the original estimate.

The giant Sakhalin-2 liquefied natural gas project off the east coast of Russia has been beset by a range of problems, the company said, including the rising cost of raw materials, a shortage of contractors, Russian inflation and currency exchange rate fluctuations.

The project had already been delayed by environmental concerns, which forced the company to re-route a pipeline to avoid whale feeding grounds.

'Unfortunately, it is now clear that the Sakhalin project budget and schedule were significantly underestimated when it was approved in 2003, especially given the project's scale, its complexity and the frontier nature of execution,' said Malcolm Brinded, executive director for Shell's exploration and production unit.

The massive cost overrun will hurt the profitability of one of Shell's most important new projects and could hit its overall production of oil and gas in 2008.

Source: 'Shell's Sakhalin-2 gas project hit by eight-month delay and $10bn cost rise', *Financial Times*, 15 July 2005, FT.com

Figure 9.5 The planning and control process

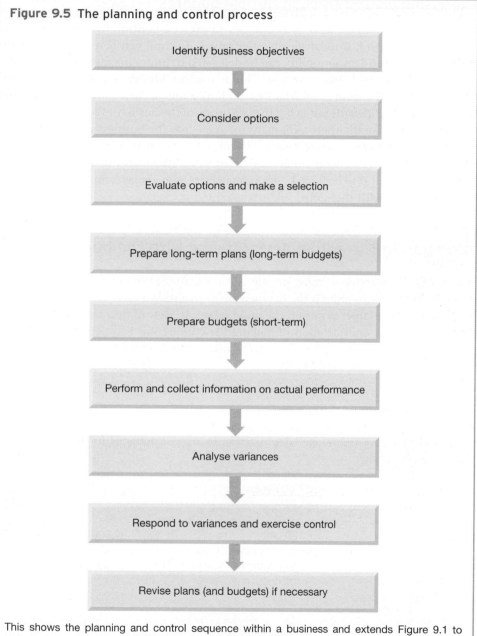

This shows the planning and control sequence within a business and extends Figure 9.1 to include the control aspect. Once the objectives have been determined, the various options that can fulfil these objectives must be evaluated in order to prepare the long-term plan. The budget is a short-term plan set within the framework of the long-term plan. Control can be exercised through a comparison of budgeted and actual performance. Where a significant divergence emerges, some form of corrective action should be taken. If the budget figures prove to be based on incorrect assumptions about the future, it may be necessary to revise the budget.

Exercising control through flexible budgets

Flexible budgets may be used by businesses to exercise control. By having a system of budgetary control, through flexible budgets, a position can be established where decision making and responsibility can be delegated to junior management, yet senior management can still retain control. This is because senior managers can use the budgetary control system to ascertain which junior managers are meeting targets and therefore working towards achieving the objectives of the business. (We should remember that budgets are the short-term plans for achieving the business's objectives.) This enables a management-by-exception environment to be created. Here senior management concentrates its energy on areas where things are not going according to plan (the exceptions – it is to be hoped). Junior managers who are performing to budget can be left to get on with their jobs.

Comparing the actual performance with the budget

The principal objective of most private sector businesses is to enhance their shareholders' wealth. Since profit is the net increase in wealth as a result of trading, the most important budget target to meet is the profit target. In view of this, we shall begin with that aspect in our consideration of making the comparison between the budget and the actual results. Example 9.3 shows the budgeted and actual income statements for Baxter Ltd for the month of May.

Example 9.3

The following are the budgeted and actual income statements for Baxter Ltd for the month of May:

	Budget	Actual
Output (production and sales)	1,000 units	900 units
	£	£
Sales revenue	100,000	92,000
Raw materials	(40,000) (40,000 metres)	(36,900) (37,000 metres)
Labour	(20,000) (2,500 hours)	(17,500) (2,150 hours)
Fixed overheads	(20,000)	(20,700)
Operating profit	20,000	16,900

From these figures, it is clear that the budgeted profit was not achieved. As far as May is concerned, this is a matter of history. However, the business (or at least one aspect of it) is out of control. Senior management must discover where things went wrong during May and try to ensure that these mistakes are not repeated in later months. It is not enough to know that, overall, things went wrong. We need to know where and why. The approach taken is to compare the budgeted and actual figures for the various items (sales revenue, raw materials and so on) in the above statement.

Activity 9.9

Can you see any problems in comparing the various items (sales revenue, raw materials and so on) for the budget and the actual performance of Baxter Ltd in order to draw conclusions as to which aspects were out of control?

The problem is that the actual level of output was not as budgeted. The actual level of output was 10 per cent less than budget. This means that we cannot, for example, say that there was a labour cost saving of £2,500 (that is, £20,000 − £17,500) and conclude that all is well in that area.

Flexing the budget

One practical way to overcome our difficulty is to 'flex' the budget to what it would have been had the planned level of output been 900 units rather than 1,000 units. **Flexing the budget** simply means revising it, assuming a different volume of output.

In the context of control, the budget is usually flexed to reflect the volume that actually occurred, where this is higher or lower than that originally planned. To be able to do this we need to know which items are fixed and which are variable relative to the volume of output. Once we have this knowledge, flexing is a simple operation. We shall assume that sales revenue, material cost and labour cost vary strictly with volume. Fixed overheads, by definition, will not. Whether, in real life, labour cost does vary with the volume of output is not so certain, but it will serve well enough as an assumption for our purposes.

On the basis of our assumptions regarding the behaviour of revenues and costs, the flexed budget would be as follows:

	Flexed budget
Output (production and sales)	<u>900</u> units
	£
Sales revenue	90,000
Raw materials	(36,000) (36,000 metres)
Labour	(18,000) (2,250 hours)
Fixed overheads	<u>(20,000)</u>
Operating profit	<u>16,000</u>

This is simply the original budget, with the sales revenue, raw materials and labour figures scaled down by 10 per cent (the same factor as the actual output fell short of the budgeted one).

Putting the original budget, the flexed budget and the actual for May together, we obtain the following:

	Original budget 1,000 units	Flexed budget 900 units	Actual 900 units
Output (production and sales)			
	£	£	£
Sales revenue	100,000	90,000	92,000
Raw materials	(40,000)	(36,000) (36,000 m)	(36,900) (37,000 m)
Labour	(20,000)	(18,000) (2,250 hr)	(17,500) (2,150 hr)
Fixed overheads	(20,000)	(20,000)	(20,700)
Operating profit	20,000	16,000	16,900

Flexible budgets enable us make a more valid comparison between budget (using the flexed figures) and actual. We can now see that there was a genuine labour cost saving, even after allowing for the output shortfall.

Sales volume variance

It may seem as if we are saying that it does not matter if there are volume shortfalls, because we just revise the budget and carry on as if all is well. However, this is not the case, because losing sales means losing profit. The first point we must pick up, therefore, is the loss of profit arising from the loss of sales of 100 units of the product.

Activity 9.10

What will be the loss of profit arising from the sales shortfall, assuming that everything except sales volume was as planned?

The answer is simply the difference between the original and flexed budget profit figures. The only difference between these two profit figures is the volume of sales; everything else was the same. Thus the figure is £4,000 (that is, £20,000 – £16,000).

As we saw in Chapter 7, when we considered the relationship between cost, volume and profit, selling one unit less will result in one less contribution to profit. The contribution is sales revenue less variable cost. We can see from the original budget that the unit sales revenue is £100 (that is, £100,000/1,000), raw material cost is £40 a unit (that is, £40,000/1,000) and labour cost is £20 a unit (that is, £20,000/1,000). Thus the contribution is £40 a unit (that is, £100 – (£40 + £20)).

If, therefore, 100 units of sales are lost, £4,000 (that is, 100 × £40) of contributions, and therefore profit, are forgone. This would be an alternative means of finding the sales volume variance, instead of taking the difference between the original and flexed budget profit figures; nevertheless once we have produced the flexed budget, it is generally easier simply to compare the two profit figures.

The difference between the original and flexed budget profit figures is called the *sales volume variance*.

Sales volume variance
The difference between the profit as shown in the original budget and the profit as shown in the flexed budget for the period.

Baxter Ltd's sales volume variance for May is an adverse variance because, taken alone, it has the effect of making the actual profit lower than that which was budgeted. A variance that has the effect of increasing profit above that which is budgeted is known as a favourable variance. We can therefore say that a variance is the effect of that factor (taken alone) on the budgeted profit. When looking at some particular aspect, such as sales volume, we assume that all other factors went according to plan. This is shown in Figure 9.6.

Figure 9.6 Relationship between the budgeted and actual profit

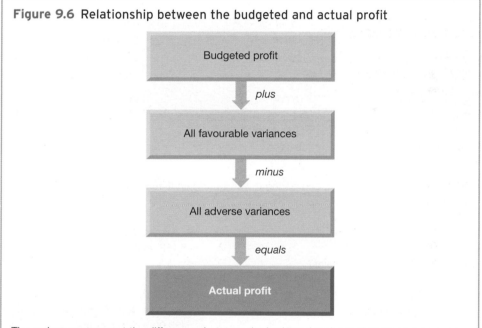

The variances represent the differences between the budgeted and actual profit, and so can be used to reconcile the two profit figures.

Activity 9.11

What else does the senior management of Baxter Ltd need to know about the May sales volume variance?

It needs to know why the volume of sales fell below the budgeted figure. Only by discovering this information will management be in a position to try to see that it does not occur again.

Who should be held accountable for this sales volume variance? The answer would probably be the sales manager. This person should know precisely why the departure from budget has occurred. This is not the same as saying that it was the sales manager's fault. The reason for the problem could easily have been that production was at fault in not having produced the budgeted quantities, meaning that there were not sufficient items to sell. What is not in doubt is that, in the first instance, the sales manager should know the reason for the problem.

The budget and actual figures for Baxter Ltd for June are given in Activity 9.12. They will be used as the basis for a series of activities that you should work through as we look at variance analysis. Note that the business had budgeted for a higher level of output for June than it did for May.

Activity 9.12

	Budget for June	Actual for June
Output (production and sales)	1,100 units	1,150 units
	£	£
Sales revenue	110,000	113,500
Raw materials	(44,000) (44,000 metres)	(46,300) (46,300 metres)
Labour	(22,000) (2,750 hours)	(23,200) (2,960 hours)
Fixed overheads	(20,000)	(19,300)
Operating profit	24,000	24,700

Try flexing the June budget, comparing it with the original June budget, and so find the sales volume variance.

	Flexed budget 1,150 units
Output (production and sales)	
	£
Sales revenue	115,000
Raw materials	(46,000) (46,000 metres)
Labour	(23,000) (2,875 hours)
Fixed overheads	(20,000)
Operating profit	26,000

The sales volume variance is £2,000 (favourable) (that is, £26,000 − £24,000). It is favourable since the original budget profit was lower than the flexed budget profit. This is because more sales were actually made than were budgeted.

Having dealt with the sales volume variance, we have picked up the profit difference caused by any variation between the budgeted and the actual volumes of sales. This means that, for the remainder of the analysis of the difference between the actual and budgeted profits, we can ignore the original budget. We can concentrate exclusively on the differences between the figures in the flexed budget and the actual figures.

Sales price variance

Starting with the sales revenue figure, we can see that for May there is a difference of £2,000 (favourable) between the flexed budget and the actual figures. This can only arise from higher prices being charged than were envisaged in the original budget, because any variance arising from the volume difference has already been 'stripped out' in the flexing process. This price difference is known as the *sales price variance*. Higher sales prices will, all other things being equal, mean more profit. So there is a favourable variance.

Sales price variance
The difference between the actual sales revenue figure for the period and the sales revenue figure as shown in the flexed budget.

Activity 9.13

Using the figures in Activity 9.12, what is the sales price variance for June?

The sales price variance for June is £1,500 (adverse) (that is, £115,000 − £113,500). Actual sales prices, on average, must have been lower than those budgeted. The actual price averaged £98.70 (that is, £113,500/1,150) whereas the budgeted price was £100. Selling output at a lower price than the budgeted one must tend to reduce profit, hence an adverse variance.

We shall now move on to look at the expenses.

Materials variances

In May, there was an overall or *total direct materials variance* of £900 (adverse) (that is, £36,900 − £36,000). It is adverse because the actual material cost was higher than the budgeted one, which has an adverse effect on profit.

Total direct materials variance
The difference between the actual direct materials cost and the direct materials cost according to the flexed budget (budgeted usage for the actual output).

Who should be held accountable for this adverse total direct materials variance? The answer depends on whether the difference arises from excess usage of the raw material, in which case it is the production manager, or whether it is a higher-than-budgeted price a metre being paid, in which case it is the responsibility of the buying manager.

Fortunately, we have the means available to go beyond this total variance. We can see from the figures that there was a 1,000 metre excess usage of the raw material (that is, 37,000 metres − 36,000 metres). All other things being equal, this alone would have led to a profit shortfall of £1,000, since clearly the budgeted price a metre is £1. The £1,000 (adverse) variance is known as the *direct materials usage variance*. Normally, this variance would be the responsibility of the production manager.

Direct materials usage variance
The difference between the actual quantity of direct materials used and the quantity of direct materials according to the flexed budget (budgeted usage for actual output). This quantity is multiplied by the budgeted direct materials cost for one unit of the direct materials.

Activity 9.14

Using the figures in Activity 9.12, what was the direct materials usage variance for June?

The direct materials usage variance for June was £300 (adverse) (that is, (46,300 − 46,000) × £1). It is adverse because more material was used than was budgeted for an output of 1,150 units. Excess usage of material will tend to reduce profit.

The other aspect of direct materials is the *direct materials price variance*. Here we simply take the actual cost of materials used and compare it with the cost that was allowed, given the quantity used. In May the actual cost of direct materials used was £36,900, whereas the allowed cost of the 37,000 metres was £37,000. Thus we have a favourable variance of £100. Paying less than the budgeted price will tend to increase profit, hence a favourable variance.

Direct materials price variance
The difference between the actual cost of the direct material used and the direct materials cost allowed (actual quantity of material used at the budgeted direct material cost).

Activity 9.15

Using the figures in Activity 9.12, what was the direct materials price variance for June?

The direct materials price variance for June was zero (that is, (£46,300 − 46,300) × £1).

As we have just seen, the total direct material variance is the sum of the usage variance and the price variance. This is illustrated in Figure 9.7.

Labour variances

Direct labour variances are similar in form to those for raw materials. The *total direct labour variance* for May was £500 (favourable) (that is, £18,000 − £17,500).

Total direct labour variance
The difference between the actual direct labour cost and the direct labour cost according to the flexed budget (budgeted direct labour hours for the actual output).

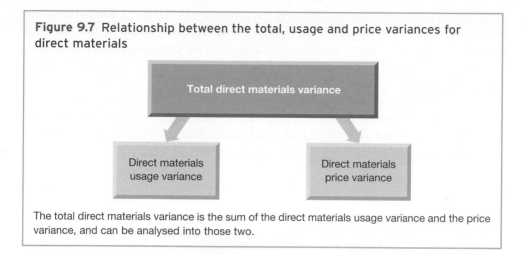

Figure 9.7 Relationship between the total, usage and price variances for direct materials

The total direct materials variance is the sum of the direct materials usage variance and the price variance, and can be analysed into those two.

This variance is favourable because £500 less was spent on labour than was budgeted for the actual level of output achieved. Again, this information is not particularly helpful, and needs to be analysed further, since the responsibility for the rate of pay lies primarily with the personnel manager, whereas the number of hours taken to complete a particular quantity of output is the responsibility of the production manager.

The *direct labour efficiency variance* compares the number of hours that would be allowed for the achieved level of production with the actual number of hours. It then costs this difference at the allowed hourly rate. Thus, for May, it was (2,250 hours − 2,150 hours) × £8 = £800 (favourable). We know that the budgeted hourly rate is £8 because the original budget shows that 2,500 hours were budgeted to cost £20,000. The variance is favourable because fewer hours were used than would have been allowed for the actual level of output. Working more quickly would tend to lead to higher profit.

Direct labour efficiency variance
The difference between the actual direct labour hours worked and the number of direct labour hours according to the flexed budget (budgeted direct labour hours for the actual output). This figure is multiplied by the budgeted direct labour rate for one hour.

Activity 9.16

Using the figures in Activity 9.12, what was the direct labour efficiency variance for June?

The direct labour efficiency variance for June was £680 (adverse) (that is, (2,960 − 2,875) × £8). It is adverse because the work took longer than the budget allowed. This would tend to lead to less profit.

The *direct labour rate variance* compares the actual cost of the hours worked with the allowed cost. For 2,150 hours worked in May, the allowed cost would be £17,200 (that is, 2,150 × £8). So, the direct labour rate variance is £300 (adverse) (that is, £17,500 − £17,200).

> **Direct labour rate variance**
> The difference between the actual cost of the direct labour hours worked and the direct labour cost allowed (actual direct labour hours worked at the budgeted labour rate).

Activity 9.17

Using the figures in Activity 9.12, what was the direct labour rate variance for June?

The direct labour rate variance for June was £480 (favourable) (that is, (2,960 × £8) − 23,200). It is favourable because a lower rate was paid than the budgeted one. Paying a lower wage rate will tend to increase profit.

Fixed overhead variance

The remaining area is that of overheads. In our example, we have assumed that all of the overheads are fixed. Variable overheads certainly exist in practice, but they have been omitted here simply to restrict the amount of detailed coverage. Variances involving variable overheads are similar in style to labour and material variances.

The *fixed overhead spending variance* is simply the difference between the flexed (or original – they will be the same) budget and the actual figures. For May, this was £700 (adverse) (that is, £20,700 − £20,000). It is adverse because more overheads cost was actually incurred than was budgeted. This would tend to lead to less profit. In theory, this is the responsibility of whoever controls overheads expenditure.

> **Fixed overhead spending variance**
> The difference between the actual fixed overhead cost and the fixed overhead cost according to the flexed (and the original) budget.

In practice, this tends to be a very slippery area, and one that is notoriously difficult to control. Of course fixed overheads (and variable ones) are usually made up of more than one type of cost. Typically, they would include such things as rent, administrative costs, salaries of managerial staff, cleaning, electricity and so on. These could be individually budgeted and the actuals recorded. This would enable individual spending variances to be identified for each element of overheads, which in turn would enable managers to identify any problem areas.

Activity 9.18

Using the figures in Activity 9.12, what was the fixed overhead spending variance for June?

The fixed overhead spending variance for June was £700 (favourable) (that is, £20,000 – £19,300). It was favourable because less was spent on overheads than was budgeted, tending to increase profit.

We are now in a position to reconcile the original May budgeted profit with the actual profit, as follows:

	£	£
Budgeted profit		20,000
Add **Favourable variances**		
Sales price	2,000	
Direct materials price	100	
Direct labour efficiency	800	2,900
		22,900
Less **Adverse variances**		
Sales volume	4,000	
Direct materials usage	1,000	
Direct labour rate	300	
Fixed overhead spending	700	6,000
Actual profit		16,900

Activity 9.19

Using the figures in Activity 9.12, try reconciling the original profit figure for June with the actual June figure.

	£	£
Budgeted profit		24,000
Add **Favourable variances**		
Sales volume	2,000	
Direct labour rate	480	
Fixed overhead spending	700	
		3,180
		27,180
Less **Adverse variances**		
Sales price	1,500	
Direct materials usage	300	
Direct labour efficiency	680	
		2,480
Actual profit		24,700

Activity 9.20

The following are the budgeted and actual income statements for Baxter Ltd for the month of July:

	Budget 1,000 units	Actual 1,050 units
Output (production and sales)		
	£	£
Sales revenue	100,000	104,300
Raw materials	(40,000) (40,000 metres)	(41,200) (40,500 metres)
Labour	(20,000) (2,500 hours)	(21,300) (2,600 hours)
Fixed overheads	(20,000)	(19,400)
Operating profit	20,000	22,400

Produce a reconciliation of the budgeted and actual operating profit, going into as much detail as possible with the variance analysis.

The original budget, the flexed budget and the actual are as follows:

	Original budget 1,000 units	Flexed budget 1,050 units	Actual 1,050 units
Output (production and sales)			
	£	£	£
Sales revenue	100,000	105,000	104,300
Raw materials	(40,000)	(42,000) (42,000 m)	(41,200) (40,500 m)
Labour	(20,000)	(21,000) (2,625 hrs)	(21,300) (2,600 hrs)
Fixed overheads	(20,000)	(20,000)	(19,400)
Operating profit	20,000	22,000	22,400

Reconciliation of the budgeted and actual operating profits for July

	£	£
Budgeted profit		20,000
Add **Favourable variances:**		
Sales volume (22,000 – 20,000)	2,000	
Direct materials usage [(42,000 – 40,500) × £1]	1,500	
Direct labour efficiency [(2,625 – 2,600) × £8]	200	
Fixed overhead spending (20,000 – 19,400)	600	4,300
		24,300
Less **Adverse variances:**		
Sales price (105,000 – 104,300)	700	
Direct materials price [(40,500 × £1) – 41,200]	700	
Direct labour rate [(2,600 × £8) – 21,300]	500	1,900
Actual profit		22,400

→ Real World 9.4 gives some indication of the extent of use of variance analysis in practice.

Accounting for control in practice

A 1993 survey of UK manufacturing businesses showed variance analysis to be very widely used: 76 per cent of all the survey respondents used it, with 83 per cent of larger businesses using it. Interestingly, 11 per cent of businesses had abandoned using variance analysis during the 10 years preceding the date of the survey. Does this imply that there is a significant shift away from its use?

The variances that are widely used, and regarded as important, are those that we have looked at in some detail in this chapter.

Though this survey was conducted some time ago, it represents the most recent such survey and is worth noting.

Source: Taken from information appearing in Drury, Braund, Osborne and Tayles (see References section at the end of the chapter)

Standard quantities and costs

We have already seen that a budget is a business plan for the short term – typically one year – and it is likely to be expressed mainly in financial terms. It is built up from standards. Standard quantities and costs (or revenues) are those planned for individual units of input or output. Thus standards are the building blocks of the budget.

We can say about Baxter Ltd's operations that:

- the standard selling price is £100 for one unit of output;
- the standard raw materials cost is £40 for one unit of output;
- the standard raw materials usage is 40 metres for one unit of output;
- the standard raw materials price is £1 a metre (that is, for one unit of input);
- the standard labour cost is £20 for one unit of output;
- the standard labour time is 2.50 hours for one unit of output;
- the standard labour rate is £8 an hour (that is, for one unit of input).

The standards, like the budgets to which they are linked, represent targets and, therefore, yardsticks by which actual performance is measured. They are derived from experience and judgements of what is a reasonable quantity of input (for labour time and materials usage) and from assessments of the market for the product (standard selling price) and the market for the inputs (labour rate and material price). These should be subject to frequent review and, where necessary, revision. It is vital, if they are to be used as part of the control process, that they represent realistic targets.

Calculation of most variances is, in effect, based on standards. For example, the material usage variance is the difference between the standard materials usage for the level of output and the actual usage, costed at the standard materials price.

Standards can have uses other than in the context of budgetary control. Standards provide the business with a database of costs, usages, selling prices and so on. These values should be broadly realistic. They are constantly being compared with actual outcomes in the monthly variance analyses and, presumably, revised where they are seen to be unrealistic. This provides managers with a ready set of information for their decision making and income measurement purposes.

Reasons for adverse variances

A constant possible reason why variances occur is that the standards against which performance is being measured are not reasonable targets. This is certainly not to say that the immediate reaction to an adverse variance should be that the standard is unreasonably harsh. On the other hand, standards that are not achievable are useless.

Activity 9.21

The variances that we have considered are:

- sales volume;
- sales price;
- direct materials usage;
- direct materials price;
- direct labour efficiency;
- direct labour rate;
- fixed overhead spending.

Ignoring the possibility that standards may be unreasonable, jot down any ideas that occur to you as possible practical reasons for adverse variances in each case.

The reasons that we thought of included the following:

Sales volume
- Poor performance by sales personnel.
- Deterioration in market conditions between the setting of the budget and the actual event.
- Lack of inventories or services to sell as a result of some production problem.

Sales price
- Poor performance by sales personnel.
- Deterioration in market conditions between the setting of the budget and the actual event.

Direct materials usage
- Poor performance by production department staff, leading to high rates of scrap.
- Substandard materials, leading to high rates of scrap.
- Faulty machinery, causing high rates of scrap.

Direct materials price
- Poor performance by the buying department staff.
- Change in market conditions between setting the standard and the actual event.

Labour efficiency
- Poor supervision.
- A low skill grade of worker taking longer to do the work than was envisaged for the correct skill grade.

- Low-grade materials, leading to high levels of scrap and wasted labour time.
- Problems with a customer for whom a service is being rendered.
- Problems with machinery, leading to labour time being wasted.
- Dislocation of materials supply, leading to workers being unable to proceed with production.

Labour rate
- Poor performance by the personnel function.
- Using a higher grade of worker than was planned.
- Change in labour market conditions between setting the standard and the actual event.

Fixed overheads
- Poor supervision of overheads.
- General increase in costs of overheads not taken into account in the budget.

Though we have tended to use the example of a manufacturing business to explain variance analysis, this should not be taken to imply that variance analysis is not equally applicable and useful in service sector businesses. It is simply that manufacturing businesses tend to have all of the variances found in practice. Service businesses, for example, may not have material variances.

Investigating variances

It is unreasonable to expect budget targets to be met precisely each month and so variances will usually occur. Whatever the reason for a variance, finding that reason will take time, and time is costly. Small variances are almost inevitable, yet investigating variances can be expensive. Management needs, therefore, to establish a policy concerning which variances to investigate and which to accept. For example, for Baxter Ltd (Example 9.3 on p. 300) the budgeted usage of materials during May was 40,000 metres at a cost of £1 a metre. Suppose that production had been the same as the budgeted quantity of output, but that 40,005 metres of material, costing £1 a metre, had actually been used. Would this adverse variance of £5 be investigated? Probably not. What, though, if the variance were £50 or £500 or £5,000?

Activity 9.22

What broad approach do you feel should be taken as to whether to spend money investigating a particular variance?

The general approach to this policy must be concerned with cost and benefit. The benefit likely to be gained from knowing why a variance arose needs to be balanced against the cost of obtaining that knowledge. The issue of balancing the benefit of having information with the cost of having it was discussed in Chapter 1.

Unfortunately, as is often the case in practice, both the cost of investigation and the value of the benefit are difficult to assess in advance of the investigation.

Knowing the reason for a variance can have a value only when it might provide management with the means to bring things back under control, enabling future targets to be met. It should be borne in mind here that variances will normally be either zero, or very close to zero. This is to say that achieving targets, give or take small variances, should be normal.

Broadly, we suggest that the following approach seems sensible:

- Significant *adverse* variances should be investigated because the continuation of the fault that they represent could be very costly. Management must decide what 'significant' means. A certain amount of science, in the form of statistical models, can be brought to bear in making this decision. Ultimately, however, it must be a matter of managerial judgement as to what is significant. Perhaps a variance of 5 per cent from the budgeted figure would be deemed to be significant.
- Significant *favourable* variances should probably be investigated as well as those that are unfavourable. Though such variances would not cause such immediate management concern as adverse ones, they still represent things not going according to plan. If actual performance is significantly better than target, it may well mean that the target is unrealistically low.
- Insignificant variances, though not triggering immediate investigation, should be kept under review. For each aspect of operations, the cumulative sum of variances, over a series of control periods, should be zero, with small adverse variances in some periods being compensated for by small favourable ones in others. This should be the case with variances that are caused by chance factors, which will not necessarily repeat themselves.

Where a variance is caused by a more systematic factor, which will repeat itself, the cumulative sum of the periodic variances will not be zero but an increasing figure. Where the increasing figure represents a set of adverse variances it may well be worth investigating the situation, even though the individual variances may be insignificant. Even where the direction of the cumulative total points to favourable variances, investigation may still be considered to be valuable.

Real World 9.5 is taken from the research of Drury, Braund, Osborne and Tayles, which was mentioned in Chapter 8. The table shows the methods used by respondents to the survey to make the decision on whether to investigate a particular variance.

Methods used to make decisions on investigation of variances

	% 'Often' or 'Always'
Decisions based on managerial judgement	75
Variance exceeds a specific monetary amount	41
Variance exceeds a given percentage of standard	36
Statistical models	3

Source: Reproduced from Table 5.7 on p. 39 of Drury, Braund, Osbourne and Tayles (see References section at the end of the chapter). Copyright © The Association of Chartered Certified Accountants.

It is interesting to note the large extent, revealed by this survey, to which decisions on whether to investigate variances are made on the basis of some, presumably subjective, judgement rather than using a more systematic approach. The survey is not very recent, but it probably provides some helpful insights to current practice.

Compensating variances

There is superficial appeal in the idea of compensating variances. This is trading off linked favourable and adverse variances against each other, without further consideration. For example, a sales manager believes that she could sell more of a particular service if prices were lowered, and that this would feed through to increased net operating profit. This would lead to a favourable sales volume variance, but also to an adverse sales price variance. On the face of it, provided that the former is greater than the latter, all would be well.

Activity 9.23

What possible reason is there why the sales manager mentioned above should not go ahead with the price reduction?

The change in policy will have ramifications for other areas of the business, including the following:

- The need for more provision of the service to be available to sell. Staff and other factors might not be able to supply this increase.
- Increased sales would involve an increased need for finance to pay for increased activity, for example to pay additional staff costs.

Thus 'trading off' variances is not automatically acceptable, without a more far-reaching consultation and revision of plans.

Making budgetary control effective

It is obvious from what we have seen of budgetary control that, if it is to be successful, a system, or a set of routines, must be established to enable the potential benefits to be gained. Most businesses that operate successful budgetary control systems tend to share some common factors. These include the following:

- A serious attitude taken to the system by all levels of management, right from the very top. For example, senior managers need to make clear to junior managers that they take notice of the monthly variance reports and base some of their actions on them.
- Clear demarcation between areas of managerial responsibility so that accountability can more easily be ascribed for any area that seems to be going out of control. It needs to be clear which manager is responsible for each aspect of the business.
- Budget targets being reasonable, so that they represent a rigorous yet achievable target. This may be promoted by managers being involved in setting their own targets. It is argued that this can increase the managers' commitment and motivation. We shall consider this in more detail shortly.
- Established data collection, analysis and dissemination routines, which take the actual results and the budget figures, and calculate and report the variances. This should be part of the business's regular accounting information system, so that the required reports are automatically produced each month.
- Reports aimed at individual managers, rather than general-purpose documents. This avoids managers having to wade through reams of reports to find the part that is relevant to them.
- Fairly short reporting periods, typically a month, so that things cannot go too far wrong before they are picked up.
- Variance reports being produced and made available to managers shortly after the end of the relevant reporting period. If it is not until the end of June that a manager is informed that the performance in May was below the budgeted level, it is quite likely that the performance for June will be below target as well. Reports on the performance in May ideally need to emerge in early June.
- Action being taken to get operations back under control if they are shown to be out of control. The report will not change things by itself. Managers need to take action to try to ensure that the reporting of significant adverse variances leads to action to put things right for the future.

Limitations of the traditional approach to control through variances and standards

Budgetary control, of the type that we have reviewed in this chapter, has obvious appeal and, judging by the wide extent of its use in practice, it has value as well. It is somewhat limited at times, however. Some of its limitations are as follows:

- Vast areas of most business and commercial activities simply do not have the same direct relationship between inputs and outputs as is the case with, say, level of output and the number of direct labour hours worked. Many of the expenses of a modern business are in areas such as training and advertising, where the expense is discretionary and not linked to the level of output in a direct way.
- Standards can quickly become out of date as a result of both technological change and price changes. This does not pose insuperable problems, but it does require that the potential problem be systematically addressed. Standards that are unrealistic are, at best, useless. At worst, they could have adverse effects on performance. A personnel manager who knows that it is impossible to meet targets on rates of pay for labour, because of general labour cost rises, may have a reduced incentive to minimise costs.
- Sometimes factors that are outside the control of the manager concerned can affect the calculation of the variance for which that manager is held accountable. This may have an adverse effect on the assessment of the manager's performance. The situation can often be overcome by a more considered approach to the calculation of the variance, resulting in those factors controllable by the manager being separated from those that are not.
- In practice, creating clear lines of demarcation between the areas of responsibility of various managers may be difficult. Thus, one of the prerequisites of good budgetary control is lost.

Behavioural aspects of budgetary control

Budgets, perhaps more than any other accounting statement, are prepared with the objective of affecting the attitudes and behaviour of managers. The point was made earlier in the chapter that budgets are intended to motivate managers, and research evidence generally shows this to be true. More specifically, the research shows:

- The existence of budgets generally tends to improve performance.
- Demanding, yet achievable, budget targets tend to motivate better than less demanding targets. It seems that setting the most demanding targets that will be accepted by managers is a very effective way to motivate them.
- Unrealistically demanding targets tend to have an adverse effect on managers' performance.
- The participation of managers in setting their targets tends to improve motivation and performance. This is probably because those managers feel a sense of commitment to the targets and a moral obligation to achieve them.

It has been suggested that allowing managers to set their own targets will lead to slack (that is, easily achievable targets) being introduced. This would make achievement of the target that much easier. On the other hand, in an effort to impress, a manager may select a target that is not really achievable. These points imply that care must be taken in the extent to which managers have unfettered choice of their own targets.

Evidence tends to suggest that where managers work in an environment in which they are expected to meet the targets represented in the budget, they will, almost irrespective of other factors, try to introduce slack into the budget. Where there is a more relaxed attitude, or other factors (for example, staff morale) are considered alongside the analysis of variances, managers are less inclined to seek to build in slack.

If a manager fails to meet a budget, care must be taken by that manager's senior in dealing with the failure. A harsh, critical approach may demotivate the manager. Adverse variances may imply that the manager needs help from the senior.

The existence of budgets gives senior managers a ready means to assess the performance of their subordinates. Where promotion or bonuses depend on the absence of variances, senior management must be very cautious.

? Self-assessment question 9.2

Toscanini Ltd makes a standard product, which is budgeted to sell at £4.00 a unit, in a competitive market. It is made by taking a budgeted 0.4 kg of material, budgeted to cost £2.40/kg, and working on it by hand by an employee, paid a budgeted £8.00/hour, for a budgeted 6 minutes. Monthly fixed overheads are budgeted at £4,800. The output for May was budgeted at 4,000 units.

The actual results for May were as follows:

	£
Sales revenue (3,500 units)	13,820
Materials (1,425 kg)	(3,420)
Labour (345 hours)	(2,690)
Fixed overheads	(4,900)
Actual operating profit	2,810

No inventories of any description existed at the beginning and end of the month.

Required:
(a) Deduce the budgeted profit for May, and reconcile it with the actual profit, through variances, in as much detail as the information provided will allow.
(b) State which manager should be held accountable, in the first instance, for each variance calculated.
(c) Assuming that the standards were all well set in terms of labour times and rates and material usage and price, suggest at least one feasible reason for each of the variances that you identified in (a), given what you know about the business's performance for May.
(d) If it were discovered that the actual total world market demand for the business's product was 10 per cent lower than estimated when the May budget was set, state how and why the variances that you identified in (a) could be revised to provide information that would be potentially more useful.

Summary

The main points of this chapter may be summarised as follows:

Budget = a short-term business plan, mainly expressed in financial terms.

- Budgets are the short-term means of working towards the business's objectives.
- Usually for 12 months with subperiods of a month.
- Uses are to:
  1 promote forward thinking;
  2 help co-ordinate the various aspects;
  3 motivate performance;
  4 provide the basis of a system of control;
  5 provide a system for authorisation.

Preparing budgets:

- There is no standard style – practicality and usefulness are the key issues.
- They are usually prepared in columnar form, with a column for each month (or similarly short period).
- Each budget must link (co-ordinate) with others.

Controlling through budgets:

- Flexing the budget to match actual volume of output.
- Variance = increase (favourable) or decrease (adverse) in profit, relative to the budgeted profit, as a result of some aspect of the business's activities taken alone.
- Budgeted profit plus all favourable variances less all adverse variances equals actual profit.
- Commonly calculated variances:
  - sales volume variance = difference between budgeted and actual volume (in units) multiplied by the contribution per unit;
  - sales price variance = difference between actual sales revenue and actual volume at the budgeted sales price per unit;
  - direct materials usage variance = difference between actual usage and budgeted usage, for the actual volume of output, multiplied by the budgeted material cost per unit of material;
  - direct material price variance = difference between the actual material cost and the actual usage multiplied by the budgeted cost per unit of material;
  - direct labour efficiency variance = difference between actual labour time and budgeted time, for the actual volume of output, multiplied by the budgeted labour rate;
  - direct labour rate variance = difference between the actual labour cost and the actual labour time multiplied by the budgeted labour rate;
  - fixed overhead spending variance = difference between the actual and budgeted spending on fixed overheads.

- Standards = budgeted physical quantities and financial values for one unit of inputs and outputs.

- Standards are useful in providing data for decision making.

- Significant and/or persistent variances need to be investigated to establish their cause.

- Good budgetary control requires establishing systems and routines to ensure such things as clear distinction between individual managers' areas of responsibility, prompt, frequent and relevant variance reporting and senior management commitment.

- Not all activities can usefully be controlled through traditional variance analysis.

- There is a behavioural aspect of control, which should be taken into account by senior managers.

→ **Key terms**

budgets p. 281
limiting factor p. 283
master budgets p. 284
control p. 287
management by exception p. 287
flexible budgets p. 300
flexing the budget p. 301

adverse variance p. 303
favourable variance p. 303
variance analysis p. 310
standard quantities and costs p. 311
investigating variances p. 313
compensating variances p. 315
budgetary control p. 316

Further reading

If you would like to explore the topics covered in this chapter in more depth, we recommend the following books:

Atkinson, R., Kaplan, R. and Young, S.M. *Management Accounting*, 4th edn, Prentice Hall, 2004, Chapter 10.

Drury, C. *Management and Cost Accounting*, 6th edn, Thomson Learning, 2004, Chapters 15, 16, 18 and 19.

Horngren, C., Datar, S. and Foster, G. *Cost Accounting: A Managerial Emphasis*, 12th edn, Prentice Hall International, 2005, Chapters 6–8.

Upchurch, A. *Management Accounting: Principles and Practice*, Financial Times/Pitman Publishing, 1998, Chapters 12–14.

References

Chittenden, F., Poutziouris, P. and Michaelis, N. *Financial Management and Working Capital Practices in UK SMEs*, Manchester Business School, 1998.

Drury, C., Braund, S., Osborne, P. and Tayles, M. *A Survey of Management Accounting Practices in UK Manufacturing Companies*, Chartered Association of Certified Accountants, 1993.

Ernst and Young *2003 Survey of Management Accounting*, Ernst and Young, 2003.

? Review questions

Answers to these questions can be found at the back of the book (pp. 494–5).

9.1 Define a *budget*. How is a budget different from a forecast?

9.2 What were the five uses of budgets that were identified in the chapter?

9.3 What is meant by a *variance*? What approaches might be used to decide whether a variance should be investigated?

9.4 What is the point in flexing the budget in the context of variance analysis? Does flexing imply that differences between budget and actual in the volume of output are ignored in variance analysis?

✷ Exercises

Exercises 9.3 to 9.5 are more advanced than Exercises 9.1 and 9.2. Those with a coloured number have an answer at the back of the book (pp. 515–17).

> If you wish to try more exercises, visit the students' side of the companion website.

9.1 You have overheard the following statements:

(a) 'A budget is a forecast of what is expected to happen in a business during the next year.'
(b) 'Budgets must be prepared with a column for each month so that you can see the whole year at a glance, month by month.'
(c) 'Budgets are OK but they stifle all initiative. No manager worth employing would work for a business which seeks to control through budgets.'
(d) 'Any sensible person would start with the sales budget and build up the other budgets from there.'

Required:
Critically discuss these statements, explaining any technical terms.

9.2 Daniel Chu Ltd, a new business, will start production on 1 April, but sales will not commence until 1 May. Planned sales for the next nine months are as follows:

→

	Sales units
May	500
June	600
July	700
August	800
September	900
October	900
November	900
December	800
January	700

The unit selling price will be a consistent £100 and all sales will be made on one month's credit. It is planned that sufficient finished goods inventories for each month's sales should be available at the end of the previous month.

Raw material purchases will be such that there will be sufficient raw materials inventories available at the end of each month to meet the following month's planned production precisely. This planned policy will operate from the end of April. Purchases of raw materials will be on one month's credit. The cost of raw material is £40 a unit of finished product.

The direct labour cost, which is variable with the level of production, is planned to be £20 a unit of finished production. Production overheads are planned to be £20,000 each month, including £3,000 for depreciation. Non-production overheads are planned to be £11,000 a month, of which £1,000 will be depreciation. Various non-current (fixed) assets costing £250,000 will be bought and paid for during April.

Except where specified otherwise, assume that all payments take place in the same month as the cost is incurred.

The business will raise £300,000 in cash from a share issue in April.

Required:
For the six months ending 30 September, draw up:

(a) a finished inventories budget, showing just physical quantities;
(b) a raw materials inventories budget, showing both physical quantities and financial values;
(c) a trade payables budget;
(d) a trade receivables budget;
(e) a cash budget.

9.3 Pilot Ltd makes a standard product, which is budgeted to sell at £5.00 a unit. It is made by taking a budgeted 0.5 kg of material, budgeted to cost £3.00 a kilogram, and working on it by hand by an employee, paid a budgeted £5.00 an hour, for a budgeted 15 minutes. Monthly fixed overheads are budgeted at £6,000. The output for March was budgeted at 5,000 units.

The actual results for March were as follows:

	£
Sales revenue (5,400 units)	26,460
Materials (2,830 kg)	(8,770)
Labour (1,300 hours)	(6,885)
Fixed overheads	(6,350)
Actual operating profit	4,455

No inventories existed at the start or end of March.

Required:

(a) Deduce the budgeted profit for March and reconcile it with the actual profit in as much detail as the information provided will allow.

(b) State which manager should be held accountable, in the first instance, for each variance calculated.

9.4 Lewisham Ltd manufactures one product line – the Zenith. Sales of Zeniths over the next few months are planned as follows:

1 Demand

	units
	units
July	180,000
August	240,000
September	200,000
October	180,000

Each Zenith sells for £3.

2 **Debtor receipts**

Credit customers (receivables) are expected to pay as follows:

70% during the month of sale
28% during the following month

The remainder of the credit customers are expected to go bad (that is, to be uncollectable).

Credit customers who pay in the month of sale are entitled to deduct a 2 per cent discount from the invoice price.

3 **Finished goods inventories**

Inventories of finished goods are expected to be 40,000 units at 1 July. The business's policy is that, in future, the inventories at the end of each month should equal 20 per cent of the following month's planned sales requirements.

4 **Raw materials inventories**

Inventories of raw materials is expected to be 40,000 kg on 1 July. The business's policy is that, in future, the inventories at the end of each month should equal 50 per cent of the following month's planned production requirements. Each Zenith requires 0.5 kg of the raw material, which costs £1.50 per kg.

Raw materials are paid for in the month after purchase.

5 **Labour and overheads**

The direct labour cost of each Zenith is £0.50. The variable overhead element of each Zenith is £0.30. Fixed overheads, including depreciation of £25,000, total £47,000 a month.

All labour and overheads are paid during the month in which they arise.

6 **Cash in hand**

The business plans to have a bank balance (in funds) at 1 August of £20,000.

Required:
Prepare the following budgets:

→

(a) Finished inventories budget (expressed in units of Zenith) for each of the three months July, August and September.

(b) Raw materials inventories budget (expressed in kg of the raw material) for the two months July and August.

(c) Cash budget for August and September.

9.5 Bradley-Allen Ltd makes one standard product. Its budgeted operating statement for May is as follows:

		£	£
Sales revenue:	(800 units)		64,000
Direct materials:	Type A	12,000	
	Type B	16,000	
Direct labour:	Skilled	4,000	
	Unskilled	10,000	
Overheads:	(All Fixed)	12,000	
			54,000
Budgeted operating profit			10,000

The standard costs were as follows:

- Direct materials: Type A   £50/kg
  -    Type B   £20/m
- Direct labour: Skilled   £10/hour
  -    Unskilled   £8/hour

During May, the following occurred:

1. 950 units were sold for a total of £73,000.
2. 310 kilos (costing £15,200) of type A material were used in production.
3. 920 metres (costing £18,900) of type B material were used in production.
4. Skilled workers were paid £4,628 for 445 hours.
5. Unskilled workers were paid £11,275 for 1,375 hours.
6. Fixed overheads cost £11,960.

There were no inventories of finished production or of work in progress at either the beginning or end of May.

Required:

(a) Prepare a statement that reconciles the budgeted to the actual profit of the business for May, through variances. Your statement should analyse the difference between the two profit figures in as much detail as you are able.

(b) Explain how the statement in (a) might be helpful to managers.

Part 3

FINANCIAL MANAGEMENT

Chapter 10

Making capital investment decisions

Introduction

In this chapter we shall look at how businesses can make decisions involving investments in new plant, machinery, buildings and similar long-term assets. Though we shall be considering this topic in the context of businesses making decisions about the type of assets that were just mentioned, the general principles can equally well be applied to investments in the shares of businesses, irrespective of whether the investment is being considered by a business or by a private individual. This chapter is the first of the three that deal with the area generally known as *business finance* or *financial management*.

Learning outcomes

When you have completed this chapter, you should be able to:

- explain the nature and importance of investment decision making;
- identify the four main investment appraisal methods used in practice;
- use each method to reach a decision on a particular practical investment opportunity;
- discuss the attributes of each of the methods.

The nature of investment decisions

The essential feature of investment decisions is *time*. Investment involves making an outlay of something of economic value, usually cash, at one point in time, which is expected to yield economic benefits to the investor at some other point in time. Usually, the outlay precedes the benefits. Also, the outlay is typically one large amount and the benefits arrive as a series of smaller amounts over a fairly protracted period.

Investment decisions tend to be of crucial importance to the business because:

- *Large amounts of resources are often involved.* Many investments made by businesses involve laying out a significant proportion of their total resources (see Real World 10.2). If mistakes are made with the decision, the effects on the businesses could be significant, if not catastrophic.
- *It is often difficult and/or expensive to 'bail out' of an investment once it has been undertaken.* It is often the case that investments made by a business are specific to its needs. For example, a hotel business may invest in a new, purposely-designed hotel complex. The specialist nature of this complex will probably lead to it having a rather limited second-hand value to another potential user with different needs. If the business found, after having made the investment, that room occupancy rates were not as buoyant as was planned, the only possible course of action might be to close down and sell the complex. This would probably mean that much less could be recouped from the investment than it had originally cost, particularly if the costs of design are included as part of the cost, as they logically should be.

Real World 10.1 gives an illustration of a major investment by a well-known business operating in the UK.

Brittany Ferries launches an investment

In the Spring of 2004, Brittany Ferries, the cross English channel ferry operator, launched a new ship. The ship had cost the business about £100 million. Though Brittany Ferries is a substantial business, this level of expenditure is significant. Clearly, the business believes that acquisition of the new ship will be profitable for it, but how would it have reached this conclusion? Presumably the anticipated future cash flows from passengers and freight operators will have been major inputs to the decision. The ship was specifically designed for Brittany Ferries, so it would be difficult for the business to recoup a large proportion of its £100 million, should these projected cash flows not materialise.

Source: Publicity material published by Brittany Ferries

The issues raised by Brittany Ferries investment will be the main subject of this chapter.

Real World 10.2 indicates the level of annual investment for a number of randomly selected, well-known UK businesses. It can be seen that the scale of investment varies

The scale of investment by UK businesses

Business	Expenditure on additional non-current (fixed) assets as a percentage of:	
	Annual sales	Start of year non-current assets
J D Wetherspoon plc	9.5	9.6
Astra-Zeneca plc	8.7	17.3
Bristol Water plc	23.2	15.2
Royal Dutch/Shell Group	6.1	11.7
Chloride plc	5.5	15.2
Yates Group plc	9.6	6.2
United Utilities	49.4	14.1
Tesco plc	7.3	15.9
J. Sainsbury plc	5.7	12.5

Source: Annual reports of the businesses concerned for the accounting years ending in 2003 or 2004

from one business to another. (It also tends to vary from one year to the next for a particular business.) In nearly all of these businesses the scale of investment is very significant.

Real World 10.2 is limited to considering the non-current (fixed) asset investment, but most non-current asset investment also requires a level of current asset investment to support it (additional inventories (stock), for example), meaning that the real scale of investment is even greater than indicated above.

Activity 10.1

When managers are making decisions involving capital investments, what should the decision seek to achieve?

Investment decisions must be consistent with the objectives of the particular business. For a private-sector business, maximising the wealth of the shareholders is usually assumed to be the key objective.

Methods of investment appraisal

Given the importance of investment decisions to investors, it is essential that proper screening of investment proposals takes place. An important part of this screening process is to ensure that the business uses appropriate methods of evaluation.

Research shows that there are basically four methods used in practice by businesses throughout the world to evaluate investment opportunities.

They are:

- accounting rate of return (ARR);
- payback period (PP);
- net present value (NPV);
- internal rate of return (IRR).

It is possible to find businesses that use variants of these four methods. It is also possible to find businesses, particularly smaller ones, that do not use any formal appraisal method, but rely more on the 'gut feeling' of their managers. Most businesses, however, seem to use one (or more) of these four methods.

We are going to assess the effectiveness of each of these methods and we shall see that only one of them (NPV) is not flawed to some extent. We shall also see how popular these four methods seem to be in practice.

To help us to examine each of the methods, it might be useful to consider how each of them would cope with a particular investment opportunity. Let us consider the following example.

Example 10.1

Billingsgate Battery Company has carried out some research that shows that the business could provide a standard service that it has recently developed.

Provision of the service would require investment in a machine that would cost £100,000, payable immediately. Sales of the service would take place throughout the next five years. At the end of that time, it is estimated that the machine could be sold for £20,000.

Sales of the service would be expected to occur as follows:

	Number of units
Next year	5,000
Second year	10,000
Third year	15,000
Fourth year	15,000
Fifth year	5,000

It is estimated that the new service can be sold for £12 a unit, and that the relevant (variable) costs will total £8 a unit.

To simplify matters, we shall assume that the cash from sales and for the costs of providing the service are paid and received, respectively, at the end of each year. (This is clearly unlikely to be true in real life. Money will have to be paid to employees (for salaries and wages) on a weekly or a monthly basis. Customers will pay within a month or two of buying the service. On the other hand, making the assumption probably does not lead to a serious distortion. It is a simplifying assumption that is often made in real life, and it will make things more straightforward for us now. We should be clear, however, that there is nothing about any of the four approaches that *demands* this assumption being made.)

Bearing in mind that each unit of the service sold will give rise to a net cash inflow of £4 (that is, £12 – £8), the total net cash flows (receipts less payments) for each year will be as follows:

Time		£000
Immediately	Cost of machine	(100)
1 year's time	Net profit before depreciation (£4 × 5,000)	20
2 years' time	Net profit before depreciation (£4 × 10,000)	40
3 years' time	Net profit before depreciation (£4 × 15,000)	60
4 years' time	Net profit before depreciation (£4 × 15,000)	60
5 years' time	Net profit before depreciation (£4 × 5,000)	20
5 years' time	Disposal proceeds from the machine	20

Note that, broadly speaking, the net profit before deducting depreciation (that is, before non-cash items) equals the net amount of cash flowing into the business. Apart from depreciation, all of this business's expenses cause cash to flow out of the business. Sales revenues lead to cash flowing in.

Having set up the example, we shall now go on to consider how each of the appraisal methods works.

Accounting rate of return (ARR)

The accounting rate of return (ARR) method takes the average accounting profit that the investment will generate and expresses it as a percentage of the average investment made over the life of the project.

Thus:

$$\text{ARR} = \frac{\text{Average annual profit}}{\text{Average investment to earn that profit}} \times 100\%$$

We can see that to calculate the ARR we need to deduce two pieces of information:

- the annual average profit;
- the average investment for the particular project.

In our example, the average annual profit *before depreciation* over the five years is £40,000 [that is, £000(20 + 40 + 60 + 60 + 20)/5]. Assuming 'straight-line' depreciation (that is, equal annual amounts), the annual depreciation charge will be £16,000 [that is, £(100,000 – 20,000)/5]. Thus the average annual profit *after depreciation* is £24,000 (that is, £40,000 – £16,000).

The average investment over the five years can be calculated as follows:

$$\text{Average investment} = \frac{\text{Cost of machine} + \text{Disposal value}}{2}$$

$$= \frac{£100{,}000 + £20{,}000}{2}$$

$$= £60{,}000$$

Thus, the ARR of the investment is:

$$\text{ARR} = \frac{£24{,}000}{£60{,}000} \times 100\%$$

$$= 40\%$$

Users of ARR should apply the following decision rules:

■ For any project to be acceptable it must achieve a target ARR as a minimum.
■ Where there are competing projects (where the business must choose between more than one project) that all seem capable of exceeding this minimum rate, the one with the higher or highest ARR would normally be selected.

To decide whether the 40 per cent return is acceptable, we need to compare this percentage return with the minimum rate required by the business.

Activity 10.2

Chaotic Industries is considering an investment in a fleet of ten delivery vans to take its products to customers. The vans will cost £15,000 each to buy, payable immediately. The annual running costs are expected to total £20,000 for each van (including the driver's salary). The vans are expected to operate successfully for six years, at the end of which period they will all have to be sold, with disposal proceeds expected to be about £3,000 a van. At present, the business uses a commercial carrier for all of its deliveries. It is expected that this carrier will charge a total of £230,000 each year for the next six years to undertake the deliveries.

What is the ARR of buying the vans? (Note that cost savings are as relevant a benefit from an investment as are net cash inflows.)

The vans will save the business £30,000 a year (that is, £230,000 − (£20,000 × 10)), before depreciation, in total.

Thus, the inflows and outflows will be:

Time		£000
Immediately	Cost of vans (10 × 15)	(150)
1 year's time	Net saving before depreciation	30
2 years' time	Net saving before depreciation	30
3 years' time	Net saving before depreciation	30
4 years' time	Net saving before depreciation	30
5 years' time	Net saving before depreciation	30
6 years' time	Net saving before depreciation	30
6 years' time	Disposal proceeds from the vans (10 × 3)	30

The total annual depreciation expense (assuming a straight-line approach) will be £20,000 (that is, (£150,000 – £30,000)/6). Thus, the average annual saving, after depreciation, is £10,000 (that is, £30,000 – £20,000).

The average investment will be.

$$\text{Average investment} = \frac{£150,000 + £30,000}{2}$$

$$= £90,000$$

Thus, the ARR of the investment is:

$$\text{ARR} = \frac{£10,000}{£90,000} \times 100\% = 11.1\%$$

ARR and ROCE

We should note that ARR and the return on capital employed (ROCE) ratio take the same approach to performance measurement, in that they both relate accounting profit to the cost of the assets invested to generate that profit. We saw in Chapter 6 that ROCE is a popular means of assessing the performance of a business, as a whole, *after* it has performed. ARR is an approach that assesses the potential performance of a particular investment, taking the same approach as ROCE, *before* it has performed.

As we have just seen, managers using ARR will require that any investment undertaken must achieve a target ARR as a minimum. Perhaps the minimum target would be based on the rate that previous investments had actually achieved (as measured by ROCE). Perhaps it would be the industry-average ROCE.

Since private-sector businesses are normally seeking to increase the wealth of their owners, ARR may seem to be a sound method of appraising investment opportunities. Profit can be seen as a net increase in wealth over a period, and relating it to the size of investment made to achieve it seems a logical approach.

ARR is said to have a number of advantages as a method of investment appraisal. It was mentioned earlier that ROCE seems to be a widely used measure of business performance. Shareholders seem to use this ratio to evaluate management performance, and sometimes the financial objective of a business will be expressed in terms of a target ROCE. It therefore seems sensible to use a method of investment appraisal that is consistent with this overall approach to measuring business performance. It also gives the result expressed as a percentage. It seems that some managers feel comfortable with using measures expressed in percentage terms.

Problems with ARR

Activity 10.3

ARR suffers from a very major defect as a means of assessing investment opportunities. Can you reason out what this is? Consider the three competing projects whose cash flows are shown below. All three of these involve investment in a machine that is expected to have no residual value at the end of the five years. Note that all of the projects have the same total net profits over the five years.

		Project		
		A	B	C
Time		£000	£000	£000
Immediately	Cost of machine	(160)	(160)	(160)
1 year's time	Net profit after depreciation	20	10	160
2 years' time	Net profit after depreciation	40	10	10
3 years' time	Net profit after depreciation	60	10	10
4 years' time	Net profit after depreciation	60	10	10
5 years' time	Net profit after depreciation	20	160	10

(*Hint*: The defect is not concerned with the ability of the decision maker to forecast future events, though this too can be a problem. Try to remember what the essential feature of investment decisions was that we identified at the beginning of this chapter.)

The problem with ARR is that it almost completely ignores the time factor. In this example, exactly the same ARR would have been computed for each of the three projects.

Since the same total profit over the five years arises in all three of these projects (that is, £200,000) and the average investment in each project is £80,000 (that is, £160,000/2), this means that each case will give rise to the same ARR of 50 per cent (that is, £40,000/£80,000).

Given a financial objective of increasing the wealth of the owners of the business, any rational decision maker faced with a choice between the three projects, set out in Activity 10.3, would strongly prefer Project C. This is because most of the benefits from the investment arise within 12 months of investing the £160,000 to establish the project. Project A would rank second, and Project B would come a poor third in the rankings. Any appraisal technique that is not capable of distinguishing between these three situations is seriously flawed. We shall look in more detail at the reason for timing being so important later in the chapter.

There are further problems associated with the use of ARR. Example 10.2 illustrates a paradox that may arise when using this method. This paradox results from the approach taken to derive the average investment in a project.

Example 10.2

To illustrate the daft results that ARR can produce, let us assume that we have put forward an investment proposal to our superior based on the following information:

Cost of equipment	£200,000
Estimated residual value of equipment	£40,000
Average annual profit before depreciation	£48,000
Estimated life of project	10 years
Annual straight-line depreciation charge	£16,000 [that is (£200,000 – £40,000)/10]

The ARR of the project will be:

$$ARR = \frac{(48,000 - 16,000)}{[(200,000 + 40,000)/2]} \times 100\% = 26.7\%$$

We are told by our superior, however, that the minimum ARR for investment projects of this nature is 27 per cent. Although we are disappointed, we realise that there is still hope. In fact, all that we have to do is to agree to give away the piece of equipment at the end of its useful life rather than to sell it. The residual value of the equipment will then be zero and the annual depreciation charge will become [(£200,000 – £0)/10] = £20,000 a year. Our revised ARR calculation will then be as follows:

$$ARR = \frac{£(48,000 - 20,000)}{[(200,000 + zero)/2]} \times 100\% = 28\%$$

ARR is based on the use of accounting profit. When measuring performance over the whole life of a project, however, it is cash flows rather than accounting profits that are important. Cash is the ultimate measure of the economic wealth generated by an investment. This is because it is cash that is used to acquire resources and for distribution to shareholders. Accounting profit, on the other hand, is more appropriate for reporting achievement on a periodic basis, as we saw in Chapters 2 and 3. It is a useful measure of productive effort for a relatively short period, such as a year, or half year. Thus, it is really a question of 'horses for courses'. Accounting profit is fine for measuring profit over a short period but cash is the appropriate measure when considering the performance over the life of a project.

The ARR method can also create problems when considering competing investments of different size.

Activity 10.4

Sinclair Wholesalers plc is currently considering opening a new sales outlet in Coventry. Two possible sites have been identified for the new outlet. Site A has a capacity of 30,000 sq. metres. It will require an average investment of £6 million, and will produce an average profit of £600,000 a year. Site B has a capacity of 20,000 sq. metres. It will

→

require an average investment of £4 million, and will produce an average profit of £500,000 a year.

What is the ARR of each investment opportunity? Which site would you select, and why?

The ARR of Site A is £600,000/£6 million = 10 per cent. The ARR of Site B is £500,000/ £4 million = 12.5 per cent. Thus, Site B has the higher ARR. However, in terms of the absolute profit generated, Site A is the more attractive. If the ultimate objective is to maximise the wealth of the shareholders of Sinclair Wholesalers plc, it might be better to choose Site A even though the percentage return is lower. It is the absolute size of the return rather than the relative (percentage) size that is important. This is a general problem of using comparative measures, like percentages, when the objective is measured in absolute ones. If businesses were seeking through their investments to generate a percentage rate of return on investment, ARR would be more helpful. The problem is that most businesses seek to achieve increases in their absolute wealth (measured in pounds, euros, dollars and so on), through their investment decisions.

Real World 10.3 illustrates how using percentage measures can lead to confusion.

Real World 10.3

Increasing road capacity by sleight of hand

During the 1970s, the Mexican government wanted to increase the capacity of a major four-lane road. It came up with the idea of repainting the lane markings so that there were six narrower lanes occupying the same space as four wider ones had previously done. This increased the capacity of the road by 50% (that is 2/4 × 100). A tragic outcome of the narrower lanes was an increase in deaths from road accidents. A year later the Mexican government had the six narrower lanes changed back to the original four wider ones. This reduced the capacity of the road by 33% (that is, 2/6 × 100). The Mexican government reported that it had increased the capacity of the road by 17% (that is 50% − 33%), despite the fact that its real capacity was identical to that which it had been originally. The confusion arose because each of the two percentages (50% and 33%) is based on different bases (four and six).

Source: Gigerenzer (see References section at end of the chapter)

Payback period (PP)

The payback period (PP) is the length of time it takes for an initial investment to be repaid out of the net cash inflows from a project. Since it takes time into account, the PP method seems to go some way to overcoming the timing problem of ARR – or at least at first glance it does.

It might be useful to consider PP in the context of the Billingsgate Battery example. We should recall that essentially the project's costs and benefits can be summarised as:

Time		£000
Immediately	Cost of machine	(100)
1 year's time	Net profit before depreciation	20
2 years' time	Net profit before depreciation	40
3 years' time	Net profit before depreciation	60
4 years' time	Net profit before depreciation	60
5 years' time	Net profit before depreciation	20
5 years' time	Disposal proceeds	20

Note that all of these figures are amounts of cash to be paid or received (we saw earlier that net profit before depreciation is a rough measure of the cash flows from the project).

As the payback period is the length of time it takes for the initial investment to be repaid out of the net cash inflows, it will be three years before the £100,000 outlay is covered by the inflows. This is still assuming that the cash flows occur at year ends. The payback period can be derived by calculating the cumulative cash flows as follows:

Time		Net cash flows £000	Cumulative cash flows £000	
Immediately	Cost of machine	(100)	(100)	
1 year's time	Net profit before depreciation	20	(80)	(−100 + 20)
2 years' time	Net profit before depreciation	40	(40)	(−80 + 40)
3 years' time	Net profit before depreciation	60	20	(−40 + 60)
4 years' time	Net profit before depreciation	60	80	(20 + 60)
5 years' time	Net profit before depreciation	20	100	(80 + 20)
5 years' time	Disposal proceeds	20	120	(100 + 20)

We can see that the cumulative cash flows become positive at the end of the third year. Had we assumed that the cash flows arise evenly over the year, the precise payback period would be:

$$2 \text{ years} + (40/60) = 2^2/_3 \text{ years}$$

where 40 represents the cash flow still required at the beginning of the third year to repay the initial outlay, and 60 is the projected cash flow during the third year. Again we must ask how to decide whether $2^2/_3$ years is acceptable.

The decision rule for using PP is:

- For a project to be acceptable it would need to have a maximum payback period.
- If there were two or more competing projects that both met the maximum payback period requirement, the decision maker should select the project with the shorter payback period.

If, for example, Billingsgate Battery had a maximum payback period of three years, the project would be acceptable. A project with a longer than three-year payback period would not be acceptable.

Activity 10.5

What is the payback period of the Chaotic Industries project from Activity 10.2?

The inflows and outflows are expected to be:

Time		Net cash flows £000	Cumulative net cash flows £000	
Immediately	Cost of vans	(150)	(150)	
1 year's time	Net saving before depreciation	30	(120)	(−150 + 30)
2 years' time	Net saving before depreciation	30	(90)	(−120 + 30)
3 years' time	Net saving before depreciation	30	(60)	(−90 + 30)
4 years' time	Net saving before depreciation	30	(30)	(−60 + 30)
5 years' time	Net saving before depreciation	30	0	(−30 + 30)
6 years' time	Net saving before depreciation	30	30	(0 + 30)
6 years' time	Disposal proceeds from the machine	30	60	(30 + 30)

The payback period here is five years; that is, it is not until the end of the fifth year that the vans will pay for themselves out of the savings that they are expected to generate.

The PP approach has certain advantages. It is quick and easy to calculate, and can be easily understood by managers. The logic of using PP is that projects that can recoup their cost quickly are economically more attractive than those with longer payback periods, that is, it emphasises liquidity. PP is probably an improvement on ARR in respect of the timing of the cash flows. PP is not, however, the whole answer to the problem.

Problems with PP

Activity 10.6

In what respect, is PP not the whole answer as a means of assessing investment opportunities? Consider the cash flows arising from three competing projects:

Time		Project 1 £000	Project 2 £000	Project 3 £000
Immediately	Cost of machine	(200)	(200)	(200)
1 year's time	Net profit before depreciation	40	10	80
2 years' time	Net profit before depreciation	80	20	100
3 years' time	Net profit before depreciation	80	170	20
4 years' time	Net profit before depreciation	60	20	200
5 years' time	Net profit before depreciation	40	10	500
5 years' time	Disposal proceeds	40	10	20

(*Hint*: Again, the defect is not concerned with the ability of the manager to forecast future events. This is a problem, but it is a problem whatever approach we take.)

The PP for each project is three years and so the PP method would regard the projects as being equally acceptable. It cannot distinguish between those projects that pay back a significant amount early in the three-year payback period and those that do not.

In addition, this method ignores cash flows after the payback period. A decision maker concerned with maximising shareholder wealth would prefer Project 3 in the table above because the cash flows come in earlier (most of the cost of the machine has been repaid by the end of the second year) and they are greater in total.

The cumulative cash flows of each project in Activity 10.6 are set out in Figure 10.1.

We can see that the PP method is not concerned with the profitability of projects; it is concerned simply with their payback period. Thus cash flows arising beyond the payback period are ignored. Whilst this neatly avoids the practical problems of forecasting cash flows over a long period, it means that relevant information may be ignored.

You may feel that, by favouring projects with a short payback period, the PP approach does at least provide a means of dealing with the problems of risk and uncertainty. However, this is a fairly crude approach to the problem. It only looks at the risk that the project will end earlier than expected. However, this is only one of many risk areas. What, for example, about the risk that the demand for the product may be less than expected? There are more systematic approaches to dealing with risk that can be used and we shall look at these later in the chapter.

The PP approach takes some note of the timing of the costs and benefits from the project. Its key deficiency, however, is that it is not linked to promoting increases in the wealth of the business. PP will tend to recommend undertaking projects that pay

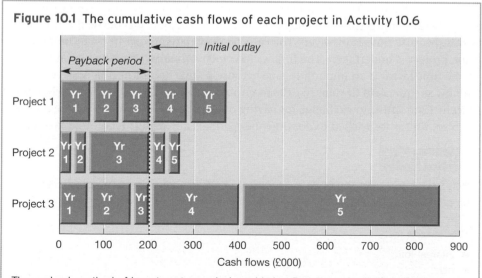

Figure 10.1 The cumulative cash flows of each project in Activity 10.6

The payback method of investment appraisal would view Projects 1, 2 and 3 as being equally attractive. In doing so, the method completely ignores the fact that Project 3 provides the payback cash earlier in the three-year period and goes on to generate large benefits in later years.

for themselves quickly. As we saw earlier, ARR ignores timing to a great extent, but it does take account of all benefits and costs.

Net present value (NPV)

To make sensible investment decisions, we need a method of appraisal that:

- considers *all* of the costs and benefits of each investment opportunity; *and*
- makes a logical allowance for the *timing* of those costs and benefits.

The net present value (NPV) method provides us with this.

Consider the Billingsgate Battery example, which we should recall can be summarised as follows:

Time		£000
Immediately	Cost of machine	(100)
1 year's time	Net profit before depreciation	20
2 years' time	Net profit before depreciation	40
3 years' time	Net profit before depreciation	60
4 years' time	Net profit before depreciation	60
5 years' time	Net profit before depreciation	20
5 years' time	Disposal proceeds	20

Given that the principal financial objective of the business is to maximise shareholder wealth, it would be very easy to assess this investment if all of the cash inflows and outflows were to occur now (all at the same time). All that we should need to do would be to add up the cash inflows (total £220,000) and compare them with the cash outflows (£100,000). This would lead us to the conclusion that the project should go ahead, because the business would be better off by £120,000. Of course, it is not as easy as this, because time is involved. The cash outflow (payment) will occur immediately if the project is undertaken. The inflows (receipts) will arise at a range of later times.

The time factor is an important issue because people do not normally see £100 paid out now as equivalent in value to £100 receivable in a year's time. If we were to be offered £100 in 12 months, in exchange for paying out £100 now, we should not be prepared to do so, unless we wished to do someone (perhaps a friend or relation) a favour.

Activity 10.7

Why would you see £100 to be received in a year's time as unequal in value to £100 to be paid immediately? (There are basically three reasons.)

The reasons are:

- interest lost;
- risk;
- effects of inflation.

We shall now take a closer look at these three reasons in turn.

Interest lost

If we are to be deprived of the opportunity to spend our money for a year, we could equally well be deprived of its use by placing it on deposit in a bank or building society. In this case, at the end of the year we could have our money back and have interest as well. Thus, unless the opportunity to invest will offer similar returns, we shall be incurring an *opportunity cost*. An opportunity cost occurs where one course of action, for example making an investment deprives us of the opportunity to derive some benefit from an alternative action, for example putting the money in the bank.

From this we can see that any investment opportunity must, if it is to make us wealthiest, do better than the returns that are available from the next best opportunity. Thus, if Billingsgate Battery Company sees putting the money in the bank on deposit as the alternative to investment in the machine, the return from investing in the machine must be better than that from investing in the bank. If the bank offered a better return, the business would become wealthier by putting the money on deposit.

Risk

Buying a machine to manufacture a product, or to provide a service, to be sold in the market, on the strength of various estimates made in advance of buying the machine, exposes the business to risk. Things may not turn out as expected.

Activity 10.8

Can you suggest some areas where things could go other than according to plan in the Billingsgate Battery Company example?

We have come up with the following:

- The machine might not work as well as expected; it might break down, leading to loss of the service.
- Sales of the service may not be as buoyant as expected.
- Labour costs may prove to be higher than was expected.
- The sale proceeds of the machine could prove to be less than was estimated.

It is important to remember that the decision as to whether or not to invest in the machine must be taken *before* any of these things are known. It is only after the machine has been purchased that we could discover that the level of sales, which had been estimated before the event, is not going to be achieved. It is not possible to wait until we know for certain whether the market will behave as we expected before we buy the machine. We can study reports and analyses of the market. We can commission sophisticated market surveys, and these may give us more confidence in the likely outcome. We can advertise strongly and try to promote sales. Ultimately, however, we have to decide whether or not to jump off into the dark and accept the risk if we want the opportunity to make profitable investments.

Normally, people expect to receive greater returns where they perceive risk to be a factor. Examples of this in real life are not difficult to find. One such example is that banks tend to charge higher rates of interest to borrowers whom the bank perceives as more risky. Those who can offer good security for a loan, and who can point to a regular source of income, tend to be charged fairly low rates of interest.

Going back to Billingsgate Battery Company's investment opportunity, it is not enough to say that we should not advise making the investment unless the returns from it are as high as those from investing in a bank deposit. Clearly we should want returns above the level of bank deposit interest rates, because the logical equivalent to investing in the machine is not putting the money on deposit but making an alternative investment that is risky.

In practice, we tend to expect a higher rate of return from investment projects where the risk is perceived as being higher. How risky a particular project is, and therefore how large this risk premium should be, are matters that are difficult to handle. It is usually necessary to make some judgement on these questions.

Inflation

If we are to be deprived of £100 for a year, when we come to spend that money it will not buy as many goods and services as it would have done a year earlier. Generally, we shall not be able to buy as many tins of baked beans or loaves of bread or bus tickets as we could have done a year earlier. This is because of the loss in the purchasing power of money, or inflation, that occurs over time. Clearly, the investor needs this loss of purchasing power to be compensated for if the investment is to be made. This is on top of a return that takes account of what could have been gained from an alternative investment of similar risk.

In practice, interest rates observable in the market tend to take inflation into account. Rates that are offered to potential building society and bank depositors include an allowance for the rate of inflation that is expected in the future.

Actions of a logical investor

To summarise, we can say that the logical investor, who is seeking to increase his or her wealth, will only be prepared to make investments that will compensate for the loss of interest and purchasing power of the money invested and for the fact that the returns expected may not materialise (risk). This is usually assessed by seeing whether the proposed investment will yield a return that is greater than the basic rate of interest (which would include an allowance for inflation) plus a risk premium.

These three factors (interest lost, risk and inflation) are set out in Figure 10.2.

Naturally, investors need at least the minimum returns before they are prepared to invest. However, it is in terms of the effect on their wealth that they should logically assess an investment project. Usually it is the investment with the highest percentage return that will make the investor most wealthy, but we shall see later in this chapter that this is not always the case. For the time being, therefore, we shall concentrate on wealth.

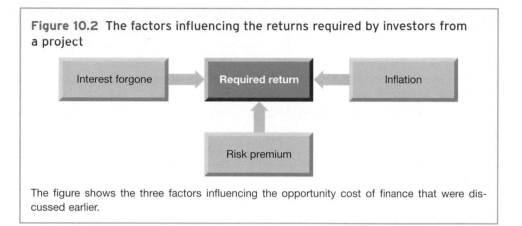

Figure 10.2 The factors influencing the returns required by investors from a project

The figure shows the three factors influencing the opportunity cost of finance that were discussed earlier.

Let us now return to the Billingsgate Battery Company example. We should recall that the cash flows expected from this investment are:

Time		£000
Immediately	Cost of machine	(100)
1 year's time	Net profit before depreciation	20
2 years' time	Net profit before depreciation	40
3 years' time	Net profit before depreciation	60
4 years' time	Net profit before depreciation	60
5 years' time	Net profit before depreciation	20
5 years' time	Disposal proceeds	20

Let us assume that, instead of making this investment, the business could make an alternative investment with similar risk and obtain a return of 20 per cent a year.

We have already seen that it is not sufficient just to compare the basic cash inflows and outflows for the investment. It would be useful if we could express each of these cash flows in similar terms, so that we could make a direct comparison between the sum of the inflows over time and the immediate £100,000 investment. Fortunately, we can do this.

Activity 10.9

We know that Billingsgate Battery Company could alternatively invest its money at a rate of 20 per cent a year. How much do you judge the present (immediate) value of the expected first year receipt of £20,000 to be? In other words, if instead of having to wait a year for the £20,000, and being deprived of the opportunity to invest it at 20 per cent, you could have some money now, what sum to be received now would you regard as exactly equivalent to getting £20,000, but having to wait a year for it?

We should obviously be happy to accept a lower amount if we could get it immediately than if we had to wait a year. This is because we could invest it at 20 per cent (in the alternative project). Logically, we should be prepared to accept the amount that, with a year's income, will grow to £20,000. If we call this amount PV (for present value) we can say:

$$PV + (PV \times 20\%) = £20,000$$

→

that is, the amount plus income from investing the amount for the year equals the £20,000.
If we rearrange this equation we find:

$$PV \times (1 + 0.2) = £20,000$$

Note that 0.2 is the same as 20 per cent, but expressed as a decimal.
Further rearranging gives:

$$PV = £20,000/(1 + 0.2) \quad ; \quad PV = £16,667$$

Thus, rational investors who have the opportunity to invest at 20 per cent a year would not mind whether they have £16,667 now or £20,000 in a year's time. In this sense we can say that, given a 20 per cent investment opportunity, the present value of £20,000 to be received in one year's time is £16,667.

If we could derive the present value (PV) of each of the cash flows associated with Billingsgate's machine investment, we could easily make the direct comparison between the cost of making the investment (£100,000) and the various benefits that will derive from it in years 1 to 5. Fortunately we can do precisely this.

We can make a more general statement about the PV of a particular cash flow. It is:

PV of the cash flow of year n = Actual cash flow of year n divided by $(1 + r)^n$

where n is the year of the cash flow (that is, how many years into the future) and r is the opportunity investing rate expressed as a decimal (instead of as a percentage).

We have already seen how this works for the £20,000 inflow for year 1. For year 2 the calculation would be:

$$PV \text{ of year 2 cash flow (that is, £40,000)} = £40,000/(1 + 0.2)^2$$
$$PV = £40,000/(1.2)^2 = £40,000/1.44 = £27,778$$

Thus the present value of the £40,000 to be received in two years' time is £27,778.

Activity 10.10

See if you can show that an investor would be indifferent to £27,778 receivable now, or £40,000 receivable in two years' time, assuming that there is a 20 per cent investment opportunity.

The reasoning goes like this:

	£
Amount available for immediate investment	27,778
Add Interest for year 1 (20% × 27,778)	5,556
	33,334
Add Interest for year 2 (20% × 33,334)	6,667
	40,001

(The extra £1 is only a rounding error.)

Thus, because the investor can turn £27,778 into £40,000 in two years, these amounts are equivalent. We can say that £27,778 is the present value of £40,000 receivable after two years (given a 20 per cent rate of return).

Now let us calculate the present values of all of the cash flows associated with the Billingsgate machine project and hence the *net present value (NPV)* of the project as a whole. The relevant cash flows and calculations are as follows:

Time	Cash flow £000	Calculation of PV	PV £000
Immediately (time 0)	(100)	$(100)/(1 + 0.2)^0$	(100.00)
1 year's time	20	$20/(1 + 0.2)^1$	16.67
2 years' time	40	$40/(1 + 0.2)^2$	27.78
3 years' time	60	$60/(1 + 0.2)^3$	34.72
4 years' time	60	$60/(1 + 0.2)^4$	28.94
5 years' time	20	$20/(1 + 0.2)^5$	8.04
5 years' time (disposal proceeds)	20	$20/(1 + 0.2)^5$	8.04
			24.19

(Note that $(1 + 0.2)^0 = 1$.)

Once again, we must ask how we can decide whether the machine project is acceptable to the business. In fact, the decision rule is simple:

If the NPV is positive we accept the project; if it is negative we reject the project.

In this case, the NPV is positive, so we should accept the project and buy the machine. The reasoning behind this decision rule is quite straightforward. Investing in the machine will make the business £24,190 better off than it would be by taking up the next best opportunity available to it. The gross benefits from investing in this machine are worth a total of £124,190 today and since the business can 'buy' these benefits for just £100,000 today, the investment should be made. If, however, the gross benefits were below £100,000, they would be less than the cost of 'buying' them.

Activity 10.11

What is the *maximum* the Billingsgate Battery Company would be prepared to pay for the machine, given the potential benefits of owning it?

The business would be prepared to pay up to £124,190 since the wealth of the owners of the business would be increased up to this price – though the business would prefer to pay as little as possible.

Using discount tables

Deducing the present values of the various cash flows is a little laborious using the approach that we have just taken. To deduce each PV we took the relevant cash flow and multiplied it by $1/(1 + r)^n$. Fortunately, there is a quicker way. Tables exist that show values of this discount factor for a range of values of r and n. Such a table is shown on page 455. Take a look at it.

Look at the column for 20 per cent and the row for one year. We find that the factor is 0.833. This means that the PV of a cash flow of £1 receivable in one year is £0.833. So a cash flow of £20,000 receivable in one year's time is £16,660 (that is, 0.833 × £20,000), the same result as we found doing it in longhand.

Activity 10.12

What is the NPV of the Chaotic Industries project from Activity 10.2, assuming a 15 per cent opportunity cost of finance (discount rate)? You should use the discount table on page 455.

Remember that the inflows and outflow are expected to be:

Time		£000
Immediately	Cost of vans	(150)
1 year's time	Net saving before depreciation	30
2 years' time	Net saving before depreciation	30
3 years' time	Net saving before depreciation	30
4 years' time	Net saving before depreciation	30
5 years' time	Net saving before depreciation	30
6 years' time	Net saving before depreciation	30
6 years' time	Disposal proceeds from the machine	30

The calculation of the NPV of the project is as follows:

Time	Cash flows	Discount factor (15% – from the table)	Present value
	£000		£000
Immediately	(150)	1.000	(150.00)
1 year's time	30	0.870	26.10
2 years' time	30	0.756	22.68
3 years' time	30	0.658	19.74
4 years' time	30	0.572	17.16
5 years' time	30	0.497	14.91
6 years' time	30	0.432	12.96
6 years' time (disposal proceeds)	30	0.432	12.96
		Net present value	(23.49)

Activity 10.13

How would you interpret this result?

The fact that the project has a negative NPV means that the present values of the benefits from the investment are worth less than the cost of entering into it. Any cost up to £126,510 (the present value of the benefits) would be worth paying, but not £150,000.

The discount tables reveal how the value of £1 diminishes as its receipt goes further into the future. Assuming an opportunity cost of finance of 20 per cent a year, £1 to be received immediately, obviously, has a present value of £1. However, as the time before it is to be received increases, its present value diminishes significantly, as is shown in Figure 10.3.

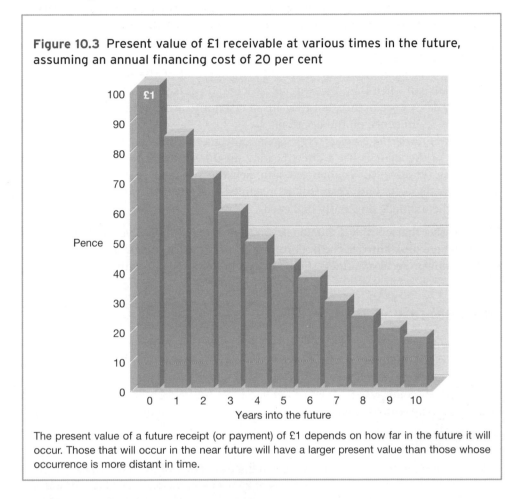

Figure 10.3 Present value of £1 receivable at various times in the future, assuming an annual financing cost of 20 per cent

The present value of a future receipt (or payment) of £1 depends on how far in the future it will occur. Those that will occur in the near future will have a larger present value than those whose occurrence is more distant in time.

The discount rate and the cost of capital

We have seen that the appropriate discount rate to use in NPV assessments is the opportunity cost of finance. This is, in effect, the cost to the business of the finance that it will use to fund the investment, should it go ahead. This will normally be the cost of the mixture of funds (shareholders' funds and borrowings) used by the business and is usually known as the cost of capital.

Why NPV is superior to ARR and PP

From what we have seen, NPV seems to be a better method of appraising investment opportunities than either ARR or PP. This is because it fully takes account of each of the following:

- *The timing of the cash flows.* By discounting the various cash flows associated with each project according to when it is expected to arise, NPV takes account of the time value of money. Associated with this is the fact that by discounting, using the opportunity cost of finance (that is, the return that the next best alternative opportunity would generate), the net benefit after financing costs have been met is identified (as the NPV of the project).
- *The whole of the relevant cash flows.* NPV includes all of the relevant cash flows, irrespective of when they are expected to occur. It treats them differently according to their date of occurrence, but they are all taken into account in the NPV, and they all have an influence on the decision.
- *The objectives of the business.* NPV is the only method of appraisal in which the output of the analysis has a direct bearing on the wealth of the shareholders of a business. (Positive NPVs enhance wealth; negative ones reduce it.) Since we assume that private-sector businesses seek to maximise shareholders' wealth, NPV is superior to the methods previously discussed.

We saw earlier that a business should take on all projects with positive NPVs, when their cash flows are discounted at the opportunity cost of finance. Where a choice has to be made among projects, a business should normally select the one with the highest NPV.

Internal rate of return (IRR)

This is the last of the four major methods of investment appraisal that are found in practice. It is quite closely related to the NPV method in that, like NPV, it also involves discounting future cash flows. The internal rate of return (IRR) of a particular investment is the discount rate that, when applied to its future cash flows, will produce an NPV of precisely zero. In essence, it represents the yield from an investment opportunity.

Activity 10.14

We should recall that, when we discounted the cash flows of the Billingsgate Battery Company machine investment opportunity at 20 per cent, we found that the NPV was a positive figure of £24,190 (see p. 345). What does the NPV of the machine project tell us about the rate of return that the investment will yield for the business?

The fact that the NPV is positive when discounting at 20 per cent implies that the rate of return that the project generates is more than 20 per cent. The fact that the NPV is a pretty large figure implies that the actual rate of return is quite a lot above 20 per cent. We should expect increasing the size of the discount rate to reduce NPV, because a higher discount rate gives a lower discounted figure.

It is somewhat laborious to deduce the IRR by hand, since it cannot usually be calculated directly. Iteration (trial and error) is the approach that must usually be adopted. Fortunately, computer spreadsheet packages can deduce the IRR with ease. The package will also use a trial and error approach, but at high speed.

Let us try a higher rate, say 30 per cent, and see what happens:

Time	Cash flow £000	Discount factor (30% – from the table)	PV £000
Immediately (time 0)	(100)	1.000	(100.00)
1 year's time	20	0.769	15.38
2 years' time	40	0.592	23.68
3 years' time	60	0.455	27.30
4 years' time	60	0.350	21.00
5 years' time	20	0.269	5.38
5 years' time (disposal proceeds)	20	0.269	5.38
			(1.88)

In increasing the discount rate from 20 per cent to 30 per cent, we have reduced the NPV from £24,190 (positive) to £1,880 (negative). Since the IRR is the discount rate that will give us an NPV of exactly zero, we can conclude that the IRR of Billingsgate Battery Company's machine project is very slightly below 30 per cent. Further trials could lead us to the exact rate, but there is probably not much point, given the likely inaccuracy of the cash flow estimates. It is probably good enough, for practical purposes, to say that the IRR is about 30 per cent.

The relationship between the NPV method discussed earlier and the IRR is shown graphically in Figure 10.4 using the information relating to the Billingsgate Battery Company.

Figure 10.4 The relationship between the NPV and IRR methods

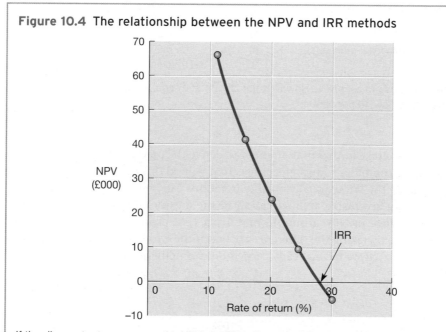

If the discount rate were zero, the NPV would be the sum of the net cash flows. In other words, no account would be taken of the time value of money. However, if we assume increasing discount rates, there is a corresponding decrease in the NPV of the project. When the NPV line crosses the horizontal axis there will be a zero NPV, and the point where it crosses is the IRR.

We can see that, where the discount rate is zero, the NPV will be the sum of the net cash flows. In other words, no account is taken of the time value of money. However, as the discount rate increases there is a corresponding decrease in the NPV of the project. When the NPV line crosses the horizontal axis there will be a zero NPV, and that represents the IRR.

Activity 10.15

What is the internal rate of return of the Chaotic Industries project from Activity 10.2? You should use the discount table on page 455. (*Hint*: Remember that you already know the NPV of this project at 15 per cent (from Activity 10.12).)

Since we know that, at a 15 per cent discount rate, the NPV is a relatively large negative figure, our next trial is using a lower discount rate, say 10 per cent:

Time	Cash flows £000	Discount factor (10% – from the table)	Present value £000
Immediately	(150)	1.000	(150.00)
1 year's time	30	0.909	27.27
2 years' time	30	0.826	24.78
3 years' time	30	0.751	22.53
4 years' time	30	0.683	20.49
5 years' time	30	0.621	18.63
6 years' time	30	0.565	16.95
6 years' time (disposal proceeds)	30	0.565	16.95
		Net present value	(2.40)

This figure is close to zero NPV. However, the NPV is still negative and so the precise IRR will be a little below 10 per cent.

We could undertake further trials in order to derive the precise IRR. In practice, most businesses have computer software packages that will do this quickly. If, however, we have to calculate the IRR manually, further iterations can be time-consuming.

We can get an acceptable approximation to the answer fairly quickly by first calculating the change in NPV arising from a 1 per cent change in the discount rate. This can be done by taking the differences between the two trials (that is, 15 per cent and 10 per cent) that we have already carried out (in Activities 10.12 and 10.15):

Trial	Discount factor	Present value £000
1	15%	(23.49)
2	10%	(2.40)
Difference	5%	21.09

The change in NPV for every 1 per cent change in the discount rate will be:

$$21.09/5 = 4.22\%.$$

The reduction in the 10% discount rate required to achieve a zero NPV would therefore be:

$$= (2.40)/4.22 = 0.57\%$$

The IRR is therefore:

$$(10.00 - 0.57) = \underline{9.43\%}$$

However, to say that the IRR is about 9 per cent is near enough for most purposes.

Note that this approach assumes a straight-line relationship between the discount rate and NPV. We can see from Figure 10.4, however, that this assumption is not strictly correct. Nevertheless, over a relatively short range, this simplifying assumption is not usually a problem and so we can still arrive at a reasonable approximation.

Users of the IRR approach should apply the following decision rules:

■ For any project to be acceptable, it must meet a minimum IRR requirement. This is often referred to as the *hurdle rate* and, logically, this should be the opportunity cost of finance.

■ Where there are competing projects (the business can choose only one of two or more viable projects) the one with the highest IRR would be selected.

IRR has certain attributes in common with NPV. All cash flows are taken into account, and their timing is logically handled.

Real World 10.4 provides some idea of IRRs sought in practice.

Real World 10.4

Rates of return

IRR rates for investment projects can vary considerably. Here are a few examples of the expected returns from investment projects of large businesses:

■ Associated British Ports, the UK's largest port operator, concentrates on projects that generate an IRR of at least 15 per cent.

■ Brascan, a Canadian property and energy business, made a bid to acquire Canary Wharf, a property estate in London, and expected to generate an IRR of at least 20 per cent if the bid price was accepted.

■ Hutchison Whampoa, a large telecommunications business, requires an IRR of at least 25 per cent from its telecom projects.

Sources: 'Brascan raises offer for Canary Wharf', *FT.com*, 13 February 2004; 'Spread of risks give ABP confident outlook', *FT.com*, 13 February 2003; Lex Column: 'Hutchison Whampoa', *Financial Times*, 31 March 2004

Problems with IRR

The main disadvantage of IRR is the fact that it does not correctly address the question of wealth generation. It could therefore lead to the wrong decision being made. This is because IRR would, for example, always see an IRR of 25 per cent being preferable to a 20 per cent IRR, assuming an opportunity cost of finance of, say, 15 per cent.

Though accepting the project with the higher percentage return will often generate more wealth, this may not always be the case. This is because IRR completely ignores the *scale of investment*. With a 15 per cent cost of finance, £15 million invested at 20 per cent (that is, $15 \times (20 - 15) = 0.75$) would make us richer than £5 million invested at 25 per cent (that is, $5 \times (25 - 15) = 0.50$). IRR does not recognise this. It should be acknowledged that it is not usual for projects to be competing where there is such a large difference in scale. Even though the problem may be rare and so, typically, IRR will give the same signal as NPV, a method (NPV) that is always reliable must be better to use than IRR. This problem with percentages is another example illustrated by the Mexican road discussed in Real World 10.3 (p. 336).

A further problem with the IRR method is that it has difficulty handling projects with unconventional cash flows. In the examples studied so far, each project has a negative cash flow arising at the start of its life and then positive cash flows thereafter. In some cases, however, a project may have both positive and negative cash flows at future points in its life. Such a pattern of cash flows can result in there being more than one IRR, or even no IRR at all.

Some practical points

When undertaking an investment appraisal, there are several practical points that we should bear in mind:

- *Past costs*. As with all decisions, we should only take account of relevant costs in our analysis. This means that only costs that vary with the decision should be considered. Thus, all past costs should be ignored as they cannot vary with the decision. In some cases, a business may incur costs (such as, development costs and market research costs) *before* the evaluation of an opportunity to launch a new product. As they have already been incurred, they should be disregarded, even though the amounts may be substantial. Costs that have already been committed, but not yet paid, should also be disregarded. Where a business has entered into a binding contract to incur a particular cost, it becomes effectively a past cost even though payment may not be due until some point in the future.
- *Common future costs*. It is not only past costs that do not vary with the decision; some future costs may also be the same. Take for example, a road haulage business that has decided that it will buy a new lorry and the decision lies between two different models. The load capacity, the fuel and maintenance costs are different for each lorry. The potential costs and revenues associated with these are all relevant items. The lorry will require a driver, so the business will need to employ one, but a suitably qualified driver could drive either lorry equally well, for the same wage. The cost of employing the driver is thus irrelevant to the decision as to which lorry to buy. This is despite the fact that this cost is a future one.

  If, however, the decision did not concern a choice between two models of lorry but rather whether to operate an additional lorry or not, the cost of employing the additional driver would be relevant. This is because it would then be a cost that would vary with the decision made.

■ *Opportunity costs.* Opportunity costs arising from benefits foregone must be taken into account. Thus, for example, when considering a decision concerning whether or not to continue to use a machine already owned by the business, the realisable value of the machine might be an important opportunity cost.

These points concerning costs are brought together in Activity 10.16 below.

Activity 10.16

A garage has an old car that it bought several months ago for £3,000. The car needs a replacement engine before it can be sold. It is possible to buy a reconditioned engine for £300. This would take seven hours to fit by a mechanic who is paid £12 an hour. At present the garage is short of work, but the owners are reluctant to lay off any mechanics or even to cut down their basic working week because skilled labour is difficult to find and an upturn in repair work is expected soon.

Without the engine, the car could be sold for an estimated £3,500. What is the minimum price at which the garage should sell the car, with a reconditioned engine fitted, to avoid making a loss? (Ignore any timing differences in receipts and payments.)

The minimum price is the amount required to cover the relevant costs of the job. At this price, the business will make neither a profit nor a loss. Any price below this amount, will result in a reduction in the wealth of the business. Thus, the minimum price is:

	£
Opportunity cost of the car	3,500
Cost of the reconditioned engine	300
Total	3,800

The original cost of the car is a past cost and is, therefore, irrelevant. However, we are told that, without the engine, the car could be sold for £3,500. This is the opportunity cost of the car, which represents real benefits foregone, and should be taken into account.

The cost of the new engine is relevant because, if the work is done, the garage will have to pay £300 for the engine; but will pay nothing if the job is not done. The £300 is a future cost that varies with the decision and should be taken into account.

The labour cost is irrelevant because the same cost will be incurred whether the mechanic undertakes the work or not. This is because the mechanic is being paid to do nothing if this job is not undertaken; thus the additional labour cost arising from this job is zero.

■ *Taxation.* Investors will be interested in the after-tax returns generated from the business and so taxation will usually be an important consideration when making an investment decision. The profits from the project will be taxed, the capital investment may attract tax relief and so on. Tax is levied on these at significant rates. This means that, in real life, unless tax is formally taken into account, the wrong decision could easily be made. The timing of the tax outflow should also be taken into account when preparing the cash flows for the project.

■ *Cash flows not profit flows.* We have seen that for the NPV, IRR and PP methods, it is cash flows rather than profit flows that are relevant to the evaluation of investment projects. In an investment appraisal requiring the application of any of these methods we may be given details of the profits for the investment period. These need to be adjusted in order to derive the cash flows. We should remember that the net profit *before* non cash items (such as depreciation) is an approximation to the cash flows for the period, and so we should work back to this figure.

When the data are expressed in profit rather than cash flow terms, an adjustment in respect of working capital may also be necessary. Some adjustment should be made to take account of changes in working capital. For example, launching a new product may give rise to an increase in the net cash investment made in trade receivables (debtors), inventories (stock) and trade payables (creditors), requiring an immediate outlay of cash. This outlay for additional working capital should be shown in the NPV calculations as part of the initial cost. At the end of the life of the project, however, the additional working capital will be released. This divestment, resulting in an inflow of cash at the end the project should also be taken into account at the point at which it is received.

■ *Year-end assumption.* In the examples above, we have assumed that cash flows arise at the end of the relevant year. This is a simplifying assumption that is used to make the calculations easier. (However, it is perfectly possible to deal more precisely with the cash flows.) The assumption is clearly unrealistic as money will have to be paid to employees on a weekly or monthly basis and customers will pay within a month or two of buying the product or service. Nevertheless, it is probably not a serious distortion. We should be clear, however, that there is nothing about any of the appraisal methods that demands that this assumption be made.

■ *Interest payments.* When using discounted cash flow techniques, interest payments should not be taken into account in deriving the cash flows for the period. The discount factor already takes account of the costs of financing and so to take account of interest charges in deriving cash flows for the period would be double counting.

■ *Other factors.* Investment decision making must not be viewed as simply a mechanical exercise. The results derived from a particular investment appraisal method will be only one input to the decision-making process. There may be broader issues connected to the decision that have to be taken into account, but which may be difficult or impossible to quantify. The reliability of the forecasts and the validity of the assumptions used in the evaluation will also have a bearing on the final decision.

Activity 10.17

The directors of Manuff (Steel) Ltd are considering closing one of the business's factories. There has been a reduction in the demand for the products made at the factory in recent years, and the directors are not optimistic about the long-term prospects for these products. The factory is situated in the north of England, in an area where unemployment is high.

The factory is leased, and there are still four years of the lease remaining. The directors are uncertain as to whether the factory should be closed immediately or at the end of the period of the lease. Another business has offered to sublease the premises from Manuff at a rental of £40,000 a year for the remainder of the lease period.

The machinery and equipment at the factory cost £1,500,000, and have a balance sheet value of £400,000. In the event of immediate closure, the machinery and equipment could be sold for £220,000. The working capital at the factory is £420,000, and could be liquidated for that amount immediately, if required. Alternatively, the working capital can be liquidated in full at the end of the lease period. Immediate closure would result in redundancy payments to employees of £180,000.

If the factory continues in operation until the end of the lease period, the following operating profits (losses) are expected:

	Year 1	Year 2	Year 3	Year 4
	£000	£000	£000	£000
Operating profit (loss)	160	(40)	30	20

The above figures include a charge of £90,000 a year for depreciation of machinery and equipment. The residual value of the machinery and equipment at the end of the lease period is estimated at £40,000.

Redundancy payments are expected to be £150,000 at the end of the lease period if the factory continues in operation. The business has an annual cost of capital of 12 per cent. Ignore taxation.

Required:

(a) Determine the relevant cash flows arising from a decision to continue operations until the end of the lease period rather than to close immediately.

(b) Calculate the net present value of continuing operations until the end of the lease period, rather than closing immediately.

(c) What other factors might the directors take into account before making a final decision on the timing of the factory closure?

(d) State, with reasons, whether or not the business should continue to operate the factory until the end of the lease period.

Your answer to this activity should be as follows:

(a) Relevant cash flows

	Years				
	0	1	2	3	4
	£000	£000	£000	£000	£000
Operating cash flows (Note 1)		250	50	120	110
Sale of machinery (Note 2)	(220)				40
Redundancy costs (Note 3)	180				(150)
Sublease rentals (Note 4)		(40)	(40)	(40)	(40)
Working capital invested (Note 5)	(420)				420
	(460)	210	10	80	380

→

Notes:

1 Each year's operating cash flows are calculated by adding back the depreciation charge for the year to the operating profit for the year. In the case of the operating loss, the depreciation charge is deducted.

2 In the event of closure, machinery could be sold immediately. Thus an opportunity cost of £220,000 is incurred if operations continue.

3 By continuing operations, there will be a saving in immediate redundancy costs of £180,000. However, redundancy costs of £150,000 will be paid in four years' time.

4 By continuing operations, the opportunity to sublease the factory will be foregone.

5 Immediate closure would mean that working capital could be liquidated. By continuing operations this opportunity is foregone. However, working capital can be liquidated in four years' time.

(b)

Discount rate 12 per cent	1.000	0.893	0.797	0.712	0.636
Present value	(460)	187.5	8.0	57.0	241.7
Net present value	34.2				

(c) Other factors that may influence the decision include:

- *The overall strategy of the business.* The business may need to set the decision within a broader context. It may be necessary to manufacture the products made at the factory because they are an integral part of the business's product range. The business may wish to avoid redundancies in an area of high unemployment for as long as possible.

- *Flexibility.* A decision to close the factory is probably irreversible. If the factory continues, however, there may be a chance that the prospects for the factory will brighten in the future.

- *Creditworthiness of sub-lessee.* The business should investigate the creditworthiness of the sub-lessee. Failure to receive the expected sublease payments would make the closure option far less attractive.

- *Accuracy of forecasts.* The forecasts made by the business should be examined carefully. Inaccuracies in the forecasts or any underlying assumptions may change the expected outcomes.

(d) The NPV of the decision to continue operations rather than close immediately is positive. Hence, shareholders would be better off if the directors took this course of action. The factory should therefore continue in operation rather than close down. This decision is likely to be welcomed by employees and would allow the business to maintain its flexibility.

Investment appraisal in practice

Many surveys have been conducted in the UK into the methods of investment appraisal used by businesses. They have tended to show the following features:

- businesses using more than one method to assess each investment decision, increasingly so over time;

- an increased use of the discounting methods (NPV and IRR) over time, with these two becoming the most popular in recent years;

- continued popularity of ARR and PP, despite their theoretical shortcomings and the rise in popularity of the discounting methods;
- a tendency for larger businesses to use the discounting methods and to use more than one method in respect of each decision.

Real World 10.5 shows the results of the most recent (1997) survey conducted of UK businesses regarding their use of investment appraisal methods.

Real World 10.5

A survey of UK business practice

Method	Percentage of businesses using the method
Net present value	80
Internal rate of return	81
Payback period	70
Accounting rate of return	56
	287

Source: Arnold and Hatzopoulos (see References section at end of chapter). Reproduced by kind permission of Blackwell Publishing Ltd

---

Activity 10.18

Earlier in the chapter we discussed the theoretical limitations of the PP method. How do you explain the fact that it still seems to be a popular method of investment appraisal among businesses?

A number of possible reasons may explain this finding:

- PP is easy to understand and use.
- It can avoid the problems of forecasting far into the future.
- It gives emphasis to the early cash flows when there is greater certainty concerning the accuracy of their predicted value.
- It emphasises the importance of liquidity. Where a business has liquidity problems, a short payback period for a project is likely to appear attractive.

PP can provide a convenient, though rough and ready, assessment of the profitability of a project, in the way that it is used in Real World 10.6.

The popularity of PP may suggest a lack of sophistication among managers concerning investment appraisal. This criticism is most often made against managers of smaller businesses. In fact, the survey discussed above, as well as other surveys, have found that smaller businesses are much less likely to use discounted cash flow methods (NPV and IRR) than larger ones.

The survey evidence suggests that many businesses use more than one method to appraise investments. The sum of percentage usage for each appraisal method in the

Real World 10.6

Space to earn

FT

SES Global is the world's largest commercial satellite operator. This means that it rents satellite capacity to broadcasters, governments, telecommunications groups and Internet service providers. It is a risky venture that few are prepared to undertake. As a result, a handful of businesses dominates the market.

Launching a satellite requires a huge initial outlay of capital, but relatively small cash outflows following the launch. Revenues only start to flow once the satellite is in orbit. A satellite launch costs around €250m. The main elements of this cost are the satellite (€120m), the launch vehicle (€80m), insurance (€40m) and ground equipment (€10m).

According to Romain Bausch, president and chief executive of SES Global, it takes three years to build and launch a satellite. However, the average lifetime of a satellite is fifteen years during which time it is generating revenues. The revenues generated are such that the payback period is around four to five years.

Source: 'Satellites need space to earn', Tim Burt, *Financial Times*, 14 July 2003, FT.com

UK survey, for example, is 287 per cent (see Real World 10.5). This survey also suggests that most businesses use one of the two discounted cash flow methods. Generally survey evidence has shown a strong increase in the rate of usage of both NPV and IRR, in the UK, over the years. Similar trends seem to prevail in most of the world.

IRR may be as popular as NPV, despite its shortcomings, because it expresses outcomes in percentage terms rather than in absolute terms. This form of expression appears to be more acceptable to managers. This may be because managers are used to using percentage figures as targets (for example, return on capital employed).

Real World 10.7 shows extracts from the 2004 annual report of a well-known business: Rolls-Royce plc, the builder of engines for aircraft and other purposes.

Real World 10.7

The use of NPV at Rolls-Royce

In its 2004 annual report and accounts, Rolls-Royce plc stated that:

> The Group continues to subject all investments to rigorous examination of risks and future cash flows to ensure that they create shareholder value. All major investments require Board approval.
>
> The Group has a portfolio of projects at different stages of their life cycles. Discounted cash flow analysis of the remaining life of projects is performed on a regular basis.

Source: Rolls-Royce plc, Annual Report and Accounts 2004

Rolls-Royce makes clear that it uses NPV (the report refers to creating shareholder value and to discounted cash flow, which strongly implies NPV). It is interesting to note that Rolls-Royce not only assesses new projects, but also reassesses existing ones.

This must be a sensible commercial approach. Businesses should not continue with existing projects unless those projects have a positive NPV based on future cash flows. Just because a project seemed to have a positive NPV before it started does not mean that this will persist, in the light of changing circumstances. Activity 10.17 (page 354) considered a decision to close down a project.

? Self-assessment question 10.1

Beacon Chemicals plc is considering buying some equipment to produce a chemical named X14. The new equipment's capital cost is estimated at £100,000. If its purchase is approved now, the equipment can be bought and production can commence by the end of this year. £50,000 has already been spent on research and development work. Estimates of revenues and costs arising from the operation of the new equipment appear below:

	Year 1	Year 2	Year 3	Year 4	Year 5
Sales price (£ per litre)	100	120	120	100	80
Sales volume (litres)	800	1,000	1,200	1,000	800
Variable costs (£ per litre)	50	50	40	30	40
Fixed costs (£000)	30	30	30	30	30

If the equipment is bought, sales of some existing products will be lost, and this will result in a loss of contribution of £15,000 a year over its life.

The accountant has informed you that the fixed costs include depreciation of £20,000 a year on the new equipment. They also include an allocation of £10,000 for fixed overheads. A separate study has indicated that if the new equipment were bought, additional overheads, excluding depreciation, arising from producing the chemical would be £8,000 a year. Production would require additional working capital of £30,000.

For the purposes of your initial calculations ignore taxation.

Required:
(a) Deduce the relevant annual cash flows associated with buying the equipment.
(b) Deduce the payback period.
(c) Calculate the net present value using a discount rate of 8 per cent.

(*Hint*: You should deal with the investment in working capital by treating it as a cash outflow at the start of the project and an inflow at the end.)

Summary

The main points of this chapter may be summarised as follows:

Accounting rate of return (ARR) is the average accounting profit from the project expressed as a percentage of the average investment.

■ Decision rule – projects with an ARR above a defined minimum are acceptable; the greater the ARR, the more attractive the project becomes.

■ Conclusion on ARR:

→

– it does not relate directly to shareholders' wealth – can lead to illogical conclusions;
– takes almost no account of the timing of cash flows;
– ignores some relevant information and may take account of some irrelevant;
– relatively simple to use;
– much inferior to NPV.

Payback period (PP) is the length of time that it takes for the cash outflow for the initial investment to be repaid out of resulting cash inflows.

■ Decision rule – projects with a PP up to defined maximum period are acceptable, the shorter the PP, the more desirable.

■ Conclusion on PP:
– does not relate to shareholders' wealth, ignores inflows after the payback date;
– takes little account of the timing of cash flows;
– ignores much relevant information;
– does not always provide clear signals and can be impractical to use;
– much inferior to NPV, but it is easy to understand and can offer a liquidity insight, which might be the reason for its widespread use.

Net present value (NPV) is the sum of the discounted values of the net cash flows from the investment.

■ Money has a time value.

■ Decision rule – all positive NPV investments enhance shareholders' wealth; the greater the NPV, the greater the enhancement and the more desirable.

■ PV of a cashflow = cashflow $\times 1/(1 + r)^n$, assuming a constant discount rate.

■ The act of discounting brings cash flows at different points in time to a common valuation basis (their present value), which enables them to be directly compared.

■ Conclusion on NPV:
– relates directly to shareholders' wealth objective;
– takes account of the timing of cash flows;
– takes all relevant information into account;
– provides clear signals and practical to use.

Internal rate of return (IRR) is the discount rate that, when applied to the cash flows of a project, causes it to have a zero NPV.

■ Represents the average percentage return on the investment, taking account of the fact that cash may be flowing in and out of the project at various points in its life.

■ Decision rule – projects that have an IRR greater than the cost of capital are acceptable; the greater the IRR, the more attractive the project.

■ Cannot normally be calculated directly; a trial and error approach is often necessary.

■ Conclusion on IRR:
– does not relate directly to shareholders' wealth; usually gives the same signals as NPV but can mislead where there are competing projects of different size;

- takes account of the timing of cash flows;
- takes all relevant information into account;
- problems of multiple IRRs when there are unconventional cash flows;
- inferior to NPV.

Use of appraisal methods in practice:

- all four methods identified are widely used;

- the discounting methods (NPV and IRR) show a steady increase in usage over time;

- many businesses use more than one method;

- larger businesses seem to be more sophisticated in their choice and use of appraisal methods than smaller ones.

→ Key terms

accounting rate of return (ARR) p. 331
payback period (PP) p. 336
net present value (NPV) p. 340
risk p. 341
risk premium p. 342

inflation p. 342
discount factor p. 346
internal rate of return (IRR) p. 348
relevant costs p. 352
opportunity cost p. 353

Further reading

If you would like to explore the topics covered in this chapter in more depth, we recommend the following books:

Drury, C. *Management and Cost Accounting*, 6th edn, Thomson Learning, 2004, Chapters 13 and 14.
Lumby, S. and Jones, C. *Investment Appraisal and Financial Decisions*, 7th edn, International Thompson Business Press, 2003, Chapters 3, 5 and 6.
McLaney, E. *Business Finance: Theory and Practice*, 7th edn, Financial Times Prentice Hall, 2006, Chapters 4–6.
Pike, R. and Neale, B. *Corporate Finance and Investment*, 4th edn, Prentice Hall International, 2002, Chapters 5, 6 and 7.

References

Arnold, G.C. and Hatzopoulos, P. 'The theory–practice gap in capital budgeting: evidence from the United Kingdom', *Journal of Business Finance and Accounting*, June/July, 2000.
Gigerenzer, G. *Reckoning with Risk*, Penguin Books, 2002.

? Review questions

Answers to these questions can be found at the back of the book (pp. 495-6).

10.1 Why is the net present value method of investment appraisal considered to be theoretically superior to other methods that are found in practice?

10.2 The payback method has been criticised for not taking the time value of money into account. Could this limitation be overcome? If so, would this method then be preferable to the NPV method?

10.3 Research indicates that the IRR method is a more popular method of investment appraisal than the NPV method. Why might this be?

10.4 Why are cash flows rather than profit flows used in the IRR, NPV and PP methods of investment appraisal?

* Exercises

Exercises 10.3 to 10.5 are more advanced than 10.1 and 10.2. Those with a coloured number have an answer at the back of the book (pp. 517-20).

If you wish to try more exercises, visit the students' side of the companion website.

10.1 The directors of Mylo Ltd are currently considering two mutually exclusive investment projects. Both projects are concerned with the purchase of new plant. The following data are available for each project:

	Project 1 £000	Project 2 £000
Cost (immediate outlay)	100	60
Expected annual net profit (loss):		
Year 1	29	18
Year 2	(1)	(2)
Year 3	2	4
Estimated residual value of the plant	7	6

The business has an estimated cost of capital of 10 per cent, and uses the straight-line method of depreciation for all non-current (fixed) assets when calculating net profit. Neither project would increase the working capital of the business. The business has sufficient funds to meet all capital expenditure requirements.

Required:

(a) Calculate for each project:
   (i)   The net present value.
   (ii) The approximate internal rate of return.
   (iii) The payback period.
(b) State which, if any, of the two investment projects the directors of Mylo Ltd should accept, and why.

(c) State, in general terms, which method of investment appraisal you consider to be most appropriate for evaluating investment projects, and why.

10.2 C. George (Controls) Ltd manufactures a thermostat that can be used in a range of kitchen appliances. The manufacturing process is, at present, semi-automated. The equipment used costs £540,000, and has a written-down (balance sheet) value of £300,000. Demand for the product has been fairly stable, and output has been maintained at 50,000 units a year in recent years.

The following data, based on the current level of output, have been prepared in respect of the product:

	Per unit	
	£	£
Selling price		12.40
Less		
Labour	3.30	
Materials	3.65	
Overheads: Variable	1.58	
Fixed	1.60	
		10.13
Profit		2.27

Although the existing equipment is expected to last for a further four years before it is sold for an estimated £40,000, the business has recently been considering purchasing new equipment that would completely automate much of the production process. The new equipment would cost £670,000 and would have an expected life of four years, at the end of which it would be sold for an estimated £70,000. If the new equipment is purchased, the old equipment could be sold for £150,000 immediately.

The assistant to the business's accountant has prepared a report to help assess the viability of the proposed change, which includes the following data:

	Per unit	
	£	£
Selling price		12.40
Less		
Labour	1.20	
Materials	3.20	
Overheads: Variable	1.40	
Fixed	3.30	
		9.10
Profit		3.30

Depreciation charges will increase by £85,000 a year as a result of purchasing the new machinery; however, other fixed costs are not expected to change.

In the report the assistant wrote:

> The figures shown above that relate to the proposed change are based on the current level of output and take account of a depreciation charge of £150,000 a year in respect of the new equipment. The effect of purchasing the new equipment will be to increase the net profit to sales ratio from 18.3 per cent to 26.6 per cent. In addition, the purchase of the new equipment will enable us to reduce our inventories level immediately by £130,000. In view of these facts. I recommend purchase of the new equipment.

The business has a cost of capital of 12 per cent.
Ignore taxation.

Required:
(a) Prepare a statement of the incremental cash flows arising from the purchase of the new equipment.
(b) Calculate the net present value of the proposed purchase of new equipment.
(c) State, with reasons, whether the business should purchase the new equipment.
(d) Explain why cash flow forecasts are used rather than profit forecasts to assess the viability of proposed capital expenditure projects.

10.3 The accountant of your business has recently been taken ill through overwork. In his absence his assistant has prepared some calculations of the profitability of a project, which are to be discussed soon at the board meeting of your business. His workings, which are set out below, include some errors of principle. You can assume that the statement below includes no arithmetical errors.

	Year 1 £000	Year 2 £000	Year 3 £000	Year 4 £000	Year 5 £000	Year 6 £000
Sales revenue		450	470	470	470	470
Less Costs						
Materials		126	132	132	132	132
Labour		90	94	94	94	94
Overheads		45	47	47	47	47
Depreciation		120	120	120	120	120
Working capital	180					
Interest on working capital		27	27	27	27	27
Write-off of development costs		30	30	30		
Total costs	180	438	450	450	420	420
Profit/(loss)	(180)	12	20	20	50	50

$$\frac{\text{Total profit (loss)}}{\text{Cost of equipment}} = \frac{(£28,000)}{£600,000} = \text{Return on investment (4.7\%)}$$

You ascertain the following additional information:

■ The cost of equipment contains £100,000, being the book value of an old machine. If it were not used for this project it would be scrapped with a zero net realisable value. New equipment costing £500,000 will be purchased on 31 December Year 0. You should assume that all other cash flows occur at the end of the year to which they relate.
■ The development costs of £90,000 have already been spent.
■ Overheads have been costed at 50 per cent of direct labour, which is the business's normal practice. An independent assessment has suggested that incremental overheads are likely to amount to £30,000 a year.
■ The business's cost of capital is 12 per cent.

Ignore taxation in your answer.

Required:
(a) Prepare a corrected statement of the incremental cash flows arising from the project. Where you have altered the assistant's figures you should attach a brief note explaining your alterations.

(b) Calculate:
    (i) the project's payback period;
    (ii) the project's net present value as at 31 December Year 0.
(c) Write a memo to the board advising on the acceptance or rejection of the project.

10.4 Newton Electronics Ltd has incurred expenditure of £5 million over the past three years researching and developing a miniature hearing aid. The hearing aid is now fully developed, and the directors are considering which of three mutually exclusive options should be taken to exploit the potential of the new product. The options are as follows:

1 The business could manufacture the hearing aid itself. This would be a new departure, since the business has so far concentrated on research and development projects. However, the business has manufacturing space available that it currently rents to another business for £100,000 a year. The business would have to purchase plant and equipment costing £9 million and invest £3 million in working capital immediately for production to begin.

    A market research report, for which the business paid £50,000, indicates that the new product has an expected life of five years. Sales of the product during this period are predicted as follows:

	Predicted sales for the year ended 30 November				
	Year 1	Year 2	Year 3	Year 4	Year 5
Number of units (000s)	800	1,400	1,800	1,200	500

The selling price per unit will be £30 in the first year but will fall to £22 in the following three years. In the final year of the product's life, the selling price will fall to £20. Variable production costs are predicted to be £14 a unit, and fixed production costs (including depreciation) will be £2.4 million a year. Marketing costs will be £2 million a year.

    The business intends to depreciate the plant and equipment using the straight-line method and based on an estimated residual value at the end of the five years of £1 million. The business has a cost of capital of 10 per cent a year.

2 Newton Electronics Ltd could agree to another business manufacturing and marketing the product under licence. A multinational business, Faraday Electricals plc, has offered to undertake the manufacture and marketing of the product, and in return will make a royalty payment to Newton Electronics Ltd of £5 per unit. It has been estimated that the annual number of sales of the hearing aid will be 10 per cent higher if the multinational business, rather than if Newton Electronics Ltd, manufactures and markets the product.

3 Newton Electronics Ltd could sell the patent rights to Faraday Electricals plc for £24 million, payable in two equal instalments. The first instalment would be payable immediately and the second at the end of two years. This option would give Faraday Electricals the exclusive right to manufacture and market the new product.

Ignore taxation.

Required:
(a) Calculate the net present value (as at 1 January Year 1) of each of the options available to Newton Electronics Ltd.
(b) Identify and discuss any other factors that Newton Electronics Ltd should consider before arriving at a decision.
(c) State what you consider to be the most suitable option, and why.

10.5   Chesterfield Wanderers is a professional football club that has enjoyed considerable success in both national and European competitions in recent years. As a result, the club has accumulated £10 million to spend on its further development. The board of directors is currently considering two mutually exclusive options for spending the funds available.

The first option is to acquire another player. The team manager has expressed a keen interest in acquiring Basil ('Bazza') Ramsey, a central defender, who currently plays for a rival club. The rival club has agreed to release the player immediately for £10 million if required. A decision to acquire 'Bazza' Ramsey would mean that the existing central defender, Vinnie Smith, could be sold to another club. Chesterfield Wanderers has recently received an offer of £2.2 million for this player. This offer is still open but will only be accepted if 'Bazza' Ramsey joins Chesterfield Wanderers. If this does not happen, Vinnie Smith will be expected to stay on with the club until the end of his playing career in five years' time. During this period, Vinnie will receive an annual salary of £400,000 and a loyalty bonus of £200,000 at the end of his five-year period with the club.

Assuming 'Bazza' Ramsey is acquired, the team manager estimates that gate receipts will increase by £2.5 million in the first year and £1.3 million in each of the four following years. There will also be an increase in advertising and sponsorship revenues of £1.2 million for each of the next five years if the player is acquired. At the end of five years, the player can be sold to a club in a lower division and Chesterfield Wanderers will expect to receive £1 million as a transfer fee. During his period at the club, 'Bazza' will receive an annual salary of £800,000 and a loyalty bonus of £400,000 after five years.

The second option is for the club to improve its ground facilities. The west stand could be extended and executive boxes could be built for businesses wishing to offer corporate hospitality to clients. These improvements would also cost £10 million and would take one year to complete. During this period, the west stand would be closed, resulting in a reduction of gate receipts of £1.8 million. However, gate receipts for each of the following four years would be £4.4 million higher than current receipts. In five years' time, the club has plans to sell the existing grounds and to move to a new stadium nearby. Improving the ground facilities is not expected to affect the ground's value when it comes to be sold. Payment for the improvements will be made when the work has been completed at the end of the first year. Whichever option is chosen, the board of directors has decided to take on additional ground staff. The additional wages bill is expected to be £350,000 a year over the next five years.

The club has a cost of capital of 10 per cent.

Ignore taxation.

Required:

(a) Calculate the incremental cash flows arising from each of the options available to the club.

(b) Calculate the net present value of each of the options.

(c) On the basis of the calculations made in (b) above, which of the two options would you choose and why?

(d) Discuss the validity of using the net present value method in making investment decisions for a professional football club.

Chapter 11

Managing working capital

Introduction

In this chapter we consider the factors that must be taken into account when managing the working capital of a business. Each element of working capital will be identified, and the major issues surrounding them will be discussed. As we saw in Chapter 10, working capital represents a significant investment for many businesses and so its proper management and control can be vital. We saw in Chapter 10 that an investment in working capital is typically an important aspect of new investment proposals. Some useful tools in the management of working capital are financial ratios, which were considered in Chapter 6 and budgets, which we examined in Chapter 9.

Learning outcomes

When you have completed this chapter, you should be able to:

- identify the main elements of working capital;
- discuss the purpose of working capital and the nature of the working capital cycle;
- explain the importance of establishing policies for the control of working capital;
- explain the factors that have to be taken into account when managing each element of working capital.

The nature and purpose of working capital

→ Working capital is usually defined as current assets less current liabilities.
The major elements of current assets are:

- inventories (stock);
- trade receivables (debtors);
- cash (in hand and at bank).

The major elements of current liabilities are:

- trade payables (creditors);
- bank overdrafts.

The size and composition of working capital can vary between industries. For some types of business, the investment in working capital can be substantial. For example, a manufacturing business will typically invest heavily in raw material, work in progress and finished goods, and will normally sell its goods on credit, giving rise to trade receivables. A retailer, on the other hand, will hold only one form of inventories (finished goods), and will usually sell goods for cash. Many service businesses hold no inventories. Most businesses buy goods and/or services on credit, giving rise to trade payables. Few, if any, businesses operate without a cash balance; though in some cases it is a negative one (bank overdraft).

Working capital represents a net investment in short-term assets. These assets are continually flowing into and out of the business, and are essential for day-to-day operations. The various elements of working capital are interrelated, and can be seen as part of a short-term cycle. For a manufacturing business, the working capital cycle can be depicted as shown in Figure 11.1.

For a retailer the situation would be as in Figure 11.1, except that there would be no work in progress and the raw materials and the finished inventories would be the same. For a purely service business, the working capital cycle would also be similar to that depicted in Figure 11.1, except that there would be no inventories of raw materials and finished goods. There may well be work in progress, however, since many services, for example a case handled by a firm of solicitors, will take some time to complete and costs will build up before the client is billed for them.

Managing working capital

The management of working capital is an essential part of the business's short-term planning process. It is necessary for management to decide how much of each element should be held. As we shall see later in this chapter, there are costs associated with holding either too much or too little of each element. Management must be aware of these costs, which include opportunity costs, in order to manage effectively. Hence, the potential benefits must be weighed against the likely costs in an attempt to achieve the optimum investment.

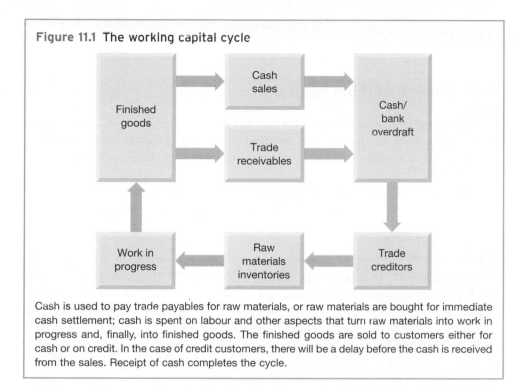

Figure 11.1 The working capital cycle

Cash is used to pay trade payables for raw materials, or raw materials are bought for immediate cash settlement; cash is spent on labour and other aspects that turn raw materials into work in progress and, finally, into finished goods. The finished goods are sold to customers either for cash or on credit. In the case of credit customers, there will be a delay before the cash is received from the sales. Receipt of cash completes the cycle.

The working capital needs of a particular business are likely to change over time as a result of changes in the business environment. This means that working capital decisions are constantly being made. Managers must try to identify changes in an attempt to ensure that the level of investment in working capital is appropriate.

Activity 11.1

What kind of changes in the commercial environment might lead to a decision to change the level of investment in working capital? Try to identify four possible changes that could affect the working capital needs of a business.

These may include the following:

- changes in interest rates;
- changes in market demand;
- changes in the seasons;
- changes in the state of the economy.

You may have also thought of others.

In addition to changes in the external environment, changes arising within the business could alter the required level of investment in working capital. Examples of such internal changes include using different production methods (resulting, perhaps, in a need to hold less inventories) and changes in the level of risk that managers are prepared to take.

The scale of working capital

We might imagine that, compared with the scale of investment in non-current assets by the typical business, the amounts involved with working capital are pretty trivial. This would be unrealistic – the scale of the working capital elements for most businesses is vast.

Real World 11.1 gives some impression of the working capital involvement for five UK businesses that are either very well known by name, or whose products are

Real World 11.1

A summary of the balance sheets of five UK businesses

Business:	Next plc	British Airways plc	Pilkington plc	Tesco plc	Severn Trent plc
Balance sheet date:	29.1.05	31.3.05	31.3.05	26.2.05	31.3.05
	%	%	%	%	%
Non-current (fixed) assets	71	102	86	118	111
Current assets					
Inventories	48	1	18	9	1
Trade receivables	54	8	17	–	5
Other receivables	12	5	6	7	4
Cash and near cash	11	20	7	8	2
	125	34	48	24	12
Current liabilities					
Trade payables	24	11	12	20	1
Tax and dividends	29	1	8	6	5
Other short-term liabilities	40	17	10	13	8
Overdrafts and short-term loans	3	7	4	3	9
	96	36	34	42	23
Working capital	29	(2)	14	(18)	(11)
Total long-term investment	100	100	100	100	100

Source: The table was constructed from information appearing in the annual reports of the five businesses concerned

The non-current assets, current assets and current liabilities are expressed as a percentage of the total net investment (equity plus non-current liabilities) of the business concerned. The businesses were randomly selected, except that they were deliberately taken from different industries. Next is a major retail and home shopping business. British Airways (BA) is a major airline. Pilkington is a glass-making business, whose products are to be found in many buildings and vehicles. Tesco is one of the major UK supermarkets. Severn Trent (ST) is a major supplier of water, sewerage services and waste management, mainly in the UK.

everyday commodities for most of us. These businesses were randomly selected, except that each one is high profile and from a different industry. For each business the major balance sheet items are expressed as a percentage of the total investment by the providers of long-term finance.

The totals for current assets are pretty large when compared with the total long-term investment. This is particularly true of Next and Pilkington. The amounts vary considerably from one type of business to the next. When we look at the nature of working capital held we can see that Next, Pilkington and Tesco, which produce and/or sell goods, are the only ones that hold significant amounts of inventories. The other two businesses are service providers and so inventories are not a significant item. We can see from the table that Tesco does not sell on credit and very few of BA's and ST's sales are on credit as these businesses have little or nothing invested in trade receivables. It is interesting to note that Tesco's trade payables are much higher than its inventories. Since most of these payables will be suppliers of inventories, it means that the business is able, on average, to have the cash from a particular sale in the bank before it needs to pay for the goods concerned.

These types of variation in the amounts and types of working capital elements are typical of other businesses.

In the sections that follow, we shall consider each element of working capital separately and how they might be properly managed. It seems from the evidence presented in Real World 11.2 that there is much scope for improvement in working capital management among UK businesses.

Real World 11.2

Capital not working hard enough!

According to a survey of 250 of the UK's largest businesses, conducted in 2004 by REL Consultancy Group, working capital is not as well managed as it could be. It is estimated that larger UK businesses have £76 billion tied up in working capital that could be released with better management of the inventories, receivables, payables and cash. Were the businesses able to manage their working capital more efficiently, REL estimate that they would increase their net profit by a staggering 19 per cent on average.

It appears that businesses in other European countries tend to be even less efficient in their management of working capital than those in the UK.

Source: Information taken from 'UK lags in cash management gains', Salamander Davoudi, *Financial Times*, 30 August 2004. The survey referred to is REL Consultancy Group's Seventh Annual Working Capital Survey Europe

---

Managing inventories (stock)

A business may hold inventories for various reasons, the most common of which is to meet the immediate day-to-day requirements of customers and production. However, a business may hold more than is necessary for this purpose if it is believed that future supplies may be interrupted or scarce. Similarly, if the business believes that the cost of inventories will rise in the future, it may decide to stockpile.

For some types of business the inventories held may represent a substantial proportion of the total assets held. For example, a car dealership that rents its premises may have nearly all of its total assets in the form of inventories. Inventories levels of manufacturers tend to be higher than in many other types of business as it is necessary to hold three kinds of inventories: raw materials, work-in-progress and finished goods. Each form of inventories represents a particular stage in the production cycle. For some types of business, the level of inventories held may vary substantially over the year owing to the seasonal nature of the industry. An example of such a business is a greetings card manufacturer. For other businesses, inventories levels may remain fairly stable throughout the year.

Where a business holds inventories simply to meet the day-to-day requirements of its customers and for production, it will normally seek to minimise the amount of inventories held. This is because there are significant costs associated with holding inventories. These include:

- storage and handling costs;
- financing costs;
- the costs of pilferage and obsolescence;
- the cost of opportunities forgone in tying up funds in this form of asset.

However, a business must also recognise that, if the level of inventories held is too low, there will also be associated costs.

Activity 11.2

What costs might a business incur as a result of holding too low a level of inventories? Try to jot down at least three types of cost.

In answering this activity you may have thought of the following costs:

- loss of sales, from being unable to provide the goods required immediately;
- loss of goodwill from customers, for being unable to satisfy customer demand;
- high transport costs incurred to ensure that inventories are replenished quickly;
- lost production due to shortage of raw materials;
- inefficient production scheduling due to shortages of raw materials;
- purchasing inventories at a higher price than might otherwise have been possible in order to replenish inventories quickly.

Before we go on to deal with the various approaches that can be taken to managing inventories, Real World 11.3 provides an example of how badly things can go wrong if inventories is not adequately controlled.

To try to ensure that the inventories are properly managed, a number of procedures and techniques may be used. These are reviewed below.

Pallets lost at Brambles

Brambles Industries plc (BI) is an Anglo-Australian industrial services business, formed in 2001 when the industrial services subsidiary of GKN plc, the UK engineering business, was merged with the Australian business Brambles Ltd.

BI uses 'pallets' on which it delivers its products to customers. These are returnable by customers so BI holds a 'pool' of pallets. Each pallet costs the business about £10. Unfortunately, BI lost 14 million pallets during the year ended in June 2002 as a result of poor control and this led to a significant decline in the business's profits and share price.

At BI's annual general meeting in Sydney, Australia, one of the shareholders was quoted as saying: 'Running a pallet pool is not rocket science. I can teach one of my employees about pallets in 20 minutes.'

Source: Information taken from an article appearing in the *Financial Times*, 27 November 2002

Budgeting future demand

One of the best means of a business trying to ensure that there will be inventories available to meet future production and sales requirements is to make appropriate plans. The budgets should deal with each product that the business makes and/or sells. It is important that every attempt is made to ensure that plans are realistic, as they will determine future ordering and production levels. The budgets may be derived in various ways. They may be developed using statistical techniques such as time series analysis, or they may be based on the judgement of the sales and marketing staff. We considered inventories budgets and their link to production and sales budgets in Chapter 9.

Real World 11.4 provides an example how things went wrong on inventories at a major and well-known retailer.

Dreaming of a bright Christmas

Wal-Mart is the world's largest retailer and has extremely sophisticated inventories planning and control systems. Nevertheless, things can still go wrong. During 2002, there was a rise in sales revenue of 12 per cent and a rise in inventories levels of 10 per cent. The large rise in inventories in relation to the rise in sales revenue was unplanned and was largely due to sales revenue over the Christmas period falling below expectations. This represents poor inventories management by Wal-Mart standards. The business, however, expects to get back on track and to ensure that inventories grow by less than half the rate of sales revenue in the future.

Source: Information taken from Lex Column, *Financial Times*, 19 February 2003

Financial ratios

One ratio that can be used to help monitor inventories levels is the average inventories turnover period, which we examined in Chapter 6. As we should recall, this ratio is calculated as follows:

$$\text{Average inventories turnover period} = \frac{\text{Average inventories held}}{\text{Cost of sales}} \times 365$$

This will provide a picture of the average period for which inventories are held, and can be useful as a basis for comparison. It is possible to calculate the average inventories turnover period for individual product lines as well as for inventories as a whole.

Recording and reordering systems

The management of inventories in a business of any size requires a sound system of recording inventories movements. There must be proper procedures for recording inventories purchases and usages. Periodic inventories checks may be required to ensure that the amount of physical inventories held is consistent with what is indicated by the inventories records.

There should also be clear procedures for the reordering of inventories. Authorisation for both the purchase and the issue of inventories should be confined to a few senior staff. This should avoid problems of duplication and lack of co-ordination. To determine the point at which inventories should be reordered, information will be required concerning the lead time (that is, the time between the placing of an order and the receipt of the goods) and the likely level of demand.

Activity 11.3

An electrical retailer stocks a particular type of light switch. The annual demand for the light switch is 10,400 units, and the lead time for orders is four weeks. Demand for the light switch is steady throughout the year. At what quantity of the light switch should the business reorder, assuming that it is confident of the information given above?

The average weekly demand for the switch is 10,400/52 = 200 units. During the time between ordering new switches and receiving them, the quantity sold will be 4 × 200 units = 800 units. So the business should reorder no later than when the level held reaches 800 units, in order to avoid a 'stockout'.

In most businesses, there will be some uncertainty surrounding the above factors and so a buffer or safety inventories level may be maintained in case problems occur. The amount of the buffer to be held is really a matter of judgement. This judgement will depend on:

- the degree of uncertainty concerning the above factors;
- the likely costs of running out of the item concerned;
- the cost of holding the buffer inventories.

The effect of holding a buffer inventory will be to raise the inventories level (the re-order point) at which an order for new inventories is placed.

Activity 11.4

Assume the same facts as in Activity 11.3 above. However, we are also told that the business maintains a buffer inventory of 300 units. At what level should the business reorder?

The reorder point = the expected level of demand during the lead time,
plus the level of buffer inventories.
= 800 + 300
= 1,100 units

Carrying buffer inventories will increase the cost of holding inventories; however, this must be weighed against the cost of running out of inventories, in terms of lost sales, production problems and so on.

Real World 11.5 provides an example of how small businesses can use technology in inventories reordering to help compete against their larger rivals.

Real World 11.5

Taking on the big boys

The use of technology in inventories recording and reordering may be of vital importance to the survival of small businesses that are being threatened by larger rivals. One such example is that of small independent bookshops. Technology can come to their rescue in two ways. First, electronic point-of-sale (EPOS) systems can record books as they are sold and can constantly update inventories held. Thus, books that need to be re-ordered can be quickly and easily identified. Second, the re-ordering process can be improved by using web-based technology, which allows books to be ordered in real time. Many large book wholesalers provide free web-based software to their customers for this purpose and try to deliver books ordered during the next working day. This means that a small bookseller, with limited shelf space, may keep one copy only of a particular book but maintain a range of books that competes with that of a large bookseller.

Source: Information taken from 'Small stores keep up with the big boys', *Financial Times*, 5 February 2003, FT.com

Levels of control

Senior managers must make a commitment to the management of inventories. However, the cost of controlling inventories must be weighed against the potential benefits. It may be possible to have different levels of control according to the nature of the inventories held. The ABC system of inventories control is based on the idea of selective levels of control.

A business may find that it is possible to divide its inventories into three broad categories: A, B and C. Each category will be based on the value of inventories held, as is illustrated in Example 11.1.

Example 11.1

Alascan Products plc makes door handles and door fittings. It makes them in brass, in steel and in plastic. The business finds that brass fittings account for 10 per cent of the physical volume of the finished inventories that it holds, but these represent 65 per cent of its total value. This is treated as Category A inventories. There are sophisticated recording procedures, tight control is exerted over inventories movements and there is a high level of security at the inventories' location. This is economic because the inventories represent a relatively small proportion of the total volume.

The business finds that steel fittings account for 30 per cent of the total volume of finished inventories and represent 25 per cent of its total value. This is treated as Category B inventories, with a lower level of recording and management control being applied.

The remaining 60 per cent of the volume of inventories is plastic fittings, which represent the least valuable items that account for only 10 per cent of the total value of finished inventories held. This is treated as Category C inventories, so the level of recording and management control would be lower still. Applying to these inventories, the level of control that is applied to Category A or even Category B inventories would be uneconomic.

Categorising inventories in this way seeks to direct management effort to the most important areas, and tries to ensure that the costs of controlling inventories are appropriate to its importance.

Figure 11.2 shows the logic of the ABC approach to inventories control.

Inventories management models

It is possible to use decision models to help manage inventories. The economic order quantity (EOQ) model is concerned with answering the question 'How much inventories should be ordered?' In its simplest form, the EOQ model assumes that demand is constant, so that inventories will be depleted evenly over time, and replenished just at the point that it runs out. These assumptions would lead to a 'saw tooth' pattern to represent inventories' movements, as shown in Figure 11.3.

The EOQ model recognises that the key costs associated with inventories management are the costs of holding it and the cost of ordering it. The model can be used to calculate the optimum size of a purchase order by taking account of both of these cost elements. The cost of holding inventories can be substantial, and so management may try to minimise the average amount of inventories held. However, by reducing the level of inventories held, and therefore the holding costs, there will be a need to increase the number of orders during the period, and so ordering costs will rise.

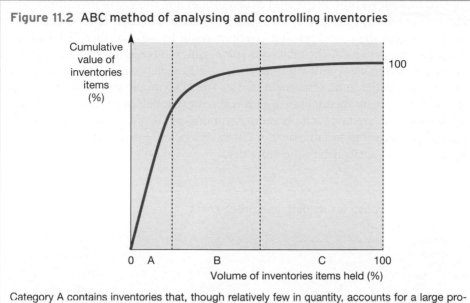

Figure 11.2 ABC method of analysing and controlling inventories

Category A contains inventories that, though relatively few in quantity, accounts for a large proportion of the total value. Category B inventories consists of those items that are less valuable
but more numerous. Category C comprises those inventories items that are very numerous but
relatively low in value. Different inventories control rules would be applied to each category. For
example, only Category A inventories would attract the more expensive and sophisticated controls.

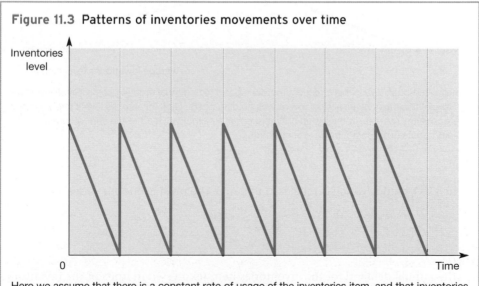

Figure 11.3 Patterns of inventories movements over time

Here we assume that there is a constant rate of usage of the inventories item, and that inventories
are reduced to zero just as new inventories arrive. At time 0 there is a full level of inventories. This
is steadily used as time passes; just as it falls to zero it is replaced. This pattern is then repeated.

Figure 11.4 shows how, as the level of inventories and the size of inventories orders increase, the annual costs of placing orders will decrease because fewer orders will be placed. However, the cost of holding inventories will increase, as there will be higher average inventories levels. The total costs curve, which is based on the sum of holding costs and ordering costs, will fall until the point E, which represents the minimum total cost. Thereafter, total costs begin to rise. The EOQ model seeks to identify point E at which total costs are minimised. This will represent half of the optimum amount that should be ordered on each occasion. Assuming, as we are doing, that inventories are used evenly over time and that they fall to zero before being replaced, the average inventories level equals half of the order size.

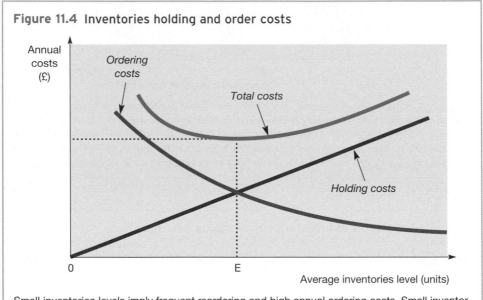

Figure 11.4 Inventories holding and order costs

Small inventories levels imply frequent reordering and high annual ordering costs. Small inventories levels also imply relatively low inventories holding costs. High inventories levels imply exactly the opposite. There is, in theory, an optimum order size that will lead to the sum of ordering and holding costs (total costs) being at a minimum.

The EOQ model, which can be used to derive the most economic order quantity, is:

$$EOQ = \sqrt{\frac{2DC}{H}}$$

where:

D = the annual demand for the inventories item (expressed in units of the inventories item);

C = the cost of placing an order;

H = the cost of holding one unit of inventories for one year.

Activity 11.5

HLA Ltd sells 2,000 bags of cement each year. It has been estimated that the cost of holding one bag of cement for a year is £4. The cost of placing an order for new inventories is estimated at £250.

Calculate the EOQ for bags of cement.

Your answer to this activity should be as follows:

$$EOQ = \sqrt{\frac{2 \times 2,000 \times 250}{4}}$$

$$= 500 \text{ units}$$

This will mean that the business will have to order bags of cement four times each year so that sales demand can be met.

Note that the cost of the inventories concerned, which is the price paid to the supplier, does not directly impact on the EOQ model. The EOQ model is only concerned with the administrative costs of placing each order and the costs of looking after the inventories. Where the business operates an ABC system of inventories control, however, more expensive inventory items will have greater holding costs. So the cost of the inventories may have an indirect effect on the economic order size that the model recommends.

The basic EOQ model has a number of limiting assumptions. In particular, it assumes that:

- demand for the product can be predicted with accuracy;
- demand is constant over the period and does not fluctuate through seasonality or other reasons;
- no 'buffer' inventories are required;
- there are no discounts for bulk purchasing.

However, the model can be developed to accommodate the problems of each of these limiting assumptions. Many businesses use this model (or a development of it) to help in the management of inventories.

Materials requirement planning systems

A materials requirement planning (MRP) system takes planned sales demand as its starting point. It then uses a computer package to help schedule the timing of deliveries of bought-in parts and materials to coincide with production requirements. It is a co-ordinated approach that links materials and parts deliveries to the scheduled time of their input to the production process. By ordering only those items that are necessary to ensure the flow of production, inventory levels are likely to be reduced. MRP is really a 'top-down' approach to inventories management, which recognises that inventories ordering decisions cannot be viewed as being independent of production decisions. In recent years, this approach has been extended so as to provide a fully integrated approach to production planning. The approach also takes account of other manufacturing resources such as labour and machine capacity.

Just-in-time inventories management

In recent years, many businesses have tried to eliminate the need to hold inventories by adopting 'just-in-time' (JIT) inventories management. This approach was first used in the United States defence industry during the Second World War, but was first used on a wide scale by Japanese manufacturing businesses. The essence of JIT is, as the name suggests, to have supplies delivered to a business just in time for them to be used in the production process or in a sale. By adopting this approach the inventories holding costs rest with suppliers rather than with the business itself. On the other hand, a failure by a particular supplier to deliver on time could cause enormous problems and costs to the business. Thus JIT can save cost, but it tends to increase risk.

For JIT to be successful, it is important that the business informs suppliers of its inventories requirements in advance, and that suppliers, in their turn, deliver materials of the right quality at the agreed times. Failure to do so could lead to a dislocation of production or supply to customers and could be very costly. Thus a close relationship is required between the business and its suppliers.

This close relationship enables suppliers to schedule their own production to that of their customers. This should mean that between supplier and customer there should be a net saving in the amount of inventories needed to be held, relative to that that would apply were JIT not in operation.

Though a business that applies JIT will not have to hold inventories, there may be other costs associated with this approach. As the suppliers will be required to hold inventories for the business, they may try to recoup this additional cost through increased prices. The close relationship necessary between the business and its suppliers may also prevent the business from taking advantage of cheaper sources of supply if they become available.

Many people view JIT as more than simply an inventories control system. The philosophy underpinning this approach is concerned with eliminating waste and striving for excellence. There is an expectation that suppliers will always deliver inventories on time and that there will be no defects in the items supplied. There is also an expectation that, for manufacturers, the production process will operate at maximum efficiency. This means there will be no production breakdowns and the queuing and storage times of products manufactured will be eliminated, as only that time spent directly on processing the products is seen as adding value. While these expectations may be impossible to achieve, they do help to create a culture that is dedicated to the pursuit of excellence and quality.

Real Worlds 11.6 and 11.7 show how two very well-known businesses operating in the UK (one a retailer, the other a manufacturer) use JIT to advantage.

Real World 11.6

JIT at Boots

The Boots Company plc, the UK's largest healthcare retailer, has recently improved the inventories management at its stores. The business is working towards a JIT system where delivery from its one central warehouse in Nottingham will be made every day to each retail branch, with nearly all of the inventories lines being placed directly on to the sales shelves, not into a branch stock room. The business says that this will bring significant savings of stores staff time and lead to significantly lower levels of inventories being held, without any lessening of the service offered to customers. The new system is expected to lead to major economic benefits for the business.

Source: Information taken from The Boots Company plc annual report and accounts for 2005

Real World 11.7

JIT at Nissan

Nissan Motors UK Limited, the UK manufacturing arm of the world famous Japanese car business has a plant in Sunderland in the NE of England. Here it operates a well-developed JIT system. Sommer supplies carpets and soft interior trim from a factory close to the Nissan plant. It makes deliveries to Nissan once every 20 minutes on average, so as to arrive exactly as they are needed in production. This is fairly typical of all of the 200 suppliers of components and materials to the Nissan plant.

Source: Information taken from Partnership Sourcing Best Practice Case Study (www.pslcbi.com/studies/docnissan.hmt)

Managing receivables (debtors)

Selling goods or services on credit will result in costs being incurred by a business. These costs include credit administration costs, bad debts, and opportunities forgone in using the funds for more profitable purposes. However, these costs must be weighed against the benefits of increased sales resulting from the opportunity for customers to delay payment.

Selling on credit is very widespread, and appears to be the norm outside the retail trade. When a business offers to sell its goods or services on credit, it must have clear policies concerning:

- which customers should receive credit;
- how much credit should be offered;
- what length of credit it is prepared to offer;
- whether discounts will be offered for prompt payment;
- what collection policies should be adopted;
- how the risk of non-payment can be reduced.

In this section, we shall consider each of these issues.

Which customers should receive credit?

A business offering credit runs the risk of not receiving payment for goods or services supplied. Thus, care must be taken over the type of customer to whom credit facilities are offered. When considering a proposal from a customer for the supply of goods or services on credit, the business must take a number of factors into account. The following five Cs of credit provide a business with a useful checklist.

- *Capital*. The customer must appear to be financially sound before any credit is extended. Where the customer is a business, its financial statements should be examined. Particular regard should be given to the customer's likely future profitability and liquidity. In addition, any major financial commitments (for example, capital expenditure, contracts with suppliers) must be taken into account.
- *Capacity*. The customer must appear to have the capacity to pay amounts owing. Where possible, the payment record of the customer to date should be examined. If the customer is a business, the type of business operated and the physical resources of the business will be relevant. The value of goods that the customer wishes to buy on credit must be related to the customer's total financial resources.
- *Collateral*. On occasions, it may be necessary to ask for some kind of security for goods supplied on credit. When this occurs, the business must be convinced that the customer is able to offer a satisfactory form of security.
- *Conditions*. The state of the industry in which the customer operates, and the general economic conditions of the particular region or country, may have an important influence on the ability of a customer to pay the amounts outstanding on the due date.
- *Character*. It is important for a business to make some assessment of the customer's character. The willingness to pay will depend on the honesty and integrity of the individual with whom the business is dealing. Where the customer is a limited company this will mean assessing the characters of its directors. The business must feel satisfied that the customer will make every effort to pay any amounts owing.

It is clear from the above that the business will need to gather information concerning the ability and willingness of the customer to pay the amounts owing at the due dates.

Activity 11.6

Assume that you are the credit manager of a business and that a limited company approaches you with a view to buying goods on credit. What sources of information might you decide to use to help assess the financial health of the potential customer?

There are various possibilities. You may have thought of some of the following:

- *Trade references*. Some businesses ask potential customers to supply them with references from other suppliers who have made sales on credit to them. This may be extremely useful, provided that the references supplied are truly representative of the opinions of a customer's suppliers. There is a danger that a potential customer will attempt to be selective when giving details of other suppliers, in order to gain a more favourable impression than is deserved.

- *Bank references*. It is possible to ask the potential customer for a bank reference. Though banks are usually prepared to supply references, the contents of such references are not always very informative. If customers are in financial difficulties, the bank may be unwilling to add to their problems by supplying poor references. It is worth remembering that the bank's loyalty is likely to be with the customer rather than the enquirer. There will usually be a fee, charged by the bank, for providing a reference.
- *Published financial statements*. A limited company is obliged by law to file a copy of its annual financial statements with the Registrar of Companies. These financial statements are available for public inspection and provide a useful source of information. Apart from the information contained in the financial statements, company law requires public limited companies to state in the directors' report the average time taken to pay suppliers. The annual reports of many companies are available on their own websites or on computer-based information systems (for example, FAME).
- *The customer*. Interviews with the directors of the customer business and visits to its premises may be carried out to gain some impression about the way that the customer conducts its business. Where a significant amount of credit is required, the business may ask the customer for access to internal budgets and other unpublished financial information to help assess the level of risk involved.
- *Credit agencies*. Specialist agencies exist to provide information that can be used to assess the creditworthiness of a potential customer. The information that a credit agency supplies may be gleaned from various sources, including the financial statements of the customer and news items relating to the customer from both published and unpublished sources. The credit agencies may also provide a credit rating for the business.
- *Register of County Court Judgements*. Any money judgements given against the business or an individual in a County Court will be maintained on the register for six years. This register is available for inspection by any member of the public for a small fee.
- *Other suppliers*. Similar business will often be prepared to exchange information concerning slow payers or defaulting customers through an industry credit circle. This can be a reliable and relatively cheap way of obtaining information.

Length of credit period

A business must determine what credit terms it is prepared to offer its customers. The length of credit offered to customers can vary significantly between businesses, and may be influenced by such factors as:

- the typical credit terms operating within the industry;
- the degree of competition within the industry;
- the bargaining power of particular customers;
- the risk of non-payment;
- the capacity of the business to offer credit;
- the marketing strategy of the business.

The last point identified may require some explanation. The marketing strategy of a business may have an important influence on the length of credit allowed. For example, if a business wishes to increase its market share it may decide to be more generous in its credit policy in an attempt to stimulate sales. Potential customers may be attracted by the offer of a longer credit period. However, any such change in policy must take account of the likely costs and benefits arising.

To illustrate this point, consider Example 11.2.

Example 11.2

Torrance Ltd produces a new type of golf putter. The business sells the putter to wholesalers and retailers and has an annual turnover of £600,000. The following data relate to each putter produced.

	£	£
Selling price		40
Variable costs	20	
Fixed cost apportionment	6	26
Net profit		14

The business's cost of capital is estimated at 10 per cent a year.

Torrance Ltd wishes to expand the sales volume of the new putter. It believes that offering a longer credit period can achieve this. The business's average receivables collection period is currently 30 days. It is considering three options in an attempt to increase sales revenue. These are as follows:

	Option		
	1	*2*	*3*
Increase in average collection period (days)	10	20	30
Increase in sales revenue (£)	30,000	45,000	50,000

To enable the business to decide on the best option to adopt, it must weigh the benefits of the options against their respective costs. The benefits arising will be represented by the increase in profit from the sale of additional putters. From the cost data supplied we can see that the contribution (that is, selling price (£40) less variable costs (£20)) is £20 a putter, that is, 50 per cent of the selling price. So, whatever increase there may be in sales revenue, the additional contributions will be half of that figure. The fixed costs can be ignored in our calculations, as they will remain the same whichever option is chosen.

The increase in contribution under each option will therefore be:

	Option		
	1	*2*	*3*
50% of the increase in sales revenue (£)	15,000	22,500	25,000

The increase in receivables under each option will be as follows:

	Option		
	1	*2*	*3*
	£	£	£
Projected level of receivables			
40 × £630,000/365 (Note 1)	69,041		
50 × £645,000/365		88,356	
60 × £650,000/365			106,849
Less Current level of receivables			
30 × £600,000/365	49,315	49,315	49,315
Increase in receivables	19,726	39,041	57,534

The increase in receivables that results from each option will mean an additional finance cost to the business.

The net increase in the business's profit arising from the projected change is:

	Option		
	1	2	3
	£	£	£
Increase in contribution (see above)	15,000	22,500	25,000
Less Increase in finance cost (Note 2)	1,973	3,904	5,753
Net increase in profits	13,027	18,596	19,247

The calculations show that Option 3 will be the most profitable one.

Notes:

1 If the annual sales revenue total £630,000 and 40 days' credit are allowed (both of which will apply under Option 1), the average amount that will be owed to the business by its customers, at any point during the year, will be the daily sales revenue (that is, £630,000/365) multiplied by the number of days that the customers take to pay (that is 40).

   Exactly the same logic applies to Options 2 and 3 and to the current level of receivables.

2 The increase in the finance cost for Option 1 will be the increase in receivables (£19,726) × 10 per cent. The equivalent figures for the other options are derived in a similar way.

Example 11.2 illustrates the way in which a business should assess changes in credit terms. However, if there is a risk that, by extending the length of credit, there will be an increase in bad debts, this should also be taken into account in the calculations, as should any additional receivable collection costs that will be incurred.

Real World 11.8 provides some insight into the typical length of credit taken by UK businesses.

Real World 11.8

Credit where it's due

The average collection period for receivables in the UK is around 60 days, according to survey evidence from Experian, the information services business.

   Where the credit customers are large UK businesses the average time that the supplier has to wait for the cash is about 78 days.

Source: Information taken from 'Legislation fails to curb late payment problems', Jonathon Moules, *Financial Times*, 28 July 2004, FT.com

An alternative approach to evaluating the credit decision

It is possible to view the credit decision as a capital investment decision. Granting trade credit involves an outlay of resources in the form of cash (which has been temporarily foregone) in the expectation that future cash flows will be increased (through higher sales) as a result. A business will usually have choices concerning the level of investment to be made in credit sales and the period over which credit is granted. These choices will result in different returns and different levels of risk. There is no reason in principle why the NPV investment appraisal method, which we considered in Chapter 10, should not be used to evaluate these choices. We have seen that the NPV method takes into account both the time value of money and the level of risk involved.

Cash discounts

A business may decide to offer a cash discount in an attempt to encourage prompt payment from its credit customers. The size of any discount will be an important influence on whether a customer decides to pay promptly.

From the business's viewpoint, the cost of offering discounts must be weighed against the likely benefits in the form of a reduction both in the cost of financing receivables and in the amount of bad debts.

In practice, there is always the danger that a customer may be slow to pay and yet may still take the discount offered. Where the customer is important to the business it may be difficult to insist on full payment. An alternative to allowing the customer to take discounts by reducing payment is to agree in advance to provide discounts for prompt payment through quarterly credit notes. As credit notes will only be given for those debts paid on time, the customer will often make an effort to qualify for the discount.

? Self-assessment question 11.1

Williams Wholesalers Ltd at present requires payment from its customers by the end of the month after the month of delivery. On average, customers take 70 days to pay. Sales revenue amounts to £4 million a year and bad debts to £20,000 a year.

It is planned to offer customers a cash discount of 2 per cent for payment within 30 days. Williams estimates that 50 per cent of customers will accept this facility but that the remaining customers, who tend to be slow payers, will not pay until 80 days after the sale. At present the business has an overdraft facility at an interest rate of 13 per cent a year. If the plan goes ahead, bad debts will be reduced to £10,000 a year and there will be savings in credit administration expenses of £6,000 a year.

Should Williams Wholesalers Ltd offer the new credit terms to customers? You should support your answer with any calculations and explanations that you consider necessary.

Collection policies

A business offering credit must ensure that amounts owing are collected as quickly as possible. Various steps can be taken to achieve this, including the following.

Develop customer relationships

For major customers it is often useful to cultivate a relationship with the key staff responsible for paying sales invoices. By so doing, the chances of prompt payment may be increased. For less important customers, the business should at least identify key staff responsible for paying invoices, who can be contacted in the event of a payment problem.

Publicise credit terms

The credit terms of the business should be made clear in all relevant correspondence, such as order acknowledgements, invoices and statements. In early negotiations with the prospective customer, credit terms should be openly discussed and an agreement reached.

Issue invoices promptly

An efficient collection policy requires an efficient accounting system. Invoices (bills) must be sent out promptly to customers, as must regular monthly statements. Reminders must also be dispatched promptly to customers who are late in paying. If a customer fails to respond to a reminder, the accounting system should alert managers so that a stop can be placed on further deliveries.

Monitor outstanding debts

Management can monitor the effectiveness of collection policies in a number of ways. One method is to calculate the average settlement period for receivables ratio, which we met in Chapter 6. This ratio, we should recall, is calculated as follows:

$$\text{Average settlement period for receivables} = \frac{\text{Trade receivables}}{\text{Credit sales}} \times 365$$

Though this ratio can be useful, it is important to remember that it produces an *average* figure for the number of days for which debts are outstanding. This average may be badly distorted by a few large customers who are very slow or very fast payers.

Produce an ageing schedule of receivables

A more detailed and informative approach to monitoring receivables may be to produce an ageing schedule of receivables. Debts are divided into categories according to the length of time the debt has been outstanding. An ageing schedule can be produced, on a regular basis, to help managers see the pattern of outstanding debts. An example of an ageing schedule is set out in Example 11.3.

Example 11.3

Ageing schedule of receivables at 31 December

Customer	Days outstanding				Total
	1 to 30 days £	31 to 60 days £	61 to 90 days £	More than 90 days £	£
A Ltd	20,000	10,000	–	–	30,000
B Ltd	–	24,000	–	–	24,000
C Ltd	12,000	13,000	14,000	18,000	57,000
Total	32,000	47,000	14,000	18,000	111,000

This shows a business's trade receivables figure at 31 December, which totals £111,000. Each customer's balance is analysed according to how long the debt has been outstanding. (This business has just three credit customers.)

Thus we can see from the schedule that A Ltd has £20,000 outstanding for 30 days or less (that is, arising from sales during December) and £10,000 outstanding for between 31 and 60 days (arising from November sales). This information can be very useful for credit control purposes.

Many accounting software packages now include this ageing schedule as one of the routine reports available to managers. Such packages often have the facility to put customers on 'hold' when they reach their credit limits. Putting a customer 'on hold' means that no further credit sales will be made to that customer, until debts arising from past sales have been settled.

Answer queries quickly

It is important for relevant staff to deal with customer queries on goods and services supplied quickly and efficiently. Payment is unlikely to be made by customers until their queries have been dealt with.

Deal with slow payers

It is almost inevitably the case that a business making significant sales on credit will sometimes be faced with customers who do not pay. When this occurs, there should be agreed procedures for dealing with the situation. However, the cost of any action to be taken against delinquent credit customers must be weighed against the likely returns. For example, there is little point in taking legal action against a customer, incurring large legal expenses, if there is evidence that the customer does not have the necessary resources to pay. Where possible, an estimate of the cost of bad debts should be taken into account when setting prices for products or services.

As a footnote to our consideration of managing receivables, Real World 11.9 outlines some of the excuses that long-suffering credit managers must listen to when chasing payment for outstanding debt.

It's in the post

Accountants' noses should be growing, if we're to believe a new survey listing the bizarre excuses given by businesses that fail to pay their debts.

'The director's been shot' and 'I'll pay you when God tells me to' are just two of the most outrageous excuses listed in a survey published by the Credit Services Association, the debt collection industry body.

The commercial sector tends to blame financial problems, and excuses such as 'you'll get paid when we do' and 'the finance director is off sick' are common. However, those in the consumer sector apparently feel no shame in citing personal relationship problems as the reason for not paying the bill.

Source: Accountancy, April 2000, p. 18

Managing cash

Why hold cash?

Most businesses hold a certain amount of cash. The amount of cash held tends to vary considerably between businesses.

Activity 11.7

Why do you think a business may decide to hold at least some of its assets in the form of cash? (*Hint*: There are broadly three reasons.)

The three are:

1 To meet day-to-day commitments, a business requires a certain amount of cash. Payments for wages, overhead expenses, goods purchased and so on must be made at the due dates. Cash has been described as the lifeblood of a business. Unless it circulates through the business and is available for the payment of maturing obligations, the survival of the business will be at risk. Profitability is not enough, a business must have sufficient cash to pay its debts when they fall due.

2 If future cash flows are uncertain for any reason, it would be prudent to hold a balance of cash. For example, a major customer that owes a large sum to the business may be in financial difficulties. Given this situation, the business can retain its capacity to meet its obligations by holding a cash balance. Similarly, if there is some uncertainty concerning future outlays, a cash balance will be required.

3 A business may decide to hold cash to put itself in a position to exploit profitable opportunities as and when they arise. For example, by holding cash, a business may be able to acquire a competitor's business that suddenly becomes available at an attractive price.

How much cash should be held?

Though cash can be held for each of the reasons identified, this may not always be necessary. If a business is able to borrow quickly, the amount of cash it needs to hold can be reduced. Similarly, if the business holds assets that can easily be converted to cash (for example, marketable securities such as shares in Stock Exchange listed businesses or government bonds), the amount of cash held can be reduced.

The decision as to how much cash a particular business should hold is a difficult one. Different businesses will have different views on the subject.

Activity 11.8

What do you think are the major factors that influence how much cash a business will hold? See if you can think of five possible factors.

You may have thought of the following:

- *The nature of the business*. Some businesses such as utilities (for example, water, electricity and gas suppliers) may have cash flows that are both predictable and reasonably certain. This will enable them to hold lower cash balances. For some businesses, cash balances may vary greatly according to the time of year. A seasonal business may accumulate cash during the high season to enable it to meet commitments during the low season.
- *The opportunity cost of holding cash*. Where there are profitable opportunities it may not be wise to hold a large cash balance.
- *The level of inflation*. Holding cash during a period of rising prices will lead to a loss of purchasing power. The higher the level of inflation, the greater will be this loss.
- *The availability of near-liquid assets*. If a business has marketable securities or inventories that may easily be liquidated, the amount of cash held may be reduced.
- *The availability of borrowing*. If a business can borrow easily (and quickly) there is less need to hold cash.
- *The cost of borrowing*. When interest rates are high, the option of borrowing becomes less attractive.
- *Economic conditions*. When the economy is in recession, businesses may prefer to hold cash so that they can be well placed to invest when the economy improves. In addition, during a recession, businesses may experience difficulties in collecting debts. They may therefore hold higher cash balances than usual in order to meet commitments.
- *Relationships with suppliers*. Too little cash may hinder the ability of the business to pay suppliers promptly. This can lead to a loss of goodwill. It may also lead to discounts being forgone.

Controlling the cash balance

Several models have been developed to help control the cash balance of the business. One such model proposes the use of upper and lower control limits for cash balances and the use of a target cash balance. The model assumes that the business will invest in marketable investments that can easily be liquidated. These investments will be purchased or sold, as necessary, in order to keep the cash balance within the control limits.

The model proposes two upper and two lower control limits (see Figure 11.5). If the business exceeds an *outer* limit, the managers must decide whether or not the cash balance is likely to return to a point within the *inner* control limits set, over the next few days. If this seems likely, then no action is required. If, on the other hand, it does not seem likely, management must change the cash position of the business by either lending or borrowing (or possibly by buying or selling marketable securities).

In Figure 11.5 we can see that the lower outer control limit has been breached for four days. If a four-day period is unacceptable, managers must sell marketable securities to replenish the cash balance.

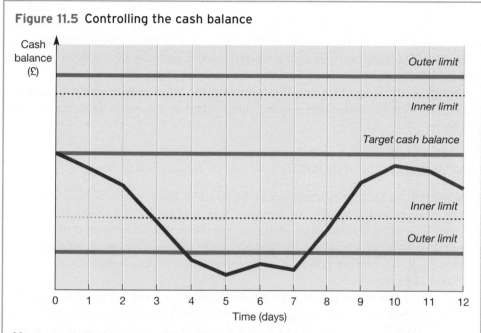

Figure 11.5 Controlling the cash balance

Management sets the upper and lower limits for the business's cash balance. When the balance goes beyond either of these limits, unless it is clear that the balance will return fairly quickly to within the limit, action will need to be taken. If the upper limit is breached, some cash will be placed on deposit or used to buy some marketable securities. If the lower limit is breached, the business will need to borrow some cash or sell some securities.

The model relies heavily on management judgement to determine where the control limits are set and the time period within which breaches of the control limits are acceptable. Past experience may be useful in helping managers decide on these issues. There are other models, however, that do not rely on management judgement. Instead, these use quantitative techniques to determine an optimal cash policy. One model proposed, for example, is the cash equivalent of the inventories economic order quantity model, discussed earlier in the chapter.

Cash budgets and managing cash

To manage cash effectively, it is useful for a business to prepare a cash budget. This is a very important tool for both planning and control purposes. Cash budgets were considered in Chapter 9, and so we shall not consider them again in detail. However, it is worth repeating the point that these statements enable managers to see the expected outcome of planned events on the cash balance. The cash budget will identify periods when cash surpluses and cash deficits are expected.

When a cash surplus is expected to arise, managers must decide on the best use of the surplus funds. When a cash deficit is expected, managers must make adequate provision by borrowing, liquidating assets or rescheduling cash payments or receipts to deal with this. Projected cash flow statements are useful in helping to control the cash held. The actual cash flows can be compared with the planned, cash flows for the period. If there is a significant divergence between the budgeted and the actual cash flows, explanations must be sought and corrective action taken where necessary.

To refresh your memory on cash budgets, it would probably be worth looking back at page 289, Chapter 9.

Though cash budgets are prepared primarily for internal management purposes, prospective lenders sometimes require them when a loan to a business is being considered.

Operating cash cycle (OCC)

When managing cash, it is important to be aware of the operating cash cycle (OCC) of the business. For a retailer, for example, this may be defined as the time period between the outlay of cash necessary for the purchase of inventories and the ultimate receipt of cash from the sale of the goods. In the case of a business, for example, a wholesaler, that purchases goods on credit for subsequent resale on credit, the OCC is as shown in Figure 11.6.

Figure 11.6 shows that payment for goods acquired on credit occurs some time after those goods have been purchased, and therefore no immediate cash outflow arises from the purchase. Similarly, cash receipts from credit customers will occur some time after the sale is made, and so there will be no immediate cash inflow as a result of the sale. The OCC is the time period between the payment made to the supplier for goods concerned and the cash received from the credit customer. Though Figure 11.6 depicts the position for a retailing or wholesaling business, the precise definition of the OCC can easily be adapted for both service and manufacturing businesses.

The OCC is important because it has a significant influence on the financing requirements of the business: the longer the cycle, the greater the financing requirements of the business and the greater the financial risks. For this reason, a business is likely to want to reduce the OCC to the minimum possible period.

For the type of business mentioned above, which buys and sells on credit, the OCC can be calculated from the financial statements by the use of certain ratios. It is calculated as shown in Figure 11.7.

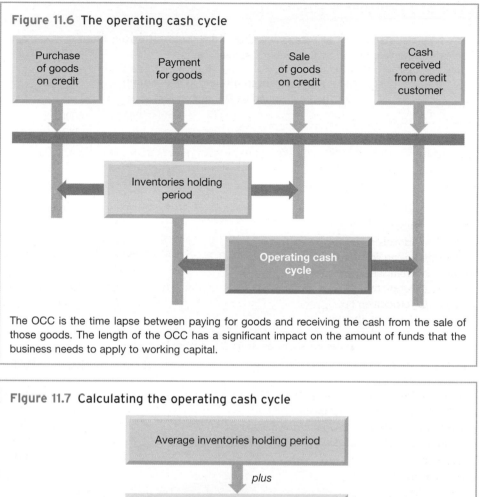

Figure 11.6 The operating cash cycle

The OCC is the time lapse between paying for goods and receiving the cash from the sale of those goods. The length of the OCC has a significant impact on the amount of funds that the business needs to apply to working capital.

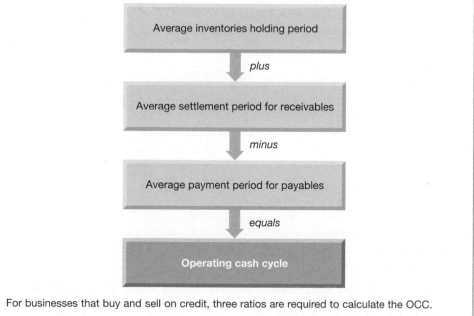

Figure 11.7 Calculating the operating cash cycle

For businesses that buy and sell on credit, three ratios are required to calculate the OCC.

Activity 11.9

The financial statements of Freezeqwik Ltd, a distributor of frozen foods, are set out below for the year ended 31 December last year.

**Income statement (profit and loss account)
for the year ended 31 December last year**

	£000	£000
Sales revenue		820
Less Cost of sales		
Opening inventories	142	
Purchases	568	
	710	
Less Closing inventories	166	544
Gross profit		276
Administration expenses	(120)	
Selling and distribution expenses	(95)	
Financial expenses	(32)	(247)
Net profit		29
Corporation tax		(7)
Net profit after tax		22

Balance sheet as at 31 December last year

	£000	£000	£000
Non-current assets			
Property, plant and equipment			
Freehold premises at valuation			180
Fixtures and fittings at written-down value			82
Motor vans at written-down value			102
			364
Current assets			
Inventories		166	
Trade receivables		264	
Cash		24	
		454	
Less **Current liabilities**			
Trade payables	159		
Corporation tax	7	166	288
			652
Equity			
Ordinary share capital			300
Preference share capital			200
Retained profit			152
			652

All purchases and sales are on credit. There has been no change in the level of receivables or payables over the period.

> Calculate the length of the OCC for the business and go on to suggest how the business may seek to reduce this period.

The OCC may be calculated as follows:

Average inventories holding period: *No. of days*

$$\frac{(\text{Opening inventories} + \text{Closing inventories})/2}{\text{Cost of sales}} \times 365 = \frac{(142 + 166)/2}{544} \times 365 \qquad 103$$

Average settlement period for receivables:

$$\frac{\text{Trade receivables}}{\text{Credit sales}} \times 365 = \frac{264}{820} \times 365 \qquad \underline{118}$$
$$221$$

Less

Average settlement period for payables:

$$\frac{\text{Trade payables}}{\text{Credit purchases}} \times 365 = \frac{159}{568} \times 365 \qquad \underline{102}$$

OCC $\underline{119}$

The business can reduce the length of the OCC in a number of ways. The average inventories holding period seems quite long. At present, average inventories held represent more than three months' sales. Lowering the level of inventories held will reduce this. Similarly, the average settlement period for receivables seems long, at nearly four months' sales. Imposing tighter credit control, offering discounts, charging interest on overdue accounts and so on, may reduce this. However, any policy decisions concerning inventories and receivables must take account of current trading conditions.

Extending the period of credit taken to pay suppliers could also reduce the OCC. However, for reasons that will be explained later, this option must be given careful consideration.

Cash transmission

A business will normally wish to benefit from receipts from customers at the earliest opportunity. The benefit is immediate where payment is made in cash. However, when payment is made by cheque, there is normally a delay of three to four working days before the cheque can be cleared through the banking system. The business must therefore wait for this period before it can benefit from the amount paid in. In the case of a business that receives large amounts in the form of cheques, the opportunity cost of this delay can be very significant.

To avoid this delay, a business could require payments to be made in cash. This is not usually very practical, mainly because of the risk of theft and/or the expense of conveying cash securely. Another option is to ask for payment to be made by standing order or by direct debit from the customer's bank account. This should ensure that the amount owing is always transferred from the bank account of the customer to the bank account of the business on the day that has been agreed.

It is also possible for funds to be transferred directly to a business's bank account. As a result of developments in computer technology, customers can pay for items by using debit cards, which results in the appropriate account being instantly debited and seller's bank account being instantly credited with the required amount. This method of payment is widely used by large retail businesses, and may well extend to other types of business.

Bank overdrafts

Bank overdrafts are simply negative bank current accounts that contain a negative amount of cash. They are a type of bank loan. We shall look at these in Chapter 12, in the context of short-term bank lending (p. 439). They can be a useful tool in managing the business's cash flow requirements.

Managing trade payables (creditors)

Trade credit arises from the fact that most businesses buy their goods and service requirements on credit. In effect, suppliers are lending the business money, interest free, on a short-term basis. Trade payables are the other side of the coin from trade receivables. One business's trade payable is another one's trade receivable, in respect of a particular transaction. Trade payables are an important source of finance for most businesses. It has been described as a 'spontaneous' source, as it tends to increase in line with the increase in the level of activity achieved by a business. Trade credit is widely regarded as a 'free' source of finance and, therefore, a good thing for a business to use. There may be real costs associated with taking trade credit, however.

Firstly, customers who take credit may not be as well treated as those who pay immediately. For example, when goods are in short supply, credit customers may receive lower priority when allocating the goods available. In addition, credit customers may be less favoured, in terms of delivery dates or the provision of technical support services. Sometimes, the goods or services provided may be more costly if credit is required. However, in most industries trade credit is the norm. As a result, the above costs will not apply except, perhaps, to customers that abuse the credit facilities. A business purchasing supplies on credit will normally have to incur additional administration and accounting costs in dealing with the scrutiny and payment of invoices, maintaining and updating payables' accounts, and so on.

In some cases, delaying payment to payables can be a sign of financial distress. One such example is given in Real World 11.10.

Where a supplier offers a discount for prompt payment, the business should give careful consideration to the possibility of paying within the discount period. An example may be useful to illustrate the cost of forgoing possible discounts.

Real World 11.10

Can't pay; won't pay

Kmart, a large US retailer, suffered a cash crisis during 2001. The crisis was largely as a result of one manager ordering $850m worth of inventories, which was later described in an internal report as 'excessive'. To conserve cash, the business implemented Project Slow It Down. This involved systematically delaying or reducing payments to trade payables. The project also involved denying payables access to records of the amounts owed by Kmart and giving false reasons as to why they had not been paid on time.

Source: Information taken from 'Kmart's fall is tale of poor governance', *Financial Times*, 29 January 2003

Example 11.4

Hassan Ltd takes 70 days to pay for goods from its supplier. To encourage prompt payment, the supplier has offered the business a 2 per cent discount if payment for goods is made within 30 days.

Hassan Ltd is not sure whether it is worth taking the discount offered.

If the discount is taken, payment could be made on the last day of the discount period (that is, the 30th day). However, if the discount is not taken, payment will be made after 70 days. This means that by not taking the discount the business will receive an extra 40 days' (that is, 70 minus 30) credit. The cost of this extra credit to the business will be the 2 per cent discount forgone. If we annualise the cost of this discount forgone, we have:

$$365/40 \times 2\% = 18.3\%*$$

We can see that the annual cost of forgoing the discount is very high, and it may be profitable for the business to pay the supplier within the discount period, even if it means that it will have to borrow to enable it to do so.

* This is an approximate annual rate. For the more mathematically minded, the precise rate is:

$$(((1 + 2/98)^{9.125}) - 1) \times 100\% = 20.2\%$$

The above points are not meant to imply that taking credit is a burden to a business. There are of course real benefits that can accrue. Provided that trade credit is not abused, it can represent a form of interest-free loan. It can be a much more convenient method of paying for goods and services than paying by cash, and during a period of inflation there will be an economic gain by paying later rather than sooner for goods and services purchased. For most businesses, these benefits will exceed the costs involved.

Controlling trade payables

To help monitor the level of trade credit taken, management can calculate the average settlement period for payables. As we saw in Chapter 6, this ratio is as follows:

$$\text{Average settlement period} = \frac{\text{Trade payables}}{\text{Credit purchases}} \times 365$$

Once again this provides an average figure, which could be misleading. A more informative approach would be to produce an ageing schedule for payables. This would look much the same as the ageing schedule for receivables described earlier.

Since, as was pointed out earlier in this section, one business's trade payable is another one's trade receivable, the information contained in Real World 11.8 provides some indication of typical lengths of trade credit taken by UK businesses.

Summary

The main points of this chapter may be summarised as follows:

Working capital (WC):

- Working capital is the difference between current assets and current liabilities
- That is, inventories + receivables + cash – payables – bank overdrafts.
- An investment in WC cannot be avoided in practice – typically large amounts are involved.

Inventories:

- There are costs of holding inventories, which include:
    - lost interest;
    - storage cost;
    - insurance cost;
    - obsolescence.

- There are also costs of not holding sufficient inventories, which include:
    - loss of sales and customer goodwill;
    - production dislocation;
    - loss of flexibility – cannot take advantage of opportunities;
    - reorder costs – low inventories imply more frequent ordering.

- Practical points on inventories management include:
    - identify optimum order size – models can help with this;
    - set inventories reorder levels;
    - use budgets;
    - keep reliable inventories records;
    - use accounting ratios (for example, inventories turnover period ratio);
    - establish systems for security of inventories and authorisation;
    - consider just-in-time (JIT) inventories management.

Trade receivables:

- When assessing which customers should receive credit, the five Cs of credit can be used:
  - capital;
  - capacity;
  - collateral;
  - condition;
  - character.

- The costs of allowing credit include:
  - lost interest;
  - lost purchasing power;
  - costs of assessing customer creditworthiness;
  - administration cost;
  - bad debts;
  - cash discounts (for prompt payment).

- The costs of denying credit include:
  - loss of customer goodwill.

- Practical points on receivables management:
  - establish a policy;
  - assess and monitor customer creditworthiness;
  - establish effective administration of receivables;
  - establish a policy on bad debts;
  - consider cash discounts;
  - use financial ratios (for example, average settlement period for receivables ratio);
  - use ageing summaries.

Cash:

- The costs of holding cash include:
  - lost interest;
  - lost purchasing power.

- The costs of holding insufficient cash include:
  - loss of supplier goodwill if unable to meet commitments on time;
  - loss of opportunities;
  - inability to claim cash discounts;
  - costs of borrowing (should an obligation need to be met at short notice).

- Practical points on cash management:
  - establish a policy;
  - plan cash flows;
  - make judicious use of bank overdraft finance – it can be cheap and flexible;
  - use short-term cash surpluses profitably;
  - bank frequently;
  - operating cash cycle (for a retailer) = length of time from buying inventories to receiving cash from receivables less payables' payment period (in days);
  - transmit cash promptly;

→

- An objective of WC management is to limit the length of the OCC, subject to any risks that this may cause.

Trade payables:

- The costs of taking credit include:
  - higher price than purchases for immediate cash settlement;
  - administrative costs;
  - restrictions imposed by seller.

- The costs of not taking credit include:
  - lost interest-free borrowing;
  - lost purchasing power;
  - inconvenience – paying at the time of purchase can be inconvenient.

- Practical points on payables management:
  - establish a policy;
  - exploit free credit as far as possible;
  - use accounting ratios (for example, average settlement period ratio).

→ Key terms

working capital p. 368
lead time p. 374
ABC system of inventories control
  p. 375
economic order quantity (EOQ) p. 376
materials requirement planning (MRP)
  system p. 379
just-in-time (JIT) inventories
  management p. 380

five Cs of credit p. 382
cash discount p. 386
average settlement period for
  receivables p. 387
ageing schedule of receivables p. 387
operating cash cycle (OCC) p. 392
average settlement period for
  payables p. 398

Further reading

If you would like to explore the topics covered in this chapter in more depth, we recommend the following books:

Arnold, G. *Corporate Financial Management*, 2nd edn, Financial Times Prentice Hall, 2002, Chapter 13.

Brealey, B. and Myers, S. *Principles of Corporate Finance*, 7th edn, McGraw-Hill, 2003, Chapters 30–32.

McLaney, E. *Business Finance: Theory and Practice*, 7th edn, Financial Times Prentice Hall, 2006, Chapter 13.

Pike, R. and Neale, B. *Corporate Finance and Investment*, 4th edn, Prentice Hall International, 2002, Chapters 14 and 15.

? Review questions

Answers to these questions can be found at the back of the book (pp. 496–7).

11.1 Tariq is the credit manager of Heltex plc. He is concerned that the pattern of monthly sales receipts shows that credit collection is poor compared with budget. Heltex's sales director believes that Tariq is to blame for this situation, but Tariq insists that he is not. Why might Tariq not be to blame for the deterioration in the credit collection period?

11.2 How might each of the following affect the level of inventories held by a business?
- An increase in the number of production bottlenecks experienced by the business.
- A rise in the level of interest rates.
- A decision to offer customers a narrower range of products in the future.
- A switch of suppliers from an overseas business to a local business.
- A deterioration in the quality and reliability of bought-in components.

11.3 What are the reasons for holding inventories? Are these reasons different from the reasons for holding cash?

11.4 Identify the costs of holding:
(a) too little cash;
(b) too much cash.

* Exercises

Exercises 11.4 and 11.5 are more advanced than 11.1 to 11.3. Those with a coloured number have an answer at the back of the book (pp. 520–2).

> If you wish to try more exercises, visit the students' side of the companion website.

11.1 Hercules Wholesalers Ltd has been particularly concerned with its liquidity position in recent months. The most recent income statement and balance sheet of the business are as follows:

Income statement for the year ended 31 December last year

	£000	£000
Sales revenue		452
Less Cost of sales		
Opening inventories	125	
Add purchases	341	
	466	
Less Closing inventories	143	323
Gross profit		129
Expenses		132
Net loss for the period		(3)

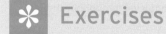

Balance sheet as at 31 December last year

	£000	£000	£000
Non-current assets			
Property, plant and equipment			
Freehold premises at valuation			280
Fixtures and fittings at cost less depreciation			25
Motor vehicles at cost less depreciation			52
			357
Current assets			
Inventories		143	
Receivables		163	
		306	
Less **Current liabilities**			
Trade payables	145		
Bank overdraft	140	285	21
			378
Less **Non-current liabilities**			
Loans			120
			258
Equity			
Ordinary share capital			100
Retained profit			158
			258

The receivables and payables were maintained at a constant level throughout the year.

Required:
(a) Explain why Hercules Wholesalers Ltd is concerned about its liquidity position.
(b) Calculate the operating cash cycle for Hercules Wholesalers Ltd based on the information above. (Assume a 360-day year.)
(c) State what steps may be taken to improve the operating cash cycle of the business.

11.2 International Electric plc at present offers its customers 30 days' credit. Half the customers, by value, pay on time. The other half takes an average of 70 days to pay. The business is considering offering a cash discount of 2 per cent to its customers for payment within 30 days.

The credit controller anticipates that half of the customers who now take an average of 70 days to pay (that is, a quarter of all customers) will pay in 30 days. The other half (the final quarter) will still take an average of 70 days to pay. The scheme will also reduce bad debts by £300,000 a year.

Annual sales revenue of £365 million is made evenly throughout the year. At present the business has a large overdraft (£60 million) with its bank at a cost of 12 per cent a year.

Required:
(a) Calculate the approximate equivalent annual percentage cost of a discount of 2 per cent, which reduces the time taken by credit customers to pay from 70 days to 30 days. (*Hint*: This part can be answered without reference to the narrative above.)
(b) Calculate receivables outstanding under both the old and new schemes.

(c) How much will the scheme cost the business in discounts?

(d) Should the business go ahead with the scheme? State what other factors, if any, should be taken into account.

(e) Outline the controls and procedures that a business should adopt to manage the level of its receivables.

11.3 The managing director of Sparkrite Ltd, a trading business, has just received summary sets of financial statements for last year and this year:

Sparkrite Ltd
Income statements for years ended 30 September last year and this year

	Last year		This year	
	£000	£000	£000	£000
Sales revenue		1,800		1,920
Less Cost of sales				
Opening inventories	160		200	
Purchases	1,120		1,175	
	1,280		1,375	
Less Closing inventories	200		250	
		1,080		1,125
Gross profit		720		795
Less Expenses		680		750
Net profit		40		45

Balance sheets as at 30 September last year and this year

	Last year		This year	
	£000	£000	£000	£000
Non-current assets		950		930
Current assets				
Inventories	200		250	
Receivables	375		480	
Bank	4		2	
	579		732	
Less Current liabilities	195		225	
		384		507
		1,334		1,437
Equity				
Fully paid £1 ordinary shares		825		883
Reserves		509		554
		1,334		1,437

The finance director has expressed concern at the increase in inventories and receivables levels.

Required:

(a) Show, by using the data given, how you would calculate ratios that could be used to measure inventories and receivables levels during last year and this year.

(b) Discuss the ways in which the management of Sparkrite Ltd could exercise control over:

(i) inventories levels;

(ii) receivables levels.

11.4 Mayo Computers Ltd has an annual turnover of £20 million before taking into account bad debts of £0.1 million. All sales made by the business are on credit, and, at present, credit terms are negotiable by the customer. On average, the settlement period for trade receivables is 60 days. Trade receivables are financed by an overdraft bearing a 14 per cent rate of interest per year. The business is currently reviewing its credit policies to see whether more efficient and profitable methods could be employed. Only one proposal has so far been put forward concerning the management of trade credit.

The credit control department has proposed that customers should be given a $2\frac{1}{2}$ per cent discount if they pay within 30 days. For those who do not pay within this period, a maximum of 50 days' credit should be given. The credit department believes that 60 per cent of customers will take advantage of the discount by paying at the end of the discount period, and the remainder will pay at the end of 50 days. The credit department believes that bad debts can be effectively eliminated by adopting the above policies and by employing stricter credit investigation procedures, which will cost an additional £20,000 a year. The credit department is confident that these new policies will not result in any reduction in sales revenue.

Required:

Calculate the net annual cost (savings) to the business of abandoning its existing credit policies and adopting the proposals of the credit control department. (*Hint*: To answer this question you must weigh the costs of administration and cash discounts against the savings in bad debts and interest charges.)

11.5 Boswell Enterprises Ltd is reviewing its trade credit policy. The business, which sells all of its goods on credit, has estimated that sales revenue for the forthcoming year will be £3 million under the existing policy. Credit customers representing 30 per cent of trade receivables are expected to pay one month after being invoiced and 70 per cent are expected to pay two months after being invoiced. These estimates are in line with previous years' figures.

At present, no cash discounts are offered to customers. However, to encourage prompt payment, the business is considering giving a $2\frac{1}{2}$ per cent cash discount to credit customers who pay in one month or less. Given this incentive, the business expects that credit customers accounting for 60 per cent of trade receivables to pay one month after being invoiced and those accounting for 40 per cent of trade receivables to pay two months after being invoiced. The business believes that the introduction of a cash discount policy will prove attractive to some customers and will lead to a 5 per cent increase in total sales revenue.

Irrespective of the trade credit policy adopted, the gross profit margin of the business will be 20 per cent for the forthcoming year and three months' inventories will be held. Fixed monthly expenses of £15,000 and variable expenses (excluding discounts), equivalent to 10 per cent of sales revenue, will be incurred and will be paid one month in arrears. Trade payables will be paid in arrears and will be equal to two months' cost of sales. The business will hold a fixed cash balance of £140,000 throughout the year, whichever trade credit policy is adopted. No dividends will be proposed or paid during the year. Ignore taxation.

Required:

(a) Calculate the investment in working capital at the end of the forthcoming year under:
    (i) the existing policy;
    (ii) the proposed policy.

(b) Calculate the expected net profit for the forthcoming year under:
    (i) the existing policy;
    (ii) the proposed policy.

(c) Advise the business as to whether it should implement the proposed policy.

(*Hint*: The investment in working capital will be made up of inventories, receivables and cash, *less* trade payables and any unpaid expenses at the year end.)

Chapter 12

Financing the business

Introduction

In this final chapter we examine various aspects of financing the business. We begin by considering the main sources of finance available. Some of these sources have already been touched upon when we discussed the structure of limited companies in Chapter 4 and the management of working capital in Chapter 11. In this chapter we shall discuss these in more detail as well as discussing other sources of finance that have not yet been mentioned. The factors to be taken into account when choosing an appropriate source of finance are also considered.

Following our consideration of the main sources of finance, we shall go on to examine various aspects of the capital markets including the role of the Stock Exchange, the financing of smaller businesses and the ways in which share capital may be issued.

Learning outcomes

When you have completed this chapter, you should be able to:

- identify the main sources of finance available to a business and explain the advantages and disadvantages of each source;
- outline the ways in which share capital may be issued;
- explain the role and nature of the Stock Exchange;
- discuss the ways in which smaller businesses may seek to raise finance.

Sources of finance

When considering the various sources of finance available to a business, it is useful to distinguish between *internal* and *external* sources of finance. By internal sources we mean sources that do not require the agreement of anyone beyond the directors and managers of the business. Thus, retained profit is considered an internal source because the directors of the business have power to retain profits without the agreement of the shareholders, whose profits they are. Finance from an issue of new shares, on the other hand, is an external source because it requires the compliance of potential shareholders.

Within each of the two categories just described, we can further distinguish between *long-term* and *short-term* sources of finance. There is no agreed definition concerning each of these terms but, for the purpose of this chapter, long-term sources of finance are defined as sources of finance that are expected to provide finance for at least one year. Short-term sources typically provide finance for a shorter period. As we shall see, often sources that are seen as short-term ones when first used by the business actually prove to be used for quite long periods.

In the sections that immediately follow, we consider the various sources of internal finance. We shall then go on to consider the various sources of external finance available. This is probably an appropriate order to deal with these since, in practice, businesses tend to look first to internal sources before going outside for new funds.

Internal sources of finance

Internal sources of finance usually have the advantage that they are flexible. They may also be obtained quickly – particularly from working capital sources – and need not require the compliance of other parties. The main sources of internal funds are described below, and are summarised in Figure 12.1.

Long-term sources of internal finance

Retained profits

Retained profit is the major source of finance for most businesses. By retaining profits within the business rather than distributing them to shareholders in the form of dividends, the funds of the business are increased.

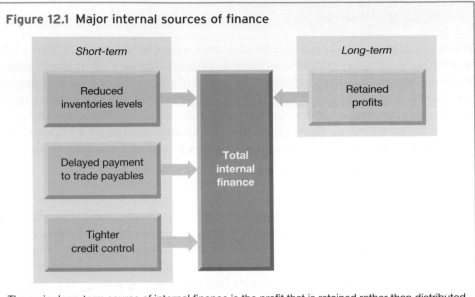

Figure 12.1 Major internal sources of finance

The major long-term source of internal finance is the profit that is retained rather than distributed to shareholders. The major short-term sources of internal finance involve reducing the level of receivables (debtors) and inventories (stocks) and increasing the level of payables (creditors).

Activity 12.1

Are retained profits a free source of finance to the business?

It is tempting to think that retained profits are a 'cost-free' source of funds for a business. However, this is not the case. If profits are reinvested rather than distributed to shareholders, those shareholders cannot invest the profits made in other forms of investment. They will therefore expect a rate of return from the profits reinvested that is equivalent to what they would have received had the funds been invested in another opportunity with the same level of risk.

The reinvestment of profits rather than the issue of new shares can be a useful way of raising capital from ordinary share investors. There are no issue costs associated with retaining profits, and the amount raised is certain, once the profit has been made. When issuing new shares, the issue costs may be substantial, and there may be uncertainty over the success of the issue. (We shall look at these two problem areas later in the chapter.)

Retaining profits will have no effect on the control of the business by existing shareholders, whereas new shares may be issued to outside investors leading to some dilution of control.

The decision to retain profits rather than pay them out as dividends to the shareholders is made by the directors. They may find it easier simply to retain profits rather than ask investors to subscribe to a new share issue. Retained profits are already held by the business, and so it does not have to wait to receive the funds. Moreover, there is often less scrutiny when profits are being retained for reinvestment purposes than when new shares are being issued. Investors and their advisers will closely examine the reasons for any new share issue. A problem with the use of profits as a source of finance, however, is that the timing and level of future profits cannot always be reliably estimated.

Some shareholders may prefer profits to be retained by the business, rather than be distributed in the form of dividends. By ploughing back profits, it may be expected that the business will expand, and that share values will increase as a result. In the UK, not all capital gains are liable for taxation. (For the tax year 2005/6, an individual with capital gains totalling less than £8,500 would not be taxed on those gains.) A further advantage of capital gains over dividends is that the shareholder has a choice as to when the shares are sold and the gain is realised. Research indicates that investors may be attracted to particular businesses according to the dividend/retention policies that they adopt.

It would be wrong to gain the impression that all businesses either retain all of their profit or pay it all out as a dividend. Where businesses pay dividends, and most larger ones do pay dividends, they typically pay no more than 50 per cent of the profit, retaining the remainder to fund expansion.

Retained profit is much the most important source of new finance for UK businesses, on average, in terms of value of funds raised.

Short-term sources of internal finance

Tighter credit control

By exerting tighter control over trade receivables (debtors) it may be possible for a business to reduce the proportion of assets held in this form and so release funds for other purposes. Having funds tied up in trade debts represents an opportunity cost in that those funds could be used for profit generating activities. As we saw in Chapter 11, it is important, however, to weigh the benefits of tighter credit control against the likely costs in the form of lost customer goodwill and lost sales. To remain competitive, a business must take account of the needs of its customers and the credit policies adopted by rival businesses within the industry.

Activity 12.2

H. Rusli Ltd provides a car valet service for car-hire businesses when their cars are returned from hire. Details of the service costs are as follows:

	Per car	
	£	£
Car valet charge		20
Less Variable costs	14	
Fixed costs	4	18
Net profit		2

Sales revenue is £10 million a year and is all on credit. The average credit period taken by the car-hire businesses is 45 days, although the terms of credit state that payment should be made within 30 days. Bad debts are currently £100,000 a year. Receivables are financed by a bank overdraft costing 10 per cent a year.

The credit control department of H. Rusli Ltd believes it can eliminate bad debts and can reduce the average credit period to 30 days if new credit control procedures are implemented. These will cost £50,000 a year, and are likely to result in a reduction in sales revenue of 5 per cent a year.

Should the business implement the new credit control procedures? (*Hint*: To answer this activity it is useful to compare the current cost of trade credit with the costs under the proposed approach.)

The current annual cost of trade credit is:

	£
Bad debts	100,000
Overdraft interest [(£10m × 45/365) × 10%]	123,288
	223,288

The annual cost of trade credit under the new policy will be:

	£
Overdraft interest [(95% × (10m) × (30/365)) × 10%]	78,082
Cost of control procedures	50,000
Net cost of lost sales [(£(£10m/£20) × 5%) × (20 – 14*)]	150,000
	278,082

* The loss will be the contribution per unit (that is, the difference between the selling price and the variable costs).

The above figures reveal that the business will be worse off if the new policies are adopted.

Reducing inventories (stock) levels

This is an internal source of funds that may prove attractive to a business. If it has a proportion of its assets in the form of inventories there is an opportunity cost, as the funds tied up cannot be used for other purposes. By holding less inventories, funds become available for those opportunities. However, a business must try to ensure that there is sufficient inventories available to meet likely future sales demand. Failure to do so will result in lost customer goodwill and lost sales revenue.

As we saw in Chapter 11, the nature and condition of the inventories held will determine whether it is possible to exploit this form of finance. A business may have too much inventories as a result of poor buying decisions in the past. This may mean that a significant proportion of the inventories held are slow moving or obsolete and cannot, therefore, be reduced easily.

Delaying payment to trade payables (creditors)

By providing a period of credit, suppliers are effectively offering a business an interest-free loan. If the business delays payment, the period of the 'loan' is extended and funds can be retained within the business. As we saw in Chapter 11, this can be a cheap form of finance for a business, although this is not always the case. If a business fails to pay within the agreed credit period, there may be significant costs. For example, the business may find it difficult to buy on credit when it has a reputation as a slow payer.

These so-called short-term sources are short term to the extent that can be reversed at short notice. For example, a reduction in the level of trade receivables can be reversed within a couple of weeks. Typically, however, once a business has established a reduced receivable collection period, a reduced inventory holding period and/or an expanded payables payment period, it will tend to maintain these new levels.

Sources of external finance

Figure 12.2 summarises the main sources of long-term and short-term external finance.

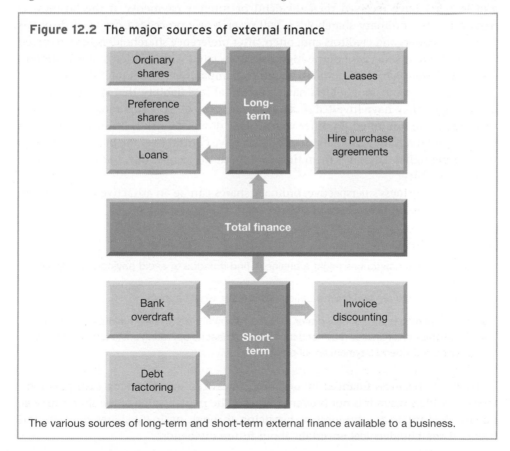

Figure 12.2 The major sources of external finance

The various sources of long-term and short-term external finance available to a business.

Long-term sources of external finance

As Figure 12.2 reveals, the major forms of long-term external finance are:

- ordinary shares;
- preference shares;
- loans;
- leases, that is, finance leases, including sale-and-leaseback arrangements;
- hire-purchase agreements.

We shall now discuss each of the sources identified.

Ordinary shares

As we saw in Chapter 4, ordinary shares form the backbone of the financial structure of a business. Ordinary share capital represents the business's risk capital. There is no fixed rate of dividend, and ordinary shareholders will receive a dividend only if profits available for distribution still remain after other investors (preference shareholders and lenders) have received their dividend or interest payments. If the business is wound up, the ordinary shareholders will receive any proceeds from asset disposals only after lenders and creditors and, often, after preference shareholders have received their entitlements. Because of the high risks associated with this form of investment, ordinary shareholders will normally require a comparatively high rate of return.

Though ordinary shareholders have a potential loss liability that is limited to the amount that they have invested or agreed to invest, the potential returns from their investment are unlimited. In other words, their downside risk is limited, while their upside potential is not. Ordinary shareholders have control over the business, through their voting rights. This gives them the power both to elect the directors and to remove them from office.

From the business's perspective, ordinary shares can be an attractive form of financing as, at times, it is useful to be able to avoid paying a dividend.

Activity 12.3

Under what circumstances might a business find it useful to avoid paying a dividend?

We feel that there are two main situations where this would apply:

- An expanding business may prefer to retain funds in order to help fuel future growth.
- A business in difficulties may need the funds to meet its operating costs and so may find making a dividend payment a real burden.

Though a business financed by ordinary shares can avoid making cash payments to shareholders when it is not prudent to do so, the market value of the shares may go down. The cost to the business of financing through ordinary shares may become higher if shareholders feel uncertain about future dividends.

It is also worth pointing out that the business does not obtain any tax relief on dividends paid to shareholders, whereas interest on borrowings is tax deductible. This makes it more expensive to the business to pay £1 of dividend than £1 of loan interest on borrowings.

Preference shares

Preference shares offer investors a lower level of risk than ordinary shares. Provided there are sufficient profits available, preference shares will normally be given a fixed rate of dividend each year, and preference shareholders will be paid the first slice of any dividend paid. Should the business be wound up, preference shareholders may be given priority over the claims of ordinary shareholders. (The business's particular documents of incorporation will state the precise rights of preference shareholders in this respect.)

Activity 12.4

Would you expect the returns on preference shares to be higher or lower than those of ordinary shares?

We expect returns on preference shareholders to be lower than those on ordinary shares. This is because of the lower level of risk associated with this form of investment (preference shareholders have priority over ordinary shareholders regarding dividends).

Preference shares are no longer an important source of new finance. A major reason for this is that dividends paid to preference shareholders, like those paid to ordinary shareholders, are not allowable against taxable profits, whereas interest on loan capital is an allowable expense. From the business's point of view, preference shares and loans are quite similar, so the tax deductibility of loan interest is an important issue.

Activity 12.5

Would you expect the market price of ordinary shares or preference shares to be the more volatile? Why?

The share price, which reflects the expected future returns from the share, will normally be less volatile for preference shares than for ordinary shares. The dividends of preference shares tend to be fairly stable over time, and there is usually an upper limit on the returns that can be received.

Both preference shares and ordinary shares are, in effect, *redeemable*. The business is allowed to buy back the shares from shareholders at any time.

Loans

Most businesses rely on loans as well as share capital to finance operations. Lenders enter into a contract with the business in which the rate of interest, dates of interest payments, capital repayments and security for the loan are clearly stated. In the event that the interest payments or capital repayments are not made on the due dates, the lender will usually have the right, under the terms of the contract, to seize the assets on which the loan is secured and sell them in order to repay the amount outstanding. Security for a loan may take the form of a fixed charge on particular assets of the business (freehold land and premises are often favoured by lenders) or a floating charge on the whole of its assets. A floating charge will 'float' over the assets and will only fix on particular assets in the event that the business defaults on its loan obligations.

Activity 12.6

What do you think is the advantage for the business of having a floating charge rather than a fixed charge on its assets?

A floating charge on assets allows the managers greater flexibility in their day-to-day operations than a fixed charge. Individual assets can be sold without reference to the lenders.

Term loans

→ One form of long-term loan is the term loan. This type of loan is offered by banks and other financial institutions, and is usually tailored to the needs of the client business. The amount of the loan, the time period, the repayment terms and the interest payable are all open to negotiation and agreement, which can be very useful. For example, where all of the funds to be borrowed are not required immediately, a business may agree with the lender that funds are drawn only as and when required. This means that interest will be paid only on amounts drawn and the business will not have to pay interest on amounts borrowed that are temporarily surplus to requirements. Term loans tend to be cheap to set up (from the borrower business's perspective) and can be quite flexible as to conditions.

Loan stocks and debentures

→ Another form of long-term loan finance is the loan stock. Loan stock is frequently divided into units (rather like share capital), and investors are invited to purchase the number of units they require. The loan stock may be redeemable or irredeemable. Loan stocks of public limited companies are often traded on the Stock Exchange, and their listed value will fluctuate according to the fortunes of the business, movements in interest rates and so on.

→ Debentures are simply loan stocks that are evidenced by a trust deed. Loan stocks and debentures are usually referred to as *bonds* in the USA and, increasingly, in the UK.

Eurobonds

→ **Eurobonds** are unsecured loan stocks denominated in a currency other than the home currency of the business that issued them. Eurobonds are issued by businesses (and other large organisations) in various countries, and the finance is raised on an international basis. They are often issued in US dollars, but many are issued in other major currencies. Interest is normally paid on an annual basis. Eurobonds are part of an ever-expanding international capital market, and they are not subject to regulations imposed by authorities in particular countries. Numerous financial institutions throughout the world have created a market for eurobonds, where holders of eurobonds are able to sell them to would-be holders. Eurobonds are usually issued by the business concerned making them available to large banks and other financial institutions, which may either retain them as an investment or sell them to their clients.

The extent of borrowing, by UK businesses, in currencies other than sterling has expanded massively in recent years. Businesses are often attracted to issue eurobonds because of the size of the international capital market. Access to a large number of international investors is likely to increase the chances of a successful issue. In addition, the lack of regulation in the eurobond market means that national restrictions regarding loan issues may be overcome.

Real World 12.1, which is an extract from an article in the *Financial Times*, provides an example of a eurobond issue by a well-known UK business.

Real World 12.1

Taking off with eurobonds

FT

A growing number of companies are entering the euro bond market for the first time, encouraged by the opportunity to reach new investors with low financing costs. . . . This week BAA, the operator of Heathrow and six other airports in the UK, raised €750m ($913m) from its first euro-denominated bond . . .

'This deal gave the company access to capital at a similar cost to what it could have done in sterling,' said Jean-Marc Mercier at HSBC's corporate syndicate desk, which managed the deal with BNP Paribas and Deutsche Bank.

'In addition, two-thirds of the investors in the deal were new to the company,' he added.

Diversifying the investor base is important for companies, as it increases their flexibility to raise capital when they need to.

Source: 'New appetite develops for Eurobonds', *Financial Times*, 18 September 2004, FT.com

Activity 12.7

Would you expect the returns to loan capital to be higher or lower than those of preference shares?

Investors are usually prepared to accept a lower rate of return. This is because they will normally view loans as being less risky than preference shares. Lenders have priority over any claims from preference shareholders, and will usually have security for their loans.

The risk return characteristics of loan, preference share and ordinary share finance are shown graphically in Figure 12.3.

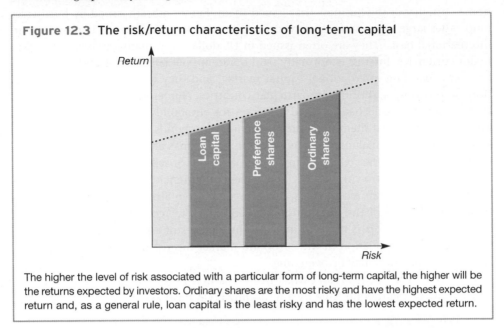

Figure 12.3 The risk/return characteristics of long-term capital

The higher the level of risk associated with a particular form of long-term capital, the higher will be the returns expected by investors. Ordinary shares are the most risky and have the highest expected return and, as a general rule, loan capital is the least risky and has the lowest expected return.

Interest rates and deep discount bonds

Interest rates on loan finance may be either floating or fixed. A floating rate means that the rate of return required by lenders will rise and fall with market rates of interest. However, the market value of the lender's investment in the business is likely to remain fairly stable over time. The converse will normally be true for fixed-interest loans and debentures. The interest payments will remain unchanged with rises and falls in market rates of interest, but the value of the loan investment will fall when interest rates rise and will rise when interest rates fall.

A business may issue redeemable loan capital that offers a rate of interest below the market rate. In some cases, the loan capital may have a zero rate of interest. Such loans are issued at a discount to their redeemable value and are referred to as deep discount bonds. Thus loan capital may be issued at, say, £80 for every £100 of nominal value. Although lenders will receive little or no interest during the period of the loan, they will receive a gain when the loan is finally redeemed at the full £100. The redemption yield, as it is referred to, is often quite high and, when calculated on an annual basis, may compare favourably with returns from other forms of loan capital with the same level of risk. Deep discount bonds may have particular appeal to businesses with short-term cash flow problems. Such businesses receive an immediate injection of cash, and there are no significant cash outflows associated with the loan until the maturity date. Deep discount bonds are likely to appeal to investors who do not have short-term cash flow needs, since they must wait for the loan to mature before receiving a cash return.

Convertible loan stocks

→ Convertible loan stocks (or convertible debentures or convertible bonds) give investors the right, but not the obligation, to exchange the loan stock for ordinary shares in the business at a specified price (the 'exercise' price) on a given future specified date or within a range of specified dates. The exercise price is usually higher than the market price of those ordinary shares at the time of issue of the convertible loan stock. In effect the investor swaps the loan stock for a particular number of shares. The investor remains a lender to the business, and will receive interest on the amount of the loan until such time as the conversion takes place. The investor is not obliged to convert to ordinary shares. This will be done only if the market price of the shares at the conversion date exceeds the specified conversion price.

An investor may find this form of investment a useful hedge against risk. This may be particularly useful when investment in a new business is being considered. Initially the investment is in the form of a loan, and regular interest payments will be made. If the business is successful, the investor can then decide to convert the investment into ordinary shares.

The business may also find this form of financing useful. If the business is successful, the loan becomes self-liquidating, as investors will exercise their option to convert. The business may also be able to offer a lower rate of interest to investors because they expect future benefits to arise from conversion. There will be, however, some dilution of both control and earnings for existing shareholders if holders of convertible loans exercise their option to convert.

Real World 12.2 details one particular convertible loan issue.

Real World 12.2

The answer is blowin' in the wind

In June 2003, Scottish Power plc issued convertible bonds to help finance research into new methods of creating energy, including the development of wind farms. The business initially intended to raise £343m from the issue, but the popularity of the bonds among investors allowed the business to raise $700m (£420m). The bonds were sold to specialist investors, mostly financial institutions. The investors can convert the bonds into 90 million ordinary shares in the future, which represent 5 per cent of Scottish Power's total share capital. Thus, there will not be a significant dilution of control for existing shareholders if the bonds are converted. The share price at which the bonds may be converted is 460 pence and, at the time of the issue, the market price of Scottish Power's shares was 372 pence.

Source: 'Generating cash from bonds', *Accountancy Age*, 17 July 2003, p. 7

Public issues of ordinary shares, preference shares and loan stocks

Real World 12.3 provides an impression of the relative importance of the three principal types of public issue.

Real World 12.3

New issues by listed businesses

Figure 12.4 plots the issues of capital made by UK listed businesses (excluding financial businesses such as banks) in recent years. The chart reveals that loan capital and ordinary shares are the major sources of long-term external finance. Preference shares are a much less important source of new finance.

Figure 12.4 Capital issues of UK Stock Exchange listed businesses (excluding financial businesses), 1992-2002

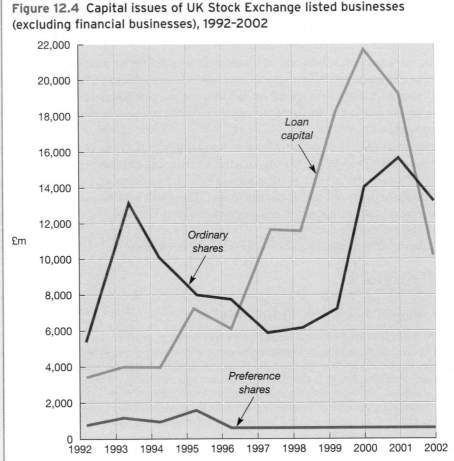

At times, the popularity of ordinary shares and that of loan capital seem to move counter to one another. When ordinary shares are popular loan capital is unpopular, and vice versa. This tends to reflect the level of interest rates and business confidence. However, in recent years, ordinary share issues and loan capital issues have both moved in the same direction. Preference shares have dwindled to virtually nothing, in terms of new issues. The chart, of course, is not the whole story. Most finance from ordinary shareholders comes from profit retentions rather than share issues. In addition, bank loans are not included.

Source: Based on information from *Financial Statistics*, Office for National Statistics, October 2005. Copyright © 2005 Crown copyright. Reproduced with the permission of the controller of HMSO.

Warrants

→ Holders of warrants have the right, but not the obligation, to acquire ordinary shares in a particular business at a given price (the 'exercise' price). As with convertible loan stocks, the price at which shares may be acquired is usually higher than the market price of those ordinary shares at the time of the issue of the warrants. The warrant will usually state the number of shares that the holder may purchase and the time limit within which the option to buy shares can be exercised. Occasionally, perpetual warrants are issued that have no set time limits. Warrants do not confer voting rights or entitle the holders to make any claims on the assets of the business. Warrants are themselves neither shares nor loan stocks.

Share warrants are often provided as a 'sweetener' to accompany the issue of loan capital, that is, an incentive to potential lenders. The issue of warrants in this way may enable the business to offer lower rates of interest on the loan or to negotiate less restrictive loan conditions. Sometimes businesses sell share warrants without there being a link to a loan stock issue. Warrants enable investors to benefit from any future increases in the business's ordinary share price, without having to buy the shares themselves. On the other hand, if the share price remains below the exercise price, the warrant cannot be used and the investor will lose out as a result.

Activity 12.8

Under what circumstances will the holders of share warrants exercise their option to purchase?

Holders will exercise this option only if the market price of the shares exceeds the exercise price within the time limit specified. If the exercise price is higher than the market price, it would be cheaper for the investor to buy the shares in the market.

To the business issuing the warrants, they represent a source of funds (the proceeds of selling the warrants). Alternatively, they represent an encouragement for the issue of another source of funds (a loan stock issue) to be successful.

Share warrants issued with a loan may be *detachable*, which means that they can be sold separately from the loan capital. The warrants of businesses whose shares are listed on the Stock Exchange are often themselves listed, providing a ready market for buying and selling the warrants.

It is probably worth mentioning the difference in status within a business between holders of convertible loan capital and holders of loans with share warrants attached if both groups decide to exercise their right to convert. Convertible loan stock holders become ordinary shareholders and are no longer lenders to the business. They will have used the value of the loan stocks to 'buy' the shares. Warrant holders become ordinary shareholders by paying cash for the shares. If the warrant holders held loan stocks, this will be unaffected by their exercising their right to buy the shares bestowed by the warrant.

→ Both convertibles and warrants are examples of financial derivatives. These are any form of financial instrument, based on share or loan capital, that can be used by investors to increase their returns or reduce risk.

Mortgages

→ A mortgage is a form of loan that is secured on an asset, typically freehold property. Financial institutions such as banks, insurance businesses and pension funds are often prepared to lend to businesses on this basis. The mortgage may be over a long period (20 years or more).

Loan covenants

→ Lenders often impose certain obligations and restrictions on borrowers in an attempt to protect themselves. Loan covenants (as they are called) often form part of a loan agreement, and may deal with such matters as:

- *Financial statements*. The lender may require access to the financial statements of the borrowing business on a regular basis.
- *Other loans*. The lender may require the business to ask the lender's permission before taking on further loans from other sources.
- *Dividend payments*. The lender may require dividend payments to be limited during the period of the loan.
- *Liquidity*. The lender may require the business to maintain a certain level of liquidity during the period of the loan. This would typically be a requirement that the borrower business's current ratio is maintained at, or above, a specified level.

Any breach of these restrictive covenants can have serious consequences for the business. The lender may require immediate repayment of the loan in the event of a material breach.

Real World 12.4 shows how one well-known UK business was at risk of breaching the covenants imposed by its lenders.

Real World 12.4

Bulmer warns of breach of covenants

HP Bulmer, the cidermaker crippled by over-ambitious expansion plans, yesterday admitted for the first time that the new management might have to put up a 'for sale' sign.

The company, which leads the UK cider market with its Strongbow brand, also warned that deteriorating trading conditions might lead to a breach of its banking covenants in April.

But Miles Templeman, chief executive, said he was fully aware of the reality of the situation when he took up the post at the beginning of this month. His appointment followed the loss of the former chief executive and finance director as the company's problems unfolded.

'It may have got a little worse,' said Mr Templeman. 'But I still believe this is a good business and it is better for us to turn it round and build the value back in ourselves.'

In a statement on its working capital requirements, the company said that October and November had been difficult months for sales of its cider to pub-goers in the UK. At the same time the decision to quit the international businesses and to stop product innovation was proving more expensive than previously estimated.

In addition, margins in the take-home trade were still being squeezed, and the loss of a third-party contract for packing at the company's Belgian plant had cost £800,000. As a result, the company, which only in November announced that it had agreed new financing arrangements with its banks until November this year, was at risk of breaching its covenants.

Mr Templeman said the board would be examining all options, including initiating talks with potential buyers if necessary. It would also consider selling the Beer Seller, the company's whole-sale business that specialises in supplies to independent pubs and restaurants, or a rights issue*.

Regarded as an expert on brands, Mr Templeman wants to focus on the UK cider business, particularly Strongbow. Bulmer has about two-thirds of the UK market, and also owns Woodpecker and Scrumpy Jack.

Source: 'Bulmer warns of breach of covenants', *Financial Times*, 25 January 2003, FT.com

As a postscript to this story, Bulmer was unsuccessful in its bid to save itself and was acquired later in 2003 by Scottish and Newcastle plc, the major UK drinks business.

* We met rights issues in Chapter 4. They are share issues made to existing shareholders in proportion to the number of shares already owned by each shareholder.

Activity 12.9

Both preference shares and loan capital are forms of finance that require the business to provide a particular rate of return to investors. What are the factors that may be taken into account by a business when deciding between these two sources of finance?

The main factors are as follows:

- Preference shares have a higher rate of return than loan capital. From the investor's point of view, preference shares are more risky. The amount invested cannot be secured, and the return is paid after the returns paid to lenders.
- A business has a legal obligation to pay interest and make capital repayments on loans at the agreed dates. It will usually make every effort to meet its obligations because failure to do so can have serious consequences. (These consequences have been mentioned earlier.) Failure to pay a preference dividend, on the other hand, is less important. There is no legal obligation to pay if profits are not available for distribution. Failure to pay a preference dividend may prove an embarrassment for the business, however. It may make it difficult to persuade investors to take up future preference share issues.
- It was mentioned above that the taxation system in the UK permits interest on loans to be allowable against profits for taxation, whereas preference dividends are not. As a result, the cost of servicing loan capital is usually much less for a business than the cost of servicing preference shares.
- The issue of loan capital may result in the management of a business having to accept some restrictions on its freedom of action. We saw earlier that loan agreements often contain covenants that can be onerous. However, preference shareholders can impose no such restrictions.

A further point is that preference shares issued form part of the permanent capital base of the business. If they are redeemed, the law requires that they be replaced, either by a new issue of shares or by a transfer from revenue reserves, so that the business's capital base stays intact. Loan capital, however, is not viewed in law as part of the business's permanent capital base, and therefore there is no legal requirement to replace any loan capital that has been redeemed.

Finance leases and sale and leaseback arrangements

When a business needs a particular asset (for example, an item of plant), instead of buying it direct from a supplier, the business may decide to arrange for another business (typically a bank) to buy it and then lease it to the first business. The business that owns the asset and leases it out is known as a 'lessor'. The one that uses it is known as the 'lessee'.

A finance lease, as such an arrangement is known, is, in essence, a form of lending. This is because, had the lessee borrowed the funds and then used them to buy the asset itself, the effect would be much the same. The lessee would have use of the asset, but have a financial obligation to the lender – much the same position as the leasing arrangement would lead to.

Though, with finance leasing, legal ownership of the asset rests with the financial institution (the lessor), a finance lease agreement transfers to the user (the lessee) virtually all the rewards and risks that are associated with the item being leased. The finance lease agreement covers a significant part of the life of the item being leased, and often cannot be cancelled.

Real World 12.5 gives an example of the use of finance leasing in a leading airline business.

Real World 12.5

Finance leasing at BA

Many airline businesses use finance leasing as a means of acquiring new aeroplanes. The financial statements for British Airways plc (BA) for the year ended 31 March 2005 reveal that approximately 26 per cent (totalling £1,742 million) of the net book value of its fleet of aircraft had been acquired through this method.

Source: British Airways plc, Annual Report and Accounts, year ended 31 March 2005

A finance lease can be contrasted with an operating lease, where the rewards and risks of ownership stay with the owner and where the lease is short term. An example of an operating lease is where a builder hires some earthmoving equipment for a week to carry out a particular job.

In recent years, some important benefits associated with finance leasing have disappeared. Changes in UK tax law no longer make it such a tax-efficient form of financing, and changes in accounting disclosure requirements no longer make it possible to conceal this form of 'borrowing' from investors. Nevertheless, the popularity of finance leases has continued. Other reasons must therefore exist for businesses to adopt this form of financing. These reasons are said to include the following:

- *Ease of borrowing*. Leasing may be obtained more easily than other forms of long-term finance. Lenders normally require some form of security and a profitable track record before making advances to a business. However, a lessor may be prepared to lease assets to a new business without a track record, and to use the leased assets as security for the amounts owing.

- *Cost.* Leasing agreements may be offered at reasonable cost. As the asset leased is used as security, standard lease arrangements can be applied and detailed credit checking of lessees may be unnecessary. This can reduce administrative costs for the lessor and, thereby, help in providing competitive lease rentals.
- *Flexibility.* Leasing can help provide flexibility where there are rapid changes in technology. If an option to cancel can be incorporated into the lease, the business may be able to exercise this option and invest in new technology as it becomes available. This will help the business to avoid the risk of obsolescence.
- *Cash flows.* Leasing, rather than purchasing an asset outright, means that large cash outflows can be avoided. The leasing option allows cash outflows to be smoothed out over the asset's life. In some cases, it is possible to arrange for low lease payments to be made in the early years of the asset's life, when cash inflows may be low, and for these to increase over time as the asset generates positive cash flows.

Real World 12.6 provides some impression of the importance of finance leasing over recent years.

Real World 12.6

Finance leasing 1999-2003

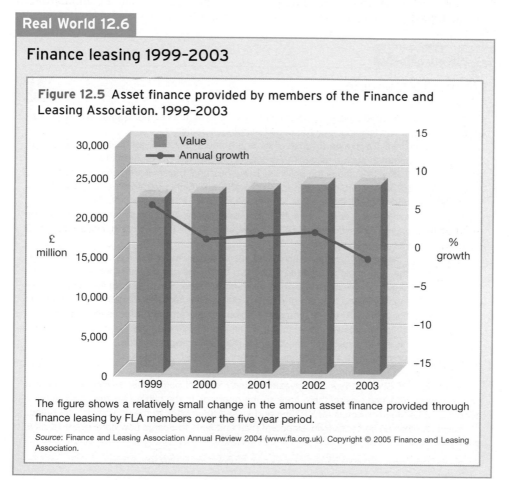

Figure 12.5 Asset finance provided by members of the Finance and Leasing Association. 1999-2003

The figure shows a relatively small change in the amount asset finance provided through finance leasing by FLA members over the five year period.

Source: Finance and Leasing Association Annual Review 2004 (www.fla.org.uk). Copyright © 2005 Finance and Leasing Association.

→   A sale-and-leaseback arrangement involves a business raising finance by selling an asset to a financial institution. The sale is accompanied by an agreement to lease the asset back to the business to allow it to continue to use the asset. The lease payment is allowable against profits for taxation purposes. There are usually reviews at regular intervals throughout the period of the lease, and the amounts payable in future years may be difficult to predict. At the end of the lease agreement, the business must either try to renew the lease or find an alternative asset. Although the sale of the asset will result in an immediate injection of cash for the business, it will lose benefits from any future capital appreciation on the asset. Where a capital gain arises on the sale of the asset to the financial institution, a liability for taxation may also arise. Freehold property is often the asset that is the subject of such an arrangement. Many of the well-known UK high-street retailers (for example, Boots, Debenhams, Marks and Spencer and Sainsbury) have recently sold off their store sites under sale and leaseback arrangements.

A sale-and-leaseback agreement can be used to help a business focus on its core areas of competence. Real World 12.7 reveals how sale-and-leaseback agreements can help hotel businesses to become purely hotel operators rather than a combination of hotel operators and owners.

Real World 12.7

Rooms to manoeuvre   **FT**

Travelodge, the UK budget hotel operator owned by Permira, the venture capital firm, is to raise £400m via a sale and leaseback of 136 of its freehold properties.

The deal will see Travelodge dispose of its entire freehold estate, the first time a UK hotel operator has attempted such a move. The group has appointed CB Richard Ellis, the hotel and property consultancy, to manage the process. Thirty potential buyers have been targeted.

Sale and leasebacks were popular a few years ago with hotel operators ranging from Hilton to Le Meridien opting to sell their assets to release capital and then lease them back.

But, while several operators continue to be asset-heavy, the popularity of the financing mechanism appeared to have waned. The Travelodge deal will be the first significant sale and leaseback this year once completed.

Grant Hearn, the chain's chief executive, said in an interview with the *Financial Times* that the proceeds from the sale would be used to pay down debt. The group is still looking to buy new hotels but will take on any new properties on a leasehold basis. 'I suppose we are being opportunistic and taking advantage of buoyant property prices,' he said. 'CB Richard Ellis has told us there's £8bn chasing property at the moment. It doesn't make any sense for us to hang on to it.'

It is unclear which groups will invest in the scheme but there are several property funds and banks with an interest in acquiring freehold hotels that deliver regular yields.

Hilton Group raised more than £335m two years ago when it sold 10 of its UK hotels to a limited partnership vehicle that included Bank of Scotland.

Royal Bank of Scotland has also invested heavily in hotel purchases, buying 10 properties from Hilton in 2001 and leasing them back to the operator. In the same year the Scottish bank acquired 12 Le Meridien hotels for £1.25bn and leased them back to the upmarket hotel brand.

Travelodge has an aggressive development plan and aims to open a new hotel every 10 days during the next 12 months.

Source: 'Travelodge to raise £400m via sale and leaseback plan', *Financial Times*, 12 July 2004, FT.com

Hire purchase

Hire purchase is a form of credit used to acquire an asset. Under the terms of a hire-purchase (HP) agreement a customer pays for an asset by instalments over an agreed period. Normally, the customer will pay an initial deposit (downpayment) and then make instalment payments at regular intervals (perhaps monthly) until the balance outstanding has been paid. The customer will usually take possession of the asset after payment of the initial deposit, although legal ownership of the asset will not be transferred until the final instalment has been paid.

Hire-purchase agreements will often involve three parties:

- the supplier;
- the customer;
- a financial institution.

3 parties

Although the supplier will deliver the asset to the customer, the financial institution will buy the asset from the supplier and then enter into a hire purchase agreement with the customer. This intermediary role played by the financial institution enables the supplier to receive immediate payment for the asset but allows the customer a period of extended credit.

Real World 12.8 describes how one well-known holiday operator uses hire purchase to help finance its assets.

Real World 12.8

Paying by instalments

Holidaybreak plc has a camping division that includes well-known brands such as Eurocamp and Keycamp. The division provides mobile homes for holidaymakers, and the company's 2004 annual report revealed that the cost of mobile homes held was £82.6m. The financing of the mobile homes involves hire purchase agreements with a number of financial institutions, with just over half the annual cost of acquiring mobile homes being financed in this way.

Sources: Based on information contained in Holidaybreak plc, Annual report 2004, and a company press release on the 2004 results

HP agreements are similar to finance leases insofar that they allow a customer to obtain immediate possession of the asset without paying its full cost. Under the terms of an HP agreement, however, the customer will eventually become the legal owner of the asset, whereas under the terms of a finance lease, ownership will stay with the lessor.

Gearing and the long-term financing decision

In Chapter 6 we saw that financial gearing occurs when a business is financed, at least in part, by contributions from fixed-charge capital (preference shares and loans). We also saw that the level of gearing associated with a business is often an important factor in assessing the risk and returns to ordinary shareholders. In Example 12.1, we consider the implications of making a choice between a geared and an ungeared approach to raising long-term finance.

Example 12.1

The following are the summarised financial statements of Woodhall Engineers plc:

Woodhall Engineers plc
Income statement for the year ended 31 December

	Year 1	Year 2
	£m	£m
Revenue	47	50
Operating costs	(42)	(48)
Operating profit	5	2
Interest payable	(1)	(1)
Profit on ordinary activities before tax	4	1
Taxation on profit on ordinary activities	–	–
Profit on ordinary activities after tax	4	1
Dividends paid	(1)	(1)
Profit retained for the financial year	3	–

Balance sheet at 31 December

	Year 1	Year 2
	£m	£m
Non-current assets (less depreciation)	21	20
Current assets		
Inventories	10	18
Receivables	16	17
Cash at bank	3	1
	29	36
Current liabilities		
Short-term loans	(5)	(11)
Trade payables	(10)	(10)
	(15)	(21)
Total assets *less* current liabilities	35	35
Non-current liabilities		
Long-term loans (secured)	(15)	(15)
	20	20
Equity		
Called-up share capital 25p ordinary shares	16	16
Retained profit	4	4
	20	20

The business is making plans to expand its premises. New plant will cost £8 million, and an expansion in output will increase working capital by £4 million. Over the

15 years' life of the project, incremental profits arising from the expansion will be £2 million a year before interest and tax. In addition, Year 3's profits before interest and tax from its existing activities are expected to return to Year 1 levels.

Two possible methods of financing the expansion have been discussed by Woodhall's directors. The first is the issue of £12 million, 10 per cent loan capital repayable in Year 18. The second is a rights issue of 40 million 25p ordinary shares, which will give the business 30p per share after expenses.

The business has substantial tax losses, which can be offset against future profits, so taxation can be ignored in the calculations. The Year 3 dividend per share is expected to be the same as that for Year 2.

Prepare a forecast of Woodhall's projected income statement (excluding revenue and operating costs) for the year ended 31 December Year 3, and of its capital and reserves, long-term loans and number of shares outstanding at that date, assuming that the business issues:

- loan capital;
- ordinary shares.

The first part of the example requires the preparation of a forecast income statement (profit and loss account) under each financing option. These will be as follows:

Projected income statement for the year ended 31 December Year 3

	Loan issue £m	Share issue £m
Profit before interest and taxation (5.0 + 2.0)	7.0	7.0
Loan interest	(2.2)	(1.0)
Profit before tax	4.8	6.0
Taxation	–	–
Profit after tax	4.8	6.0
Dividends paid	(1.0)	(1.6)
Retained profit for the year	3.8	4.4

The capital structure of the business under each option as at the end of Year 3 will be as follows:

	Loan issue £m	Share issue £m
Equity		
Share capital 25p ordinary shares	16.0	26.0
Share premium account*	–	2.0
Retained profit	7.8	8.4
	23.8	36.4
Number of shares in issue (25p shares)	64 million	104 million

* This represents the amount received from the issue of shares that is above the nominal value of the shares. The amount is calculated as follows:

$$40m \text{ shares} \times (30p - 25p) = £2m$$

Activity 12.10

Compute Woodhall's interest cover and earnings per share for the year ended 31 December Year 3 and its gearing on that date, assuming that the business issues:

(a) loan capital;
(b) ordinary shares.

Your answer should be as follows:

	(a) Loan issue	(b) Share issue

Interest cover ratio

$$\frac{\text{Profit before interest and tax}}{\text{Interest payable}} = \frac{7.0}{2.2} \quad = \frac{7.0}{1.0}$$

$$= 3.2 \text{ times} \quad = 7.0 \text{ times}$$

Earning per share

$$\frac{\text{Earning available to equity}}{\text{Number of ordinary shares}} = \frac{£4.8m}{64m} \quad = \frac{£6.0m}{104m}$$

$$= 7.5p \quad = 5.8p$$

Gearing ratio

$$\frac{\text{Non-current liabilities}}{\text{Share capital + Reserves + Non-current liabilities}} = \frac{£27m}{£23.8m + £27m} \quad = \frac{£15m}{£36.4m + £15m}$$

$$= 53.1\% \quad = 29.2\%$$

Activity 12.11

What would your views of the proposed schemes be in each of the following circumstances?

(a) If you were a banker and you were approached for a loan.
(b) If you were an ordinary share investor in Woodhall and you were asked to subscribe to a rights issue.

(a) A banker may be unenthusiastic about lending money to the business. The gearing ratio of 53.1 per cent is rather high, and would leave the bank in an exposed position. The existing loan is already secured on the business's assets, and it is not clear whether the business is in a position to offer an attractive form of security for the new loan. The interest cover ratio of 3.2 times is also rather low. If the business is unable to achieve the expected returns from the new project, or if it is unable to restore profits from the remainder of its operations to Year 1 levels, this ratio would be even lower.

(b) Ordinary share investors may need some convincing that it would be worthwhile to make further investments in the business. The return on ordinary shareholders' funds in

> Year 1 was 20 per cent (£4m/£20m). The incremental profit from the new project is £2 million and the investment required is £12 million, which represents a return of 16.7 per cent. Thus, the returns from the project are expected to be lower than for existing operations. In making their decision, investors should discover whether the new investment is of a similar level of risk to their existing investment and how the returns from the investment compare with those available from other opportunities with similar levels of risk.

Share issues

A business may issue shares in a number of ways. These may involve direct appeals to investors, or the use of financial intermediaries. The most common methods of share issues for cash are:

- rights issues;
- offers for sale and public issue;
- private placing.

These are discussed below.

Rights issues

As we saw in Chapter 4, rights issues are made when businesses that have been established for some time seek to raise additional share capital for expansion, or even to solve a liquidity problem (cash shortage) by issuing additional shares for cash. Company law gives existing shareholders the first right of refusal on these new shares, so the new shares would be offered to shareholders in proportion to their existing holding. Thus existing shareholders are each given the right to buy some new shares. Only where the existing shareholders agree to waive their right would the shares be offered to the investing public generally. Rights issues are now the most common form of share issue. The business (in effect, the existing shareholders) would typically prefer that existing shareholders buy the shares through a rights issue, irrespective of the legal position. This is for two reasons:

- The ownership (and, therefore, control) of the business remains in the same hands.
- The costs of making the issue (advertising, complying with various company law requirements) tend to be less if the shares are to be offered to existing shareholders.

To encourage existing shareholders to take up their 'rights' to buy some new shares, those shares are always offered at a price below the current market price of the existing ones.

Activity 12.12

In Chapter 4 (Example 4.2, p. 114) the point was made that issuing new shares at below their current worth was to the advantage of the new shareholders at the expense of the old ones. In view of this, does it matter that rights issues are always made at below the current value of the shares?

The answer is that it does not matter *in these particular circumstances*, because, in a rights issue, the existing shareholders and the new shareholders are exactly the same people. Moreover, the shareholders will hold the new shares in the same proportion as they currently hold the existing shares. Thus, shareholders will gain on the new shares exactly as much as they lose on the existing ones: in the end, no one is better or worse off as a result of the rights issue being made at a discount.

Calculating the value of the rights offer received by shareholders is quite straightforward, as shown in Example 12.2.

Example 12.2

Shaw Holdings plc has 20 million ordinary shares of 50p in issue. These shares are currently valued on the Stock Exchange at £1.60 per share. The directors have decided to make a one-for-four issue (that is, one new share for every four shares held) at £1.30 per share.

The first step in the valuation process is to calculate the price of a share following the rights issue. This is known as the *ex-rights price*, and is simply a weighted average of the price of shares before the issue of rights and the price of the rights shares. In the above example, we have a one-for-four rights issue. The theoretical ex-rights price is therefore calculated as follows:

	£
Price of four shares before the rights issue (4 × £1.60)	6.40
Price of taking up one rights share	1.30
	7.70

$$\text{Theoretical ex-rights price} = \frac{7.70}{5} = £1.54$$

As the price of each share, in theory, should be £1.54 following the rights issue and the price of a rights share is £1.30, the value of the rights offer will be the difference between the two:

$$£1.54 - £1.30 = £0.24 \text{ per share}$$

Market forces will usually ensure that the actual and theoretical price of rights will be fairly close.

Activity 12.13

An investor with 2,000 shares in Shaw Holdings plc (see Example 12.2) has contacted you for investment advice. She is undecided whether to take up the rights issue, sell the rights or allow the rights offer to lapse.

Calculate the effect on the net wealth of the investor of each of the options being considered.

	£
Before the rights issue the investor had shares worth (2,000 × £1.60)	3,200

If she takes up the rights issue, she will be in the following position:

	£
Value of holding after rights issue [(2,000 + 500) × £1.54]	3,850
Less Cost of buying the rights shares (500 × £1.30)	650
	3,200

If the investor sells the rights, she will be in the following position:

	£
Value of holding after rights issue (2,000 × £1.54)	3,080
Sale of rights (500 × £0.24)	120
	3,200

If the investor lets the rights offer lapse, she will be in the following position:

	£
Value of holding after rights issue (2,000 × £1.54)	3,080

As we can see, the first two options should leave her in the same position concerning net wealth as she was before the rights issue. Before the rights issue she had 2,000 shares worth £1.60 each or £3,200. However, she will be worse off if she allows the rights offer to lapse than under the other two options. In practice, however, the business may sell the rights, on behalf of the investor, and pass on the proceeds in order to ensure that she is not worse off as a result of the issue.

When considering a rights issue, the directors must first consider the amount of funds that needs to be raised. This will depend on the future plans and commitments of the business. The directors must then decide on the issue price of the rights shares. Normally, this decision is not critical. In Example 12.2 above, the business made a one-for-four issue with the price of the rights shares set at £1.30. However, it could have raised the same amount by making a one-for-two issue and setting the rights price at £0.65, a one-for-one issue and setting the price at £0.325, and so on. The issue price that is finally decided upon will not affect the value of the underlying assets of the business or the proportion of the underlying assets and earnings to which each shareholder is entitled. The directors must ensure that the issue price is not above the current market price of the shares, however, or the issue will be unsuccessful.

Real World 12.9 describes how Prudential plc, the insurance business, made a rights issue.

Real World 12.9

The rights stuff

In November 2004 Prudential plc, the UK's second largest life insurance business, made a one-for-six rights issue that raised £1 billion. Shareholders took up 92 per cent of the issue, leaving underwriters to take up the remaining 8 per cent.

The new finance was raised to fund growth in the UK market for the business's products.

Source: Taken from 'Prudential gets high take up in rights issue', Andrea Felstead, *FT.com*, 11 November 2004

Offer for sale and public issue

An offer for sale involves a business, trading as a public limited company, selling a new issue of shares to a financial institution known as an issuing house. However, shares that are already in issue may also be sold to an issuing house. In this case, existing shareholders agree to sell their shares to the issuing house. The issuing house will, in turn, sell the shares, purchased from either the business or its shareholders, to the public. The issuing house will publish a prospectus that sets out details of the business and the type of shares to be sold and investors will be invited to apply for shares. The advantage of this type of issue, from the business's viewpoint, is that the sale proceeds of the shares are certain.

A public issue involves the business making a direct invitation to the public to purchase its shares. Typically, this is done through a newspaper advertisement. The shares may, once again, be a new issue or those already in issue. An offer for sale and a public issue will both result in a widening of share ownership in the business.

In practical terms, the net effect on the business is much the same whether there is an offer for sale or a public issue.

Issues by tender

When making an issue of shares, the business or the issuing house will usually set a price for the shares. Establishing this may not be an easy task, however, particularly where the market is volatile or where the business has unique characteristics. One way of dealing with this issue-price problem is to make a tender issue of shares. This involves the investors determining the price at which the shares are issued. Though the business (or issuing house) may publish a reserve price to help guide investors, it will be up to the individual investor to determine the number of shares to be purchased and the price the investor is prepared to pay. Once the offers from investors have been received, a price at which all the shares can be sold will be established (known as the *striking price*). Investors who have made offers at, or above, the striking price will be issued shares at the striking price; offers received below the striking price will be rejected. Note that all of the shares will be issued at the same price, irrespective of the prices actually offered by individual investors. Though this form of issue is adopted occasionally, it is not popular with investors, and is therefore not in widespread use.

Private placings

A private placing does not involve an invitation to the public to subscribe for shares. Instead the shares are 'placed' with selected investors, such as large financial institutions. This can be a quick and relatively cheap form of raising funds, because savings can be made in advertising and legal costs. However, it can result in the ownership of the business being concentrated in a few hands. Usually, unlisted businesses seeking relatively small amounts of cash will make this form of issue.

Real World 12.10 describes how Tesco plc, the supermarket chain, used a placing to raise finance.

Real World 12.10

Tesco well placed

Tesco on Tuesday revealed better than expected trading over the Christmas period and announced it was planning to raise £810m ($1.5bn) through a placing of shares.

Tesco said the placing, which will see it put 315m new ordinary shares into the market, equivalent to 4.4 per cent of its issued share capital, would give it the flexibility and firepower to take advantage of further opportunities to grow.

The placing also includes an over allotment option of 45m new ordinary shares.

As part of its expansion plans, Tesco will be using the money to accelerate its non-food offering, introducing more Tesco Extra formats allowing it to expand further into clothing and health and beauty.

As well as concentrating on the larger end of the market, the group said it would be increasing its presence in the convenience market, with the expansion of the Tesco Express brand.

Tesco said it would be well placed to buy some of the Safeway stores up for sale following Morrison's acquisition of the chain.

Terry Leahy, chief executive, said: 'Now is the right time to strengthen our finances further so we can take full advantage of the opportunities available.'

Source: 'Tesco raises £810m in placing as sales rise', *Financial Times*, 13 January 2004, FT.com

---

Bonus issues

We should recall from Chapter 4 that bonus issues are not means of raising finance. They are simply converting one part of the owners' claim (reserves) into another (ordinary shares). No cash changes hands; this benefits neither the business nor the shareholders.

The role of the Stock Exchange

Earlier we considered the various forms of long-term capital that are available to a business. In this section, we examine the role that the Stock Exchange plays in the provision of finance for businesses. The Stock Exchange acts as an important *primary* and *secondary* market in capital for businesses. As a primary market, its function is to enable businesses to raise new capital. As a secondary market, its function is to enable investors to sell their securities (including shares and loan capital) with ease. Thus, it provides a 'second-hand' market where shares and loan capital already in issue may be bought and sold.

In order to issue shares or loan capital through the Stock Exchange, a business must be 'listed'. This means that the business must meet fairly stringent requirements concerning size, profit history, information disclosure and so on. Some share issues on the Stock Exchange arise from the initial listing of the business, often known as an *initial public offering (IPO)*. Other share issues are undertaken by businesses that are already listed and that are seeking additional finance from investors.

Real World 12.11 describes how Jessops plc, the high street camera retailer, made a major IPO.

Real World 12.11

Jessops goes public

Jessops plc was floated in October 2004 through an IPO. The business operates 263 stores throughout the UK. It planned to use much of the funds raised to reduce its debt (and, therefore, its capital gearing) by about £95 million.

Source: Taken from 'Jessps IPO below target value range', Kevin Allison, *Financial Times*, 29 October 2004

Real World 12.12 explains how new issues are not always good investments for those who take up the shares concerned.

Real World 12.12

New issues but old problems   **FT**

It seems that we should be cautious when invited to subscribe to a new issue of shares arising from an initial listing on the Stock Exchange. The following extract from the *Financial Times* tells us why investing in new business flotations may be bad for our wealth.

Back in 1940 Benjamin Graham and David Dodd, the fathers of security analysis, wrote: 'the odds are so strongly against the man who buys into these new flotations that he might as well throw three-quarters of the money out the window and keep the rest in the bank.'

Now confirmation of the poor record of recent new issues comes from an Ernst and Young survey. The accountancy group looked at the records of 200 companies that floated on the UK market between 1998 and 2002. It found that only 39% of the sample had increased profits since flotation (although 82% had seen their sales grow).

This should not come as too much of a surprise. Companies are most likely to float on the market when their recent trading record is impressive. But periods of rapid growth can be very dangerous for a company – costs and management ambitions can get out of hand.

Furthermore, no business can grow rapidly forever, and there is a risk that the flotation occurs just at the moment when the decline is beginning.

And, as Ernst and Young points out, the very act of flotation incurs significant costs and can divert management focus from the business. The money raised can also burn a hole in the management's pockets, leading to a flurry of spending that would disgrace a football manager.

All this is slightly discouraging, given that the primary role of the stock market is to allow growing businesses to raise capital. But perhaps a certain amount of investor greed (and gullibility) is necessary if industry is to gain access to finance. New issue investors have been fooled before; they will be fooled again.

Source: *Financial Times*, 8 August 2003, p. 22

Advantages of a listing

The secondary market role of the Stock Exchange means that shares and other financial claims are easily transferable. Furthermore, the prices of shares and other financial claims are constantly under scrutiny by investors and skilled analysts. This helps to ensure that the prices quoted for a particular share reflect its true worth. These factors can bring real benefits to a business.

Activity 12.14

What kind of benefits might a business gain from its shares being listed?

If investors know that their shares can easily be sold for prices that reflect the true worth of the shares, they will have more confidence to invest. The business may benefit from this greater investor confidence by finding it easier to raise long-term finance and by obtaining this finance at a lower cost, as investors will view their investment as being less risky.

It is worth pointing out that investors are not obliged to use the Stock Exchange as the means of transferring shares in a listed business. However, it is usually the most convenient way of buying or selling shares.

The Stock Exchange can be a useful vehicle for a successful entrepreneur wishing to realise the value of the business that has been built up. By floating (listing) the shares on the Stock Exchange, and thereby making the shares available to the public, the entrepreneur will usually benefit from a gain in the value of the shares held and will be able to realise that gain easily, if required, by selling some shares. Real Worlds 12.13 and 12.14 give examples of businesses 'floating' on the Stock Exchange and making their owners a lot of money.

Real World 12.13

Privatised stationer 'to float'

Ray Peck is an entrepreneur who runs a business that was the government's former stationery division. Newspaper reports revealed that he wished to float the business on the Stock Exchange and that stock market investors were likely to value the business at around £80m to £100m. Mr Peck, his senior managers and a financial institution bought the whole business for about £10m two years before the intention to float the business was reported. At the time, Ray Peck owned 20% of the shares of the business, which means that his stake in the business would be valued somewhere between £16m and £20m, assuming that predictions concerning the value of the business were accurate.

Source: Sunday Times, Business Section, 30 June 2002, p. 3

Real World 12.14

Cashing in

Mark Mills, a 33-year-old entrepreneur, made himself a fortune in the form of the value of shares worth £4.6m, when his business (Cardpoint) was floated. The business owns 1,900 cash dispensing machines installed in garages and other locations. Everyone using the machines is charged £1.50 to withdraw cash. The business also owns 3,600 mobile phone top-up terminals.

Cardpoint was not Mark Mills' first business venture. He started young, selling bags of broken biscuits to his friends at age 6. At 18 he was in business as a party organiser. He then moved on to selling payphone systems to publicans, then to selling advertising to go on the outside of post boxes. These businesses had mixed success, but he really hit the jackpot with Cardpoint.

Source: Based on information in Sunday Times, Business Section, 11 January 2004, p. 11

Disadvantages of a listing

A Stock Exchange listing can have certain disadvantages for a business. These include:

- Strict rules are imposed on listed businesses, including requiring additional levels of financial disclosure to that already imposed by law (for example, the listing rules require that half-yearly financial reports are published).
- Financial analysts, financial journalists and others closely monitor the activities of listed businesses. Such scrutiny may not be welcome, particularly if the business is dealing with sensitive issues or is experiencing operational problems.
- It is often suggested that listed businesses are under pressure to perform well over the short term. This pressure may detract from undertaking projects that will only

yield benefits in the longer term. If the market becomes disenchanted with the business, and the price of its shares falls, this may make it vulnerable to a takeover bid from another business.

■ The costs of obtaining a listing are vast and this may be a real deterrent for some businesses.

To make an initial public offering (IPO), a business will rely on the help of various specialists such as lawyers, accountants and bankers. However, their services do not come cheap. Real World 12.15 provides an example.

Real World 12.15

Floating under heavy fees

Benfield has earmarked almost 10 per cent of the proceeds from its initial public offering on fees and commissions for a host of bankers, lawyers and accountants.

The reinsurance broker is seeking to raise £100m through a global institutional offering as part of a plan to float on the London Stock Exchange later this month.

However, it has emerged that £9.2m of that sum will be swallowed up by the dozen companies involved in the flotation. . . .

Source: 'Benfield earmarks almost 10 per cent for fees in £100m flotation', *Financial Times* Business, 9 June 2003, p. 26

Real World 12.16 explains how the larger businesses tend to dominate investment on the London Stock Exchange.

Real World 12.16

Big is beautiful

There are more than 2,000 listed businesses on the London Stock Exchange. However, the 100 largest businesses account for more than 80 per cent of the value of the market and it is these large companies that provide the main focus of interest for investors. Smaller businesses often claim that they are overlooked, particularly by large institutional investors. These investors are normally only interested in large businesses because of the size of the investments that they make in each business. It has been suggested that businesses valued at less than £100m are unlikely to be of interest. This makes it hard for smaller businesses to raise new capital, unless, perhaps, they can convince investors that they are fast growing. Thus, for some small businesses the advantages of listing are outweighed by the disadvantages.

Source: Based on information in 'Climbing aboard the flight from flotation', Philip Coggan, *Financial Times*, 6 September 2003

Real World 12.17 provides an analysis of the ownership of shares in UK listed businesses at the end of 2004.

Real World 12.17

Ownership of UK listed shares

At the end of 2004, the proportion of shares of UK listed businesses held by various groups are as shown in Figure 12.6 below.

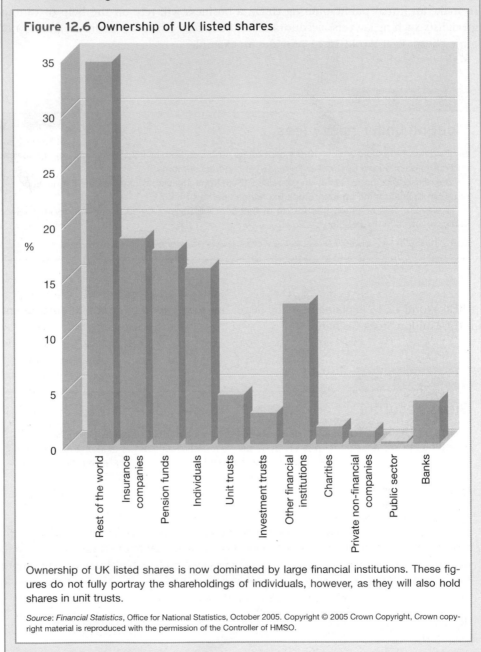

Figure 12.6 Ownership of UK listed shares

Ownership of UK listed shares is now dominated by large financial institutions. These figures do not fully portray the shareholdings of individuals, however, as they will also hold shares in unit trusts.

Source: Financial Statistics, Office for National Statistics, October 2005. Copyright © 2005 Crown Copyright, Crown copyright material is reproduced with the permission of the Controller of HMSO.

Short-term sources of external finance

Short-term, in this context, is usually taken to mean up to one year. Figure 12.2 revealed that the major sources of short-term external finance were:

- bank overdrafts;
- debt factoring;
- invoice discounting.

These are discussed below.

Bank overdrafts

A bank overdraft enables a business to maintain a negative balance on its bank account. It represents a very flexible form of borrowing as the size of the overdraft can (subject to bank approval) be increased or decreased according to the financing requirements of the business. It is relatively inexpensive to arrange, and interest rates are often very competitive, though often higher than those for a term loan. As with all loans, the rate of interest charged on an overdraft will vary, however, according to how creditworthy the customer is perceived to be by the bank. It is also fairly easy to arrange – sometimes an overdraft can be agreed by a telephone call to the bank. In view of these advantages, it is not surprising that this is an extremely popular form of short-term finance.

Banks prefer to grant overdrafts that are self-liquidating: that is, the funds applied will result in cash inflows that will extinguish the overdraft balance. The banks may ask for a cash budget (projected cash flow statement) from the business to see when the overdraft will be repaid and how much finance is required. The bank may also require some form of security on amounts advanced. One potential drawback with this form of finance is that it is repayable on demand. This may pose problems for a business that is illiquid. However, many businesses operate for many years using an overdraft, simply because the bank remains confident of their ability to repay and the arrangement suits the businesses. Thus the bank overdraft, though in theory regarded as short term, often becomes a long-term source of finance.

Debt factoring

Debt factoring is a service offered by a financial institution (known as a 'factor'). Many of the large factors are subsidiaries of commercial banks. Debt factoring involves the factor taking over the business's debt collection. In addition to operating normal credit control procedures, a factor may offer to undertake credit investigations and to provide protection for approved credit sales. The factor is usually prepared to make an advance to the business of a maximum of 80 per cent of approved trade receivables. The charge made for the factoring service is based on total sales revenue, and is often 2 to 3 per cent of sales revenue. Any advances made to the business by the factor will attract a rate of interest similar to the rate charged on bank overdrafts.

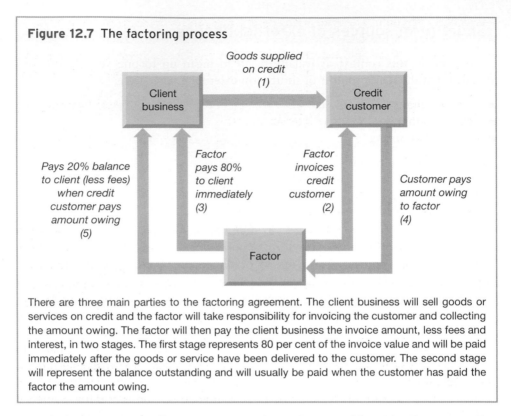

Figure 12.7 The factoring process

Goods supplied on credit (1)

Client business

Credit customer

Pays 20% balance to client (less fees) when credit customer pays amount owing (5)

Factor pays 80% to client immediately (3)

Factor invoices credit customer (2)

Customer pays amount owing to factor (4)

Factor

There are three main parties to the factoring agreement. The client business will sell goods or services on credit and the factor will take responsibility for invoicing the customer and collecting the amount owing. The factor will then pay the client business the invoice amount, less fees and interest, in two stages. The first stage represents 80 per cent of the invoice value and will be paid immediately after the goods or service have been delivered to the customer. The second stage will represent the balance outstanding and will usually be paid when the customer has paid the factor the amount owing.

Debt factoring is, in effect, outsourcing the trade receivables control to a specialist subcontractor. Many businesses find a factoring arrangement very convenient. It can result in savings in credit management and create more certain cash flows. It can also release the time of key personnel for more profitable activities. This may be extremely important for smaller businesses that rely on the talent and skills of a few key individuals. However, there is a possibility that some will see a factoring arrangement as an indication that the business is experiencing financial difficulties. This may have an adverse effect on confidence. For this reason, some businesses try to conceal the factoring arrangement by collecting debts on behalf of the factor. When considering a factoring agreement, the costs and likely benefits arising must be identified and carefully weighed.

Figure 12.7 shows the factoring process diagrammatically.

Invoice discounting

Invoice discounting involves a factor or other financial institution providing a loan based on a proportion of the face value of a business's credit sales outstanding. The amount advanced is usually 75 to 80 per cent of the value of the approved sales invoices outstanding. The business must agree to repay the advance within a relatively short period – perhaps 60 or 90 days. The responsibility for collecting the trade receivables outstanding remains with the business, and repayment of the advance is not dependent on the trade receivables being collected. Invoice discounting will not result in such a close relationship developing between the business and the financial institution as factoring. It may be a short-term arrangement whereas debt factoring usually involves a longer-term relationship.

Invoice discounting is a much more important source of funds than factoring (see Figure 12.8). There are three main reasons for this:

- It is a confidential form of financing that the business's customers will know nothing about.
- The service charge for invoice discounting is generally only 0.2 to 0.3 per cent of sales revenue, compared with 2.0 to 3.0 per cent for factoring.
- Many businesses are unwilling to relinquish control of their customers' records. Customers are an important resource of the business, and many wish to retain control over all aspects of their relationship with their customers.

Real World 12.18 shows the relative importance of invoice discounting and factoring.

Factoring and invoice discounting are forms of asset-based finance, as the asset of receivables is in effect used as security for the cash advances received by the business.

Long-term versus short-term borrowing

Having decided that some form of borrowing is required to finance the business, managers must then decide whether it should be long-term or short-term in form. There are many issues that should be taken into account when making this decision. These include the following:

- *Matching.* The business may attempt to match the type of borrowing with the nature of the assets held. Thus, long-term borrowing might finance assets that form part of the permanent operating base of the business, including non-current assets and a certain level of current assets. This leaves assets held for a short period, such as current assets held to meet seasonal increases in demand, to be financed by short-term borrowing, because short-term borrowing tends to be more flexible in that funds can be raised and repaid at short notice. Figure 12.9 shows this funding division graphically.

  A business may wish to match the asset life exactly with the period of the related loan; however, this may not be possible because of the difficulty of predicting the life of many assets.
- *Flexibility.* Short-term borrowing may be a useful means of postponing a commitment to taking on a long-term loan. This may be seen as desirable if interest rates are high and it is forecast that they will fall in the future. Short-term borrowing does not usually incur penalties if there is early repayment of the amount outstanding, whereas some form of financial penalty may arise if long-term debt is repaid early.
- *Refunding risk.* Short-term borrowing has to be renewed more frequently than long-term borrowing. This may create problems for the business if it is already in financial difficulties, or if there is a shortage of funds available for lending.

Real World 12.18

The popularity of invoice discounting and factoring

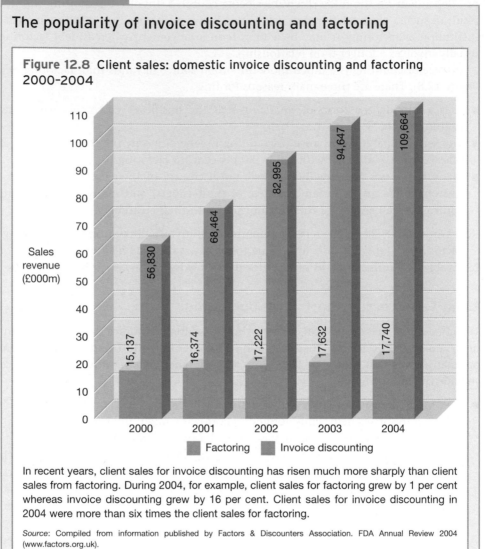

Figure 12.8 Client sales: domestic invoice discounting and factoring 2000–2004

Factoring ■   Invoice discounting ■

In recent years, client sales for invoice discounting has risen much more sharply than client sales from factoring. During 2004, for example, client sales for factoring grew by 1 per cent whereas invoice discounting grew by 16 per cent. Client sales for invoice discounting in 2004 were more than six times the client sales for factoring.

Source: Compiled from information published by Factors & Discounters Association. FDA Annual Review 2004 (www.factors.org.uk).

■ *Interest rates*. Interest payable on long-term debt is often higher than for short-term debt, as lenders require a higher return where their funds are locked up for a long period. This fact may make short-term borrowing a more attractive source of finance for a business. However, there may be other costs associated with borrowing (arrangement fees, for example) to be taken into account. The more frequently borrowings must be renewed, the higher these costs will be.

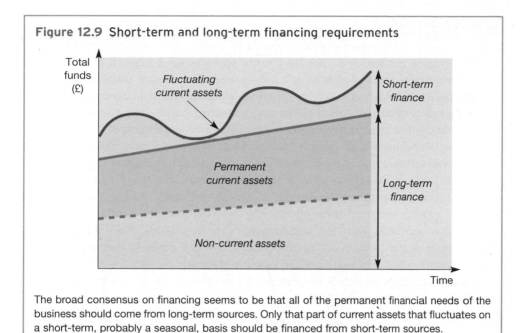

Figure 12.9 Short-term and long-term financing requirements

The broad consensus on financing seems to be that all of the permanent financial needs of the business should come from long-term sources. Only that part of current assets that fluctuates on a short-term, probably a seasonal, basis should be financed from short-term sources.

Activity 12.15

Some businesses may take up a less cautious financing position than that shown in Figure 12.9, and others may take up a more cautious one. How would the diagram differ under each of these options?

A less cautious position would mean relying on short-term finance to help fund part of the permanent capital base. A more cautious position would mean relying on long-term finance to help finance the fluctuating assets of the business.

Providing long-term finance for the small business

Though the Stock Exchange provides an important source of long-term finance for large businesses, it is not really suitable for small businesses. The aggregate market value of shares that are to be listed on the Stock Exchange must be at least £700,000 and, in practice, the amounts are much higher because of the high costs of listing. Thus, small businesses must look elsewhere for help in raising long-term finance. The more important sources of finance that are available to small businesses are private equity (venture capital and business angels) and government assistance. We shall now consider these.

Venture capital

→ Venture capital is long-term capital provided to small and medium-sized businesses wishing to grow but which do not have ready access to stock markets because of the prohibitively large costs of obtaining a listing. The businesses of interest to the venture capitalist will have higher levels of risk than would normally be acceptable to traditional providers of finance, such as the major clearing banks. The attraction for the venture capitalist of investing in higher-risk businesses is the prospect of higher returns.

Many small businesses are designed to provide the owners with a particular lifestyle and with job satisfaction. These kinds of businesses are not of interest to venture capitalists, as they are unlikely to provide the desired financial returns. Instead, venture capitalists look for businesses where the owners are seeking significant sales revenue and profit growth and need some outside help in order to achieve this.

The risks associated with the business can vary in practice. They are often due to the nature of the products or the fact that it is a new business that either lacks a trading record or has new management or both of these.

Venture capitalists provide long-term capital in the form of share and loan finance for different situations, including:

- *Start-up capital*. This is available to businesses that are not fully developed. They may need finance to help refine the business concept or to engage in product development or initial marketing. They have not yet reached the stage where they are trading.
- *Early stage capital*. This is available for businesses that are ready to commence trading.
- *Expansion capital*. This is aimed at providing additional funding for existing, growing businesses.
- *Buy-out or buy-in capital*. This is used to fund the acquisition of a business either by the existing management team ('buy-out') or by a new management team ('buy-in'). Management buy-outs (MBOs) and buy-ins (MBIs) often occur where a large business wishes to divest itself of one of its operating units or where a family business wishes to sell out because of succession problems.

The venture capitalist will often make a substantial investment in the business, and this will often take the form of ordinary shares. However, some of the funding may be in the form of preference shares or loan capital. To keep an eye on the sum invested, the venture capitalist will usually require a representative on the board of directors as a condition of the investment. The venture capitalist may not be looking for a quick return, and may well be prepared to invest in a business for five years or more. The return may take the form of a capital gain on the realisation of the investment (typically selling the shares).

Though venture capital is extremely important for some small businesses, the vast majority of small businesses obtain their finance from other sources. Real World 12.19 below shows the main sources of finance for small businesses in the UK.

Business angels

→ Business angels are often wealthy individuals who have been successful in business. They are usually willing to invest, through a shareholding, somewhere between £10,000

Real World 12.19

Small business funding

Bank finance, such as overdrafts and loans, is the main source of external finance as the pie chart in Figure 12.10 shows.

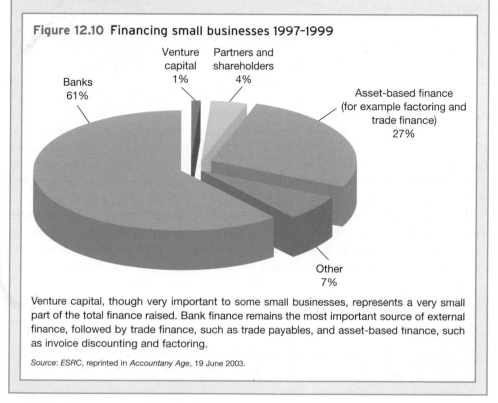

Figure 12.10 Financing small businesses 1997–1999

Venture capital 1%

Partners and shareholders 4%

Banks 61%

Asset-based finance (for example factoring and trade finance) 27%

Other 7%

Venture capital, though very important to some small businesses, represents a very small part of the total finance raised. Bank finance remains the most important source of external finance, followed by trade finance, such as trade payables, and asset-based finance, such as invoice discounting and factoring.

Source: ESRC, reprinted in Accountany Age, 19 June 2003.

and £100,000 in a start-up business or in a business that is at an early stage of development. They will often invest for a period of between three and five years, and sometimes even longer. They normally have a minority stake in the business and do not become involved in its day-to-day management. Business angels fill an important gap in the market as the size and the nature of the investment that they find appealing will not often appeal to venture capitalists.

Business angels may be attractive to small businesses for a number of reasons, including:

- They may be able to make investment decisions quickly, particularly if they are familiar with the industry in which the new business operates.
- They may also be able to offer a wealth of business experience to budding tycoons.
- Some may be prepared to accept lower financial returns than those required from venture capitalists in order to have the opportunity to become involved in a new and interesting project.

Business angels offer an informal source of share finance and it is not always easy for owners of small businesses to identify a suitable angel. However, numerous business angel networks have now developed to help owners of small businesses find their 'perfect partner'.

Government assistance

One of the most effective ways in which the UK government assists small businesses is through the Small Firms Loan Guarantee Scheme. This scheme aims to help small businesses that have viable business plans but lack the security to obtain a loan. The scheme guarantees loans made over a two- to ten-year period to small businesses from lending institutions for sums of £5,000 to £100,000 (increased to £250,000 for businesses that have been trading for at least two years). The government will guarantee up to 70 per cent (increased to 85 per cent for businesses that have been trading for at least two years) of the amount borrowed. In addition to other forms of financial assistance, such as government grants and tax incentives for investors to buy shares in small businesses, the government also helps by providing information concerning the sources of finance available.

Real World 12.20 records the financing phases of a very well-known dotcom retailer. The business started (as many businesses do) with the owner putting in personal savings and borrowings, to start it up. This led in stages to major Stock Exchange listed issues of shares and bonds (loan stocks) during 1997 and 1998.

Real World 12.20

Financing of Amazon.com – the early years

Amazon.com is an online retailer that has enjoyed considerable growth in recent years. The following table shows the key financing stages in the early years of the business.

Financing of Amazon.com (1994–1998)

Dates		Share price	Source of funds
1994:	July to Nov	$0.0010	*Founder*: Jeff Bezos starts Amazon.com with $10,000; borrows $44,000
1995:	Feb to July	$0.1717	*Family*: founder's father and mother invest $245,000
1995:	Aug to Dec	$0.1287–0.3333	*Business angels*: two angels invest $54,408
1995/96:	Dec to May	$0.3333	*Business angels*: 20 angels invest $937,000
1996:	May	$0.3333	*Family*: founder's siblings invest $20,000
1996:	June	$2.3417	*Venture capitalists*: two venture capital funds invest $8m
1997:	May	$18.00	*IPO**: 3m shares issued raising $49.1m
1997/98:	Dec to May	$52.11	*Bond issue*: $26m bond issue

* Initial public offering of shares

Source: Van Osnabrugge and Robinson 2000. Reprinted in *Financial Times*, 6 November 2000

? Self-assessment question 12.1

Helsim Ltd is a wholesaler and distributor of electrical components. The most recent financial statements of the business revealed the following:

Income statement (profit and loss account) for the year

	£m	£m
Sales revenue		14.2
Opening stock	3.2	
Purchases	8.4	
	11.6	
Closing stock	(3.8)	(7.8)
Gross profit		6.4
Administration expenses	(3.0)	
Selling and distribution expenses	(2.1)	
Finance charges	(0.8)	(5.9)
Net profit before taxation		0.5
Corporation tax		(0.2)
Net profit after taxation		0.3

Balance sheet as at the end of the year

	£m	£m	£m
Non-current assets			
Land and buildings			3.8
Equipment			0.9
Motor vehicles			0.5
			5.2
Current assets			
Inventories		3.8	
Trade receivables		3.6	
Cash at bank		0.1	
		7.5	
Less **Current liabilities**			
Trade payables	1.8		
Bank overdraft	3.6	5.4	2.1
			7.3
Less **Non-current liabilities**			
Debentures (secured on freehold land)			3.5
			3.8
Equity			
Ordinary £1 shares			2.0
Retained profit			1.8
			3.8

Notes
1 Land and buildings are shown at their current market value. Equipment and motor vehicles are shown at their written-down values (that is, cost less accumulated depreciation).
2 No dividends have been paid to ordinary shareholders for the past three years.

→

In recent months, trade payables have been pressing for payment. The managing director has therefore decided to reduce the level of trade payables to an average of 40 days outstanding. To achieve this, he has decided to approach the bank with a view to increasing the overdraft. The business is currently paying 12 per cent a year interest on the overdraft.

Required:

(a) Comment on the liquidity position of the business.

(b) Calculate the amount of finance required to reduce trade payables, from the level shown on the balance sheet, to an average of 40 days outstanding.

(c) State, with reasons, how you consider the bank would react to the proposal to grant an additional overdraft facility.

(d) Identify four sources of finance (internal or external, but excluding a bank overdraft) that may be suitable to finance the reduction in trade payables, and state, with reasons, which of these you consider the most appropriate.

Summary

The main points in this chapter may be summarised as follows:

Sources of finance:

■ Internal sources of finance do not require the agreement of anyone beyond the directors and managers of the business, whereas external sources of finance do require the compliance of 'outsiders'.

■ Long-term sources of finance are not due for repayment within one year whereas short-term sources are due for repayment within one year.

■ The higher the level of risk associated with investing in a particular form of finance, the higher the level of return that will be expected by investors.

Internal sources of finance:

■ The major internal source of long-term finance is retained profits.

■ The main short-term sources of internal finance are tighter credit control of receivables (debtors), reducing inventories (stock) levels and delaying payments to trade payables (creditors).

External sources of finance:

■ The main external, *long-term* sources of finance are ordinary shares, preference shares, loans, leases and hire purchase agreements.

■ Ordinary shares are normally considered to be the most risky form of investment and, therefore, provide the highest expected returns. Loan capital is normally the least risky and provides the lowest expected returns to investors.

■ Leases and hire-purchase agreements allow a business to obtain immediate possession of an asset without having to pay the cost of acquiring the asset.

■ The level of gearing associated with a business is often an important factor in assessing the level of risk and returns to ordinary shareholders.

- The main sources of external *short-term* finance are bank overdrafts, debt factoring and invoice discounting.
- When considering the choice between long-term and short-term sources of borrowing, factors such as matching the type of borrowing with the nature of the assets held, the need for flexibility, refunding risk and interest rates should be taken into account.

Share issues:

- Share issues that involve the payment of cash by investors can take the form of a rights issue, public issue, offer for sale or a private placing.
- A rights issue is made to existing shareholders. Most share issues are of this type as the law requires that shares that are to be issued for cash must first be offered to existing shareholders.
- A public issue involves a direct issue to the public and an offer for sale involves an indirect issue to the public.
- A private placing is an issue of shares to selected investors.

The Stock Exchange:

- The Stock Exchange is an important primary and secondary market in capital for large businesses. However, obtaining a Stock Exchange listing can have certain drawbacks for a business.

Small businesses:

- Venture capital is long-term capital for small or medium-sized businesses that are not listed on the Stock Exchange. These businesses often have higher levels of risk but provide the venture capitalist with the prospect of higher levels of return.
- Business angels are wealthy individuals who are willing to invest in businesses at an early stage of development.
- The government assists small businesses through guaranteeing loans and by providing grants and tax incentives.

→ **Key terms**

Further reading

If you would like to explore the topics covered in this chapter in more depth, we recommend the following books:

Arnold, G. *Corporate Financial Management*, 2nd edn, Financial Times Prentice Hall, 2002, Chapters 11 and 12.

Brealey, R. and Myers, S. *Principles of Corporate Finance*, 7th edn, McGraw-Hill, 2003, Chapters 23, 25 and 26.

McLaney, E. *Business Finance: Theory and Practice*, 7th edn, Financial Times Prentice Hall, 2006, Chapter 8.

Pike, R. and Neale, B. *Corporate Finance and Investment*, 4th edn, Prentice Hall International, 2003, Chapters 16 and 18.

? Review questions

Answers to these questions can be found at the end of the book (pp. 497-8).

12.1 What are the benefits to a business of issuing share warrants?

12.2 Why might a business that has a Stock Exchange listing revert to being unlisted?

12.3 Distinguish between an offer for sale and a public issue of shares.

12.4 Distinguish between invoice discounting and factoring.

✱ Exercises

Exercises 12.3 to 12.5 are more advanced than 12.1 and 12.2. Those with a coloured number have an answer at the back of the book (pp. 523-4).

If you wish to try more exercises, visit the students' side of the companion website.

12.1 H. Brown (Portsmouth) Ltd produces a range of central heating systems for sale to builders' merchants. As a result of increasing demand for the business's products, the directors have decided to expand production. The cost of acquiring new plant and machinery and the increase in working capital requirements are planned to be financed by a mixture of long-term and short-term borrowing.

Required:
(a) Discuss the major factors that should be taken into account when deciding on the appropriate mix of long-term and short-term borrowing necessary to finance the expansion programme.
(b) Discuss the major factors that a lender should take into account when deciding whether to grant a long-term loan to the business.
(c) Identify three conditions that might be included in a long-term loan agreement, and state the purpose of each.

12.2 Carpets Direct plc wishes to increase the number of its retail outlets in the south of England. The board of directors has decided to finance this expansion programme by raising the funds from existing shareholders through a one-for-four rights issue. The most recent income statement of the business is as follows:

Income statement for the year ended 30 April

	£m
Sales revenue	164.5
Profit before interest and taxation	12.6
Interest	(6.2)
Profit before taxation	6.4
Corporation tax	(1.9)
Profit after taxation	4.5
Ordinary dividends paid	(2.0)
Retained profit for the year	2.5

The share capital consists of 120 million ordinary shares with a par value of £0.50 a share. These are currently being traded on the Stock Exchange at a price/earnings ratio of 22 times and the board of directors has decided to issue the new shares at a discount of 20 per cent on the current market value.

Required:
(a) Calculate the theoretical ex-rights price of an ordinary share in Carpets Direct plc.
(b) Calculate the price at which the rights in Carpet Direct plc are likely to be traded.
(c) Identify and evaluate, at the time of the rights issue, each of the options arising from the rights issue to an investor who holds 4,000 ordinary shares before the rights announcement.

(*Hint*: To answer Part (a), first calculate the earnings per share and then use this and the P/E ratio to calculate the marker value per share.)

12.3 Raphael Ltd is a small engineering business that has annual credit sales revenue of £2.4 million. In recent years, the business has experienced credit-control problems. The average collection period for credit sales has risen to 50 days even though the stated policy of the business is for payment to be made within 30 days. In addition, 1.5 per cent of sales are written off as bad debts each year.

The business has recently been in talks with a factor, which is prepared to make an advance to the business equivalent to 80 per cent of receivables, based on the assumption that customers will, in future, adhere to a 30-day payment period. The interest rate for the advance will be 11 per cent a year. The trade receivables are currently financed through a bank overdraft, which has an interest rate of 12 per cent a year. The factor will take over the credit-control procedures of the business and this will result in a saving to the business of £18,000 a year; however, the factor will make a charge of 2 per cent of sales revenue for this service. The use of the factoring service is expected to eliminate the bad debts incurred by the business.

Required:
Calculate the net cost of the factor agreement to the business and state whether or not the business should take advantage of the opportunity to factor its trade debts.

(*Hint*: To answer this question, compare the cost of existing trade policies – cost of investment in trade receivables and cost of bad debts – with the cost of using a factor – interest and other charges less the credit control savings.)

12.4   Gainsborough Fashions Ltd operates a small chain of fashion shops in North Wales. In recent months the business has been under pressure from its suppliers to reduce the average credit period taken from three months to one month. As a result, the directors have approached the bank to ask for an increase in the existing overdraft for one year to be able to comply with the suppliers' demands. The most recent financial statements of the business are as follows:

Balance sheet as at 31 May

	£	£	£
Non-current assets			
Property, plant and equipment			
Fixtures and fittings at cost		90,000	
Less Accumulated depreciation		23,000	67,000
Motor vehicles at cost		34,000	
Less Accumulated depreciation		27,000	7,000
			74,000
Current assets			
Inventories at cost		198,000	
Trade receivables		3,000	
		201,000	
Current liabilities			
Trade payables	(162,000)		
Accrued expenses	(10,000)		
Bank overdraft	(17,000)		
Taxation	(5,000)		
		(194,000)	7,000
			81,000
Non-current liabilities			
Debentures repayable in just over one			
year's time			(40,000)
			41,000
Equity			
£1 ordinary shares			20,000
General reserve			4,000
Retained profit			17,000
			41,000

Abbreviated income statement for the year ended 31 May

	£
Sales revenue	740,000
Net profit before interest and taxation	38,000
Interest charges	(5,000)
Net profit before taxation	33,000
Taxation	(10,000)
Net profit after taxation	23,000
Dividend paid	(10,000)
Retained profit for the year	13,000

Notes

1 The debentures are secured by personal guarantees from the directors.
2 The current overdraft bears an interest rate of 12 per cent a year.

Required:

(a) Identify and discuss the major factors that a bank would take into account before deciding whether or not to grant an increase in the overdraft of a business.

(b) State whether, in your opinion, the bank should grant the required increase in the overdraft for Gainsborough Fashions Ltd. You should provide reasoned arguments and supporting calculations where necessary.

12.5 Telford Engineers plc, a medium-sized Midlands manufacturer of automobile components, has decided to modernise its factory by introducing a number of robots. These will cost £20 million and will reduce operating costs by £6 million a year for their estimated useful life of 10 years starting next year (Year 10). To finance this scheme, the business can raise £20 million either:

1 by the issue of 20 million ordinary shares at 100p; or
2 by loan capital at 14 per cent interest a year, capital repayments of £3 million a year commencing at the end of Year 11.

Extracts from Telford Engineers' financial statements appear below:

Summary of balance sheet at 31 December

	Year 6	Year 7	Year 8	Year 9
	£m	£m	£m	£m
Non-current assets	48	51	65	64
Current assets	55	67	57	55
Current liabilities				
Trade payables	(20)	(27)	(25)	(18)
Bank overdraft	(5)	–	(6)	(8)
	78	91	91	93
Equity	48	61	61	63
Non-current liabilities	30	30	30	30
	78	91	91	93
Number of issued 25p shares	80 million	80 million	80 million	80 million
Share price	150p	200p	100p	145p

Summary of income statements for years ended 31 December

	Year 6	Year 7	Year 8	Year 9
	£m	£m	£m	£m
Sales revenue	152	170	110	145
Profit before interest and taxation	28	40	7	15
Interest payable	(4)	(3)	(4)	(5)
Profit before taxation	24	37	3	10
Taxation	(12)	(16)	(0)	(4)
Profit after taxation	12	21	3	6
Dividends paid	(6)	(8)	(3)	(4)
Retained profit	6	13	0	2

→

For your answer you should assume that the corporate tax rate for Year 10 is 30 per cent, that sales revenue and operating profit will be unchanged except for the £6 million cost saving arising from the introduction of the robots, and that Telford Engineers will pay the same dividend per share in Year 10 as in Year 9.

Required:

(a) Prepare, for each financing arrangement, Telford Engineers' projected income statement for the year ending 31 December Year 10 and a statement of its share capital, reserves and loans on that date.

(b) Calculate Telford's projected earnings per share for Year 10 for both schemes.

(c) Which scheme would you advise the business to adopt? You should give your reasons and state what additional information you would require.

Present value table

Present value of £1, that is, $1/(1 + r)^n$

where r = discount rate
n = number of periods until payment

Periods (n)					Discount rates (r)						
	1%	2%	3%	4%	5%	6%	7%	8%	9%	10%	
1	0.990	0.980	0.971	0.962	0.952	0.943	0.935	0.926	0.917	0.909	1
2	0.980	0.961	0.943	0.925	0.907	0.890	0.873	0.857	0.842	0.826	2
3	0.971	0.942	0.915	0.889	0.864	0.840	0.816	0.794	0.772	0.751	3
4	0.961	0.924	0.888	0.855	0.823	0.792	0.763	0.735	0.708	0.683	4
5	0.951	0.906	0.863	0.822	0.784	0.747	0.713	0.681	0.650	0.621	5
6	0.942	0.888	0.837	0.790	0.746	0.705	0.666	0.630	0.596	0.564	6
7	0.933	0.871	0.813	0.760	0.711	0.665	0.623	0.583	0.547	0.513	7
8	0.923	0.853	0.789	0.731	0.677	0.627	0.582	0.540	0.502	0.467	8
9	0.914	0.837	0.766	0.703	0.645	0.592	0.544	0.500	0.460	0.424	9
10	0.905	0.820	0.744	0.676	0.614	0.558	0.508	0.463	0.422	0.386	10
11	0.896	0.804	0.722	0.650	0.585	0.527	0.475	0.429	0.388	0.350	11
12	0.887	0.788	0.701	0.625	0.557	0.497	0.444	0.397	0.356	0.319	12
13	0.879	0.773	0.681	0.601	0.530	0.469	0.415	0.368	0.326	0.290	13
14	0.870	0.758	0.661	0.577	0.505	0.442	0.388	0.340	0.299	0.263	14
15	0.861	0.743	0.642	0.555	0.481	0.417	0.362	0.315	0.275	0.239	15

	11%	12%	13%	14%	15%	16%	17%	18%	19%	20%	
1	0.901	0.893	0.885	0.877	0.870	0.862	0.855	0.847	0.840	0.833	1
2	0.812	0.797	0.783	0.769	0.756	0.743	0.731	0.718	0.706	0.694	2
3	0.731	0.712	0.693	0.675	0.658	0.641	0.624	0.609	0.593	0.579	3
4	0.659	0.636	0.613	0.592	0.572	0.552	0.534	0.516	0.499	0.482	4
5	0.593	0.567	0.543	0.519	0.497	0.476	0.456	0.437	0.419	0.402	5
6	0.535	0.507	0.480	0.456	0.432	0.410	0.390	0.370	0.352	0.335	6
7	0.482	0.452	0.425	0.400	0.376	0.354	0.333	0.314	0.296	0.279	7
8	0.434	0.404	0.376	0.351	0.327	0.305	0.285	0.266	0.249	0.233	8
9	0.391	0.361	0.333	0.308	0.284	0.263	0.243	0.225	0.209	0.194	9
10	0.352	0.322	0.295	0.270	0.247	0.227	0.208	0.191	0.176	0.162	10
11	0.317	0.287	0.261	0.237	0.215	0.195	0.178	0.162	0.148	0.135	11
12	0.286	0.257	0.231	0.208	0.187	0.168	0.152	0.137	0.124	0.112	12
13	0.258	0.229	0.204	0.182	0.163	0.145	0.130	0.116	0.104	0.093	13
14	0.232	0.205	0.181	0.160	0.141	0.125	0.111	0.099	0.088	0.078	14
15	0.209	0.183	0.160	0.140	0.123	0.108	0.095	0.084	0.074	0.065	15

Glossary of key terms

ABC system of inventories control A method of applying different levels of inventories control, based on the value of each category of inventories. *p. 375*

accounting The process of identifying, measuring and communicating information to permit informed judgements and decisions by users of the information. *p. 2*

accounting conventions Accounting rules that have evolved over time in order to deal with practical problems rather than to reflect some theoretical ideal. *p. 46*

accounting information system The system used within a business to identify, record, analyse and report accounting information. *p. 9*

accounting rate of return (ARR) The average profit from an investment, expressed as a percentage of the average investment made. *p. 331*

accruals accounting The system of accounting that follows the accruals convention. This is the system followed in drawing up the income statement and balance sheet. *p. 76*

accruals convention The convention of accounting that asserts that profit is the excess of revenue over expenses, not the excess of cash receipts over cash payments. *p. 76*

accrued expenses Expenses that are outstanding (unpaid) at the end of the accounting period. *p. 72*

acid test ratio A liquidity ratio that relates the current assets (less inventories) to the current liabilities. *p. 188*

activity-based costing (ABC) A technique for more accurately relating overheads to specific production or provision of a service. It is based on acceptance of the fact that overheads do not just occur but are caused by activities, such as holding products in stores, that 'drive' the costs. *p. 269*

adverse variance A difference between planned and actual performance, usually where the difference will cause the actual profit to be lower than the budgeted one. *p. 303*

ageing schedule of receivables A report dividing receivables into categories, depending on the length of time outstanding. *p. 387*

assets Resources held by a business that have certain characteristics. *p. 31*

asset-based finance A form of financing where assets are used as security for cash advances to the business. Factoring and invoice discounting, where the security is trade receivables, are examples of asset-based finance. *p. 441*

auditors   Professional accountants whose main duty is to prepare a report for share-holders stating whether, in their opinion, the financial statements of a business show a true and fair view of financial position and performance. *p. 128*

authorised share capital   The maximum amount of share capital that directors are authorised to by the shareholders to issue. *p. 117*

average inventories turnover period   An efficiency ratio that measures the average period for which inventories are held by a business. *p. 180*

average settlement period for payables   The average time taken for a business to pay its trade payables. *pp. 182 and 398*

average settlement period for receivables   The average time taken for customers to pay the amounts owing. *pp. 181 and 387*

bad debt   Amount owed to the business that is considered to be irrecoverable. *p. 90*

balance sheet   A statement of financial position that shows the assets of a business and the claims on those assets. *p. 26*

bank overdraft   A flexible form of borrowing that allows an individual or business to have a negative current account balance. *p. 439*

batch costing   A technique for identifying full cost, where the production of many types of goods and services, particularly goods, involves producing in a batch of identical or nearly identical units of output, but where each batch is distinctly different from other batches. *p. 265*

bonus shares   Shares that have been created from the reserves of a company and which are distributed 'free' to shareholders in proportion to their existing share-holdings. *p. 115*

break-even analysis   The activity of deducing the break-even point of some activity through analysing costs and revenues. *p. 222*

break-even chart   A graphical representation of the costs and revenues of some activity, at various levels, which enables the break-even point to be identified. *p. 223*

break-even point (BEP)   A level of activity where revenue will exactly equal total cost, so there is neither profit nor loss. *p. 223*

budgets   Financial plans for the short term, typically one year. *p. 281*

budgetary control   Using the budget as a yardstick against which the effectiveness of actual performance may be assessed. *p. 316*

business angels   Investors, typically wealthy individuals, who are prepared to make investments, normally equity ones, in small businesses. Often business angels take a close interest in the running of the business(es) in which they invest. *p. 444*

business entity convention   The convention that holds that, for accounting purposes, the business and its owner(s) are treated as quite separate and distinct. *p. 46*

capital   The owner's claim on the assets of the business. *p.33*

capital reserves Reserves that arise from a 'capital' profit or gain rather than from normal trading activities. *p. 113*

cash discount A reduction in the amount due for goods or services sold on credit in return for prompt payment. *p. 386*

cash flow statement A statement that shows the sources and uses of cash for a period. *p. 26*

claims Obligation on the part of the business to provide cash or some other benefit to outside parties. *p. 31*

Combined Code A code of corporate governance that applies to companies listed on the London Stock Exchange. Directors of these companies are obliged to comply with the provisions of the code or explain to shareholders why they have failed to comply. *p. 109*

common costs Another name for indirect costs or overheads. These are costs that do not directly relate and are not measurable in respect of particular units of output, but relate to all output. *p. 252*

comparability The requirement that items that are basically the same should be treated in the same manner for measurement and reporting purposes. Lack of comparability will limit the usefulness of accounting information. *p. 7*

compensating variances The situation that exists when two variances, one adverse the other favourable, are of equal size and therefore cancel out. *p. 315*

consistency convention The accounting convention that holds that when a particular method of accounting is selected to deal with a transaction, this method should be applied consistently over time. *p. 89*

contribution Sales revenue less variable costs. *p. 228*

control Compelling events to conform to plan. *p. 287*

convertible loan stocks Loan capital that can be converted into equity share capital at the option of the holders. *p. 417*

corporate governance Systems for directing and controlling a company. *p. 107*

corporation tax Taxation that a limited company is liable to pay on its profits. *p. 106*

cost behaviour The manner in which costs alter with changes in the level of activity. *p. 254*

cost centre Some area, object, person or activity for which costs are separately collected. *p. 264*

cost driver An activity that causes costs. *p. 269*

cost of sales The cost of the goods sold during a period. Cost of sales can be derived by adding the opening inventories held to the inventories purchased during the period and then deducting the closing inventories held. *p. 66*

cost pool The sum of the overhead costs that are seen as being caused by the same cost driver. *p. 270*

cost units The objects for which the cost is being deduced, usually individual products or services. *p. 255*

cost-plus pricing An approach to pricing output that is based on full cost, plus a percentage profit loading. *p. 272*

creative accounting Adopting accounting policies to achieve a particular view of performance and position that preparers of financial reports would like users to see, rather than what is a true and fair view. *p. 129*

current assets Assets that are held for the short-term. They include cash itself and other assets that are held for sale or consumption in the normal course of a business's operating cycle. *p. 39*

current liabilities Amounts due for repayment to outside parties in the short term, usually within 12 months of the balance sheet date or the normal course of a business's operating cycle. *p. 41*

current ratio A liquidity ratio that relates the current assets of the business to the current liabilities. *p. 187*

debenture A long-term loan, usually made to a business, evidenced by a trust deed. *pp. 118 and 414*

debt factoring A service offered by a financial institution (a factor) that involves the factor taking over the management of the trade receivables of the business. The factor is often prepared to make an advance to the business based on the amount of trade receivables outstanding. *p. 439*

deep discount bond Redeemable loan capital offering a rate of interest below the market rate and so issued at a discount to its redeemable value. *p. 416*

depreciation A measure of that portion of the cost, or fair value, (less residual value) of a non-current asset that has been consumed during an accounting period. *p. 76*

direct costs Costs that can be identified with specific cost units, to the extent that the effect of the cost can be measured in respect of each particular unit of output. *p. 251*

direct method An approach to deducing the cash flows from operating activities, in a cash flow statement, by analysing the business's cash records. *p. 149*

directors Individuals who are elected to act as the most senior level of management of a business. *p. 107*

directors' report A report containing information of a financial and non-financial nature that the directors must produce as part of the annual financial report to shareholders. *p. 128*

discount factor The rate applied to future cash flows to derive the present value of those cash flows. *p. 346*

dividend A transfer of assets made by a business to its shareholders. *p. 111*

dividend cover ratio An investment ratio that relates the earnings available for dividends to the dividend paid, to indicate how many times the former covers the latter. *p. 196*

dividend payout ratio   An investment ratio that relates the dividends announced for the period to the earnings available for dividends that were generated in that period. *p. 195*

dividend per share   An investment ratio that relates the dividends paid for a period to the number of shares in issue. *p. 197*

dividend yield ratio   An investment ratio that expresses a business's dividend per share as a percentage of its current share price. It provides users with some measure of the dividend returns that the share generates. *p. 196*

dual aspect convention   The accounting convention that holds that each transaction has two aspects, and that each aspect must be reflected in the financial statements. *p. 49*

earnings per share   An investment ratio that relates the earnings generated by the business during a period, and available to shareholders, to the number of shares in issue. *p. 197*

economic order quantity (EOQ)   The quantity of a particular item of inventories that should be purchased with each order, in an attempt to minimise total inventories costs. *p. 376*

equity   Ordinary shares and reserves of a company. *p. 111*

eurobonds   A form of long-term bonds issued in a currency that is not that of the country in which the bonds are issued. *p. 415*

expense   A measure of the outflow of assets (or increase in liabilities) that is incurred as a result of generating revenues. *p. 62*

fair values   The values ascribed to assets as an alternative to historic cost. It is usually the current market value (that is, the exchange values in arms-length transactions). *p. 52*

favourable variance   A difference between planned and actual performance, usually where the difference will cause the actual profit to be higher than the budgeted one. *p. 303*

final accounts   The income statement, cash flow statement and balance sheet taken together. *p. 29*

finance   The raising, investment and management of funds. *p. 2*

finance lease   A financial arrangement whereby the asset title remains with the owner (the lessor) but the lease agreement transfers virtually all the rewards and risks to the business that uses the asset (the lessee). *p. 422*

financial accounting   The measuring and reporting of accounting information for external users (those users other than the managers of the business). *p. 13*

financial derivatives   Any form of financial instrument, based on share or loan capital, which can be used by investors to either increase their returns or decrease their exposure to risk. *p. 419*

financial gearing   The existence of fixed payment bearing securities (for example, loans) in the capital structure of a business. *p. 189*

financial management   A subject area concerned with the financing and investing decisions of businesses. *p. 15*

first in, first out (FIFO)   A method of inventories valuation that assumes that the earlier inventories are to be sold first. *p. 86*

five Cs of credit   A checklist of factors to be taken into account when assessing the creditworthiness of a customer. *p. 382*

fixed cost   A cost that stays the same when changes occur to the volume of activity. *p. 218*

flexible budgets   Budgets that are adjusted to reflect what they would have been had the planned level of output been different. This different level may be the actual level of output achieved. *p. 300*

flexing the budget   Revising the budget to what it would have been had the planned level of output been different. *p. 301*

full cost   The total direct and indirect (overhead) costs of pursuing some activity or objective. *p. 250*

full costing   Deducing the total direct and indirect (overhead) costs of pursuing some activity or objective. *p. 250*

gearing ratio   A ratio that relates the contribution of long-term lenders to the total long-term capital of the business. *p. 192*

going concern convention   The accounting convention that assumes that the business will continue operations for the foreseeable future, unless the opposite is known to be true. In other words, there is no intention or need to liquidate the business. *p. 48*

gross profit   The amount remaining (if positive) after trading expenses (for example, cost of sales) have been deducted from trading revenue (for example, sales revenue). *p. 65*

gross profit margin ratio   A profitability ratio relating the gross profit for the period to the sales revenue for the period. *p. 178*

hire purchase   A method of acquiring an asset by paying the purchase price by instalments over a period. Normally, control of the asset will pass as soon as the hire-purchase contract is signed and the first instalment is paid, whereas ownership will pass on payment of the final instalment. *p. 425*

historic cost convention   The accounting convention that holds that assets should be recorded at their historic (acquisition) cost. *p. 48*

income statement   A financial statement that measures and reports the profit (or loss) the business has generated during a period. It is derived by deducting from total revenue for a period, the total expenses associated with those revenues. Also known as a profit and loss account. *pp. 26 and 63*

indirect costs (or overheads)   All costs except direct costs, that is, those that cannot be directly measured in respect of each particular unit of output. *p. 252*

indirect method   An approach to deducing the cash flows from operating activities, in a cash flow statement, by analysing the business's financial statements. *p. 149*

inflation   A tendency for a currency to lose value over time owing to increasing prices of goods and services. *p. 342*

intangible assets   Assets that do not have a physical substance (for example, patents, goodwill and receivables). *p. 33*

interest cover ratio   A gearing ratio that divides the net profit before interest and taxation by the interest payable for a period. *p. 193*

internal rate of return (IRR)   The discount rate for a project that will have the effect of producing a zero NPV. *p. 348*

International Financial Reporting Standards   Transnational accounting rules that have been adopted or developed by the International Accounting Standards Board and which should be followed in preparing the published financial statements of limited companies. *p. 127*

invoice discounting   A loan provided by a financial institution based on a proportion of the face value of credit sales outstanding. *p. 440*

issued share capital   That part of the authorised share capital that has been issued to shareholders. Also known as allotted share capital. *p. 117*

job costing   A technique for identifying the full cost per unit of output, where that unit of output is not similar to other units of output. *p. 252*

just-in-time (JIT) inventories management   A system of inventories management that aims to have supplies delivered to production just in time for their required use. *p. 380*

last in, first out (LIFO)   A method of inventories valuation that assumes that the latest inventories are the first to be sold. *p. 86*

lead time   The time lapse between placing an order for something, usually an item of inventories, and its delivery to the required location. *p. 374*

liabilities   Claims of individuals and organisations, apart from the owner, that have arisen from past transactions or events such as supplying goods or lending money to the business. *p. 34*

limited company   An artificial legal person that has an identity separate from that of those who own and manage it. *p. 101*

limited liability   The restriction of the legal obligation of shareholders to meet all of the company's debts. *p. 104*

limiting factor   Some aspect of the business (for example, lack of sales demand) that will prevent it from achieving its objectives to the maximum extent. *p. 283*

loan covenants   Conditions contained within a loan agreement that are designed to protect the lenders. *p. 420*

loan stock   Long-term loan made by businesses. *pp. 118 and 414*

management accounting   The measuring and reporting of accounting information for the managers of a business. *p. 13*

management by exception   A system of control, based on a comparison of planned and actual performance, that allows managers to focus on areas of poor performance rather than dealing with areas where performance is satisfactory. *p. 287*

margin of safety   The extent to which the planned level of output or sales revenue lies above the break-even point. *pp. 121 and 228*

marginal analysis   The activity of decision making through analysing variable costs and revenues, ignoring fixed costs. *p. 236*

marginal cost   The additional cost of producing one more unit. This is often the same as the variable cost. *p. 236*

master budgets   A summary of the individual budgets, usually consisting of a budgeted income statement, a budgeted balance sheet and a budgeted cash flow statement. *p. 284*

matching convention   The accounting convention that holds that, in measuring income, expenses should be matched to revenues that they helped generate, in the same accounting period as those revenues were realised. *p. 71*

materiality   The requirement that material information should be disclosed to users in financial statements. *p. 8*

materiality convention   The accounting convention that states that, where the amounts involved are immaterial, only what is expedient should be considered. *p. 75*

materials requirement planning (MRP) system   A computer-based system of inventories control that schedules the timing of deliveries of bought-in parts and materials to coincide with production requirements to meet demand. *p. 379*

money measurement convention   The accounting convention that holds that accounting should deal only with those items that are capable of being expressed in monetary terms. *p. 46*

mortgage   A loan secured on property. *p. 420*

net present value (NPV)   A method of investment appraisal based on the present value of all relevant cash flows associated with the project. *p. 340*

net profit   The amount remaining (if positive) after the total expenses for a period have been deducted from total revenue. *p. 65*

net profit margin ratio   A profitability ratio relating the net profit for the period to the sales revenue for the period. *p. 177*

nominal value   The face value of a share in a company. Also known as par value. *p. 111*

non-current assets   Assets held that do not meet the criteria of current assets. They are held for the long-term operations of the business rather than continuously circulating within the business. *p. 40*

non-current liabilities Those amounts due to other parties that are not current liabilities. *p. 41*

objectivity convention The accounting convention that holds that, in so far as is possible, the financial statements prepared should be based on objective verifiable evidence rather than on matters of opinion. *p. 50*

offer for sale An issue of shares that involves a public limited company (or its shareholders) selling the shares to a financial institution that will, in turn, sell the shares to the public. *p. 432*

operating cash cycle (OCC) The period between the outlay of cash to purchase supplies and the ultimate receipt of cash from the sale of goods. *p. 392*

operating gearing The relationship between the total fixed and the total variable costs for some activity. *p. 229*

operating lease A short-term arrangement, where a business hires an asset for a short time. Hiring an asset under an operating lease tends to be an operating, rather than a financing, decision. *p. 422*

operating profit The profit achieved during a period after all operating expenses have been deducted from revenues from operations. Financing expenses are deducted after the calculation of operating profit. *p. 124*

opportunity cost The cost incurred when one course of action prevents an opportunity to derive some benefit from another course of action. *p. 353*

ordinary shares Shares of a company owned by those who are due the benefits of the company's activities after all other stakeholders have been satisfied. *p. 112*

outsourcing Arranging for another business to undertake some activity, on a subcontract basis, that could be carried out 'in house'. *p. 240*

overhead (or indirect cost) Any cost except a direct cost; a cost that cannot be directly measured in respect of each particular unit of output. *p. 252*

overhead absorption (recovery) rate The rate at which overheads are charged to cost units (jobs), usually in a job costing system. *p. 256*

payback period (PP) The time taken for the initial investment in a project to be repaid from the net cash inflows of the project. *p. 336*

preference shares Shares of a company owned by those who are entitled to the first part of any dividend that the company might pay. *p. 112*

prepaid expenses Expenses that have been paid in advance, at the end of the accounting period. *p. 75*

price/earnings ratio An investment ratio that relates the market value of a share to the earnings per share. *p. 198*

private company A limited company for which the directors can restrict the ownership of its shares. *p. 104*

private equity Equity finance primarily for small and medium-sized businesses provided by venture capitalists and/or business angels. *p. 443*

private placing   An issue of shares that involves a limited company arranging for the shares to be sold to the clients of particular issuing houses or stockbrokers, rather than to the general investing public. *p. 433*

process costing   A technique for deriving the full cost per unit of output, where the units of output are exactly similar or it is reasonable to treat them as being so. *p. 251*

profit   The increase in wealth attributable to the owners of a business that arises through business operations. *p. 62*

profit–volume (PV) chart   A graphical representation of the contributions (revenues less variable costs) of some activity, at various levels, which enables the break-even point, and the profit at various activity levels, to be identified. *p. 232*

property, plant and equipment   Those non-current assets that have a physical substance (for example, plant and machinery, motor vehicles). *p. 52*

prudence convention   The accounting convention that holds that financial statements should err on the side of caution. The prudence convention represents a pessimistic rather than an optimistic view of financial position. *p. 49*

public company   A limited company for which the directors cannot restrict the ownership of its shares. *p. 104*

public issue   An issue of shares that involves a public limited company making a direct invitation to the public to purchase shares in the company. *p. 432*

reducing-balance method   A method of calculating depreciation that applies a fixed percentage rate of depreciation to the written-down value of an asset in each period. *p. 80*

relevance   The ability of accounting information to influence decisions. Relevance is regarded as a key characteristic of useful accounting information. *p. 6*

relevant cost   A cost that is relevant to a particular decision. *p. 352*

reliability   The requirement that accounting should be free from material error or bias. Reliability is regarded as a key characteristic of useful accounting information. *p. 7*

reserves   Part of the owners' claim on a limited company that has arisen from profits and gains, to the extent that these have not been distributed to the shareholders. *p. 110*

residual value   The amount for which a non-current asset is sold when the business has no further use for it. *p. 78*

return on capital employed (ROCE)   A profitability ratio expressing the relationship between the net profit (before interest and taxation) and the long-term capital invested in the business. *p. 175*

return on ordinary shareholders' funds (ROSF)   A profitability ratio that compares the amount of profit for the period available to the ordinary shareholders with their stake in the business. *p. 174*

revenue A measure of the inflow of assets (for example, cash or amounts owed by trade receivables), or a reduction in liabilities, which arise as a result of trading activities. *p. 62*

revenue reserve Part of the owners' claim of a company that arises from realised profits and gains, including after-tax trading profits and gains from disposals of non-current assets. *p. 111*

rights issues Issues of shares for cash to existing shareholders on the basis of the number of shares already held. *p. 429*

risk The likelihood and extent that what is projected to occur will not actually occur. *p. 341*

risk premium A rate of return in excess of that which would be expected from a risk-free investment, to compensate the investor for bearing risk. *p. 342*

sale and leaseback An agreement to sell an asset (usually property) to another party and simultaneously to lease the asset back in order to continue using the asset. *p. 424*

sales revenue per employee ratio An efficiency ratio that relates the sales revenue generated during a period to the average number of employees of the business. *p. 184*

sales revenue to capital employed ratio An efficiency ratio that relates the sales revenue generated during a period to the capital employed. *p. 183*

semi-fixed (semi-variable) cost A cost that has an element of both fixed and variable cost. *p. 222*

shares Portions of the ownership, or equity, of a company. *p. 101*

share premium account A reserve that shows any amount above the nominal value of shares issued that is paid for those shares. *p. 114*

stable monetary unit convention The accounting convention that holds that money, which is the unit of measurement in accounting, will not change in value over time. *p. 50*

standard quantities and costs Planned quantities and costs (or revenues) for individual units of input or output. Standards are the building blocks used to produce the budget. *p. 311*

stepped fixed cost A fixed cost that does not remain fixed over all levels of output but which changes in steps as a threshold level of output is reached. *p. 220*

Stock Exchange A market where 'second-hand' shares may be bought and sold and new capital raised. *p. 433*

straight-line method A method of accounting for depreciation that allocates the amount to be depreciated evenly over the useful life of the asset. *p. 79*

tangible assets Those assets that have a physical substance (for example, plant and machinery, motor vehicles). *p. 33*

tender issue An issue of shares that involves a public limited company inviting the investing public to make offers for the shares, rather than the company setting the price itself. *p. 432*

term loan   Finance provided by financial institutions, like banks and insurance companies, under a contract with the borrowing business that indicates the interest rate and dates of payments of interest and repayment of the loan. The loan is not normally transferable from one lender to another. *p. 414*

total cost   The sum of the variable and fixed costs of pursuing some activity. *p. 255*

understandability   The requirement that accounting information should be capable of being understood by those for whom the information is primarily compiled. Lack of understandability will limit the usefulness of accounting information. *p. 7*

variable cost   A cost that varies according to the volume of activity. *p. 218*

variance   The financial effect, on the budgeted profit, of the particular factor under consideration being more or less than budgeted. *p. 310*

variance analysis   Carrying out calculations to find the area of the business's operations that has caused the budgets not to have been met. *p. 304*

venture capital   Long-term capital provided by certain institutions to small and medium-sized businesses to exploit relatively high-risk opportunities. *p. 444*

warrants   A document giving the holder the right, but not the obligation, to acquire ordinary shares in a company at an agreed price. *p. 419*

weighted average cost (AVCO)   A method of valuing inventories that assumes that inventories entering the business lose their separate identity and any issues of inventories reflect the weighted average cost of the inventories held. *p. 86*

working capital   Current assets less current liabilities. *p. 386*

written-down value   The difference between the cost (or revalued amount) of a non-current asset and the accumulated depreciation relating to the assets. The written down-value is also referred to as the net book value (NBV). *p. 79*

Relevant websites

General websites

Biz/ed   **www.bized.ac.uk**

This website is maintained by the Biz/ed team at the University of Bristol. It provides a free, online service for students and others on various business related areas, including accounting and finance. Whilst some specific pages are given below, in the context of individual chapters, you may well find the homepage a useful start in finding resources relating to your studies in other subjects.

Search engines that are helpful in finding accounting/finance/business websites:

www.ananova.com/business
www.business.com
www.uk.biz.yahoo.com
uk.finance.yahoo.com
www.cranfield.ac.uk/cils/library/subject/finance.htm
www.financeprofessor.com
www.utk.edu/~jwachowi/wacho_world.html

Websites containing relevant articles and other useful information:

Accountancy Age	**www.accountancyage.com**
The Association of Chartered Certified Accountants	**www.accaglobal.com/publications**
Financial Times	**news.ft.com/home/uk/**
The Economist	**www.economist.com**
Guardian	**www.guardian.co.uk/money**
Business Finance Magazine	**www.bfmag.com**
Bamboo Web	**www.bambooweb.com**
Board Member Europe	**www.boardmembereurope.com**

Chapter 1

The websites of the businesses featured in this chapter are:

Gap	**www.gap.com**
Marks and Spencer plc	**www.marksandspencer.com**
Morrisons Supermarket plc	**www.morrisons.co.uk**
Nike Inc	**www.nike.com**

The websites of businesses tend to be 'menu driven'. They typically have a lot of information on the business's products as well as sections dealing with finance and accounting issues about themselves, including their annual financial statements. The sites often refer to the latter sections as 'shareholder' or 'corporate' information.

Chapter 2

The websites of the businesses featured in this chapter are:

Cementbouw BV	www.cementbouw.nl
CRH	www.crh.ie
Marks and Spencer plc	www.marksandspencer.com
Newcastle United plc	www.nufc.co.uk
Unilever plc	www.unilever.co.uk
O_2 plc	www.o2.plc

Chapter 3

The websites of the businesses featured in this chapter are:

Brandon Hire plc	www.brandontoolhire.co.uk
Euro-Disney SCA	www.disneylandparis.com
Hyder Consulting plc	www.hyderconsulting.com
Newcastle United plc	www.nufc.co.uk
O_2 plc	www.o2.plc
Tate and Lyle plc	www.tateandlyle.com
Thorntons plc	www.thorntons.co.uk

Chapter 4

The Biz/ed site (see General websites, above) has pages that provide useful learning resources on company financial statements:

Company report database	www.bized.ac.uk/cgi-bin/ratios/ratiodata.pl
Company case studies	www.bized.ac.uk/compfact/comphome.htm

The UK and international accounting standards bodies have sites that provide information on their activities and on individual accounting standards:

Accounting Standards Board (UK)	www.asb.org.uk
International Accounting Standards Board	www.iasb.org.uk

This site, maintained by the *Financial Times* enables you to order annual reports and accounts of many listed businesses including some overseas ones:

www.ft.ar.wilink.com

This site maintained by the Department of Trade and Industry (a UK government department) gives access to the addresses of all UK companies so that they can be contacted to ask for a copy of their annual report and accounts:

www.companieshouse.gov.uk/info/

Hemscott's site will allow you to extract lots of information about Stock Exchange listed companies, including individual business's share prices over time:

www.hemscott.co.uk/hemscott/

Most major businesses have a copy of their annual report and financial statements on their websites. If you open any of the websites for the businesses that are listed above or below, you can use the menu to get to the financial statements (income statement and so on). These can be read online or downloaded.

The websites of the businesses featured in this chapter are:

Asda plc	www.asda.co.uk
Carlton Communications plc	www.carlton.co.uk
Clinton Cards plc	www.clintoncards.co.uk
Enron	www.enron.com
Global Crossing	www.globalcrossing.com
Granada Media plc	www.granadamedia.com
Monotub Industries plc	www.monotub.co.uk
Morrisons Supermarket plc	www.morrisons.co.uk
J Sainsbury plc	www.j-sainsbury.com
SSL	www.ssl.com
Tesco plc	www.tesco.com
Wal-Mart Stores Inc	www.walmart.com

Chapter 5

The websites of the businesses featured in this chapter are:

Eurotunnel plc	www.eurotunnel.com
Rolls-Royce plc	www.rollsroyce.com
Waterford Wedgewood plc	www.waterfordwedgewood.com

Chapter 6

The Biz/ed site (see General websites, above) has pages that provide information and a useful set of exercises on accounting ratios:

www.bized.ac.uk/compfact/ratios/

The websites of the businesses featured in this chapter are:

British Petroleum plc	www.bp.com
British Sky Broadcasting plc	www.sky.com

Deutsche Bank AG	www.db.com
Imperial Chemical Industries plc	www.ici.com
Marks and Spencer plc	www.marksandspencer.com
Rolls-Royce plc	www.rollsroyce.com
Royal Dutch Shell	www.shell.com
Sony Corp	www.sony.net
Tesco plc	www.tesco.com
Vodafone Group plc	www.vodafone.com
Volkswagen AG	www.vw.com
J D Wetherspoon plc	www.jdwetherspoon.co.uk

Chapter 7

The websites of the businesses featured in this chapter are:

The Boots Company plc	www.boots-plc.com
British Airways plc	www.britishairways.com
easyJet plc	www.easyjet.com
Ford Motor Company	www.ford.com
Jaguar	www.jaguar.com
Ryanair Holdings plc	www.ryanair.com

Chapter 9

The website of the business featured in this chapter is:

Royal Dutch Shell	www.shell.com

Chapter 10

The websites of the businesses featured in this chapter are:

Associated British Ports Holdings plc	www.abports.co.uk
Astra-Zeneca plc	www.astrazeneca.com
Brascam Corp	www.brascam.be
Brittany Ferries	www.brittany-ferries.com
Bristol Water plc	www.bristol-water.co.uk
Chloride Group plc	www.cloridepower.com
Hutchison Whampoa Ltd	www.hutchison-whampoa.com
Rolls-Royce plc	www.rollsroyce.com
Royal Dutch Shell	www.shell.com
J Sainsbury plc	www.j-sainsbury.com
SEC Global	www.sec-global.com
Tesco plc	www.tesco.com
United Utilities plc	www.unitedutilities.com
J D Wetherspoon plc	www.jdwetherspoon.co.uk
Yates Group plc	www.yates-group.com

Chapter 11

Some sites that provide information on the management of trade debtors are:

www.moodys.com
www.standardandpoor.com
www.payontime.co.uk

The websites of the businesses featured in this chapter are:

The Boots Company plc	www.boots-plc.com
Brambles Industries plc	www.brambles.com
British Airways plc	www.britishairways.com
Kmart Corp	www.kmart.com
Next plc	www.next.co.uk
Nissan Motors UK Ltd	www.nissan.co.uk
Pilkington plc	www.pilkington.com
REL Consultancy Group	www.relconsult.com
Severn Trent plc	www.severntrent.com
Tarkett Sommer plc	www.tarkett.com
Tesco plc	www.tesco.com
Wal-Mart Stores Inc	www.walmart.com

Chapter 12

The site for the London Stock Exchange contains a lot of information and statistics about the exchange:

www.londonstockexchange.com

This provides access to Bank of England statistics and to various publications, including regular reports on the financing of businesses, particularly small ones, which can be downloaded:

www.bankofengland.co.uk/

The British Venture Capital Association's website provides information about venture capital:

www.bvca.co.uk

The National Business Angels Network site is:

www.bestmatch.co.uk

The Finance and Leasing Association site is:

www.fla.org.uk

The 3i Group plc (a leading venture capital business) site is:

www.3i.com

The websites of the businesses featured in this chapter are:

Amazon.com Inc	www.amazon.com
Benfield Group plc	www.benfieldgroup.com
BNP Paribas	www.bnpparibas.com
BAA plc	www.baa.co.uk
British Airways plc	www.britishairways.com
H P Bulmer plc	www.bulmer.com
Cardpoint Group plc	www.cardpointplc.com
Deutsche Bank AG	www.db.com
Hilton Group plc	www.hiltongroup.com
Holidaybreak plc	www.holidaybreak.co.uk
Jessops plc	www.jessops.com
Le Meridien Hotels and Resorts Ltd	www.lemeridien.com
Permira Advisors Ltd	www.permira.com
Prudential plc	www.prudential.co.uk/plc
Scottish Power plc	www.scottishpower.co.uk
Tesco plc	www.tesco.com
Travelodge	www.travelodge.co.uk

Appendix A: Solutions to self-assessment questions

Chapter 2

2.1 Simonson Engineering

The balance sheet you prepare should be set out as follows:

Balance sheet as at 30 September 2005

	£	£	£
Non-current assets			
Freehold premises			72,000
Plant and machinery			25,000
Motor vehicles			15,000
Fixtures and fittings			9,000
			121,000
Current assets			
Inventories		45,000	
Trade receivables		48,000	
Cash in hand		1,500	
		94,500	
Current liabilities			
Trade payables	(18,000)		
Bank overdraft	(26,000)		
		(44,000)	
			50,500
Total assets less current liabilities			171,500
Non-current liabilities			
Loan			(51,000)
Net assets			120,500
Capital			
Opening balance			117,500
Add Profit			18,000
			135,500
Less Drawings			15,000
			120,500

Chapter 3

3.1

TT and Co
Balance sheet as at 31 December 2005

Assets	£	Claims	£
Delivery van (12,000 – 2,500)	9,500	Capital (50,000 + 26,900)	76,900
Inventories (143,000 + 12,000	65,000	Trade payables	22,000
– 74,000 – 16,000)		(143,000 – 121,000)	
Trade receivables (152,000 –	19,600	Accrued expenses (630 + 620)	1,250
132,000 – 400)			
Cash at bank (50,000 – 25,000 –	750		
500 – 1,200 – 12,000 – 33,500 –			
1,650 – 12,000 + 35,000 – 9,400			
+ 132,000 – 121,000)			
Prepaid expenses (5,000 + 300)	5,300		
	100,150		100,150

Income statement for the year ended 31 December 2005

	£	£
Sales revenue (152,000 + 35,000)		187,000
Less Cost of sales (74,000 + 16,000)		90,000
Gross profit		97,000
Less		
Rent	20,000	
Rates (500 + 900)	1,400	
Wages (33,500 + 630)	34,130	
Electricity (1,650 + 620)	2,270	
Bad debts	400	
Van depreciation [(12,000 – 2,000)/4]	2,500	
Van expenses	9,400	
		70,100
Net profit for the year		£26,900

The balance sheet could now be rewritten in a more stylish form as follows:

TT and Co
Balance sheet as at 31 December 2005

	£	£	£
Non-current assets			
Motor van			9,500
Current assets			
Inventories	65,000		
Trade receivables	19,600		
Prepaid expenses	5,300		
Cash	750		
		90,650	
Less **Current liabilities**			
Trade payables	22,000		
Accrued expenses	1,250		
		23,250	
			67,400
			76,900
Capital			
Original			50,000
Retained profit			26,900
			76,900

Chapter 4

4.1

Pear Limited
Income statement for the year ended 30 September 2006

	£000	£000
Revenue (1,456 + 18)		1,474
Cost of sales		(768)
Gross profit		706
Less Expenses		
Salaries	220	
Depreciation (249 + 12)	261	
Other operating costs (131 + 2)	133	(614)
Operating profit		92
Interest payable (15 + 15)		(30)
Profit before taxation		62
Taxation (62 × 30%)		(19)
Profit after taxation		43
Dividend proposed		(25)
		18

Balance sheet as at 30 September 2006

	£000	£000
Non-current assets		
Property, plant and equipment		
Cost (1,570 + 30)	1,600	
Depreciation (690 + 12)	702	
		898
Current assets		
Inventories	207	
Trade receivables (182 + 18)	200	
Cash at bank	21	
	428	
Less Current liabilities		
Trade payables	88	
Other payables (20 + 30 + 15 + 2)	67	
Taxation	19	
Dividend approved	25	
Bank overdraft	105	
	304	
Net current assets		124
Less Non-current liabilities		
10% debenture – repayable 2013		(300)
		722
Equity		
Share capital		300
Share premium account	300	
Retained profit at beginning of year	104	
Profit for year	18	422
		722

Chapter 5

5.1
Touchstone plc
Cash flow statement for the year ended 31 December 2006

	£m	£m
Cash flows from operating activities		
Net profit, after interest, before taxation (Note 1)	60	
Adjustments for:		
Depreciation	16	
Interest expense (Note 2)	4	
	80	
Increase in trade receivables (26 − 16)	(10)	
Decrease in trade payables (38 − 37)	(1)	
Decrease in inventories (25 − 24)	1	
Cash generated from operations	70	
Interest paid	(4)	
Corporation tax paid (Note 3)	(12)	
Dividend paid	(18)	
Net cash from operating activities		36
Cash flows from investing activities		
Payments to acquire tangible non-current assets (Note 4)	(41)	
Net cash used in investing activities		(41)
Cash flows from financing activities		
Issue of debenture stock (40 − 20)	20	
Net cash used in financing activities		20
Net increase in cash and cash equivalents		15
Cash and cash equivalents at 1 January 2006:		
Cash		4
Cash and cash equivalents at 31 December 2006:		
Cash		4
Treasury bills		15
		19

To see how this relates to the cash of the business at the beginning and end of the year it can be useful to provide a reconciliation as follows:

Analysis of cash and cash equivalents during the year ended 31 December 2006

	£m
Cash and cash equivalents at 1 January 2006	4
Net cash inflow	15
Cash and cash equivalents at 31 December 2006	19

Notes:

1 This is simply taken from the income statement for the year.
2 Interest payable expense must be taken out, by adding it back to the profit figure. We subsequently deduct the cash paid for interest payable during the year. In this case the two figures are identical.
3 Companies pay tax of 50 per cent during their accounting year and the other 50 per cent in the following year. Thus the 2006 payment would have been half the tax on the 2005 profit (that is, the figure that would have appeared in the current liabilities at the end of 2005), plus half of the 2006 tax charge (that is, $4 + (1/2 \times 16) = 12$).

4 Since there were no disposals, the depreciation charges must be the difference between the start and end of the year's non-current asset values, adjusted by the cost of any additions.

	£m
Book value, at 1 January 2006	147
Add Additions (balancing figure)	41
	188
Less Depreciation (6 + 10)	16
Book value, at 31 December 2006	172

Chapter 6

6.1 Ali plc and Bhaskar plc

In order to answer this question you may have used the following ratios:

	Ali plc	*Bhaskar plc*
Current ratio	$= \dfrac{853.0}{422.4} = 2.0$	$= \dfrac{816.5}{293.1} = 2.8$
Acid test ratio	$= \dfrac{(853.0 - 592.0)}{422.4} = 0.6$	$= \dfrac{(816.5 - 403.0)}{293.1} = 1.4$
Gearing ratio	$= \dfrac{190}{(687.6 + 190)} \times 100 = 21.6\%$	$= \dfrac{250}{(874.6 + 250)} \times 100 = 22.2\%$
Interest cover ratio	$= \dfrac{151.3}{19.4} = 7.8 \text{ times}$	$= \dfrac{166.9}{27.5} = 6.1 \text{ times}$
Dividend payout ratio	$= \dfrac{135.0}{99.9} \times 100 = 135\%$	$= \dfrac{95.0}{104.6} \times 100 = 91\%$
Price/earnings ratio	$= \dfrac{£6.50}{31.2p} = 20.8 \text{ times}$	$= \dfrac{£8.20}{41.8p} = 19.6 \text{ times}$

Ali plc has a much lower current ratio and acid test ratio than Bhaskar plc. The reasons for this may be partly due to the fact that Ali plc has a lower average settlement period for receivables. The acid test ratio of Ali plc is substantially below 1.0: this may suggest a liquidity problem.

The gearing ratio of each business is quite similar. Neither business has excessive borrowing. The interest cover ratio for each business is also similar. The respective ratios indicate that both businesses have good profit coverage for their interest charges.

The dividend payout ratio for each business seems very high. In the case of Ali plc, the dividends announced for the year are considerably higher than the earnings generated during the year that are available for dividend. As a result, part of the dividend was paid out of retained profits from previous years. This is an unusual occurrence; although it is quite legitimate, such action may nevertheless suggest a lack of prudence on the part of the directors.

The P/E ratio for both businesses is high, which indicates market confidence in their future prospects.

Chapter 7

7.1 Khan Ltd

(a) The break-even point if only the Alpha service were rendered would be:

$$\frac{\text{Fixed costs}}{\text{Sales revenue per unit} - \text{Variable cost per unit}}$$

$$= \frac{\pounds40,000}{\pounds30 - \pounds(15 + 6)} = 4,445 \text{ units (a year)}$$

(Strictly, it is 4,444.44 but 4,445 is the smallest number of units of the service that must be rendered to avoid a loss.)

(b)

	Product:		
	Alpha	Beta	Gamma
	(per unit)	(per unit)	(per unit)
	£	£	£
Selling price	30	39	20
Variable materials	(15)	(18)	(10)
Variable production costs	(6)	(10)	(5)
Contribution	9	11	5
Staff time (hr/unit)	2	3	1
Contribution/staff-hour	£4.50	£3.67	£5.00
Order of priority	2nd	3rd	1st

(c)

	Hours		Contribution
			£
Render:			
5,000 Gamma using	5,000	generating (that is, 5,000 × £5 =)	25,000
2,500 Alpha using	5,000	generating (that is, 2,500 × £9 =)	22,500
	10,000		47,500
		Less Fixed costs	40,000
		Profit	7,500

Leaving a demand for 500 units of Alpha and 2,000 units of Beta unsatisfied.

Chapter 8

8.1 Promptprint Ltd

(a) The budget may be summarised as:

	£	
Sales revenue	196,000	
Direct materials	(38,000)	
Direct labour	(32,000)	
Total overheads	(77,000)	(that is, 2,400 + 3,000 + 27,600 + 36,000 + 8,000)
Profit	49,000	

The job may be priced on the basis that both overheads and profit should be apportioned to it on the basis of direct labour cost, as follows:

	£	
Direct materials	4,000	
Direct labour	3,600	
Overheads	8,663	(that is, £77,000 × 3,600/32,000)
Profit	5,513	(that is, £49,000 × 3,600/32,000)
	21,776	

This answer assumes that variable overheads vary in proportion to direct labour cost.

Various other bases of charging overheads and profit loading the job could have been adopted. For example, materials cost could have been included (with direct labour) as the basis for profit-loading, or even apportioning overheads.

(b) This part of the question is, in effect, asking for comments on the validity of 'full cost-plus' pricing. This approach can be useful as an indicator of the effective long-run cost of doing the job. On the other hand, it fails to take account of relevant opportunity costs as well as the state of the market and other external factors. For example, it ignores the price that a competitor printing business may quote.

Chapter 9

9.1 Antonio Ltd

(a) (i) Raw materials inventories budget for the six months ending 31 December (physical quantities):

	July units	Aug units	Sept units	Oct units	Nov units	Dec units
Opening inventories (current month's production)	500	600	600	700	750	750
Purchases (balance figure)	600	600	700	750	750	750
	1,100	1,200	1,300	1,450	1,500	1,500
Less Issued to production (from question)	500	600	600	700	750	750
Closing inventories (next month's production)	600	600	700	750	750	750

Raw materials' inventories budget for the six months ending 31 December (in financial terms), that is, the physical quantities × £8:

	July £	Aug £	Sept £	Oct £	Nov £	Dec £
Opening inventories	4,000	4,800	4,800	5,600	6,000	6,000
Purchases	4,800	4,800	5,600	6,000	6,000	6,000
	8,800	9,600	10,400	11,600	12,000	12,000
Less Issued to production	4,000	4,800	4,800	5,600	6,000	6,000
Closing inventories	4,800	4,800	5,600	6,000	6,000	6,000

(ii) Payables budget for the six months ending 31 December:

	July £	Aug £	Sept £	Oct £	Nov £	Dec £
Opening balance (current month's payment)	4,000	4,800	4,800	5,600	6,000	6,000
Purchases (from raw materials inventories budget)	4,800	4,800	5,600	6,000	6,000	6,000
	8,800	9,600	10,400	11,600	12,000	12,000
Less Payments	4,000	4,800	4,800	5,600	6,000	6,000
Closing balance (next month's payment)	4,800	4,800	5,600	6,000	6,000	6,000

(iii) Cash budget for the six months ending 31 December:

	July £	Aug £	Sept £	Oct £	Nov £	Dec £
Inflows						
Receipts:						
Receivables (40% of sales revenue of two months previous)	2,800	3,200	3,200	4,000	4,800	5,200
Cash sales revenue (60% of current month's sales)	4,800	6,000	7,200	7,800	8,400	9,600
Total inflows	7,600	9,200	10,400	11,800	13,200	14,800
Outflows						
Payables (from payables budget)	(4,000)	(4,800)	(4,800)	(5,600)	(6,000)	(6,000)
Direct costs	(3,000)	(3,600)	(3,600)	(4,200)	(4,500)	(4,500)
Advertising	(1,000)	–	–	(1,500)	–	–
Overheads: 80%	(1,280)	(1,280)	(1,280)	(1,280)	(1,600)	(1,600)
20%	(280)	(320)	(320)	(320)	(320)	(400)
New plant			(2,200)	(2,200)	(2,200)	
Total outflows	(9,560)	(10,000)	(12,200)	(15,100)	(14,620)	(12,500)
Net inflows (outflows)	(1,960)	(800)	(1,800)	(3,300)	(1,420)	2,300
Balance carried forward	5,540	4,740	2,940	(360)	(1,780)	520

The balances carried forward are deduced by deducting the deficit (net outflows) for the month from (or adding the surplus for the month to) the previous month's balance.

Note how budgets are linked; in this case the inventories budget to the payables budget and the payables budget to the cash budget.

(b) The following are possible means of relieving the cash shortages revealed by the budget:
- Make a higher proportion of sales on a cash basis.
- Collect the money from credit customers more promptly, for example during the month following the sale.
- Hold lower inventories, both of raw materials and of finished goods.
- Increase the payables payment period.

- Delay the payments for advertising.
- Obtain more credit for the overhead costs; at present only 20% are on credit.
- Delay the payments for the new plant.

9.2 Toscanini Ltd

(a) and (b)

	Budget		
	Original	*Flexed*	*Actual*
Output (units)	4,000	3,500	3,500
(prod'n and sales)			
	£	£	£
Sales revenue	16,000	14,000	13,820
Raw materials	(3,840)	(3,360) (1,400 kg)	(3,420) (1,425 kg)
Labour	(3,200)	(2,800) (350 hr)	(2,690) (345 hr)
Fixed overheads	(4,800)	(4,800)	(4,900)
Operating profit	4,160	3,040	2,810

	£	*Manager accountable*
Sales volume variance	(1,120) (A)	Sales
(4,160 – 3,040)		
Sales price variance	(180) (A)	Sales
(14,000 – 13,820)		
Materials price variance	0	–
(1,425 × 2.40) – 3,420		
Materials usage variance	(60) (A)	Production
[(3,500 × 0.4) – 1,425] × £2.40		
Labour rate variance	70 (F)	Personnel
(345 × £8) – 2,690		
Labour efficiency variance	40 (F)	Production
[(3,500 × 0.10) – 345] × £8		
Fixed overhead spending	(100) (A)	Various depending on the nature of the
(4,800 – 4,900)		overheads
Total net variances	(1,350) (A)	
Budgeted profit	4,160	
Less Total net variance	1,350	
Actual profit	2,810	

(c) Feasible explanations include the following:

- Sales volume – unanticipated fall in world demand would account for 400 × £2.24 = £896 of this variance (£2.24 is the budgeted contribution per unit). The remainder is probably caused by ineffective marketing, though a lack of availability of inventories to sell may be a reason.
- Sales price – ineffective selling seems the only logical reason.
- Materials usage – inefficient usage of material, perhaps because of poor performance by labour or substandard materials.
- Labour rate – less overtime worked or lower production bonuses paid as a result of lower volume of activity.
- Labour efficiency – more effective working.
- Overheads – ineffective control of overheads.

(d) Clearly, not all of the sales volume variance can be attributed to poor marketing, given a 10% reduction in demand.

It will probably be useful to distinguish between that part of the variance that arose from the shortfall in general demand (a planning variance) and a volume variance, which is more fairly attributable to the manager concerned. Thus accountability will be more fairly imposed.

	£
Planning variance (10% × 4,000) × £2.24	896
'New' sales volume variance [4,000 − (10% × 4,000) − 3,500] × £2.24	224
Original sales volume variance	1,120

Chapter 10

10.1 Beacon Chemicals plc

(a) Relevant cash flows are as follows:

	Year 0 £000	Year 1 £000	Year 2 £000	Year 3 £000	Year 4 £000	Year 5 £000
Sales revenue	−	80	120	144	100	64
Loss of contribution		(15)	(15)	(15)	(15)	(15)
Variable costs		(40)	(50)	(48)	(30)	(32)
Fixed costs (Note 1)		(8)	(8)	(8)	(8)	(8)
Operating cash flows		17	47	73	47	9
Working capital	(30)					30
Capital cost	(100)					
Net relevant cash flows	(130)	17	47	73	47	39

Notes:

1 Only the fixed costs that are incremental to the project (only existing because of the project) are relevant. Depreciation is irrelevant because it is not a cash flow.

2 The research and development cost is irrelevant since it has been spent irrespective of the decision on X14 production.

(b) The payback period is as follows:

	Year 0 £000	Year 1 £000	Year 2 £000	Year 3 £000
Cumulative cash flows	(130)	(113)	(66)	7

Thus the equipment will have repaid the initial investment by the end of the third year of operations.

(c) The net present value is as follows:

	Year 0 £000	Year 1 £000	Year 2 £000	Year 3 £000	Year 4 £000	Year 5 £000
Discount factor	1.000	0.926	0.857	0.794	0.735	0.681
Present value	(130)	15.74	40.28	57.96	34.55	26.56
Net present value	45.09	(that is, the sum of the present values for years 0 to 5)				

Chapter 11

11.1 Williams Wholesalers Ltd

	£	£
Existing level of receivables (£4m × 70/365)		767,123
New level of receivables: £2m × 80/365	438,356	
£2m × 30/365	164,384	602,740
Reduction in receivables		164,383
Costs and benefits of policy		
Cost of discount (£2m × 2%)		40,000
Less Savings		
Interest payable (£164,383 × 13%)	21,370	
Administration costs	6,000	
Bad debts (20,000 − 10,000)	10,000	37,370
Net cost of policy		2,630

The above calculations reveal that the business will be worse off by offering the discounts.

Chapter 12

12.1 Helsim Ltd

(a) The liquidity position may be assessed by using the liquidity ratios discussed in Chapter 6:

$$\text{Current ratio} = \frac{\text{Current assests}}{\text{Current liabilities}}$$

$$= \frac{£7.5\text{m}}{£5.4\text{m}}$$

$$= 1.4$$

$$\text{Acid test ratio} = \frac{\text{Current assets (excluding inventory)}}{\text{Current liabilities}}$$

$$= \frac{£3.7\text{m}}{£5.4\text{m}}$$

$$= 0.7$$

These ratios reveal a fairly weak liquidity position. The current ratio seems quite low and the acid test ratio very low. This latter ratio suggests that the business does not have sufficient liquid assets to meet its maturing obligations. It would, however, be useful to have details of the liquidity ratios of similar businesses in the same industry in order to make a more informed judgement. The bank overdraft represents 67 per cent of the current liabilities and 40 per cent of the total liabilities of the business. The continuing support of the bank is therefore important to the ability of the business to meet its commitments.

(b) The finance required to reduce trade payables to an average of 40 days outstanding is calculated as follows:

	£m
Trade payables at balance sheet date	1.80
Trade payables outstanding based on 40 days' credit	
40/365 × £8.4m (that is, credit purchases)	(0.92)
Finance required	0.88 (say £0.9m)

(c) The bank may not wish to provide further finance to the business. The increase in overdraft will reduce the level of trade payables but will increase the exposure of the bank. The additional finance invested by the bank will not generate further funds and will not therefore be self-liquidating. The question does not make it clear whether the business has sufficient security to offer the bank for the increase in overdraft facility. The profits of the business will be reduced and the interest cover ratio, based on the profits generated during the most recent year, would reduce to less than 2.0 times (see note below) if the additional overdraft was granted (based on interest charged at 10% each year). This is very low and means that only a small decline in profits would leave interest charges uncovered.

Note:
Existing bank overdraft (3.6) + extension of overdraft to cover reduction in trade payables (0.9) + debentures (3.5) = £8.0m. Assuming a 10% interest rate means a yearly interest payment of £0.8m. Before interest, the profit was £1.3m (that is, 6.4 – 3.0 – 2.1). Interest cover would be 1.63 (that is, 1.3/0.8).

(d) A number of possible sources of finance might be considered. Four possible sources are as follows:

■ *Issue equity shares.* This option may be unattractive to investors. The return on equity is fairly low at 7.9 per cent (that is, net profit after tax (0.3)/share capital and reserves (3.8)) and there is no evidence that the profitability of the business will improve. If profits remain at their current level the effect of issuing more equity will be to reduce further the returns to equity.

■ *Issue loans.* This option may also prove unattractive to investors. The effect of issuing further loans will have a similar effect to that of increasing the overdraft. The profits of the business will be reduced and the interest cover ratio will decrease to a low level. The gearing ratio of the business is already quite high at 48 per cent (that is, debentures (3.5)/(debentures + capital and reserves (3.5 + 3.8)) and it is not clear what security would be available for the loan. The gearing ratio would be much higher if the overdraft were to be included.

■ *Chase receivables.* It may be possible to improve cash flows by reducing the level of credit outstanding from receivables. At present, the average settlement period is 93 days (that is, (receivables (3.6)/sales revenue (14.2)) × 365), which seems quite high. A reduction in the average settlement period by approximately one-quarter would generate the funds required. However, it is not clear what effect this would have on sales.

■ *Reduce inventories.* This appears to be the most attractive of the four options. At present, the average inventories holding period is 178 days (that is, (closing inventories (3.8)/cost of sales (7.8)) × 365), which seems very high. A reduction in this period by less than one-quarter would generate the funds required. However, if the business holds a large amount of slow-moving and obsolete inventories, it may be difficult to reduce inventories levels.

Chapter 1

1.1 The objective of providing accounting information is to enable users to make more informed decisions and judgements about the organisation concerned. Accounting has no other valid purpose or justification.

1.2

Students	Whether to enrol on a course of study. This would probably involve an assessment of the university's ability to continue to operate and to fulfil students' needs.
Other universities and colleges	How best to compete against the university. This might involve using the university's performance in various aspects as a 'benchmark' when evaluating their own performance.
Employees	Whether to take up or to continue in employment with the university. Employees might assess this by considering the ability of the business to continue to provide employment and to reward employees adequately for their labour.
Government/ Funding authority	How efficient the university is in undertaking its various activities.
Local community representatives	Whether to allow/encourage the university to expand its premises. To assess this, the university's ability to continue to provide employment for the community, to use community resources and to help fund environmental improvements might be considered.
Suppliers	Whether to continue to supply the university at all; also whether to supply on credit. This would involve an assessment of the university's ability to pay for any goods and services supplied.
Lenders	Whether to lend money to the university and/or whether to require repayment of any existing loans. To assess this, the university's ability to meet its obligations to pay interest and to repay the principal would be considered.
Board of governors and other managers (Faculty deans and so on)	Whether the performance of the business requires improvement. Here performance to date would be compared with earlier plans or some other 'benchmark' to decide whether action needs to be taken. Whether there should be a change in the university's future direction. In making such decisions management will need to look at the university's ability to perform and at the opportunities available to it.

1.3 Most businesses are far too large and complex for managers to be able to see and assess everything that is going on in their own areas of responsibility merely by personal observation. Managers need information on all aspects within their control. Management accounting reports can provide them with this information, to a greater or lesser extent. These reports can be seen, therefore, as acting as the eyes and ears of the managers, providing insights not necessarily obvious without them.

1.4 Since we can never be sure what is going to happen in the future, the best that we can do is to make judgements on the basis of past experience. Thus information concerning flows of cash and of wealth in the recent past is likely to be a useful source on which to base judgements about possible future outcomes.

Chapter 2

2.1 The confusion arises because the owner seems unaware of the business entity convention in accounting. This convention requires a separation of the business from the owner(s) of the business for accounting purposes. The business is regarded as a separate entity and the balance sheet is prepared from the perspective of the business rather than that of the owner. As a result, funds invested in the business by the owner will be regarded as a claim that the owner has on the business. In a balance sheet prepared using the horizontal format, this claim will be shown alongside other claims on the business from outsiders.

2.2 A balance sheet does not show what a business is worth for two major reasons:

- the money measurement convention ensures that only those items that can be measured reliably are shown on the balance sheet. Thus, things of value such as the reputation for product quality, skills of employees and so on will not normally appear in the balance sheet;
- the historic cost convention results in assets being recorded at their outlay cost rather than their current value. In the case of certain assets, the difference between historic cost and current value may be significant.

2.3 The balance sheet equation is simply the relationship between a business's assets, liabilities and capital. In the 'horizontal' form it is:

Assets (current and non-current) = Capital plus Liabilities (current and non-current)

In the 'vertical' form, the equation is rearranged to:

Non-current assets + (Current assets − Current liabilities) − Non-current liabilities = Capital

2.4 Some object to the idea of humans being treated as assets for inclusion on the balance sheet. It can be seen as demeaning for humans to be listed alongside inventories, plant and machinery and other assets. However, others argue that humans are often the most valuable resource of a business and by placing a value on this resource will help bring to the attention of managers the importance of nurturing and developing this 'asset'. There is a saying in management that 'the things that count are the things that get counted'. As the value of the 'human assets' is not stated in the financial statements, there is a danger that managers will treat these 'assets' less favourably than other assets that are on the balance sheet.

Humans are likely to meet the first criterion of an asset listed in the chapter, that is, a probable future benefit exists. There would be little point in employing people if this were not the case. The second criterion concerning exclusive right of control is more problematic. Clearly a business cannot control humans in the same way as most other assets. However, a business can have the exclusive right to the employment services that a person provides. This distinction between control over the services provided, rather than control over the person, makes it possible to argue that the second criterion can be met.

Humans sign a contract of employment with the business normally and so the third criterion is normally met. The difficulty, however, is with the fourth criterion, that is, whether the value of humans (or their services) can be measured with any degree of reliability. To date, none of the measurement methods proposed enjoy widespread acceptance.

Chapter 3

3.1 At the time of preparing the income statement, it is not always possible to determine accurately the expenses that need to be matched to the sales revenue figure for the period. It will only be at some later point in time that the true position becomes clear. However, it is still necessary to try to include all relevant expenses in the income statement and so estimates of the future will have to be made. Examples of estimates that may have to be made include:

- Expenses accrued at the end of the period such as the amount of telephone expenses incurred since the last quarter's bill.
- The amount of depreciation based on estimates of the life of the non-current asset and future residual value.
- The amount of bad and doubtful debts incurred.

3.2 Depreciation attempts to allocate the cost (less any residual value) of the asset over its useful life. Depreciation does not attempt to measure the fall in value of the asset during the period. Thus, the written-down value of the asset appearing on the balance sheet normally represents the unexpired cost of the asset rather than its current market value.

3.3 The convention of consistency is designed to provide a degree of uniformity concerning the application of accounting policies. We have seen that, in certain areas, there may be more than one method of accounting for an item, for example, inventories valuation. The convention of consistency states that, having decided on a particular accounting policy, a business should continue to apply the policy in successive periods. Whilst this policy helps to ensure that users can make valid comparisons concerning business performance *over time* it does not ensure that valid comparisons can be made *between businesses*. This is because different businesses may consistently apply different accounting policies.

3.4 An expense is that element of the cost incurred that is used up during the accounting period. An asset is that element of cost which is carried forward on the balance sheet and which will normally be used up in future periods. Thus, both assets and expenses arise from costs being incurred. The major difference between the two is the period over which the benefits (resulting from the costs incurred) accrue.

Chapter 4

4.1 It does not differ. In both cases they are required to meet their debts to the full extent that there are assets available. To this extent they both have a liability that is limited to the extent of their assets. This is a particularly important fact for the shareholders of a limited company because they know that those owed money by the company cannot demand that the shareholders contribute additional funds to help meet debts. Thus the liability of the shareholders is limited to the amount that they have paid for their shares, or have agreed to pay in the case of partially unpaid shares. This contrasts with the position of the owner or part owner of an unincorporated (non-company) business. Here all of the individual's assets could be required to meet the unsatisfied liabilities of the business.

4.2 A private limited company may place restrictions on the transfer of its shares; that is, the directors can veto an attempt by a shareholder to sell his or her shares to another person to whom the directors object. Thus, in effect, the majority can avoid having as a shareholder someone that they would prefer not to have. A public company cannot do this.

A public limited company must have authorised share capital of at least £50,000. There is no minimum for a private limited company.

The main advantage of being a public limited company is that they may offer their shares and debentures to the general public; private companies cannot make such an offer.

4.3 A reserve is that part of the equity (owners' claim) of a company that is not share capital. Reserves represent gains or surpluses that enhance the claim of the shareholders above the nominal value of their shares. For example, the share premium account is a reserve that represents the excess over the nominal value of shares that is paid for them on a share issue. The retained profit balance is a reserve that arises from ploughed-back profits earned by the company.

4.4 A preference share represents part of the ownership of a company. Preference shares entitle their owners to the first part of any dividend paid by the company, up to a maximum amount. The maximum is usually expressed as a percentage of the nominal or par value of the preference shares.

(a) They differ from ordinary shares to the extent that they only entitle their holders to dividends to a predetermined maximum value. Dividends to ordinary shareholders have no predetermined maximum. Usually preference shares attract a maximum payout equal to their nominal value on liquidation, the ordinary shareholders receive the residue after all other claimants, including the preference shareholders.

(b) They differ from debentures in that these represent a loan to the company, where normally holders have a contract with the company that specifies the rate of interest, interest payment dates and redemption date. They are often secured on the company's assets. Preference shareholders have no such contract.

Chapter 5

5.1 People and organisations will normally only accept cash in settlement of their claims against the business. If a business wants to employ people it must pay them in cash. If it wants to buy a new non-current asset to exploit a business opportunity, the supplier will normally insist on being paid in cash, normally after a short period of credit. Claimants against the business will not normally accept inventories in settlement of their claims.

When businesses fail, it is their inability to find the cash to pay claimants that actually drives them under. Thus cash is the pre-eminent business asset and, therefore, the one that analysts and others watch carefully in trying to assess the ability of the business to survive and/or to take advantage of commercial opportunities as they arise.

5.2 With the 'direct method', the business's cash records are analysed for the period concerned. The analysis reveals the amounts of cash, in total, that have been paid and received in respect of each category of the cash flow statement. This is not difficult in principle, or in practice if it is done by computer as a matter of routine.

The 'indirect method' takes the approach that, while the net profit (loss) is not equal to the net inflow (outflow) of cash from operations, they are fairly closely linked to the extent that appropriate adjustment of the profit (loss) figure will produce the correct cash flow one. The adjustment is concerned with depreciation and interest charges for the period and movements in relevant working capital items over the period.

5.3 (a) *cash flows from operating activities*. This would normally be positive, even for a business with small profits or even losses. The fact that depreciation (typically a major expense) is not a cash flow tends to lead to positive cash flows in this area in most cases.

(b) *cash flows from investing activities*. Normally this would be negative in cash flow terms since assets become worn out and need to be replaced in the normal course of business. This means that, typically, old items of property, plant and equipment are generating less cash on their disposal than is having to be paid out to replace them.

(c) *cash flows from financing activities*. There is a tendency for businesses either to expand or to fail. In either case, this is likely to mean that over the years more finance will be raised than will be redeemed or retired.

5.4 There are several reasons for this. These include the following:

- Changes in inventories, receivables and payables. For example, an increase in receivables during an accounting period would mean that the cash received from credit sales would be less than the credit sales revenue for the same period.
- Cash may have been spent on new non-current assets or received from disposals of old ones; these would not directly affect profit.
- Cash may have been spent to redeem or repay a financial claim or received as a result of the creation or the increase of a claim. These would not directly affect profit.

The tax charged in the income statement would not be the same tax that is paid (and reflected in the cash flow statement) during the same accounting period.

Chapter 6

6.1 The fact that a business operates on a low profit margin indicates that a small percentage of profit is being produced for each £1 of sales revenue generated. However, this does not mean necessarily that the return on capital employed will be low as a result. If the business is able to generate a large amount of sales revenue during a period, the total profit may be very high even though the net profit per £1 of sales revenue is low. If the net profit generated is high, this can lead, in turn, to a high return on capital employed, since it is the total net profit that is used as the numerator (top part of the fraction) in this ratio. Many profitable businesses (including supermarkets) pursue a strategy of 'low margin, high turnover'.

6.2 The balance sheet is drawn up at a single point in time – the end of the financial period. As a result, the figures shown on the balance sheet represent the position at that single point in time and may not be representative of the position during the period. Wherever appropriate and possible, average figures (perhaps based on monthly figures) should be used. However, an external user may only have access to the opening and closing balance sheets for the year and so a simple average based on these figures may be all that is possible to calculate. Where a business is seasonal in nature or is subject to cyclical changes, this simple averaging may not be sufficient.

6.3 Three possible reasons for a high inventories turnover period are:

- Poor inventories controls, leading to excessive investment in inventories.
- Inventories hoarding in anticipation of price rises or shortages.
- Inventories building in anticipation of increased future sales.

A low inventories turnover period may be due to:

- Tight inventories controls, thereby reducing excessive investment in inventories and/or limiting the amount of obsolete and slow moving inventories.
- An inability to finance the required amount of inventories to meet sales demand.
- A difference in the mix of inventories carried by similar businesses (for example, greater investment in perishable goods which are held for a short period only).

6.4 The P/E ratio may vary between businesses within the same industry for the following reasons:

- *Accounting conventions*. Differences in the methods used to compute profit (for example, inventories valuation and depreciation) can lead to different profit figures and, therefore, different P/E ratios.
- *Different prospects*. One business may be regarded as having a much brighter future due to factors, such as, the quality of management, the quality of products, location and so on. This will affect the market price investors are prepared to pay for the share and, hence, the P/E ratio.
- *Different asset structure*. The business's underlying asset base may be much higher and this may affect the market price of the shares.

Chapter 7

7.1 A fixed cost is one that is the same irrespective of the level of activity or output. Typical examples of costs that are fixed, irrespective of the level of production or provision of a service, include rent of business premises, salaries of supervisory staff and electricity charges for heating and lighting.

A variable cost is one that varies with the level of activity or output. Examples include raw materials and labour, where labour is rewarded in proportion to the level of output.

Note particularly that it is relative to the level of activity that costs are fixed or variable. Fixed costs may be affected by inflation and they will usually be greater for a longer period than for a shorter one.

For a particular product or service, knowing which costs are fixed and which variable enables managers to predict the total cost for any particular level of activity. It also enables them to concentrate only on the variable costs in circumstances, where a decision will not alter the fixed costs.

7.2 The break-even point is the level of activity, either measured in physical units or in value of sales revenue, at which the sales revenue exactly covers all of the costs, both fixed and variable.

Break-even point is calculated as:

$$BEP = Fixed\ costs/(sales\ revenue\ per\ unit - variable\ costs\ per\ unit)$$

which may alternatively be expressed as:

$$BEP = Fixed\ costs/contribution\ per\ unit.$$

Thus break even will occur when the contributions for the period are sufficient to cover the fixed costs for the period.

Break-even point tends to be useful as a comparison with planned level of activity in an attempt to assess the riskiness of the activity.

7.3 Operating gearing refers to the extent of fixed costs relative to variable costs in the total costs of some activity. Where the fixed costs form a relatively high proportion of the total, we say that the activity has high operating gearing.

Typically, high operating gearing is present in environments where there is a relatively high level of mechanisation (that is, capital intensive). This is because such environments tend simultaneously to involve relatively high fixed costs of depreciation, maintenance and so on and relatively low variable costs.

High operating gearing tends to mean that the effects of increases or decreases in the level of activity have an accentuated effect on operating profit. For example, a 20% decrease in output of a particular service will lead to a greater than 20% decrease in operating profit, assuming no cost or price changes.

7.4 In the face of a restricting scarce resource, profit will be maximised by using the scarce resource on output where the contribution per unit of the scarce resource is maximised.

This means that the contribution per unit of the scarce resource (for example, hour of scarce labour, unit of scarce raw material and so on) for each competing product or service needs to be identified. It is then a question of allocating the scarce resource to the product or service that provides the highest contribution per unit of the particular scarce resource.

The logic of this approach is that the scarce resource is allocated to the activity that uses it most effectively, in terms of contribution and, therefore, profit.

Chapter 8

8.1 In process costing, the total production costs for a period are divided by the number of completed units of output for the period to deduce the full cost. Where there is work in progress at the beginning and/or the end of the period complications arise.

The problem is that some of the output completed during a period incurred costs in the preceding period. Similarly some of the costs incurred in the current period lead to completed production in the subsequent period. Account needs to be taken of these facts, if reliable full cost information is to be obtained.

8.2 The only reason for distinguishing between direct and indirect costs is to help to deduce the full cost of a unit of output in a job-costing environment. In an environment where all units of output are identical, or can reasonably be regarded as being so, a process costing approach will be taken. This avoids the need for identifying direct and indirect costs separately.

Direct costs form that part of the total costs of pursuing some activity that can, unequivocally, be associated with that particular activity. Examples of direct costs in the typical job-costing environment include direct labour and direct materials.

Indirect costs are the remainder of the costs of pursuing some activity. Identifying direct costs reduces the extent to which costs must be related to individual jobs on a, more or less, arbitrary basis. In practice, knowledge of the direct costs tends to provide the basis used to charge overheads to jobs.

The distinction between direct and indirect costs is irrelevant for any other purpose.

Directness and indirectness is dictated by the nature of that which is being costed, as much as the nature of the cost.

8.3 The notion of direct and indirect costs is concerned only with the extent to which particular costs can unequivocally be related to and measured in respect of a particular cost unit, usually a product or service. The distinction between direct and indirect costs is made exclusively for the purpose of deducing the full cost of some cost unit, in an environment where each cost unit is not identical, or close enough to being identical for it to be treated as such. Thus, it is typically in the context of job costing, or some variant of it, that the distinction between direct and indirect costs is usefully made.

The notion of variable and fixed costs is concerned entirely with how costs behave in the face of changes in the volume of output. The value of being able to distinguish between fixed and variable costs is that predictions can be made of what total costs will be at particular levels of volume and/or what reduction or addition to costs will occur if the volume of output is reduced or increased.

Thus the notion of direct and indirect costs, on the one hand, and that of variable and fixed costs, on the other, are not connected with one another. Though it is true that, in most contexts, some direct costs are variable, other direct costs are fixed. Similarly, indirect costs might be fixed or variable.

8.4 The full cost includes all of the costs of pursuing the cost objective, including a 'fair' share of the overheads. Generally the full cost represents an average cost of the various elements, rather than a cost that arises because the business finds itself in a particular situation.

The fact that the full cost reflects all aspects of cost should mean that, were the business to sell its output at a price exactly equal to the full cost, the sales revenue for the period would exactly cover all of the costs and the business would break even, that is make neither profit nor loss.

Chapter 9

9.1 A budget can be defined as a business plan for a future period of time. Thus it sets out the intentions which management has for the period concerned. Achieving the budget plans should help to achieve the long-term plans of the business. Achievement of the long-term plans should mean that the business is successfully working towards its objectives.

A budget differs from a forecast in that a forecast is a statement of what is expected to happen without the intervention of management, perhaps because they cannot intervene as with a weather forecast. A plan is an intention to achieve.

Normally management would take account of reliable forecasts when making its plans.

9.2 The five uses of budgets are:

1 They tend to promote forward thinking and the possible identification of short-term problems. Managers must plan and the budgeting process tends to force them to do so. In doing so they are likely to encounter potential problems. If the potential problems can be identified early enough solutions might be easily found.
2 They can be used to help co-ordination between various sections of the business. It is important that the plans of one area of the business fit in with those of other areas; a lack of co-ordination could have disastrous consequences. Having formal statements of plans for each aspect of the business enables a check to be made that plans are complimentary.
3 They can motivate managers to better performance. It is believed that people are motivated by having a target to aim for. Provided that the inherent goals are achievable, budgets can provide an effective motivational device.
4 They can provide a basis for a system of control. Having a plan against which actual performance can be measured provides a potentially useful tool of control.
5 They can provide a system of authorisation. Many managers have 'spending' budgets, like research and development, staff training and so on. For these people, the size of their budget defines their authority to spend.

9.3 A variance is the effect on budgeted profit of the particular aspect of the business that is being considered. Thus it is the difference between the budgeted profit and what the actual profit would have been, had all other matters except the one under consideration, gone according to budget. From this it must be the case that:

Budgeted profit + favourable variances − unfavourable variances = actual profit.

The objective of analysing and assessing variances is to identify whether, and if so where, things are not going according to plan. If this can be done it may well be possible to find out the actual cause of things going out of control. If this can be discovered, it may be possible to put thing right for the future.

The broad approach that is taken to investigating variances is balancing the cost of investigation against the economic benefits of knowing the cause of a variance and being in a position to correct things for the future.

9.4 Where the budgeted and actual volumes of output do not coincide it is impossible to make valid comparison of 'allowed' and actual expenses and revenues. Flexing the original budget to reflect the actual output level enables a more informative comparison to be made.

Flexing certainly does not mean that output volume differences do not matter. Flexing will show (as the difference between flexed and original budget profits) the effect on profit of output volume differences.

Chapter 10

10.1 NPV is usually considered the best method of assessing investment opportunities because it takes account of:

- *The timing of the cash flows.* By *discounting* the various cash flows associated with each project according to when it is expected to arise, it recognises the fact that cash flows do not all occur simultaneously. Associated with this is the fact that, by discounting, using the opportunity cost of finance (that is, the return which the next best alternative opportunity would generate), the net benefit after financing costs have been met is identified (as the NPV).
- *The whole of the relevant cash flows.* NPV includes all of the relevant cash flows irrespective of when they are expected to occur. It treats them differently according to their date of occurrence, but they are all taken account of in the NPV and they all have, or can have, an influence on the decision.
- *The objectives of the business.* NPV is the only method of appraisal where the output of the analysis has a direct bearing on the wealth of the business. (Positive NPVs enhance wealth; negative ones reduce it.) Since most private sector businesses seek to increase their value and wealth, NPV clearly is the best approach to use.

NPV provides clear decision rules concerning acceptance/rejection of projects and the ranking of projects. It is fairly simple to use, particularly with the availability of modern computer software that takes away the need for routine calculations to be done manually.

10.2 The payback method, in its original form, does not take account of the time value of money. However, it would be possible to modify the payback method to accommodate this requirement. Cash flows arising from a project could be discounted, using the cost of finance as the appropriate discount rate, in the same way as the NPV method. The discounted payback approach is used by some businesses and represents an improvement on the original approach described in the chapter. However, it still retains the other flaws of the original payback approach that were discussed. For example, it ignores relevant data after the payback period. Thus, even in its modified form, the PP method cannot be regarded as superior to NPV.

10.3 The IRR method does appear to be preferred to the NPV method among practising managers. The main reasons for this appear to be as follows:

■ A preference for a percentage return ratio rather than an absolute figure as a means of expressing the outcome of a project. This preference for a ratio may reflect the fact that other financial goals of the business are often set in terms of ratios; for example, return on capital employed.

■ A preference for ranking projects in terms of their percentage return. Managers feel it is easier to rank projects on the basis of percentage returns (though NPV outcomes should be just as easy for them). We saw in the chapter that the IRR method could provide misleading advice on the ranking of projects and the NPV method was preferable for this purpose.

10.4 Cash flows must be used, not profit flows, because cash is the ultimate measure of economic wealth. Cash is used to acquire resources and for distribution to shareholders. When cash is invested in an investment project an opportunity cost is incurred, as the cash cannot be used in other investment projects. Similarly, when positive cash flows are generated by the project it can be used to re-invest in other investment projects.

Profit, on the other hand, is relevant to reporting the productive effort for a period. Profit will not usually be the same as cash flows for a particular business for a particular period. The conventions of accounting may lead to the recognition of gains and losses in one period with the relevant cash inflows and outflows occurring in another period.

Chapter 11

11.1 Though the credit manager is responsible for ensuring that receivables pay on time, Tariq may be right in denying blame. Various factors may be responsible for the situation described which are beyond the control of the credit manager. These include:

■ a downturn in the economy leading to financial difficulties among credit customers;

■ a decision made by other managers (for example sales managers) to liberalise credit policy in order to stimulate sales;

■ an increase in competition among suppliers offering credit that is being exploited by customers;

■ disputes with customers over the quality of goods or services supplied;

■ problems in the delivery of goods leading to delays.

You may have thought of others.

11.2 Inventories levels could be affected in the following ways:

■ An increase in production bottlenecks is likely to result in an increase in raw materials and work-in-progress being processed within the plant. Therefore, inventories levels should rise.

- A rise in interest rates will make the cost of holding inventories more expensive. This may, in turn, lead to a decision to reduce inventories levels.
- The decision to reduce the range of products should result in lower inventories being held. It would no longer be necessary to hold certain items in order to meet customer demand. The decision on the narrower range may partly have been made with inventories holding cost savings as one of the objective.
- Switching to a local supplier may reduce the lead time between ordering an item and receiving it. This should, in turn, reduce the need to carry such high levels of the particular item.
- A deterioration in the quality of bought-in items may result in the purchase of higher quantities of inventories to take account of the defective element in inventories acquired and, perhaps, an increase in the inspection time for items received. This would lead to a rise in inventories levels.

11.3 Inventories are held:

- to meet customer demand;
- to avoid the problems of running out of inventories;
- to take advantage of profitable opportunities (for example, buying a product which is expected to rise steeply in price in the future).

These reasons are similar to the transactionary, precautionary and speculative motives that were used to explain why cash is held by a business.

11.4 (a) The costs of holding too little cash are:

- a failure to meet obligations when they fall due which can damage the reputation of the business and may, in the extreme, lead to the business being wound up;
- having to borrow and thereby incur interest charges;
- an inability to take advantage of profitable opportunities.

(b) The costs of holding too much cash are:

- failure to use the funds available for more profitable purposes; and
- loss of value during a period of inflation.

Chapter 12

12.1 Share warrants may be particularly useful for young expanding businesses that wish to attract new investors. They can help provide a 'sweetener' for the issue of debentures. By attaching warrants it may be possible to agree a lower rate of interest or less restrictive loan covenants. If the business is successful, the warrants will provide a further source of finance. Investors will exercise their option to acquire shares if the market price of the shares exceeds the exercise price of the warrant. However, this will have the effect of diluting the control of existing shareholders.

12.2 A listed business may wish to revert to unlisted status for a number of possible reasons. These include:

- *Cost.* Maintaining a stock exchange listing can be costly, as the business must adhere to certain administrative regulations and financial disclosures. These go beyond what is required to obtain the original listing.
- *Scrutiny.* Listed companies are subject to close scrutiny by analysts and this may not be welcome if the business is engaged in sensitive negotiations or controversial business activities.
- *Take-over risk.* The shares of the business may be purchased by an unwelcome bidder and this may result in a take-over.
- *Investor profile.* If the business is dominated by a few investors who wish to retain their interest in the business and do not wish to raise further capital by public issues, the benefits of a listing are few.

12.3 An offer for sale involves an issuing house buying the shares in the business and then, in turn, selling the shares to the public. The issue will be advertised by the publication of a prospectus, which will set out details of the business and the issue price of the shares (or reserve price if a tender issue is being made). The shares issued by the issuing house may be either new shares or shares previously which have been purchased from existing shareholders.

A public issue is where the business undertakes direct responsibility for issuing shares to the public. If an issuing house is used it will usually be in the role of adviser and administrator of the issue. However, the issuing house may also underwrite the issue. A public issue runs the risk that the shares will not be taken up and is a less popular form of issue for businesses.

12.4 Invoice discounting is a service offered to businesses by a financial institution where the institution is prepared to advance a sum equivalent to 75% to 80% of outstanding receivables. The amount advanced is usually payable to the business within 60 to 90 days. The business retains responsibility for collecting the amounts owing from customers and the advance must be repaid irrespective of whether or not the these amounts have been collected.

Factoring is a service that is also offered to businesses by financial institutions. In this case, the factor will take over the sales records (sales ledger) of the business and will undertake to collect amounts owed on behalf of the client business. The factor makes an advance of 80% to 85% of approved debts that is repayable from the amounts received from customers.

The service charge for invoice discounting is up to 0.5% of turnover, whereas the service charge for factoring is up to 3% of turnover. This difference explains, in part, why businesses have shown a preference for invoice discounting rather than factoring in recent years (and why financial institutions prefer to factor!).

Appendix C: Solutions to selected exercises

Chapter 2

2.1

Paul
Cash flow statement for day 4

	£
Opening balance (from day 3)	59
Cash from sale of wrapping paper	47
	106
Cash paid to purchase wrapping paper	(53)
Closing balance	53

Income statement for day 4

	£
Sales revenue	47
Cost of goods sold	(33)
Profit	14

Balance sheet at the end of day 4

	£
Cash	53
Inventories for resale (23 + 53 − 33)	43
Total business wealth	96

2.2

Helen
Income statement for day 1

	£
Sales revenue (70 × £0.80)	56
Cost of sales (70 × £0.50)	(35)
Profit	21

Cash flow statement for day 1

	£
Opening balance	40
Add Cash from sales	56
	96
Less Cash for purchases (80 × £0.50)	40
Closing balance	56

Balance sheet as at end of day 1

	£
Cash balance	56
Inventories of unsold goods (10 × £0.50)	5
Helen's business wealth	61

Income statement for day 2

	£
Sales revenue (65 × £0.80)	52.0
Cost of sales (65 × £0.50)	(32.5)
Profit	19.5

Cash flow statement for day 2

	£
Opening balance	56.0
Add Cash from sales	52.0
	108.0
Less Cash for purchases (60 × £0.50)	30.0
Closing balance	78.0

Balance sheet as at end of day 2

	£
Cash balance	78.0
Inventories of unsold goods (5 × £0.50)	2.5
Helen's business wealth	80.5

Income statement for day 3

	£
Sales revenue (20 × £0.80) + (45 × £0.40)	34.0
Cost of sales (65 × £0.50)	(32.5)
Profit	1.5

Cash flow statement for day 3

	£
Opening balance	78.0
Add Cash from sales	34.0
	112.0
Less Cash for purchases (60 × £0.50)	30.0
Closing balance	82.0

Balance sheet as at end of day 3

	£
Cash balance	82.0
Inventories of unsold goods	–
Helen's business wealth	82.0

2.4 (a)

Crafty Engineering Ltd
Balance sheet as at 30 June last year

	£000	£000	£000
Non-current assets			
Freehold premises			320
Machinery and tools			207
Motor vehicles			38
			565
Current assets			
Inventories		153	
Receivables		185	
		338	
Less **Current liabilities**			
Payables	86		
Bank overdraft	116	202	
			136
			701
Less **Non-current liabilities**			
Loan from Industrial Finance Co.			260
			441
Capital (missing figure)			441

(b) The balance sheet reveals a high level of investment in non-current assets. In percentage terms, we can say that more than 60 per cent of the total investment in assets (565/903) has been in non-current assets. The nature of the business may require a heavy investment in non-current assets. The investment in current assets exceeds the current liabilities by a large amount (approximately 1.7 times). As a result, there is no obvious sign of a liquidity problem.

However, the balance sheet reveals that the business has no cash balance and is therefore dependent on the continuing support of the bank (in the form of a bank overdraft) in order to meet obligations when they fall due. When considering the long-term financing of the business, we can see that about 37 per cent [260/(260 + 441)] of the total long-term finance for the business has been supplied by loan capital and about 63 per cent [441/(260 + 441)] by the owners. This level of borrowing seems quite high but not excessive.

However, we would need to know more about the ability of the business to service the loan capital (that is, make interest payments and loan repayments) before a full assessment could be made.

Chapter 3

3.1 (a) Capital does increase as a result of the owners introducing more cash into the business, but it will also increase as a result of introducing other assets (for example, a motor car) and by the business generating revenue by trading. Similarly, capital decreases not only as a result of withdrawals of cash by owners but also by withdrawals of other assets (for example, inventories for the owners' personal use) and through trading expenses being incurred. For the typical business in a typical accounting period, capital will alter much more as a result of trading activities than for any other reason.

(b) An accrued expense is not one that relates to next year. It is one that needs to be matched with the revenue of the accounting period under review, but that has yet to be met in terms of cash payment. As such, it will appear on the balance sheet as a current liability.

(c) The purpose of depreciation is not to provide for asset replacement. Rather, it is an attempt to allocate the cost, or fair value, of the asset (less any residual value) over its useful life. Depreciation is an attempt to provide a measure of the amount of the non-current asset that has been consumed during the period. This amount will then be charged as an expense for the period in deriving the profit figure. Depreciation is a book entry (the outlay of cash normally occurs when the asset is purchased) and does not normally entail setting aside a separate amount of cash for asset replacement. Even if this were done, there would be no guarantee that sufficient funds would be available at the end of the asset's life for its replacement. Factors such as inflation and technological change may mean that the replacement cost is higher than the original cost of the asset.

(d) In the short term, it is possible for the current value of a non-current asset to exceed its original cost. However, nearly all non-current assets will wear out over time as a result of being used to generate wealth for the business. This will be the case for freehold buildings. As a result, some measure of depreciation should be calculated to take account of the fact that the asset is being consumed. Some businesses revalue their freehold buildings where the current value is significantly different from the original cost. Where this occurs, the depreciation charged should be based on the revalued amount. This will normally result in higher depreciation charges than if the asset remained at its historic cost.

3.3 The existence of profit and downward movement in cash may be for various reasons, which include the following:

- The purchase of assets for cash during the period (for example, motor cars and inventories), which were not all consumed during the period and are therefore not having as great an effect on expenses as they are on cash.
- The payment of an outstanding liability (for example, a loan), which will have an effect on cash but not on expenses in the income statement.
- The withdrawal of cash by the owners from the capital invested, which will not have an effect on the expenses in the income statement.
- The generation of revenue on credit where the cash has yet to be received. This will increase the sales revenue for the period but will not have a beneficial effect on the cash balance until a later period.

3.4

WW Company
Balance sheet as at 31 December 2005

Assets	£	Claims	£
Machinery		Capital	
(+25,300 + 6,000 +	21,840	(+48,900 − 23,000 + 26,480)	52,380
9,000 − 13,000 +	(see note below)		
3,900 − 9,360)			
Inventories		Trade payables	
(+12,200 + 143,000 + 12,000	15,200	(+16,900 + 143,000 − 156,000)	3,900
− 127,000 − 25,000)			
Trade receivables		Accrued expenses	
(+21,300 + 211,000 − 198,000)	34,300	(+1,700 − 1,700 + 860)	860
Cash at bank (overdraft)	−19,700		
(+8,300 − 23,000 − 25,000 −			
2,000 − 6,000 − 23,800 −			
2,700 − 12,000 + 42,000			
+ 198,000 − 156,000 − 17,500)			
Prepaid expenses			
(+400 − 400 + 500 + 5,000)	5,500		
	57,140		57,140

Note:

	£
Cost less accumulated depreciation at 31 December 2004	25,300
Less Book value of machine disposed of (£13,000 − £3,900)	9,100
	16,200
Add Cost of new machine	15,000
	31,200
Depreciation for 2005 (£31,200 × 30%)	9,360
Net book value of machine at 31 December 2005	21,840

Income statement for the year ended 31 December 2005

	£	£
Sales revenue (+211,000 + 42,000)		253,000
Less Cost of inventories sold (+127,000 + 25,000)		152,000
Gross profit		101,000
Less		
Rent (+20,000)	20,000	
Rates (+400 + 1,500)	1,900	
Wages (−1,700 + 23,800 + 860)	22,960	
Electricity (+2,700)	2,700	
Machinery depreciation (+9,360)	9,360	
Loss on disposal of the old machinery (+13,000 − 3,900 − 9,000)	100	
Van expenses (+17,500)	17,500	
		74,520
Net profit for the year		26,480

The loss on disposal of the old machinery is the book value (cost less depreciation) less the disposal proceeds. Since the machinery had only been owned for one year, with a depreciation rate of 30%, the depreciation on it so far is £3,900 (that is, £13,000 × 30%). The effective disposal proceeds were £9,000 because, as a result of trading it in, the business saved £9,000 on the new asset.

The depreciation expense for 2005 is based on the cost less accumulated depreciation of the assets owned at the end of 2005. Accumulated depreciation must be taken into account because the business uses the reducing-balance method.

The balance sheet could now be rewritten in a more stylish form as follows:

WW Company
Balance sheet as at 31 December 2005

	£	£	£
Non-current assets			
Machinery			21,840
Current assets			
Inventories	15,200		
Trade receivables	34,300		
Prepaid expenses	5,500		
		55,000	
Less Current liabilities			
Trade payables	3,900		
Accrued expenses	860		
Bank overdraft	19,700		
		24,460	30,540
			52,380
Capital			
Original			48,900
Profit			26,480
			75,380
Less Drawings			23,000
			52,380

Chapter 4

4.1 Limited companies can no more set a limit on the amount of debts they will meet than can human beings. They must meet their debts up to the limit of their assets, just as we as individuals must. In the context of owners' claim, 'reserves' mean part of the owners' claim against the assets of the company. These assets may or may not include cash. The legal ability of the company to pay dividends is not related to the amount of cash that it has.

Preference shares do not carry a guaranteed dividend. They simply guarantee that the preference shareholders have a right to the first slice of any dividend that is paid. Shares of many companies can, in effect, be bought by one investor from another through the Stock Exchange. Such a transaction has no direct effect on the company, however. These are not new shares being offered by the company, but existing shares that are being sold 'second-hand'.

4.2 (a) The first part of the quote is incorrect. Bonus shares should not, of themselves, increase the value of the shareholders' wealth. This is because reserves, belonging to the shareholders, are used to create bonus shares. Thus, each shareholder's stake in the company has not increased.

(b) This statement is incorrect. Shares can be issued at any price, provided that it is not below the nominal value of the shares. Once the company has been trading profitably for a period, the shares will not be worth the same as they were (the nominal value) when the company was first formed. In such circumstances, issuing shares at above their nominal value would not only be legal, but essential to preserve the wealth of the existing shareholders relative to any new ones.

(c) This statement is incorrect. From a legal perspective, the company is limited to a maximum dividend of the current extent of its revenue reserves. This amounts to any after-tax profits or gains realised that have not been eroded through, for example, payments of previous dividends. Legally, cash is not an issue; it would be perfectly legal for a company to borrow the funds to pay a dividend – although whether such an action would be commercially prudent is another question.

(d) This statement is partly incorrect. Companies do indeed have to pay tax on their profits. Depending on their circumstances, shareholders might also have to pay tax on their dividends.

4.4

Chips Limited
Balance sheet as at 30 June 2006

	Cost	Depreciation	
	£000	£000	£000
Non-current assets			
Property, plant and equipment			
Buildings	800	(112)	688
Plant and equipment	650	(367)	283
Motor vehicles (102 – 8); (53 – 5 + 19)	94	(67)	27
	1,544	(546)	998
Current assets			
Inventories		950	
Trade receivables (420 – 16)		404	
Cash at bank (16 + 2)		18	
		1,372	
Less **Current liabilities**			
Trade payables (361 + 23)		(384)	
Other payables (117 + 35)		(152)	
Taxation		(26)	
		(562)	
Net current assets			810
Less **Non-current liabilities**			
Secured 10% loan			(700)
			1,108
Equity			
Ordinary shares of £1, fully paid			800
Reserves at 1 July 2005		248	
Retained profit for year		60	308
			1,108

Income statement for the year ended 30 June 2006

	£000	£000
Revenue (1,850 – 16)		1,834
Cost of sales (1,040 + 23)		1,063
Gross profit		771
Less Depreciation [220 – 2 – 5 + 8 + (94 × 20%)]	(240)	
Other operating costs	(375)	
		(615)
Operating profit		156
Interest payable (35 + 35)		(70)
Profit before taxation		86
Taxation (86 × 30%)		(26)
Profit after taxation		60

Chapter 5

5.1 (a) An increase in the level of inventories would ultimately have an adverse effect on cash.

(b) A rights issue of ordinary shares will give rise to a positive cash flow, which will be included in the 'financing' section of the cash flow statement.

(c) A bonus issue of ordinary shares has no cash flow effect.

(d) Writing off some of the value of the inventories has no cash flow effect.

(e) A disposal for cash of a large number of shares by a major shareholder has no cash flow effect as far as the business is concerned.

(f) Depreciation does not involve cash at all. Using the indirect method of deducing cash flows from operating activities involves the depreciation expense in the calculation, but this is simply because we are trying to find out from the profit (after depreciation) figure what the profit before depreciation must have been.

5.3

Torrent plc
Cash flow statement for the year ended 31 December 2006

	£m	£m
Cash flows from operating activities		
Net profit, after interest, before taxation (Note 1)	170	
Adjustments for:		
Depreciation (Note 2)	78	
Interest expense (Note 3)	26	
	274	
Decrease in inventories (41 − 35)	6	
Increase in trade receivables (145 − 139)	(6)	
Decrease in trade payables (54 − 41)	(13)	
Cash generated from operations	261	
Interest paid	(26)	
Corporation tax paid (Note 4)	(41)	
Dividend paid	(60)	
Net cash from operating activities		134
Cash flows from investing activities		
Payments to acquire plant and machinery	(67)	
Net cash used in investing activities		(67)
Cash flows from financing activities		
Redemption of debenture stock (250 − 150) (Note 5)	(100)	
Net cash used in financing activities		(100)
Net decrease in cash and cash equivalents		(33)
Cash and cash equivalents at 1 January 2006		
Bank overdraft		(56)
Cash and cash equivalents at 31 December 2006		
Bank overdraft		(89)

To see how this relates to the cash of the business at the beginning and end of the year it can be useful to provide a reconciliation as follows:

Analysis of cash and cash equivalents during
the year ended 31 December 2006

	£m
Cash and cash equivalents at 1 January 2006	(56)
Net cash outflow	(33)
Cash and cash equivalents at 31 December 2006	(89)

Notes:

1 This is simply taken from the income statement for the year.

2 Since there were no disposals, the depreciation charges must be the difference between the start and end of the year's plant and machinery values, adjusted by the cost of any additions.

	£m
Book value, at 1 January 2006	325
Add Additions	67
	392
Less Depreciation (balancing figure)	78
Book value, at 31 December 2006	314

3 Interest payable expense must be taken out, by adding it back to the profit figure. We subsequently deduct the cash paid for interest payable during the year. In this case the two figures are identical.

4 Companies pay 50 per cent tax during their accounting year and 50 per cent in the following year. Thus the 2006 payment would have been half the tax on the 2005 profit (that is, the figure that would have appeared in the current liabilities at the end of 2005), plus half of the 2006 tax charge (that is, $23 + (^1/_2 \times 36) = 41$).

5 It is assumed that the cash payment to redeem the debentures was simply the difference between the two balance sheet figures.

It seems that there was a bonus issue of ordinary shares during the year. These increased by £100 million. At the same time, the share premium account balance reduced by £40 million (to zero) and the revaluation reserve balance fell by £60 million.

5.5

Blackstone plc
Cash flow statement for the year ended 31 March 2006

	£m	£m
Cash flows from operating activities		
Net profit, after interest, before taxation (see Note 1 below)	1,853	
Adjustments for:		
Depreciation (Note 2)	1,289	
Interest expense (Note 3)	456	
	3,598	
Increase in inventories (2,410 – 1,209)	(1,201)	
Increase in trade receivables (1,173 – 641)	(532)	
Increase in trade payables (1,507 – 931)	576	
Cash generated from operations	2,441	
Interest paid	(456)	
Corporation tax paid (see Note 4 below)	(300)	
Dividend paid	(400)	
Net cash from operating activities		1,285
Cash flows from investing activities		
Proceeds of disposals	54	
Payment to acquire intangible non-current asset	(700)	
Payments to acquire property, plant and equipment	(4,578)	
Net cash used in investing activities		(5,224)
Cash flows from financing activities		
Bank loan	2,000	
Net cash from financing activities		2,000
Net decrease in cash and cash equivalents		(1,939)
Cash and cash equivalents at 1 April 2005		
Cash at bank		123
Cash and cash equivalents at 31 March 2006		
Bank overdraft		(1,816)

To see how this relates to the cash of the business at the beginning and end of the year it can be useful to provide a reconciliation as follows:

Analysis of cash and cash equivalents during the year ended 31 March 2006

	£m
Cash and cash equivalents at 1 April 2005	123
Net cash outflow	(1,939)
Cash and cash equivalents at 31 March 2006	1,816

Notes:

1 This is simply taken from the income statement for the year.

2 The full depreciation charge was that stated in the table in Note 3 to the question (£1,251m), plus the deficit on disposal of the non-current assets. According to the table, these non-current assets had originally cost £581m and had been depreciated by £489m (that is, a net book value of £92m). They were sold for £54m, leading to a deficit on disposal of £38m. Thus the full depreciation expense for the year was £1,289m (that is, £1,251m + £38m).

3 Interest payable expense must be taken out, by adding it back to the profit figure. We subsequently deduct the cash paid for interest payable during the year. In this case the two figures are identical.

4 Companies pay tax at 50 per cent during their accounting year and the other 50 per cent in the following year. Thus the 2006 payment would have been half the tax on the 2005 profit (that is, the figure that would have appeared in the current liabilities at 31 March 2004), plus half of the 2006 tax charge (that is, $105 + (^1/_2 \times 390) = 300$).

Chapter 6

6.1   Jiang (Western) Ltd

The effect of each of the changes on ROCE is not always easy to predict.

(i)   On the face of it, an increase in the gross profit margin would tend to lead to an increase in ROCE. An increase in the gross profit margin may, however, lead to a decrease in ROCE in particular circumstances. If the increase in the margin resulted from an increase in price, which in turn led to a decrease in sales revenue, a fall in ROCE can occur. A fall in sales revenue can reduce the net profit (the numerator in ROCE) if the overheads of the business did not decrease correspondingly.

(ii)   A reduction in sales revenue can reduce ROCE for the reasons mentioned above.

(iii)   An increase in overhead expenses will reduce the net profit and this in turn will result in a reduction in ROCE.

(iv)   An increase in inventories held would increase the amount of capital employed by the business (the denominator in ROCE) where long-term funds are employed to finance the inventories. This will, in turn, reduce ROCE.

(v)   Repayment of the loan at the year end will reduce the capital employed and this will increase the ROCE, assuming that the year-end capital employed figure has been used in the calculation. Since the net profit was earned during a period in which the loan existed, there is a strong argument for basing the capital employed figure on what was the position during the year, rather than at the end of it.

(vi)   An increase in the time taken for credit customers (receivables) to pay will result in an increase in capital employed if long-term funds are employed to finance the receivables. This increase in long-term funds will, in turn, reduce ROCE.

6.2 Amsterdam Ltd and Berlin Ltd

The ratios for Amsterdam Ltd and Berlin Ltd reveal that the receivables turnover ratio for Amsterdam Ltd is three times that for Berlin Ltd. Berlin Ltd is therefore much quicker in collecting amounts outstanding from customers. On the other hand, there is not much difference between the two businesses in the time taken to pay trade payables.

It is interesting to compare the difference in the receivables and payables collection periods for each business. As Amsterdam Ltd allows an average of 63 days' credit to its customers, yet pays suppliers within 50 days, it will require greater investment in working capital than Berlin Ltd, which allows an average of only 21 days to its credit customers but takes 45 days to pay its suppliers.

Amsterdam Ltd has a much higher gross profit percentage than Berlin Ltd. However, the net profit percentage for the two businesses is identical. This suggests that Amsterdam Ltd has much higher overheads (as a percentage of sales revenue) than Berlin Ltd. The inventories turnover period for Amsterdam Ltd is more than twice that of Berlin Ltd. This may be due to the fact that Amsterdam Ltd maintains a wider range of goods in inventories in an attempt to meet customer requirements. The evidence therefore suggests that Amsterdam Ltd is the one that prides itself on personal service. The higher average settlement period for receivables is consistent with a more relaxed attitude to credit collection (thereby maintaining customer goodwill) and the high overheads are consistent with incurring the additional costs of satisfying customers' requirements. Amsterdam Ltd's high inventories levels are consistent with maintaining a wide range of inventories, with the aim of satisfying a range of customer needs.

Berlin Ltd has the characteristics of a more price-competitive business. Its gross profit margin is much lower than that of Amsterdam Ltd, that is, a much lower gross profit for each £1 of sales revenue. However, overheads have been kept low, the effect being that the net profit percentage is the same as Amsterdam Ltd's. The low inventories turnover period and average collection period for receivables are consistent with a business that wishes to minimise investment in current assets, thereby reducing costs.

6.5 Bradbury Ltd

(a)

			2005	2006
(i)	Net profit margin			
	914/9,482 × 100%		9.6%	
	1,042/11,365 × 100%			9.2%
(ii)	ROCE			
	914/11,033 × 100%		8.3%	
	1,042/13,943 × 100%			7.5%
(iii)	Current ratio			
	4,926/1,508		3.3:1	
	7,700/5,174			1.5:1
(iv)	Gearing ratio			
	1,220/11,033 × 100%		11.1%	
	3,675/13,943 × 100%			26.4%
(v)	Days receivables			
	(2,540/9,482) × 365		98 days	
	(4,280/11,365) × 365			137 days
(vi)	Sales revenue to capital employed			
	9,482/11,033		0.9 times	
	11,365/13,943			0.8 times

(b) The net profit margin was slightly lower in 2006 than in 2005. Though there was an increase in sales revenue in 2006, this could not prevent a slight fall in ROCE in 2006. The lower net profit margin and increases in sales revenue may well be due to the new contract. The capital employed of the company increased in 2006 by a larger percentage than the increase in revenue. Hence, the sales revenue to capital employed ratio decreased over the period. The increase in capital during 2006 is largely due to an increase in borrowing. However, the gearing ratio is probably still low in comparison with other businesses. Comparison of the freehold premises and loans figures indicates possible unused debt capacity.

The major cause for concern has been the dramatic decline in liquidity during 2006. The current ratio has more than halved during the period. There has also been a similar decrease in the acid test ratio, from 1.7:1 in 2005 to 0.8:1 in 2006. The balance sheet shows that the business now has a large overdraft and the trade payables outstanding have nearly doubled in 2006.

The trade receivables outstanding and inventories have increased much more than appears to be warranted by the increase in sales revenue. This may be due to the terms of the contract that has been negotiated and may be difficult to influence. If this is the case, the business should consider whether it is overtrading. If the conclusion is that it is, increasing its long-term funding may be a sensible policy.

Chapter 7

7.3 Products A, B and C

(a) Total time required on cutting machines:

$$(2,500 \times 1.0) + (3,400 \times 1.0) + (5,100 \times 0.5) = 8,450 \text{ hours}$$

Total time available on cutting machines is 5,000 hours. Therefore, this is a limiting factor. Total time required on assembling machines:

$$(2,500 \times 0.5) + (3,400 \times 1.0) + (5,100 \times 0.5) = 7,200 \text{ hours}$$

Total time available on assembling machines is 8,000 hours. Therefore, this is not a limiting factor.

	Product:		
	A (per unit)	B (per unit)	C (per unit)
	£	£	£
Selling price	25	30	18
Variable materials	(12)	(13)	(10)
Variable production costs	(7)	(4)	(3)
Contribution	6	13	5
Time on cutting machines	1.0 hour	1.0 hour	0.5 hour
Contribution per hour on cutting machines	£6	£13	£10
Order of priority	3rd	1st	2nd

Therefore, produce: 3,400 product B using   3,400 hours
3,200 product C using   1,600 hours
5,000 hours

(b) Assuming that the business would make no saving in variable production costs by subcontracting, it would be worth paying up to the contribution per unit (£5) for product C, which would therefore be £5 × (5,100 − 3,200) = £9,500 in total.

Similarly it would be worth paying up to £6 per unit for product A – that is, £6 × 2,500 = £15,000 in total.

7.4 Darmor Ltd

(a) Contribution per hour of skilled labour of product X is:

$$\frac{£(30 - 6 - 2 - 12 - 3)}{6/12} = £14$$

Given the scarcity of skilled labour, if the management is to be indifferent between the products, the contribution per skilled labour hour must be the same. Thus for product Y the selling price must be:

$$£(14 × (9/12)) + 9 + 4 + 25 + 7 = £55.50$$

(that is, the contribution plus the variable costs), and for product Z the selling price must be:

$$£(14 × (3/12)) + 3 + 10 + 14 + 7 = £37.50$$

(b) The business could pay up to £26 an hour (£12 + £14) for additional hours of skilled labour. This is the potential contribution per hour, before taking account of the labour rate of £12 an hour.

7.5 Gandhi Ltd

(a) Given that the spare capacity could not be used by other services, the standard service should continue to be offered. This is because it renders a positive contribution.

(b) The standard service renders a contribution per unit of £15 (that is, £80 – £65), or £30 during the time it would take to render one unit of the nova service. The nova service would provide a contribution of only £25 (that is, £75 – £50).

The nova service should, therefore, not replace the standard service.

(c) Under the original plans, the following contributions would be rendered by the basic and standard services:

		£
Basic:	11,000 × (£50 – £25) =	275,000
Standard:	6,000 × (£80 – £65) =	90,000
		365,000

If the basic were to take the standard's place, 17,000 units (that is, 11,000 + 6,000) of them could be produced in total. To generate the same total contribution, each unit of the standard service would need to provide £21.47 (that is, £365,000/17,000) of contribution. Given the basic's variable cost of £25, this would mean a selling price of £46.47 each (that is £21.47 + £25.00).

Chapter 8

8.1 All three of these costing techniques are means of deducing the full cost of some activity. The distinction between them lies essentially with the difference in the style of the production of the goods or services involved.

- *Job costing* is used where each unit of output or 'job' differs from others produced by the same business. Because the jobs are not identical, it is not normally useful or acceptable to those who are likely to use the cost information to treat the jobs as if they are identical. This means that costs need to be identified, job by job. For this purpose, costs fall into two categories: direct costs and indirect costs (or overheads).

Direct costs are those that can be measured directly in respect of the specific job, such as the amount of labour that was directly applied to the job or the amount of material that has been incorporated in it. To this must be added a share of the indirect costs. This is usually done by taking the total overheads for the period concerned and charging part of them to the job. This, in turn, is usually done according to some measure of the job's size and/or importance, relative to the other jobs done during the period. The number of direct labour hours worked on the job is the most commonly used measure of size and/or importance.

The main problem with job costing tends to be the method of charging indirect costs to jobs. Indirect costs, by definition, cannot be related directly to jobs, and so must, if full cost is to be deduced, be charged on a basis that is more or less arbitrary. If indirect costs accounted for a small proportion of the total, the arbitrariness of charging them would probably not matter. Indirect costs, in many cases, however, form the majority of total costs, so arbitrariness is a problem.

- *Process costing* is the approach taken where all output is of identical units. These can be treated, therefore, as having identical cost. Sometimes a process costing approach is taken even where the units of output are not strictly identical. This is because process costing is much simpler and cheaper to apply than the only other option, job costing. Provided that users of the cost information are satisfied that treating units as identical when they are not strictly so is acceptable, the additional cost and effort of job costing is not justified.

In process costing, the cost per unit of output is found by dividing total costs for the period by the total number of units produced in the period. Note that the distinction between direct and indirect costs is not of any importance in process costing.

The main problem with process costing tends to be that at the end of any period/beginning of the next period, there will probably be partly completed units of output. An adjustment needs to be made for this work in progress if the resulting figures for cost per unit are not to be distorted.

- *Batch costing* is really an extension of job costing. Batch costing tends to be used where production is in batches. A batch consists of more than one, perhaps many, identical units of output. The units of output differ from one batch to the next. For example, a clothing manufacturing business may produce 500 identical jackets in one batch. This is followed by a batch of 300 identical skirts.

Each batch is costed, as one job, using a job costing approach. The full cost of each garment is then found by dividing the cost of the batch by the number of garments in the batch.

The main problem of batch costing is exactly that of job costing, of which it is an extension. This is the problem of dealing with overheads.

8.4 Kaplan plc

(a) At present, the business makes each model of suitcase in a batch. The direct materials and labour costs will be recorded for each batch. To these costs will be added a share of the overheads of the business for the period in which production of the batch takes place. The basis of the batch absorbing overheads is a matter of managerial judgement. Direct labour hours spent working on the batch, relative to total direct labour hours worked during the period, is a popular method. This is not the 'correct' way, however. There is no correct way. If the activity is capital intensive, some machine-hour basis of dealing with overheads might be more appropriate, though still not 'correct'. Overheads might be collected, department by department, and charged to the batch as it passes through each department. Alternatively, all of the overheads for the entire production facility might be totalled and the overheads dealt with more globally. It is only in restricted circumstances that overheads charged to batches will be affected by a decision to deal with them departmentally, rather than globally.

Once the 'full cost' (direct costs plus a share of indirect costs) has been ascertained for the batch, the cost per suitcase can be established by dividing the batch cost by the number in the batch.

(b) The uses to which full cost information can be put have been identified as:

■ *For pricing purposes.* In some industries and circumstances, full costs are used as the basis of pricing. Here the full cost is deduced and a percentage is added on for profit. This is known as cost-plus pricing. A solicitor handling a case for a client probably provides an example of where cost-plus pricing tends to apply in practice.

In many circumstances, however, suppliers are not in a position to deduce prices on a cost-plus basis. Where there is a competitive market, a supplier will probably need to accept the price that the market offers – that is, most suppliers are 'price takers' not 'price makers'. This may well be true of suitcases.

■ *For income-measurement purposes.* To provide a valid means of measuring a business's income, it is necessary to match expenses with the revenue realised in the same accounting period. Where manufactured inventories are made or partially made in one period but sold in the next, or where a service is partially rendered in one accounting period but the revenue is realised in the next, the full cost (including an appropriate share of overheads) must be carried from one accounting period to the next. Unless we are able to identify the full cost of work done in one period, which is the subject of a sale in the next, the profit figures of the periods concerned will become meaningless.

Unless all related production costs are charged in the same accounting period as the sale is recognised in the income statement, distortions will occur that will render the income statement much less useful. Thus it is necessary to deduce the full cost of any production undertaken completely or partially in one accounting period but sold in a subsequent one.

(c) Whereas the traditional approach to dealing with overheads is just to accept that they exist and deal with them in a fairly broad manner, ABC takes a much more enquiring approach. ABC takes the view that overheads do not just 'occur', but that they are caused or 'driven' by 'activities'. It is a matter of finding out which activities are driving the costs and how much cost they are driving.

For example, a significant part of the costs of making suitcases of different sizes might be resetting machinery to cope with a batch of a different size from its predecessor batch. Where a particular model is made in very small batches, because it has only a small market, ABC would advocate that this model is charged directly with its machine-setting costs. The traditional approach would be to treat machine setting as a general overhead that the individual suitcases (irrespective of the model) might bear equally. ABC, it is claimed, leads to more accurate costing and thus to more accurate assessment of profitability.

(d) The other advantage of pursuing an ABC philosophy and identifying cost drivers is that, once the drivers have been identified, they are likely to become much more susceptible to being controlled. Thus the ability of management to assess the benefit of certain activities against their cost becomes more feasible.

8.5

Offending phrase	*Explanation*
'Necessary to divide the business up into departments'	This can be done but it will not always be of much benefit. Only in quite restricted circumstances will it give significantly different job costs.
'Fixed costs (or overheads)'	This implies that fixed costs and overheads are the same thing. They are not really connected with one another. 'Fixed' is to do with how costs behave as the level of output is raised or lowered; 'overheads' are to do with the extent to which costs can be directly measured in respect of a particular unit of output. Though it is true that many overheads are fixed, not all are. Also, direct labour is usually a fixed cost. All of the other references to fixed and variable costs are wrong. The person should have referred to indirect and direct costs.
'Usually this is done on the basis of area'	Where overheads are apportioned to departments, they will be apportioned on some logical basis. For certain costs, for example rent, the floor area may be the most logical; for others, such as machine maintenance costs, the floor area would be totally inappropriate.
'When the total fixed costs for each department have been identified, this will be divided by the number of hours that were worked'	Where overheads are dealt with on a departmental basis, they may be divided by the number of direct labour hours to deduce a recovery rate. However, this is only one basis of applying overheads to jobs. For example, machine hours or some other basis may be more appropriate to the particular circumstances involved.
'It is essential that this approach is taken in order to deduce a selling price'	It is relatively unusual for the 'job cost' to be able to dictate the price at which the manufacturer can price its output. For many businesses, the market dictates the price.

Chapter 9

9.3 Pilot Ltd

(a) and (b)

	Original	Flexed		Actual	
		Budget			
Output (units)	5,000	5,400		5,400	
(production and sales)					
	£	£		£	
Sales revenue	25,000	27,000		26,460	
Raw materials	(7,500)	(8,100)	(2,700 kg)	(8,770)	(2,830 kg)
Labour	(6,250)	(6,750)	(1,350 hr)	(6,885)	(1,300 hr)
Fixed overheads	(6,000)	(6,000)		(6,350)	
Operating profit	5,250	6,150		4,455	

		£	Manager accountable
Sales volume variance			
(5,250 – 6,150)		= 900 (F)	Sales
Sales price variance			
(27,000 – 26,460)		= (540) (A)	Sales
Materials price variance			
(2,830 × 3) – 8,770		= (280) (A)	Buyer
Materials usage variance			
[(5,400 × 0.5) – 2,830] × £3		= (390) (A)	Production
Labour rate variance			
(1,300 × £5) – 6,885		= (385) (A)	Personnel
Labour efficiency variance			
[(5,400 × 0.25) – 1,300] × £5		= 250 (F)	Production
Fixed overhead spending			
(6,000 – 6,350)		= (350) (A)	Various – depends on the nature of the overheads

Total net variances	£795 (A)

Budgeted profit	£5,250
Less Total net variance	795
Actual profit	£4,455

9.4 Lewisham Ltd

(a) Finished goods inventories budget for the three months ending 30 September (in units of production):

	July '000 units	Aug '000 units	Sept '000 units
Opening inventories (Note 1)	40	48	40
Production (Note 2)	188	232	196
	228	280	236
Less Sales (Note 3)	180	240	200
Closing inventories	48	40	36

(b) Raw materials inventories budget for the two months ending 31 August (in kg):

	July '000 kg	Aug '000 kg
Opening inventories (Note 1)	40	58
Purchases (Note 2)	112	107
	152	165
Less Production (Note 4)	94	116
Closing inventories	58	49

(c) Cash budget for the two months ending 30 September:

	Aug £	Sept £
Inflows		
Credit customers: Current month (Note 5)	493,920	411,600
Preceding month (Note 6)	151,200	201,600
Total inflows	645,120	613,200
Outflows		
Payments to suppliers (Note 7)	168,000	160,500
Labour and overheads (Note 4)	185,600	156,800
Fixed overheads	22,000	22,000
Total outflows	375,600	339,300
Net inflows/(outflows)	269,520	273,900
Balance brought forward	20,000	289,520
Balance carried forward	289,520	563,420

Notes:

1 The opening balance is the same as the closing balance from the previous month.
2 This is a balancing figure.
3 This figure is given in the question.
4 This figure derives from the finished inventories budget.
5 This is 98 per cent of 70 per cent of the current month's sales revenue.
6 This is 28 per cent of the previous month's sales.
7 This figure derives from the raw materials inventories budget.

9.5 Bradley-Allen Ltd

(a)

	Original	Budget Flexed	Actual		
Output (units) (production and sales)	800	950	950		
	£	£		£	
Sales revenue	64,000	76,000		73,000	
Raw materials – A	(12,000)	(14,250)	(285 kg)	(15,200)	(310 kg)
– B	(16,000)	(19,000)	(950 m)	(18,900)	(920 m)
Labour – skilled	(4,000)	(4,750)	(475 hr)	(4,628)	(445 hr)
– unskilled	(10,000)	(11,875)	(1,484.375 hr)	(11,275)	(1,375 hr)
Fixed overheads	(12,000)	(12,000)		(11,960)	
Operating profit	10,000	14,125		11,037	

Sales variances

Volume	£(10,000 − 14,125) = £4,125 (F)
Price	£(76,000 − 73,000) = £3,000 (A)

Direct materials A variances

Usage	[(950 × 0.3) − 310] × £50 = £1,250 (A)
Price	(310 × £50) − £15,200 = £300 (F)

Direct materials B variances

Usage	[(950 × 1) − 920] × £20 = £600 (F)
Price	(920 × £20) − £18,900 = £500 (A)

Skilled direct labour variances

Efficiency	[(950 × 0.5) − 445] × £10 = £300 (F)
Rate	(445 × £10) − £4,628 = £178 (A)

Unskilled direct labour variances

Efficiency	[(950 × 1.5625) − 1,375] × £8 = £875 (F)
Rate	(1,375 × £8) − £11,275 = £275 (A)

Fixed overhead variances

Spending:	£(12,000 − 11,960) = £40 (F)

	£		£
Budgeted profit			10,000
Sales: Volume	4,125	(F)	
Price	(3,000)	(A)	1,125
Direct material A: Usage	(1,250)	(A)	
Price	300	(F)	(950)
Direct material B: Usage	600	(F)	
Price	(500)	(A)	100
Skilled labour: Efficiency	300	(F)	
Rate	(178)	(A)	122
Unskilled labour: Efficiency	875	(F)	
Rate	(275)	(A)	600
Fixed overheads: Expenditure			40
Actual profit			£11,037

(b) The statement in (a) is useful to management because it enables them to see where there have been failures to meet the original budget and to be able to quantify the extent of such failures. This means that junior managers can be held accountable for the performance of their particular area of responsibility.

Chapter 10

10.1 Mylo Ltd

(a) The annual depreciation of the two projects is:

$$\text{Project 1: } \frac{(£100,000 − £7,000)}{3} = £31,000$$

$$\text{Project 2: } \frac{(£60,000 − £6,000)}{3} = £18,000$$

Project 1

(i)

	Year 0 £000	Year 1 £000	Year 2 £000	Year 3 £000
Net profit(loss)		29	(1)	2
Depreciation		31	31	31
Capital cost	(100)			
Residual value				7
Net cash flows	(100)	60	30	40
10% discount factor	1.000	0.909	0.826	0.751
Present value	(100.00)	54.54	24.78	30.04
Net present value	9.36			

(ii) Clearly the IRR lies above 10 per cent; try 15 per cent:

15% discount factor	1.000	0.870	0.756	0.658
Present value	(100.00)	52.20	22.68	26.32
Net present value	1.20			

Thus, the IRR lies a little above 15 per cent, perhaps around 16 per cent.

(iii) To find the payback period, the cumulative cash flows are calculated:

Cumulative cash flows	(100)	(40)	(10)	30

Thus, the payback will occur after three years if we assume year-end cash flows.

Project 2

(i)

	Year 0 £000	Year 1 £000	Year 2 £000	Year 3 £000
Net profit (loss)		18	(2)	4
Depreciation		18	18	18
Capital cost	(60)			
Residual value				6
Net cash flows	(60)	36	16	28
10% discount factor	1.000	0.909	0.826	0.751
Present value	(60.00)	32.72	13.22	21.03
Net present value	6.97			

(ii) Clearly the IRR lies above 10 per cent; try 15 per cent:

15% discount factor	1.000	0.870	0.756	0.658
Present value	(60.00)	31.32	12.10	18.42
Net present value	1.84			

Thus, the IRR lies a little above 15 per cent; perhaps around 17 per cent.

(iii) The cumulative cash flows are:

Cumulative cash flows	(60)	(24)	(8)	20

Thus, the payback will occur after three years (assuming year-end cash flows).

(b) Presuming that Mylo Ltd is pursuing a wealth-maximisation objective, Project 1 is preferable since it has the higher NPV. The difference between the two NPVs is not significant, however.

(c) NPV is the preferred method of assessing investment opportunities because it fully addresses each of the following:

- *The timing of the cash flows.* Discounting the various cash flows associated with each project, according to when they are expected to arise, takes account of the fact that cash flows do not all occur simultaneously. Associated with this is the fact that by discounting, using the opportunity cost of finance (namely the return that the next-best alternative opportunity would generate), the net benefit, after financing costs have been met, is identified (as the NPV).
- *The whole of the relevant cash flows.* NPV includes all of the relevant cash flows irrespective of when they are expected to occur. It treats them differently according to their date of occurrence, but they are all taken into account in the calculation of the NPV and they all have, or can have, an influence on the decision.
- *The objectives of the business.* NPV is the only method of appraisal where the output of the analysis has a direct bearing on the wealth of the business. (Positive NPVs enhance wealth; negative NPVs reduce it.) Since most private-sector businesses seek to increase their value and wealth, NPV clearly is the best approach to use.

10.4 Newton Electronics Ltd

(a) **Option 1**

	Year 0 £m	Year 1 £m	Year 2 £m	Year 3 £m	Year 4 £m	Year 5 £m
Plant and equipment	(9.0)					1.0
Sales revenue		24.0	30.8	39.6	26.4	10.0
Variable costs		(11.2)	(19.6)	(25.2)	(16.8)	(7.0)
Fixed costs (ex. dep'n)		(0.8)	(0.8)	(0.8)	(0.8)	(0.8)
Working capital	(3.0)					3.0
Marketing costs		(2.0)	(2.0)	(2.0)	(2.0)	(2.0)
Opportunity costs		(0.1)	(0.1)	(0.1)	(0.1)	(0.1)
	(12.0)	9.9	8.3	11.5	6.7	4.1
Discount factor 10%	1.000	0.909	0.826	0.751	0.683	0.621
Present value	(12.0)	9.0	6.9	8.6	4.6	2.5
NPV	19.6					

Option 2

	Year 0	Year 1	Year 2	Year 3	Year 4	Year 5
Royalties	–	4.4	7.7	9.9	6.6	2.8
Discount factor 10%	1.000	0.909	0.826	0.751	0.683	0.621
Present value	–	4.0	6.4	7.4	4.5	1.7
NPV	24.0					

Option 3

	Year 0	Year 1	Year 2
Instalments	12.0		12.0
Discount factor 10%	1.000		0.826
Present value	12.0		9.9
NPV	21.9		

(b) Before making a final decision, the board should consider the following factors:

- The long-term competitiveness of the business may be affected by the sale of the patents.
- At present, the business is not involved in manufacturing and marketing products. Would a change in direction be desirable?

- The business will probably have to buy in the skills necessary to produce the product itself. This will involve costs, and problems will be incurred. Has this been taken into account?
- How accurate are the forecasts made and how valid are the assumptions on which they are based?

(c) Option 2 has the highest NPV and is therefore the most attractive to shareholders. However, the accuracy of the forecasts should be checked before a final decision is made.

10.5 Chesterfield Wanderers

(a) and (b)

Player option

	Year 0 £000	Year 1 £000	Year 2 £000	Year 3 £000	Year 4 £000	Year 5 £000
Sale of player	2,200					1,000
Purchase of Bazza	(10,000)					
Sponsorship and so on		1,200	1,200	1,200	1,200	1,200
Gate receipts		2,500	1,300	1,300	1,300	1,300
Salaries paid		(800)	(800)	(800)	(800)	(1,200)
Salaries saved		400	400	400	400	600
Net cash received (paid)	(7,800)	3,300	2,100	2,100	2,100	2,900
Discount factor 10%	1.000	0.909	0.826	0.751	0.683	0.621
Present values	(7,800)	3,000	1,735	1,577	1,434	1,801
NPV	1,747					

Ground improvement option

	Year 1 £000	Year 2 £000	Year 3 £000	Year 4 £000	Year 5 £000
Ground improvements	(10,000)				
Increased gate receipts	(1,800)	4,400	4,400	4,400	4,400
	(11,800)	4,400	4,400	4,400	4,400
Discount factor 10%	0.909	0.826	0.751	0.683	0.621
Present values	(10,726)	3,634	3,304	3,005	2,732
NPV	1,949				

(c) The ground improvement option provides the higher NPV and is therefore the preferable option, based on the objective of shareholder wealth maximisation.

(d) A professional football club may not wish to pursue an objective of shareholder wealth maximisation. It may prefer to invest in quality players in an attempt to enjoy future sporting success. If this is the case, the NPV approach will be less appropriate because the club is not pursuing a strict wealth-maximisation objective.

Chapter 11

11.1 Hercules Wholesalers Ltd

(a) The liquidity ratios of the business seem low. The current ratio is only 1.1:1 (that is, 306/285) and its acid test ratio is 0:1:6 (that is, 163/285). This latter ratio suggests that the business has insufficient liquid assets to pay its short-term obligations. A cash flow projection for the next period would provide a better insight into the liquidity position of the business. The bank overdraft seems high and it would be useful to know whether the bank is pressing for a reduction and what overdraft limit has been established for the business.

(b) The operating cash cycle can be calculated as follows:

No. of days

Average inventories holding period:

$$\frac{[(\text{Opening inventories} + \text{Closing inventories})/2] \times 360}{\text{Cost of sales}}$$

$$= \frac{[(125 + 143)/2] \times 360}{323} \qquad\qquad = 149$$

Add Average settlement period for receivables:

$$\frac{\text{Trade receivables} \times 360}{\text{Credit sales revenue}} = \frac{163}{452} \times 360 \qquad\qquad = \underline{130}$$

$$= 279$$

Less Average settlement period for payables:

$$\frac{\text{Trade payables} \times 360}{\text{Credit purchases}} - \frac{145}{341} \times 360 \qquad\qquad = \underline{153}$$

$$= \underline{126}$$

(c) The business can reduce the operating cash cycle in a number of ways. The average inventories holding period seems quite long. At present, average inventories held represent almost five months' sales. Reducing the level of inventories held can reduce this period. Similarly, the average settlement period for receivables seems long at more than four months' sales revenue. Imposing tighter credit control, offering discounts, charging interest on overdue accounts, and so on, may reduce this. However, any policy decisions concerning inventories and receivables must take account of current trading conditions.

Extending the period of credit taken to pay suppliers would also reduce the operating cash cycle. However, for the reasons mentioned in the chapter, this option must be given careful consideration.

11.4

Mayo Computers Ltd
New proposals from credit control department

	£000	£000
Current level of investment in receivables		
[£20m × (60/365)]		3,288
Proposed level of investment in receivables		
[(£20m × 60%) × (30/365)]	(986)	
[(£20m × 40%) × (50/365)]	(1,096)	(2,082)
Reduction in level of investment		1,206

The reduction in overdraft interest as a result of the reduction in the level of investment will be £1,206,000 × 14% = £169,000.

	£000	£000
Cost of cash discounts offered (£20m × 60% × 2½%)		300
Additional cost of credit administration		20
		320
Bad debt savings	(100)	
Interest charge savings (see above)	(169)	(269)
Net cost of policy each year		51

These calculations show that the business would incur additional annual costs if it implemented this proposal. It would therefore be cheaper to stay with the existing credit policy.

11.5 Boswell Enterprises Ltd

(a)

	Current policy		New policy	
	£000	£000	£000	£000
Receivables				
(£3m × 1/12 × 30%) +				
(£3m × 2/12 × 70%)		425.0		
(£3.15m × 1/12 × 60%) +				
(£3.15m × 2/12 × 40%)				367.5
Inventories				
[£3m − (£3m × 20%)] × 3/12		600.0		
[£3.15m − (£3.15m × 20%)] × 3/12				630.0
Cash (fixed)		140.0		140.0
		1,165.0		1,137.5
Payables				
£3m − (£3m × 20%) × 2/12	(400.0)			
[£3.15m − (£3.15m × 20%)] × 2/12			(420.0)	
Accrued variable expenses				
£3m × 1/12 × 10%	(25.0)			
£3.15m × 1/12 × 10%			(26.3)	
Accrued fixed expenses	(15.0)	(440.0)	(15.0)	(461.3)
Investment in working capital		725.0		676.2

(b) The expected net profit for the year

	Current policy		New policy	
	£000	£000	£000	£000
Sales revenue		3,000.0		3,150.0
Cost of goods sold		(2,400.0)		(2,520.0)
Gross profit (20%)		600.0		630.0
Variable expenses (10%)	(300.0)		(315.0)	
Fixed expenses	(180.0)		(180.0)	
Discounts (£3.15m × 60% × 2½%)	–	(480.0)	(47.3)	542.3
Net profit		120.0		87.7

(c) Under the proposed policy we can see that the investment in working capital will be slightly lower than under the current policy. However, profits will be substantially lower as a result of offering discounts. The increase in sales revenue resulting from the discounts will not be sufficient to offset the additional costs of making the discounts to customers. It seems that the business should, therefore, stick with its current policy.

Chapter 12

12.1 H. Brown (Portsmouth) Ltd

(a) The main factors to take into account are:

- *Risk.* If a business borrows, there is a risk that, at the maturity date of the loan, the business will not have the funds to repay the amount owing and will be unable to find a suitable form of replacement borrowing. With short-term loans, the maturity dates will arrive more quickly, and the type of risk outlined will occur at more frequent intervals.

- *Matching.* A business may wish to match the life of an asset with the maturity date of the borrowing. In other words, long-term assets will be purchased with long-term loan funds. A certain level of current assets, which form part of the long-term asset base of the business, may also be funded by long-term borrowing. Short-term borrowing will fund those current assets that fluctuate owing to seasonality and so on. This approach to funding assets will help reduce risks for the business.

- *Cost.* Interest rates for long-term loans may be higher than for short-term loans as investors may seek extra compensation for having their funds locked up for a long period. However, issue costs may be higher for short-term loans as there will be a need to refund at more frequent intervals.

- *Flexibility.* Short-term loans may be more flexible. It may be difficult to repay long-term loans before the maturity period.

(b) When deciding to grant a loan, a lender should consider the following factors:

- security;
- purpose of the loan;
- ability of the borrower to repay;
- loan period;
- availability of funds;
- character and integrity of the senior managers.

(c) Loan conditions may include:

- the need to obtain permission before borrowing more money from any source;
- the need to maintain a certain level of liquidity during the loan period;
- a restriction on the level of dividends and directors' pay.

12.2 Carpets Direct plc

(a) Earnings per share (EPS):

$$\frac{\text{Profit after taxation}}{\text{Number of ordinary shares}} = \frac{£4.5m}{120m} = £0.0375$$

Current market value per share:

$$\text{Earnings per share} \times \text{P/E} = £0.0375 \times 22 = £0.825$$

The rights issue price will be £0.825, less 20% discount = £0.66.
Theoretical ex-rights price:

	£
Original shares (4 @ £0.825)	3.30
Rights share (1 @ £0.66)	0.66
Value of five shares following rights issue	3.96

Therefore, the value of one share following the rights issue:

$$\frac{£3.96}{5} = 79.2p$$

(b)

Value of one share after rights issue	79.2p
Cost of a rights share	(66.0p)
Value of rights to shareholder	13.2p

(c) (i) *Taking up rights issue*

	£
Shareholding following rights issue [(4,000 + 1,000) × 79.2p]	3,960
Less Cost of rights shares (1,000 × 66p)	(660)
Shareholder wealth	3,300

(ii) *Selling the rights*

Shareholding following rights issue (4,000 × 79.2p)	3,168
Add Proceeds from sale of rights (1,000 × 13.2p)	132
Shareholder wealth	3,300

(iii) *Doing nothing*

As the rights are neither purchased nor sold, the shareholder wealth following the rights issue will be:

Shareholding (4,000 × 79.2p)	3,168

We can see that the investor will have the same wealth under the first two options. However, by the investor doing nothing, the rights offer will lapse and so the investor will lose the value of the rights and will be worse off.

12.3 Raphael Ltd

The existing credit policies have the following costs:

	£
Cost of investment in trade receivables [(50/365) × £2.4m × 12%]	39,452
Cost of bad debts (1.5% × £2.4m)	36,000
Total cost	75,452

Using the services of a factor will result in the following costs and savings:

	£
Charges of the factor (2% × £2.4m)	48,000
Interest charges on advance [(30/365) × (80% × £2.4m) × 11%]	17,359
Interest charges on overdraft [(30/365) × (20% × £2.4m) × 12%]	4,734
Total cost	70,093
Less Credit control savings	(18,000)
Net cost	52,093

We can see that the net cost of factoring is lower than the existing costs, so there would be a benefit gained from entering into an agreement with the factor.

Index

Note: Page numbers in **bold** indicate highlighted **key terms** and their glossary definitions.